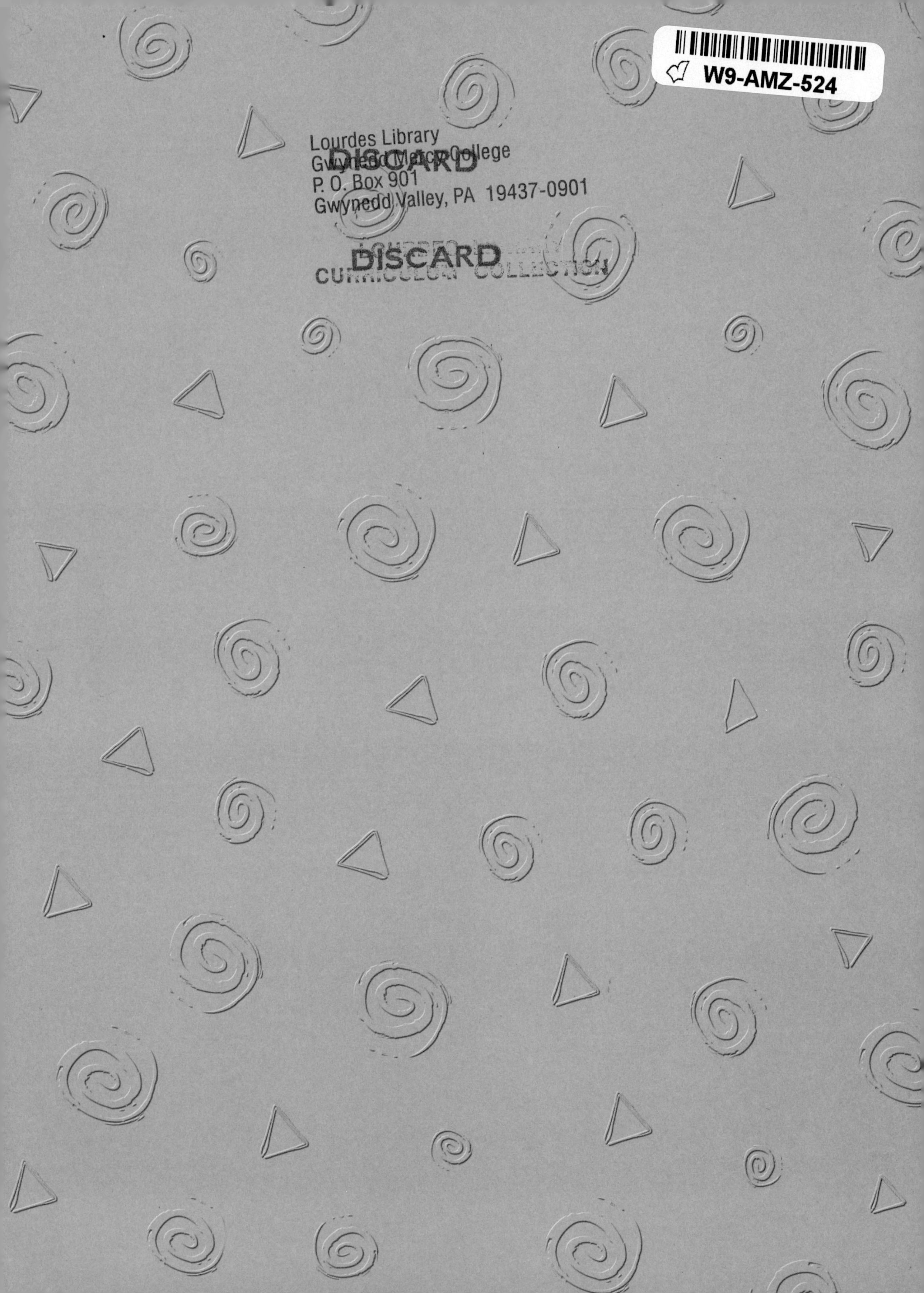

McGraw-Hill Mathematics

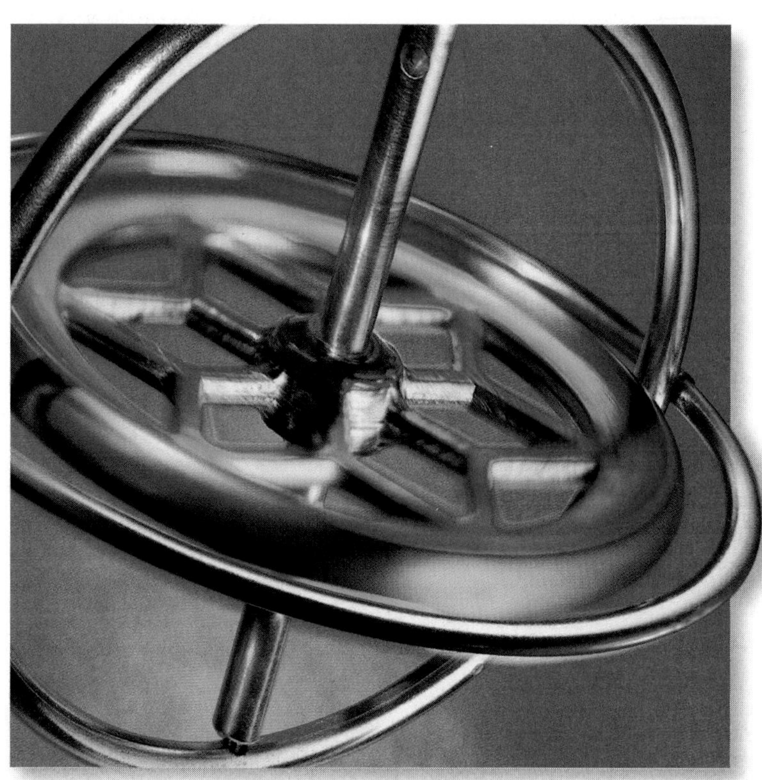

McGraw-Hill School Division
New York Farmington

Senior Program Authors

Gunnar Carlsson, Ph.D.
Professor of Mathematics
Stanford University
Stanford, California

Ralph L. Cohen, Ph.D.
Professor of Mathematics
Stanford University
Stanford, California

Program Authors

Douglas H. Clements, Ph.D.
Professor of Mathematics Education
State University of New York at Buffalo
Buffalo, New York

Carol E. Malloy, Ph.D.
Assistant Professor of Mathematics Education
University of North Carolina at Chapel Hill
Chapel Hill, North Carolina

Lois Gordon Moseley, M.S.
Mathematics Consultant
Houston, Texas

Robyn R. Silbey, M.S.
Montgomery County Public Schools
Rockville, Maryland

McGraw-Hill School Division

A Division of The ***McGraw-Hill*** *Companies*

McGraw-Hill School Division
Two Penn Plaza
New York, New York 10121-2298

Printed in the United States of America
ISBN 0-02-100128-6
1 2 3 4 5 6 7 8 9 027/043 05 04 03 02 01 00

Contributing Authors

Mary Behr Altieri, M.S.
Mathematics Teacher
1993 Presidential Awardee
Lakeland Central School District
Shrub Oak, New York

Nadine Bezuk, Ph.D.
Professor of Mathematics Education
San Diego State University
San Diego, California

Pam B. Cole, Ph.D.
Associate Professor of
Middle Grades English Education
Kennesaw State University
Kennesaw, Georgia

Barbara W. Ferguson, Ph.D.
Assistant Professor of Mathematics
and Mathematics Education
Kennesaw State University
Kennesaw, Georgia

Carol P. Harrell, Ph.D.
Professor of English and English Education
Kennesaw State University
Kennesaw, Georgia

Donna Harrell Lubcker, M.S.
Assistant Professor of Education
and Early Childhood
East Texas Baptist University
Marshall, Texas

Chung-Hsing OuYang, Ph.D.
Assistant Professor of Mathematics
California State University, Hayward
Hayward, California

Marianne Weber, M.ED.
National Mathematics Consultant
St. Louis, Missouri

Contents

Chapter 1: Place Value: Add and Subtract Whole Numbers and Decimals

Theme: World Records

Chapter 2: Multiply Whole Numbers and Decimals

Theme: Faraway Places

Chapter 3: Divide Whole Numbers and Decimals

Theme: Wonderful Wildlife

Chapter 4: Data, Statistics, and Graphs

Theme: Inventions

Chapter 5: Number Theory and Fraction Concepts

Theme: Performing Arts

Chapter 6: Add and Subtract Fractions

Theme: Careers

Chapter 7: Multiply and Divide Fractions

Theme: Hobbies

Chapter 8: Measurement

Theme: Communication

Chapter 9: Algebra & functions Integers

Theme: Science

Chapter 10: Expressions and Equations

Theme: Our Environment

Chapter 11: Geometry

Theme: Art and Design

Chapter 12: Perimeter, Area and Volume

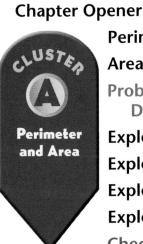

Theme: Architecture

Chapter 13: Ratio and Probability

Theme: Running a Business

Chapter 14: Percents

Theme: Sports and Games

WORLD

CHAPTER 1

Place Value, Add and Subtract Whole Numbers and Decimals

Theme: World Records

Use the Data

Top 5 Movie-Producing Countries

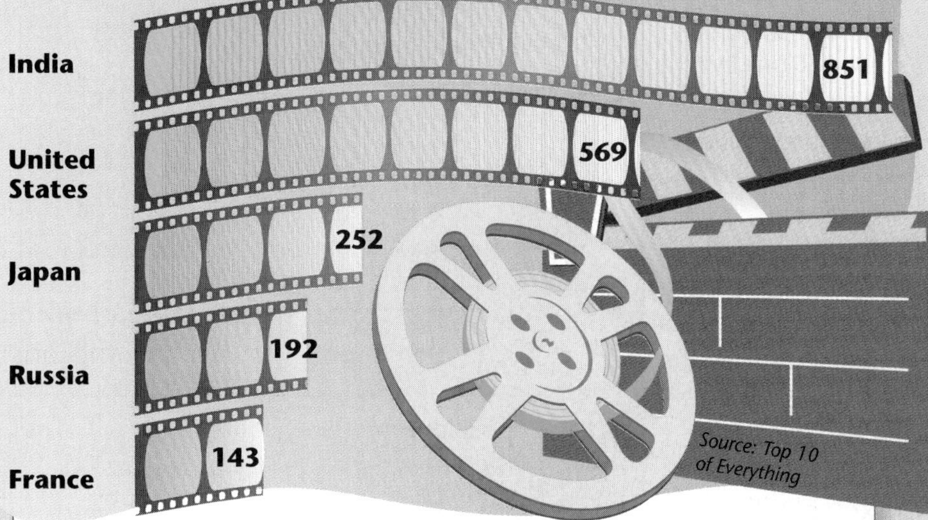

- About how many more movies are produced each year in India than in the United States?

What You Will Learn

In this chapter you will learn how to

- compare and order whole numbers and decimals.
- add and subtract whole numbers and decimals.
- estimate sums and differences.
- use strategies to solve problems.

Objective: Review the place value of whole numbers.

1•1 Place Value Through Billions

Learn

The Shanghai Bank in Hong Kong is the most expensive building ever made. Its total costs were $1,032,398,705! What is the word name for that dollar amount?

Math Words

whole number any one of the numbers 0, 1, 2, 3, and so on

period each group of three digits in a place value chart

place the position of a digit in a number

value the product of a digit multiplied by its place

standard form the usual or common way to write a number

expanded form a way of writing a number as the sum of the values of its digits

Example

A place value chart helps you read **whole numbers**. This chart is divided into 4 **periods**: billions, millions, thousands, and ones.

Billions			Millions			Thousands			Ones		
H	T	O	H	T	O	H	T	O	H	T	O
		1	0	3	2	3	9	8	7	0	5

- ▶ The **place** of the digit 1 is billions.
- ▶ The **value** of the digit 1 is 1,000,000,000.

Standard form: 1,032,398,705

Short word name: 1 billion, 32 million, 398 thousand, 705

Read: one billion, thirty-two million, three hundred ninety-eight thousand, seven hundred five

Expanded form:

1,000,000,000 + 30,000,000 + 2,000,000 + 300,000 + 90,000 + 8,000 + 700 + 5

Try It

Name the place and write the value of the underlined digit.

1. <u>7</u>1,964,083,720
2. 451,<u>6</u>97,743,508
3. 123,456,<u>7</u>89,000

How would you write the short word name for 613,284,953,846?

Practice

Name the place and write the value of each underlined digit.

4. 1,2<u>6</u>8 5. 1<u>5</u>,807 6. <u>4</u>93,269 7. 7<u>8</u>3,002,000

Write each number in standard form.

8. 67 million, 854 thousand, 912
9. 243 billion, 907 million, 430
10. 750 billion, 621 thousand, 245

Write the numbers in expanded form.

11. 64,900 12. 1,467,000 13. 623,408,009 14. 23,906,700,043

Use place value to answer each question.

15. What is the value of the 4 in 294,506,893,613?
16. In the number 4,523,158,973, what digit is in the ten-millions place?
17. What number is 1,000,000 more than 3,458,910,326?
★18. What number is 1,111,111 less than 4,581,293?

Problem Solving

Use data from the chart for problems 19–21.

19. Which length has a 6 in the thousands place? Which country has that number?
20. How do you read the length of Denmark and China's bridges?
★21. Which country's bridge is six hundred miles longer than four thousand, twenty-six?
22. An average of 130,700,000 people in Japan go to the movies each year. How do you read that number?

Longest Suspension Bridges in the World

Location	Country	Length in Feet
AkasHi-Kaiko, Kobe-Naruto	Japan	6,529
Great Belt	Denmark	5,328
Jiangyin	China	5,328
Humber Estuary	United Kingdom	4,626

23. **Social Studies:** The Pacific Ocean covers an area of 64,185,629 square miles. How would you write that number in expanded form?

Spiral Review and Test Prep

Use the numbers 3, 10, 6, 7, 6, 12, and 9 for problems 24–26.

24. Find the range. 25. Find the median. 26. Find the mode.

Choose the correct answer.

27. What is 12 more than 4×9?
A. 144 C. 48
B. 72 D. Not Here

28. What is $3 \times 9 \times 16$?
F. 27 H. 432
G. 310 J. 561

Extra Practice, page 37

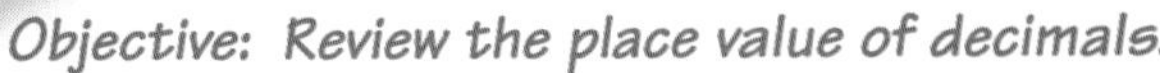

Objective: Review the place value of decimals.

1·2 Explore Decimal Place Value

Learn

You can use 10-by-10 grids to explore decimal place value.

Math Words

decimal a number with a decimal point in it, such as 8.37 or 0.05, that represents a number between two whole numbers

fraction a number, such as $\frac{3}{4}$, that names part of a whole or part of a group

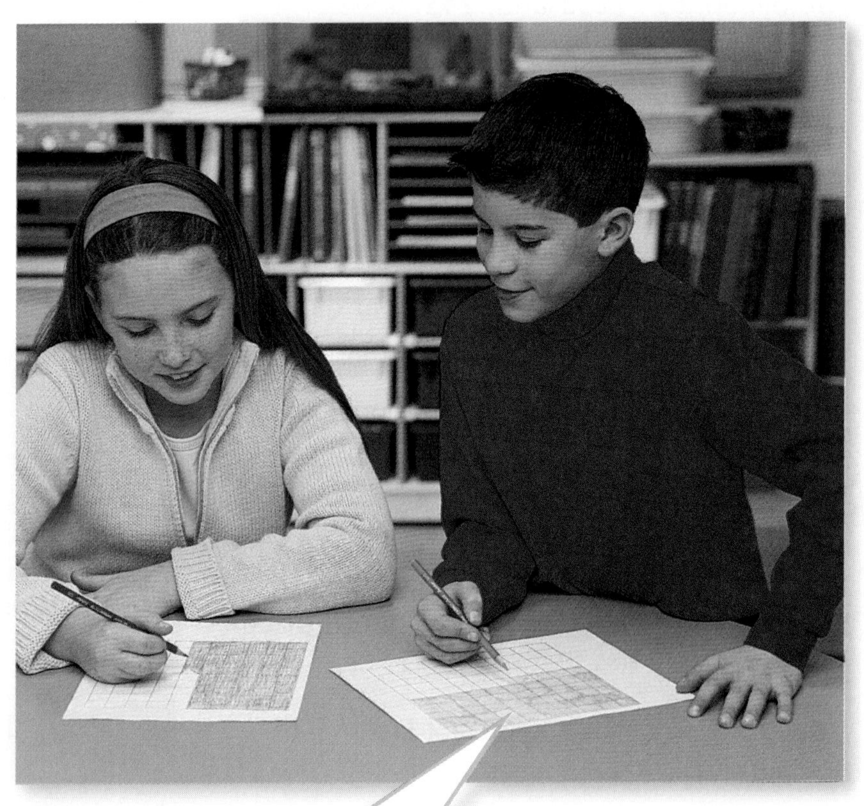

Work Together

You Will Need

- **10-by-10 grids**

▶ You can use 10-by-10 grids to model **decimals**. Model 1.58.

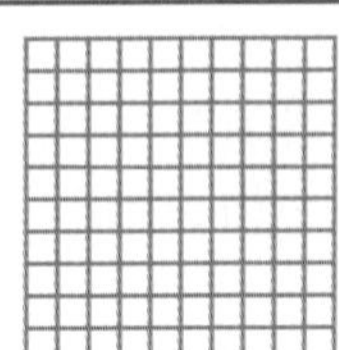

Each small square represents 1 hundredth, or 0.01. Each row or column is 1 tenth, or 0.10.

A completely shaded grid represents 1.

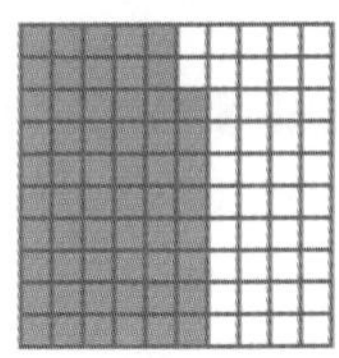

A grid with 58 squares shaded represents 58 hundredths, or 0.58, or $\frac{58}{100}$.

▶ Use 10-by-10 grids to model the decimals. Record your work.

0.5 4.58 2.65 0.08 1.10

Make Connections

You can change **fractions** to decimals and decimals to fractions. You can write numbers shown on grids as decimals or fractions.

	Using Models	**Using Paper and Pencil**	
17 hundredths can be written as 0.17 or $\frac{17}{100}$.	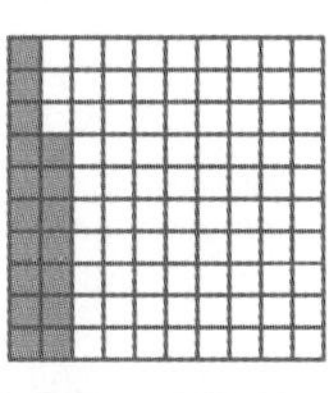	Decimal 0.17	Fraction $\frac{17}{100}$
1 and 82 hundredths can be written as 1.82 or $1\frac{82}{100}$.	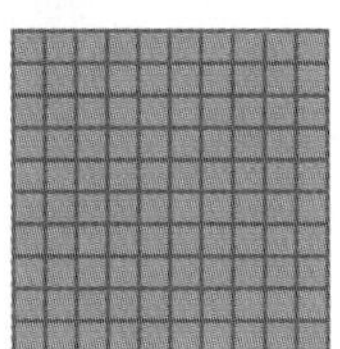	Decimal 1.82	Fraction $1\frac{82}{100}$

Try It **Write the decimal and the fraction.**

1. 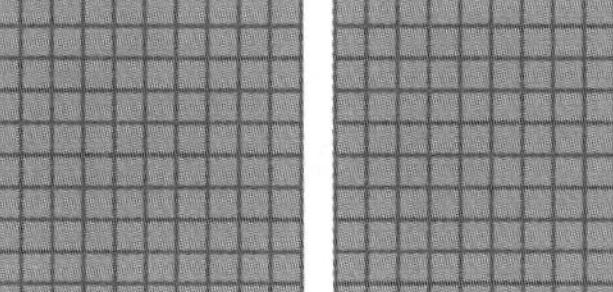
2. 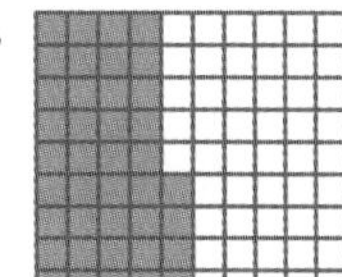
3. 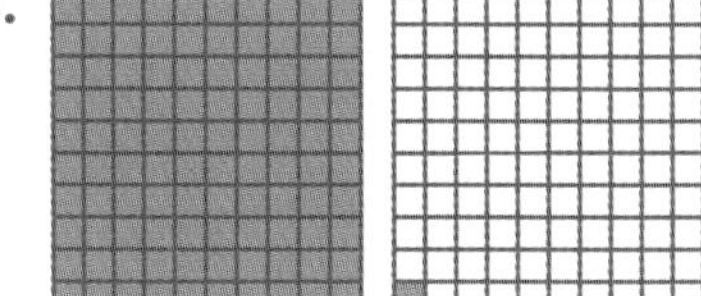

Sum it Up Explain how you would use 10-by-10 grids to model 2.03.

Practice **Write the decimal and the fraction.**

4. 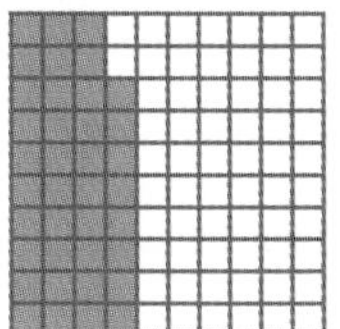
5. 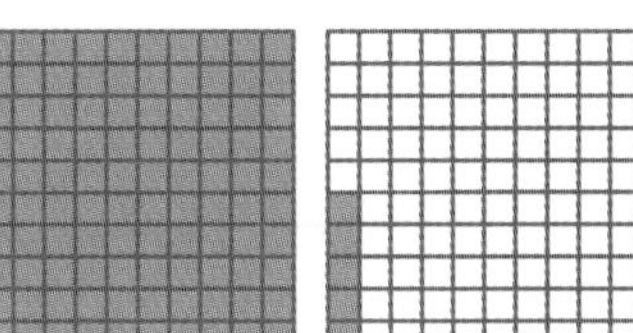
6. 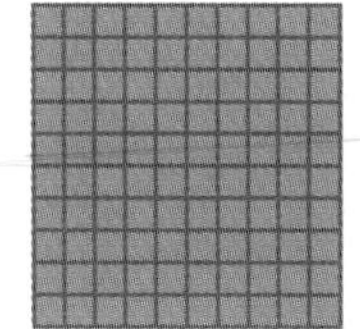 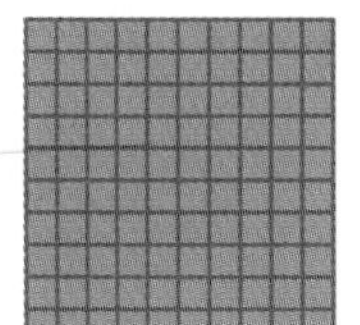
7. 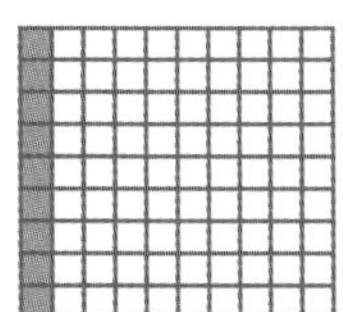
8. 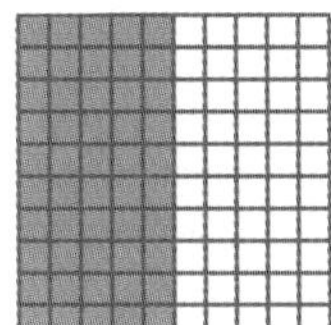
9. 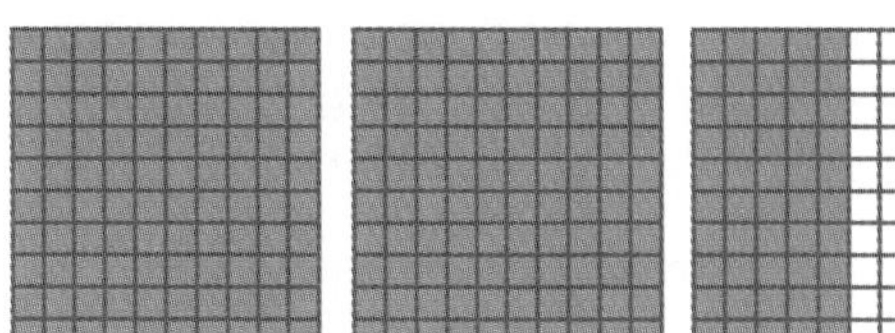
10. **Analyze:** How many 10-by-10 grids would you need to model $199.99?
11. Draw a 10-by-10 grid that shows 0.63.

Objective: Review the place value of decimals.

1•3 Decimal Place Value

Learn

Math Word
equivalent decimals decimals that name the same number

Florence Griffith-Joyner earned the title "World's Fastest Woman" in 1988 when she ran 100 meters in 10.61 seconds. How can you read and write that amount?

World record time: 10.61 seconds

Example 1

Place value models and number lines can help you read and write decimal numbers such as 10.61.

1 Model 10.61 using 10-by-10 grids.

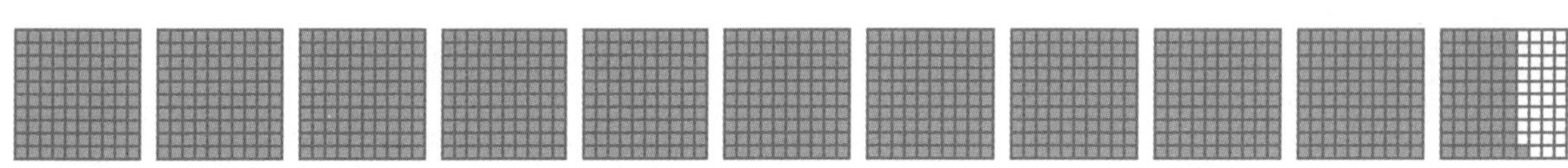

2 Show the number on a number line.

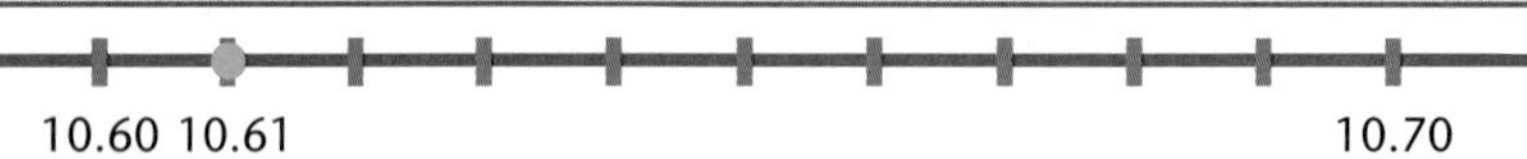

Tens	Ones		Tenths	Hundredths
1	0	.	6	1

Standard form: 10.61
Short word name: 10 and 61 hundredths
Read: ten and sixty-one hundredths
Expanded form: 10 + 0.6 + 0.01

Think: The last digit is in the hundredths place. To read the decimal part of a number, use the place value of the last digit in the number.

Florence Griffith-Joyner ran the 100-meter race in 10 and 61 hundredths of a second.

In 1989 Alain Ferte, a French race-car driver, set the record for the fastest race-lap speed ever—150.429 miles per hour. How do you read that number?

Example 2

The place value chart can be extended to the right for decimals. Each section to the right of the decimal point represents part of a whole number. Decimal places extend to the right forever. After the thousandths comes ten-thousandths, hundred-thousandths, millionths, and so on.

Hundreds	Tens	Ones		Tenths	Hundredths	Thousandths
1	5	0	.	4	2	9

Standard form: 150.429
Short word name: 150 and 429 thousandths
Expanded form: 100 + 50 + 0.4 + 0.02 + 0.009
Read: one hundred fifty and four hundred twenty-nine thousandths

Alain Ferte raced at one hundred fifty and four hundred twenty-nine thousandths miles per hour.

Are 0.2 and 0.20 equivalent?

Example 3

Two decimals are equivalent if they represent the same amount.

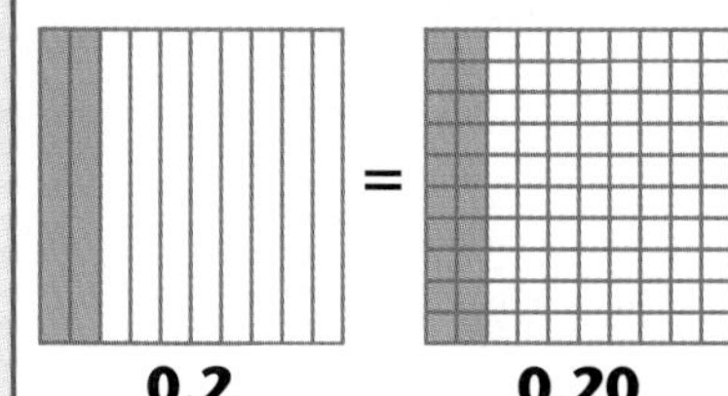

0.2 is equivalent to 0.20.
0.200 and 0.2000 are also equivalent to 0.2.

Note: Placing zeros to the right of the last digit of a decimal does not change the value of the decimal.

0.2 and 0.20 are **equivalent decimals**.

Try It **Write the place of the underlined digit.**

1. 5.0<u>4</u>3
2. 30.128<u>6</u>
3. 30.<u>0</u>07
4. <u>1</u>.0001

Write two equivalent decimals for each.

5. 6.7
6. 0.8
7. 7.95
8. 0.120

Write the number 345.8632 in a place-value chart. What is the word name for this decimal?

Practice

Name the place of the underlined digit.

9. $31.\underline{4}8$
10. $0.0\underline{8}2$
11. $9.75\underline{6}$
12. $0.007\underline{3}$
13. $1,\underline{4}78.02$
14. $34.222\underline{2}$
15. $5.\underline{1}06$
16. $5.11\underline{0}3$

Write in standard form.

17. four and two tenths
18. sixteen and thirty four hundredths
19. eight and twenty-five thousandths
★20. nine and eleven ten-thousandths

Write the word name and expanded form.

21. 8.20
22. 47.034
23. 111.1110

Match each number with the number line that shows its location.

24. $\frac{4}{10}$
25. 0.04
26. 0.89

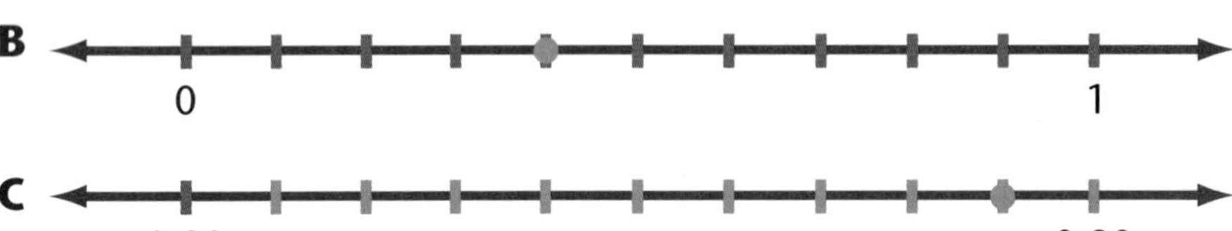

Name an equivalent decimal.

27. 0.7
28. 1.16
29. 305.08
★30. 4,110.32
31. 15.09
32. 0.01
33. 26.30
34. 1.000

35.

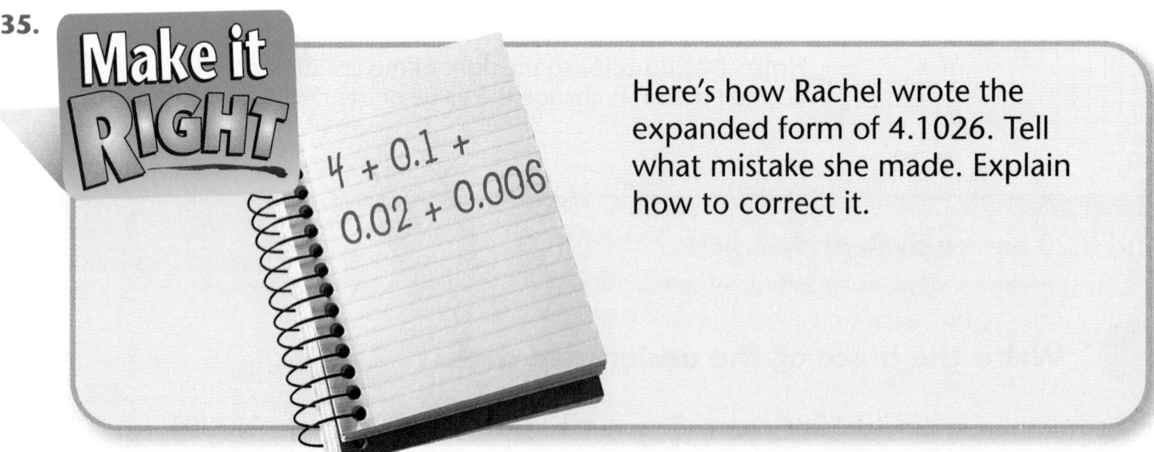

Here's how Rachel wrote the expanded form of 4.1026. Tell what mistake she made. Explain how to correct it.

Problem Solving

36. Julian hears that an athlete completed a race in twelve and thirty-one hundredths seconds. Write this number.

37. The official timer at an Olympic event reads 11.041 seconds. Write an equivalent decimal for this number.

38. **Measurement:** Marco wrote a paper on Alain Ferte. He wrote that Ferte reached a speed of 15.0429 miles per hour. How do you say the speed that Marco wrote in his paper? How can you tell that 15.0429 miles per hour is a mistake?

39. **Social Studies:** Chuck Yeager first broke the sound barrier in his Bell XS-1 plane in 1947. He flew at 822.18 miles per hour. What is the place value of the 1 in the number? Write an equivalent decimal for Yeager's speed.

40. Dave Campos holds the motorcycle speed record of 322.15 miles per hour. If one newspaper reports the speed to be 322.15 and another reports a speed of 322.150, did the papers report the same number? Explain.

41. The world land speed record is held by Andy Green. He drove the car, ThrustSSC, at a maximum speed of 763.04 miles per hour. Write the words needed to say this number.

42. **Science:** The cheetah is the fastest land animal on Earth. It can run up to sixty-five and zero tenths miles per hour over long distances. Write this number in standard form.

43. The display on an Olympic stopwatch shows Florence Griffith-Joyner's record time as 010.6100. Is this number equivalent to her time of 10.61? Explain why or why not.

44. Name all of the places where the number 5 appears in the number 345,533,075.

45. **Summarize:** How do you know if two decimals are equivalent?

46. **Create a problem** about a track race that involves decimals. Solve it and give it to another student to solve.

★47. **Spatial Reasoning:** If the cube at the right represents 1 whole unit, what would one tenth look like? one hundredth? one thousandth? Draw a picture of the place value block model for each value.

Spiral Review and Test Prep

Complete each fact family.

48. $9 \times 7 = \blacksquare$
$7 \times \blacksquare = 63$
$\blacksquare \div 9 = 7$
$63 \div \blacksquare = 9$

49. $3 \times \blacksquare = 24$
$8 \times 3 = \blacksquare$
$24 \div 8 = \blacksquare$
$\blacksquare \div 3 = 8$

50. $6 \times \blacksquare = 42$
$\blacksquare \times 6 = 42$
$\blacksquare \div 6 = 7$
$42 \div 7 = \blacksquare$

Choose the correct answer.

51. $6 + 6 + 6 + 6 + 6$

A. 9×3
B. 6×1
C. 6×6
D. 6×5

52. $314 - 297$

F. 17
G. 117
H. 314
J. 611

Extra Practice, page 37

Objective: Review comparing and ordering whole numbers and decimals.

1-4 Compare and Order Whole Numbers and Decimals

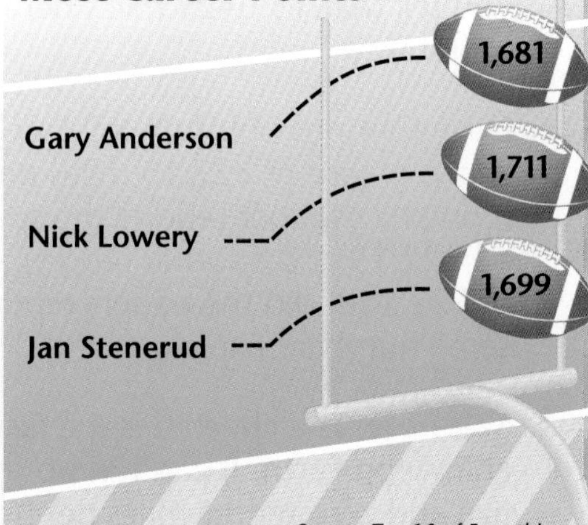

Learn

Gary Anderson, Nick Lowery, and Jan Stenerud are listed in the top ten highest-scoring football players ever. Who has more career points, Gary Anderson or Jan Stenerud?

There's more than one way!

Method A

You can you use a number line to compare 1,681 and 1,699.

1,681 ... 1,699

1,680 1,682 1,684 1,686 1,688 1,690 1,692 1,694 1,696 1,698 1,700

Think: 1,699 is to the right of 1,681. So, 1,699 > 1,681.

Remember: < means less than, > means greater than

You can also compare numbers by looking at the digits.

Method B

1 Line up the ones digits.

1,699

1,681

2 Compare the digits in the same place from left to right. If the digits are the same, compare the digits in the next place to the right.

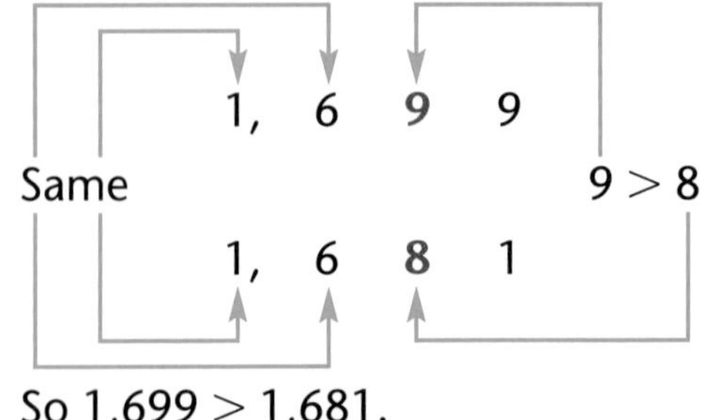

So 1,699 > 1,681.

Jan Stenerud has more career points.

Baseball's Addie Joss has a career earned run average (ERA) of 1.89, compared to Ed Walsh's ERA of 1.82. Whose ERA is less?

Example

You can order decimals by comparing their digits.

1 Line up the decimal points.

1.89
1.82

2 Compare the digits in the greatest place.

1.89
1.82

The ones digits are the same.

3 Compare the digits in the next greater place.

1.89
1.82

The tenths digits are the same.

4 Compare the digits in the least place.

1.89
1.82

$2 < 9$

So $1.82 < 1.89$.

Ed Walsh's ERA is less.

More Examples

A Order from least to greatest: 0.3335, 0.3330, and 0.3328

0.3335
0.3330
0.3328

$2 < 3$
So 0.3328 is less than 0.3335 and 0.3330.

0.3335
0.3330

$0 < 5$
So 0.3330 is less than 0.3335.

least → 0.3328
0.3330
greatest → 0.3335

B Compare. Write >, <, or =.

23,068,634,221 ● 23,068,934,221
$6 < 9$
So 23,068,634,221 < 23,068,934,221.

C Compare. Write >, <, or =.

5.176 ● 5
5.176 ● 5.000
$0 < 1$
So $5.176 > 5$.

Try It **Compare. Write >, <, or =.**

1. 19.107 ● 19.196
2. 0.565 ● 0.510
3. 8.01 ● 8.001
4. 0.201 ● 2.01
5. 99.9 ● 9.99
6. 2.221 ● 2.222
7. 1.4 ● 1.40
8. 0.11 ● 11
9. 8.76 ● 8.67

Explain how to compare 38.06 and 38.12.

Practice

Compare. Write >, <, or =.

10. 24,907 ● 249,007 **11.** 11,111,999 ● 8,952,665 **12.** 316,820,705 ● 316,830,705

13. 1.5 ● 1.45 **14.** 5.780 ● 5.708 **15.** 40.900 ● 40.9

Order from least to greatest.

16. 524,620; 8,843; 97,624

17. 104,600; 104,600.4; 104,060

18. 5.285; 5.825; 5.5; 5.28; 5

19. 0.56; 0.6; 0.509; 0.523; 0.556

20. 10.500; 0.500; 0.050; 1.050; 0.005

★**21.** 1.11; 1.1; 1.1111; 1.111; 1; 11.11

Find two numbers between the numbers given.

22. 2,022 and 2,023 **23.** 67.5 and 68 ★**24.** 7.05 and 7.06 ★**25.** 0.089 and 0.1

Algebra & functions **Find a missing digit that makes each sentence true.**

26. $7{,}058 > 7{,}0\blacksquare 8$ **27.** $23.\blacksquare 6 > 23.56$ **28.** $65{,}081 < 65.0\blacksquare 1$

29. $0.00\blacksquare 2 > 0.002$ **30.** $16.265 > 16.2\blacksquare$ **31.** $8{,}124.\blacksquare < 8{,}124.68$

32.

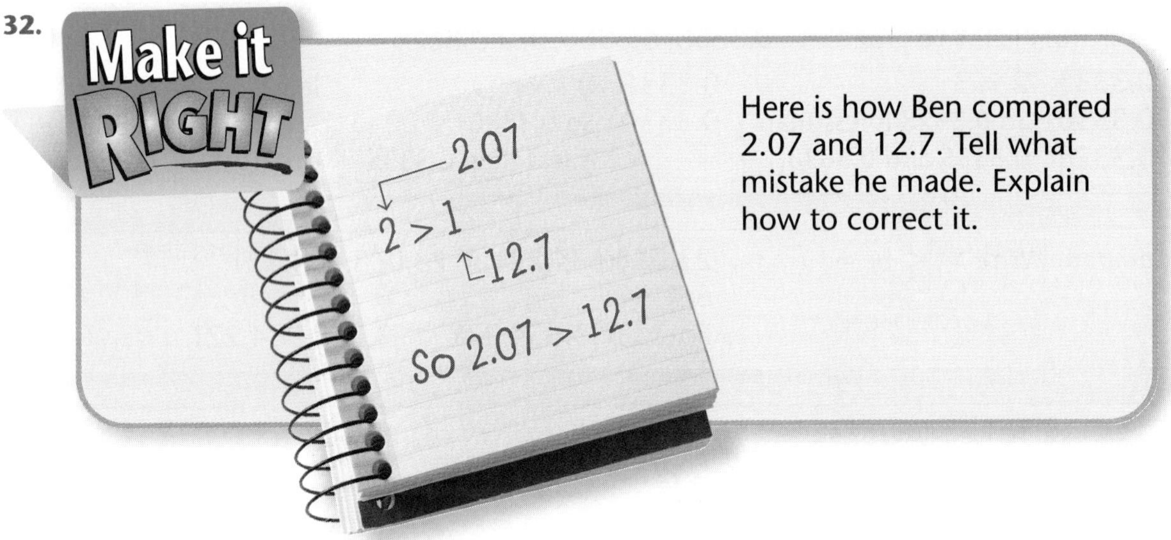

Here is how Ben compared 2.07 and 12.7. Tell what mistake he made. Explain how to correct it.

Problem Solving

33. The three largest sports stadiums are Strahov (Czech Republic), Maracana Municipa (Rio de Janeiro), and Rungrado (Pyungyang). They seat 240,000; 205,000; and 150,000 people, respectively. Which is the largest stadium?

34. **Logical Reasoning:** Leigh is on her school's speed skating team. She wants to be in first place on her team. The current top 3 records set by her teammates are 20.06 miles per hour, 20.20 miles per hour, and 20.31 miles per hour. What is the maximum speed Leigh must skate to be in first place?

35. Super Bowl XVI had a TV audience rating of 49.1. Super Bowl XVII had a rating of 48.6, and Super Bowl XX had a rating of 48.3. Which Super Bowl had the largest audience?

36. **Generalize:** How can you order three whole numbers with different numbers of digits without comparing the digits? Give an example.

Paralympics Swimming Records

	Butterfly	Freestyle	Freestyle (severely disabled)	Freestyle (very severely disabled)	Backstroke
Men	1 min. 2.44 sec.	56.4 sec.	1 min. 31.35 sec.	2 min. 41.94 sec.	1 min. 4.1 sec.
Women	1 min. 8.88 sec.	1 min. 8.16 sec.	1 min. 36.23 sec.	3 min. 9 sec.	1 min. 26.41 sec.

Use data from the table for problems 37–42.

37. Is the men's or women's time in the severely disabled freestyle category shorter?

38. Which race category has the shortest swim time?

39. What is the longest race time? For what event is that?

40. Rank the women's records from the slowest time to the fastest time.

41. **Create a problem** that can be answered by using the table. Include comparing and ordering numbers in your problem.

★42. If the women's severely disabled freestyle time were shortened by 5 seconds, would the men still have a faster time? Explain.

Spiral Review and Test Prep

Complete.

43. $8 \times 10 = \blacksquare$
$8 \times 100 = \blacksquare$
$8 \times 1{,}000 = \blacksquare$
$8 \times 10{,}000 = \blacksquare$

44. $3 \times \blacksquare = 30$
$3 \times \blacksquare = 300$
$3 \times \blacksquare = 3{,}000$
$3 \times \blacksquare = 30{,}000$

45. $\blacksquare \times 10 = 50$
$5 \times 100 = \blacksquare$
$5 \times 1{,}000 = \blacksquare$
$5 \times \blacksquare = 50{,}000$

Choose the correct answer.

46. Find a number that when multiplied by 12 gives you a product of 72.

A. 12
B. 9
C. 6
D. Not Here

47. Which of the following is not equal to 360?

F. 45×8
G. 120×3
H. 360×1
J. 60×8

Objective: Review using the four-step process to solve problems.

1·5

Problem Solving: Reading for Math

Use the Four-Step Process

World's Tallest Buildings

Read These three famous American buildings have all held the tallest building title at one time—the Empire State Building (1,250 feet), the Chrysler Building (1,046 feet), and the Sears Tower (1,450 feet). List these skyscrapers from tallest to shortest.

READING SKILL ▶

Steps in a Process

A **process** is a series of steps. The four-step process will help you solve problems. The steps are read, plan, solve, and look back.

- **What do you know?** The height of each building
- **What do you need to find?** The buildings listed from tallest to shortest

MATH SKILL ▶

Use the Four-Step Process

- Read the problem. Identify what you need to find.
- Decide what actions you will take and in what order.
- Follow your plan to solve the problem.
- Look back to see that you have answered the question. Check that the answer is reasonable.

Plan Compare the heights of the buildings.

Solve

Compare the Empire State Building and Chrysler Building.

$1,250 > 1,046$

Compare the Empire State Building and the Sears Tower.

$1,250 < 1,450$

The order from tallest to shortest is Sears Tower, Empire State Building, Chrysler Building.

Look Back Did you answer the question?

How did using the four-step process help you solve the problem?

Solve. Use the four-step process.

1. The John Hancock Building in Chicago is 1,127 feet tall. Another skyscraper in Chicago, the Amoco Building, is 1,136 feet tall. Which building is taller?
2. First Interstate Plaza in Houston is 973 feet tall. Central Plaza in Hong Kong is 1,227 feet tall. List these two buildings and the Chrysler Building from shortest to tallest.

Use data from the table for problems 3–7.

3. List the Smith Tower, the Equitable Building, and Philadelphia's City Hall from tallest to shortest.
4. List the Woolworth, Equitable, and Travelers Insurance buildings from shortest to tallest.
5. Which of the buildings was built first?
6. Which two buildings are about the same height?
7. Is it true that every new skyscraper built before 1920 was taller than those built earlier? Explain.

Buildings Constructed Before 1920 (Height in Feet)

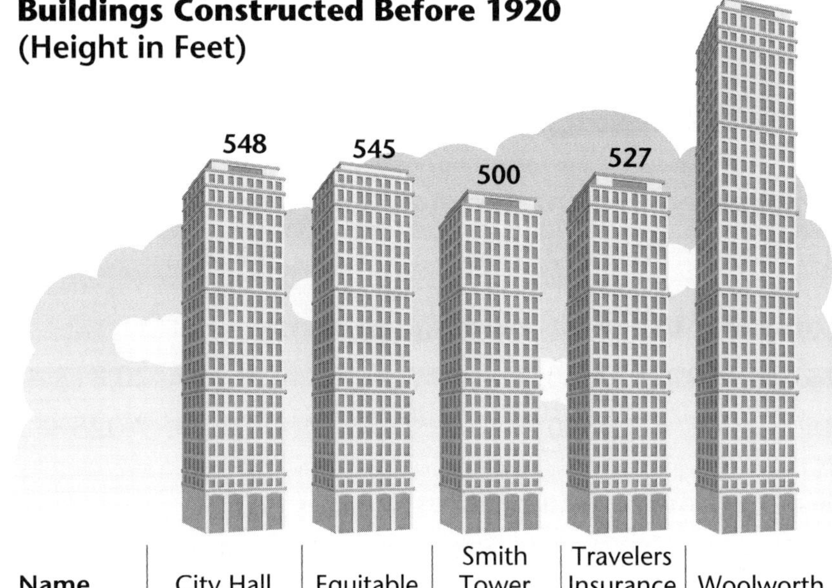

Name	City Hall	Equitable	Smith Tower	Travelers Insurance	Woolworth
City	Philadelphia	New York	Seattle	Hartford	New York
Year Built	1901	1915	1914	1919	1913

Source: World's Tallest Buildings—Marshall Gerometta's Hot 500

8. **Create a problem** about tall buildings that you would solve using the four-step process. Give it to another student to solve.

Spiral Review and Test Prep

Choose the correct answer.

The Bank of China Building in Hong Kong is 1,209 feet tall and the Texas Commerce Tower in Houston is 1,002 feet tall. Which building is taller?

9. Which statement is true?
   - A. Both buildings are in China.
   - B. The Texas Commerce Tower is 1,202 feet tall.
   - C. The Bank of China Building is 1,209 feet tall.
   - D. Texas is in China.
10. According to the four-step process, what follows reading the problem?
    - F. See if the answer is reasonable.
    - G. Check the answer.
    - H. Decide what actions you will take to solve the problem.
    - J. Follow your plan.

Extra Practice, page 38

Check Your Progress A

Name the place and write the value of each underlined digit. **(pages 2–3)**

1. 47,834,009 2. 204,000,652,956 3. 385,857,373,000 4. 1,000,000,001
5. 7.4538 6. 4.1907 7. 9.5671 8. 0.0311

Write the decimal and the fraction. **(pages 4–5)**

9. 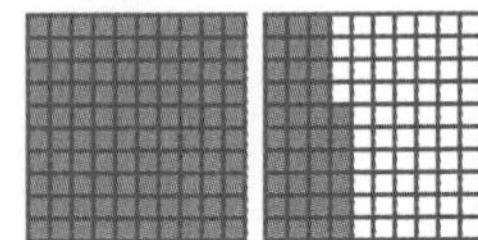
10. 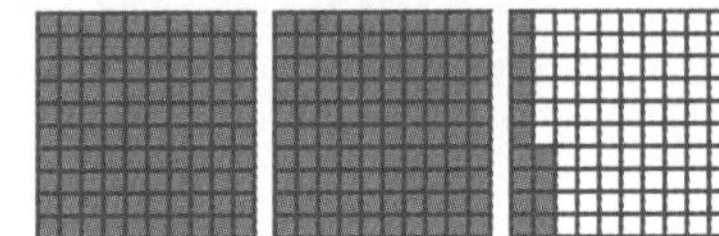
11. 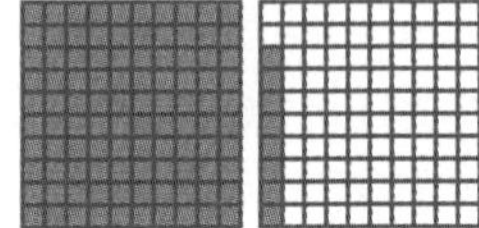

Name an equivalent decimal. **(pages 6–9)**

12. 1.5 13. 0.307 14. 4 15. 2.05

Compare. Use >, <, or =. **(pages 10–13)**

16. 145,191 ● 145,051
17. 20,813,467,006 ● 20,843,978,356
18. 3.4067 ● 3.4580
19. 7.025 ● 7.0206

Order from least to greatest. **(pages 10–13)**

20. 80,745,631; 76,003,471; 76,356,812; 79,956,431
21. 2.0287; 0.287; 1.8954; 1.0287; 2.2087
22. 0.04; 4.00; 0.40; 0.004; 0.44

Solve. **(pages 2–15)**

23. Since 1991 Japan has put 325,000 robots to work in industrial plants. What is the place and value of the 3 in this number?

24. The fastest speed ever reached by a standing person on a skateboard was 55.43 miles per hour. The fastest luge was recorded at 85.38 miles per hour and the fastest water skier went 143.08 miles per hour. The fastest a horse ever galloped was 43.26 miles per hour. Order these speeds from fastest to slowest.

25. The oldest person ever to compete in the Olympics was athlete Patrick McDonald. He won a medal in 1920 at the age of 42 years and 26 days. He won his medal in an event called the 25.4-kilogram weight throw. Find an equivalent decimal for that weight. Explain.

Use Place-Value Models to Compare Decimals

Hannah ran 2.442 miles and Jon ran 2.434 miles. Who ran the farthest?

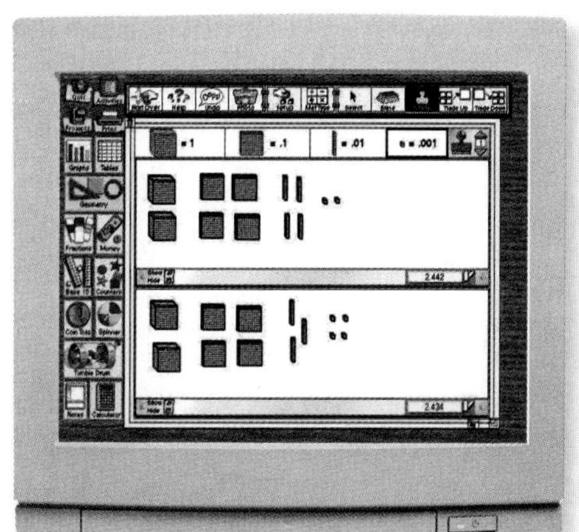

You can build a model of the number of miles each person ran using place-value or base-ten models.

- Use a mat with two sections open.
- In the top section, start with the ones and stamp out 2.442.
- In the bottom section, start with the ones and stamp out 2.434.

The number boxes keep count as you stamp.

Who ran the farthest?

Use the computer to model each number. Then name the greater number.

1. 4.145 and 4.154
2. 6.207 and 6.203
3. 5.038 and 5.049
4. 7.034 and 7.304

Solve.

5. Ramón paid $1.569 for a gallon of gas and Kendra paid $1.589. Who paid the most?
6. Nanci's home is 3.672 kilometers from the library. Carman's home is 3.583 kilometers from the library. Whose home is closest to the library?
7. **Analyze:** How does using the model help you decide which number is greater?

For more practice, use Math Traveler™.

Objective: Review adding and subtracting whole numbers and decimals.

1·6 Add and Subtract Whole Numbers and Decimals

Math in ACTION

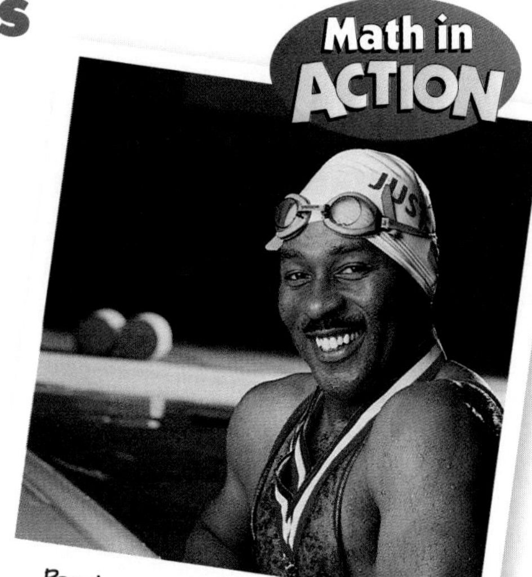
Paralympic athlete Curtis Lovejoy

Learn

Curtis Lovejoy earned the fastest 50-meter breaststroke race time ever at the Paralympic Swimming Trials, the Olympic trials for disabled athletes. Suppose an athlete training for the trials swims each lap of a four-lap race in the times of 54.73, 54.56, 54.32, and 54.54 seconds. What is the total time?

Example 1

Add the four numbers.

Remember: When you regroup, you rename numbers in a different way. For example, you can rename 10 ones as 1 ten.

1 Line up the decimal points. Write an equivalent decimal if necessary.

```
  54.73
  54.56
  54.32
 +54.54
```

2 Add the decimal places first, from right to left. Regroup if necessary.

```
    1
  54.73
  54.56
  54.32
 +54.54
    .15
```

3 Add the whole numbers. Write the decimal point.

```
  1 2 1
  54.73
  54.56
  54.32
 +54.54
 218.15
```

The total time would be 218.15 seconds.

More Examples

A

```
   2 11
 $4,624
    829
 +  556
 $6,009
```

B

```
  2 12
  2.995
  0.867
 +0.929
  4.791
```

C

```
  1
  2.16
  1.30
 +0.83
  4.29
```

Greg Louganis shares the record for the most Olympic medals in diving—five. In the 1984 Olympics, he scored an all-time record of 754.41 points. In 1988 he earned a total of 730.8. How much higher did he score in 1984 than in 1988?

Example 2

Find: 754.41 − 730.8

1 Line up the decimal points. Write an equivalent decimal if necessary.

$$\begin{array}{r} 754.41 \\ -730.80 \\ \hline \end{array}$$

2 Write the decimal point. Subtract the decimals from right to left. Regroup if necessary.

$$\begin{array}{r} 754.41 \\ -730.80 \\ \hline .61 \end{array}$$

3 Subtract the whole numbers from right to left. Regroup if necessary.

$$\begin{array}{r} 754.41 \\ -730.80 \\ \hline \mathbf{23.61} \end{array}$$

Check by adding: 23.61 + 730.80 = 754.41.

Louganis earned 23.61 more points in 1984 than in 1988.

More Examples

D

$$\begin{array}{r} 6{,}284 \\ -1{,}839 \\ \hline 4{,}445 \end{array}$$

E

$$\begin{array}{r} 8{,}628.000 \\ -\quad 1.090 \\ \hline 8{,}626.910 \end{array}$$

F

$$\begin{array}{r} \$14.50 \\ -\quad 1.35 \\ \hline \$13.15 \end{array}$$

Try It **Add or subtract.**

1. $\begin{array}{r} 9.4 \\ +5.72 \\ \hline \end{array}$
2. $\begin{array}{r} 3{,}824 \\ +\ 739 \\ \hline \end{array}$
3. $\begin{array}{r} \$16.25 \\ +\ 5.08 \\ \hline \end{array}$
4. $\begin{array}{r} 2{,}458 \\ -\ 506 \\ \hline \end{array}$
5. $\begin{array}{r} 15.1 \\ -\ 7.37 \\ \hline \end{array}$
6. 1.6 + 0.89
7. 2.005 − 0.123
8. 7,336 − 2,984
9. $3.58 − $0.73
10. 2.45 − 1.3
11. 21 + 4.51
12. 0.34 − 0.04
13. 3.11 + 2.31 + 0.35

Why is it necessary to line up decimal points when adding or subtracting decimals?

Practice **Add or subtract.**

14. $\begin{array}{r} 18{,}721 \\ -14{,}657 \\ \hline \end{array}$
15. $\begin{array}{r} 29{,}238 \\ +51{,}698 \\ \hline \end{array}$
16. $\begin{array}{r} 215{,}075 \\ +\quad 6{,}025 \\ \hline \end{array}$
17. $\begin{array}{r} 800{,}000 \\ -411{,}132 \\ \hline \end{array}$
18. $\begin{array}{r} 382{,}500 \\ -\quad 17{,}986 \\ \hline \end{array}$

19. $\begin{array}{r} 80.123 \\ +91.608 \\ \hline \end{array}$
20. $\begin{array}{r} 3.7 \\ -0.96 \\ \hline \end{array}$
21. $\begin{array}{r} 43.906 \\ -\quad 0.387 \\ \hline \end{array}$
22. $\begin{array}{r} \$317.21 \\ +\ 113.75 \\ \hline \end{array}$
23. $\begin{array}{r} 31.0678 \\ -\quad 0.1678 \\ \hline \end{array}$

24. $\begin{array}{r} 509{,}378{,}226 \\ +478{,}302{,}886 \\ \hline \end{array}$
25. $\begin{array}{r} 33.782 \\ -21.0712 \\ \hline \end{array}$
26. $\begin{array}{r} 206{,}781{,}100 \\ -188{,}990{,}357 \\ \hline \end{array}$

27. 16.1265 + 0.847
★28. 79,000 − 658
★29. 107.55 − 78.268

Choose the sum that is greater.

30. A. 4,590 + 380
    B. 4,375 + 206

31. A. 230,000 + 170,000
    B. 250,000 + 210,000

32. A. 1.223 + 0.256
    B. 15.05 + 0.89

★33. A. 30,600 + 7,200 + 4,000
    B. 1,050 + 2,050 + 8,380

Identify the symbol that makes the number sentence true.

34. 18.431 ● 6.89 = 11.541
35. 3.703 ● 1.45 = 2.253
36. 1.587 ● 0.609 = 2.196
★37. 7.048 + 6.978 ● 14.926

38.

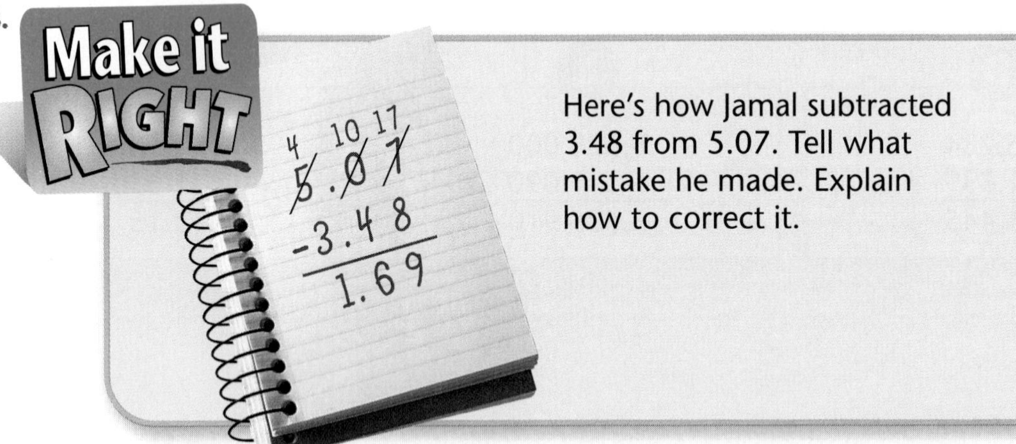

Here's how Jamal subtracted 3.48 from 5.07. Tell what mistake he made. Explain how to correct it.

Problem Solving

39. Emma George holds both the indoor and outdoor women's pole vault records. She vaulted 4.55 meters indoors and 4.58 meters outdoors. How much higher did she vault outdoors than indoors?

40. **Health:** Olympic athletes—and all people—can strengthen their hearts with exercise. The average male's heart weighs 11.1 ounces. The average female's heart weighs 9.3 ounces. How much more does the average male's heart weigh than the average female's?

Use data from the table for problems 41–49.

Olympic Event Ticket Prices

Event	Gymnastics	Figure Skating	Downhill Racing	Ski Jumping
Adult	$37.50	$42.75	$62.25	$58.75
Child	$25.50	$32.25	$52.00	$47.75

41. Order the adult events from least expensive to most expensive.
42. Which is the least expensive event for a child? the most expensive?
43. Find the cost of two adult tickets for the figure skating event.
44. How much more does an adult's ski jumping ticket cost than a child's?
45. How much would it cost one adult to attend each of the 4 events?
46. How much would it cost for one child to go to all of the events?
47. A family of 5 has $300 to spend on ski jump tickets. If there are 2 adults and 3 children, how much money will they have left over?
48. **Create a problem** using the information from the table. Solve it, and give it to another student to solve.

★ 49. **Number Sense:** Two adults want to go to an event together. They have $100 to spend on tickets. Which events can they go to? Why?

50. **Compare:** How are adding and subtracting decimals alike?

Spiral Review and Test Prep

51. $\frac{1}{2} + \frac{1}{2}$
52. $\frac{2}{5} + \frac{4}{5}$
53. $\frac{1}{5} + \frac{1}{6}$
54. $3 + \frac{6}{5}$

Choose the correct answer.

55. Simplify this expression and choose a number that is equal to it. $6 + (4 \times 7)$
    - A. 15
    - B. 17
    - C. 34
    - D. Not Here

56. A dozen eggs has 5 brown ones and 7 white ones. What fraction of the eggs is brown?
    - F. $\frac{5}{12}$
    - G. $\frac{7}{12}$
    - H. $\frac{5}{7}$
    - J. $\frac{12}{5}$

Objective: Review estimating sums and differences of whole numbers and decimals.

1·7 Estimate Sums and Differences

Learn

Math Words

round to find the nearest value of a number based on a given place value

estimate to find a number that is close to the exact answer

People will often do interesting things to set a world record. In 1987, John Kenmuir ate 14 hard-boiled eggs in 14.42 seconds. How do you round this number to the nearest tenth?

14 eggs in 14.42 seconds

Example 1

You can use a number line to help you **round** 14.42.

Think: 14.42 is closer to 14.4 than to 14.5

14.42

14.40 14.45 14.50

You can round 14.42 to the nearest tenth without a number line.

1 Underline the place to which you want to round.

14.<u>4</u>2

2 Look at the digit to the right.

14.<u>4</u>**2**

3 If the digit is 5 or greater, round up. If the digit is less than 5, round down.

14.4

Think: Since 2 < 5, round down to 14.4.

Kenmuir's record is 14.4 seconds, rounded to the nearest tenth.

More Examples

A

Round to the nearest ten: 2,378

2,3<u>7</u>8

8 > 5 Round up.

2,378 → 2,380

B

Round to the nearest dollar: $178.39

$17<u>8</u>.39

3 < 5 Round down.

$178.39 → $178.00

C

Round to the nearest hundredth: 6.955

6.9<u>5</u>5

5 = 5 Round up.

6.955 → 6.96

You can round to **estimate** sums and differences of whole numbers and decimals.

Example 2

Estimate: 6,138 + 7, 315

Round to the nearest thousand.
Add the rounded numbers.

$$\begin{array}{rcr} 6{,}138 & \rightarrow & 6{,}000 \\ +7{,}315 & \rightarrow & +7{,}000 \\ \hline & & 13{,}000 \end{array}$$

6,138 and 7,315 is about 13,000.

Example 3

Estimate: 8.23 − 1.87

Round to the nearest whole number.
Subtract the rounded numbers.

$$\begin{array}{rcr} 8.23 & \rightarrow & 8 \\ -1.87 & \rightarrow & -2 \\ \hline & & 6 \end{array}$$

8.23 − 1.87 is about 6.

More Examples

You must use the context of the problem to decide which place to round to.

How accurate you want the estimate to be will determine to which place you round. In general, larger numbers can round to places such as tens or hundreds. Smaller numbers can round to places such as ones or tens. Decimals can be rounded to tenths or whole numbers.

Estimate the difference.

$$\begin{array}{rcr} 283.476 & \rightarrow & 300 \\ -\ 62.733 & \rightarrow & -\ 60 \\ \hline & & 240 \end{array}$$

Think: Round 283.476 to the nearest hundred. Round 62.733 to the nearest ten.

E

Estimate the sum.

$$\begin{array}{rcr} 344.27 & \rightarrow & 344 \\ 1{,}866.082 & \rightarrow & 1{,}866 \\ +\ 135.466 & & +\ 135 \\ \hline & & 2{,}345 \end{array}$$

Think: Round to the nearest whole number.

F

Estimate the difference.

$$\begin{array}{rcr} 2{,}117.1 & \rightarrow & 2{,}117 \\ -112.62 & \rightarrow & -\ 113 \\ \hline & & 2{,}004 \end{array}$$

Think: Round to the nearest whole number.

Try It

Round to the underlined place.

1. $\underline{7}$,560
2. $\underline{1}$1.029
3. 28.4$\underline{4}$13
4. \$2,21$\underline{5}$.42
5. 9.$\underline{3}$069

Estimate each sum or difference. Show your work.

6. $\begin{array}{r} 33.56 \\ +0.67 \\ \hline \end{array}$
7. $\begin{array}{r} 25.21 \\ -22.843 \\ \hline \end{array}$
8. $\begin{array}{r} 40.23 \\ +26.46 \\ \hline \end{array}$
9. $\begin{array}{r} \$116.86 \\ +\ \ 54.31 \\ \hline \end{array}$

Explain how you would estimate the sum of 412.3 and 81.6.

Practice

Round to the underlined place.

10. $\underline{4}$,501 **11.** 64,8$\underline{7}$5 **12.** 91.$\underline{4}$4 **13.** 25,7$\underline{0}$4 **14.** 43.3$\underline{9}$2

15. 13.$\underline{8}$6 **16.** 83,48$\underline{6}$,096 **17.** 1.00$\underline{1}$8 ★**18.** 2,395.$\underline{9}$8 ★**19.** 0.$\underline{9}$701

Round to the place indicated.

20. 756 (hundreds) **21.** 4,831 (thousands) **22.** 17.787 (tenths)

23. $5.57 (dollar) **24.** 1.015 (hundredths) **25.** $17.787 (cent)

26. 59.9999 (ones) ★**27.** 30,904 (ten thousands) ★**28.** 4.0372 (thousandths)

Estimate each sum or difference. Show your work.

29. $\begin{array}{r} 6.24 \\ +0.09 \\ \hline \end{array}$ **30.** $\begin{array}{r} 0.85 \\ +1.095 \\ \hline \end{array}$ **31.** $\begin{array}{r} 34.38 \\ -12.831 \\ \hline \end{array}$ **32.** $\begin{array}{r} \$24.86 \\ -\ 12.49 \\ \hline \end{array}$

33. 53.9 + 6.9 **34.** 834 − 518 **35.** 1,394 − 623 **36.** 74 + 82 + 96

37. 7.6 + 3.37 + 5.4 **38.** 18.8 − 9.93 **39.** 2.83 + 5.91 **40.** 9.06 − 6.7

★**41.** 457 + 25 ★**42.** 102.3 – 5.6 ★**43.** 0.84 + 5.77 ★**44.** 9.06 − 0.13

Use the numbers in the box. Estimate to find two numbers that have:

45. A sum of about 600.

46. A difference of about 400.

47. A sum of about 1,100.

★**48.** A difference of about 700.

49.

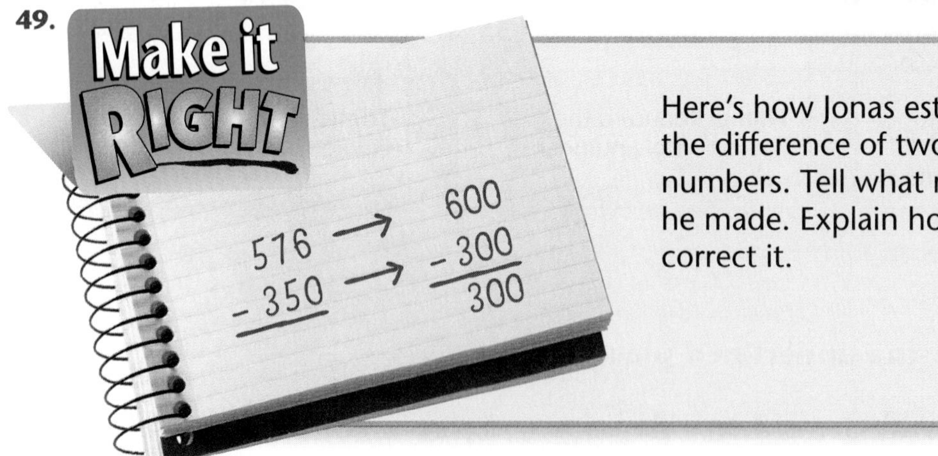

Here's how Jonas estimated the difference of two numbers. Tell what mistake he made. Explain how to correct it.

Problem Solving

50. Science: The African bush elephant weighs between 4.4 and 7.7 tons. What is the least and greatest weight, rounded to the nearest ton?

51. Art: Pablo Picasso's *Self-Portrait* is one of the most expensive paintings to be sold in the United States. It sold for $43,500,000 in 1989. Write the price in expanded form.

52. **Explain:** Two students estimated 22,376 + 5,780. One student's estimate was 28,000. The other student's estimate was 30,000. Explain how each student might have estimated.

53. In 1999 Michael Flatley was the theater's best-paid actor. He earned $83,215 each week for his performances. About how much did he earn in one month?

54. In 1986 Tony Dowdeswell ate 3 pounds, 6 ounces of unmelted ice cream in 31.46 seconds. Round the time to the nearest tenth of a second.

55. In 1986 Peter Dowdeswell ate 300 feet of spaghetti in 12.02 seconds. Round the time to the nearest tenth of a second.

56. **Analyze:** Estimate the sum of 527 + 341. Will the estimated sum be greater or less than the exact sum? Explain why.

★ 57. **Explain** why money amounts are often rounded to the hundredths place.

Use data from *Did You Know?* for problems 58–61.

58. About how long was *The Mousetrap* performed at the Ambassadors Theater in London?

59. About how long was it performed at St. Martin's Theater through 1998?

60. For about how many years did the play run at these two theaters in London combined?

61. Estimate the number of performances given at St. Martin's Theater through 1998.

62. **Create a problem** about estimation. Solve it and give it to another student to solve.

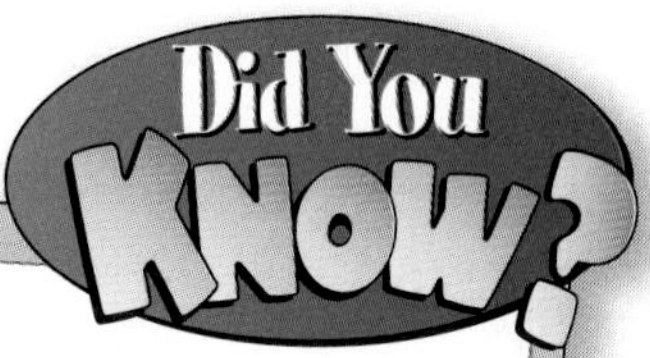

The Mousetrap, a play by Agatha Christie, opened at the Ambassadors Theater, London, in 1952. In 1974, after 8,862 performances, it moved next door to St. Martin's Theater. By 1998 the 18,944th performance took place.

Spiral Review and Test Prep

63. 65 × 212

64. 1,875 ÷ 125

65. 47 × 111

66. 912 ÷ 12

67. 21 × 21

68. 480 ÷ 15

Choose the correct answer.

69. Which of the following is not a part of the 7 × 8 fact family?
   - A. 56 ÷ 7 = 8
   - B. 7 + 8 = 15
   - C. 8 × 7 = 56
   - D. 56 ÷ 8 = 7

70. Seven more than a number is 18. What is the number?
   - F. 7
   - G. 11
   - H. 18
   - J. 25

Objective: Solve problems by finding a pattern.

Problem Solving: Strategy
Find a Pattern

Stefka Kostadinnova

Read

Read the problem carefully.

When a high jumper practices, the bar is raised a small amount after each successful jump. If the bar starts at 5 feet, 6 inches and increases 0.5 inch after each successful jump, how high will the bar be on the 5th jump?

- **What do you know?** The bar starts at 5 feet, 6 inches and is raised 0.5 inch each time.
- **What are you asked to find?** How high the bar will be after 5 successful jumps

Plan

One way to solve the problem is to find a pattern.

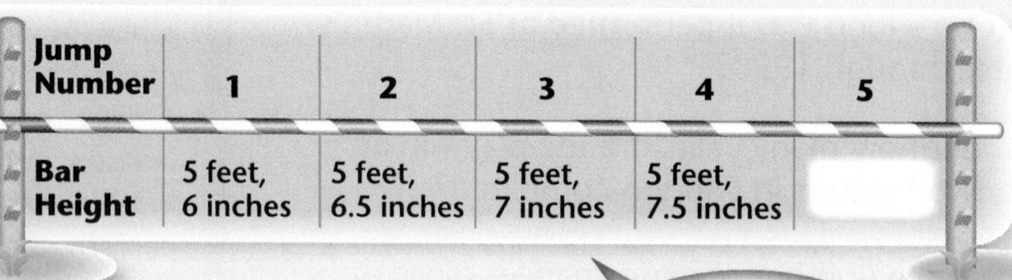

Jump Number	1	2	3	4	5
Bar Height	5 feet, 6 inches	5 feet, 6.5 inches	5 feet, 7 inches	5 feet, 7.5 inches	

The pattern is add 0.5 inch each time.

Think:
6 inches + 0.5 inch = 6.5 inches
6.5 inches + 0.5 inch = 7 inches

Solve

Continue the pattern to predict the height for the fifth jump.

Jump 5: 5 feet, 7.5 inches + 0.5 inch = 5 feet, 8 inches

The bar will be set at 5 feet, 8 inches for the fifth jump.

Note: This type of pattern is called a linear pattern. Linear patterns involve adding or subtracting the same amount at each step.

Look Back

Is the answer reasonable? How can you check the answer?

Would it make sense to continue the pattern forever? Explain.

Practice Find a pattern to solve.

1. A high school student practices the high jump, starting the bar at 3 feet, 4 inches and raising the bar 0.5 inch after each successful jump. How high will the bar be after 4 jumps?

2. A college high jumper starts the bar at 4 feet and raises it 0.25 inch after each jump. How high will the bar be after 3 jumps?

3. An Olympic athlete starts the bar at 5 feet 4 inches and raises it 0.25 inch after each jump. How high will the bar be after 9 jumps?

4. Like high jumpers, pole vaulters also raise the bar with each successful vault. If the bar begins at 10 feet, 8 inches and raises 1 inch with each vault, how high will the bar be after 6 successful attempts?

Problem Solving

Mixed Strategy Review

5. **Number Sense:** What are three consecutive whole numbers whose sum is 63?

6. An equilateral triangle has a perimeter of 24 meters. What is the length of each side of the triangle?

7. A group of friends playing "Limbo" decide to lower the bar 1 inch after each successful pass under the bar. If the bar starts at 4 feet, what height will the bar be after 3 successful passes?

8. Kayla balanced twice as many glasses as Petra. Petra balanced 80 glasses fewer than Chico. Chico balanced 230 glasses. How many glasses did Kayla balance?

CHOOSE A STRATEGY
- Logical Reasoning
- Draw a Diagram
- Make a Graph
- Make a Table or List
- Find a Pattern
- Guess and Check
- Write an Equation
- Work Backward
- Solve a Simpler Problem
- Conduct an Experiment

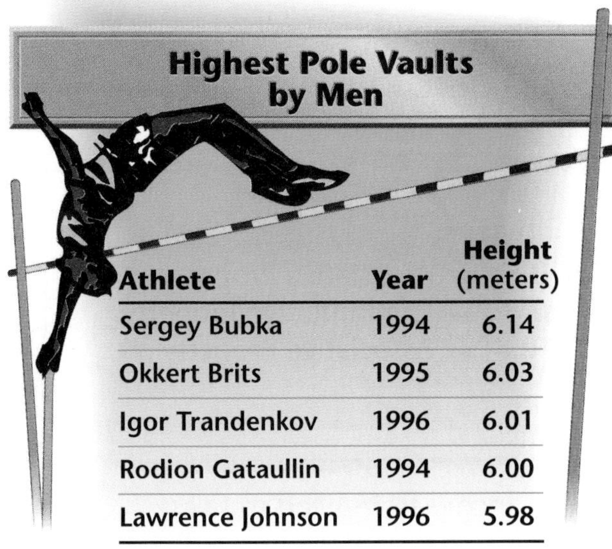

Highest Pole Vaults by Men

Athlete	Year	Height (meters)
Sergey Bubka	1994	6.14
Okkert Brits	1995	6.03
Igor Trandenkov	1996	6.01
Rodion Gataullin	1994	6.00
Lawrence Johnson	1996	5.98

Use data from the table for problems 9–10.

9. Which vaulter holds the record for the highest pole vault by a man?

10. Do you think any male athlete will pole vault higher than 7 meters before the year 2010? Use logical reasoning to explain.

Extra Practice, page 39

1•9

Objective: Review properties of addition. Review using mental math strategies to add and subtract.

Properties of Addition

Algebra & functions

Learn

Math Words

Commutative Property

Associative Property

Identity Property

Compensation process by which you change the values of numbers to add or subtract mentally

The world's smallest rodent is the pygmy mouse. How long is the pygmy mouse from head to tail?

You can use the properties of addition to solve the problem.

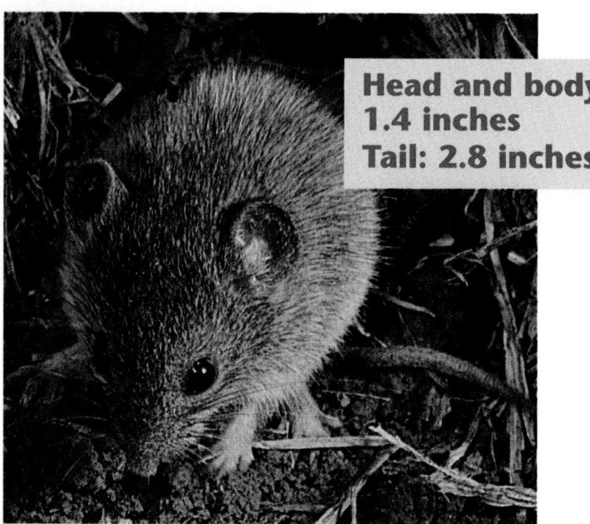

Commutative Property

The order of the addends does not change the sum.

$3 + 4 = 4 + 3$

Associative Property

The way the addends are grouped does not change the sum.

$(6 + 7) + 3 = 6 + (7 + 3)$

Identity Property

The sum of any number and 0 equals the number.

$5 + 0 = 5$

Example 1

Think: $1.4 = 1 + 0.4$
$2.8 = 2 + 0.8$

$1.4 + 2.8$

$$\begin{aligned}1.4 + 2.8 &= (1 + 0.4) + (2 + 0.8) \\ &= 1 + (0.4 + 2) + 0.8 && \leftarrow \text{Associative Property} \\ &= 1 + (2 + 0.4) + 0.8 && \leftarrow \text{Commutative Property} \\ &= (1 + 2) + (0.4 + 0.8) && \leftarrow \text{Associative Property} \\ &= 3 + 1.2 \\ &= 4.2\end{aligned}$$

The pygmy mouse measures 4.2 inches from head to tail.

The world's smallest true primate is called the pygmy mouse lemur (not to be confused with the pygmy mouse). Its head and body measures 2.4 inches and its tail reaches 5.3 inches. How long is the animal from head to tail?

Example 2

Sometimes you can use **compensation** to add mentally.

Think: To use compensation for addition, add a number to one addend and subtract the number from the other.

2.4	+	5.3		
↓− 0.4		↓ + 0.4		
2.0	+	5.7	=	7.7

The pygmy mouse lemur measures 7.7 inches from head to tail.

Example 3

You can also use compensation to subtract mentally.

Find: 3.9 − 1.3

Think: To use compensation to subtract, add the same amount to both numbers.

3.9	−	1.3		
↓ + 0.7		↓ + 0.7		
4.6	−	2.0	=	2.6

3.9 − 1.3 = 2.6

More Examples

A

298	+	515		
↓ + 2		↓ − 2		
300	+	513	=	813

B

362	−	297		
↓ + 3		↓ + 3		
365	−	300	=	65

Try It **Add or subtract. Describe your work.**

1. 29 + 15 + 11
2. 98 + 64
3. 62 − 19
4. 375 − 96
5. 3.38 + 4.7
6. 29.5 − 1.78
7. 82.9 + 3.7
8. 4.54 − 2.46
9. 18 + 24
10. 4.9 − 1.1
11. 3.2 + 1.5
12. 2 − 0.9

Explain how you could use compensation to find 497 + 325.

Practice

Identify the addition property used to rewrite each problem.

13. $7 + 65 + 13 = 7 + 13 + 65$
14. $(4 + 0.75) + 0.25 = 4 + (0.75 + 0.25)$
15. $223 + 150 + 27 = 27 + 223 + 150$
16. $(22 + 37) + 13 = 22 + (37 + 13)$
17. $349 + (21 + 51) = (349 + 21) + 51$
18. $598 + 202 = 202 + 598$
19. $65.13 + 11 + 0.87 = 65.13 + 0.87 + 11$
20. $15 + 12 + 5 = 15 + 5 + 12$
21. $43 + (57 + 27) = (43 + 57) + 27$
22. $\$3.25 + \$7.50 = \$7.50 + \$3.25$
23. $678 + 0 = 678$

★24. $42 + 9 + 8 + 1 = (42 + 8) + (9 + 1)$

Add or subtract. Describe your work.

25. $46 + 31$
26. $537 + 98$
27. $598 + 202$
28. $39 + 45$
29. $759 - 401$
30. $193 - 68$
31. $\$136 - \$98$
32. $27 + 42$
33. $5.89 + 3.07$
34. $45.08 - 32.02$

★35. $69.1 - 28.09$

★36. $2 - 1.88$

Algebra & functions **Find the number that makes each sentence true.**

37. $8.3 + 0.5 = 8.0 + \square$
38. $7 + 9 + 3 = \square + 10$
39. $13 + 0 + 37 = 37 + \square$
40. $123 = \square + 123$
41. $\square + 2.5 = 2.0 + 0.8$
42. $(8 + 1.6) + 0.4 = 8 + (\square + 0.4)$
43.

Here's how Lee used compensation to add 129 + 67 mentally. Tell what mistake he made. Explain how to correct it.

Problem Solving

44. The top 3 countries with the most Asian elephants are India (24,000), Myanmar (6,000), and Indonesia (4,500). Use the Associative Property to group these numbers and find the total number of elephants in these three countries.

45. Faisal collects data on the number of threatened bird species. The top 5 countries have the following number of threatened species—104, 103, 90, 86, and 73. He then adds to find the total. Does the order in which he adds the numbers affect the outcome? Explain.

46. **Compare:** How is the Commutative Property different from the Associative Property?

Use data from the table for problems 47–48.

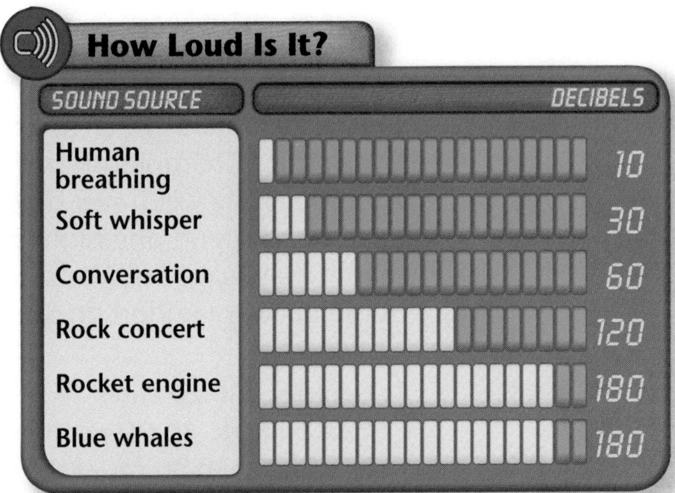

How Loud Is It?	
SOUND SOURCE	DECIBELS
Human breathing	10
Soft whisper	30
Conversation	60
Rock concert	120
Rocket engine	180
Blue whales	180

47. **Science:** Blue whales communicate with low-frequency pulses of up to 180 decibels. This is the loudest sound made by a living animal. How much louder do whales communicate than humans?

48. How much louder is a conversation than a soft whisper?

Use data from *Did You Know?* for problems 49–50.

49. How do you write 17,056 in expanded form?

50. What is the height of the area in which the Tibetan loach has been found, rounded to the nearest thousand feet?

Did You
KNOW?
The highest-living fish is the Tibetan loach, which has been found in the Himalayan Mountains at an altitude of 17,056 feet.

51. **Science:** The greatest difference in size between a male and female of the same species is with the *Bonella viridis*, a type of spoon worm. The female reaches lengths up to 36 inches, while the male is only 0.05 inches. What is the difference in size?

52. **Analyze:** If you had no paper and pencil, how would you find \$53.70 + \$46.55? Explain your steps.

53. **Collect Data:** Make a list of five animals. Ask 20 people to choose their favorite from the animals on your list. Graph your results.

Spiral Review and Test Prep

54. Order from least to greatest: $\frac{1}{2}, \frac{1}{3}, \frac{1}{4}$.

55. Order from greatest to least: $\frac{6}{8}, \frac{2}{5}, \frac{4}{7}$.

Choose the correct answer.

56. What is the value of 4 dimes and 5 nickels?
    - A. 45 cents
    - B. 55 cents
    - C. 65 cents
    - D. 70 cents

57. What time is 1 hour after 5:30?
    - F. 4:30
    - G. 5:29
    - H. 5:31
    - J. 6:30

Objective: Apply addition and subtraction to making decisions.

Problem Solving: Application

Decision Making

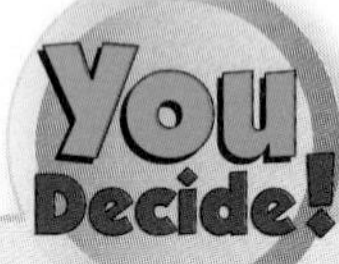

Which hotel should they stay in to keep within their budget for the trip?

Tony and Tamara Green are representing their school at the World Gymnastics Championship. Their combined budget for the trip is $300.00. They will travel by bus, purchase souvenir T-shirts and meals, and spend one night in a hotel. A parent must accompany them. They leave for Weston at 10:00 A.M. on Saturday and arrive home in New London on Sunday at 11:00 A.M.

T-shirts: $10.25 each
Meal budget: $5.00 per meal, per person
Bus fare: $45.30 for each round-trip bus ticket from New London to Weston

WESTON AREA ACCOMMODATIONS

Accommodations	Basic rate per room for 2 people	Charge for each extra person	Transportation from hotel to tournament
Motel Weston	$70.00 per night	$15.00 per night	$30.00 by taxi —total for all
Weston Inn	$89.00 per night	No charge	$20.00 by taxi —total for all
Travel Inn at Weston	$75.00 per night	$5.00 per night	$25.00 by taxi —total for all
Weston Hotel and Convention Center	$85.00 per night	$10.00 per night	No charge—tournament being held in convention center

Read for Understanding

1. How many people in the Green family need to go to the tournament?
2. Does the $300 budget apply to Tony, Tamara, or both?
3. How many different expenses do Tony and Tamara have to plan for? What are they?
4. If the Greens leave after breakfast on Saturday, how many meals will they eat on their trip?
5. Of the accommodations in Weston, which has the lowest basic room rate?
6. Do the Greens need taxi transportation at all the hotels?

Problem Solving

Make Decisions

7. How many round-trip bus tickets will the Greens need to buy?
8. What will be the total cost of bus transportation for the trip?
9. How much will the Greens need to budget for meals for each person for the trip?
10. How much money can the Greens expect to pay in total for meals on their trip?
11. How many T-shirts do the Greens need to buy? What will the total cost be for them?
12. Sister Susie wants to go to the tournament and stay in the same hotel room. What expenses will she have?
13. If Susie wants to go on the trip, how much more money should they add to the budget?
14. What do you need to add to the basic room rate to find the total cost of the room for three people?
15. Which accommodations offer the least expensive room rate for three people?
16. In choosing accommodations, what other factors should the Greens consider?
17. How much will the Greens spend on the room, the charge for an extra person, and taxi transportation if they stay at the Travel Inn at Weston?
18. How much will it cost the Greens to stay at the Motel Westin including the cost of an extra person and taxi transportation?
19. If the Greens stay at the Weston Inn, they will need taxi transportation. How much will it cost to stay in this hotel and take a taxi to the tournament?
20. Which one of the hotel options, including the costs of taxi transportation, will be the least expensive for the Greens?

Your Decision!

Where do you recommend that the Greens stay in Weston? Will they stay within their budget? Explain.

Objective: Apply addition and subtraction to investigate science concepts.

Problem Solving: Math and Science
How fast are you?

You Will Need
- **meterstick**

Quick! A soccer ball is coming at you. How will you react?

In order to react to the ball, your body must

- notice what is happening
- tell your brain about it
- decide what to do
- let your brain tell your muscles what to do.
- follow those instructions

The amount of time it takes for you to react is called reaction time.

In this activity, you will measure your reaction time.

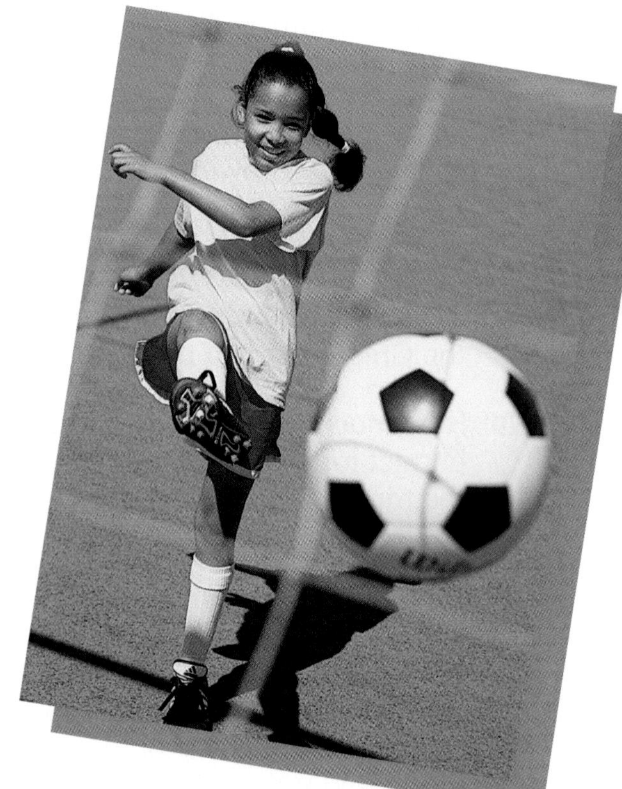

Hypothesize

Estimate your reaction time for catching a ball.

Procedure

1. Work with a partner. Take turns.
2. Have your partner hold a meterstick from the top, with the bottom a few feet above the floor.
3. Hold your fingers near the 50-centimeter (cm) mark, but don't touch the stick.
4. Without warning, your partner will let go of the meterstick. You should catch it with your fingers as fast as you can.
5. Record the mark where you grabbed the meterstick (round to the nearest centimeter).
6. Repeat the activity two more times.

Data

Copy and complete the chart to record your observations. Record the finishing mark and find the difference. Use the "Reaction Time" chart to find the reaction time.

	Starting Mark	Finishing Mark	Difference	Reaction Time
1	50 cm			
2	50 cm			
3	50 cm			

Reaction Time	
Difference	Time
10 cm	0.14 s
11 cm	0.15 s
12 cm	0.16 s
13 cm	0.16 s
14 cm	0.17 s
15 cm	0.17 s
16 cm	0.18 s
17 cm	0.19 s
18 cm	0.19 s

Reaction Time	
Difference	Time
19 cm	0.20 s
20 cm	0.20 s
21 cm	0.21 s
22 cm	0.21 s
23 cm	0.22 s
24 cm	0.22 s
25 cm	0.23 s
26 cm	0.23 s
27 cm	0.23 s

Reaction Time	
Difference	Time
28 cm	0.24 s
29 cm	0.24 s
30 cm	0.25 s
31 cm	0.25 s
32 cm	0.26 s
33 cm	0.26 s
34 cm	0.26 s
35 cm	0.27 s
36 cm	0.27 s

Reaction Time	
Difference	Time
37 cm	0.27 s
38 cm	0.28 s
39 cm	0.28 s
40 cm	0.29 s
41 cm	0.29 s
42 cm	0.29 s
43 cm	0.30 s
44 cm	0.30 s
45 cm	0.30 s

Conclude and Apply

- What was your fastest reaction time?
- Did your 3 reaction times differ by a lot or a little? Explain why.
- How does your fastest time compare with that of your partner?
- Compare your reaction times above to your times for the activities below. Are they slower, faster, or about the same? tying your shoe; jumping off the ground; eating a piece of toast
- Use *Did You Know?* to decide if catching a ball is an example of a **reflex**. Why or why not?

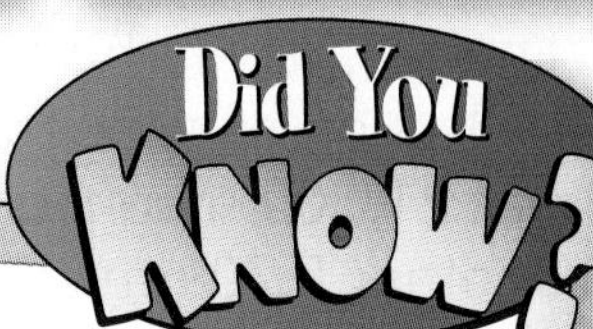

Sometimes you react without your brain being involved. These reactions are called reflexes. An example of a reflex is when you bang your knee and automatically kick your foot.

Going Further

1. Repeat the activity with someone much younger and someone much older than you. Does reaction time change with age?
2. Write a story about a fifth-grader playing soccer who discovers that his or her reaction time is suddenly 100 times slower.

Check Your Progress B

Add or subtract. **(pages 18–21)**

1. $\begin{array}{r} 8.9651 \\ -0.752 \\ \hline \end{array}$ 2. $\begin{array}{r} 788.9651 \\ -245.9131 \\ \hline \end{array}$ 3. $\begin{array}{r} 133{,}622.2 \\ +\ 29{,}877.5 \\ \hline \end{array}$ 4. $\begin{array}{r} 0.2678 \\ +0.5929 \\ \hline \end{array}$

Estimate by rounding to the highest place value. **(pages 22–25)**

5. 6.898 + 88.77 6. 88,711 + 21,988 7. 686 + 155

Estimate sums and differences by rounding to the place indicated. **(pages 22–25)**

8. $\underline{9}1$, 998,877 + $\underline{4}3$,999,999 9. 2.8$\underline{9}$44 − 1.2$\underline{3}$65 10. 4,$\underline{5}$71 − 4,$\underline{1}$62

Identify the addition property used to rewrite each problem. **(pages 28–31)**

11. 63 + 29 + 5 = 63 + 5 + 29 12. 50,145,144 + 0 = 50,145,144

13. 47 + (3 + 93) = (47 + 3) + 93

Add or subtract. **(pages 28–31)**

14. 47 + 56 15. 7,540 − 1,290 16. 4.53 + 6.34

Solve. **(pages 18–31)**

17. Louise Greenfarb has the world's largest collection of refrigerator magnets. She has 21,500 magnets. If Louise collects another 5,709 magnets, about how many magnets will she have?

18. Ted Hoz has the world's largest collection of golf balls. He has 43,824 golf balls. If he has room for 31,886 more golf balls in his storage cabinets, how many golf balls will Ted have if he fills his cabinets?

19. The most successful *trainspotter*, or person who keeps track of all the trains he or she sees, is Bill Curtis. He has spotted 60,000 locomotives, 11,200 electric units, and 8,300 diesel units. How many trains has he spotted in all?

20. **Analyze:** Sharon collected 7 baseball cards in January, 11 baseball cards in February, 15 baseball cards in March, and 19 baseball cards in April. If this pattern continues, how many baseball cards will she collect in December? Explain the pattern and tell how you got your answer.

Extra Practice

Place Value Through Billions (pages 2–3)

Name the place and write the value of the underlined digit.

1. 875,320,5<u>4</u>3,000
2. <u>1</u>56,904,229,107
3. 8<u>7</u>,402,777
4. 222,0<u>5</u>2,356,119
5. 3,999,<u>6</u>21,871
6. 33,005,299,<u>4</u>22

Write each number in standard form.

7. 83 billion, 102 thousand, 405
8. 642 million, 85 thousand, 911
9. 202 billion, 5 thousand, 277
10. 909 million, 624 thousand, 25

Use place value to answer each question.

11. What number is 1,000,000 more than 8,766,042,759?
12. What is the value of the 8 in the number 825,907,653,012?

Explore Decimal Place Value (pages 4–9)

Name the place of the underlined digit.

1. 29.8<u>7</u>98
2. 879.003<u>4</u>
3. 0.<u>9</u>765
4. 4.11<u>2</u>6
5. 467.7<u>2</u>51
6. 62.<u>1</u>866
7. 2.34<u>5</u>
8. 88.976<u>7</u>

Write in standard form.

9. six and forty-nine hundredths
10. twenty-five and eight tenths
11. one and sixteen ten-thousandths
12. two and nine thousandths

Write the word name and expanded form.

13. 0.91
14. 67.89
15. 1.05
16. 6.6
17. 32.06
18. 5.701
19. 6.881
20. 1,118.14

Name an equivalent decimal.

21. 1.05
22. 22.9
23. 8.350
24. 5.124
25. 9.004
26. 467.012
27. 10.010
28. 963.0003

Solve.

29. In the 1986 Olympics, Marina Styepanova ran the 400-meter hurdles in 52.94 seconds. What is the place and value of the digit 9 in that number?
30. In 1978 Franklin Jacobs jumped a height of 2.32 meters. How do you read that number?

Extra Practice

Compare and Order Whole Numbers and Decimals (pages 10–13)

Order from least to greatest.

1. 2.042; 2.402; 2.420
2. 687,931,516,726; 687,931,516,267; 687,931,516,627
3. 55.987; 55.459; 56.987
4. 2,917,384.32; 2,917,484.32; 2,916,384.32

Compare. Write >, <, or =.

5. 231,654,042 ● 231,654,142
6. 6.0 ● 6.078
7. 70.09 ● 70.090
8. 342,000,616 ● 342,000,661
9. 387.837 ● 387.378
10. 15,115.015 ● 115,115.015

Problem Solving: Reading for Math Use the Four-Step Process (pages 14–15)

Solve. Use the four-step process.

1. China and France are two of the five countries with the most movie theaters. China has 4,639 theaters, and France has 4,365 theaters. Which country has more movie theaters? Which place determines which number is greater?
2. Latvia has 101.7 movie screens for every one million people. Sweden has 137.8 movie screens for every one million people, and the United States has 105.9 movie screens for every one million people. List these countries in order from the greatest to the least number of movie screens for every one million people.

Add and Subtract Whole Numbers and Decimals (pages 18–21)

Add or subtract.

1. $4,299.22 + 667.99$
2. $262,882,114 + 31,422,611$
3. $65.9852 + 5.4221$
4. $788,011.877 - 0.688$
5. $11.87709 - 8.20065$
6. $291.643 - 114.843$
7. $326,864,798 + 482,092,305$
8. $4,273.98 - 2,809.23$
9. $27,633.082 - 2,187.620$
10. $6,983.729 + 9,860.198$
11. $12.0744 - 3.1816$
12. $101.6083 - 96.1872$

Estimate Sums and Differences (pages 22–25)

Round to the underlined place.

1. $\underline{1}$,957
2. 97,1$\underline{8}$5
3. $\underline{4}$10,268
4. 6,45$\underline{6}$,456
5. 71,$\underline{5}$95,791
6. 78.$\underline{1}$3
7. 5.0$\underline{0}$458
8. 7.09$\underline{8}$53
9. 10$\underline{2}$.6785
10. 67.$\underline{8}$191

Round to the place indicated.

11. 5,642 (hundreds)
12. 25,601 (ten thousands)
13. 15.1285 (thousandths)
14. $686.2198 (hundredths)
15. 1,870 (hundreds)
16. 97.511 (ones)

Estimate the sum or difference by rounding.

17. 2.8 + 3.09
18. $8,599 + $677
19. 9.8 + 5.009
20. 39.067 − 7.812
21. 985,601,000 − 5,429,68
22. $456.67 − $22.43

Solve.

23. Leonardo's *The Codex Hammer* was sold at an auction for $30,800,000 in 1994. Audubon's *The Birds of America* was sold at an auction for $3,600,000 in 1989. About how much more was paid for *The Codex Hammer* than for *The Birds of America*?

Problem Solving: Strategy Find a Pattern (pages 26–27)

What could the pattern be?

1. The table shows four of the top five highest jumps ever made. Use a pattern to predict how high Sotomayor jumped.

Jumper	Height in Meters
Sotomayor	■
Sjoberg	2.42
Paklin	2.41
Povarnitsyn	2.40
Jianhua	2.39

Algebra: Properties of Addition (pages 28–31)

Identify the addition property used to rewrite each problem.

1. 5 + 114 + 95 = 5 + 95 + 114
2. 0.78 + (0.22 + 19.6) = (0.78 + 0.22) + 19.6
3. 7,054,687 + 0 = 7,054,687
4. 0.7 + 54 + 3.3 + 46 = (0.7 + 3.3) + (54 + 46)

Add or subtract. Describe your work.

5. 811 + 500
6. 211 + 0.0678 + 9
7. 6.2 + 6.05
8. 42.1 + 12 + 3.9

Chapter Study Guide

Language and Math

Math Words

standard form
period
decimal
whole number
round
expanded form
place
estimate

Complete. Use a word from the list.

1. To find the next highest or lowest value of a number based on a given place value is to ____ the number.
2. 300 + 20 + 5 is the ____ of the number 325.
3. To find a number that is close to the exact answer to a problem is to ____.
4. In the number 2,781,806, the digits 7, 8, and 1 are in the hundreds ____.
5. 9.67 is an example of a ____.

Skills and Applications

Compare and order whole numbers and decimals. (pages 2–13)

Example

Which number is greater, 3.25 or 3.28?

Solution

Line up the decimal points.

3.25
3.28

Compare the ones. 3 = 3

Compare the tenths. 2 = 2

Compare the hundredths. 8 > 5

3.28 is greater than 3.25.

Compare. Write >, <, or =.

6. 1,903,484 ● 1,903,574
7. 16.015 ● 16.04

Order from least to greatest.

8. 54,710; 54,071; 54,107
9. 5.0124; 5.041; 5.005
10. 927,618,013; 927,678,009; 927,618,109

Add and subtract whole numbers and decimals. (pages 18–21)

Example

Find: 65.09 + 2.145

Solution

$$\begin{array}{r} \overset{1}{6}5.090 \\ +\ 2.145 \\ \hline 67.235 \end{array}$$

65.09 + 2.145 = 67.235

Add or subtract.

11. 899.4894 − 87.6226
12. 813,648,785 + 87,231,682
13. 14.0214 + 9.475
14. Lana is practicing the long jump. Her first jump is 13.55 feet. Her second jump is 12.44 feet. How much longer is her first jump than her second jump?

Estimate sums and differences. (pages 22–25)

Example

Estimate:

4,678.11 + 29.99

Solution

4,678.11 + 29.99

↓ ↓

4,680 + 30 = 4,710

Round to the underlined place.

15. 76,666
16. 11.618
17. 18.628
18. 198,826

Estimate the sum or difference by rounding.

19. 8.56 + 4.89
20. 25,429 − 22,167
21. 0.7854 − 0.236
22. Sam had $66.51 in his bank at home. He adds $2.68 in change. About how much does he now have?

Use stategies to solve problems. (pages 14–15, 26–27)

Example

Lee starts a new exercise program. He exercises 23 minutes the first week, 28 minutes the second week, and 33 minutes the third week. If he continues this pattern, how long will he exercise the fourth week?

Solution

What could the pattern be?

Week	Number of Minutes
1	23
2	28
3	33
4	▪

The pattern is add 5. Lee will exercise 38 minutes the fourth week.

Solve.

23. The top 3 best-selling albums in the United States are The Eagles' *Greatest Hits 1971–1975,* Michael Jackson's *Thriller,* and Pink Floyd's *The Wall.* The Eagles sold 24,000,000 copies, Michael Jackson sold 25,000,000 copies, and Pink Floyd sold 22,000,000 copies. Order these numbers from greatest to least.
24. Erika starts a new jogging program. She jogs 1 mile the first month, 5 miles the second month, and 9 miles the third month. If she continues this pattern, how long will she jog the fifth month?
25. Five members of the Jade High School track team are over 5 feet 9 inches tall. Ken is 6 feet 2 inches, Margo is 5 feet 10 inches, Jenny is 6 feet 3 inches, Joe is 5 feet 11 inches and Karen is 5 feet 11 inches. Order each member from least to greatest in height.

Chapter Test

Write the word name.

1. 7,562,849,302
2. 541.014

Write in standard form.

3. 89 ten-thousandths
4. 65 billion, 100 thousand
5. 508 thousand and 2 hundredths

Compare. Write >, <, or =.

6. 4,233 ● 4,322
7. 23.4 ● 23.34

Order from least to greatest.

8. 583,621; 583,260; 558,924
9. 0.0181; 0.0081; 0.0818; 0.0811

Round to the underlined place.

10. 34$\underline{7}$,890,345
11. $\underline{1}$97,382,481,402
12. 89\underline{4}$.47
13. 1.20$\underline{8}$9

Estimate the sum or difference by rounding.

14. 653 + 721
15. 12,308 − 975
16. 0.2145 + 0.457
17. 2.47 − 1.210

Add or subtract.

18. $\begin{array}{r} 5{,}000 \\ -3{,}967 \\ \hline \end{array}$
19. $\begin{array}{r} 358{,}201 \\ +527{,}230 \\ \hline \end{array}$
20. 7.98 + 12.56
21. 14.34 − 8.55

Solve.

22. Bonnie Blair won a gold medal in the 500-meter speed skating event in 1992. Her time was 40.33 seconds. In 1994 she won the same event with a time that was 1.08 seconds faster. What was her time in 1994?
23. Thirty students from the Netherlands set up a record 1,500,000 dominoes. Of these, 1,138,101 were toppled by one push. How many dominoes remained standing after that push?
24. The largest bird that can fly is the great bustard. It weighs 20.9 kilograms. The ostrich cannot fly, but it is the largest bird at 156.5 kilograms. How much more does the ostrich weigh than the great bustard?
25. The top speed at which a man has ever traveled is 24,791 miles per hour, achieved by the *Apollo 10* crew. The top speed traveled by a woman is 17,864 miles per hour, by Kathryn Sullivan on the *Discovery* shuttle mission. About how much faster did *Apollo 10* travel than *Discovery?*

Performance Assessment

Along with the Olympic record for most points in diving, Greg Louganis also holds the record for the most national championships. He won 47 during his career. To reach this high level of performance, athletes must train very hard and keep track of their progress. What if you collected this data for the diving team and want to organize it for the team coach?

Diving: 3-Meter Springboard

Name	Dive 1	Dive 2	Total
Megan	32.64	38.53	
Chris	29.99	35.61	
Erica	36.05	34.12	
Tom	30.02	37.50	

Complete the chart.

- Find the total for each diver's first two dives.
- Order the four divers from lowest total to highest.
- Estimate the difference between the highest and lowest totals.
- Find the exact difference.

A Good Answer

- has a complete chart showing point totals.
- shows how you found the total time for each swimmer.
- shows the steps you used to estimate and find the difference between high and low scores.
- gives explanations for how you solved each problem.

You may want to save this work in your portfolio.

Assessment

Enrichment

Roman Numerals

The ancient Romans devised a numbering system that used seven letters as symbols to name numbers.

Roman Numeral	I	V	X	L	C	D	M
Value	1	5	10	50	100	500	1,000

Roman numerals use combinations of these seven letters. No letter is repeated more than 3 times in a row.

To find the value of a Roman numeral, add or subtract.

- When a letter has a value that is less than or equal to the value of the letter to its left, add.

  VIII = 5 + 1 + 1 + 1 = 8

  LXI = 50 + 10 + 1 = 61

  CCXXV = 100 + 100 + 10 + 10 + 5 = 225

  MDCLXXVI = 1,000 + 500 + 100 + 50 + 10 + 10 + 5 + 1 = 1,676

- When a letter has a value that is greater than the value of the letter to its left, subtract.

  IX = 10 − 1 = 9

  XC = 100 − 10 = 90

  CIX = 100 + (10 − 1) = 109

  MCCXLIX = 1,000 + 100 + 100 + (50 − 10) + (10 − 1) = 1,249

Write each number.

1. III **2.** XX **3.** XV **4.** LXV **5.** CLXX

6. IV **7.** XCVII **8.** MCDXXXVI **9.** MCMLV **10.** MDCXXIV

Write each Roman numeral.

11. 35 **12.** 2,501 **13.** 1,575 **14.** 264 **15.** 929

16. 49 **17.** 362 **18.** 958 **19.** 2,054 **20.** 1,781

21. Work with a partner. Take turns. Write a Roman numeral and have your partner write the number. Have your partner write a number and you write the Roman numeral.

Test-Taking Tips

When taking a multiple-choice test, it can be helpful to **find an answer** to the problem on your own first. Then, check the answer choices given to see if your answer is there. If it is not, you should double check your work.

Round 419,867 to the nearest hundred.

A. 419,900 C. 420,900
B. 420,900 D. 421,000

Find the answer on your own before looking at the answer choices.

- Underline the digit in the place to which you are rounding. 419,<u>8</u>67
- Look at the digit to the right of the underlined digit.

  419,<u>8</u>67 **Think:** $6 > 5$

  Round up to 419,900.
- Now look at the answer choices to see if there is one that matches your answer. If there is not one that matches, go back and check your work again.

  419,900 matches choice A.

  The correct answer is A.

Check for Success

Before turning in a test, go back one last time to check.

☑ I understood and answered the questions asked.
☑ I checked my work for errors.
☑ My answers make sense.

Practice **Read each problem. First find an answer on your own. Choose the answer that matches yours. If your answer is not one of the choices, double-check your work.**

1. Round 2,840,983 to the nearest thousand.
   A. 3,000,000 C. 2,841,000
   B. 2,841,980 D. 2,840,000

2. A $124.49 skateboard has been discounted by $19.99. What is the discounted price of the skateboard?
   F. $99.99 H. $104.59
   G. $104.50 J. $119.49

3. Round 25.08475 to the nearest tenth.
   A. 25.0 C. 25.1
   B. 25.08 D. 30

4. Steph spends $9.95 on a gymnastics uniform and $3.95 on tights. How much does she spend?
   F. $13.90 H. $6.00
   G. $12.80 J. Not Here

Spiral Review and Test Prep

Chapter 1

Choose the correct answer.

Number Sense

1. 1.01 more than 23.062 is ____.
   A. 24.163 C. 24.072
   B. 24.162 D. 23.163

2. What is 98,343 rounded to the nearest hundred?
   F. 99,000 H. 98,300
   G. 98,400 J. 98,000

3. 4 + 0.03 + 0.002 = ■
   A. 43.2 C. 4.302
   B. 4.32 D. 4.032

4. In 1991 Mike Powell jumped a long-jump distance of 8.95 feet. That same year Carl Lewis jumped a long-jump distance of 8.87 feet. Who jumped farther?
   F. Lewis H. They jumped the same
   G. Powell J. Not Here

Measurement and Geometry

5. What is the name of this figure?

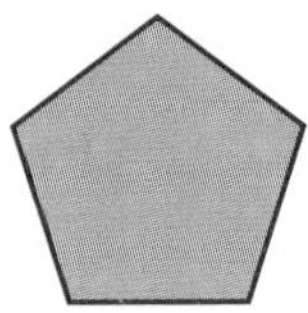

   A. Quadrilateral C. Hexagon
   B. Pentagon D. Octagon

6. What is the name of this figure?

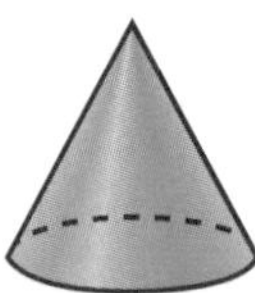

   F. Cone H. Cylinder
   G. Cube J. Sphere

7. What is the area?

   A. 12 square feet C. 32 square feet
   B. 24 square feet D. 40 square feet

8. What is the perimeter?

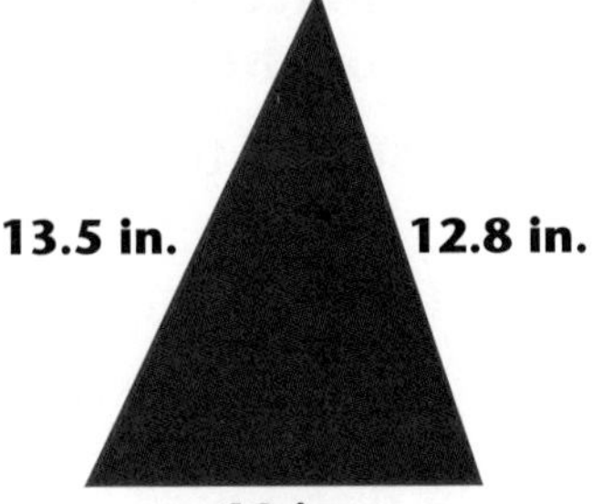

   F. 26.13 inches H. 35.13 inches
   G. 27.3 inches J. 36.3 inches

Statistics, Data Analysis, and Probability

Use data from the table for problems 9–12.

9. Which month had the most rainfall?
   A. March C. May
   B. April D. June

10. Which month had the least rainfall?
   F. April H. June
   G. May J. July

11. How much more rain fell in April than in May?
   A. 1.8 inches C. 2.8 inches
   B. 2.2 inches D. Not Here

12. How many inches of rain altogether fell in the months of March, April, and May?
   F. 36.7 inches H. 34 inches
   G. 34.2 inches J. 32.8 inches

Algebra and Functions

13. Which is the correct solution of $x + 12 = 45$?
   A. 24 C. 40
   B. 33 D. 57

14. What number is missing from the chart?

Rule: Multiply by 14	
3	42
8	112
13	182
18	■
23	322

   F. 222 H. 242
   G. 232 J. 252

15. Which property of addition shows that $23 + (17 + 4) = (23 + 17) + 4$?
   A. Identity Property
   B. Commutative Property
   C. Associative Property
   D. Addition Property

16. List 3 different ways you can combine coins to equal exactly 45 cents.

Multiply Whole Numbers and Decimals

Theme: Faraway Places

Use the Data

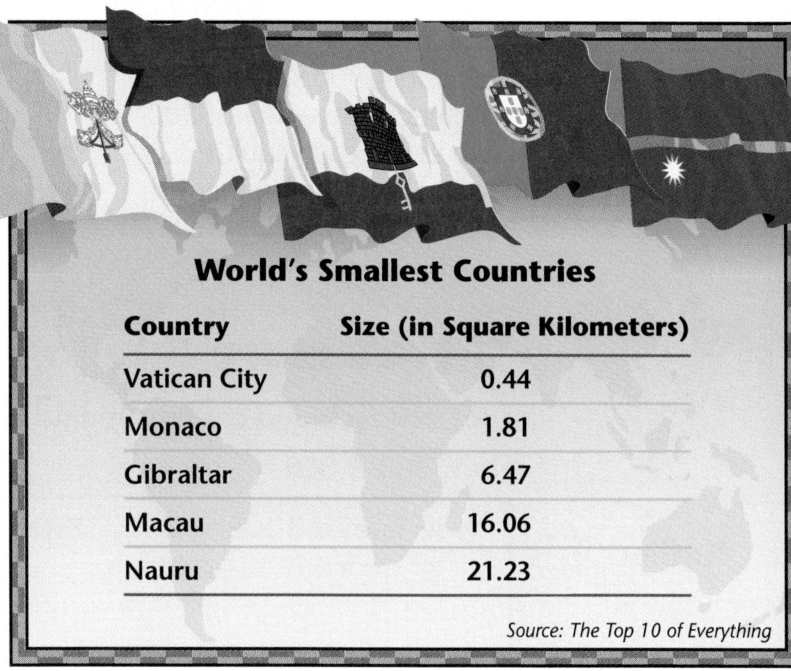

World's Smallest Countries

Country	Size (in Square Kilometers)
Vatican City	0.44
Monaco	1.81
Gibraltar	6.47
Macau	16.06
Nauru	21.23

Source: The Top 10 of Everything

- Which country is about 8 times as large as Monaco?

What You Will Learn

In this chapter you will learn how to

- multiply whole numbers and decimals.
- estimate products of whole numbers and decimals.
- use properties of multiplication.
- evaluate expressions with exponents.
- use strategies to solve problems.

Objective: Multiply whole numbers by multiples of 10.

2•1 Patterns of Multiplication

Learn

Math Words

product the answer in a multiplication problem

factor a number multiplied to give a product; for example, 3 and 5 in 3 x 5

Vitoria-Gasteiz is a district capital in the Basque Country, a group of regions in the Pyrenees Mountains between France and Spain. The city covers about 300 square kilometers. An average of 800 people live in each square kilometer. About how many people live in Vitoria-Gasteiz?

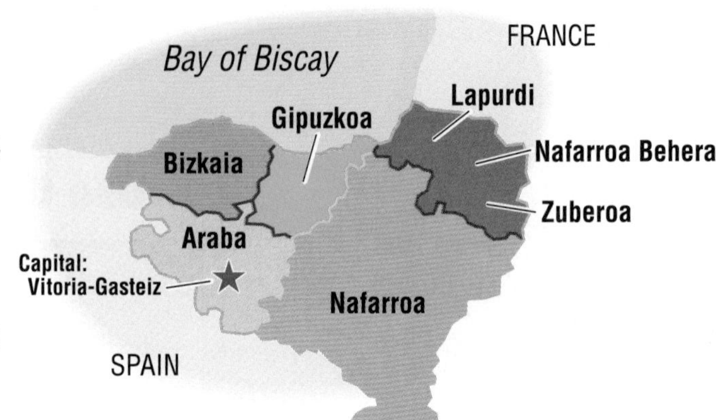

There's more than one way!

Use basic facts and patterns to find **products**.

Find: 300×800

Think: 3 x 8 tens = 24 tens = 240

Method A

Basic fact → $3 \times 8 = 24$ Pattern → $3 \times 80 = 240$

$3 \times 800 = 2{,}400$

$30 \times 800 = 24{,}000$

$300 \times 800 = 240{,}000$

You can count zeros in the **factors**.

Method B

1. Find the basic fact.

   $3 \times 8 = 24$

2. Count the number of zeros in each factor.

   300×800

   2 zeros + 2 zeros = 4 zeros

3. Write the zeros to the right of the product in Step 1.

   240,000

Think: Sometimes there is an extra zero in the product. For example: 5 x 6 = 30

About 240,000 people live in Vitoria-Gasteiz.

Try It

Multiply.

1. 4×400 **2.** 6×50 **3.** 100×12

How many zeros will be in the product of 500 and 4,000? Explain.

Practice Copy and complete.

4. $3 \times 2 = 6$
$3 \times 20 = 60$
$3 \times 200 = \blacksquare$
$3 \times 2{,}000 = \blacksquare$

5. $7 \times 3 = 21$
$7 \times 30 = \blacksquare$
$7 \times 300 = 2{,}100$
$7 \times 3{,}000 = \blacksquare$

6. $2 \times 9 = \blacksquare$
$20 \times 9 = \blacksquare$
$200 \times 9 = \blacksquare$
$2{,}000 \times 9 = \blacksquare$

7. $1 \times \$30 = \$30$
$10 \times \$30 = \$300$
$100 \times \$30 = \blacksquare$
$1{,}000 \times \$30 = \blacksquare$

8. $3 \times 12 = \blacksquare$
$30 \times 12 = 360$
$300 \times 12 = \blacksquare$
$3{,}000 \times 12 = \blacksquare$

★9. $8 \times 50 = \blacksquare$
$80 \times 50 = 4{,}000$
$800 \times 50 = \blacksquare$
$8{,}000 \times 50 = \blacksquare$

Multiply.

10. 7×40
11. $6 \times 2{,}000$
12. 300×8
13. $20 \times \$50$
14. 160×10
15. $65 \times 1{,}000$
★16. $40 \times 50 \times 10$
★17. $900 \times 50 \times 0$

Problem Solving

18. Sandi is reading a book about the Basque Country. She reads an average of 20 pages each day. She has 6 days to finish her book. How many pages can she read in the next 6 days? Will she be able to finish the last 113 pages? Explain.

19. **Art:** The Guggenheim Museum in Bilbao opened in 1998. It exhibits the work of artists from the Basque Country and around the world. If a square painting measures 0.45 meters on each side, what is the distance around the painting?

20. **Social Studies:** Mr. Lesh says, "complete this multiplication sentence, and you will know the length in miles of the Pyrenees mountain chain: $3 \times 90 = \blacksquare$." How long are the Pyrenees?

21. **Language Arts:** Most Basque words end in the letters *s, n, r, t,* or *l*. Each verb can have up to 24 different forms. If the Basque language has about 1,200 verbs, about how many verb forms could there be?

22. **Generalize:** How does using basic facts help you find 600×800 mentally? Explain how would find the product.

23. **Create a problem** about the Basque Country that can be solved using patterns of multiplication. Solve it, and give it to another student to solve.

Spiral Review and Test Prep

Round each number to the underlined place.

24. $67.8\underline{7}59$
25. $4,\underline{6}92$
26. $\$45.8\underline{7}2$
27. $67\underline{3}.243$

Choose the correct answer.

28. Find the sum of 687 + 478 + 269.
A. 1,334
B. 1,434
C. 1,444
D. 1,544

29. How is $\frac{8}{10}$ written as a decimal?
F. 8.0
G. 0.08
H. 0.8
J. Not Here

Objective: Use the distributive property to multiply.

2·2 Explore the Distributive Property

Learn

Math Words

array a group of objects separated in rows and columns

Distributive Property states that to multiply a sum by a number, you can multiply each addend by the number, and then add those products together

You can use counters to explore the Distributive Property.

Work Together

You Will Need
- counters

▶ You can model multiplication by making an **array** with counters.

Make an array to model 6 × 14.

Think: 6 rows with 14 in each row models 6 × 14.

$6 \times 14 = 84$

Then change your array into two separate arrays. One array should model 6 × 10. The other array should model 6 × 4.

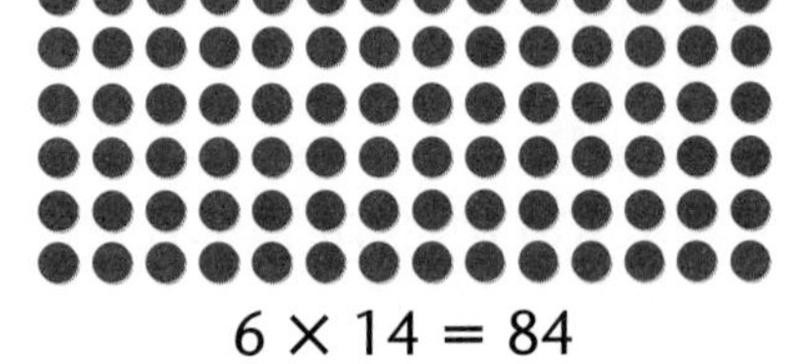

$6 \times 10 = 60$ $6 \times 4 = 24$

Add the two products to find the product of 6 × 14. Record your work.

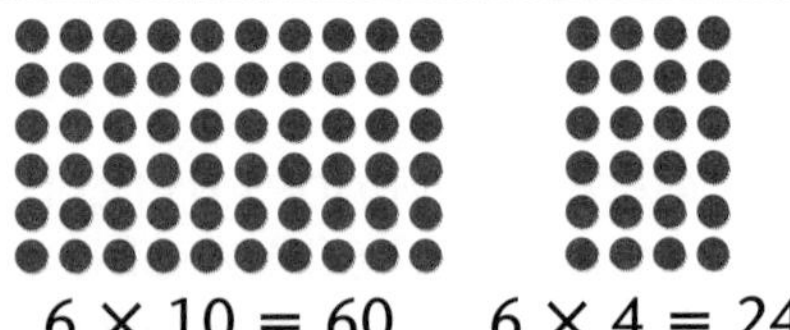

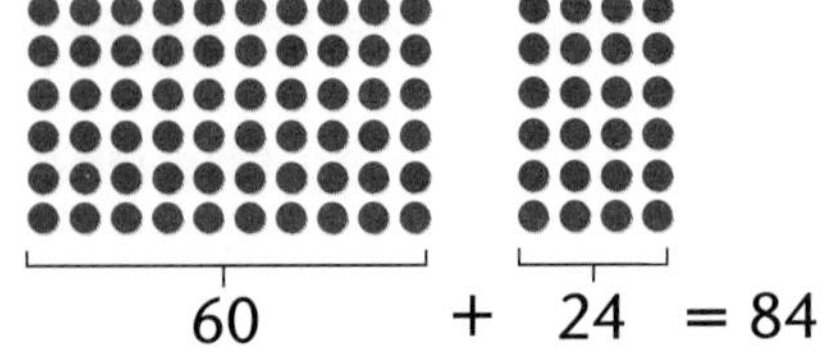

$60 + 24 = 84$

▶ Use counters to multiply. Record your work.

3×11 6×15 8×15 5×23

Make Connections

You can use the **Distributive Property** to make it easier to find products.

Distributive Property
To multiply a sum by a number, you can multiply each addend by the number, and then add those products together.

Find: 3×14

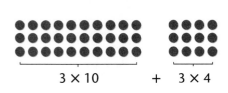

Using Models	Using Paper and Pencil
$3 \times 10 + 3 \times 4$	$3 \times 14 = 3\,(10 + 4)$ $3 \times 14 = (3 \times 10) + (3 \times 4)$ $3 \times 14 = 30 + 12$ $3 \times 14 = 42$

Try It

Multiply.

1. 8×35
2. 5×21
3. 8×65
4. 7×22
5. 8×16
6. 9×14
7. 4×86
8. 3×52
9. 6×29

How can you use the Distributive Property to find the product of 5×34?

Practice

Multiply.

10. 6×24
11. 9×39
12. 21×9
13. 5×27
14. 2×97
15. 6×81
16. 3×96
17. 8×47
18. 7×52
19. 6×16
20. 23×5
21. 5×41
22. 75×4
23. 45×8
24. 5×35
25. 4×115
26. 7×233
27. 8×399

Rewrite each problem using the Distributive Property.

28. 6×47
29. 7×19
30. 9×86
31. 8×145
32. 5×93
33. 4×83
34. 9×24
35. 6×57
36. **Analyze:** Is it easier to rewrite 5×673 as $(5 \times 600) + (5 \times 70) + (5 \times 3)$ or as $(5 \times 129) + (5 \times 544)$? Explain.

Extra Practice, page 91

Objective: Multiply up to 5-digit numbers.

2·3 Multiply Whole Numbers

Learn

The East African nation of Tanzania has both the largest lake (Victoria) and the tallest mountain (Mount Kilimanjaro) on the African continent. Erica and Nicole help their parents run safari trips in Tanzania. If they make the 465-mile trip between Dar es Salaam and Lake Victoria 4 times, how many miles would they travel?

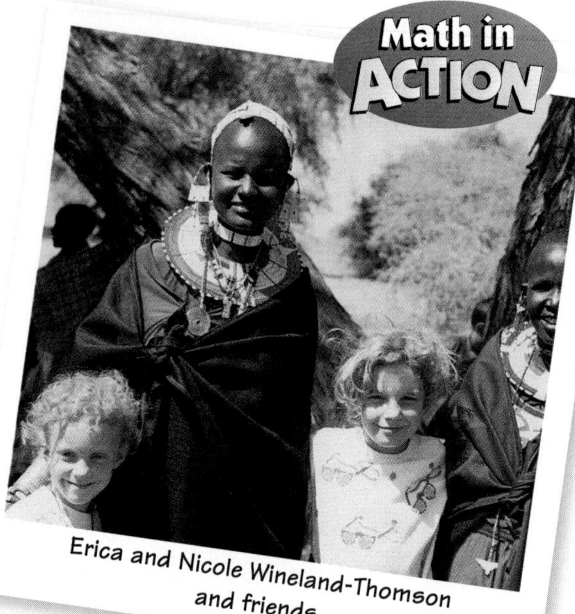

Erica and Nicole Wineland-Thomson and friends

Example 1

Find: 4×465

1 Multiply the ones. Regroup if necessary.

$$\begin{array}{r} 465 \\ \times \quad 4 \\ \hline 0 \end{array}$$

Think:
$4 \times 5 = 20$ ones

2 Multiply the tens. Add any new tens. Regroup if necessary.

$$\begin{array}{r} 465 \\ \times \quad 4 \\ \hline 60 \end{array}$$

Think:
$4 \times 6 = 24$ tens
$24 + 2 = 26$ tens

3 Multiply the hundreds. Add any new hundreds. Regroup if necessary.

$$\begin{array}{r} 465 \\ \times \quad 4 \\ \hline 1{,}860 \end{array}$$

Think:
$4 \times 4 = 16$ hundreds
$16 + 2 = 18$ hundreds

Nicole and Erica would travel 1,860 miles.

More Examples

A

$$\begin{array}{r} 455 \\ \times \quad 6 \\ \hline 2{,}730 \end{array}$$

B

$$\begin{array}{r} 3{,}006 \\ \times \quad 4 \\ \hline 12{,}024 \end{array}$$

C

$$\begin{array}{r} 42{,}163 \\ \times \quad 8 \\ \hline 337{,}304 \end{array}$$

The island of Zanzibar is separated from the mainland of Tanzania by a 22-mile-wide channel of water. If a boat crosses this channel 123 times, how many miles does it travel?

Example 2

Find: 22 × 123

1 Multiply the ones.

```
  123
×  22
  246
```

Think:
2 × 123 = 246 ones

2 Multiply the tens.

```
  123
×  22
  246
 2460
```

Think:
2 × 123 = 246 tens

3 Add.

```
   123
×   22
   246
+2 460
 2,706
```

The boat travels 2,706 miles.

More Examples

D

```
   253
×  361
   253
 15180
 75900
91,333
```

E

```
 $5,024
×    18
 40 192
 50 24
$90,432
```

F

237 × 95 × 13

```
   237
×   95
 1 185
21 330
22,515  →   22,515
          ×     13
            67 545
           225 150
           292,695
```

Try It

Multiply.

1. 7,093 × 6
2. 534 × 67
3. 3,956 × 48
4. $43,782 × 21
5. 9 × 4,501
6. 87 × 914
7. 16 × 11 × 6,090
8. 32 × 412 × 7

Explain how to multiply 27 × 416.

Practice **Multiply.**

9. 2 × 634
10. 86 × 32
11. 276 × 49
12. 93 × 82
13. 903 × 54
14. 1,903 × 27
15. 34 × 7,658
16. 365 × 9
17. 46 × 9,148
18. 38,651 × 19
★19. 8 × 372,507
★20. 1,427,000 × 20
21. $\begin{array}{r} 324 \\ \times \ \ 8 \\ \hline \end{array}$
22. $\begin{array}{r} 222 \\ \times \ 14 \\ \hline \end{array}$
23. $\begin{array}{r} 48 \\ \times 56 \\ \hline \end{array}$
24. $\begin{array}{r} 3,256 \\ \times \quad 72 \\ \hline \end{array}$
25. $\begin{array}{r} 12,473 \\ \times \qquad 6 \\ \hline \end{array}$
26. $\begin{array}{r} 43,111 \\ \times \quad 19 \\ \hline \end{array}$
27. $\begin{array}{r} 1,295 \\ \times \quad 66 \\ \hline \end{array}$
★28. $\begin{array}{r} 3,964 \\ \times 6,394 \\ \hline \end{array}$

Compare. Write >, <, or =.

29. 23 × 156 ● 1,723 × 589
30. 75 × 3,954 ● 73,589 × 4
31. 35 × 852 ● 12,300 + 14,329
32. 299 × 35 ● 157 × 69
33. 7 × 78 × 22 ● 115 × 21 × 3
34. 16 × 21 × 11 ● 9 × 123 × 17

35.

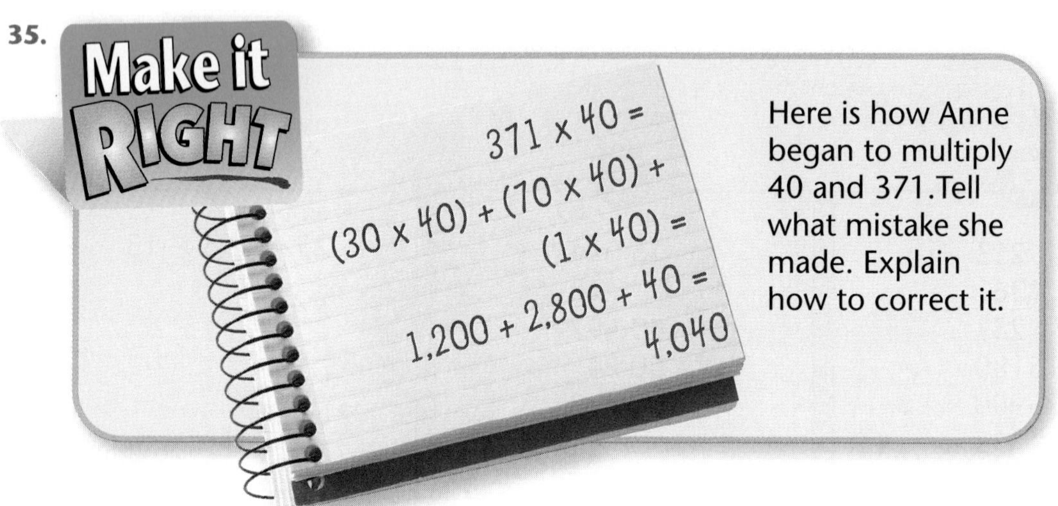

Here is how Anne began to multiply 40 and 371. Tell what mistake she made. Explain how to correct it.

Problem Solving

Use data from the table for problems 36–37.

Miles Between Cities in Tanzania			
	Musoma	Sumbawanga	Tabora
Musoma	*	480	260
Sumbawanga	480	*	220
Tabora	260	220	*

36. If a delivery truck made 20 one-way trips between Musoma and Sumbawanga, how many miles would it travel?

★37. When you travel from Sumbawanga to Musoma, are you traveling more or less than twice the distance between Tabora and Musoma? Explain.

38. **Collect Data:** The Serengeti Plain in Tanzania is home to hundreds of wonderful animal species. Make a list of 5 animals you might see on the Serengeti Plain. Ask 20 people to choose their favorite animal. Display the results in a pictograph.

39. **Spatial Reasoning:** The Tanzanian flag is a rectangle with a diagonal black stripe going from the bottom left corner to the upper right corner. There is a thin yellow stripe on each side of the black stripe. The triangle above the stripes is green and the triangle below the stripes is blue. Draw a picture of the flag.

40. **Literature:** *The Snows of Kilimanjaro* is a short story by Ernest Hemingway. He wrote it after a safari in 1932. At 19,340 feet, Kilimanjaro is the highest peak in Africa. What is its height rounded to the nearest ten thousand?

41. A large group of tourists is taking tours of the Serengeti National Park. There are 16 seats in each of 25 tour buses. Are there enough seats for 365 tourists? Explain.

42. **Explain** how you can use the Distributive Property to multiply 321 by 50. Show your work.

43. If it costs $1,089 to fly round trip from New York City to Tanzania, what would it cost for 4 round-trip tickets?

Use data in the chart for problems 44–47.

44. Which country has the longest border with Tanzania? the shortest?

45. How much longer is the Burundi border than the Zambia border?

46. What is the total length of Tanzania's land border?

★ 47. Tanzania's coastline is one kilometer less than 3 times the Malawi border. How long is the coastline?

Boundary Lengths with Tanzania

Country	Distance (in Kilometers)
Burundi	451
Kenya	769
Malawi	475
Mozambique	756
Rwanda	217
Uganda	396
Zambia	338

48. In Tanzania, 9,570 square miles of land are available for farming. Forests and woodlands cover 13 times this amount. How many square miles of forests and woodlands are in Tanzania?

★49. **Social Studies:** The total land area of Tanzania is 945,090 square kilometers. The total water area is 59,050 square kilometers. How many square kilometers is the entire country?

Spiral Review and Test Prep

50. 13.3 + 8.5

51. 87.26 + 9.5

52. 46.5 − 23.4

53. 21.4 − 7.9

Choose the correct answer.

54. What is the value of the 7 in 371,982?
   A. 700
   B. 7,000
   C. 70,000
   D. Not Here

55. Which has a 4 in the thousands place?
   F. 10,452
   G. 14,052
   H. 15,042
   J. 45,012

Extra Practice, page 91

Objective: Use the properties of multiplication.

2·4 Properties of Multiplication

Learn

You can use the Properties of Multiplication to help you multiply.

Math Words

Properties of Multiplication

- Distributive
- Associative
- Commutative
- Identity
- Zero

Distributive Property of Multiplication over Addition

Multiplying a sum by a number is the same as multiplying each addend by the number and then adding the products.

$6 \times (12 + 9) = (6 \times 12) + (6 \times 9)$

Zero Property

The product of any factor and 0 equals 0.

$65 \times 0 = 0$

Commutative Property

The order of the factors does not change a product.

$6 \times 8 = 8 \times 6$

Associative Property

The way factors are grouped does not change a product.

$(11 \times 3) \times 4 = 11 \times (3 \times 4)$

Identity Property

The product of any factor and 1 equals the factor.

$56 \times 1 = 56$

Distributive Property of Multiplication over Subtraction

To multiply a difference of two numbers by a third number, you can multiply the first two numbers by the third, and then find the difference of the products.

$7 \times (23 - 9) = (7 \times 23) - (7 \times 9)$

Example

Find: $(2 \times 16) \times 5$

Think: It is easier to multiply 2×5 first.

$(2 \times 16) \times 5 = (16 \times 2) \times 5$ ← **Think:** Use the Commutative Property to reorder the factors.

$= 16 \times (2 \times 5)$ ← **Think:** Use the Associative Property to regroup the factors.

$= 16 \times 10$

$= 160$

The answer is 160.

There's more than one way!

Find: 5×95

Method A

You can use the Distributive Property of Multiplication over Addition to multiply.

$$\begin{aligned} 5 \times 95 &= 5 \times (90 + 5) \\ &= (5 \times 90) + (5 \times 5) \\ &= 450 + 25 \\ &= 475 \end{aligned}$$

Method B

Sometimes it is easier to use the Distributive Property of Multiplication over Subtraction to multiply.

$$\begin{aligned} 5 \times 95 &= 5 \times (100 - 5) \\ &= (5 \times 100) - (5 \times 5) \\ &= 500 - 25 \\ &= 475 \end{aligned}$$

The answer is 475.

More Examples

A

$$\begin{aligned} 8 \times 56 &= 8 \times (50 + 6) \\ &= (8 \times 50) + (8 \times 6) \\ &= 400 + 48 \\ &= 448 \end{aligned}$$

B

$$\begin{aligned} 6 \times 89 &= 6 \times (90 - 1) \\ &= (6 \times 90) - (6 \times 1) \\ &= 540 - 6 \\ &= 534 \end{aligned}$$

Try It **Multiply. Name the property you used.**

1. 3×45
2. $4 \times (25 \times 13)$
3. 1×53
4. $(345 \times 0) \times 2$
5. 5×48

How would you use the Distributive Property of Multiplication over Subtraction to multiply 6 times 98 mentally?

Practice

Multiply. Name the property you used.

6. 4×48
7. 0×36
8. $5 \times (4 \times 95)$
9. 3×39
10. $(28 \times 12) \times 5$
11. $54{,}127 \times 4533 \times 0$
12. $89{,}425 \times 1$
13. $(25 \times 1) \times 4$
14. 8×97
15. $(5 \times 18) \times 52$
16. 12×29
★17. 50×612

Algebra & functions **Find the number that makes each sentence true.**

18. $712 \times 5 = 5 \times n$
19. $50 \times (2 \times 12) = (50 \times n) \times 12$
20. $546 \times n = 0$
21. $6 \times (80 - 2) = (6 \times n) - (6 \times 2)$
22. $464 \times n = 464$
23. $4 \times 79 = (4 \times 80) - (n \times 1)$
24. $(6 \times 4) \times 2 = 4 \times (6 \times n)$
25. $18 \times 4 \times 1 = 1 \times 18 \times n$
26. $812 \times n = 812$
27. $2{,}146 \times 0 = n$
28. $16 \times (8 \times 4) = n \times (16 \times 4)$
29. $4 \times 6 \times n = 24$
30. $n \times 1 = 47$
31. $(5 \times 72) = (5 \times n) + (5 \times 2)$
32. $29 \times (70 + 3) = (n \times 70) + (29 \times 3)$
33. $30 \times 212 = (30 \times 200) + (30 \times n) + (30 \times 2)$

34.

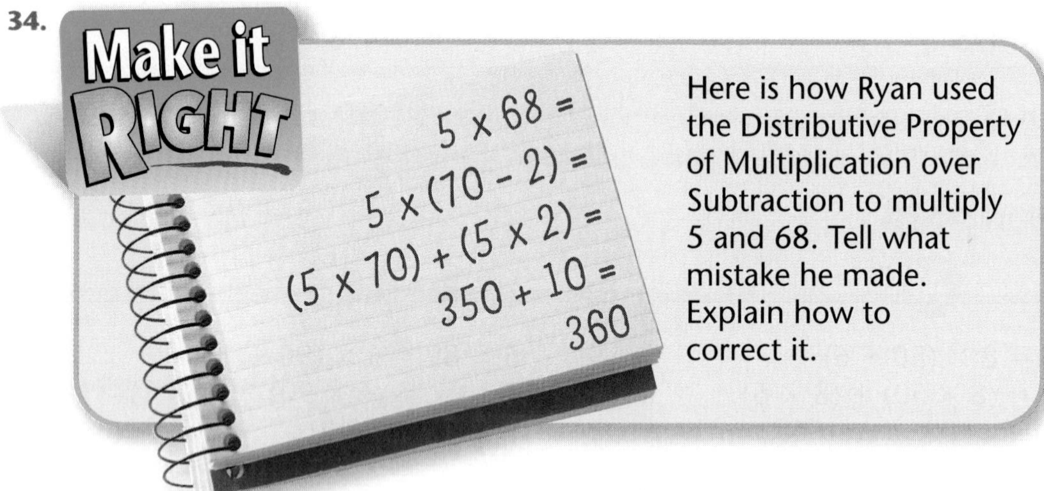

Here is how Ryan used the Distributive Property of Multiplication over Subtraction to multiply 5 and 68. Tell what mistake he made. Explain how to correct it.

Problem Solving

35. The New Zealand flag includes four 5-pointed stars in the center of the flag that represent the Southern Cross constellation. If a flag company makes 25 New Zealand flags each day, how many stars must they make for one month (assume 20 work days each month)?

36. Mount Cook is the highest point in New Zealand. Its peak is 12,349 feet high. Mount Kosciusko in Australia is 7,310 feet high. Is Mount Cook greater or less than twice as high as Mount Kosciusko? By how many feet?

37. In New Zealand, 8 of every 10 people live in cities. Write this number as a decimal.

Use data from the map for problems 38–40.

38. If you travel by helicopter from Christchurch to Wellington and Wellington to Auckland, how many miles would you travel altogether?

39. Juan traveled round-trip from Christchurch to Auckland. On his return trip only, he traveled through Wellington. How many miles did he travel?

★40. If you biked 25 miles a day for 21 days, would you be able to ride from Wellington to Auckland? Explain.

New Zealand

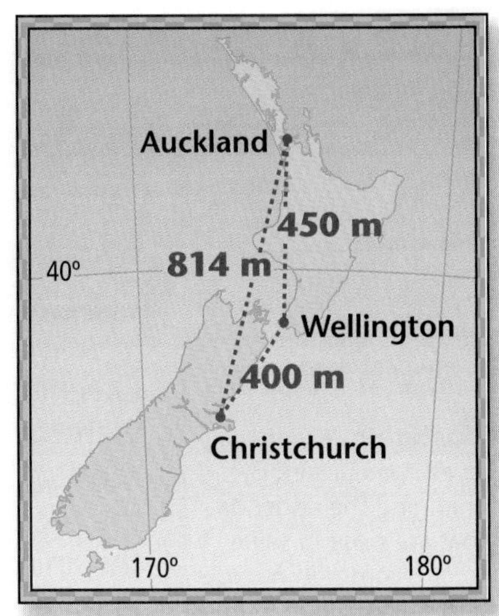

Use data from *Did You Know?* for problems 41–42.

41. About how many square miles is Colorado? Round to the nearest 1,000 square miles.

42. How much larger is the South Island than the North Island?

43. **Language Arts:** A "centennial" celebrates the 100 year anniversary of an event. New Zealand gained independence from The United Kingdom in 1907. When will it celebrate its centennial?

Journal 44. **Compare:** Would you use the Commutative Property or the Distributive Property of Multiplication over Subtraction to find 8×59 mentally? Explain. Then solve.

New Zealand is about the same size as Colorado. New Zealand's North Island has an area of 44,281 square miles. Its South Island has an area of 58,093 square miles.

Spiral Review and Test Prep

Compare. Write >, < or =.

45. 1.20 ● 1.02   46. 0.510 ● 0.5100   47. 0.908 ● 0.098   48. 1.53 ● 1.5 + 0.3

Choose the correct answer.

49. Bill bought a T-shirt for $9.99, a stuffed whale for $25.00, and a pen for $1.49. He gave the clerk $40.00. If there is no sales tax, how much change should he get back?

A. $6.48   C. $28.27
B. $3.52   D. $2.48

50. Delilah finds 6 quarters. How much money did she find?

F. $0.60   H. $6.00
G. $0.25   J. Not Here

Objective: Estimate products of whole numbers and decimals.

2·5 Estimate Products of Whole Numbers and Decimals

Learn

Math Word

clustering a way to estimate a sum by changing the addends that are close in value to one common number and multiplying by the number of addends

Greenland is the largest island in the world, and most of it lies north of the Arctic Circle. One of the animals that thrive in this icy climate is the harp seal. Estimate how many harp seals live on a 192-square-mile coastal area.

About 13 seal pups in each square mile.

Example 1

Estimate: 13×192

You can use these general rules as a guide.

- Small numbers: Round to the nearest ten.
- Large numbers: Round to the nearest hundred or thousand.
- Decimals: Round to the nearest whole number.

1	Decide the place to which you will round each factor.	Round 13 to the nearest 10. Round 192 to the nearest 100.
2	Round each factor.	13 rounds to 10. 192 rounds to 200.
3	Multiply.	$10 \times 200 = 2{,}000$

Note: You could also round 192 to 190.

There are about 2,000 harp seals in a 192-square-mile area.

Suppose the number of harp seal pups born in Greenland for each of the three years that data is collected is 539, 487, and 511. About how many pups were born in all?

Example 2

You can also use rounding and multiplication patterns to estimate sums. This is called **clustering**.

Think: All three addends are close to 500.

Estimate: 539 + 487 + 511

$$539 + 487 + 511 \rightarrow 500 + 500 + 500 = 3 \times 500 = 1{,}500$$

So 539 + 487 + 511 is about 1,500.

More Examples

A Estimate: 177 × 4.23

$$177 \times 4.23 \rightarrow 180 \times 4 = 720$$

B Estimate: 0.83 × 1.12

$$0.83 \times 1.12 \rightarrow 1 \times 1 = 1$$

C Estimate: 2.4 + 2.1 + 1.9

$$2.4 + 2.1 + 1.9 \rightarrow 2 + 2 + 2 = 3 \times 2 = 6$$

D Estimate: 108 + 98 + 138

$$108 + 98 + 138 \rightarrow 100 + 100 + 100 = 3 \times 100 = 300$$

Try It **Estimate by rounding.**

1. 342 × 13
2. 67 × 832
3. 129 × 1,842
4. 4.2 × 81

Estimate by clustering.

5. 134 + 129 + 131
6. 51.2 + 51.4 + 50.9
7. 832 + 759 + 848
8. 43 + 43.4 + 39

Sum it Up Explain one way to estimate 63.2 × 142.

Practice

Estimate by rounding.

9. 8.9 × 10
10. 12 × 76
11. 432 × 285
12. 87 × 1.02
13. 43 × 65
14. 3,095 × 23
15. 84 × 52
16. 96 × 505
17. 4.24 × 74
18. 2.31 × 5.9
19. 3.54 × 108
20. 732.45 × 50
21. 6.8 × 10.06
22. 10.05 × 10
★23. 42 × 10.2 × 89
★24. 143.5 × 3,923
25. 1.37 × 343
26. 946 × 8
27. 456 × 392
28. 65 × 9.3
29. 11.7 × 0.9
30. 2.4 × 48
31. 1.1 × 9.9
32. 208 × 31
33. 77 × 7
34. 0.8 × 0.7

Estimate by clustering.

35. 455 + 493 + 503
36. 76.6 + 79.9 + 81.2
37. 1,254 + 1,194 + 999
38. 939 + 924 + 911
39. 12,486 + 11,450 + 9,432
40. 3.204 + 3.032 + 3.423

Estimate by rounding. Write > or <.

41. 42.88 × 1.9 ● 75.69
42. 48.91 × 11.89 ● 20 × 20
43. $200 ● $76.32 × 2.9
44. 69.3 × 3.5 ● 71 + 68 + 72
46. 8.6 × 5 ● 18 × 4.1
46. 108 × 27 ● 8 × 185

47.

Here is how Zoe estmated 4.3 × 12. Tell what mistake she made. Explain how to correct it.

Problem Solving

48. **Summarize** the steps you take to estimate the product of two decimals.

49. **Analyze:** Sue said that 423 × 11 is about 4,000. Felipe said the estimate is 4,200. Who is correct? Explain.

50. **Social Studies:** Greenland is an independent part of Denmark that uses the Danish krone for money. Marco exchanges 15 U.S. dollars for Danish krones. Each U.S. dollar is worth 7.03 krones. About how many krones does Marco receive?

★51. **Science:** The ice sheet that covers Greenland can be as thick as 14,000 feet in some places. The highest peak on the island is Mount Gunnbjorn at 12,139 feet. How much thicker is the maximum depth of the ice sheet compared to the highest peak?

Use data from *Did You Know?* for problems 52–53.

52. About how many pounds of food would 100 adult seals eat in 1 day?

53. Estimate how many pounds of fish a seal eats every year.

54. **Number Sense:** A scientific journal reports that only about one hundred and twenty-three thousand square miles of Greenland has no ice cap covering. Write this number in standard form.

55. **Social Studies:** In 1814 the Treaty of Kiel put Greenland under the protective rule of Denmark. How long has Greenland been a protectorate of Denmark?

56. **Explain** how to estimate the product of 4.9 and 0.8. What is the product?

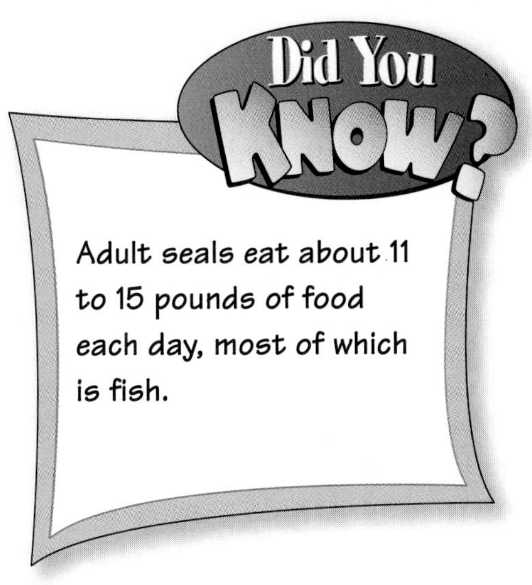
Did You
Know?
Adult seals eat about 11 to 15 pounds of food each day, most of which is fish.

Spiral Review and Test Prep

Find the number that makes each sentence true.

57. $68 + (4 + 5) = (68 + 4) + \blacksquare$

58. $365 + \blacksquare = 365$

59. $8 \times (4 + 3) = (8 \times \blacksquare) + (8 \times 3)$

60. $473 + \blacksquare = 656 + 473$

Choose the correct answer.

61. If Iris saw 24 seals in one day, 39 seals the next day, and 100 the third day, how many seals did she see altogether?

A. Between 150 and 160

B. Between 160 and 170

C. Between 170 and 180

D. Not Here

62. If $(69 - 8) + 8 = 69$, what would the missing number be in $(578 - \blacksquare) + 42 = 578$?

F. 8

G. 42

H. 578

J. 42,578

Extra Practice, page 91

Objective: Determine if a problem needs an estimate or exact answer.

2·6 Problem Solving: Reading for Math

Estimate or Exact Answer

Students Receive Books from Paraguay

Read

Mountain View Elementary trades used books with a school in Paraguay so the students can learn each other's languages better. The school in Paraguay is sending 4 boxes with 32 books in each box. How many book covers should the students make?

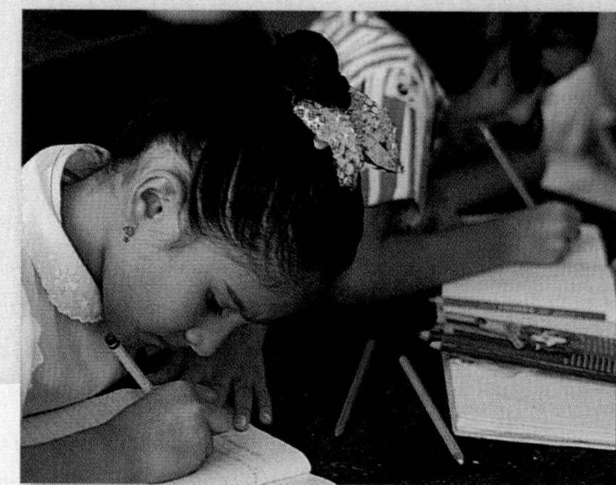

READING SKILL

Form a Conclusion

When you combine details and facts with your own knowledge and common sense to make a decision, you form a conclusion.

- **What do you know?** The number of boxes; the number of books in each box
- **What do you need to find?** How many covers to make

MATH SKILL

Estimate or Exact Answer

- Some problems need an exact answer. Others only need an estimate.
- You can use an estimate when you do not need to know the exact number or when an exact number is too difficult to find.
- Sometimes a problem will use words like *about* or *approximately* to indicate that only an estimate is needed to solve for the problem.

Plan

You need to know how many books are coming from Paraguay. In this problem, you need an exact answer.

Solve

$4 \times 32 = 128$

Look Back

Is your answer reasonable?

Explain some advantages of using an exact or approximate answer.

Solve. State whether the problem requires an estimate or an exact answer to solve.

1. Students plan to send books to another school. They must pay a customs duty when they send the books. The fee is $4 for each box. How much must they pay for 18 boxes?

2. A restaurant in Paraguay can make 695 dinners each night. The restaurant has been sold out for 7 straight nights. About how many dinners were served during this week?

3. About 3,600,000 of Paraguay people speak a language called Guarani. If 4,000,000 people live in Paraguay, how many speak other languages?

4. Members of the Paraguayan Senate serve 5-year terms. If a Senator has served 5 terms, how many years has the Senator been in office?

Use data from *Did You Know?* for problems 5–7.

5. A hiker wants to know if he can reach the top of Cerro San Rafael before noon. If he can climb about 400 meters each hour and leaves at 9 A.M., will he reach the top on time? Explain whether you need an estimate or an exact answer.

6. What is the total length of Paraguay's land border? Do you think these measurements are estimates or exact?

7. A group goes rafting on the Paraná River. Each raft carries 14 people. There are 8 rafts. How many people go rafting? Is your answer exact or an estimate?

8. A class is making a presentation about Paraguay to the school. An encyclopedia says that Paraguay is 406,750 square kilometers. Do you think this number is exact or an estimate?

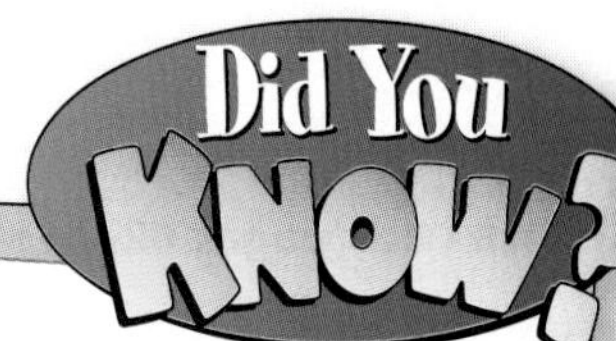

Paraguay is a landlocked country in South America. It shares an 1,880-kilometer border with Argentina, a 1,290-kilometer border with Brazil, and a 750-kilometer border with Bolivia. The highest point is called Cerro San Rafael at 850 meters. The lowest point can be found where the Paraguay and the Paraná rivers meet at a height of 46 meters.

Spiral Review and Test Prep

Choose the correct answer.

Wonders of the World Tours took 6 busloads of tourists to Asunción, the capital of Paraguay. Each bus held 48 tourists. About 300 people went on the tour.

9. Which of the following is true?
   A. Each bus contained 48 tourists.
   B. There were 48 buses.
   C. Exactly 300 people went on the tour.
   D. A total of 48 buses traveled to Asunción.

10. When you estimate an answer, you
   F. ignore all facts given in the problem.
   G. don't have to check your answer.
   H. find a number that is close to the exact answer.
   J. simply guess at the answer.

Extra Practice, page 92

Check Your Progress A

Multiply. **(pages 50–51, 54–57)**

1. 8×40
2. 30×400
3. 50×60
4. 80×700
5. 6×32
6. 5×21
7. 4×44
8. 3×121
9. 13×16
10. 23×33
11. 43×21
12. 12×18
13. 65×29
14. 81×384
15. 287×455
16. $432 \times 1{,}306$

Multiply. Name the property you used. **(pages 52–53, 58–61)**

17. $(45 \times 5) \times 4$
18. 325×8
19. 67×4
20. $(835 \times 2) \times 5$

Estimate. **(pages 62–65)**

21. 67×123
22. $4{,}903 \times 9$
23. 98×67
24. 8×212
25. 23×314
26. $8{,}624 \times 27$

Solve. **(pages 50–67)**

27. A plane ticket to the island of Borneo costs $987. How much will 4 tickets cost?
28. Megan is touring the Scottish highlands. Each day she travels 100 miles. How many miles does she travel in 14 days?
29. Explain how to use the Distributive Property to multiply 5×79.
30. Julie fills the 45 pages of her photo album with travel pictures. If she puts 4 photos on each page, how many are in the album? Explain if you need an estimate or exact answer.
31. Four busloads of tourists visit an art museum. If each bus holds 65 people, how many tourists visit the museum?
32. Is $4 \times 6 \times 3$ equal to $6 \times 3 \times 4$? Explain.

33. John buys 3 rolls of film that have 36 frames in each. Jill buys 4 rolls with 24 frames in each. Who has more frames? Explain.

Use Place Value Models to Multiply

The cost of a one-week trip to Washington, D.C., is $1,232.

How much will the trip cost for 6 people?

You can build a model of 6 groups of 1,232 dollars using place-value or base-ten models.

- Choose multiplication for the mat type.
- Stamp out 1 thousand, 2 hundreds, 3 tens, and 2 ones in each of the 6 sections at the top of the mat.

The number boxes keep count as you stamp.

How much will the trip cost for 6 people?

Use the computer to model each multiplication problem. Then write the product.

1. 5×458
2. $7 \times 1{,}076$
3. $3 \times 3{,}108$
4. $8 \times 1{,}186$
5. 321×4
6. 105×6
7. $2{,}119 \times 2$
8. $3{,}075 \times 9$

Solve.

9. Northeast Elementary School received a grant to purchase 5 new computer systems. Each system costs $1,468. What was the cost for all 5 systems?
10. A theatre has 2,450 seats, and tickets for all of the seats have been sold for all 3 performances. How many tickets have been sold?
11. **Analyze:** How does modeling the problem help you multiply?

For more practice, use Math Traveler™.

Objective: Multiply whole numbers by decimals.

2·7 Multiply Whole Numbers by Decimals

1 U.S. dollar = 0.7 dinar

Learn

The country of Jordan sits between Israel and Saudi Arabia in the Middle East. The local currency is called the Jordan dinar. On the day of an exchange, 1 U.S. dollar can be exchanged for 0.7 dinar. What is the value in dinars of 9 U.S. dollars?

There's more than one way!

Find: 9×0.7

Estimate: 9×0.7
$\downarrow \quad \downarrow$
$9 \times 1 = 9$

A

Use models.

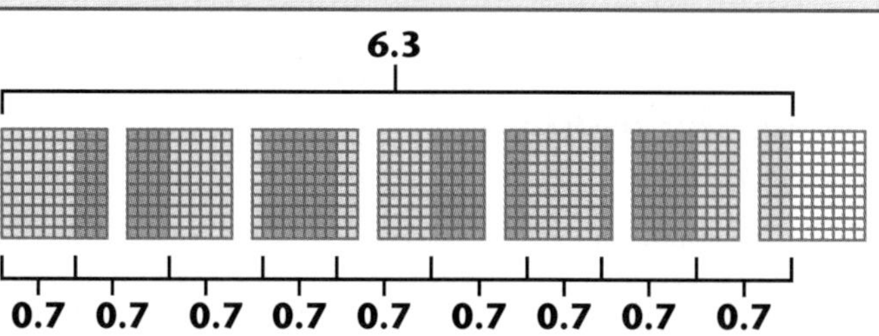

B

1. Multiply as with whole numbers.

$$\begin{array}{r} 0.7 \\ \times\ 9 \\ \hline 63 \end{array}$$

2. You can use the estimate to place the decimal point.

$$\begin{array}{r} 0.7 \\ \times\ 9 \\ \hline 6.3 \end{array}$$

Think: 6.3 is close to 9.

C

1. Multiply as with whole numbers.

$$\begin{array}{r} 0.7 \\ \times\ 9 \\ \hline 63 \end{array}$$

2. Count the total number of digits after the decimal point in each factor

$0.7 \leftarrow$ 1 digit

$\times 9 \leftarrow$ 0 digits

3. Add the digits. Count in that many places from the right in the product

$$\begin{array}{r} 0.7 \\ \times\ 9 \\ \hline 63 \end{array}$$

Think: count in 1 digit from the right

So 9 U.S. dollars equals 6.3 dinars.

You can use patterns to multiply decimals by multiples of 10.

Example 1

Find: $12.5 \times 1,000$

$$1 \times 12.5 = 12.5$$
$$10 \times 12.5 = 125$$
$$100 \times 12.5 = 1,250$$
$$1,000 \times 12.5 = 12,500$$

Think: the number of zeros in the multiple of 10 tells you how many places to move the decimal point to the right.

So $12.5 \times 1,000$ equals 12,500.

The product of a decimal and a multiple of 10 may also be a decimal.

Example 2

Find: 0.004×100

$$1 \times 0.004 = 0.004$$
$$10 \times 0.004 = 0.04$$
$$100 \times 0.004 = 0.4$$

So 0.004×100 is 0.4.

More Examples

A

$$\begin{array}{r} 5.8 \\ \times 29 \\ \hline 522 \\ 1160 \\ \hline 168.2 \end{array}$$

B

$$\begin{array}{r} 4.82 \\ \times \quad 3 \\ \hline 14.46 \end{array}$$

C

$$\begin{array}{r} \$5.35 \\ \times \quad 5 \\ \hline \$26.75 \end{array}$$

D

$$\begin{array}{r} 10.25 \\ \times \ 100 \\ \hline 1,025 \end{array}$$

Try It **Multiply.**

1. $\begin{array}{r} 2.3 \\ \times \ 3 \\ \hline \end{array}$

2. $\begin{array}{r} 5.1 \\ \times \ 3 \\ \hline \end{array}$

3. $\begin{array}{r} \$6.80 \\ \times \quad 3 \\ \hline \end{array}$

4. $\begin{array}{r} 0.9 \\ \times 10 \\ \hline \end{array}$

5. $\begin{array}{r} 1,000 \\ \times \ 14.7 \\ \hline \end{array}$

Will the product of 3.5 and 3 be 105 or 10.5? How can you tell without finding the exact answer?

Practice

Multiply.

6. 7.5 × 6
7. 16.3 × 9
8. 5.94 × 65
9. 75.21 × 8
10. 4.05 × 100
11. 5.4 × 4
12. 0.6 × 2
13. 3.05 × 5
14. 1.23 × 3
15. 0.03 × 10
16. 0.8 × 3
17. $0.92 × 6
18. 6.3 × 100
19. 9 × 2.8
20. 1,000 × $7.88
21. 9.68 × 8
22. 2 × 16.4
23. 25.8 × 4
24. 51.25 × 10
25. 123.3 × 2
26. 11.97 × 100
27. 50.025 × 10

Find the multiple of 10 that makes each statement true.

28. 2.3 × ■ = 230
29. ■ × 1.5 = 1,500
30. 0.69 × ■ = 6.9
31. 0.0044 × ■ = 44
32. 324.6 × ■ = 32,460
33. ■ × 0.003 = 0.03
34. $54.67 × ■ = $546.70
★35. 1.55 × ■ = 15,500
★36. 0.0004 × ■ = 40

Compare. Write >, <, or =.

37. 4.5 × 2 ● 0.9 × 10
38. 4.6 × 8 ● 9 × 3.7
39. 12.2 × 3 ● 0.9 × 5
40. 1.5 × 10 ● 100 × 0.15
41. 1.64 × 4 ● 6 × 1.1
42. 100 × 100 ● 10 × 1,000
43. 5.5 × 5 ● 3.3 × 6
44. 2.04 × 9 ● 0.9 × 20.4
45. 0.0015 × 1,000 ● 10 × 1.5
46. 0.01 × 10 ● 0.05 × 2
47. 4.5 × 4 ● 0.2 × 100
48. 12.9 × 1 ● 1,000 × 0.0129

49.

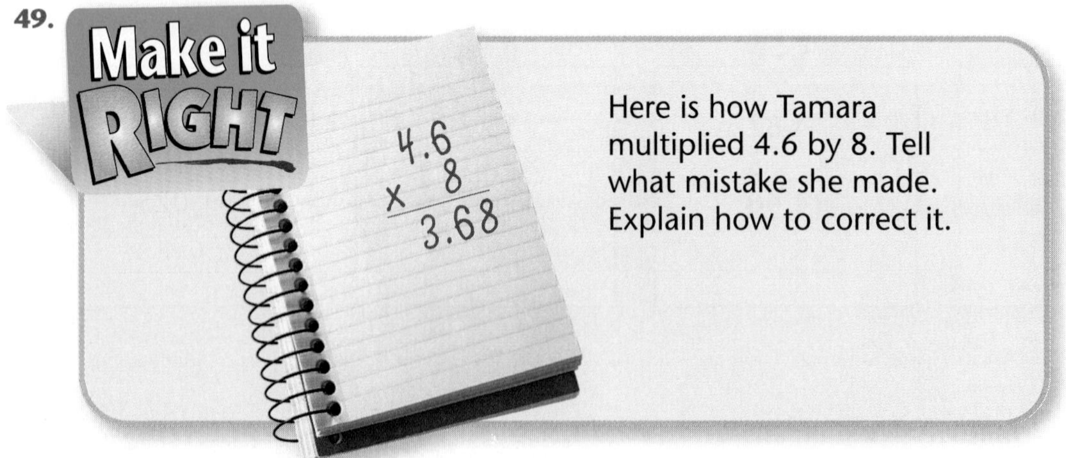

Here is how Tamara multiplied 4.6 by 8. Tell what mistake she made. Explain how to correct it.

Problem Solving

50. Will exchanges 100 U.S. dollars for Jordanian dinars. If the exchange rate is 0.7 dinar for each dollar, how many dinars does he receive?

51. At the same time, Alana exchanges 5 U.S. dollars for Jordan dinars. How many dinars does she receive?

52. **What if** 1,000 tourists each pay $5.25 to view an exhibit of artifacts from the ruins at Petra? How much money do they pay altogether?

53. Mrs. Carpenter buys 4 copies of a travel book about Jordan. Each book costs $29.90. How much does she spend?

Use data from the table for problems 54–57.

54. Which country has the most people?

55. Which country has about 1 million more people than Jordan?

56. Which country has about 3 times as many people as Israel?

57. If the fruit in an open-air market in Jordan costs 3 dinars for each kilogram, how much does 0.6 kilogram cost?

Population of Jordan and Its Neighbors

Country	Population (Rounded to the Nearest Thousand)
Jordan	4,561,000
Israel	5,750,000
Syria	17,214,000
Saudi Arabia	21,505,000
Iraq	22,427,000

58. **Social Studies:** The lowest place on earth is the Dead Sea. It is a very salty sea located between Israel and Jordan. It is 1,292 feet below sea level. What is this number rounded to the nearest hundred?

59. **Summarize:** How does estimating help you know where to place the decimal point in a product?

Spiral Review and Test Prep

60. $\begin{array}{r} 969.76 \\ 115.45 \\ +\ 58.37 \\ \hline \end{array}$

61. $\begin{array}{r} 74.43 \\ -\ 7.85 \\ \hline \end{array}$

62. $\begin{array}{r} 97.13 \\ +\ 8.88 \\ \hline \end{array}$

63. $\begin{array}{r} 206.888 \\ -108.913 \\ \hline \end{array}$

64. What fraction of the square is shaded?

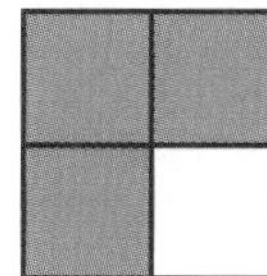

A. $\frac{1}{4}$ C. $\frac{3}{4}$

B. $\frac{2}{4}$ D. $\frac{4}{4}$

65. If a tour through the ruins of Petra costs $22 for each person, how much will it cost for a group of 20 people?

F. $44 H. $440

G. $40 J. $444

Extra Practice, page 92

Objective: Multiply decimals by decimals.

2·8 Explore Multiplying Decimals by Decimals

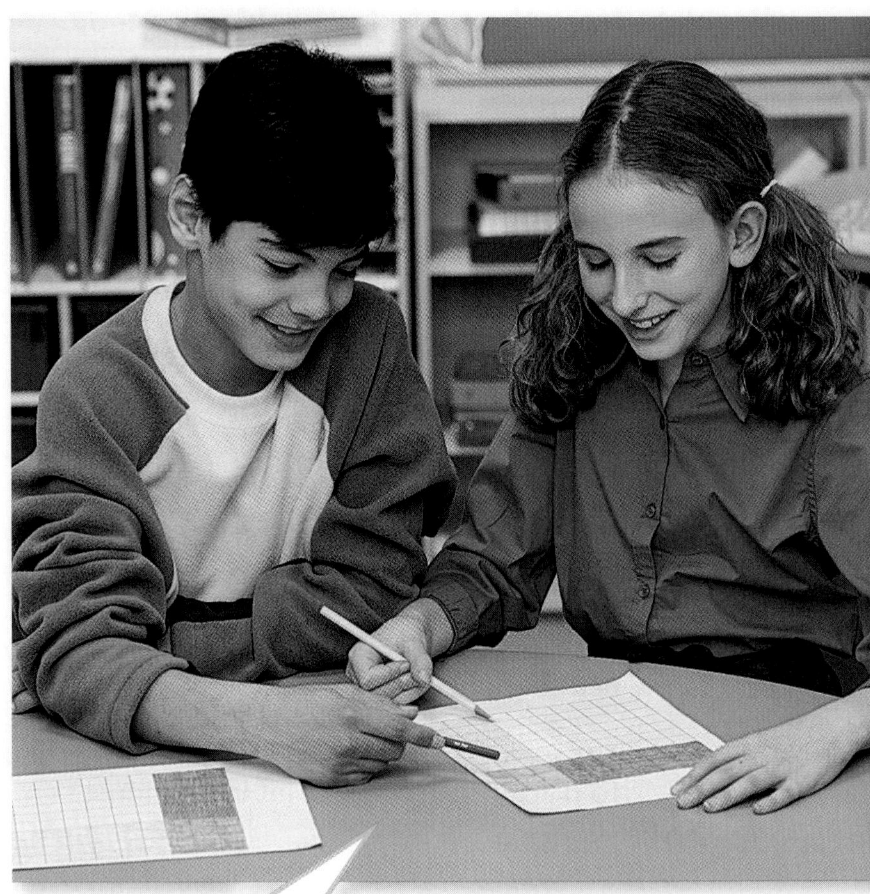

Learn

You can use graph paper and markers to explore multiplying decimals by decimals.

Work Together

Find: 0.4 × 0.3

You Will Need
- graph paper
- 2 markers

▶ Use 10-by-10 grids to model the multiplication of decimals. Each square represents 0.01.

- Shade the grid to show 0.4, the first factor.
- Using a different color, shade the grid to show 0.3, the second factor.
- Count the squares that are shaded twice.
- Record your work.

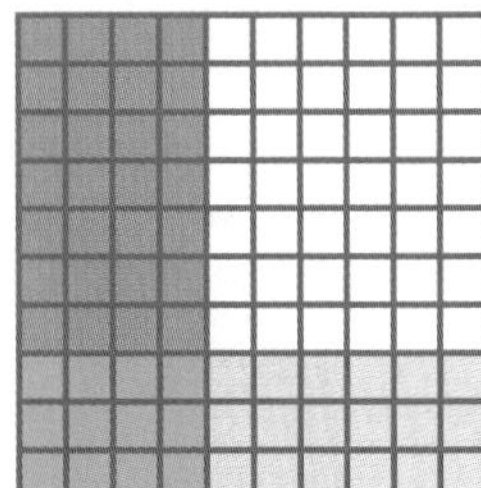

▶ Shade 10-by-10 grids to multiply. Record your work.

0.6 × 0.8	0.2 × 0.4	0.3 × 0.5	0.1 × 0.9
0.2 × 0.5	0.3 × 0.9	0.8 × 0.1	0.2 × 0.1

Make Connections

	Using Models	Using Paper and Pencil
Multiply: 0.6 × 0.3 Eighteen squares are shaded twice.		$\begin{array}{r} 0.3 \\ \times 0.6 \\ \hline 0.18 \end{array}$ Think: Place the decimal point so the product will be 18 hundredths.
Multiply: 0.5 × 0.8 Forty squares are shaded twice.		Think: Place the decimal point so the product will be 40 hundredths. $\begin{array}{r} 0.8 \\ \times 0.5 \\ \hline 0.40 \end{array}$

Try It **Multiply. You can use 10-by-10 grids.**

1. 0.4 × 0.6
2. 0.9 × 0.3
3. 0.5 × 0.4
4. 0.2 × 0.9
5. 0.3 × 0.3
6. 0.2 × 0.8
7. 0.8 × 0.7
8. 0.6 × 0.6

Explain how you would use 10-by-10 grids to find 0.8 × 0.7. What is the product?

Practice **Multiply.**

9. 0.7 × 0.5
10. 0.2 × 0.3
11. 0.3 × 0.8
12. 0.9 × 0.9
13. 0.7 × 0.7
14. 0.5 × 0.1
15. 0.4 × 0.7
16. 0.3 × 0.6
17. $\begin{array}{r} 0.5 \\ \times 0.9 \\ \hline \end{array}$
18. $\begin{array}{r} 0.6 \\ \times 0.7 \\ \hline \end{array}$
19. $\begin{array}{r} 0.1 \\ \times 0.7 \\ \hline \end{array}$
20. $\begin{array}{r} 0.8 \\ \times 0.8 \\ \hline \end{array}$
21. $\begin{array}{r} 0.3 \\ \times 0.7 \\ \hline \end{array}$
22. $\begin{array}{r} 0.1 \\ \times 0.9 \\ \hline \end{array}$
23. $\begin{array}{r} 0.4 \\ \times 0.4 \\ \hline \end{array}$
24. $\begin{array}{r} 0.5 \\ \times 0.6 \\ \hline \end{array}$
25. **Summarize** how to multiply 0.8 × 0.6.

Objective: Multiply decimals by decimals.

2·9 Multiply Decimals by Decimals

Learn

Nepal, home of Mount Everest and the Himalaya mountains, has spectacular nature views. One tour group walks a 4.3-kilometer trail 2.5 times before stopping for a rest. How far did they walk altogether?

There's more than one way!

Find: 4.3×2.5

Method A

1. Estimate the product.

4.3×2.5
$\downarrow \quad \downarrow$
$4 \times 3 = 12$

2. Multiply as with whole numbers.

$$\begin{array}{r} 4.3 \\ \times 2.5 \\ \hline 1075 \end{array}$$

3. Use your estimate to place the decimal point.

$$\begin{array}{r} 4.3 \\ \times 2.5 \\ \hline 10.75 \end{array}$$

Think: 10.75 is close to 12.

Method B

1. Multiply as with whole numbers.

$$\begin{array}{r} 4.3 \\ \times 2.5 \\ \hline 1075 \end{array}$$

2. Add the decimal places in the factors. Put that many decimal places in the product.

$$\begin{array}{rl} 4.3 & \leftarrow \text{1 decimal place} \\ \times 2.5 & \leftarrow \text{1 decimal place} \\ \hline 10.75 & \leftarrow \text{2 decimals places.} \end{array}$$

The group walked 10.75 kilometers.

Example 1

$$\begin{array}{rl} 0.2 & \leftarrow \text{1 decimal place} \\ \times 0.3 & \leftarrow \text{1 decimal place} \\ \hline 0.06 & \leftarrow \text{2 decimals places.} \end{array}$$

Think: Sometimes you need a zero as a place holder.

You can multiply any decimal by any other decimal. They do not need to have the same number of decimal places.

Example 2

Find: 3.7×12.79

Estimate: 3.7×12.79

$\downarrow \quad \downarrow$

$4 \times 13 = 52$

1 Multiply as with whole numbers.

$$\begin{array}{r} 12.79 \\ \times \quad 3.7 \\ \hline 47323 \end{array}$$

2 Count the decimal places in the factors.

$$\begin{array}{rl} 12.79 & \leftarrow \text{2 decimal places} \\ \times \quad 3.7 & \leftarrow \text{1 decimal place} \\ \hline 47.323 & \leftarrow \text{The product has 3 decimal places.} \end{array}$$

3 Check that your answer is reasonable. 47.323 is close to the estimate of 52, so the answer is reasonable.

So, $3.7 \times 12.79 = 47.323$

More Examples

A

$$\begin{array}{r} 1.243 \\ \times \quad 2.8 \\ \hline 3.4804 \end{array}$$

B

$$\begin{array}{r} 2.4 \\ \times 0.5 \\ \hline 1.20 \end{array}$$

C

$$\begin{array}{r} 0.005 \\ \times \ 0.06 \\ \hline 0.00030 \end{array}$$

Try It **Multiply.**

Remember: Estimate to check for reasonableness.

1. $\begin{array}{r} 0.9 \\ \times 0.3 \\ \hline \end{array}$
2. $\begin{array}{r} 0.2 \\ \times 0.4 \\ \hline \end{array}$
3. $\begin{array}{r} 1.7 \\ \times 0.6 \\ \hline \end{array}$
4. $\begin{array}{r} 2.46 \\ \times \ 0.8 \\ \hline \end{array}$
5. $\begin{array}{r} 3.54 \\ \times \ 2.8 \\ \hline \end{array}$
6. $\begin{array}{r} 0.29 \\ \times 0.05 \\ \hline \end{array}$
7. $\begin{array}{r} 3.05 \\ \times \ 0.4 \\ \hline \end{array}$
8. $\begin{array}{r} 18.4 \\ \times 0.01 \\ \hline \end{array}$
9. $\begin{array}{r} 2.165 \\ \times \ 0.25 \\ \hline \end{array}$
10. $\begin{array}{r} 310 \\ \times 1.4 \\ \hline \end{array}$

If you multiply 7.31×1.6, how many decimal places will there be in the product? How do you know?

Remember:
Estimate to check for reasonableness.

Practice Multiply.

11. 5.82×1.3
12. 72.68×8.3
13. 10.09×0.4
14. 1.11×2.2
15. 5.73×6.85
16. 234.813×0.3
17. 5.03×9.6
18. 12.4×1.63
★19. 413.12×33.7
★20. 3.429×0.84
21. 3.7×0.8
22. 4.9×0.6
23. 34.5×0.7
24. 82.49×0.6
25. 104.28×0.3
26. 1.8×3.6
27. 2.03×1.6
28. 0.091×2.8

Algebra & functions Find the number that makes each problem true.

29. $2.3 \times 1.4 = 3.\square 2$
30. $0.9 \times 0.06 = 0.\square 54$
31. $2.2 \times 0.2 = \square.44$
32. $0.2 \times 0.\square = 0.12$
★33. $1.\square 4 \times 0.4 = 0.776$

Compare. Write >, <, or =.

34. 0.92×0.5 ● 0.46
35. 1.7×0.8 ● 3.207
36. 0.065×7 ● $0.236 + 0.219$
37. 0.9×7 ● 0.7×9
38. 8.6×5 ● 4.31×3
39. 1.8×6.2 ● $5.05 + 5.05$

40.

Here is how Kelly multiplied 0.7 and 29.64. Tell what mistake she made. Explain how to correct it.

Problem Solving

41. The tallest mountain in the world is Mount Everest in Nepal. It reaches 8,796 meters. Climbers must let their bodies adjust to the thin air at high altitudes before attempting to reach the summit. If climbers rest at a base camp at 5,200 meters, how much farther must they climb to reach the top?

42. Nepal has two kinds of weather. The dry season runs from October to May. The wet season runs from June to September, when monsoons often flood the land. How many months does each season last? If each month in the wet season receives an average of 6.9 inches of rain, how much rain will fall during the wet season?

43. The population of the capital of Nepal, Kathmandu, is about 700,000. The population of the rest of the country is about 30 times greater. Estimate the population of Nepal.

44. The Nepalese rupee is the money unit of Nepal. If a person buys 2.5 pounds of fruit that costs 6.7 rupees per pound, how much does he spend?

Use data from the chart for problems 45–48.

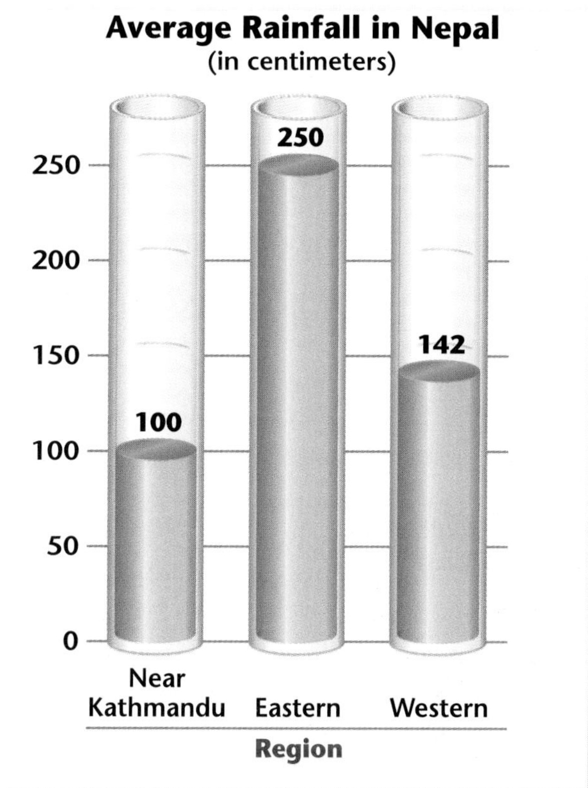

45. Does the Eastern region receive more or less rain than the other two regions together?

46. Order the three regions from most rainfall to least.

47. If 0.8 of the total rainfall comes during monsoon season, how much rain does the Western region receive during this time?

48. About how much rain will the area near Kathmandu receive in 15 years?

49. **Summarize** the steps you take to multiply a decimal by a decimal.

50. **Create a problem** that includes decimals as factors. Solve it. Then give your problem to another student to solve.

Spiral Review and Test Prep

51. 34.05 + 1.2 52. 1.4 + 0.5 53. 45.09 − 6.05 54. 1.23 − 0.66

Choose the correct answer.

55. The 6 in 412,809.87609 is in which place?

A. Hundredths C. Thousandths
B. Thousands D. Ones

56. Find the distance around the square.

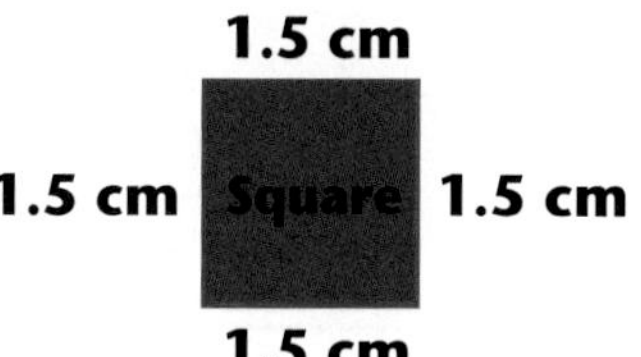

F. 28 cm H. 6 cm
G. 15cm J. 1.5 cm

Extra Practice, page 92

Objective: Solve problems by using the guess-and-check strategy.

2·10 Problem Solving: Strategy
Guess and Check

Bactrian camel

Read **Read the problem carefully.**

Camels live in many places across the globe, including Africa, Arabia, Australia, Asia, and South America. There are two kinds of camels. The Bactrian camel has two humps, while the Dromedary camel has just one. If you count 19 animals with a total of 27 humps, how many camels of each type did you see?

- **What do you know?** Bactrian camels have two humps; Dromedary camels have one; there are 19 camels and 27 humps.
- **What are you asked to find?** How many of each camel there are

Plan One way to solve the problem is to make a guess, check it, and adjust your guess until you find the correct answer.

Solve

Guess: 10 Bactrian camels and 9 Dromedary camels
Check: $10 \times 2 = 20$ humps → **20 humps + 9 humps = 29 humps**
$9 \times 1 = 9$ humps — **Too high. Adjust your guess: Try fewer Bactrian camels.**

Guess: 7 Bactrian and 12 Dromedary
Check: $7 \times 2 = 14$ humps → **14 humps + 12 humps = 26 humps**
$12 \times 1 = 12$ humps — **Too low. Adjust your guess: Try more Dromedary.**

Guess: 8 Bactrian and 11 Dromedary
Check: $8 \times 2 = 16$ humps → **16 humps + 11 humps = 27 humps**
$11 \times 1 = 11$ humps

There are 8 Bactrian and 11 Dromedary camels.

Look Back Does your answer seem reasonable? How would you check your answer?

How does the guess and check stategy help you solve problems?

Practice Use the guess-and-check strategy to solve.

1. Marla counts 11 camels with 18 humps. How many Bactrian and Dromedary camels did she see?

2. Sanjay sends letters and postcards to tell about his camel-riding adventure. A letter costs $0.33, and a postcard costs $0.20 to mail. He writes to 8 friends and spends $1.86. How many letters and postcards did he send?

3. Sanjay also sends letters and postcards to his teachers. He spends $0.93 on postage. How many teachers will receive mail from Sanjay?

4. Lonnie travels to Saudi Arabia. She spends $12.50 for a souvenir camel and a T-shirt. If the T-shirt costs $2.50 more than the camel, how much does the shirt cost?

Mixed Strategy Review

5. Misako works at the Historical Museum. She sets up tables for a group of visitors. The square tables seat two people on each side. How many people can she seat at 8 square tables pushed together end-to-end?

6. Jacob spent $700.00 on his trip to Tunisia. His expenses included $40.00 for bus fares, $15 for souvenirs, and $73.50 for hotels and food. His only other expense was his airfare. How much did his airfare cost?

7. A vending machine sells drinks for $1.50 and accepts only quarters. Carl has $1.55 in nickels and quarters. If there are 11 coins, does Carl have enough quarters to buy a drink from the vending machine? Explain.

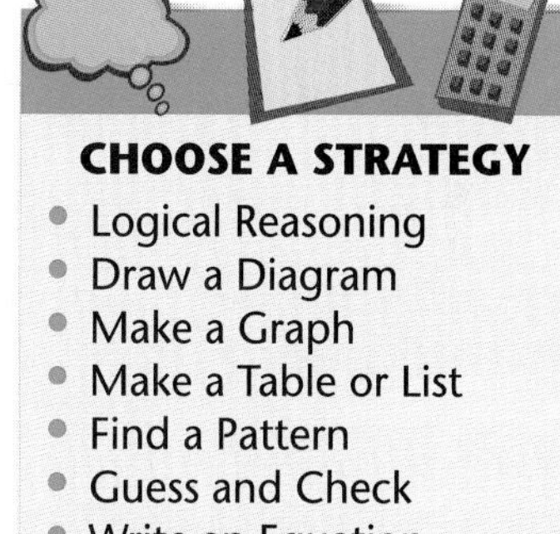

CHOOSE A STRATEGY
- Logical Reasoning
- Draw a Diagram
- Make a Graph
- Make a Table or List
- Find a Pattern
- Guess and Check
- Write an Equation
- Work Backward
- Solve a Simpler Problem
- Conduct an Experiment

8. The library charges $0.10 for the first three days of overdue books. It charges $0.05 for every day after that. Molly owed the library $1.50. How many days overdue was her book?

9. Each letter in this problem stands for a number. Find the number to replace each letter to make the problem true.

```
  SUN
 +FUN
 SWIM
```

Use data from the bar graph for problems 10–12.

10. Is it true or false that twice as many runners were from England than from France? Explain.

11. How many more runners live in Greece than in Spain and Italy combined?

12. Would it be correct to say that there were more runners from Greece and Switzerland than all other countries combined?

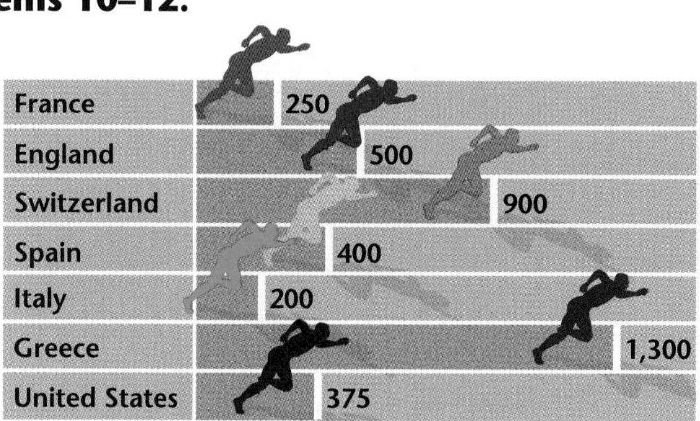

Runners From Each Country

Problem Solving

Extra Practice, page 93

Objective: Evaluate expressions with exponents.

2·11 Exponents

Learn

Math Words

base the number that is to be raised to a given exponent

exponent the number that tells how many times the base is used as a factor

power a number obtained by raising a base to an exponent

Although Easter Island is one of the most isolated places on Earth, people lived there thousands of years ago. A group of historians plans a trip to Easter Island. They make a phone tree so that each person calls two more people. If the first historian starts the phone tree, how many people can be reached in 5 rounds of phone calls?

Moais on Easter Island

Example 1

You can use a multiplication pattern to find the answer.

Round of phone calls	1	2	3	4	5
Number of people	2	2×2	$2 \times 2 \times 2$	$2 \times 2 \times 2 \times 2$	$2 \times 2 \times 2 \times 2 \times 2$

Multiply: $2 \times 2 \times 2 \times 2 \times 2 = 32$

You can use a **base** and an **exponent** to rewrite the problem.

$$2 \times 2 \times 2 \times 2 \times 2 = 2^5 = 32$$

Read: 2 to the 5th power.

exponent ↓

$2^5 = 32$

↑ base ↑ **power**

So 32 people can be reached.

More Examples

A

$3 \times 3 = 3^2 = 9$

3^2 is read "three squared."

B

$7 \times 7 \times 7 = 7^3 = 343$

7^3 is read "seven cubed."

C

$1 \times 1 \times 1 \times 1 \times 1 \times 1 = 1^6 = 1$

The number 1 raised to any exponent always equals 1.

You can use patterns to find the value of 2^1 and 2^0.

Example 2

What is the value of 2^1 and 2^0?

$2^5 = 2 \times 2 \times 2 \times 2 \times 2 = 32$
$2^4 = 2 \times 2 \times 2 \times 2 \quad = 16 = 32 \div 2$
$2^3 = 2 \times 2 \times 2 \quad = 8 = 16 \div 2$
$2^2 = 2 \times 2 \quad = 4 = 8 \div 2$
$2^1 = 2 \quad = 2 = 4 \div 2$
$2^0 = 1 \quad = 1 = 2 \div 2$

Think: Divide by 2 each time.

This pattern works for any base. You can try a base of 3.

$3^4 = 3 \times 3 \times 3 \times 3 = 81$
$3^3 = 3 \times 3 \times 3 \quad = 27 = 81 \div 3$
$3^2 = 3 \times 3 \quad = 9 = 27 \div 3$
$3^1 = 3 \quad = 3 = 9 \div 3$
$3^0 = 1 \quad = 1 = 3 \div 3$

Think: Divide by 3 each time.

Any base raised to the exponent 1 equals the base. So $2^1 = 2$.
Any base raised to the exponent 0 equals 1. So $2^0 = 3^0 = 1$.

Example 3

You can write some numbers using an exponent and a base.
Write 9 using an exponent and a base.

If possible, find a number that can be multiplied by itself a certain number of times to give the number you want.
$9 = 3 \times 3$

Write the factors with a base and an exponent.
$9 = 3 \times 3 = 3^2$

Try It

Rewrite using a base and an exponent.

1. 5×5 **2.** $10 \times 10 \times 10 \times 10$ **3.** $9 \times 9 \times 9 \times 9 \times 9 \times 9 \times 9$

Write in standard form.

4. 3^3 **5.** 5^1 **6.** 4^0 **7.** 10^5 **8.** 1^9

How are a base and an exponent used in place of a multiplication expression?

Extra Practice, page 93

Practice

Rewrite using a base and exponent.

9. 8×8
10. $3 \times 3 \times 3 \times 3$
11. $5 \times 5 \times 5 \times 5 \times 5 \times 5$
12. $2 \times 2 \times 2 \times 2 \times 2 \times 2 \times 2 \times 2$
13. $10 \times 10 \times 10 \times 10$
14. $4 \times 4 \times 4 \times 4$
★15. $(6 \times 6 \times 6 \times 6 \times 6 \times 6) \times 6$

Write in standard form.

16. 9^2
17. 4^3
18. 2^6
19. 3^7
20. 8^0
21. 3^6
22. 10^7
23. 12^2
24. 4^1
25. 8^2
26. 1^0
27. 1^1
★28. 11^3
★29. $(0.6)^3$
★30. $(0.03)^2$

Algebra & functions **Find each missing number.**

31. $3^{■} = 9$
32. $5^{■} = 125$
33. $14^{■} = 14$
34. $■^4 = 16$
35. $7^{■} = 1$
★36. $■^2 = 64$

37.

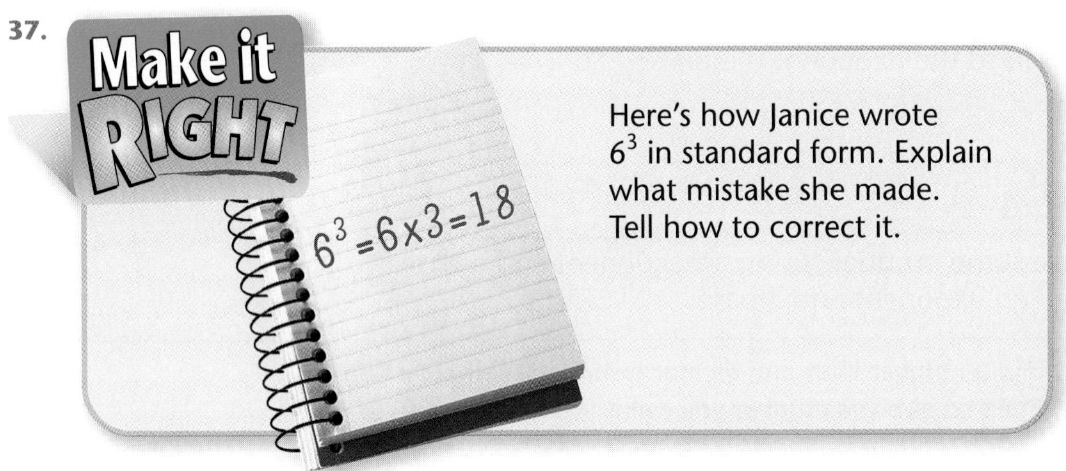

Here's how Janice wrote 6^3 in standard form. Explain what mistake she made. Tell how to correct it.

Problem Solving

38. The group traveling to Easter Island decides that each person will call three people instead of two. How many people can be reached in 4 rounds of phone calls?

39. **Mental Math:** If each rock sculpture on Easter Island weighs about 40 tons and there are about 60 sculptures, how many tons of rock sculpture are there on the island?

40. **Time:** The tour group gets on the bus at 8:20 A.M. The ride to the coast takes 3 hours 40 minutes. They spend $2\frac{1}{2}$ hours there, then ride the same bus back. What time do they return?

41. **Number Sense:** A scientist reads that the population of Easter Island was once estimated at 2×10^3. Write this number in standard form.

42. On Easter Island, a biologist collects 216 snail samples to take back to the lab for study. Write this number using a base and an exponent. Use 6 as the base.

43. Science: Some bacteria reproduce by splitting in two. Suppose the number of bacteria doubles every hour. If there are 2 bacteria to start with, how many bacteria will there be after 6 hours?

Use data in *Did You Know?* for problems 44–46.

44. If the stone carvers moved a Moai to the coast and then returned to the carving site, how many miles did they travel?

45. There are 2,000 pounds in each ton. How many pounds would a 50-ton Moai weigh? Write this number as a base and an exponent. Use 10 as a base.

★ **46.** How many times taller than a 5-foot fifth-grade student is the Moai found lying in the quarry?

47. Create a problem that can be solved using a base and exponent. Solve it. Ask others to solve it too.

48. Just 4 plane flights fly to and from Easter Island each week. How many flights occur during a year?

49. Compare: 3^2 and 2^3. How are they the same? How are they different?

★ **50. Explain** why 6 raised to the zero power equals 1.

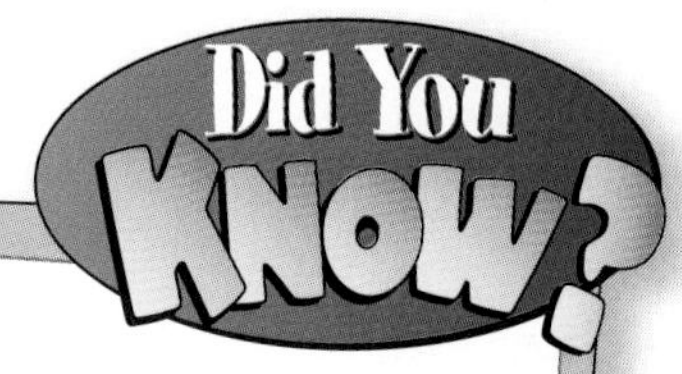

The giant rock sculptures on Easter Island are called Moai. The island people who carved them moved the Moais as much as 14 miles to the coast after making them. One sculpture, found still lying in its quarry, was 70 feet long. Many of the stones weigh up to 50 tons.

Spiral Review and Test Prep

51. $78 + 96$

52. $6{,}610 + 65$

53. $12.054 + 0.3$

54. $34.67 + 0.05$

Choose the correct answer.

55. Which number is 5 tenths greater than 64.327?

A. 64.377
B. 64.827
C. 69.327
D. 114.327

56. The product of 4 and 9 is

F. less than 30.
G. between 30 and 35.
H. greater than 30.
J. Not Here

Extra Practice, page 93

Objective: Apply multiplication to making decisions.

Problem Solving: Application

Decision Making

The German Club is planning a fund-raiser to send an exchange student to Germany. They have $69.70 to spend on supplies that they cannot obtain from school.

Which event should the German Club hold to raise funds?

Option 1 **Bake Sale**

Estimated Costs:		Baked Goods to Sell:
Baking Supplies	$55.00	20 dozen cookies
Bags/Labels	13.00	14 loaves of bread
Total	$68.00	22 pies
		18 cakes

Time needed to complete fund-raiser: 4 days

German Club Bake Sale

Bread	$2.50
Cookies	$3.50 per dozen
Pie	$4.00
Cake	$5.00

German Club Car Wash

Option 2 **Car Wash**

Estimated Costs:	
Soap	$8.00
Sponges	5.00
Wax	13.50
Total	$26.50

Time needed to complete fund-raiser: 1 day

Read for Understanding

1. How much will the bake sale cost? the car wash?
2. Which fund-raising event will cost the most?
3. Which fund-raiser will take more time?
4. If the German Club decides to double the number of cookies to 40 dozen, how many cookies will there be?

Problem Solving

Make Decisions

5. Suppose the price of car wax is 10 times what was estimated. What would the car wax cost?
6. **What if** the German Club sells $283 worth of baked goods? How much would their profit be?
7. How much would the German Club make if they wash 10 cars?
8. The German Club believes they can wash 4 dozen cars in one day. What would their profits be?
9. The German Club determines that they have enough supplies to hold a two-day car wash. What would their profit be?
10. How much would it cost the club to hold both a bake sale and a car wash? Can they afford to do this?
11. If the club receives a donation of $75.00, can they hold both fund-raisers? Explain.
12. How many cars must be washed to cover the cost of expenses?
13. About how many times more does it cost to hold a bake sale than a car wash? Round to the nearest whole number.
14. If the club could only wash and wax 10 cars with their supplies, how much profit will they make washing and waxing 10 cars?
15. What are the advantages to the car wash fund-raiser?
16. What are the disadvantages of holding a car wash?
17. What are the advantages of holding a bake sale?
18. What are the disadvantages of holding the bake sale?

What is your recommendation for the German Club? Explain.

Objective: Apply multiplication to investigate science concepts.

Problem Solving: Math and Science

Build a Model of the Solar System

Suppose you could drive a really fast car to Pluto. Did you know that it would take over 6,600 years for you to arrive?

The solar system is big! The distance from Earth to the sun equals 150 million kilometers (a distance also called an astronomical unit). To get a sense of the scale of the solar system, you can make a model.

You Will Need

- **paper**
- **tape**
- **pencil**
- **ruler**
- **meterstick (optional)**

Hypothesize

Draw a picture that shows the sun and nine planets. Put a dot for each planet to show where you think it will be in relation to the sun.

Procedure

1. Work with a small group.
2. Let 2 centimeters equal one astronomical unit.
3. Use the chart to calculate how many centimeters each planet should be placed from the sun in your model.
4. Draw dots for the sun and nine planets so that they have the proper distances from each other on the paper (you may need to tape a few sheets together).

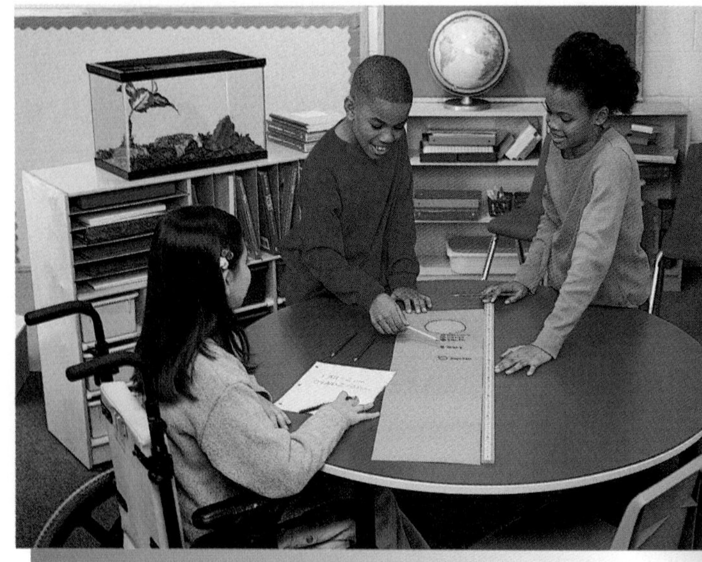

Data

Copy and complete the chart to record your calculations. Multiply the distance from the sun in astronomical units by 2 to calculate the distance for the model. Use the data to make the model.

Planet	Mercury	Venus	Earth	Mars	Jupiter	Saturn	Uranus	Neptune	Pluto
Distance from the sun (in astronomical units)	0.4	0.7	1.0	1.5	5.2	9.6	19.2	30.1	39.5
Distance in your model (in centimeters)			2.0						

Problem Solving

Conclude and Apply

- Compare and contrast your model with your drawing.
- Did your model use a good scale (2 cm = 1 astronomical unit)? Why or why not?
- If you could make the model again, what scale would you choose? Explain your choice.
- Use data from *Did You Know?* to explain why the *period of revolution* for Mercury lasts 88 days, but that of Pluto lasts 248 years?
- **Challenge:** Use the distances in the chart to find the period of revolution in years for each planet. Round to the nearest hundredth.

The time it takes a planet to go around the sun is called the period of revolution. The farther away the planet is from the sun, the longer it takes to go around. The period of revolution for Earth is one year. The period of revolution is related to distance by the formula $P^2 = D^3$, where P equals the period in years and D equals the distance in astronomical units.

Going Further

1. Look up the diameter of each planet, and make a scale model of the size of the planets. (Note: the sun, Jupiter, and Saturn may be too big to actually make.)
2. Explain why it is very difficult to make a model that shows both planet size and distance from the sun in the same scale.

Check Your Progress B

Multiply. **(pages 70–79)**

1. 0.3×3
2. 4.58×0.3
3. 6.8×10
4. 6.3×9.5
5. 0.05×2
6. $754.22 \times 1{,}000$
7. 3×17.54
8. 3.7×100
9. 8.002×4
10. 60.2×4.7
11. 4.64×7.8
12. 0.79×8.02
13. 0.005×100

Rewrite using a base and an exponent. **(pages 82–85)**

14. $2 \times 2 \times 2$
15. 3×3
16. $7 \times 7 \times 7 \times 7$
17. $9 \times 9 \times 9$
18. $4 \times 4 \times 4 \times 4$
19. $1 \times 1 \times 1$
20. $5 \times 5 \times 5$
21. $3 \times 3 \times 3 \times 3 \times 3$

Write in standard form. **(pages 82–85)**

22. 5^3
23. 7^2
24. 1^5
25. 8^0
26. 2^8
27. 3^4
28. 4^2
29. 6^3

Solve. **(pages 70–85)**

30. Stacy and 5 friends go to a movie. They each pay \$4.75 for each ticket. How much do they pay altogether?

31. Mr. Wood is taking a 10-day bike trip across Germany. He will bike 55.5 miles each day. How many miles will he bike altogether?

32. Vivian reads that about 10^3 people visit a certain museum each year. How many people is that?

33. Billy buys souvenir shirts. Long-sleeve shirts cost \$8 and short-sleeves cost \$6. He buys shirts for 10 friends and spends a total of \$70. How many of each kind of shirt does he buy?

Extra Practice

Patterns of Multiplication (pages 50–51)

Multiply.

1. 13×100
2. 420×10
3. $5 \times 1{,}000$
4. 203×100

The Distributive Property (pages 52–53)

Rewrite each problem using the Distributive Property.

1. 8×14
2. 22×6
3. 13×54
4. 145×7

Multiply Whole Numbers (pages 54–57)

Multiply.

1. $4{,}034 \times 8$
2. $86{,}114 \times 3$
3. 321×64
4. $71{,}044 \times 28$
5. $89{,}572 \times 7$
6. $54{,}987 \times 62$
7. 878×518
8. 495×104
9. $99{,}726 \times 99$

Solve.

10. Mr. Garcia buys 14 bus tickets for his students to go on a field trip. Each ticket cost $102. What is the total?

Properties of Multiplication (pages 58–61)

Multiply. Use mental math. Name the property you used.

1. 5×81
2. $1 \times 32{,}514$
3. $5 \times (4 \times 63)$
4. 901.24×0
5. 6×88
6. $(39 \times 6) \times 5$
7. $5 \times (12 \times 3.6)$
8. 5×5.9

Estimate Products (pages 62–65)

Estimate.

1. 9×781
2. 8×97.6
3. 27×521
4. 81×815
5. $1{,}821 \times 3.6$
6. 312×259
7. 883×429
8. $8{,}347 \times 98$
9. $5{,}733 \times 21$

Solve.

10. The Grand Canyon in Arizona is about 217 miles long. The Great Barrier Reef off the coast of Australia is about 6 times as long as the Grand Canyon. Estimate the length of the Great Barrier Reef.

Extra Practice

Estimate or Exact Answer
Problem Solving: Reading for Math (pages 66–67)

Solve. State whether your answer is an estimate or an exact answer.

1. Suppose 1,000 people are traveling to Egypt. One 747 airplane can carry 420 passengers. Will two 747s be able to carry 1,000 people?
2. What is the greatest number of people that seven 747s can carry?

Multiply Whole Numbers by Decimals (pages 70–73)

Multiply.

1. 5×2.2
2. 8×4.1
3. 0.7×6
4. 9.3×6
5. 3.8×1.2
6. 7.4×5
7. 3×10.3
8. 4×11.6
9. 8×15.5
10. 16.3×2

Solve.

11. Nadema fished for 3.5 hours a day for 4 days. How many hours did she fish?
12. The lake in which Nadema fished was 0.65 miles from her campsite. She walked to the lake and back each of the 4 days. How many miles did she walk altogether?

Multiply Decimals by Decimals (pages 76–79)

Multiply.

1. 0.6×0.4
2. 0.7×0.7
3. 1.3×0.8
4. 2.4×0.5
5. 0.4×0.2
6. 4.03×0.2
7. 6.22×1.9
8. 5.18×3.6
9. 2.5×6.3
10. 21.6×1.1
11. 42.2×0.3
12. 58.06×3.5
13. 87.88×9.4
14. 0.02×0.3

Solve.

15. A bus ticket to Florence, Italy, costs $75.50. How much will 6 bus tickets cost?
16. The students spent 3.75 hours riding gondolas in Venice. They walked 4 times longer than they rode in gondolas. How much time did they spend walking in Venice?

Extra Practice

Problem Solving: Strategy Guess and Check (pages 80–81)

Use guess and check to solve.

1. Kevin ran 120 minutes in Golden Gate Park in 2 days. He ran 20 more minutes the second day than the first. How many minutes did he run each day?
2. Suzanne bought 2 postcards of cable cars, and received $1.35 back in change in quarters and dimes. If she got 6 coins back, how many of each coin did she get back?
3. A ferry ride to Sausalito costs $7.50 for cars and $12.50 for trucks. In one trip $390.00 is collected from 40 vehicles. How many cars and trucks rode the ferry?
4. The sum of two numbers is 20. Their product is 96. What are the two numbers?

Exponents (pages 82–85)

Rewrite using a base and an exponent.

1. 8×8
2. $1 \times 1 \times 1 \times 1$
3. $4 \times 4 \times 4 \times 4 \times 4 \times 4 \times 4 \times 4 \times 4$
4. 2×2
5. $4 \times 4 \times 4$
6. $6 \times 6 \times 6 \times 6 \times 6 \times 6 \times 6$

Write in standard form.

7. 9^2
8. 3^4
9. 10^7
10. 1^5
11. 2^6
12. 6^3
13. 2^4
14. 9^0
15. 4^1
16. 5^4

Write each number using a base and an exponent.

17. 9
18. 32
19. 25
20. 27
21. 100

Solve.

22. A travel journal reports that the number of visitors to a city rose by 1,000 people the past year. Write this number with a base and an exponent.
23. Can the number 81 be written with a base and an exponent? Explain.

Chapter Study Guide

Language and Math

Complete. Use a word from the list.

1. In the expression 5^3, 5 is the ____.
2. In the expression 5×3, 5 and 3 are ____.
3. A number that is found after multiplying two or more numbers is called the ____.
4. A number that tells how many times a base number is used as a factor is called an ____.

Math Words
- array
- base
- exponent
- factors
- product

Skills and Applications

Multiply whole numbers and decimals. (pages 54–57, 70–79)

Example

Find: 8.7×60.9

Solution

$$\begin{array}{r l} 60.9 & \leftarrow 1 \text{ decimal place} \\ \times\ 8.7 & \leftarrow 1 \text{ decimal place} \\ \hline 426\ 3 & \\ 487\ 20 & \\ \hline 529.83 & \leftarrow 2 \text{ decimal places} \end{array}$$

Multiply.

5. $\begin{array}{r} 23 \\ \times 40 \\ \hline \end{array}$
6. $\begin{array}{r} 194 \\ \times\ 78 \\ \hline \end{array}$
7. $\begin{array}{r} 5,403 \\ \times\ 27 \\ \hline \end{array}$
8. $\begin{array}{r} 41.4 \\ \times\ 5.2 \\ \hline \end{array}$
9. $\begin{array}{r} 1.32 \\ \times\ 0.6 \\ \hline \end{array}$
10. $\begin{array}{r} 4.08 \\ \times\ 6.5 \\ \hline \end{array}$
11. 25.04×7.8
12. 0.03×0.2

Estimate products of whole numbers and decimals. (pages 62–65)

Example

Estimate: 63.2×27.9

Solution

Estimate by rounding.

$$\begin{array}{c c c} 63.2 & \times & 27.9 \\ \downarrow & & \downarrow \\ 60 & \times & 30 = 1,800 \end{array}$$

Estimate.

13. 33.33×74.8
14. 498×331
15. 362×986
16. $76,886 \times 6.4$
17. 54.98×17.2
18. $\$32.70 \times 20$

Use properties of multiplication. (pages 52–53, 58–61)

Example
Multiply: $4 \times 6 \times 25$

Solution
You can use the Commutative and Associative properties to reorder and regroup the factors.
$4 \times 6 \times 25 = (4 \times 25) \times 6 = 600$

Multiply. Name the property you used.

19. $5 \times 3 \times 20$
20. 16×8
21. 98×8
22. 537×0

Evaluate expressions with exponents. (pages 82–85)

Example
Rewrite using a base and exponent.

$3 \times 3 \times 3 \times 3$

Solution
3^4 ← **exponent**
↑
base

Rewrite using a base and an exponent.

23. $10 \times 10 \times 10$
24. $5 \times 5 \times 5 \times 5 \times 5$
25. $2 \times 2 \times 2 \times 2 \times 2 \times 2 \times 2$

Write in standard form.

26. 10^4
27. 1^8
28. 65^0
29. 15^1

Solve problems. (pages 66–67, 80–81)

Example
The admission to the Maritime Museum in Greece is \$5 for adults and \$3 for children ages 6–12. It costs a total of \$37 for 9 people. How many adults and children were in the group?

Solution
Guess: 7 adults, 2 children = \$41 too high
Guess: 5 adults, 2 children = \$31 too low
Guess: 5 adults, 4 children = \$37

There were 5 adults and 4 children in the group.

Solve.

30. There are 15 students taking a bus tour in Greece. Each student pays \$35.15 for the tour. How much does it cost for the 15 students altogether? Is your answer an estimate or an exact answer?

31. A group of 171 tourists go to Greece and separates into 3 groups. A group of 86 goes to the Parthenon. A group that is 25 tourists fewer goes to the Acropolis. The third group has a picnic on the beach. How many people are in this last group?

32. An adult and a child ticket cost \$10 total. The adult ticket is 3 times more than the child ticket. How much does each ticket cost?

33. Gary sees 14 wheels on a total of 6 bicycles and tricycles at the park. How many bicycles and tricycles does he see?

Chapter Test

Multiply.

1. 5×30
2. 2.7×10
3. 400×500
4. 0.4×0.6
5. 0.1×0.2
6. $6 \times 25 \times 3$

Estimate. Then multiply.

7. $\begin{array}{r} 289 \\ \times \quad 6 \\ \hline \end{array}$
8. $\begin{array}{r} 48 \\ \times 12 \\ \hline \end{array}$
9. $\begin{array}{r} 3{,}456 \\ \times \quad 28 \\ \hline \end{array}$
10. $\begin{array}{r} \$42.86 \\ \times \quad 34 \\ \hline \end{array}$
11. $\begin{array}{r} 2.7 \\ \times 6.2 \\ \hline \end{array}$
12. $\begin{array}{r} 40.23 \\ \times \quad 1.6 \\ \hline \end{array}$

13. 389×12
14. 6.12×0.9
15. 72.3×18

Multiply. Name the property you used.

16. $4 \times 8 \times 25$
17. 22×9
18. 97×6
19. $3{,}254 \times 1$

Rewrite using a base and an exponent.

20. $5 \times 5 \times 5 \times 5$
21. $9 \times 9 \times 9$
22. 7
23. $2 \times 2 \times 2 \times 2 \times 2$

Write in standard form.

24. 4^2
25. 6^4
26. 10^0
27. 9^1
28. 3^3

Solve.

29. Judy makes \$6.75 an hour. About how much did she make last week if she worked 39.5 hours? Is your answer an estimate or an exact number?

30. Scott plans to hike 16 miles in New Zealand in two days. If he hikes 2 miles farther the first day, how far will he hike each day?

31. A lemonade stand at a stop on the Tour de France has 40 quarts of lemonade in 12 containers. Some containers hold 4 quarts and some hold 2 quarts. How many of each are there?

32. The cost of 1 roll of film, including developing, is \$12.75. What is the cost of 15 rolls of film?

33. Each page of a photo album holds 6 pictures. Tom has filled 14 pages so far. How many photos are in the album?

Performance Assessment

Your class wants to earn enough money to buy an atlas with maps of all the countries of the world and a globe. The atlas costs $125, and the globe costs $100. You decide to sell snacks as a fund-raiser.

Complete the chart and use it to answer the question below.

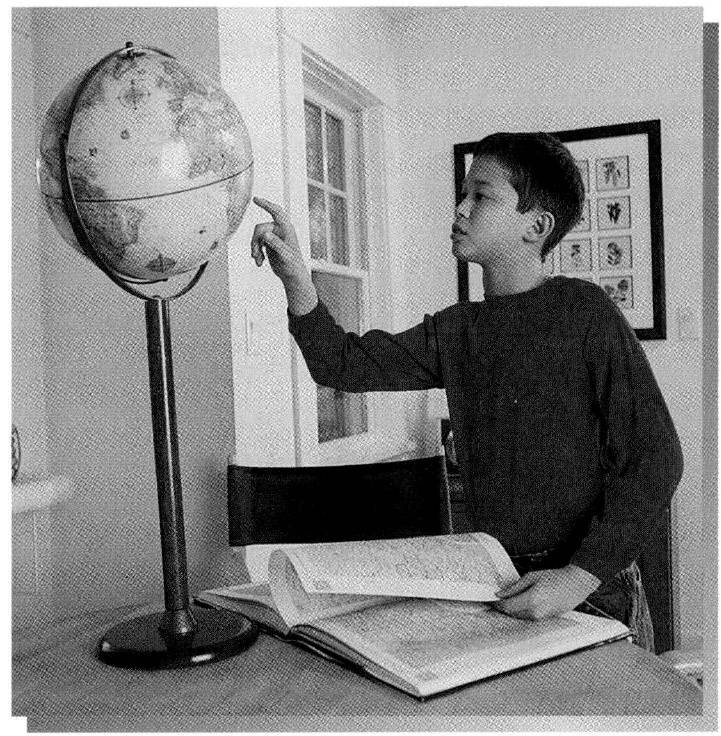

	Popcorn	Pretzels	Total Cost of Snacks
Number bought:	11 cases at $2.99 each case (6 boxes in a case)	3 cases at $11.99 each case (48 bags in a case)	
Total spent:	▮	▮	▮
Selling price:	$1.25 each box	$0.65 each bag	
Number sold:	65 boxes	140 bags	
Total earned:	▮	▮	▮
Total profit:	▮	▮	▮

- Can the class buy the globe or the atlas? Explain.

A Good Answer

- has a complete chart with each total.
- clearly shows how you found the totals for each snack.
- shows the steps you used to answer the question.

You may want to save this work in your portfolio.

Assessment

Enrichment

Use Compensation

Sometimes you can use compensation to multiply mentally.

Example

Multiply: 14×25

$14 \times 25 =$
$(14 \div 2) \times (25 \times 2) =$
$7 \times 50 = 350$

If you divide one factor by 2 and multiply the other factor by 2, the answer stays the same.

Note: You can multiply one of the factors by a number that is a divisor of the other factor.

So $14 \times 25 = 350$.

More Examples

A

$50 \times 68 =$
$(50 \times 2) \times (68 \div 2) =$
$100 \times 34 = 3{,}400$

B

$250 \times 12 =$
$(250 \times 2) \times (12 \div 2) =$
$500 \times 6 = 3{,}000$

C

$2.5 \times 16 =$
$(2.5 \times 4) \times (16 \div 4) =$
$10 \times 4 = 40$

D

$200 \times 43 =$
$(200 \div 2) \times (43 \times 2) =$
$100 \times 86 = 8{,}600$

Complete.

1. $50 \times 32 =$
   $(50 \times 2) \times (32 \div \blacksquare) =$
   $100 \times \blacksquare = 1{,}600$

2. $25 \times 84 =$
   $(25 \times \blacksquare) \times (84 \div 4) =$
   $\blacksquare \times 21 = \blacksquare$

3. $20 \times 15 =$
   $(20 \times 5) \times (15 \div \blacksquare) =$
   $\blacksquare \times 3 = \blacksquare$

4. $25 \times 12 =$
   $(\blacksquare \times 4) \times (12 \div \blacksquare) =$
   $100 \times \blacksquare = \blacksquare$

5. $300 \times 14 =$
   $(300 \div \blacksquare) \times (14 \times \blacksquare) =$
   $100 \times 42 =$
   $4{,}200$

6. $2.5 \times 64 =$
   $(2.5 \times \blacksquare) \times (64 \div 4) =$
   $10 \times \blacksquare =$
   160

Use compensation to solve.

7. 4×16
8. 3×27
9. 5×440
10. 25×884
11. 20×165
12. 50×64
13. 3×333
14. 25×36
15. 5×220

Test-Taking Tips

S.O.S.

When taking a multiple-choice test, be sure to read each question and the answer choices carefully. **Be aware of small words like *only, always, all, sometimes,* and *never.*** These words indicate there may be an exception to a general rule that you should consider before choosing your answer.

When you multiply two multiples of 10, the product will

A. always have the same number of zeros as the factors combined.
B. always have one less zero than the factors combined.
C. never have the same number of zeros as the factors combined.
D. always have the same number of zeros or one more zero than the factors combined.

If you can find even one exception to a rule, then the answers with *never* and *always* must be false.

If a rule is always or never true, then the answers with sometimes must be false.

Choice A is incorrect since $50 \times 60 = 3{,}000$.

Choice B is incorrect since $50 \times 60 = 3{,}000$.

Choice C is incorrect since $40 \times 80 = 3{,}200$.

The correct answer is Choice D.

You can also use these ideas to help answer true/false questions.

Check for Success

Before turning in a test, go back one last time to check.

- ☑ I understood and answered the questions asked.
- ☑ I checked my work for errors.
- ☑ My answers make sense.

Choose the correct answer.

1. The product of two multiples of 10 do not have the same number of zeros as the factors combined
   A. when the product of the basic fact ends with a 5.
   B. when the product of the basic fact ends with a 0.
   C. when one of the factors is 10.
   D. when one of the factors is 20.

2. When you multiply a decimal by a whole number, the product is
   F. always a whole number.
   G. always a decimal.
   H. always zero.
   J. Not Here.

3. The only time you should estimate is when you have no pencil, paper, or calculator, and the numbers are too large to multiply mentally.
   A. True. B. False.

4. When multiplying decimals, the decimal points will sometimes line up.
   F. True. G. False.

5. When you multiply two factors that do not end in zero, the product will never end in a zero.
   A. True. B. False.

Spiral Review and Test Prep

Chapters 1–2

Choose the correct answer.

Number Sense

1. If the 3 in 536,789 is changed to a 5, by how much will this increase the value of the number?
   A. 8 C. 20,000
   B. 2,000 D. 80,000

2. What is the standard form of 6,000 + 500 + 7?
   F. 6,507 H. 6,057
   G. 657 J. 6,570

3. What is 74.803 rounded to the nearest tenth?
   A. 74.8 C. 74.9
   B. 74 D. Not Here

4. What is the value of the underlined digit? 12,4<u>7</u>9,083,492
   F. 7 H. 70
   G. 70,000 J. 70,000,000

Mathematical Reasoning

5. Joanie has 24 marbles. If each marble has a mass of 2 grams, what is the total mass of Joanie's marbles?
   A. 12 grams C. 48 grams
   B. 18 grams D. 576 grams

6. Each egg carton holds 12 eggs. Marial has 18 egg cartons. Which number sentence tells the number of eggs in all?
   F. $18 - 12$ H. 18×12
   G. $18 \div 12$ J. 12^{18}

7. Signs on the Evergreen Trail show the distances to different lakes.

   How much farther is it to Long Lake than to Pine Lake?
   A. 1.7 miles C. 15 miles
   B. 2.5 miles D. 25 miles

8. If 1 plane ticket costs $457.25, how much will 17 tickets cost?
   F. $777 H. $7,773
   G. $7,000 J. $7,773.25

Statistics, Data Analysis, and Probability

Use data from the table for problems 9–12.

Height of Mountains	
Mountain	Height in Feet
Everest	29,028
Makalu	27,789
Pobedy Peak	24,406
McKinley	20,320
Whitney	14,494

9. How much higher is Mount Makalu than Mount Whitney?
   A. 13,295 feet C. 42,283 feet
   B. 14,534 feet D. 16,309 feet

10. There are 5,280 feet in one mile. About how many miles high is the peak of Mount Everest?
   F. 3 H. 4.5
   G. 6 J. 10

11. How much higher is the highest mountain listed than the lowest mountain listed?
   A. 1,239 feet C. 43,522 feet
   B. 12,390 feet D. 14,534 feet

12. Which mountain is more than twice as high as Mount Whitney?
   F. Makalu H. Pobedy Peak
   G. McKinley J. Everest

Algebra and Functions

13. $\blacksquare - 75.4 = 20.6$
   A. 54.8 C. 96
   B. 100 D. 96.8

14. Which property is illustrated in the equation?
   $89.5 + 0 = 89.5$
   F. Identity Property
   G. Commutative Property
   H. Associative Property
   J. Distributive Property

15. Complete.
   $50 \times 98 = (50 \times \blacksquare) - (50 \times 2)$
   A. 8 C. 16
   B. 100 D. 90

16. Describe the dimensions of all the rectangles that can be formed from 12 square tiles. Use all of the tiles for each rectangle.

Spiral Review and Test Prep

Divide Whole Numbers and Decimals

Theme: Wonderful Wildlife

Use the Data

Maximum Beetle Lengths

Goliath Beetle	110 millimeters
Asian Long-Horned Beetle	32 millimeters
Black Turpentine Beetle	8 millimeters
Pink Spotted Lady Beetle	6 millimeters

Source: Fantastic Book of 1001 Lists

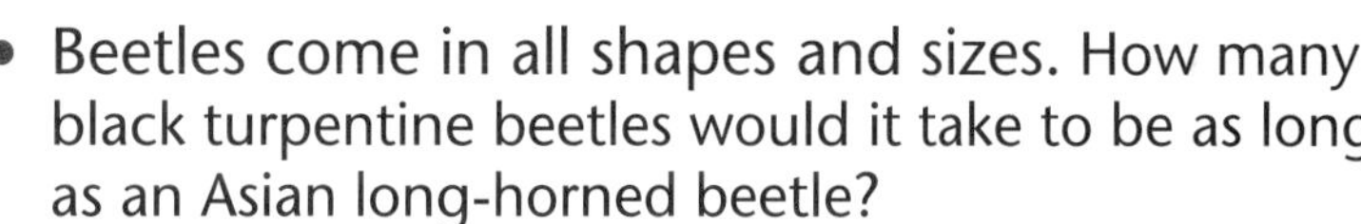

- Beetles come in all shapes and sizes. How many black turpentine beetles would it take to be as long as an Asian long-horned beetle?

What You Will Learn

In this chapter you will learn how to
- divide by 10, 100, and 1,000.
- divide whole numbers and decimals.
- estimate quotients.
- use strategies to solve problems.

Objective: Use the relationship of division to multiplication to solve division problems.

Relate Multiplication and Division

Learn

Math Words

dividend a number to be divided

divisor the number by which a dividend is divided

quotient the answer to a division problem

fact family a group of related facts using the same numbers

The spiny anteater does not have to move much to catch its prey. It can extend its tongue up to 6 inches to reach and eat insects. How many times longer is the spiny anteater's body than its tongue?

Example

Divide 18 by 6 to solve the problem.

A **fact family** shows how multiplication and division are related. The fact family for the numbers 3, 6, and 18 is:

$3 \times 6 = 18$
$6 \times 3 = 18$
$18 \div 6 = 3$
$18 \div 3 = 6$

18	÷	6	=	3
dividend		**divisor**		**quotient**

$6\overline{)18}$ with quotient 3

Think:
The quotient times the divisor equals the dividend.

If your body were 3 times longer than your tongue, you would only be about 1 foot tall. The spiny anteater's body is three times longer than its tongue!

Try It

Divide.

1. $24 \div 4$ **2.** $16 \div 2$ **3.** $30 \div 6$ **4.** $36 \div 4$ **5.** $56 \div 8$

6. $3\overline{)24}$ **7.** $7\overline{)49}$ **8.** $8\overline{)48}$ **9.** $12\overline{)72}$ **10.** $6\overline{)30}$

Explain how you can use a fact family to help you divide.

Practice Copy and complete.

11. $4 \times 5 = 20$
$5 \times 4 = 20$
$■ \div 5 = 4$
$■ \div 4 = 5$

12. $2 \times ■ = 12$
$6 \times 2 = 12$
$12 \div 6 = ■$
$12 \div 2 = 6$

13. $5 \times 3 = 15$
$3 \times ■ = 15$
$15 \div ■ = 5$
$15 \div 5 = 3$

14. $12 \times 7 = 84$
$7 \times 12 = 84$
$84 \div ■ = 12$
$■ \div 12 = 7$

Divide.

15. $45 \div 9$ 16. $42 \div 7$ 17. $24 \div 8$ 18. $81 \div 9$ 19. $48 \div 6$

20. $15 \div 5$ 21. $14 \div 2$ 22. $54 \div 9$ 23. $24 \div 6$ 24. $60 \div 5$

25. $5\overline{)30}$ 26. $8\overline{)32}$ 27. $6\overline{)42}$ 28. $4\overline{)36}$ 29. $7\overline{)49}$

30. $12\overline{)84}$ 31. $3\overline{)21}$ 32. $7\overline{)14}$ 33. $9\overline{)54}$ 34. $6\overline{)36}$

Problem Solving

35. There are two types of spiny anteater. The long-nosed variety can weigh up to 16 pounds, while the short-nosed can weigh up to 8 pounds. How many times heavier is the long-nosed than the short-nosed?

36. After a spiny anteater hatches from the egg, it remains in its mother's pouch. (At this stage, it is called a "puggle.") In the pouch, it can gain about 7 grams each day. How many grams does it gain in a week?

37. **Analyze:** Can you use a fact family to solve $216 \div 3$? Explain why or why not.

★38. **Science:** A 3-kilogram spiny anteater can eat up to 80 grams of ants in 4 minutes. How many grams of ants can it eat in one minute?

Did You Know?

The duck-billed platypus uses its rubbery bill to find food. Its total body length, including tail and bill, is about 63 centimeters. The bill extends about 9 centimeters, and the tail about 18 centimeters.

Use data from *Did You Know?* for problems 39–40.

39. How much longer is the platypus's tail than its bill?

40. How many times longer is the entire platypus than its bill?

Spiral Review and Test Prep

Name the value of the underlined digit.

41. $3\underline{2}6$ 42. $5.3\underline{6}6$ 43. $326.\underline{9}82$

Choose the correct answer.

44. What is the same as six and four tenths?
A. 1.64 C. 6.04
B. 6.4 D. Not Here

45. What is 19.23 rounded to the nearest tenth?
F. 19.22 H. 19.3
G. 19.2 J. 19

Objective: Divide by 1-digit numbers.

3•2 Explore Dividing by 1-Digit Divisors

Math Word

remainder in division, a number left after the quotient is found

Learn

You can use place-value models to explore dividing by 1-digit divisors.

Work Together

▶ Use place-value models to find 142 ÷ 4.

You Will Need
- **place-value models**

Show 142 as 1 hundred, 4 tens, and 2 ones.

Regroup the 1 hundred as 10 tens.

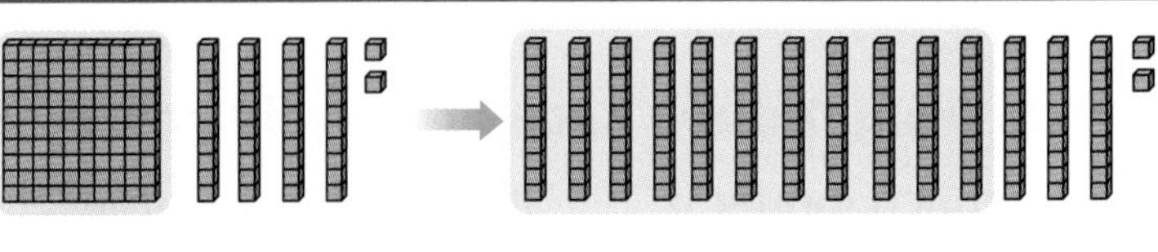

Divide the tens into 4 equal groups.

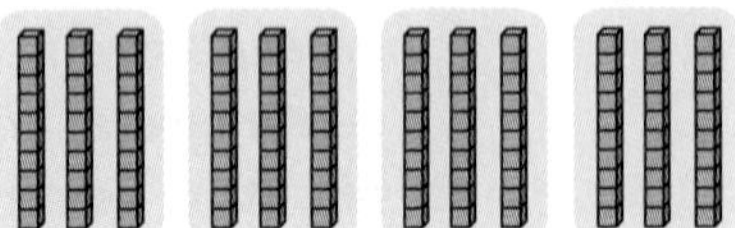

Regroup the extra tens as ones.

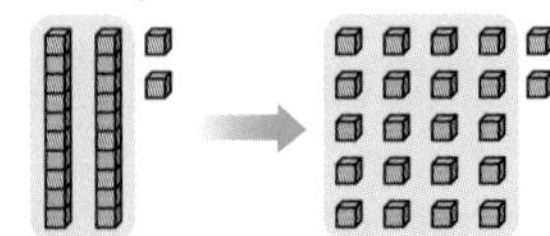

Divide the ones into 4 equal groups. Keep the **remainder** separate.

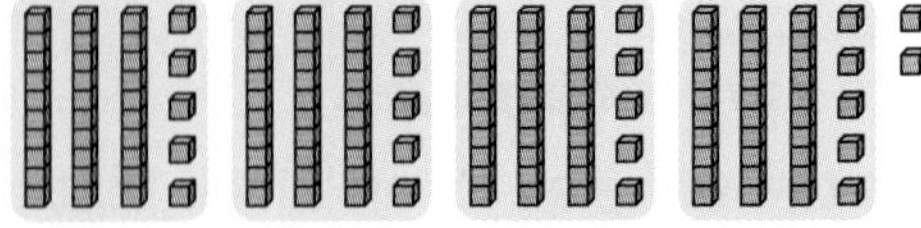

▶ Use place-value models to divide. Record your work.

119 ÷ 3   243 ÷ 5   150 ÷ 7   109 ÷ 4

Make Connections

Find: $35 \div 2$

	Using Models	Using Paper and Pencil
1 Set up the problem: 35 is the total to be divided into 2 equal groups.	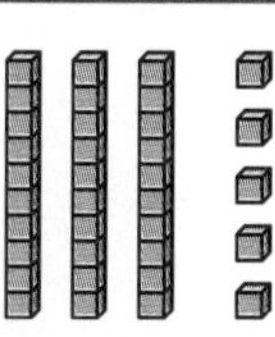	$2\overline{)35}$
2 Place one ten in each group. There is 1 ten and 5 ones still left.	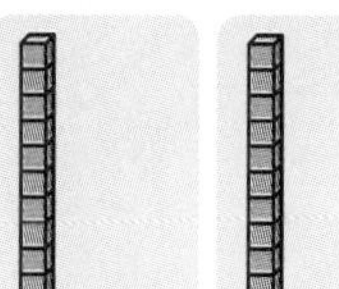	$\begin{array}{r} 1 \\ 2\overline{)35} \\ \underline{-2} \\ 1 \end{array}$ ← 1 ten in each group ← 2 tens used ← 1 ten left over
3 Regroup the remaining ten into ones.	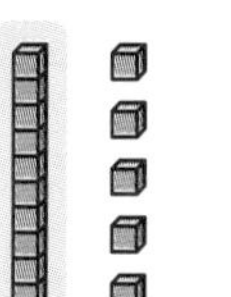	$\begin{array}{r} 1 \\ 2\overline{)35} \\ \underline{-2\downarrow} \\ 15 \end{array}$ Bring down 5 ones ← 15 ones in all
4 Place 7 ones in each group.	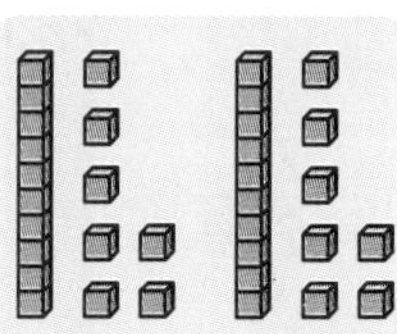	$\begin{array}{r} 17 \\ 2\overline{)35} \\ \underline{-2} \\ 15 \\ \underline{-14} \\ 1 \end{array}$ ← 7 ones in each group ← 14 ones used ← The 1 left is the **remainder.**

There are two groups of 17, and 1 left over. So $35 \div 2 = 17$ R1.

Try It **Divide. You may use place-value models.**

1. $97 \div 4$
2. $125 \div 6$
3. $7\overline{)118}$
4. $9\overline{)210}$

Explain how to use place-value models to find $116 \div 5$.

Practice **Divide.**

5. $3\overline{)67}$
6. $4\overline{)99}$
7. $5\overline{)207}$
8. $4\overline{)109}$
9. $200 \div 7$
10. $270 \div 8$
11. $184 \div 6$
12. $274 \div 7$
13. **Analyze:** How do models help you solve $121 \div 6$?

Objective: Divide whole numbers by 1-digit divisors.

3•3 Divide by 1-Digit Divisors

Learn

Wombats are fast-running, burrow-digging marsupials. They can live in a home area of about 6 hectares or about the size of 10 city blocks. How many wombats could live in a 4,250-hectare area?

Wombat home area: 6 hectares

Example

Find 4,250 ÷ 6 to solve this problem.

1 Decide where to place the first digit in the quotient.

$$\begin{array}{r} x \\ 6\overline{)4{,}250} \end{array}$$

Think: Estimate: 4,200 ÷ 6 = 700. The first digit of the quotient will be in the hundreds place.

The first digit will be in the hundreds place.

2 Divide the hundreds.

$$\begin{array}{r} 7 \\ 6\overline{)4{,}250} \\ -4\,2 \\ \hline 0 \end{array}$$

Multiply: $7 \times 6 = 42$

Subtract: $42 - 42 = 0$

Compare: $0 < 6$

3 Bring down the tens. Divide the tens.

$$\begin{array}{r} 70 \\ 6\overline{)4{,}250} \\ -4\,2\downarrow \\ \hline 05 \end{array}$$

Think: $6 > 5$. There are not enough tens to divide. Place a zero in the quotient.

4 Bring down the ones. Divide the ones. Write the remainder.

$$\begin{array}{r} 708 \text{ R2} \\ 6\overline{)4{,}250}\phantom{\text{ R2}} \\ -4\,2\downarrow\downarrow\phantom{\text{ R2}} \\ \hline 50\phantom{\text{ R2}} \\ -48\phantom{\text{ R2}} \\ \hline 2\phantom{\text{ R2}} \end{array}$$

Check your answer. Multiply the quotient and divisor. Add the remainder. 708 × 6 = 4,248; 4,248 + 2 = 4,250

It would be possible for about 708 wombats to live in the area.

Try It

Divide. Check your answer.

1. $4\overline{)185}$
2. $3\overline{)2{,}390}$
3. 9,783 ÷ 8
4. 47,902 ÷ 6

Sum it Up! Explain the steps you would take to find 436 ÷ 8. What are the quotient and the remainder?

Practice Divide. Check your answer.

5. $4\overline{)395}$
6. $6\overline{)932}$
7. $5\overline{)206}$
8. $8\overline{)270}$
9. $3\overline{)285}$
10. $7\overline{)698}$
11. $5\overline{)8{,}481}$
12. $8\overline{)2{,}893}$
13. 24,794 ÷ 9
14. 82,563 ÷ 6
15. 30,583 ÷ 4
16. 58,011 ÷ 7
17. 42,053 ÷ 2
18. 28,749 ÷ 8
★19. 912,872 ÷ 2
★20. 472,286 ÷ 5

Algebra & functions Find a number that makes each sentence true.

21. 325 ÷ ■ = 65
★22. 9,264 ÷ ■ = 1,852 R4
★23. 19,264 ÷ 9 = 2,140 R■

Problem Solving

Use data from the table for problems 24–25.

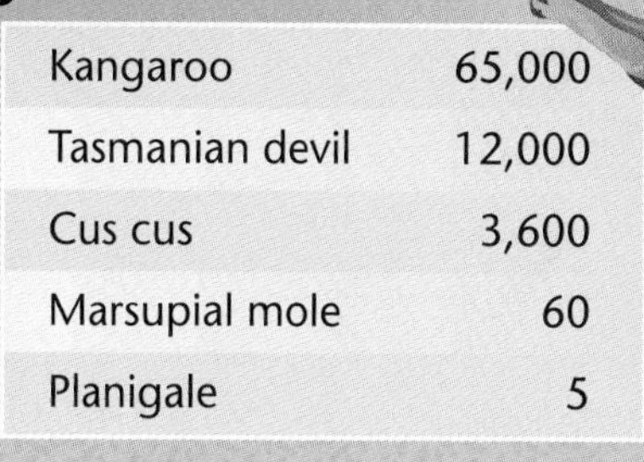

Approximate Weight of Marsupials, in grams

Animal	Weight
Kangaroo	65,000
Tasmanian devil	12,000
Cus cus	3,600
Marsupial mole	60
Planigale	5

24. Which animal weighs 720 times more than a planigale?
25. How many times more does a Tasmanian devil weigh than a marsupial mole?
26. **Explain** how you can use multiplication to check a division problem.
27. **Language Arts**: In the *Winnie the Pooh* books, Kanga and Roo are kangaroos. Kanga is the parent and Roo is the baby, or "joey." A grown kangaroo can weigh 145 pounds. A joey weighs about 5 pounds. How much more does the parent weigh than the joey?
★28. **Science:** Marsupial moles live in warm areas underground. They can live in an environment no warmer than 27°C. They will begin to shiver from the cold at 15°C. What is the maximum temperature range these moles can tolerate?

Spiral Review and Test Prep

Estimate the sum or difference.

29. 41.3 + 46.5
30. 1,226 − 647
31. 3,793 + 28
32. 1.152 + 4.777

Choose the correct answer.

33. Which of the following answers is the best estimate of 7.58 − 3.44?
   A. 11
   B. 4
   C. 5
   D. 0
34. The sum of two numbers is 15. Their product is 56. Which numbers are they?
   F. 5 and 10
   G. 5 and 6
   H. 15 and 56
   J. Not Here

Objective: Divide whole numbers by 2-digit and 3-digit divisors.

Divide by 2-Digit and 3-Digit Divisors

Can live at a depth of 2,620 feet

Learn

This fearsome fish is called melanoceutus johnsonii. It lives deep in the ocean. How many times deeper is its home than a 14-foot deep swimming pool?

Example 1

Find: 2,620 ÷ 14

1 Decide where to place the first digit in the quotient.

```
       x
14)2,620
```

The first digit will be in the hundreds place.

2 Divide the hundreds.

```
       2
14)2,620
   -28
```

Try 2.
Multiply: $2 \times 14 = 28$
Compare: $28 > 26$
Too high. Try 1.

```
       1
14)2,620
   -14
```

Multiply: $1 \times 14 = 14$
Subtract: $26 - 14 = 12$
Compare: $12 < 14$

3 Bring down the tens. Divide the tens.

```
      18
14)2,620
   -1 4↓
    1 22
   -1 12
      10
```

Multiply:
$8 \times 14 = 112$
Subtract:
$122 - 112 = 10$
Compare:
$10 < 12$

4 Bring down the ones. Divide the ones. Write the remainder.

```
     187 R2
14)2,620
   -1 4
    1 22
   -1 12↓
     100
     -98
       2
```

Multiply:
$7 \times 14 = 98$
Subtract:
$100 - 98 = 2$
Compare:
$2 < 14$

Check your answer. $187 \times 14 = 2{,}618$; $2{,}618 + 2 = 2{,}620$.

The melanoceutus johnsonii fish lives at depths over 187 times deeper than a 14-foot swimming pool.

You can also divide whole numbers by 3-digit divisors.

Example 2

Find: $9{,}945 \div 195$

Decide where to place the first digit in the quotient.

```
        x
195)9,945
```

The first digit will be in the tens place.

2 Divide the tens.

```
        5
195)9,945
    -9 75
       19
```

Multiply:
$5 \times 195 = 975$

Subtract:
$994 - 975 = 19$

Compare: $19 < 195$

3 Bring down the ones. Divide the ones.

```
       51
195)9,945
    -9 75
      195
     -195
        0
```

Multiply:
$1 \times 195 = 195$

Subtract:
$195 - 195 = 0$

Check your answer: $195 \times 51 = 9{,}945$.
So $9{,}945 \div 195 = 51$.

More Examples

```
    211 R14
19)4,023
  -3 8↓
    22
   -19↓
     33
    -19
     14
```

B

```
     51 R23
25)1,298
  -1 25↓
      48
     -25
      23
```

C

```
    301 R3
16)4,819
  -4 8↓↓
     019
     -16
       3
```

Try It **Divide. Check your answer.**

1. $11\overline{)3{,}479}$
2. $31\overline{)5{,}087}$
3. $86\overline{)7{,}852}$
4. $126\overline{)39{,}573}$

Explain how you would find $4{,}567 \div 15$.

Practice

Divide. Check your answer.

5. $24\overline{)4,613}$ 6. $71\overline{)9,106}$ 7. $392\overline{)2,045}$ 8. $317\overline{)5,488}$

9. $85\overline{)3,007}$ 10. $52\overline{)6,169}$ 11. $290\overline{)9,545}$ 12. $915\overline{)2,018}$

13. 75,058 ÷ 38 14. 39,428 ÷ 47 15. 1,258 ÷ 243 16. 61,945 ÷ 837

17. 31,506 ÷ 65 ★18. 80,020 ÷ 90 ★19. 25,462 ÷ 724 ★20. 346,898 ÷ 956

Find each dividend.

21. Quotient: 35 R2
Divisor: 17

22. Quotient: 291 R6
Divisor: 32

23. Quotient: 401 R20
Divisor: 123

Decide whether the first digit of the quotient is too high or too low. Then complete.

24. $\begin{array}{r} 5 \\ 49\overline{)2,406} \end{array}$ 25. $\begin{array}{r} 7 \\ 35\overline{)2,971} \end{array}$ 26. $\begin{array}{r} 6 \\ 56\overline{)39,401} \end{array}$ 27. $\begin{array}{r} 2 \\ 114\overline{)20,857} \end{array}$

Algebra & functions **Copy and complete.**

	Rule: Divide by 13	
	Input	Output
28.	654	■
29.	5,710	■
30.	12,687	■

	Rule: Divide by 26	
	Input	Output
31.	654	■
32.	5,710	■
33.	■	487 R25

	Rule: Divide by 216	
	Input	Output
34.	654	■
35.	■	26 R94
36.	12,687	■

37. 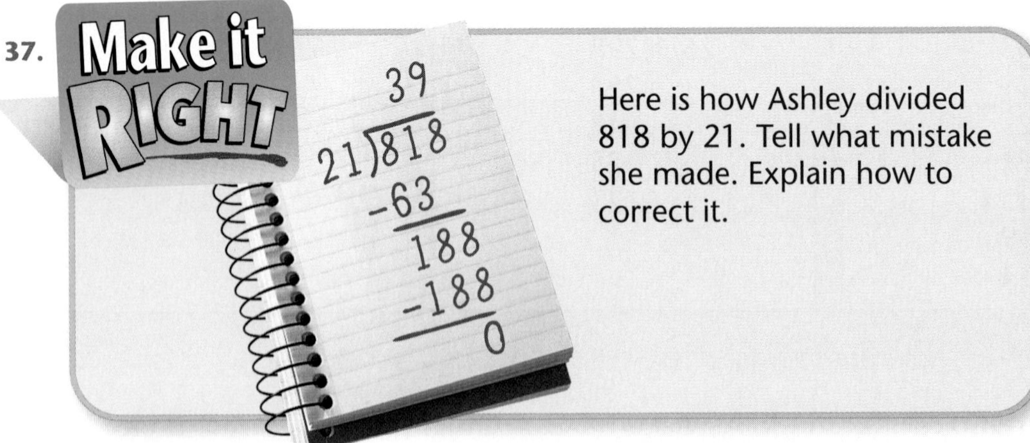

Here is how Ashley divided 818 by 21. Tell what mistake she made. Explain how to correct it.

Problem Solving

38. **Compare:** How is dividing by 2-digit divisors like dividing by 3-digit divisors? How is it different?

39. A flying fish can leap out of the water to avoid predators. It can "fly" about 20 seconds. If it leaps 14 times, how long will it spend in the air?

40. **Science:** The sea lamprey is a long, thin parasitic fish that attaches itself to another fish and feeds on the skin and blood of the other fish. If a population survey indicates that 5,692 lampreys live in an area covering 126 square miles, how many of these fish live in each square mile?

41. **Literature:** *The Shark Callers* by Eric Campbell tells the story of two boys who leave Papua New Guinea in boats and travel though shark-infested waters. The heaviest shark is the whale shark, weighing 46,297 pounds. How many times heavier is this shark than an 85-pound student?

42. **Science:** Electric eels can give an electric shock up to 650 volts. The source of the shock is nearly 6,000 elements concentrated in a 150-millimeter region behind the head. How many elements are found in each millimeter?

43. The porcupine fish is covered with tiny spikes, or quills. When threatened, it can inflate itself to appear larger. If a fish 75 millimeters across inflates to 190 millimeters, how many millimeters does it grow?

★44. The threespine stickleback fish is named for the three large spines that stick out from its back. It usually lives near the sea, but one fish was found 400 kilometers upriver from the nearest sea. The fish measured 40 millimeters in length. How many times its own body length did the fish swim upstream? Hint: 400 kilometers = 400,000,000 millimeters.

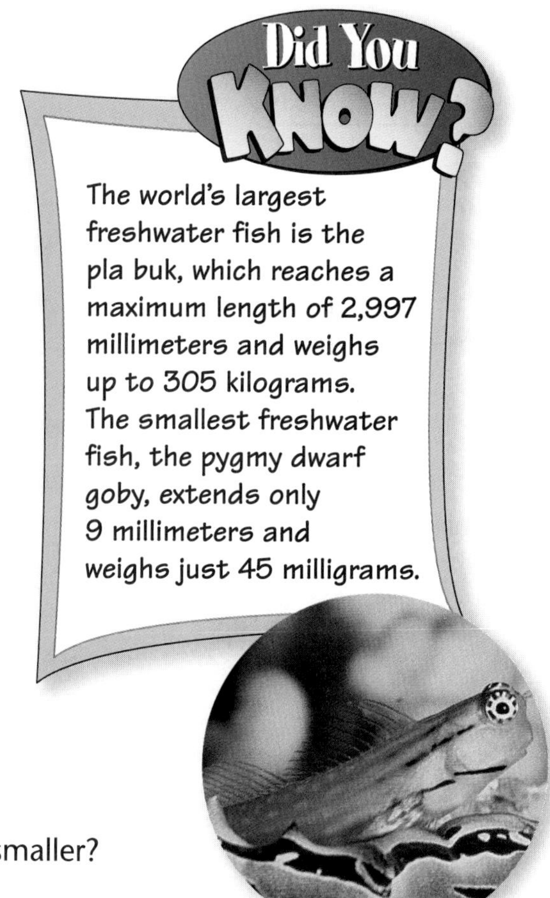

The world's largest freshwater fish is the pla buk, which reaches a maximum length of 2,997 millimeters and weighs up to 305 kilograms. The smallest freshwater fish, the pygmy dwarf goby, extends only 9 millimeters and weighs just 45 milligrams.

Use data from *Did You Know?* for problems 45–46.

45. How many times longer is the largest fish than the smallest?

46. How many times heavier is the largest fish than the smaller? Hint: 305 kilograms = 305,000,000 milligrams

Spiral Review and Test Prep

47. 253 + 57

48. 0.567 − 0.448

49. 1.43 + (3.12 + 0.57)

50. 2.629 − 0.05

Choose the correct answer.

51. Which has the same sum as 49.6 + 57.8?
   - A. 50 + 60
   - B. 50.0 + 58.0
   - C. 50.0 + 57.4
   - D. 50.0 + 56.2

52. Marty says that 4 + (6 + 2) equals (4 + 6) + 2. Nan says that it equals (2 + 4) + 6. Who is correct?
   - F. Neither Marty nor Nan
   - G. Nan
   - H. Both Marty and Nan
   - J. Marty

Objective: Divide by multiples of 10, 100, 1,000, and 10,000 and use compatible numbers to estimate quotients.

Estimate Quotients

Elizabeth Ford

Learn

Math Word

compatible numbers
numbers that can be divided mentally, without a remainder

Elizabeth Ford trains capuchin monkeys to assist physically-challenged people. In the wild, capuchin monkeys live in troops of about 9 monkeys. If a nature preserve is home to 27,000 monkeys, about how many troops live there?

There's more than one way!

Find: 27,000 ÷ 9

Method A

Find division patterns by using place value.

27 ones ÷ 9 = 3 ones ⟷ 27 ÷ 9 = 3
27 tens ÷ 9 = 3 tens ⟷ 270 ÷ 9 = 30
27 hundreds ÷ 9 = 3 hundreds ⟷ 2,700 ÷ 9 = 300
27 thousands ÷ 9 = 3 thousands ⟷ 27,000 ÷ 9 = 3,000

Method B

Find division patterns by using fact families.

3 × 9 = 27 So 27 ÷ 9 = 3
30 × 9 = 270 So 270 ÷ 9 = 30
300 × 9 = 2,700 So 2,700 ÷ 9 = 300
3,000 × 9 = 27,000 So 27,000 ÷ 9 = 3,000

So 27,000 ÷ 9 = 3,000. There would be about 3,000 troops.

You can also divide by multiples of 10, 100, 1,000, and 10,000.

Example 1

20 ÷ 4 = 5
200 ÷ 40 = 5
2,000 ÷ 400 = 5
20,000 ÷ 4,000 = 5
200,000 ÷ 40,000 = 5

Think: Placing the same numbers of zeros in the divisor and dividend does not change the quotient.

You can use division patterns and **compatible numbers** to estimate a quotient.

Example 2

Estimate: 212 ÷ 41

Think: 212 is close to 200. 41 is close to 40.

200 ÷ 40 = 5	200 can be evenly divided by 40 200 and 40 are compatible numbers	So to estimate 212 ÷ 41, think 200 ÷ 40 = 5.

So 212 ÷ 41 is about 5.

You can cross out zeros to make it easier to divide.

Example 3

Find: 56,000 ÷ 700

Cross out the same number of zeros in both the dividend and divisor. Then divide.	56,0~~00~~ ÷ 7~~00~~ 560 ÷ 7 = 80

So 56,000 ÷ 700 = 80.

More Examples

Estimate.

A

23,501 ÷ 5
↓
25,000 ÷ 5 = 5,000

B

3,562 ÷ 72
↓
3,500 ÷ 70 = 50

C

$195\overline{)15{,}678}$
↓
$\begin{array}{r}80\\ 200\overline{)16{,}000}\end{array}$

D

3,20~~0~~ ÷ 4~~0~~
↓
320 ÷ 4 = 80

Try It

Copy and complete.

1.
12 ÷ 3 = 4
120 ÷ 3 = ■
1,200 ÷ ■ = 400
■ ÷ 3 = 4,000

2.
28 ÷ 4 = 7
■ ÷ 4 = 70
2,800 ÷ ■ = 700
■ ÷ 4 = 7,000

3.
15 ÷ 5 = 3
150 ÷ ■ = 3
■ ÷ 500 = 3
15,000 ÷ 5,000 = ■

Estimate. Use compatible numbers.

4. 485 ÷ 7 **5.** 711 ÷ 9 **6.** 2,441 ÷ 58 **7.** 38,917 ÷ 45

Explain how you would use compatible numbers to estimate 368 ÷ 9.

Practice

Copy and complete.

8.
15 ÷ 3 = 5
150 ÷ 3 = ■
1,500 ÷ 3 = ■
15,000 ÷ 3 = ■

9.
63 ÷ 7 = 9
■ ÷ 7 = 90
6,300 ÷ ■ = 900
63,000 ÷ 7 = ■

10.
48 ÷ 4 = ■
480 ÷ 4 = 120
4,800 ÷ 4 = ■
48,000 ÷ ■ = 12,000

11.
180 ÷ 60 = ■
1,800 ÷ ■ = 30
18,000 ÷ 60 = ■
180,000 ÷ 60 = ■

12.
640 ÷ ■ = 80
6,400 ÷ 80 = ■
64,000 ÷ 80 = ■
■ ÷ 80 = 8,000

★13.
1,080 ÷ 120 = 9
■ ÷ 1,200 = 9
108,000 ÷ 1,200 = ■
1,080,000 ÷ ■ = 900

Divide.

14. 250 ÷ 5 **15.** 36,000 ÷ 9 **16.** 300,000 ÷ 5 **17.** 160 ÷ 40

18. 60,000 ÷ 10 **19.** 600 ÷ 20 **20.** 36,000 ÷ 12 **21.** 64,000 ÷ 80

22. 2,400 ÷ 30 **23.** 490 ÷ 70 **24.** 24,000 ÷ 600 **25.** 2,500 ÷ 500

★26. 280,000 ÷ 700 **★27.** 800,000 ÷ 800 **★28.** 3,500 ÷ 500 **★29.** 450,000 ÷ 900

Estimate. Use compatible numbers.

30. 753 ÷ 9 **31.** 512 ÷ 7 **32.** 3,465 ÷ 8 **33.** 16,101 ÷ 3

34. $62\overline{)371}$ **35.** $35\overline{)274}$ **36.** $48\overline{)2{,}867}$ **37.** $93\overline{)46{,}749}$

38. $481\overline{)1{,}859}$ **★39.** $852\overline{)26{,}043}$ **★40.** $528\overline{)33{,}842}$ **★41.** $167\overline{)472{,}217}$

42.

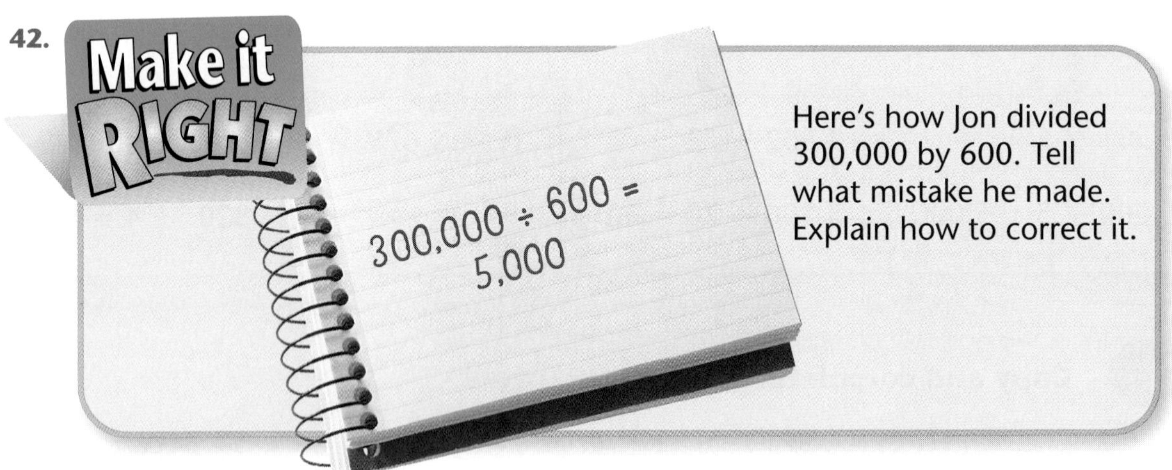

Here's how Jon divided 300,000 by 600. Tell what mistake he made. Explain how to correct it.

Problem Solving

43. Only about 400 golden lion tamarins (a type of primate) still live in the wild. They live in small groups of about 8 animals. About how many groups still live in the wild?

44. The aye-aye is the largest nocturnal (active at night) primate. It can live up to 280 months. A newborn will stay close to its mother for about 7 months. How much longer is the lifespan than the time with its mother?

Use data from the chart for problems 45–47.

45. How many more bonobo chimpanzees are there than golden lion tamarins?

46. How many more humans are there than mountain gorillas? than orangutans?

★47. How many times more humans are there than the other four primates in the chart all together? Round your sum to the nearest ten thousand to compare.

Estimated Primate Population in the Wild

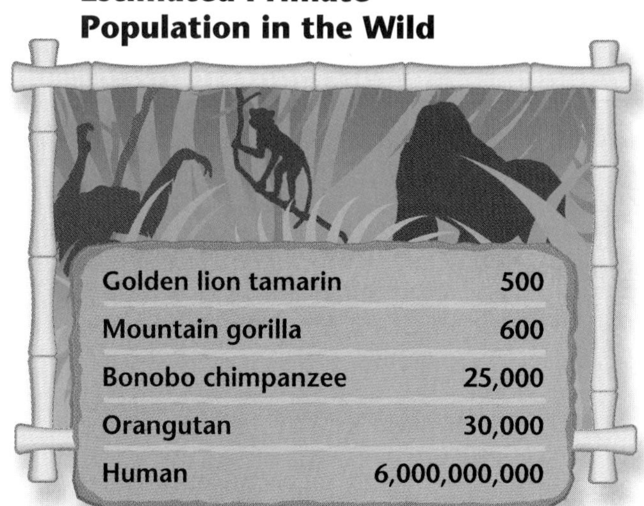

Golden lion tamarin	500
Mountain gorilla	600
Bonobo chimpanzee	25,000
Orangutan	30,000
Human	6,000,000,000

48. **Compare:** Which way of estimating 33,988 ÷ 75 is easier: Using the compatible numbers 32,000 ÷ 80, or rounding the dividend and the divisor to 34,000 ÷ 80? Explain.

★49. The White-cheeked gibbon usually lives at least 25 years. About every 5 days, it defines its territory with displays of yelling, jumping, and chasing intruders. About how many times will the gibbon make this display during its lifetime?

★50. Coquerel's sifaka, a dog-sized primate, live in small groups of 3 to 10 animals. Each group requires up to 22 acres of space. How many acres would 45 groups require?

51. **Collect Data:** Make a list of five different primates. Ask 20 classmates to choose their favorite primate from your list. Display the results of your survey in a graph.

52. **Social Studies:** The ring-tailed lemur lives on Madagascar, an island in the Indian Ocean. Madagascar extends about 1,600,000 meters from north to south. A lemur will wander about 800 meters each day. How many times longer is the island than the lemur's range?

53. **Explain:** How can you tell that 48 ÷ 6 and 4,800 ÷ 600 are equal, without doing any computation?

Spiral Review and Test Prep

Compare. Write >, <, or =.

54. 3.26 ● 3.25 55. 4.06 ● 4.13 56. 2.2 ● 2.21 57. 1.50 ● 1.05 58. 0.50 ● 0.5

Choose the correct answer.

59. Which of the following numbers is equivalent to 1.53?

A. 1.053 C. 1.530
B. 1.503 D. Not Here

60. A shape has sides that are all the same length. What shape is it?

F. Square H. Trapezoid
G. Rectangle J. Circle

Objective: Interpret remainders to solve problems.

3·6 Problem Solving: Reading for Math
Interpreting the Remainder

School Group Takes Trip

Read

A total of 190 students are going to the World of Butterflies exhibit. If each bus holds 60 students, how many buses will be needed?

READING SKILL

Make Inferences

You make an inference when you draw a conclusion from something hinted at.

- **What do you know?** **190 students will travel; each bus holds 60 students.**
- **What can you infer?** **Everyone needs a seat; the students want to use as few buses as possible.**
- **What do you need to find?** **The number of buses needed**

MATH SKILL

Interpreting the Remainder

- Sometimes only use the quotient and ignore the remainder.
- Sometimes the remainder is part of the answer.
- Sometimes you add 1 to the quotient.

Plan

Divide 190 students into groups of 60. Interpret the remainder.

Solve

$190 \div 60 = 3 \text{ R}10$ ← **The students will have 3 full buses, and 10 students in another bus.**

To make sure that every student is assigned to a bus, add 1 to the quotient. They will need 4 buses for the trip.

Look Back

- Is your answer reasonable?
- How could you check your answer?

How does making an inference help to interpret the remainder?

Practice

Solve. Tell how you interpreted the remainder.

1. Each picnic table at the World of Butterflies seats 8 people. How many tables will the 190 students need if they all eat at the same time?

2. The World of Butterflies is open for 9 hours each day. A 7-minute movie about butterflies plays continuously. How many times does the complete movie play each day? (Hint: 9 hours = 540 minutes.)

3. The theater seats only 9 students at a time. How many times will the movie be shown so that all the students can see it?

4. Only 15 students can enter the scorpion room at a time. How many groups will need to be formed if all the students want to see the scorpions?

Use data from the graph for problems 5–7. Solve. Tell how you interpreted the remainder.

5. If the students divide equally the butterfly photographs to put on 4 posters, how many photographs will be on each poster?

6. How many posters will the students need if they want to divide the moth photographs into equal groups of 12?

7. Explain a situation about a trip to a butterfly museum where you would ignore the remainder.

Insect Photographs

Number of Photographs: 0, 50, 100, 150, 200, 250

Name	Number of Photographs
Butterfly	213
Moth	89
Other Insects	42

Spiral Review and Test Prep

Choose the correct answer.

Forty-seven students plan an after-school trip to the Natural History Museum. They will travel in groups of 9 students.

8. How many parents would need to join the students if each group is accompanied by one adult?
   - A. 5 adults
   - B. 6 adults
   - C. 9 adults
   - D. 47 adults

9. How does an inference help you solve a problem?
   - F. Tells you something you already know
   - G. Gives you unnecessary information
   - H. Organizes the data into a chart
   - J. Helps you make a conclusion

Extra Practice, page 140

Check Your Progress A

Copy and complete. **(pages 104–105, 114–117)**

1. $24 \div 4 = 6$
   $240 \div 4 = ■$
   $2{,}400 \div 4 = ■$
   $■ \div 4 = 6{,}000$
   $240{,}000 \div 4 = ■$

2. $35 \div 7 = 5$
   $350 \div ■ = 5$
   $■ \div 70 = 50$
   $35{,}000 \div 70 = ■$
   $350{,}000 \div 70 = ■$

3. $48 \div 6 = 8$
   $480 \div 60 = ■$
   $4{,}800 \div 600 = ■$
   $■ \div 600 = 80$
   $480{,}000 \div 600 = ■$

Divide. **(pages 106–113)**

4. $631 \div 7$
5. $5{,}204 \div 8$
6. $40{,}687 \div 5$
7. $254 \div 15$
8. $2{,}217 \div 70$
9. $94{,}701 \div 63$
10. $344\overline{)9{,}218}$
11. $230\overline{)22{,}782}$
12. $709\overline{)81{,}375}$

Estimate. Use compatible numbers. **(pages 114–117)**

13. $8\overline{)635}$
14. $64\overline{)232}$
15. $59\overline{)3{,}454}$
16. $206\overline{)17{,}660}$

Solve. **(pages 104–119)**

17. The male platypus can be about 50 centimeters long. It has a small spur on its rear leg, which can give off venom. The spur is about 2 centimeters long. How much longer is the platypus than its spur?

18. Emus lay their eggs in nests under bushes. Each nest holds up to 12 eggs. If a population survey of a bird sanctuary finds 1,848 eggs, how many nests are there?

19. A Tasmanian devil searches for food at night. It can roam up to 16,000 meters each night. If it looks for food for 8 hours, how far does it go each hour?

20. **Compare:** Tosha used $4{,}200 \div 60$ to estimate $4{,}527 \div 57$. Greg used $4{,}800 \div 60$ to estimate the same quotient. Who is correct? Explain.

Use the Internet

Ms. Warren's class is gathering data on the highest and lowest points in different countries of the world. They need to find data for three different countries. They will use the data they collect to complete the following table. How can they use the Internet to gather the data?

Country	Highest Point	Lowest Point	Times Highest Point Is Higher Than Lowest Point

- Go to www.mhschool.com/math.
- Find the list of sites that provide world data. Click on a link.
- Find the data on land elevation of countries. Choose three countries for which data is given.
- Copy the table. Write the names of the countries you chose in your table.
- Record the elevation of the highest and lowest points for each country in the table.
- Estimate how many times higher the high point is than the low point.

1. Which country has a high point that is the greatest number of times the low point? the least?

2. **Analyze:** Why does using the Internet make more sense than using another reference source to find the data needed to complete your table?

For more practice, use Math Traveler™.

Objective: Solve a division problem using the work-backward strategy.

Problem Solving: Strategy
Work Backward

Read

Read the problem carefully.

The Nature Club raised $125 to buy and install nesting boxes for birds at a wildlife site. Each box costs $5 and the bus to the site costs $75. How many boxes can the club buy?

- What do you know? **$125 is available/ Each box costs $5/ The bus costs $75.**
- What are you asked to find? **How many boxes can be bought.**

Plan

You can work backward to find the number of boxes that can be bought. You use math operations to undo each step.

Solve

Work backward.

$\$125 - \$75 = \$50$	Undo the addition of the cost of the bus	→	**Subtract the cost of the bus.**
$\$50 \div \$5 = 10$	Undo the multiplication of the cost of the boxes	→	**Divide by the cost for each box.**

Ten boxes can be bought.

Look Back

How could you check your answer?

If the student group now has $150 and the bus costs $60, how many boxes can they buy? Show your work.

Practice

Use the work-backward strategy to solve.

1. A scientist plans to study exotic birds in the rain forest. A helicopter flight costs $499. Supplies cost $112 for each day. How many days can the scientist stay in the rainforest on a $1,283 budget?

2. The school environment club raised money to help clean up a local pond. They spent $14 for trash bags. They spent half of the remaining money on waterproof boots. The club still has $47 left over. How much did they raise?

3. Wyatt counts 16 baby birds. He also sees 53 female birds. If there are equal numbers of males and females, how many birds did he count?

4. The student government sells raffle tickets to raise money. The first 20 tickets sold cost $4 and all other tickets cost $2. They raise $216. How many tickets did they sell?

5. A student group visits a bird sanctuary. They pay $12 for each student, but receive a $34 group discount. They pay $242 for the group's admission after receiving the discount. How many students were in the group?

6. Paco, Shonda, and Mary fill jars with water samples. Shonda fills half of the jars. Mary and Paco each fill half of the remainder. They return to school with 12 jars. How many did Paco fill?

Mixed Strategy Review

CHOOSE A STRATEGY

- Logical Reasoning
- Draw a Diagram
- Make a Graph
- Make a Table or List
- Find a Pattern
- Guess and Check
- Write an Equation
- Work Backward
- Solve a Simpler Problem
- Conduct an Experiment

7. **Logical Reasoning:** Sean is thinking of a number. It has 3 ones. It has twice as many hundreds as ones, and 3 times as many tens as ones. It has 2 more thousands than hundreds. What is the number?

8. A group of 18 people wants to make one long table. Each table is a rectangle that seats 2 on the long sides and one on the short sides. If they place the short sides together, how many tables do they need?

9. Betty tells Vern to pick a number, add 17, multiply the sum by 3 and subtract 2. Vern's final answer is 103. What number did he pick?

Use data from the graph for problems 10–11.

10. About how far can a pronghorn antelope run in 1 minute?

11. How long would it take a wildebeest to run 250 miles?

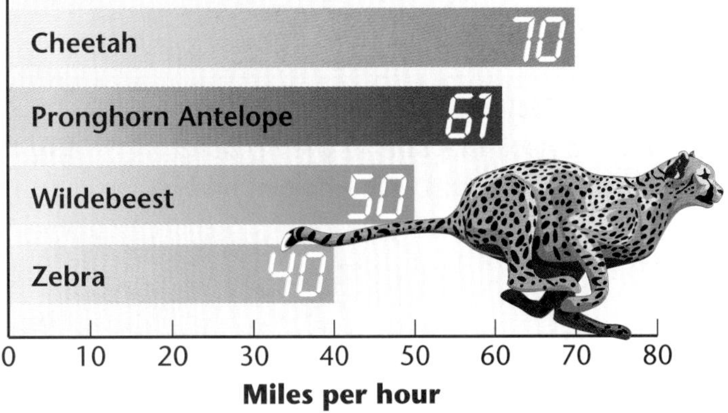

Extra Practice, page 140

Objective: Divide decimals by whole numbers.

3·8 Divide Decimals by Whole Numbers

Learn

Did you know that a sponge is actually a type of animal? Sponges live rooted to one place and filter water to get food. How many liters of water can some sponges filter in 1 hour?

Filters 26.4 liters in 4 hours

Example 1

Find 26.4 ÷ 4 to solve the problem.

Place the decimal point in the quotient above the decimal point in the dividend. Divide like you would with whole numbers.

```
    6.6
 4)26.4
  -24 ↓
    2 4
   -2 4
      0
```

Multiply the quotient and divisor to check: $6.6 \times 4 = 26.4$

Some sponges can filter up to 6.6 liters of water in one hour.

You may get a decimal quotient when you divide a whole number by a whole number.

Example 2

Find: 130 ÷ 20

You can use properties and the skills of Example 2 to show why 26.4 ÷ 4 = 6.6

Place the decimal point in the quotient above the decimal point in the dividend. Divide like you would with whole numbers.

```
       6.5
 20)130.0
   -120 ↓
     10 0
    -10 0
        0
```

$26.4 \div 4 =$

$((26.4 \times 10) \div 4) \div 10 =$

$(264 \div 4) \div 10 =$

$66 \div 10 =$

6.6

Sometimes the quotient will need to be rounded.

Example 3

Divide 139 by 26. Round the quotient to the nearest tenth.

Divide to one more place than you are rounding the quotient to.

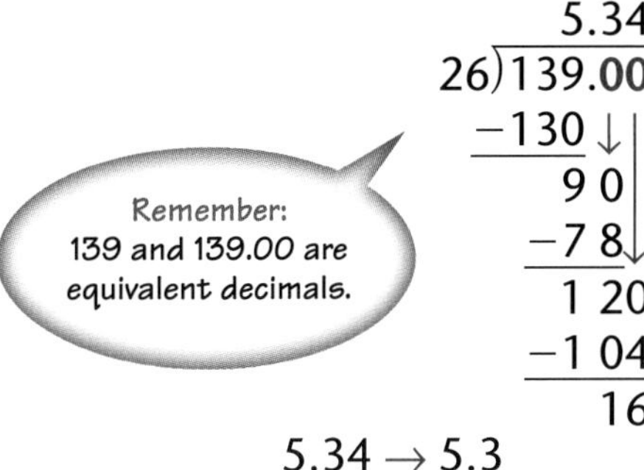

5.34 → 5.3

So 139 ÷ 26 is 5.3 to the nearest tenth.

You can use a division pattern to divide by 10, 100, and 1,000.

Example 4

Find: 29.7 ÷ 1,000

When you divide by 10, 100, and 1,000, the number of zeros in the divisor tells how many places to the left the decimal point moves in the dividend.

Move the decimal one place to the left when you divide by 10.

Move two places left when you divide by 100. Move 3 places left when you divide by 1,000.

29.7 ÷ 1 = 29.7
29.7 ÷ 10 = 2.97
29.7 ÷ 100 = **0**.297
29.7 ÷ 1,000 = **0.0**297

So 29.7 ÷ 1,000 is 0.0297.

Try It **Divide. Check your answer.**

1. 11.65 ÷ 5 **2.** 2.82 ÷ 6 **3.** 17.85 ÷ 3 **4.** 25 ÷ 10 **5.** 324.6 ÷ 100

Divide. Round the quotient to the nearest tenth.

6. 20 ÷ 7 **7.** 18 ÷ 32 **8.** 3.7 ÷ 4 **9.** 12.6 ÷ 8 **10.** 128.5 ÷ 9

Explain how to find 4.5 ÷ 5.

Practice

Divide. Round each quotient to the nearest hundredth if necessary.

Remember: Multiply to check your answers.

11. $7\overline{)9.1}$ **12.** $3\overline{)6.3}$ **13.** $4\overline{)5.2}$ **14.** $9\overline{)64.08}$

15. $5\overline{)2.7}$ **16.** $10\overline{)3.6}$ **17.** $6\overline{)7.92}$ **18.** $4\overline{)21.26}$

19. $3\overline{)1.57}$ **20.** $100\overline{)592}$ **21.** $6\overline{)27}$ **22.** $4\overline{)30}$

23. $85.7 \div 2$ **24.** $8.5 \div 4$ **25.** $25.16 \div 8$ **26.** $4.14 \div 5$

27. $78 \div 5$ **28.** $41 \div 8$ **29.** $321 \div 6$ **30.** $795 \div 2$

31. $615 \div 4$ **32.** $145 \div 4$ **33.** $21 \div 10$ **34.** $507 \div 100$

35. $18\overline{)4.14}$ **36.** $5\overline{)9.42}$ **37.** $12\overline{)25.42}$ **38.** $100\overline{)62}$

39. $280 \div 59$ **40.** $503 \div 27$ **41.** $496 \div 100$ **42.** $496 \div 15$

Copy and complete.

43.
$81.9 \div 10 = ■$
$81.9 \div 100 = 0.819$
$81.9 \div 1{,}000 = ■$

44.
$6.5 \div 10 = ■$
$6.5 \div 100 = ■$
$6.5 \div 1{,}000 = 0.0065$

45.
$75 \div 10 = ■$
$75 \div 100 = 0.75$
$75 \div 1{,}000 = ■$

46.
$28 \div 10 = ■$
$28 \div 100 = ■$
$28 \div 1{,}000 = 0.028$

★**47.**
$0.34 \div 10 = .034$
$0.34 \div 100 = ■$
$0.34 \div 1{,}000 = ■$
$0.34 \div 10{,}000 = ■$

★**48.**
$4.6 \div 10 = ■$
$4.6 \div 100 = 0.046$
$4.6 \div 1{,}000 = ■$
$4.6 \div 10{,}000 = ■$

49.

Here's how Ian found 62.4 ÷ 5. Tell what mistake he made. Explain how to correct it.

Problem Solving

50. The African giant millipede can be up to 29.7 centimeters in length. If the millipede is made of 100 segments, how long is each segment?

51. **Analyze:** If you have to round a quotient to the nearest hundredth, to what place do you need to divide?

52. **Science:** A sea star, once known as a starfish, has 5 "arms." It is covered with a spiny skin and tube feet like suction cups. How many arms would 47 sea stars have?

53. The Aussie cuttlefish, an animal closely related to the squid, can weigh up to 2.3 pounds. If a group of cuttlefish weighs 23 pounds, how many are there?

54. **Summarize:** How do you divide numbers by 10, 100, and 1,000?

★55. **Language Arts:** Although "millipede" means "1,000 legs," the most legs ever counted was 752. To find the number of legs, count the number of segments then multiply by 2 and add 6. If a millipede has 44 segments, how many legs does it have? How many body segments did the millipede with 752 legs have?

Did You Know?

It is estimated that about 170 different species of sea slugs live along the North Atlantic coast of Europe and about 1,000 species live in the West Pacific Ocean.

Use data from *Did You Know?* for problems 56–57.

56. How many more species live in the West Pacific ocean than in the North Atlantic?

★57. If scientists estimate that there is an average of 975 slugs of each species in the North Atlantic, how many animals are there altogether?

Spiral Review and Test Prep

58. $47 + 123 + 88$ 59. $205 - 66$ 60. 300×500 61. 24×83 62. $8 \times 4 \times 5$

Choose the correct answer.

63. What is the product of 39, 82, and 6?
 A. 127 C. 19,188
 B. 3.198 D. Not Here

64. The sum of two numbers is 21. Their product is 108. Which numbers could they be?
 F. 10 and 11 H. 1 and 21
 G. 4 and 27 J. 12 and 9

Objective: Divide decimals by decimals.

3·9 Explore Dividing Decimals by Decimals

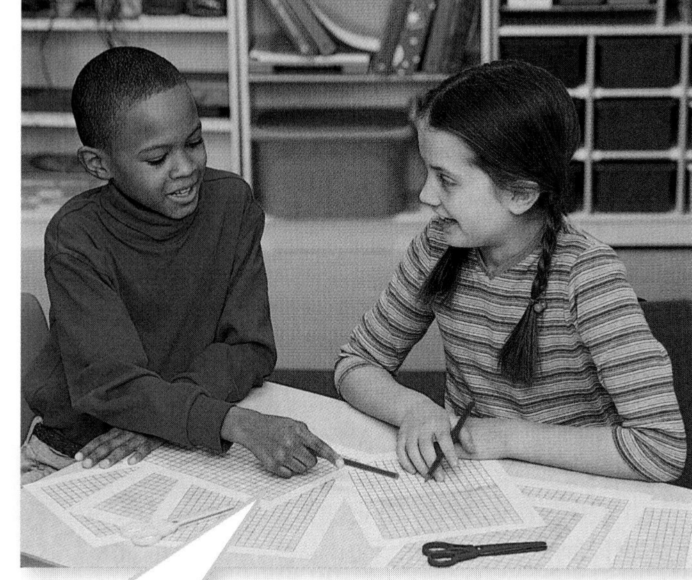

Learn

Math Word

power of 10
a number obtained by raising 10 to an exponent

Examples: $10^1 = 10$, $10^2 = 10 \times 10 = 100$

You can use graph paper to explore dividing decimals by decimals.

Work Together

You Will Need
- graph paper
- scissors

▶ Use models to find 7.5 ÷ 1.5.

- Represent 7.5 by shading 10-by-10 grids.

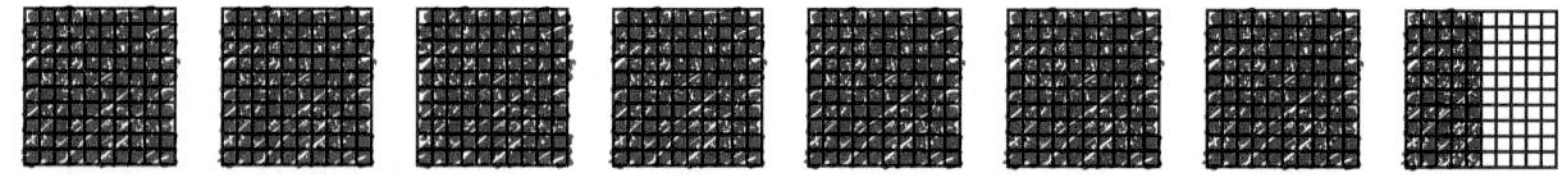

- Cut off the unshaded part.

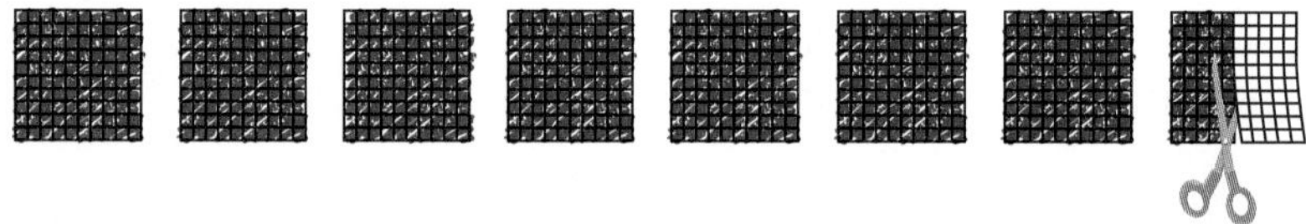

- Cut apart the 10-by-10 grids to make equal groups of 1.5.

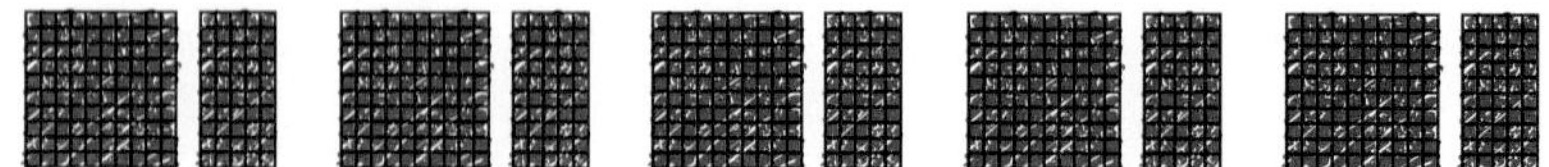

- Count the number of groups. How many are there?

▶ Use models to divide.

5.2 ÷ 1.3 　　 7.5 ÷ 2.5 　　 5.6 ÷ 0.8 　　 4 ÷ 0.4

Make Connections

Find: $1.2 \div 0.6$

You can divide 12 into 2 groups of 6.

6 6

$12 \div 6 = 2$

You can divide 1.2 into 2 groups of 0.6.

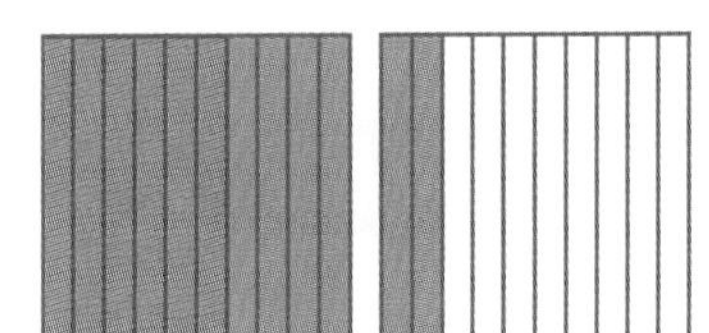

0.6 0.6

$1.2 \div 0.6 = 2$

Note: 12 is 10 times greater than 1.2 and 6 is 10 times greater than 0.6. The quotient of both division problems is 2.

You can use properties to show why $12 \div 6$ and $1.2 \div 0.6$ have the same quotient.

$$1.2 \div 0.6 =$$
$$(1.2 \times 10) \div (0.6 \times 10) =$$
$$12 \div 6 =$$
$$2$$

Think: When you multiply both the dividend and divisor by the same **power of 10**, the new division problem will have the same quotient.

Follow these steps to find $1.2 \div 0.6$

$0.6 \times 10 = 6$	Multiply the divisor by a power of 10 to make it a whole number.
$1.2 \times 10 = 12$	Multiply the dividend by the same power of 10.
$12 \div 6 = 2$	Divide as with whole numbers.

So, $1.2 \div 0.6 = 2$

Try It

Divide. You can use models.

1. $7.2 \div 1.2$ **2.** $7.6 \div 1.9$ **3.** $3.5 \div 0.7$ **4.** $4.8 \div 0.6$

Explain how to use models to find $7.8 \div 1.3$. What is the quotient?

Practice

Divide.

5. $9.2 \div 2.3$ **6.** $5.4 \div 1.8$ **7.** $8.4 \div 2.1$ **8.** $6.2 \div 3.1$

9. $5.5 \div 1.1$ **10.** $2.4 \div 2.4$ **11.** $3.9 \div 1.3$ **12.** $6.0 \div 2.0$

13. $5.8 \div 2.9$ **14.** $9.6 \div 3.2$ **15.** $3.2 \div 0.8$ **16.** $6.3 \div 0.9$

17. Analyze: Do $24 \div 6$ and $2.4 \div 0.6$ have the same quotient? Explain.

Objective: Divide decimals by decimals.

3·10 Divide Decimals by Decimals

Learn

The longest snake ever recorded was a reticulated python. The shortest-known snakes are the Brahming thread snake and the blind snake which are only 4.25 inches. How many times longer is the python than the blind snake?

Example 1

Find: $393.55 \div 4.25$

1

Multiply the divisor by a power of 10 to make it a whole number. Multiply the dividend by the same number.

$4.25\overline{)393.55}$

Multiply by 100 to make the divisor a whole number.

2

Divide until there is no remainder.

```
        92.6
425.)39,355.0
    −38 25↓
       1 105
     −   850↓
         255 0
        −255 0
             0
```

Multiply to check: $4.25 \times 92.6 = 393.55$

The python is 92.6 times longer than the blind snake.

More Examples

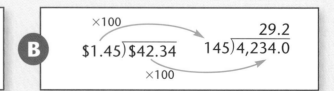

A

$3.6\overline{)24.57}$ (×10) → $36\overline{)245.700}$ (×10), quotient 6.825

B

$\$1.45\overline{)\$42.34}$ (×100) → $145\overline{)4{,}234.0}$ (×100), quotient 29.2

Sometimes you may want to round the quotient instead of dividing until there is no remainder.

Example 2

Divide: 16.4 by 3.25. Round the quotient to the nearest hundredth.

1 Multiply the dividend and the divisor by 100.

$3.25\overline{)16.40}$

2 Divide. Round the quotient to the hundredths place.

```
          5.046
325)1,640.000
   -1 625
      15 00
     -13 00
       2 000
      -1 950
          50
```

5.046→5.05

Remember: divide to one more place than you want to round to.

So 16.4 ÷ 3.25 is 5.05, rounded to the nearest hundredth.

Another Example

Round the quotient to the nearest tenth.
Find: 45.7 ÷ 2.13

21.45 rounds to 21.5.

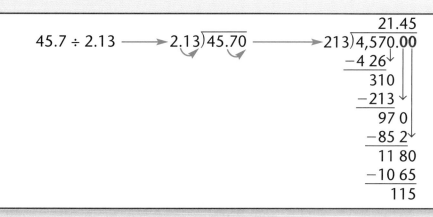

C

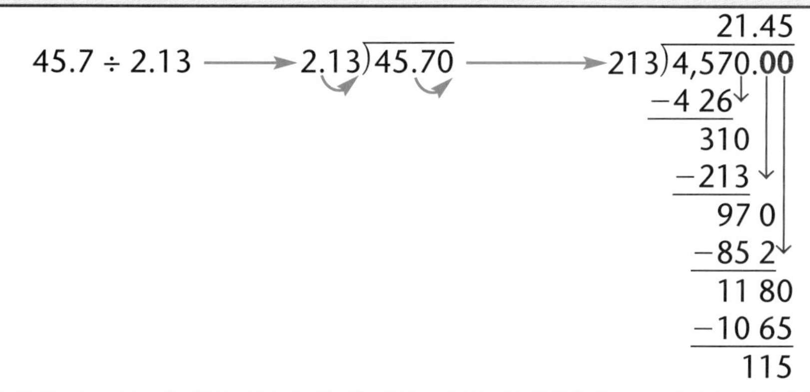

So, 45.7 ÷ 2.13 is 21.5 rounded to the nearest tenth.

Try It **Divide. Round to the nearest hundredth if necessary.**

1. $14.5\overline{)33.35}$ **2.** $12.5\overline{)79.25}$ **3.** $4.8\overline{)24.6}$ **4.** $18.25\overline{)98.55}$

How is dividing by decimals the same as dividing by whole numbers? How is it different?

Practice Divide until there is no remainder.

5. $1.2 \div 0.5 = $ ■
6. $1.36 \div 0.8 = $ ■
7. $444.5 \div 25.4 = $ ■
8. $16.5 \div 0.15 = $ ■
9. $2.037 \div 0.42 = $ ■
10. $15.6875 \div 1.25 = $ ■

Divide. Round to the nearest tenth.

11. $1.3\overline{)3.69}$
12. $7.1\overline{)82.35}$
13. $4.6\overline{)74.5}$
14. $3.7\overline{)12.45}$
15. $1.72\overline{)61}$
16. $0.45\overline{)42.35}$
17. $2.19\overline{)564.87}$
18. $3.24\overline{)9{,}412.3}$

★19. $15.78\overline{)102.67}$

★20. $13.79\overline{)54.0568}$

★21. $20.65\overline{)78.4}$

★22. $21.12\overline{)686}$

Divide. Round to the nearest hundredth.

23. $6.3\overline{)20.58}$
24. $5.1\overline{)47.91}$
25. $12.7\overline{)309.4}$
26. $46.3\overline{)120.5}$
27. $2.87\overline{)164.5}$
28. $0.36\overline{)54}$
29. $6.04\overline{)74.98}$
30. $4.11\overline{)59.62}$
31. $9.65\overline{)42}$
32. $0.15\overline{)2.3604}$

★33. $0.036\overline{)0.012}$

★34. $1.524\overline{)334.56}$

Algebra & functions **Find each missing number.**

35. $11.9 \div$ ■ $= 4.25$
36. ■ $\div 3.2 = 8.56$
37. ■ $\div 16.7 = 5.74$
38. ■ $\div 2.35 = 4.51$
39. $2.7832 \div$ ■ $= 3.92$
40. $41.477 \div$ ■ $= 7.03$

41.

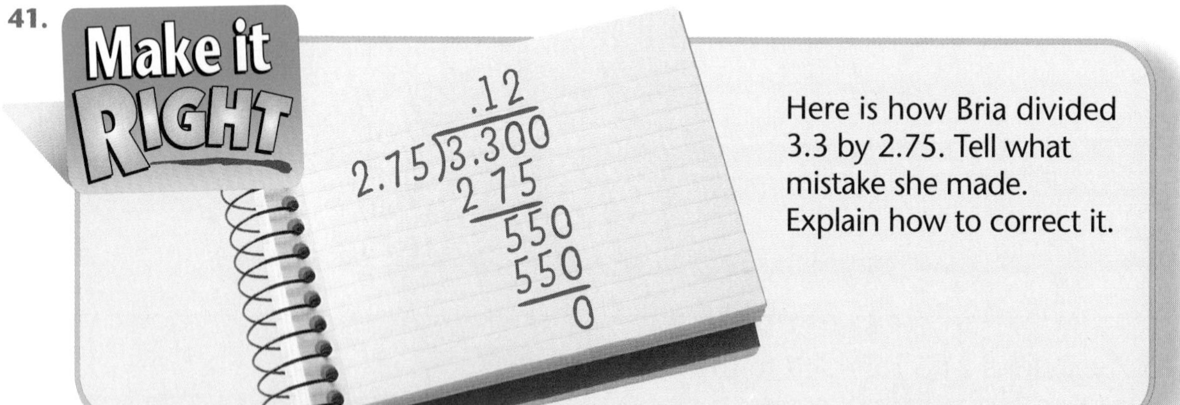

Here is how Bria divided 3.3 by 2.75. Tell what mistake she made. Explain how to correct it.

Problem Solving

42. The spotted turtle lives in wet woods, bogs, and swampy streams. Each turtle needs about 1.3 acres of land. If a group of turtles covers 11.7 acres, how many turtles are there?

43. The largest group of reptiles is the lizards with 3,100 species. Snakes, the next largest group, have 2,000 species. How many more species of lizards are there than snakes?

Use data from the chart for problems 44–46.

44. Which country has the most threatened reptile species? the most amphibian species?

45. Order the 3 countries from highest to lowest in terms of the total number of threatened reptile and amphibian species.

Country	Threatened Reptile Species	Threatened Amphibian Species
Australia	37	25
Japan	8	10
United States	28	24

46. In the three countries, what is the total number of threatened reptile and amphibian species?

47. The heaviest living Galápagos tortoise, Goliath, weighs 845 pounds. How many times heavier is Goliath than you?

48. **Analyze:** If you divide a decimal dividend by a decimal divisor, do you always get a decimal quotient? Give examples to support your answer.

49. **Generalize:** Why do you multiply the divisor and the dividend by the same number when dividing a decimal by a decimal?

★50. The leopard frog can jump up to 91.4 centimeters in one jump. If a frog jumped 1,371.6 centimeters, how many times did it jump?

51. **Create a problem** that can be solved by dividing a decimal by a decimal. Solve it and give it to another student to solve.

52. **Summarize** how you divide a decimal by a decimal. Use the words dividend, divisor, quotient, decimal point, and power of 10.

Spiral Review and Test Prep

53. 6.4 + 4.2 54. 39.5 + 2.8 55. 53.7 − 4.0 56. 18.7 − 12.7

57. 18.4 − 5.34 58. 4.03 × 8.525 59. 5.05 × 5.05 60. 465.3 × 8.6

Choose the correct answer.

61. Which pair of numbers gives a product equal to 8 × 12?
   A. 6 and 16
   B. 7 and 13
   C. 5 and 18
   D. 4 and 22

62. How many legs do 46 blue-tongued skinks have? What information do you need to answer this question?
   F. The number of tongues a skink has
   G. The number of skinks in the world
   H. The number of legs a skink has
   J. Not Here

Objective: Apply division to analyze data and make decisions.

Problem Solving: Application

Decision Making

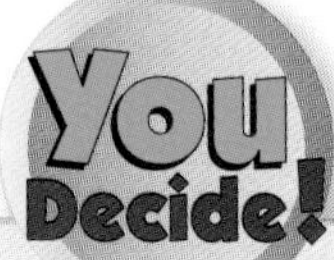

Should they buy from the computer store, the mail-order catalog, or the computer lab supply center?

Ms. Lee's class is ordering 25 copies of 3 CD-ROMs for the school computer center. One is called *Large Animals of Africa*, one is called *Strange Sea Creatures*, and one is called *Birds That Can't Fly*.

Option 1

CD-ROM Catalog
Great Bundle Offer!
3 CD-ROMs for just $63.81
Large Animals of Africa
Birds That Can't Fly
Strange Sea Creatures
Regular Shipping (7–10 days) $2.50
Overnight Delivery add $5.00

Option 2

CD-ROM Sale!

	Large Animals of Africa	was $35.00	now $29.00
	Strange Sea Creatures	was $25.00	now $15.00
	Birds That Can't Fly	was $20.00	now $18.00

Option 3

Computer Lab Supply Center

Large Animals of Africa, Strange Sea Creatures, Birds That Can't Fly

Site license — all three CD-ROMs, whole school: $1,750.00

Read for Understanding

1. How much do all three CD-ROMs cost if you order from the catalog? How much is regular shipping?

2. Suppose Ms. Lee decides that her students need the CD-ROMs right away. How much would they pay for overnight delivery, in addition to the amount for regular shipping?

3. How much does each CD-ROM cost at the store?

4. How much is a site license for all three CD-ROMs for the whole school?

Problem Solving

Make Decisions

5. What would the total cost for the three CD-ROMs be at the store?

6. The store charges $0.07 on every dollar for sales tax. How much tax will Ms. Lee's class pay if they buy from the store?

7. What would it cost to buy the CD-ROMs from the catalog, including regular shipping?

8. What would it cost to buy the CD-ROMs from the catalog, including overnight delivery?

9. If 25 teachers share the cost equally, what is the cost for each classroom if they order from the catalog, with regular delivery? Round the quotient to the nearest cent.

10. What is the cost for each student if 25 students order from the catalog, with overnight delivery?

11. Does it cost more to buy the 3 CD-ROMs from the store or the bundle from the catalog? Explain.

12. The trip to the store is 7 miles. How much would it cost to drive there and back at $0.31 for each mile?

13. What would the total cost of buying the CD-ROMs at the store be, including mileage?

14. If there are 25 classes in the school and they share the costs equally, what is the cost for each class if they buy from the store?

15. There are 625 students in the school. If everyone agrees to share equally the cost of the site license for the whole school, what is the cost for each student?

16. What is an advantage of ordering from a catalog? buying from the store? getting a site license?

What is your recommendation for Ms. Lee's class? Explain.

Objective: Apply division to investigate science concepts.

Problem Solving: Math and Science

How much trash do you make each year?

Do you know what happens to your trash after you throw it away? Every year, millions of tons of trash are burned, buried, or dumped at sea.

Because trash is a serious environmental challenge, everyone should be aware of how much they make. You probably make a lot more than you think!

You Will Need
- **trash bag**
- **mass scale**

Hypothesize

Estimate how many bags of trash you make in a year.

Procedure

1. Spend one day collecting your trash. Keep it in a large trash bag.
2. Measure how many bags you collected in one day, or estimate the fraction of a bag.
3. Calculate the number of bags you would collect each week.
4. Calculate the number of bags you would collect in a year.
5. Measure the mass of the trash bag and repeat your calculations.

Data

Copy and complete the chart to record your observations.

Trash	Number of Bags	Mass of Trash
Each day		
Each week		
Each year		

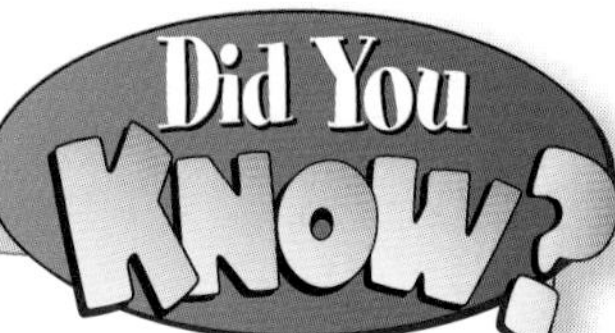

Many materials can be recycled. Metal cans, newspapers, some cardboard boxes and some types of plastics can be recycled. Paper products, clothing, and new containers are some of the things that can be made from recycled products.

Conclude and Apply

- How much trash do you make each year? Was your estimate high or low?
- Estimate the mass of trash your family makes each year. Explain your estimate.
- List other sources of trash that affect your life (for example, the trash your school cafeteria makes). How many more bags of trash do these sources add to your total?
- A family of five used to collect 250 bags of trash each year. Now they recycle and collect only 200 bags each year. How many fewer bags does the family collect *for each person*?
- Use data in *Did You Know?* to explain how **recycling** can reduce the amount of trash produced each year.

Going Further

1. Estimate the amount of trash collected by your entire school in a year. Include the cafeteria, art room, main office, each student and any other place that makes trash.
2. Make a list of at least five ways to make less trash or recycle.

Problem Solving

Check Your Progress B

Divide until there is no remainder. **(pages 124–127)**

1. $1.44 \div 12$
2. $71.5 \div 55$
3. $155 \div 62$
4. $299 \div 92$

Divide. Round to the nearest tenth. **(pages 128–133)**

5. $38.32 \div 51$
6. $964 \div 49$
7. $75\overline{)6,293}$
8. $735\overline{)4,067}$
9. $4.37 \div 9.7$
10. $3.54 \div 8.6$
11. $64.75 \div 2.2$
12. $230.83 \div 4.1$

Divide. Round to the nearest hundredth. **(pages 128–133)**

13. $57\overline{)28.79}$
14. $46\overline{)918}$
15. $2,471 \div 38$
16. $9,153 \div 486$
17. $7.65 \div 9.3$
18. $6.07 \div 5.7$
19. $48.15 \div 1.2$
20. $36.32 \div 3.1$

Solve. **(pages 118–133)**

21. Six monkeys share equally a 45-pound bag of monkey chow each week. How much does each monkey eat each week?

22. The longest lizard, the Papuan monitor lizard, is 4,750 millimeters long. The smallest lizard, the Virgin Islands gecko, is 18 millimeters long. To the nearest tenth, how many times longer is a Papuan monitor lizard than a Virgin Islands gecko?

23. A trip to the Natural History Museum costs $80 for the bus and $10 for admission of each student. The whole trip cost the school $330. How many students went on the trip?

24. **Analyze:** If you divided a decimal by a decimal will you always get a decimal quotient? Give an example to support your answer.

25. **Compare:** Matt says that 2,045 ÷ 17 is 120.3. Michael says that 2,045 ÷ 17 is 120.29. Who is correct? Explain.

Extra Practice

Relate Multiplication and Division (pages 104–105)

Copy and complete .

1. $7 \times 8 = 56$
   $8 \times 7 = ■$
   $56 \div 8 = ■$
   $56 \div 7 = ■$

2. $9 \times 6 = 54$
   $■ \times 9 = 54$
   $54 \div 6 = ■$
   $54 \div 9 = ■$

3. $4 \times 11 = 44$
   $11 \times 4 = 44$
   $44 \div 11 = ■$
   $44 \div 4 = ■$

4. $12 \times 7 = 84$
   $7 \times ■ = 84$
   $84 \div 7 = ■$
   $■ \div 12 = 7$

Divide.

5. $16 \div 2$
6. $49 \div 7$
7. $48 \div 4$
8. $32 \div 8$
9. $45 \div 5$

Divide by 1-Digit Divisors (pages 106–109)

Divide. Check your answer.

1. $6\overline{)721}$
2. $4\overline{)233}$
3. $8\overline{)519}$
4. $2\overline{)9{,}361}$
5. $9{,}723 \div 8$
6. $40{,}729 \div 3$
7. $13{,}887 \div 3$
8. $39{,}616 \div 5$
9. $4{,}372 \div 4$
10. $3{,}444 \div 6$
11. $5{,}555 \div 2$
12. $10{,}009 \div 9$

Solve.

13. Dr. Watson puts 465 fish equally into 5 tanks for study. How many fish are in each tank?

Divide by 2-Digit and 3-Digit Divisors (pages 110–113)

Divide. Check you answer.

1. $899 \div 26$
2. $236 \div 61$
3. $497 \div 31$
4. $4{,}883 \div 72$
5. $89\overline{)4{,}712}$
6. $11\overline{)33{,}771}$
7. $83\overline{)14{,}916}$
8. $49\overline{)30{,}207}$
9. $2{,}716 \div 897$
10. $6{,}807 \div 713$
11. $7{,}810 \div 318$
12. $3{,}348 \div 897$
13. $155\overline{)80{,}092}$
14. $290\overline{)13{,}107}$
15. $284\overline{)92{,}561}$
16. $215\overline{)87{,}538}$

Solve.

17. Eight teachers and 212 students travel to the Museum of Natural History. Each bus holds 55 people. How many buses are needed?

Extra Practice

Estimate Quotients (pages 114–117)

Copy and complete.

1. $72 \div 9 = 8$
   $720 \div 9 = \square$
   $7{,}200 \div 9 = \square$
   $72{,}000 \div 9 = \square$
   $720{,}000 \div 9 = \square$

2. $12 \div 3 = 4$
   $120 \div 3 = \square$
   $1{,}200 \div 3 = \square$
   $12{,}000 \div 3 = \square$
   $120{,}000 \div 3 = \square$

3. $28 \div 7 = 4$
   $280 \div 70 = 4$
   $2{,}800 \div \square = 40$
   $\square \div 70 = 400$
   $280{,}000 \div 70 = \square$

4. $18 \div 3 = 6$
   $180 \div 30 = 6$
   $1{,}800 \div \square = 60$
   $\square \div 30 = 600$
   $180{,}000 \div 30 = \square$

5. $24 \div 8 = 3$
   $240 \div 80 = \square$
   $2{,}400 \div 800 = \square$
   $24{,}000 \div \square = 30$
   $\square \div 800 = 300$

6. $72 \div 6 = 12$
   $720 \div 60 = \square$
   $7{,}200 \div 600 = \square$
   $72{,}000 \div 600 = \square$
   $\square \div 600 = 1{,}200$

Estimate. Use compatible numbers.

7. $805 \div 9$
8. $1{,}715 \div 8$
9. $2{,}702 \div 42$
10. $38{,}230 \div 73$
11. $50{,}244 \div 36$
12. $2{,}619 \div 764$
13. $72{,}517 \div 664$
14. $59{,}112 \div 759$

Solve.

15. Estimate the number of monkey family groups that will live in a nature preserve. There are 2,156 monkeys. They live in groups of 11–14.

Problem Solving: Reading for Math Interpreting the Remainder (pages 118–119)

Solve. Explain how you interpreted the remainder.

1. There are 50 students traveling in vans to an Insect Pavilion. Each van seats 8 students. How many vans are needed for all 50 students?
2. The students must travel 95 miles. The vans travel at a speed of 45 miles per hour. How long will it take to get to the Insect Pavilion?

Problem Solving: Strategy Work Backward (pages 122–123)

Work backward to solve.

1. The science club spends $22 to install a water-saving faucet in the science lab's sink. They spend half of the remaining money to print a flyer telling people how to save water at home. They have $50 left. How much was in the original budget?
2. Half of the fifth grade class volunteers to clean a local beach. The other half divides into two groups. One group will help a whale-rescue group. The 8 students in the other group will count sea birds. How many students are in the class?

Extra Practice

Divide Decimals by Whole Numbers (pages 124–127)

Divide until there is no remainder.

1. $16\overline{)14.08}$ 2. $27\overline{)62.1}$ 3. $96\overline{)396}$ 4. $85\overline{)289}$

Divide. Round to the nearest tenth.

5. $3.48 \div 14$ 6. $46.19 \div 64$ 7. $41\overline{)4{,}272}$ 8. $903\overline{)60{,}732}$

Divide. Round to the nearest hundredth.

9. $95\overline{)8.72}$ 10. $56\overline{)91.46}$ 11. $7{,}399 \div 34$ 12. $94{,}850 \div 181$

Copy and complete.

13. $15.6 \div 10 = \blacksquare$
$15.6 \div 100 = \blacksquare$
$15.6 \div 1{,}000 = \blacksquare$

14. $36.2 \div 10 = \blacksquare$
$36.2 \div 100 = \blacksquare$
$36.2 \div 1{,}000 = \blacksquare$

15. $4.95 \div 10 = \blacksquare$
$4.95 \div 100 = \blacksquare$
$4.95 \div 1{,}000 = \blacksquare$

16. $7.1 \div 10 = \blacksquare$
$7.1 \div 100 = \blacksquare$
$7.1 \div 1{,}000 = \blacksquare$

17. $92 \div 10 = \blacksquare$
$92 \div 100 = \blacksquare$
$92 \div 1{,}000 = \blacksquare$

18. $20 \div 10 = \blacksquare$
$20 \div 100 = \blacksquare$
$20 \div 1{,}000 = \blacksquare$

19. A dividend is divided by 4. The quotient is 3.25. What is the dividend?

20. Six biology students share the cost of a new microscope equally. If the microscope costs $147.90, how much does each student pay?

Divide Decimals by Decimals (pages 128–133)

Divide until there is no remainder.

1. $8.16 \div 2.4$ 2. $17.64 \div 3.92$ 3. $159.82 \div 5.24$ 4. $277.09 \div 45.8$

Divide. Round to the nearest tenth.

5. $5.76\overline{)62.786}$ 6. $88.6\overline{)49.18}$ 7. $64.2\overline{)74.076}$ 8. $72.2\overline{)38.646}$

Divide. Round to the nearest hundredth.

9. $6.07\overline{)50.29}$ 10. $8.28\overline{)25.41}$ 11. $90.4\overline{)46.71}$ 12. $48.7\overline{)153.28}$

13. Suppose a newborn animal measures 4.3 centimeters and grows to a maximum length of 24.08 centimeters. How many times longer is it at its maximum length compared to birth?

Chapter Study Guide

Language and Math

Math Words

compatible numbers
dividend
divisor
fact family
quotient
remainder

Complete. Use a word from the list.

1. When you divide, the answer is called the ____.
2. Related multiplication and division sentences are called a ____.
3. A ____ is the number left after a quotient is found.
4. When you use 450 ÷ 9 to estimate 447 ÷ 9, you are using ____.

Skills and Applications

Divide whole numbers and decimals. (pages 104–113, 124–133)

Example

Find: 238 ÷ 5

Solution

```
   47 R3
5)238
 -20↓      Multiply:   4 × 5 = 20
   38      Subtract: 23 − 20 = 3
  -35      Multiply:   7 × 5 = 35
    3      Subtract:  38 − 35 = 3
```

Divide.

5. $8\overline{)597}$
6. $9\overline{)964}$
7. $69\overline{)1,729}$
8. $41\overline{)6,428}$
9. $62\overline{)87,348}$
10. $70\overline{)36,585}$
11. 9,652 ÷ 201
12. 4,416 ÷ 107
13. 32,024 ÷ 493
14. 41,085 ÷ 358

Example

Find: 3.56 ÷ 5

Solution

```
  0.712
5)3.560
 -3 5↓↓
   06↓
  − 5↓
    10
   -10
     0
```

Place the decimal point in the quotient. Divide until there is no remainder.

Divide until there is no remainder.

15. $5\overline{)6.16}$
16. $4\overline{)7.23}$
17. $5.8\overline{)9.831}$
18. $6.2\overline{)6.975}$
19. 8.5 ÷ 25
20. 125 ÷ 40

Divide. Round to the nearest tenth.

21. 24.45 ÷ 2.7
22. 39.71 ÷ 5.8

Divide by 10, 100, 1,000. (pages 114–117)

Example

43.8 ÷ 10 = ▮
43.8 ÷ 100 = ▮
43.8 ÷ 1,000 = ▮

Solution

Use patterns or move the decimal point one place to the left for each zero in the divisor.

43.8 ÷ 1 = 43.8
43.8 ÷ 10 = 4.38
43.8 ÷ 100 = 0.438
43.8 ÷ 1,000 = 0.0438

Complete.

23. 65.2 ÷ 10 = 6.52
65.2 ÷ 100 = ▮
65.2 ÷ 1,000 = ▮

24. 9.4 ÷ 10 = 0.94
9.4 ÷ 100 = ▮
9.4 ÷ 1,000 = ▮

25. 73 ÷ 10 = ▮
73 ÷ 100 = ▮
73 ÷ 1,000 = ▮

Estimate quotients of whole numbers. (pages 114–117)

Example

Estimate the quotient: 18,199 ÷ 92

Solution

Estimate. Use compatible numbers:

18,199 ÷ 92
↓ ↓
18,000 ÷ 90

18 ÷ 9 = 2
180 ÷ 90 = 2
1,800 ÷ 90 = 20
18,000 ÷ 90 = 200

Estimate. Use compatible numbers.

26. 554 ÷ 6
27. 253 ÷ 5
28. 713 ÷ 63
29. 374 ÷ 93
30. 6,242 ÷ 31
31. 3,059 ÷ 59

Solve problems. (pages 118–119, 122–123)

Example

A student group spends $13 to make a bulletin board about endangered species. They spend half of the remainder to adopt an injured bird at the bird sanctuary. They still have $86. How much did they start with?

Solution

Work backward to solve.

$86 × 2 = $172; $172 + $13 = $185

They started with $185.

Solve.

32. The school science club raised money to clean the local beach. They spent $29 for trash bags. They spent half of the remaining money on waterproof boots. The club still has $47 leftover. How much did they raise?

33. A scientist wants to go to Antarctica to study penguins. A plane ticket costs $2,350. It also costs $435 each day for supplies. How long can the scientist study if he has $6,700?

Chapter Test

Estimate.

1. 934 ÷ 9
2. 351 ÷ 46
3. 5,587 ÷ 64
4. 2,845 ÷ 91

Divide. Show the answer with a remainder.

5. $8\overline{)917}$
6. $77\overline{)4{,}557}$
7. $45\overline{)1{,}503}$
8. 30,039 ÷ 18
9. 51,348 ÷ 314
10. 26,303 ÷ 634

Copy and complete.

11. 15.1 ÷ 10 = ■
    15.1 ÷ 100 = ■
    15.1 ÷ 1,000 = ■
12. 2.8 ÷ 10 = ■
    2.8 ÷ 100 = ■
    2.8 ÷ 1,000 = ■
13. 49 ÷ 10 = ■
    49 ÷ 100 = ■
    49 ÷ 1,000 = ■

Divide. Round to the nearest tenth.

14. 26.1 ÷ 3.4
15. 7.428 ÷ 5.01
16. $7.28\overline{)2{,}965}$
17. $804\overline{)68.001}$

Divide. Round to the nearest hundredth.

18. 57.2 ÷ 3.7
19. 140.1 ÷ 2.34
20. $4.76\overline{)9{,}026}$
21. $117\overline{)19{,}486}$

Solve.

22. A park ranger has 1,000 pamphlets describing the wild animals in the park. She divides the pamphlets evenly among 7 visitor centers. How many pamphlets does each visitor center get? Explain how you interpreted the remainder.

23. The visitor center offers guided park tours. Each tour bus holds 25 people. If 180 students want to go on a tour, how many buses will they need? Explain how you interpreted the remainder.

24. A school group spends $40 for a bus and $8 for each student to visit a natural history museum. They pay $408 for the whole trip. How many students went on the trip?

25. There are 100 students from the Friends of the Ocean club who pick up trash at beaches so that the trash will not wash into the ocean. They collect 48.5 pounds of trash in all. If each student collects the same amount of trash, how much does each student collect?

Performance Assessment

The fifth- and sixth-grade classes at Sherwood School raised money to help protect endangered species. They will "adopt" animals at bird sanctuaries and animal preserves by donating money to help pay for their care. The students research the cost of a donation for different animals to get an idea of about how many animals they can adopt.

Copy and complete a chart like the one below. Explain how you interpreted the remainder.

Use the chart to answer these questions:

- How many more Sumatran tigers can the fifth-grade class adopt than the sixth-grade class?
- If both classes adopt only screech owls, how many will be adopted?
- How much money would it cost to adopt 1 of each animal? Can the fifth or sixth grade afford this?
- If the two grades combine their money, can they adopt 5 of each kind of animal? Explain.

Animal	Cost for Each Animal for One Year	Fifth Grade Class $725.00	Sixth Grade Class $573.75
Snow leopard	$12.75		
Sumatran tiger	$45.00		
Screech owl	$72.50		
Golden eagle	$100.00		

A Good Answer

- has a complete chart that shows how many animals each class can adopt.
- shows the steps you used to find each number.
- answers the questions about the chart.

You may want to save this work in your portfolio.

Enrichment

Repeating Decimals

When you divide 3 by 4 the quotient is a **terminating decimal** because the quotient terminates, or ends.

$$\begin{array}{r} .75 \\ 4\overline{)3.00} \\ \underline{-2\,8\downarrow} \\ 20 \\ \underline{-20} \\ 0 \end{array}$$

Sometimes when you divide, the quotient does not end. This is called a **repeating decimal.**

Find: $2 \div 3$

$$\begin{array}{r} 0.666 \\ 3\overline{)2.000} \\ \underline{-1\,8} \\ 20 \\ \underline{-18} \\ 20 \\ \underline{-18} \\ 2 \end{array}$$

← If you keep dividing, you keep getting 6 in the quotient.

2 ← When you subtract you get the same number.

You can write a repeating decimal by drawing a bar over the digit or digits that repeat.

$2 \div 3 = 0.6666666666\ldots = 0.\overline{6}$

$1 \div 3 = 0.33333333333\ldots = 0.\overline{3}$

$5 \div 11 = 0.4545454545\ldots = 0.\overline{45}$

$1 \div 7 = 0.142857142857\ldots = 0.\overline{142857}$

Rewrite each repeating decimal by drawing a bar over the digits that repeat.

1. 0.555555... **2.** 0.232323... **3.** 1.472472472... **4.** 0.285714285714...

Find each quotient and tell whether it is a terminating or repeating decimal.

5. $26 \div 6$ **6.** $3 \div 5$ **7.** $10 \div 12$ **8.** $78 \div 4$

9. $23 \div 6$ **10.** $64 \div 12$ **11.** $7 \div 4$ **12.** $12 \div 18$

Test-Taking Tips

When taking a multiple-choice test, you may find that some problems have more information than you need to solve the problem. Before you solve the problem, decide which information is needed and which is not needed. This method is called **identifying extra information.**

The dwarf pygmy goby is the smallest fish in the world. There are 1,081 dwarf pygmy gobies at the aquarium. They are divided equally among 23 fish tanks. There is a tank of 15 goldfish nearby. How many dwarf pygmy gobies are in each tank?

A. 47 **C.** 1,104
B. 1,058 **D.** 24,863

Look at the information in the problem:
- The dwarf pygmy goby is the smallest fish in the world.
- There are 1,081 dwarf pygmy gobies.
- They are divided among 23 tanks.
- There is a tank of 15 goldfish nearby.

Look at the question you have to answer.
- How many dwarf pygmy gobies are in each tank?

Identify the extra information.
- The Dwarf pygmy goby is the smallest fish in the world.
- There is a tank of 15 goldfish nearby.

Ignore the extra information, and solve the problem.
- Divide the number of dwarf pygmy gobies by the number of tanks. 1,081 ÷ 23 = 47.

The correct answer is A.

Check for Success

☑ Before turning in a test, go back one last time to check.
☑ I understood and answered the question asked.
☑ I checked my work for errors.
☑ My answers make sense.

Practice

Choose the correct answer.

1. Marcie has 85 books about animals. She puts them on 5 shelves. She puts an equal number of books on each shelf. She puts 10 magazines on a table. How many books are on each shelf?

   A. 95 **C.** 17
   B. 75 **D.** 10

2. Paul takes 120 pictures of interesting animals. There are 24 pictures on each roll of film. He sends 7 postcards to his friends. How many rolls of film does he use?

   F. 5 **H.** 96
   G. 17 **J.** 144

Spiral Review and Test Prep

Chapters 1–3

Choose the correct answer.

Number Sense

1. Find a number that makes this sentence true:
   15,432 ÷ 219 = ■
   A. 74
   B. 74 R144
   C. 70
   D. 70 R102

2. Find a number that makes this sentence true:
   94.017 ÷ 3.7 = ■
   F. 2.541
   G. 25.41
   H. 254.1
   J. 2,541

3. There are 675 shelves in the library. Each shelf has 35 books. How many books are in the library?
   A. 4,870
   B. 5,400
   C. 21,205
   D. 23,625

4. José rides 15.78 miles per hour on his bike. In a year, he rides a total of 95.2 hours. How many miles does he ride in a year?
   F. 17.1
   G. 25.2
   H. 302.9
   J. 1,502.3

Measurement and Geometry

5. What is the perimeter of the rectangle?

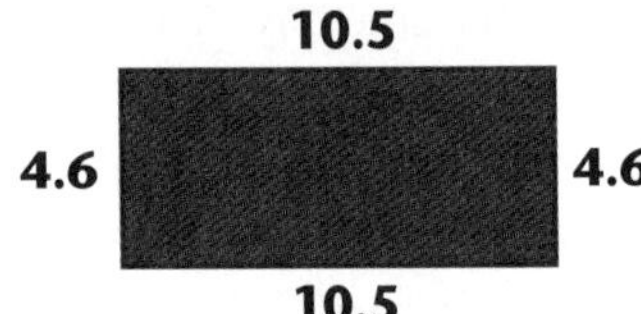

   A. 30.2
   B. 15.1
   C. 10.5
   D. 4.6

6. What kind of angle is shown?

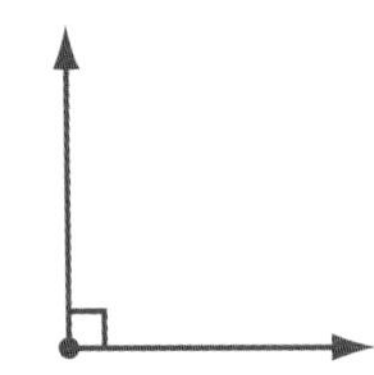

   F. Acute
   G. Obtuse
   H. Right
   J. Not Here

7. What three-dimensional figure is shown?

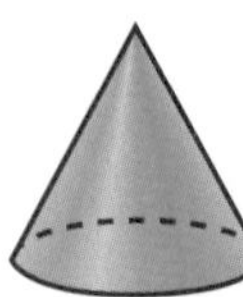

   A. Cylinder
   B. Cone
   C. Pyramid
   D. Sphere

8. What quadrilateral is shown?

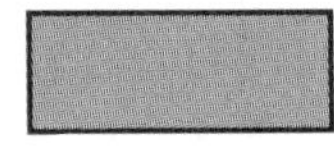

   F. Rhombus
   G. Rectangle
   H. Square
   J. Trapezoid

Statistics, Data Analysis, and Probability

Use data from the graph to answer problems 9–12.

U.S. Waterfalls (Height in Feet)

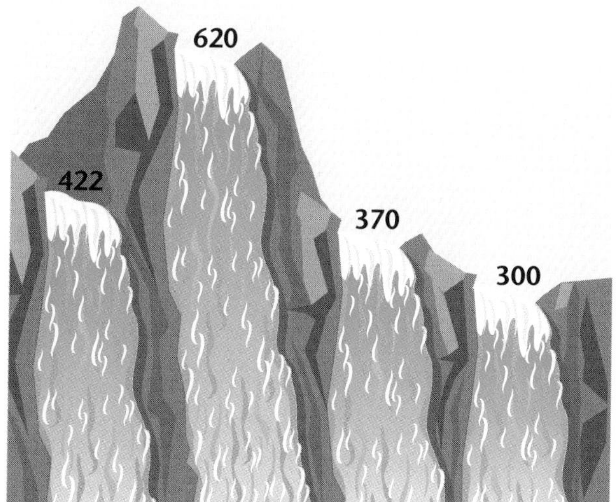

9. Which waterfall is the tallest?
   - A. Akaka
   - B. Bridal Veil
   - C. Illilouette
   - D. Sluiskin

10. Which waterfall is the shortest?
    - F. Akaka
    - G. Bridal Veil
    - H. Illilouette
    - J. Sluiskin

11. How much taller is Bridal Veil Falls than Akaka Falls?
    - A. 178 feet
    - B. 222 feet
    - C. 1,062 feet
    - D. Not Here

12. How much taller is Akaka Falls than Illiouette Falls?
    - F. 812 feet
    - G. 132 feet
    - H. 52 feet
    - J. Not Here

Mathematical Reasoning

13. There are 34 classrooms in the school. Last week 29 new students enrolled. Now there are 31 students in each classroom. How many students were in the school two weeks ago?
    - A. 1,054
    - B. 1,025
    - C. 986
    - D. 955

14. There are 15 gardens in the park. This year the gardener planted 12 new trees. Now there are 5 trees in each garden. How many trees were there last year?
    - F. 180
    - G. 75
    - H. 63
    - J. 60

15. A reindeer travels 144 miles in 4.5 hours. A zebra travels 180 miles in 4.5 hours. How far does a reindeer travel in 1 hour?
    - A. 8 miles
    - B. 32 miles
    - C. 36 miles
    - D. 40 miles

16. Cecily saw 6 people riding bicycles and tricycles in the park. She saw 15 wheels in all. How many bicycles and tricycles did she see?

Spiral Review and Test Prep

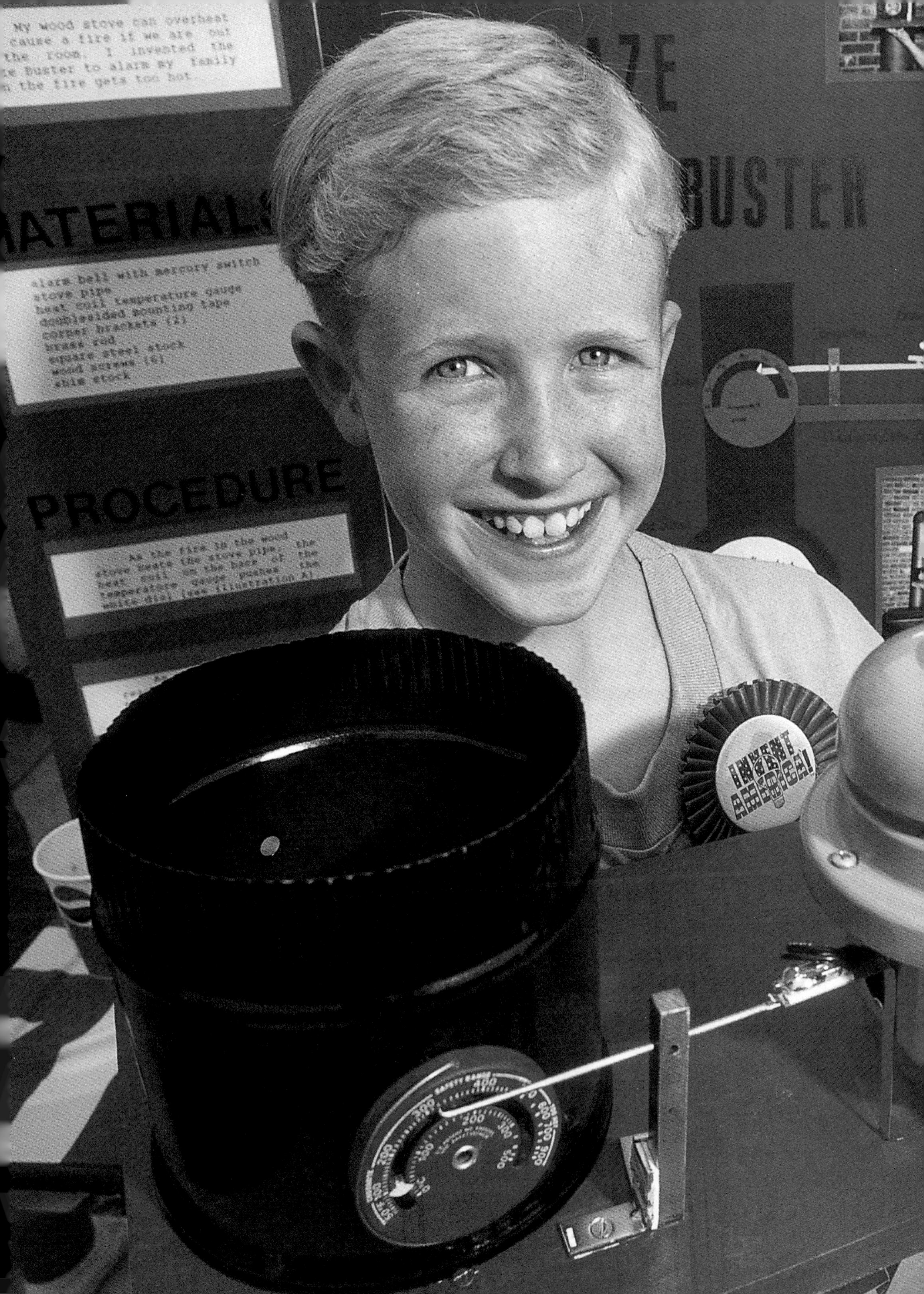
My wood stove can overheat
cause a fire if we are out
the room. I invented the
e Buster to alarm my family
n the fire gets too hot.
AZE
BUSTER
ATERIALS
alarm bell with mercury switch
stove pipe
heat coil temperature gauge
doublesided mounting tape
corner brackets (2)
brass rod
square steel stock
wood screws (6)
shim stock
PROCEDURE
As the fire in the wood
stove heats the stove pipe, the
heat coil on the back of the
temperature gauge pushes the
white dial (see illustration A).
INVENT AMERICA!
SAFETY RANGE
400
300
200
100
500

CHAPTER 4 Data, Statistics, and Graphs

Theme: Inventions

Use the Data

Patents Issued by United States Patent Office to Various Countries in 1997

Country	Number of Patents
Norway	303
Russian Federation	249
Sweden	1,980
Switzerland	1,637
Spain	370
United Kingdom	5,147

- Did Sweden receive more than 5 times the number of patents than Norway?

What You Will Learn

In this chapter you will learn how to
- read and interpret data.
- organize and display data.
- find range, mode, median, and mean.
- use strategies to solve problems.

Objective: Collect and organize data.

4·1 Explore Collecting, Organizing and Displaying Data

Math Words

data collected information

frequency table a way of organizing a set of data, showing the number of times each item or number appears

survey a method to gather data that involves asking people questions

frequency the number of times a response occurs

line plot a graph that uses columns of Xs above a number line

Learn

You can use the results of this survey to explore how to collect, organize, and display data.

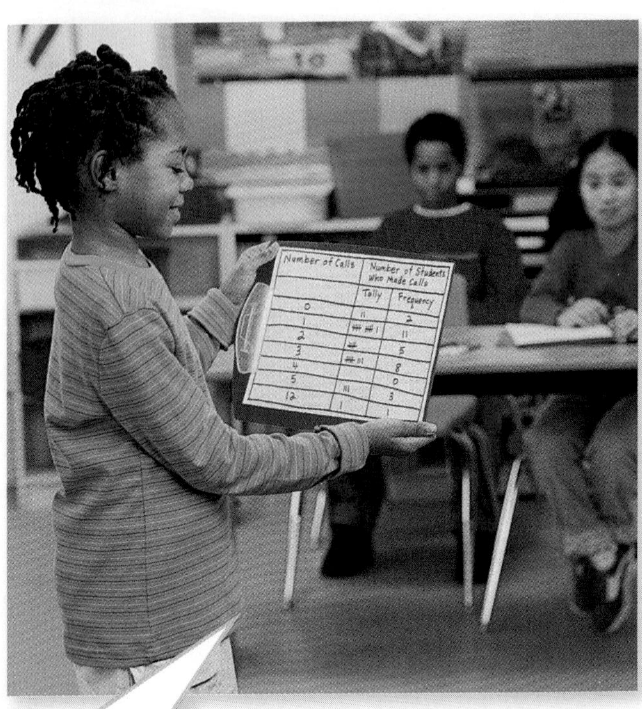

Work Together

- Work in a large group to collect **data**. This **frequency table** organizes the results. First you tally the responses. Then you total the tallies to find the frequency.
- Decide how you will collect the data. Use the following questions to **survey** your class:

Question 1 How many phone calls did you make yesterday?

Question 2 How many times in 1 week do you talk on the telephone?

Question 3 How many minutes do you use the phone each day?

Question 4 How many people in your family use the same phone that you do?

Number of Students Who Made Calls		
Number of calls	Tally	**Frequency**
0	II	2
1	卌 卌 I	11
2	卌	5
3	卌 III	8
4		0
5	III	3
12	I	1

Make Connections

Here is how to make a **line plot** of the data.
Use the data in the frequency table on page 152.

1 Draw a number line.

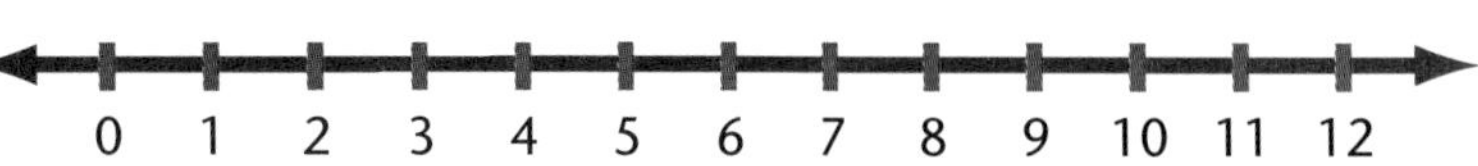

2 Stack the correct number of Xs above each number.

3 Label the line plot and give it a title.

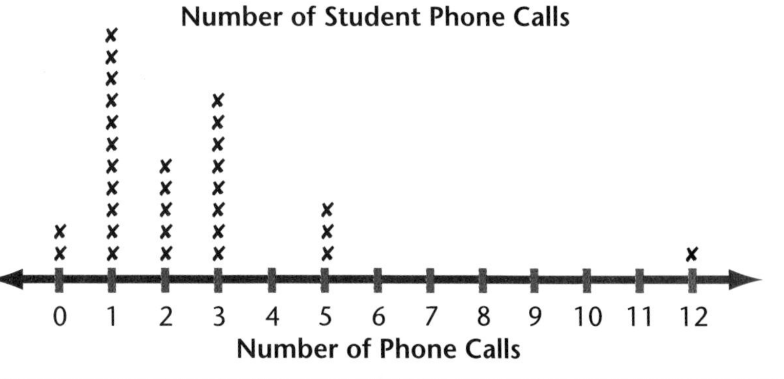

Try It **Make a line plot for each survey question.**

1. Survey Question 1
2. Survey Question 2

How do frequency tables and line plots help to organize data?

Practice **Make a line plot for each survey question.**

3. Survey Question 3
4. Survey Question 4
5. **Summarize:** Look at each of your line plots from survey questions 1 through 4. Write a sentence for each that summarizes the data.

Use data from the line plot above for problems 6–8.

6. Where does most of the data fall, or group, in the line plot? What does this tell you?
7. Explain what the gap at 4 means.
8. Andrew was planning a party. He talked to more people on the telephone than anyone else in the class. How many people did he talk to?

Extra Practice, page 187

Objective: Find and use range, mode, median, and mean.

4·2 Range, Mode, Median, and Mean

Learn

In the 1950s, the "Frisbee" flying disc was invented. A group of friends decides to collect data on how far their discs can fly. What are the range, mode, median, and mean of the data?

Name	Feet
Cheung	30
Rick	30
Art	24
Mara	24
Bob	27
Pam	37
Pablo	24

Math Words

range the difference between the greatest and the least number in a set of numbers

mode the number that occurs most often in a set of numbers

median the middle number in a set of numbers arranged in order from least to greatest

mean the quantity that is found by adding the numbers in a set of numbers and dividing their sum by the number of addends

Example 1

1 The **range** shows the spread of the data. Find the range: $37 - 24 = 13$ The range is 13 feet.

2 The **mode** is the most common number. Find the mode: Find the number that occurs most often. The mode is 24 feet.

3 The **median** is the middle number in a set of ordered data. Find the median: Arrange the data in order from least to greatest. Then find the middle number.
24, 24, 24, **27**, 30, 30, 37
The middle number is 27. The median is 27 feet.

4 The **mean** is a mathematical balance of all numbers in the data. Find the mean: Add all the numbers, then divide by the number of addends. The mean is 28 feet.

$$24 + 24 + 24 + 27 + 30 + 30 + 37 = 196$$
$$196 \div 7 = 28$$

As you can see from the data, the mode, median, and mean may be different numbers.

The range, median, and mean may or may not be one of the numbers in the original data.

Flying discs come in different sizes and weights. This data shows the weight in ounces of 5 different models.

Model	Flying Disc's Weight (Ounces)
High Flyer	9.5
The Disk	8.5
Junior	8.0
Megadisc	10.0
Light 'n Loopy	6.0

Example 2

You can find the range, mode, median and mean for decimals also.

Range:

10 − 6 = 4

The range is 4 ounces.

Mode:

No number occurs more than once.

This data has no mode.

Median:

Order the data.
6, 8, 8.5, 9.5, 10

The middle number is 8.5.

The median is 8.5 ounces.

Mean:

Add the numbers.
6 + 8 + 8.5 + 9.5 + 10 = 42

Divide. 42 ÷ 5 = 8.4

The mean is 8.4 ounces.

Some data has no mode. The mean may be a decimal not represented in the data.

A 13-inch flying disc holds the record for the "world's farthest object ever thrown." Use the data on the widths of six flying discs to find the median.

Model	Diameter (Inches)
Junior	12
Megadisc	15
Distance Disc	12
High Flyer	13
Light 'n Loopy	10
The Disc	14

Example 3

Find the median.

Note: When there is an even amount of numbers in the data, there will be two numbers in the middle.

1 Order the data: 10, 12, 12, 13, 14, 15

The numbers 12 and 13 are both in the middle.

2 To find the median of the data, find the mean of the two middle numbers.

12 + 13 = 25
25 ÷ 2 = 12.5

The median is 12.5 inches.

Try It **Find the range, mode, median, and mean.**

1. 15, 16, 19, 12, 16, 14, 13
2. 5, 7, 9, 5, 7, 3, 1, 5, 9, 8

Summarize how the mean can be found and explain what it represents about a set of data.

Practice **Find the range, mode, median, and mean.**

3. 0, 3, 0, 2, 1, 1, 4, 3, 5, 1
4. 7, 9, 6, 5, 4, 9, 10, 9
5. 23, 28, 25, 29, 25
6. 99, 101.5, 98, 100, 112.7
7. 12, 10, 13, 24, 12, 11, 13, 11
8. \$2.40, \$3.30, \$2.80, \$1.20, \$1.10, \$3.90
9. Find the range, mode, and median.

Student	Nan	Bob	Jim	Kay	Ann	Rex	Jay	Liv	Cam
Number of Discs	3	0	2	2	6	0	0	1	4

★10.

28 29 30 31 32

Distance Thrown

★11.

6 7 8 9 10 11 12 13 14 15 16

Number of Frisbees

12. **Make it RIGHT**

1+2+3+4 = 10

10÷4=2.5

Here is how Jeanne found the mean of 1, 2, 2, 3, and 4. Tell what mistake she made. Explain how to correct it.

Problem Solving

13. Marlo conducts a survey to find how long people play with flying discs when they go to the beach. She collects these answers: 20 minutes, 45 minutes, 5 minutes, 1 hour, and 15 minutes. Find the range, mode, median and mean of the data Marlo collected.
14. It takes Marlo 2 minutes to survey each person. How many people can she survey in 1 hour?
15. **Analyze:** Explain why the median is always between the greatest and least number in the data.

The Ultimate Frisbee Team scored 14, 9, 6, 11, and 9 points in their last 5 games.

16. What score would the team need in the next game to make the range 10?

17. What score would make the mode 11?

★ 18. What number would make the median 9.5?

★ 19. What number would make the mean 9?

20. Four friends decide to save money to buy a $15 flying disc. They each save $3.50 from their weekly allowance. Do they have enough money? Explain.

★ 21. **Number Sense:** There are several sizes of flying discs in a collection. The range of sizes is 8 centimeters. The median is 22 centimeters. The least number of centimeters is 16. What is the greatest sized disc in the collection?

Use data from the chart for problems 22–25.

Flying Disc	Price
Junior	$12.50
Light 'n Loopy	$18.00
Megadisc	$39.99
High Flyer	$20.00
The Disc	$15.25

22. What is the median price?

23. What is the price range?

24. What is the total cost for all 5 discs?

★ 25. What is the mean price? Round your answer to the nearest penny.

26. **Logical Reasoning:** Some data have no mode. Why? Give an example.

★ 27. The president of a toy company earns $2,000,000 a year. Each of her 40 assistants earns $40,000 a year. An advertisement for a sales assistant says that the average salary is $80,000. Is this true? How might an ad better represent the sales assistant's salary?

28. **Create a problem** about flying discs in which you would have to find the mean. Solve it, then give it to another student to solve.

Spiral Review and Test Prep

29. 55.5×2.5

30. $172.26 \div 5.4$

31. 69.3×6.3

32. $452.32 \div 8.8$

Choose the correct answer.

33. Monica earned $10.95 on Saturday and $14.14 on Sunday. How much did she earn for the weekend?
    - A. $23.09
    - B. $24.89
    - C. $23.89
    - D. Not Here

34. What is the value of 4 raised to the third power?
    - F. 12
    - G. 64
    - H. 43
    - J. 81

Extra Practice, page 187

Objective: Read and make pictographs.

4·3 Read and Make Pictographs

Learn

Math Word
pictograph
a graph that compares data by using symbols

The first novel was written in 1008 by a Japanese woman named Murasaki Shikibu. Libraries all over the world have millions of novels of all categories. This table shows the types of books you might find in a school library. How can you display the data in a graph?

Novel Type	Number of Novels
Western	20
Mystery	50
Science Fiction	40
Historical	15
Adventure	30

Example

You can use a **pictograph** to display the data.

1. Use book a  as a symbol to represent the data.
2. Let each book represent 10 novels. Divide to find the number of books you need for each type of novel.
3. Draw in the correct number of books for each category. Sometimes you must use half of a book symbol.
4. Give the pictograph a title and a key.

Number of Novels

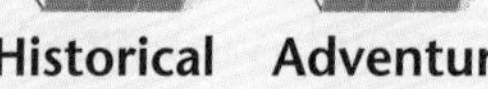

Western | Mystery | Science Fiction | Historical | Adventure

Key: [book] = 10 novels

Try It

Use data from the table about library books for problems 1–3.

1. Show a new pictograph for the data. Let each picture represent 5 novels.
2. A pictograph shows 2 pictures for mystery novels. How many novels would each picture represent?
3. Would you let each picture represent 2 novels? Explain.

Describe two different sets of data about a library for which you might use a pictograph.

Practice

4. Make a pictograph from this data.

Student	Stories Read During Summer
Matt	18
Mary	12
Mike	15
Mara	3

Use data from the pictograph for problems 5–10.

5. How many science fiction novels did students read last week?
6. How many western novels did students read last week?
7. How many more historical novels than science fiction novels did students read last week?
8. How many novels did students read altogether last week?
9. **What if** students had read a total of 8 folktale novels last week? How would the pictograph change?

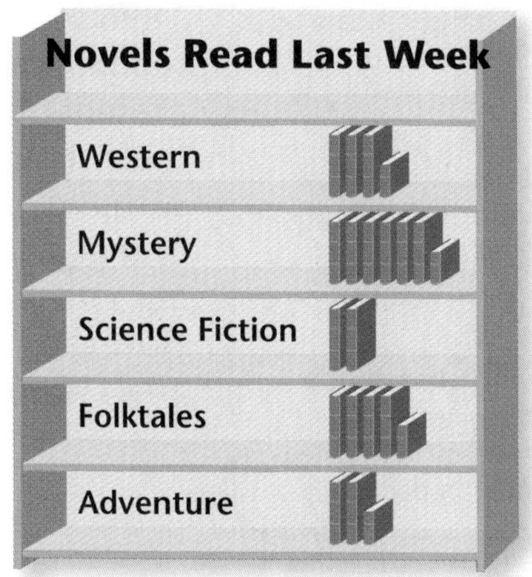

Key: = 4 novels

Problem Solving

10. **Collect Data:** Survey your class. Find each student's favorite kind of novel from the following categories: mystery, humor, adventure, and science fiction. Make a frequency table to display the data. Make a pictograph for the data.

11. **Social Studies:** The ancient library at Alexandria, Egypt, housed over 40,000 volumes before it burned down. If there were an equal number of volumes about mathematics, astronomy, mechanics, and medicine, how many volumes about each subject did the library have?

Spiral Review and Test Prep

Round each number to the underlined place.

12. $0.7\underline{3}5$
13. $22.\underline{1}7$
14. $8.\underline{9}6$
15. $36.74\underline{8}6$

Choose the correct answer.

16. Joy baked 6 dozen muffins for her class party. There are 24 students in her class. How many muffins can each student have?
    - A. 6 muffins
    - B. 5 muffins
    - C. 4.8 muffins
    - D. 3 muffins

17. Burritos cost $1.35 each. If Charlie buys 3 and pays with a five-dollar bill, how much change does he receive?
    - F. $0.95
    - G. $1.35
    - H. $4.05
    - J. $5

Extra Practice, page 187

Objective: Read and make single- and double-bar graphs.

4•4 Read and Make Bar Graphs

Learn

Math Words

bar graph a graph that compares data by using vertical or horizontal bars

axis (pl. axes) the horizontal or vertical number line on a graph

interval the distance between numbers on an axis

double-bar graph a bar graph that compares two related groups of data

The Olympic Games were first introduced by the Ancient Greeks. In 1896 the games were reorganized into the present-day event. The table shows the countries with the greatest number of medals at the 25th Summer Olympic Games. How can you display and analyze the data?

25th Summer Olympics

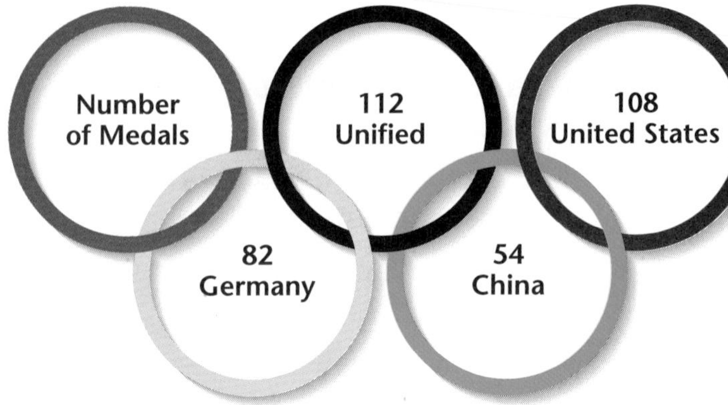

Source: *The World Almanac and Book of Facts*

Example 1

You can make a **bar graph** to display and analyze the data.

Step 1 Draw and label each **axis**.

Step 2 Choose the **intervals** for the graph: 10-medal intervals is a good choice.

Step 3 Draw a bar for each country.

Step 4 Give the graph a title.

Note: The break in the vertical axis shows that there is no data between 0 and 50.

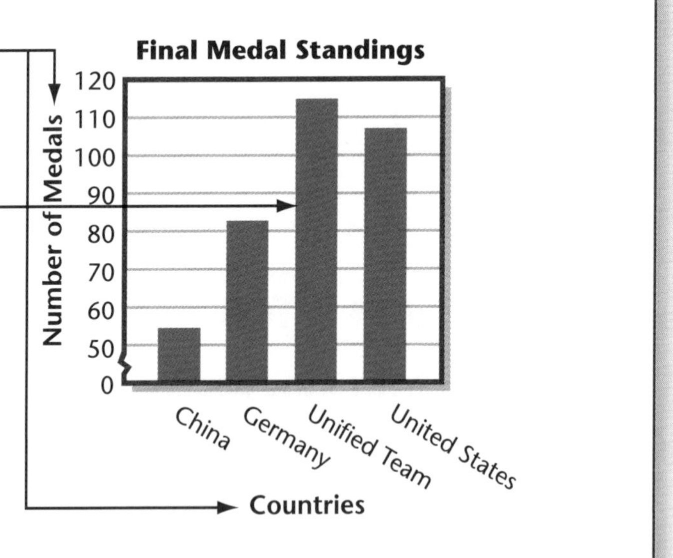

This frequency table shows the number of medals won by each individual country. A **double-bar graph** can be used to display two sets of data for the same group.

Example 2

Making a double-bar graph is similar to making a single-bar graph.

When you draw bars for each set of data, use a different color for each set. Let the bars for each group touch.

Country	Gold Medals	Silver Medals
China	16	22
Germany	33	21
Unified Team	45	38
United States	37	34

Source: *The World Almanac and Book of Facts*

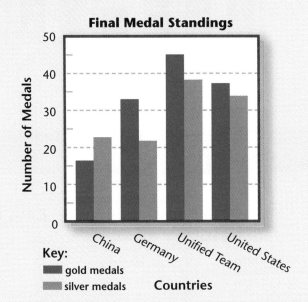

Final Medal Standings

Number of Medals: 0, 10, 20, 30, 40, 50

China, Germany, Unified Team, United States

Key:
gold medals
silver medals

Countries

Try It

The table shows other medal-winning countries at the 25th Summer Olympic Games.

1. Which country in the table had the greatest number of medals? the least number of medals?
2. What is the range of the data?
3. What is the mode of the data?
4. Make a bar graph for the data.

25th Summer Olympic Games	
Country	Number of Medals
Cuba	31
Hungary	30
South Korea	29
France	29
Australia	27
Spain	22

Describe the steps you follow to make a double-bar graph.

Practice

Use data from the graph for problems 5–8.

5. What year was the best year for the 400-meter run?

6. Which event had the most recent best year?

7. What interval is used for the dates?

★ 8. Suppose that in the year 2008, the record for the 100-meter event is broken. How will that change the graph?

9. **Explain** when you would use a double-bar graph instead of a single-bar graph.

10. Use data from the chart to make a double-bar graph.

11. **Create a problem** that can be solved by making a bar graph. Give it to another student to solve.

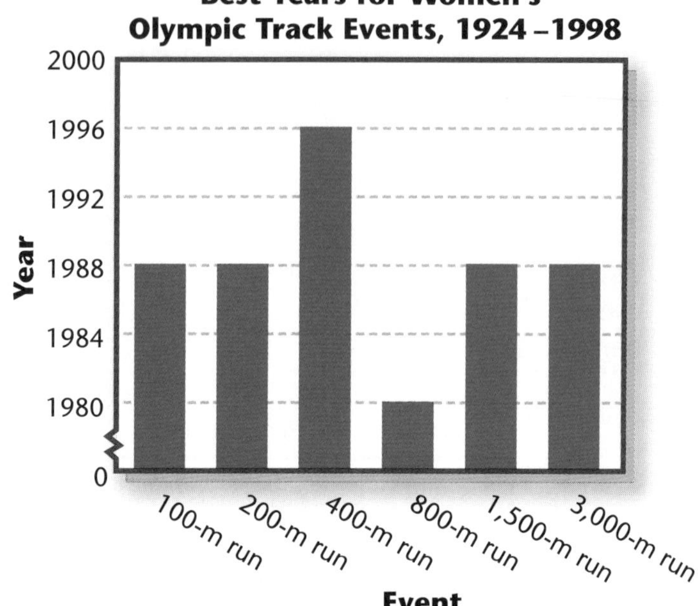

Students Participating in the East Vernon Track and Field Olympics		
Event	Number of Sixth Grade Students	Number of Fifth Grade Students
100 meter dash	12	15
High jump	13	8
Long jump	9	9
Javelin throw	4	7

12. **Make it RIGHT**

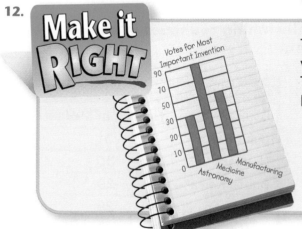

This is how Morgan drew the vertical axis of a bar graph. Tell what mistake she made. Explain how to correct it.

Problem Solving

13. Explain how single- and double-bar graphs are similar.

★14. **Health:** Running is one way to improve your physical fitness. Marcy makes a graph to show how long she ran each day. Should she make a single-bar graph or a double-bar graph? Explain.

Day	Time (In minutes)
Monday	45
Tuesday	55
Wednesday	00
Thursday	30
Friday	15
Saturday	40
Sunday	10

Use data from *Did You Know?* for problems 15–17.

15. Make a bar graph that shows the number of athletes at each game.

16. Find the mean number of students in the games from 1968 to 1975.

17. How many more athletes competed in 1975 than 1968?

18. **Compare:** How are single- and double-bar graphs the same? different?

19. **Collect Data:** Survey your friends and family about their favorite winter Olympic's sport. Collect the data in a frequency table. Make a bar graph from the data.

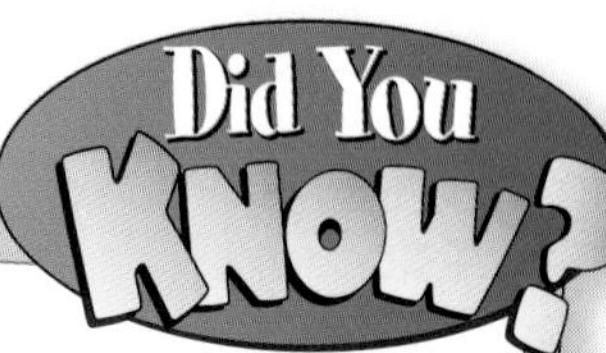

Eunice Kennedy Shriver started the International Special Olympics Games in Chicago in 1968. The number of athletes in the games is shown in this frequency table.

International Special Olympics Games		
Game	Year	Athletes
1	1968	1,000
2	1970	2,000
3	1972	2,500
4	1975	3,200

Spiral Review and Test Prep

20. 3.56 + 0.77 21. 21.094 + 5.4 22. 5.89 − 2.3 23. 0.04 − 0.029

Choose the correct answer.

24. What digit is in the hundredths place of the number 4,305.129?
A. 0 C. 3
B. 2 D. 9

25. Round 42.849 to the nearest tenth.
F. 40 H. 42.85
G. 42.8 J. 42.9

Objective: Read and make histograms.

4·5 Read and Make Histograms

Learn

The skates we use today were patented in 1819, although they were originally invented at least 3,000 years ago. City officials collected data to find the ages of skaters in their town. How can the data be presented in a histogram?

Math Word

histogram a bar graph that shows frequency of data for intervals

Age of Skaters	Number of Inline Skaters
0–5	4
6–10	26
11–15	20
16–20	17
21–25	18
26–30	15

Example

When a survey includes the frequency of data over an interval, you can make a **histogram**.

1. Decide on a scale for the vertical axis.
2. Label the axes.
3. Draw bars for each set of data. There should be no gaps between the bars.
4. Add a title.

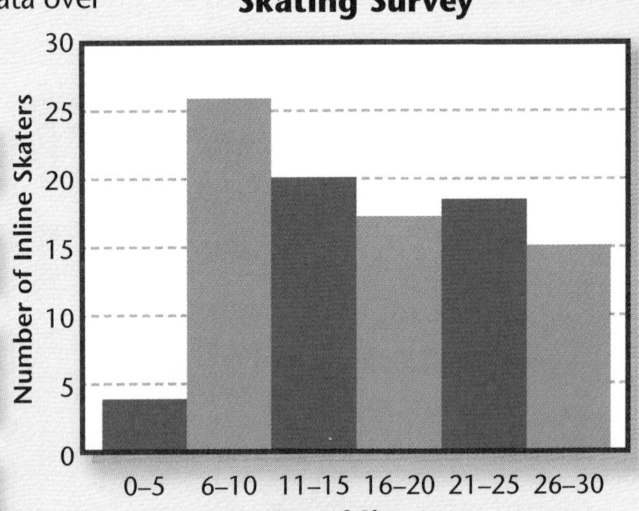

Try It

1. Use this data to make a histogram.
2. How can you tell by looking at your histogram that more people use the skate ramp from 2–6 P.M. than from 6–10 A.M.?
3. **What if** one skater arrives home late and uses the skate ramp at 7 P.M. instead of 5 P.M.? How would the histogram change?

People Using the Skate Ramp During the Day

Time	Number of Skaters
6 A.M.–10 A.M.	5
10 A.M.–2 P.M.	16
2 P.M.–6 P.M.	12
6 P.M.–10 P.M.	3

Sum it Up Explain when you would use a histogram to display data.

Practice

4. The community center holds a skate race. They record the number of skaters who complete the obstacle course in a certain time. Make a histogram using this data.

Times Through the Obstacle Course	
Time	Number of Skaters
1–2 minutes	1
2–3 minutes	5
3–4 minutes	8
4–5 minutes	4

Use data from the histogram for problems 5–7.

5. Which age group has the fewest skaters?

6. Which age group has the most skaters?

7. How many skaters were included in the survey?

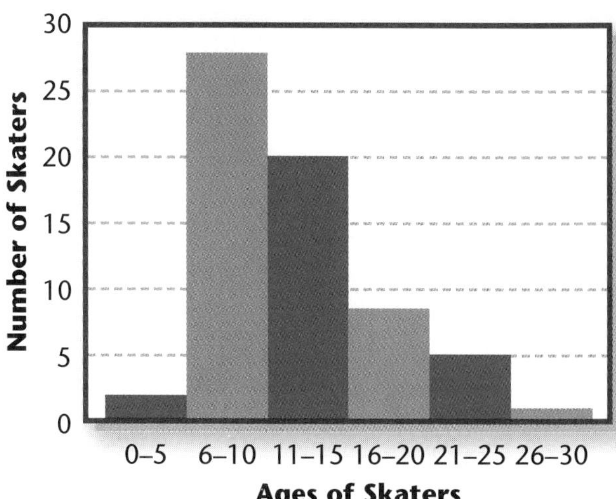

Problem Solving

Use data from the table for problem 8.

8. Make a histogram for the data.

9. If the Garcia brothers buy one pair of skates for $44.99 and another pair for $69.99, how much money do they spend?

10. **Compare:** How is a histogram like a bar graph? How is it different?

Cost of Inline Skates	
Price In Dollars	Number of Models
41–60	15
61–80	18
81–100	6
101–120	9

Spiral Review and Test Prep

Order from least to greatest.

11. 1.4, 14, 1.45, 1.405, 1.418

12. 8.5, 8.05, 8.51, 8.501, 8.15

13. 2.3, 2.083, 2.08, 2.83, 2.33

14. 7.1, 7.03, 7, 7.01, 7.3

Choose the correct answer.

15. Charlie buys an $80 pair of skates and a helmet. He spends a total of $110. How much was the helmet?

    A. $30 C. $110
    B. $80 D. $170

16. A teacher passes out 92 books among 23 students. How many does each student get?

    F. 5 H. 7
    G. 6 J. Not Here

Extra Practice, page 188

Objective: Read and make line graphs.

4·6 Read and Make Line Graphs

Learn

Math Words

coordinates the numbers in an ordered pair

ordered pair a pair of numbers that gives the location of a point on a grid

plot to graph a point on a coordinate plane

line graph a graph that uses a line to show changes in data

Who built the first motorized flying machine? Orville and Wilbur Wright's 1903 invention of the airplane changed the way people travel. How can travel destinations be located? Name the coordinates of New York, New York.

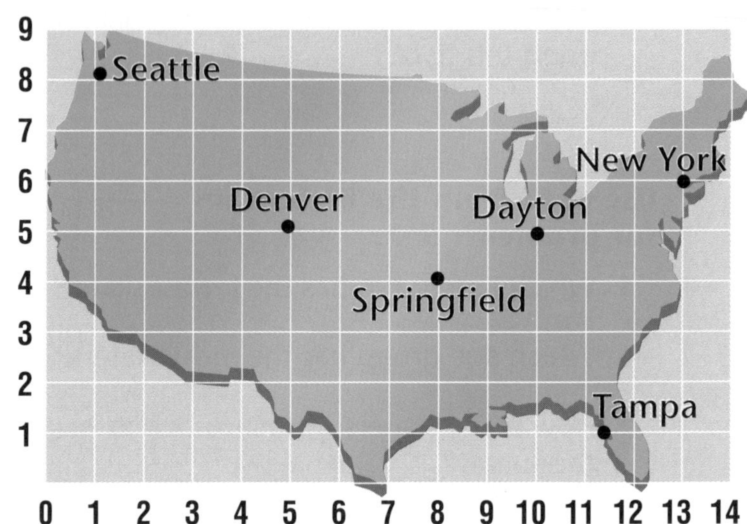

Example 1

You can use a map with a grid to find and identify locations.

You can locate a point on a map using **coordinates**.

1. Start at zero.
2. Count the number of units to the right and the number of units up to find New York.
3. Write these numbers as an **ordered pair**.

The coordinates for New York, New York are (13, 6).

Example 2

Sioux Falls is located at (6,7). **Plot** it on the graph.

1. Start at (0, 0).
2. Count 6 units to the right. From there, count 7 units up.
3. Place a point and label it Sioux Falls.

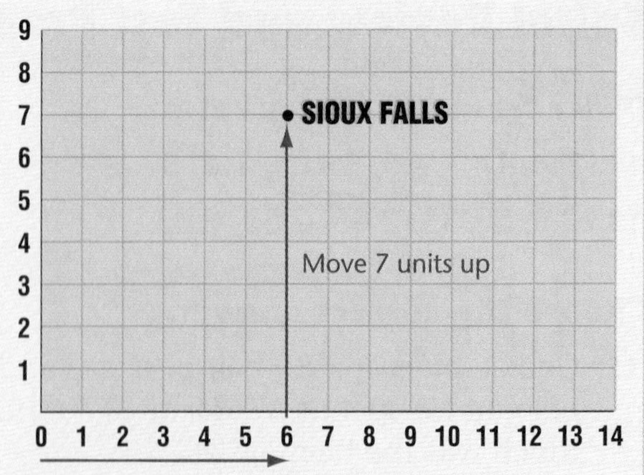

A pilot graphs the number of flights she makes each month or a year. During which months did the number of flights increase?

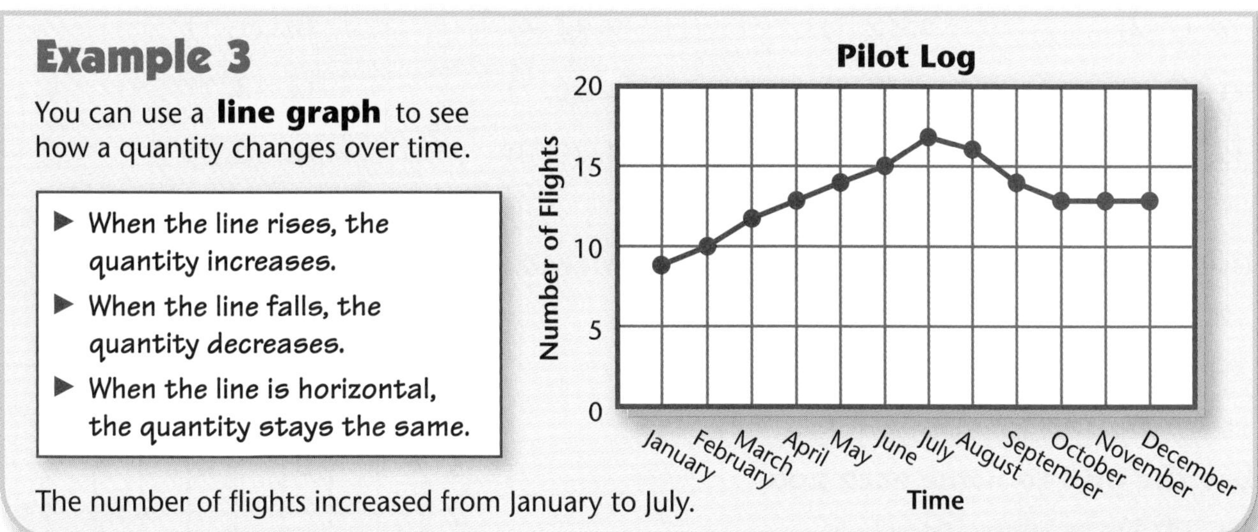

Example 3

You can use a **line graph** to see how a quantity changes over time.

- When the line rises, the quantity increases.
- When the line falls, the quantity decreases.
- When the line is horizontal, the quantity stays the same.

The number of flights increased from January to July.

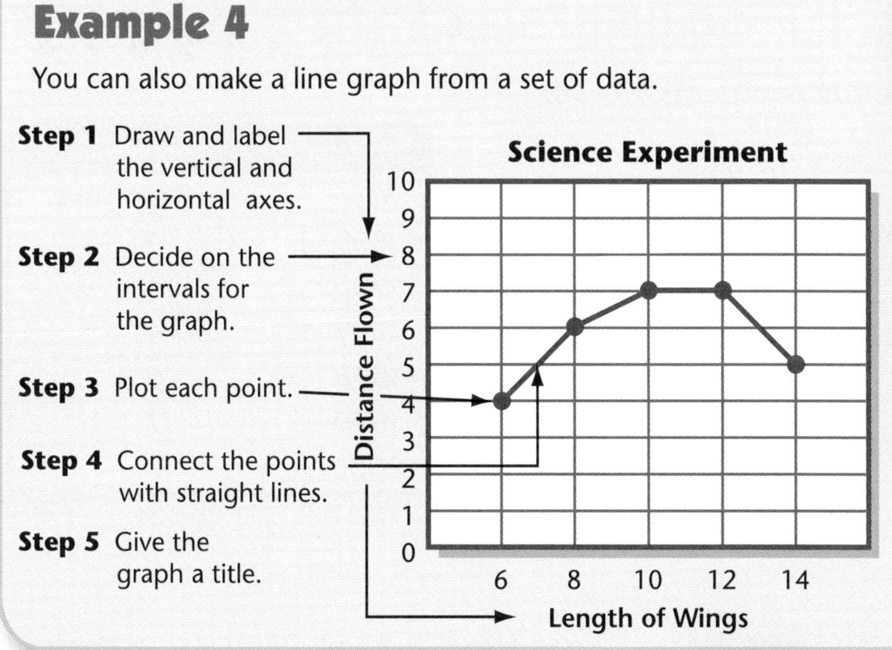

Example 4

You can also make a line graph from a set of data.

Step 1 Draw and label the vertical and horizontal axes.

Step 2 Decide on the intervals for the graph.

Step 3 Plot each point.

Step 4 Connect the points with straight lines.

Step 5 Give the graph a title.

Results of a Paper Airplane Science Experiment	
Length of Wings (Inches)	Distance Flown (Feet)
6	4
8	6
10	7
12	7
14	5

Try It

1. Use this data to make a line graph.
2. Tell which months on the graph show an increase, a decrease, and no change.

Trips to Atlanta	
Month	Number of Trips
January	16
February	15
March	14
April	14
May	16
June	18

Explain when you would use a line graph to show data.

Practice

Tell how many units to the right and how many up you would move for each coordinate pair.

3. (8, 4)	**4.** (5, 5)	**5.** (1, 6)	**6.** (3, 9)
7. (7, 2)	**8.** (5, 1)	**9.** (2, 4)	**10.** (1, 1)
11. (3, 4)	**12.** (8, 5)	**13.** (6, 7)	**14.** (3, 1)
15. (3, 3)	**16.** (6, 6)	★**17.** (0, 0)	★**18.** (0, 4)

Use the coordinate grid to name each ordered pair.

19. A **20.** B

21. C **22.** D

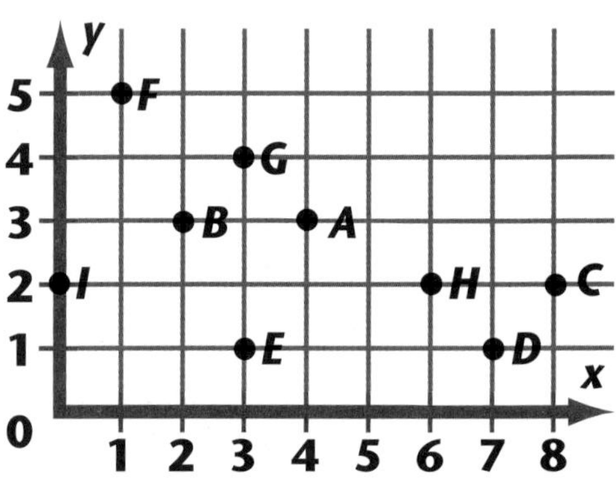

Use the grid to name each point.

23. (3, 1) **24.** (1, 5)

25. (3, 4) **26.** (6, 2)

Use data from the table for problems 27–30.

27. Make a line graph to display the data.

28. Name the years that show an increase. Name the years that show a decrease.

29. How many years did the number of trips stay the same?

30. What is the mode of the number of trips for the data shown?

International business trips	
Year	Number of trips
1995	4
1996	4
1997	4
1998	6
1999	7
2000	2

31. Make it RIGHT

This is how Anita graphed points A (0, 1) and B (2, 3). Tell what mistake she made. Explain how to correct it.

Problem Solving

32. An airplane leaves an airport at (7, 5). It lands 4 units south of that point. What are its new coordinates?

33. Jake plotted *W* (1, 3), *X* (6, 3), *Y* (1, 8), and *Z* (6, 8). Then he connected *W* and *X*, *X* and *Z*, *Z* and *Y*, and *Y* and *W*. What figure did he make?

34. A pilot leaves an airport at (2, 2) and flies to (8, 2). What direction is she flying?

35. Find four points that make a rectangle when they are plotted.

36. Compare a line graph with a bar graph. How are they alike and different?

★ 37. A point is plotted zero units to the right and zero units up. What are the coordinates of the point?

Use data from *Did You Know?* for problems 38–39.

38. Was Orville or Wilbur the older brother?

39. How old was Wilbur when he and Orville first flew a plane?

40. **Collect data:** Survey your class about how many plane trips they made in the last year. Show the data in a line graph.

★ 41. A line graph shows the number of pilots living in South Carolina over the past 5 years. The same number have lived there for the past 3 years. What will the line in this part of the graph look like?

Although few people ever discuss Wilbur or Orville Wright without talking about the other, the brothers were not twins. Wilbur lived from 1867 to 1912 and Orville lived from 1871 to 1948. They first flew a plane in 1903.

Spiral Review and Test Prep

Use data from the bar graph for problems 42–43.

42. How many people traveled on vacation last year?

43. How many more people traveled by car than by bus?

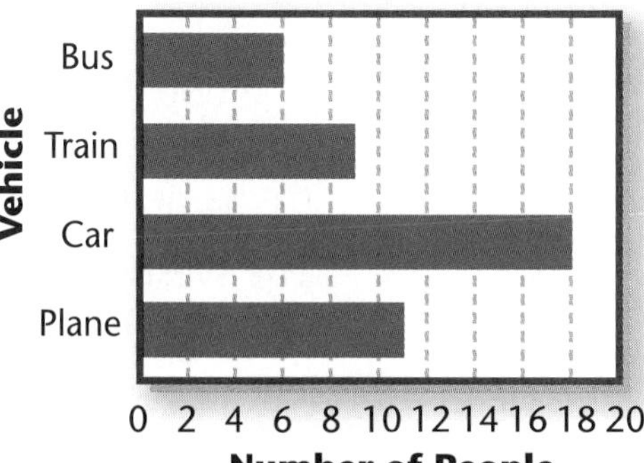

Choose the correct answer.

44. Emily used 600 ÷ 20 to estimate a quotient. She rounded the dividend to the nearest hundred and the divisor to the nearest ten. Which problem is she solving?
    - A. 635 ÷ 23
    - B. 555 ÷ 25
    - C. 575 ÷ 12
    - D. 651 ÷ 20

45. Which addition property tells you that 68 + 4 = 4 + 68?
    - F. Commutative
    - G. Associative
    - H. Identity
    - J. Not Here

Extra Practice, page 189

Objective: Change scales on graphs to identify methods of persuasion.

Problem Solving: Reading for Math

Change Scales

Debate on City Train Schedule

Read

The Train Company manager wants to add a train to each route. The West Route manager wants more than one train added to his route. Which graph supports each manager?

- **What do you know?** how many riders on each route
- **What do you need to find?** the graph for each argument

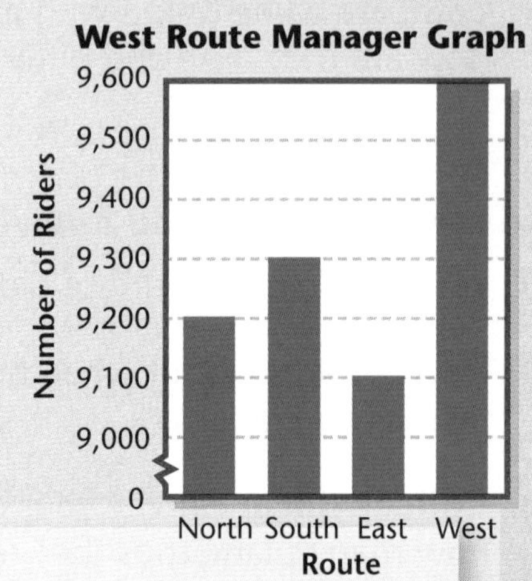

READING SKILL ▶ Identify Methods of Persuasion
Persuasion is the art of convincing someone of a point of view.

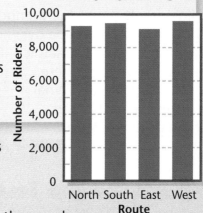

Train Company Manager Graph

10,000
8,000
6,000
4,000
2,000
0
Number of Riders
North South East West
Route

MATH SKILL ▶ Change Scales on Graphs
Small intervals can make small differences in data appear more dramatic. Large intervals can do the opposite.

Plan

Decide how the scale of the graph affects your impression of the data.

Solve

The Train Company graph uses intervals of 2,000 riders. It makes the difference in the number of riders look unimportant. It supports the idea of adding the same number of trains to each route.

The West Route graph makes the difference in riders look more dramatic by using intervals of 100 riders and a break in the vertical scale. This graph supports the need for more trains on the West Route.

Look Back

How could you make a graph so that the need for more trains on the West Route seems even more convincing?

Explain how scales can be used as a method of persuasion.

Practice **Use data from the graph for problems 1–3.**

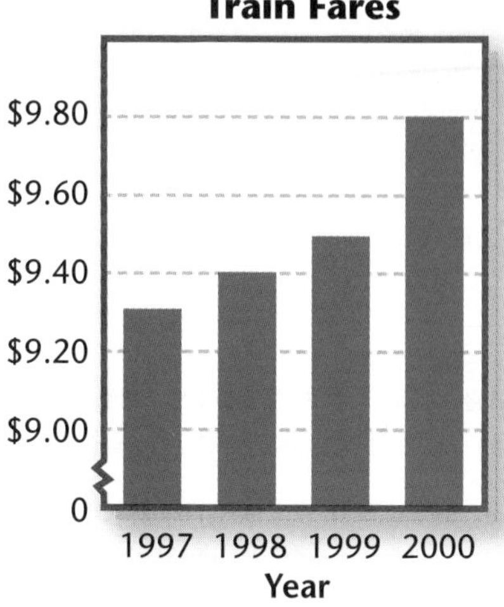

1. Without looking at the vertical axis, what does this graph appear to show about the train fares?

2. **Analyze:** Suppose the Train Company wants to increase the fares for next year. Would this graph help to convince the passengers of the need? Explain.

3. How might you change the graph to show that train fares have stayed about the same?

Use data from the chart for problems 4–5.

4. You work as a train engineer. You want to convince your boss that she should remove two cars from Train B. Make a bar graph that will support your argument.

5. Your co-worker thinks that the trains have about the same number of cars. Make a bar graph that supports this point of view.

Number of Cars on Trains	
Train	Cars
A	12
B	14
C	11
D	13

Use data from the graph for problems 6–7.

6. Without looking at the vertical axis, what does this graph appear to show about how fast a train leaves a station?

7. How might you change the graph to show that the train speeds up very quickly?

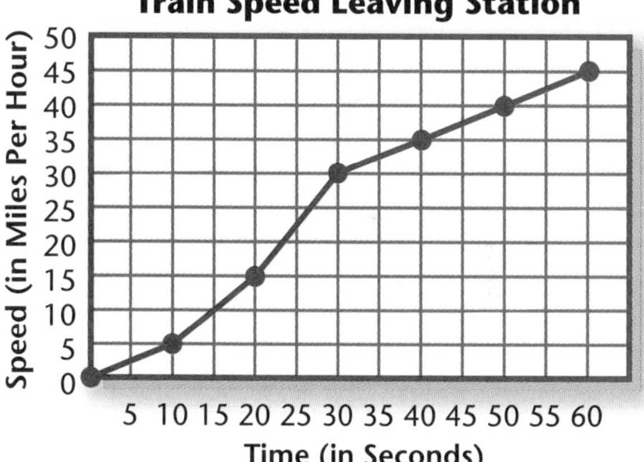

Spiral Review and Test Prep

Choose the correct answer.

The Train Company records the temperature in car 7 during the afternoon. They collect the data in the chart.

Temperature in Car 7	
Time	Temperature
1:00	72°F
2:00	70°F
3:00	71°F
4:00	72°F

8. Which of the following statements is NOT true?
   - **A.** The temperature was the same at 1:00 P.M. and 4:00. P.M.
   - **B.** The mode of the data was 72°F.
   - **C.** The temperature increased each hour during the afternoon.
   - **D.** The lowest temperature was recorded at 2:00 P.M.

Extra Practice, page 189

Problem Solving

Check Your Progress A

Find the range, mode, median, and mean. **(pages 154–157)**

1. 72, 80, 99, 95, 90, 80
2. 35, 28, 12, 19, 35, 34

Use data from the table for problems 3–5. **(pages 158–165)**

3. Make a pictograph of the number of inventions.
4. Make a bar graph of the number of inventions.
5. Make a histogram of the number of inventions.

Some Notable Inventions		
Years	Invention	Number
1750–1799	Cotton Gin, 1793 Vaccination, 1796	2
1800–1849	Steam Locomotive, 1814 Sewing Machine, 1830 Vulcanized Rubber, 1839	3
1850–1899	Dynamite, 1866 Phonograph, 1877 X rays, 1895 Radio Telegraphy, 1895	4

Source: World Magazine

Use data from the graph for problems 6–7. **(pages 166–169)**

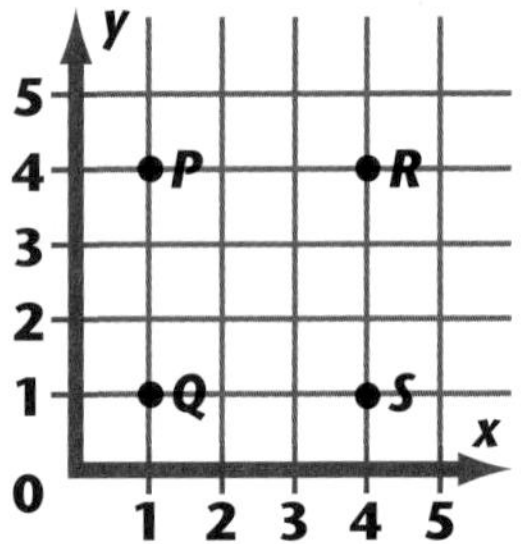

6. Name the point located at (1, 4).
7. Name the coordinates of point *S*.
8. Make a line graph from the data in the table.

Membership in the Young Inventor's Club						
Year	1995	1996	1997	1998	1999	2000
Number of Students	4	5	8	4	4	7

Use data from the table for problems 9–10. **(pages 170–171)**

9. Make a graph that the Spanish Club might use to convince the principal that they have more members and deserve a larger budget.

10. Make a graph that the soccer team might use to convince the principal that all groups deserve an equal share of the budget.

Membership	
Activity	Members
Young Inventors' Club	19
Spanish Club	23
Soccer Team	18
Science Club	18

Additional activities at
www.mhschool.com/math

Use a Table to Find Mean, Median, Mode, and Range

Ms. Reno works in the cafeteria at a local hospital. She wants to determine the mean, median, mode, and range of the amounts spent by employees in the cafeteria on Monday, Tuesday, and Wednesday. The first 6 employees on each day spent the following amounts:

Monday: $2.45; $1.75; $2.20; $2.90; $3.25; $2.05
Tuesday: $2.50; $2.85; $1.9; $2.55; $2.90; $2.50
Wednesday: $2.95; $3.20; $2.50; $2.15; $2.45; $2.15

Find the mean, median, mode, and range for each day.

You can use a spreadsheet table to find the mean, median, mode, and range.

- Click on the table key
- Label the columns *Monday, Tuesday,* and *Wednesday.*
- Enter the amounts for each day in the appropriate column.
- Click on Setup key and choose Mean, Median, Mode, and Range and click OK.

Find the mean, median, mode, and range for each day.

Enter each set of data in a spreadsheet table. Then find the mean, median, mode, and range.

1. 15, 18, 29, 15, 30, 25
2. 1.6, 1.9, 2.6, 2.8, 1.9
3. 5.89, 5.78, 6.924.36

Solve.

4. Juanita works at the library. She worked 4 days last week and checked out 36, 29, 47, and 38 books. Find the mean, median, mode, and range of the number of books she checked out.

For more practice, use Math Traveler™.

Objective: Explain which types of graphs are appropriate for various data sets.

4·8 Problem Solving: Strategy

Make a Graph

Read

Read the problem carefully.

Although ball playing has been popular for 2,000 years, the first bouncing balls were invented after 1839. In that year it was discovered that balls could be made from rubber. The table shows a day's sales of balls at a sporting goods store. Which type of graph could be used to display the data?

12 basketballs sold

Ball	Number Sold
Golf balls	8
Softballs	15
Basketballs	12
Soccer balls	10

Plan

Decide which graph best represents the data. Choose between a bar graph, double-bar graph, histogram, line graph, line plot, or pictograph.

Solve

Since you cannot use numbers on both axes, you cannot use a line graph, line plot, or histogram.

The table compares one set of data. So a double-bar graph is not a good choice.

A bar graph is a good choice for representing the data.

Look Back

What other type of graph could you use to display the data?

Explain why it is necessary to choose a certain type of graph to represent a set of data.

For problems 1–2, choose the graph that best displays the data. Explain your choice.

1. **Art:** The number of paintings by men and the number of paintings by women at a museum
   A. Line graph
   B. Bar graph
2. Number of hours radio and TV are used during each day for a week
   F. Histogram
   G. Double-bar graph
3. Which is the better data for a bar graph? Explain.
   A. Diameters of basketball, baseball, and golf ball
   B. Distance of a bowling ball from the bowler for the first 5 seconds after it has been rolled
4. **Analyze:** Which would be the best graph to display the game-day temperature data: line graph, bar graph, or pictograph? Explain.

Temperatures at Saturday's Football Game

Time	Temperature
2:00	48°F
2:30	55°F
3:00	55°F
3:30	50°F
4:00	46°F

Problem Solving

Mixed Strategy Review

CHOOSE A STRATEGY
- Logical Reasoning
- Draw a Diagram
- Make a Graph
- Make a Table or List
- Find a Pattern
- Guess and Check
- Write an Equation
- Work Backward
- Solve a Simpler Problem
- Conduct an Experiment

5. One apple and two pears cost $1.55. Two apples and two pears cost $2.30. How much does one apple cost?
6. Gary and Lily play a number game. Lily tells Gary to pick a number, add 2 to it, then multiply by 3. Gary's final answer is 30. What number did he start with?
7. Julia's address is a two-digit number. The product of the numbers is 24. The sum is 10. The numbers in the address appear from smaller to greater. What is her address?
8. Oscar helps his parents install a fence around the yard. The fence will be in the shape of a square. There will be 9 fence posts on each side. How many fence posts do they need altogether?
9. During a baseball game, the two teams scored 9 runs in all. The losing team lost by 3 runs. What was the final score?
10. Name at least two different appropriate graphs to represent these points scored by players in a basketball game: Trina, 4; Alayna, 6; Bernita, 2; Shelly, 3; Diane, 10; Justine, 7.
11. How much money could you have in pennies, nickels, dimes, and quarters, but still not be able to make exact change for a dollar? You do not need to have every type of coin.

Extra Practice, page 189

Objective: Read and make stem-and-leaf plots.

4•9 Read and Make Stem-and-Leaf Plots

Learn

The data shows how many gallons of milk a dairy farmer pasteurizes over a period of several days. How can a stem-and-leaf plot be used to organize the data?

Math Words

stem the digit or digits to the left of the ones digit of a number in a data set

leaf a ones digit in a row of a stem-and-leaf plot

stem-and-leaf-plot an arrangement of numbers that separates the ones digits from the other digits

Example 1

Think: 8 and 9 have no tens digits, so write 0 for their stem.

1 Write the **stem** by vertically writing the tens digits of the data from least to greatest.

0
1
2
3

2 Make the **leaves** by writing each ones digit, in order, to the right of its tens digit.

0	8 9
1	1 1 2 6 7 7 7
2	3 6
3	0 0 1

3 Add a title and a key.

Pasteurized Milk

Stems	Leaves
0	8 9
1	1 1 2 6 7 7 7
2	3 6
3	0 0 1

Key: 2|3=23

Try It

1. Make a stem-and-leaf plot from the data at the right.

Stores that Carry Organic Milk

County	Number of Stores
Bryen	12
Porter	8
Marks	10
Stanton	15
Fells	21

How does a stem-and-leaf plot organize data?

Practice

A farmers' cooperative keeps track of the milk produced by the cows on its members' farms each day.

Stems	Leaves
12	8 9
13	0 1 1 1 1 2 5 6 7 8 8 9
14	0 0 1 2

Use data from the stem-and-leaf plot for problems 2–8.

2. How many farmers belong to the cooperative?
3. What is the range of the gallons of milk produced?
4. What was the greatest amount of milk produced?
5. How many farms had cows that produced 138 gallons of milk?
6. What is the median amount of milk produced?
7. What is the mean amount of milk produced?
8. What type of data measurement will best represent the most frequent amount of milk produced on the farms? What is that amount?

Problem Solving

Some farmers milk their cows twice a day, every day of the year. Use this calendar rule for problems 9–11:

Thirty days hath September, April, June, and November. All the rest have thirty-one, except February, which has twenty-eight.

9. Make a stem-and-leaf plot that shows the number of days in each month.
10. How many times each year would a farmer milk the cows?
11. How could you change the stem-and-leaf plot into a bar graph? How would you label the vertical axis?

★ 12. Explain why you would or would not use a stem-and-leaf plot to show the milk produced by 100 cows.

Spiral Review and Test Prep

13. $468 + 762$

14. $976 - 57$

15. $\$14.97 + 22.44$

16. $11.55 - 2.65$

17. $9.4 - 8.55$

Choose the correct answer.

18. Forty-eight farmers in a cooperative each have about 390 cows. Estimate the number of cows in the cooperative.

    A. About 2,000 C. About 10,000
    B. About 5,000 D. About 20,000

19. A farmer's cows produce 1,344 gallons of milk during a week. What is the mean number of gallons produced each day?

    F. 176 H. 1,344
    G. 192 J. 9,408

Objective: Understand how to select a random sample.

4·10 Sampling

California inventer Krysta Morlan invented a battery-operated cooler for people wearing casts.

Learn

A school nurse wants to find out how many students have had to wear a cast in the past year. The school has 1,253 students. The nurse surveys the first 25 students to arrive at school. What are the population and sample in this survey?

Math Words

population an entire group or set about which information is wanted

sample the part of a population that is used in a survey to represent the whole population

representative sample a sample that represents the entire population

biased sample a sample that does not represent the entire population

random sample a sample where each member in the population has an equal chance of being chosen

Example 1

The **population** is the group you are interested in studying. In this case the entire student body is the population.

Since it would be very difficult to survey all of the 1,253 students, a **sample** of the population can be surveyed.

The sample is the group you actually survey. The 25 students to arrive first at school are the sample.

So the population is the entire student body, and the sample is the first 25 students to arrive at school.

Were the 25 students surveyed a **representative sample** or a **biased sample**? Was the sample a **random sample**?

Example 2

To get accurate results, you want the sample to give the same answers you would get if you surveyed the entire population. If it does, the sample is a representative sample.

Think about ways that the survey is unfair.

- The students who arrived later had no chance of being included.
- Perhaps the students who are now wearing casts arrived late because it takes them longer to get ready for school.

The best way to get a representative sample is to use a random sample. A sample that is not random is more likely to be biased. A biased sample does not represent the population fairly, and the results cannot be trusted. A random sample gives everyone in the population an equal chance of being chosen. Each member of the sample would be chosen by chance. To get a random sample, place everyone's name in a hat, and choose 125 at random.

The nurse's survey had a biased sample. It was not a representative sample and it was not random.

Try It

Name each population and sample.

1. A survey asks the fifth-grade students in an elementary school how many of them have ever thought of a possible invention.
2. A survey asks the 5 oldest students in Mr. Manfred's class if they can name a famous inventor.

Tell whether or not each sample is a random sample. Explain.

3. A student wants to know how many students in the school have ever worn a cast. She surveys the members of the soccer team.
4. The fifth-grade teachers want to select students for a field trip to the science museum. They only have 12 tickets. They put everyone's name in a hat and select 12 names without looking.

Explain a way that you could select a random sample of the fifth-grade students in your school.

Practice **Name each population and sample.**

5. In a school of 536 students, you pick 100 names from a bag. You want to find out how many students in the school own at least one bicycle.

6. Survey 20 bikers to find the most popular biking trail in town.

7. Survey all 10 cello players in the school orchestra to find how many orchestra members ride bikes to rehearsal.

8. Survey high school students in your town to find how many people own a tandem bike.

9. Athletes sometimes need to wear casts to help broken bones heal. Survey the soccer team to see how many students at school have ever worn casts.

10. Ask your friends in the fifth-grade to see how many fifth-grade students have visited the nurse during this school year.

11. Pick 25 names from the phone book to see who in town has been to an inventors' convention before.

12. You want to find out if there are many inventors in your school. You ask all the fifth-grade students named Bob to see how many have ever invented something.

A researcher wants to find out which bicycle model is the most popular in your school. Tell whether or not each sample is a random sample. Is it a representative sample? Explain.

13. A survey of every tenth fifth-grade student from an alphabetical list of the fifth grade

14. A survey of every tenth student from a list of all the students in your school

15. A survey of all of the students in Mrs. Acela's class

16. All the shoppers at a bike store

17. All of the students who ride bikes to school

18. Thirty names drawn from a hat

19. The school principal and the 5th grade teachers

★ 20. Every student in the school

Describe one way you could find a representative sample for each population.

21. All people in a town

22. Your fifth grade class

23. Your school

24. The United States

Problem Solving

25. Joanne conducts a survey to see which bike trails are the most popular in the park. She surveys bikers between 7 A.M. and 9 A.M. on a Friday morning. Is the sample a random sample? Explain.

26. Gary wants to know how many people in his town need casts each day. He surveys people at a doctor's office for one week. Is the sample a random sample? Explain.

Use data from the table for problems 27–28.

27. **What if** you turned on a radio station at random anywhere in the United States? Which type of music would you probably hear? Explain.

28. How many more Jazz stations were there than Classical stations?

29. **Collect Data:** Create a survey question to ask students in your school. Decide how to select a random sample. Survey the sample. Then make a graph to display your data.

Radio Stations

Type of Music	Number of Stations
Classical, Fine Arts	42
Jazz	90
Ethnic	565
Oldies and Classic Hits	975
Rock	782
Country	2,393

30. Bill surveys 84 people. Kwang surveys 56 people. How many times more people did Bill survey?

31. **Explain** why you usually choose a sample rather than survey the entire population.

32. Clara sees 14 tricycles and 65 bicycles at the park. How many wheels did she see?

33. A survey reveals that 32 of Dr. Kim's patients needed a cast during the winter months. In the summer months, 54 people needed casts. How many more casts were needed in the summer than in the winter?

34. Duane rides his bike 15.6 miles on Saturday and 12.9 miles on Sunday. How many miles did he ride on the weekend?

Spiral Review and Test Prep

35. $6{,}000 \div 4.8$ **36.** 64×3.2 **37.** 1.27×8.5 **38.** $4.5 \div 0.09$

39. 8.57×29.7 **40.** $8.2 \div 0.2$ **41.** 3.5×1.5 **42.** $4.3 \div 0.4$

Choose the correct answer.

43. Find the median of this set of data.
5, 6, 6, 3, 4, 16, 2

- **A.** 7
- **B.** 6
- **C.** 5.5
- **D.** Not Here

44. Which of the following is equal to 5^3?

- **F.** 3^5
- **G.** $5 \times 5 \times 5$
- **H.** $5 + 5 + 5$
- **J.** 5×3

Extra Practice, page 189

Objective: Apply data, statistics, and graphs to analyze data and make decisions. Make a decision based on information in graphs.

Problem Solving: Application

Decision Making

Will you vote for an increased, decreased, or same-sized budget?

The Oakdale Inventors' Museum is supported by the town council. Each year the council votes on a budget for the museum. In the year 2000, they voted for a budget of $75,000. As a member of this year's council, you must vote whether to increase or decrease the budget by $3,000 or leave the budget the same. The museum would like an increase. They present the following graphs to the council.

Year 2000 Budget Expenses

Expense	Amount
New Exhibits	
Books for Museum Library	
Employee Salaries	
Advertising	
Budget to Make School Visits Free	

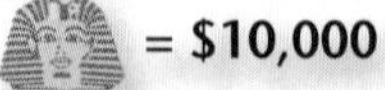
= $10,000

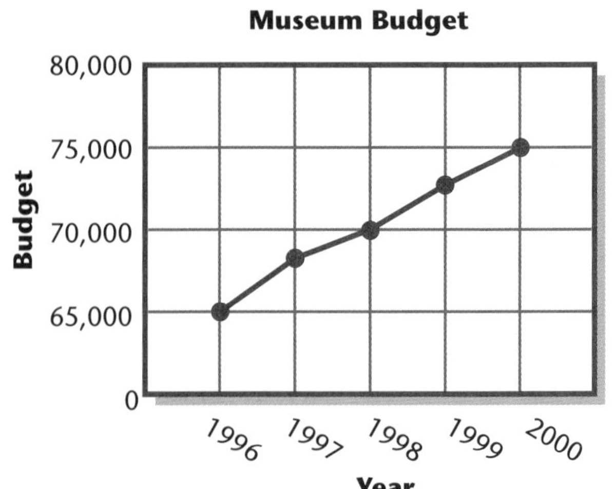

Read for Understanding

1. What is the museum's current budget?
2. How much money was spent on new exhibits?
3. How many years of data are included in the graph about the number of visitors?
4. What kind of graphs did the museum present?

Make Decisions

5. What is the range of the number of visitors to the museum?
6. Which graph shows a break in the vertical scale? What might be the purpose of this break?
7. Has the number of visitors ever decreased? If so, between which two years?
8. Describe how the number of visitors changed from 1997 to 2000.
9. About how many new visitors came to the museum between 1999 and 2000?
10. What is the largest budget the museum ever had?
11. About how much money was spent on advertising and salaries in the year 2000?
12. Did the museum stay within budget last year?
13. If each new book costs about $25, about how many books were added to the library last year?
14. How many times more money was spent on salaries than on new books last year?
15. About how much did the budget increase between 1996 and 2000?
16. About how much did the budget increase between 1999 and 2000?
17. If the museum spent $10,000 on advertising in 1999, about how much was spent on advertising per visitor?
18. Find the range, mode, median, and mean of the number of museum visitors each year.
19. Find the range, median, and mode of the year 2000 expenses.
20. List some advantages of having a museum in the town.
21. If the town has a population of about 75,000 people, about how much money was spent for each person in the year 2000?

How will you vote?

Objective: Apply graphs to investigate science concepts.

Problem Solving: Application
Math and Science

You Will Need
- **thermometer**

Which school location has the greatest difference between morning and afternoon temperatures?

Temperatures can rise a lot in the afternoon if the area receives a lot of sunlight.

You may have noticed that some places around your school get hotter than others. You may feel hot in a parking lot, but cool in a shady field. Some places heat up more than others depending on how much sunlight they receive or the materials they are made from.

In this activity you will collect temperature data from different locations around the school. Then you will decide which site has the greatest temperature difference between morning and afternoon.

Hypothesize

Which location do you think will have the greatest temperature difference between morning and afternoon? Explain.

Procedure

1. Work with a partner. Choose the location you want to study.
2. Measure the temperature at your location in the morning and afternoon.
3. Record the data.
4. Repeat every day for one week.

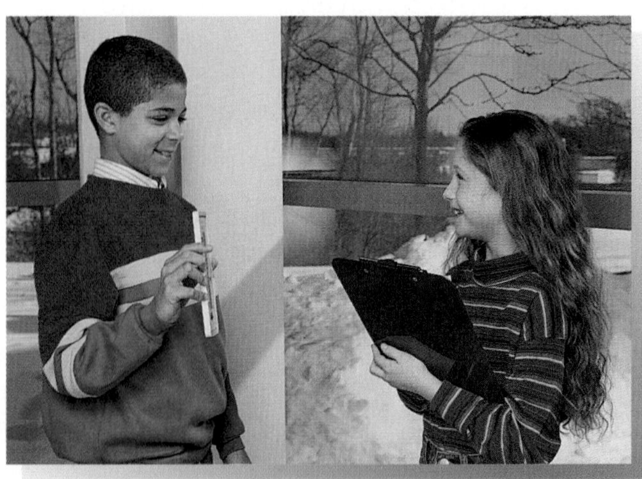

Data

Copy and complete the chart to record your observations.

Your Location		
Day	Morning Temperature	Afternoon Temperature
1		
2		
3		
4		
5		
6		
7		

Conclude and Apply

- Calculate the difference between the morning and afternoon temperatures for each day.
- Find the mean daily difference.
- Make a graph to compare the morning and afternoon temperatures at your location. Use the type of graph that you think best represents the data. Justify your choice.
- Collect the data from the entire class, then decide which location had the greatest temperature difference.
- Use data from ***Did You Know?*** to decide which locations you think are made of materials with high and low ***albedos***.

The word albedo describes how much sunlight a surface material reflects. A material with a high albedo will reflect a lot of sunlight and not heat up very much. Low albedo materials absorb a lot of sunlight and heat up much more. Although the moon seems bright, it actually has an albedo of only 7%, meaning it reflects just 7% of the sunlight it receives—about the same as a black-top parking lot.

Going Further

1. Design and complete an activity to determine which locations inside the school show the greatest temperature difference between morning and afternoon.
2. Design and complete an activity to determine which colors or materials absorb the most heat.

Check Your Progress B

Determine the graph that best represents the data. (pages 174–175)

1. Stella rides her bike 6 blocks in 10 minutes. Then she rests for 1 minute and walks the bike home in 20 minutes.
2. Fred collects data on the number of inventions patented in the last 5 decades.
3. Gillian collects data on the number of hours students talk on the phone and listen to the radio for one week.

Make a stem-and-leaf plot from the data. (pages 176–177)

4. 36 42 52 42 37 45 35 50
5. 8 15 30 26 26 19 39 2

Name the population and sample in each example. (pages 178–191)

6. The mayor wants to know if the town should build an invention museum. He surveys the first 10 people who check out books about inventors from the library.
7. A principal wants to know how many students in the school have ever invented something. She surveys the entire fifth-grade class.

Tell whether or not each sample is a random sample.
Is it a representative sample? Explain. (pages 178–191)

8. A student wants to know if radios or televisions are more popular with fifth-grade students. She asks her friends what they think.
9. A teacher wants to select a small group of students to help put up a bulletin board about inventors. She puts the names in a hat and pulls out 6 names.

10. **Generalize:** Suppose you want to graph the number of students who think the following inventions are most valuable: telephone, computer, vaccinations, steam engine, and sewing machine. Explain why a line graph is not a good graph to use. Then choose a graph and explain why you chose it.

Extra Practice

Collect, Organize, and Display Data (pages 152–153)

Make a frequency table and line plot for each survey question.

1. How many telephones do you have in your home?
2. How many different telephone numbers does your family have for one house?

Range, Mode, Median, and Mean (pages 154–157)

Find the range, mode, median, and mean.

1. 4 8 2 1 2
2. 52 23 67 9
3. 17 17 16 6 20 14 8
4. 121 100 90 95

Read and Make Pictographs (pages 158–159)

Use data from the pictograph for problems 1–4.

1. How many computers are in Library D?
2. Find the range of computers in the four libraries.
3. What is the total number of computers in the four libraries?
4. What is the mean number of computers?
5. Use the data below to make a pictograph.

Number of Computers

Number of Books in the Library on Different Inventors	
Inventor	Number of Books
Thomas Edison	30
Louis Pasteur	10
Wright Brothers	25
George Washington Carver	40

Extra Practice

Read and Make Bar Graphs (pages 160–163)

Use data from the bar graph.

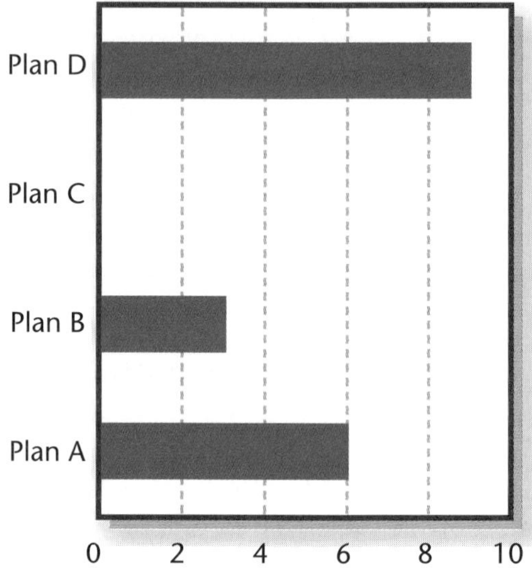

1. How many people voted for each of the plans?
2. Which plan got twice as many votes as Plan B?
3. How many people voted altogether?
4. What is the range of votes? the median number of votes?
5. Make a bar graph from the data.

Number of Inventors Students Can Name	
Student	Number
Lisa	3
Andrew	2
Lauren	4
Colton	9

Read and Make Histograms (pages 164–165)

Use data from the histogram.

Popular TV Shows

Number of Viewers: 0, 4, 8, 12, 16, 20

Age Groups: 1–5, 6–10, 11–15, 16–20

1. Which age group has the most viewers?
2. How many viewers are in this survey?
3. Which age group has the fewest viewers?
4. Describe what happens to the graph when a 7-year-old viewer turns 8. Explain.
5. Make a histogram from the data.

Number of Air Conditioners Sold At Harry's Hardware in Each Season			
Season	Number Sold	Season	Number Sold
January to March	16	July to September	34
April to June	29	October to December	4

Extra Practice

Read and Make Line Graphs (pages 166–169)

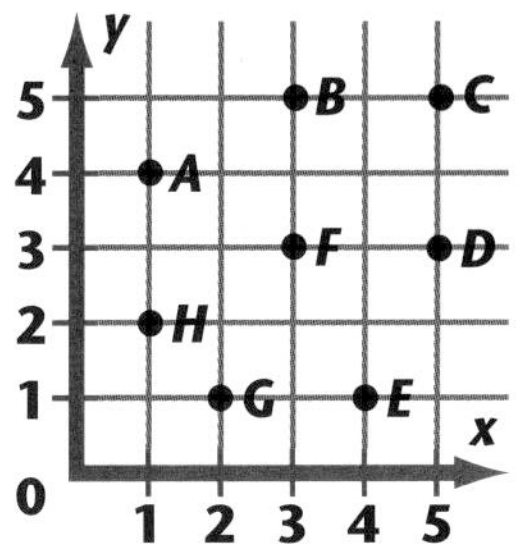

Use the graph to write an ordered pair for each point or name each ordered pair.

1. A
2. D
3. (2, 1)
4. (3, 3)

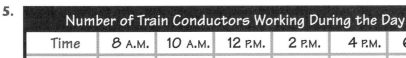

Make a line graph from the data.

5.

Number of Train Conductors Working During the Day						
Time	8 A.M.	10 A.M.	12 P.M.	2 P.M.	4 P.M.	6 P.M.
Number	26	32	23	26	28	27

6. Between which two times did the number increase the most?
7. Between which two times did the number decrease the most?

Problem Solving: Reading for Math Change Scales (pages 170–171)

Use the line graph you created above.

1. How could you change the scale to make the difference in the number of conductors seem smaller?

Problem Solving: Strategy Make a Graph (pages 174–175)

Choose pictograph, bar graph, histogram, line graph, or coordinate graph.

1. The temperature of the classroom was 68°F at 9:00 A.M., 70°F at 10:00 A.M., 72°F at 11:00 A.M., and 76°F at 12:00 P.M. Which graph best represents this data?

Read and Make Stem-and-Leaf Plots (pages 176–177)

Make a stem-and-leaf plot for each set of data.

1. 87 88 82 85 98 99 88 90
2. 34 30 25 28 30 41

Sampling (pages 178–181)

1. Suppose you want to find out which are the most useful inventions to fifth-grade students. Is surveying the first 20 people you see at the town library a good idea? Explain.
2. Suppose you want to find out how many students in your class have dreamed up a new invention. How could you find out without asking all of them?

Chapter Study Guide

Language and Math (pages 152–181)

Math Words
- **bar graph**
- **frequency**
- **histogram**
- **leaf**
- **line graph**
- **mean**
- **median**
- **random sample**
- **stem**

Complete. Use a word from the list.

1. A ____ is necessary to make an unbiased survey.
2. The ones digit of a number is a ____ in a stem-and-leaf plot.
3. A ____ shows frequency of data for intervals.
4. The middle number in a set of numbers arranged in order from least to greatest is called the ____.
5. When data is collected, the number of times a response occurs is its ____.

Skills and Applications

Find the range, mode, median, and mean. (pages 154–157)

Example

What is the range, mode, median, and mean for this set of data?

5 1 11 6 5 8

Solution

Range: $11 - 1 = 10$

Mode: 5, since it appears most often.

Median: 1, 5, 5, 6, 8, 11. The median is 5.5.

Mean: $36 \div 6 = 6$

Use this set of data for problems 6–9.

7 1 8 7 4 9 5 7

6. Find the range.
7. Find the mode.
8. Find the median.
9. Find the mean.

Read and make bar graphs and histograms. (pages 160–163)

Example

Make a histogram.

Age	Number of Students
4-6	16
7-9	13
10-12	18

Solution

20
18
16
14
12
10
0
4–6 7–9 10–12

Use data from the graph for problems 10–11.

10. A nine-year-old turns ten. Find the new range.
11. What happens to the height of the bars when a nine-year-old turns ten?

Read and make line graphs. (pages 166–169)

Example

Write the data for 4 seconds as an ordered pair.

Solution

Write the number of units to the right of 0 as the first number and the number of units up as the second number.

The data is 4 units right and 5 units up. The ordered pair is (4, 5).

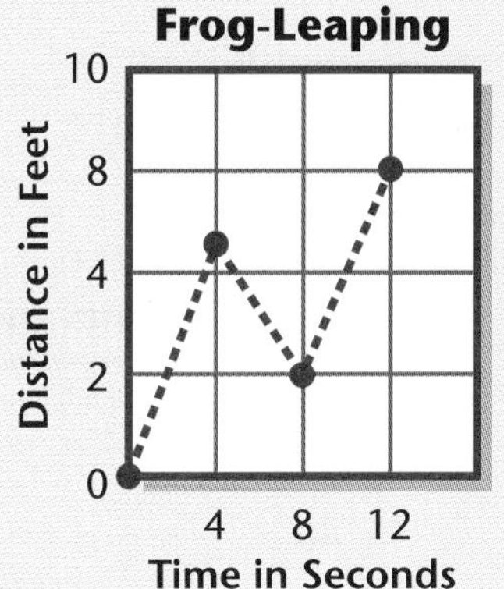

Use data from the graph for problems 12–14.

12. Write the data for 10 seconds as an ordered pair.
13. Write the data for 8 feet as an ordered pair.
14. What was the total distance the frog jumped in 12 seconds?

Read and make stem-and-leaf plots. (pages 176–177)

Example

Make a stem-and-leaf plot for this data:
14, 24, 32, 33, 25, 27,14,
16, 28, 33, 35, 23, 14

Solution

Stem	Leaves
1	4 4 4 6
2	3 4 5 7 8
3	2 3 3 5

Use data from the graph for problems 15–18.

15. In which row is 16 represented?
16. Which row has the most data?
17. Include the number 36 in the stem-and-leaf plot. Graph the new stem-and-leaf plot.
18. Suppose the number 16 was included by mistake. Explain how to remove it from the stem-and-leaf plot.

Solve problems. (pages 170–171, 174–175)

Example

Lucille measured the heights of 5 computer models at the museum. What kind of graph would best display the data?

Solution

Since the computers are separate models, the graph that would best display the heights is a bar graph with one bar for each computer.

Choose the best graph. Explain.

19. A nurse took the temperature of a patient every four hours. He wants to display the data. What kind of graph should he use?
20. A city is mapped out in square blocks. Katy rides her bicycle 3 blocks north and 2 blocks west. She wants to graph her route. What kind of graph should she use?

Study Guide

Chapter Test

Use data from the table for problems 1–2.

Month	1	2	3	4	5	6
Books Read	6	3	5	10	3	9

1. Find the range, mode, median, and mean for the number of books read.

2. Make a bar graph for the data.

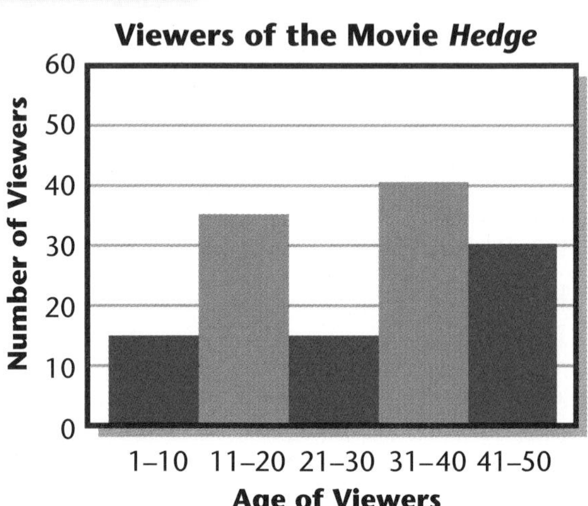

Use data from the graph for problems 3–4.

3. How many people between the ages of 11 and 20 saw *Hedge*?

4. How would the graph change if you increase the interval to 20? if you decrease the interval to 5?

Display each set of data in a stem-and-leaf plot.

5. 60 37 45 51 48 54 52 42 46 37

6. 13 18 22 10 25 26 19

Use graph paper for problems 7–8.

7. Find 4 ordered pairs that can make a square when the points are connected.

8. If you move the point (5, 2) left 1 unit, what are the new coordinates?

Use data from the table for problem 9.

9. Make a line plot for the data in the table.

Number of Telephones in Home	Frequency
1	2
2	8
3	10
4	5

10. What kind of graph would you make to display the data in the table? Explain. Make the graph.

Club membership by grade		
Grade	Science Club	French Club
First	4	6
Second	6	5
Third	3	3
Fourth	5	4
Fifth	7	6

Performance Assessment

The electrocardiograph was invented almost 100 years ago. It measures the electrical activity of the heart over time and displays it as a graph.

Collect data on your heart rate before and after 3 kinds of exercise.

You can measure your heart rate by placing two fingers (not your thumb) over the pulse on the inside of your wrist or by resting your hand over your heart.

1. Count the number of beats in 30 seconds.
2. Walk slowly around the room for 30 seconds. Measure your heart rate for 30 seconds.
3. Rest for 2 minutes.
4. Repeat steps 1–3, but do sit-ups instead of walking.
5. Repeat steps 1–3, but jog in place.

Make a table to record your data. Choose an appropriate graph to show your results. Explain why you chose the graph you did.

A Good Answer

- has an accurate, organized table of your data.
- uses an appropriate graph to display the data.
- accurately graphs the data.
- explains why you chose the graph you did.

You may want to save this work for your portfolio.

Objective: Use a random number table to select a random sample.

Enrichment

Random Number Table									
76	46	11	91	19	90	30	49	55	00
17	46	30	02	39	63	46	23	49	74
08	86	55	64	16	37	91	97	13	39
15	36	94	59	17	98	62	45	37	14
59	53	50	40	46	49	27	47	84	45
26	67	33	65	54	52	62	23	56	93
20	83	07	34	71	57	18	37	22	79
71	22	57	75	82	92	83	11	31	30
19	66	46	28	89	12	69	12	54	24
09	02	57	52	03	13	14	94	11	73

There are 100 fifth-grade students at Deering Elementary School. There are 30 seats available for a local play. The principal wants to choose 30 students fairly to go to the show. She could put all of the students' names in a hat and select 30 names, or use a random number table. A random number table displays numbers in a random order.

Here are the steps you would take to use a random number table.

Step 1 Make a table with the names of every student in the grade. Assign a number from 00 to 99 for each one.

Table of Student Names											
D. Crohn	0	F. Giano	01	L. Lau	02	B. Marks	03	S. Weir	04	A. Clay	05
C. Hyatt	06	Y. Mager	07	S. Ely	08	K. Abram	09	G. Abad	10	D. Hawks	11
N. Freed	12	H. Lee	13	S. Singh	14	Z. Hart	15	B. Tews	16	Q. Buell	17
S. Pesta	18	C. Macy	19	L. Davis	20	K. Daras	21	T. Chang	22	E. Paz	23
A. Ryles	24	X. Ruta	25	J. Starr	26	P. Loew	27	J. Lanto	28	U. Hauck	29
T. Mintz	30	O. Kim	31	S. Ruben	32	V. Sethi	33	W. Sorel	34	M. Kelly	35
A. Murat	36	S. Chan	37	M. Wend	38	O. Lee	39	L. Gill	40	L. Saki	41
J. Genet	42	W. Bram	43	C. Jaffa	44	P. Awn	45	U. Penn	46	C. Po	47
F. Fabio	48	Y. First	49	A. Jane	50	T. Brand	51	B. Rich	52	F. Spahn	53
G. Daum	54	K. Hearn	55	D. Levin	56	B. Luce	57	S. Mako	58	J. Thal	59
R. Fabio	60	N. Perm	61	F. Milch	62	A. Vera	63	C. Check	64	M. Kelly	65
L. Craig	66	P. Mick	67	H. Jenik	68	M. Yusef	69	T. Woods	70	L. Saki	71
L. Thad	72	G. Mala	73	P. Pick	74	P. Awn	75	F. Long	76	B. Reed	77
X. Pang	78	H. Oh	79	W. Sokol	80	R. Neal	81	S. Lee	82	J. Jones	83
N. Soon	84	T. Ling	85	R. Toddy	86	K. Smith	87	G. Allen	88	L. Baker	89
B. Boone	90	E. Ray	91	T. Toms	92	K. Toro	93	O. Mills	94	H. Johns	95
V. Jacob	96	L. Dixon	97	N. Clare	98	D. Costa	99				

Step 2 Starting anywhere in the random number table, select 30 consecutive numbers.

Step 3 Match the 30 numbers to the names in the student names table. Make a list of the selected names.

Practice

1. Select a random sample of 20 students to go on a field trip. Write the names of the selected students.

2. Select a random sample of 33 students. Write the names of the selected students.

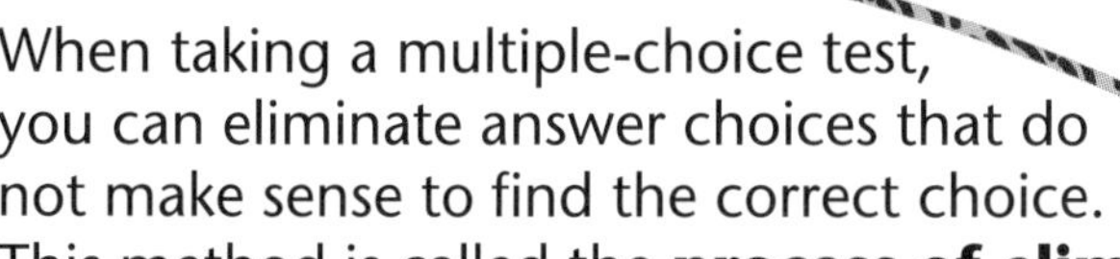

Test-Taking Tips

When taking a multiple-choice test, you can eliminate answer choices that do not make sense to find the correct choice. This method is called the **process of elimination.**

1. Which point on the number line shows about where 3×22 would be?

A. Point A **C.** Point C
B. Point B **D.** Point D

- You can eliminate answer choice A because 3×22 cannot be less than 3×20.
- You can eliminate answer choice D because 3×22 cannot be more than 3×30.
- Since 22 is closer to 20 than to 30, you can eliminate choice C.
- The correct answer choice is B.

Check for Success

Before turning in a test, go back one last time to check.

- ☑ I understood and answered the questions asked.
- ☑ I checked my work for errors.
- ☑ My answers make sense.

Choose the correct answer. Use the process of elimination.

1. Which point on the number line shows about where 2×28 would be?

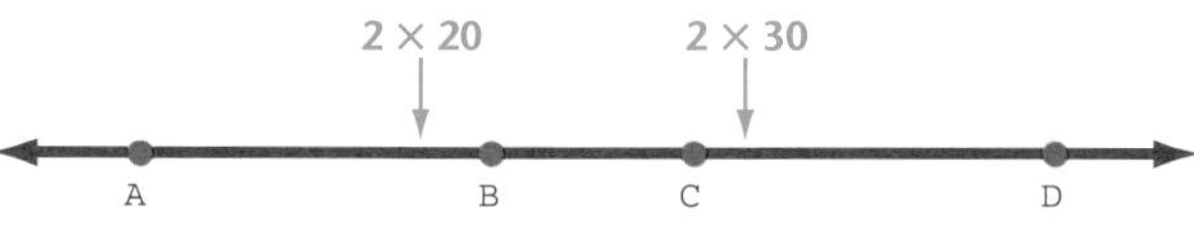

A. Point A **C.** Point C
B. Point B **D.** Point D

2. Which point on the number line shows about where 23×4 would be?

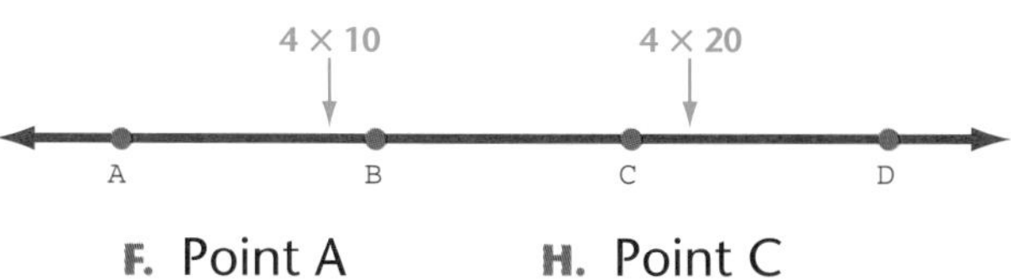

F. Point A **H.** Point C
G. Point B **J.** Point D

3. Find the number for n that makes the sentence true.

$n \times 10 = 22.1$

A. A number less than 2
B. A number equal to 2
C. A number between 2 and 3
D. A number greater than 3

4. Which of the following statements is true?

F. The sum of two odd numbers is an even number.
G. The sum of two odd numbers is an odd number.
H. The sum of two even numbers is an odd number.
J. The sum of an even number and an odd number is an even number.

Spiral Review and Test Prep

Chapters 1–4

Choose the correct answer.

Number Sense

1. Round 0.0734 to the nearest hundredth.
   A. 0.06
   B. 0.07
   C. 0.073
   D. 0.074

2. Your family rents a car. One afternoon you drive for 4 hours at the same speed. The odometer on the car shows that you drove 254.4 kilometers. How far did you drive in 1 hour?
   F. 1,017.6 kilometers
   G. 258.4 kilometers
   H. 250.4 kilometers
   J. 63.6 kilometers

3. Which is the greatest number?
   A. 1.009
   B. 1.01
   C. 1.0001
   D. 1.00001

4. Find 2^6.
   F. 12
   G. 26
   H. 36
   J. 64

Mathematical Reasoning

5. Perry divided a number into $864 and got the quotient $36. What was the divisor?
   A. 24
   B. 828
   C. 900
   D. 31,104

6. How many times does the digit 7 appear in the numbers from 50 to 100?
   F. 5
   G. 10
   H. 11
   J. 15

7. Bonnie skates every day. Each day she skates 0.1 mile farther than the day before. If she skated 1.8 miles on Wednesday, how far will she skate on Saturday?
   A. 2.2 miles
   B. 2.1 miles
   C. 1.9 miles
   D. 1.7 miles

8. On a trip to visit a cousin, Carol took everyone to a buffet lunch that cost $5.25 for each meal. She paid for 6 meals. What should she do to find the cost for 6 meals?
   F. Divide $5.25 by 6.
   G. Multiply $5.25 by 6.
   H. Divide 6 by $5.25.
   J. Not Here

Statistics, Data, and Probability

9. Sheryl's test scores in science are 92, 96, 96, and 90. Find the median score.

A. 91 **C.** 94
B. 93.5 **D.** 96

10. Find the mode of Sheryl's scores.

F. 90 **H.** 96
G. 92 **J.** Not Here

11. You want to display the results of a survey about the number of ideas that students in your school have for inventions. What would be an appropriate graph to show the data?

A. Line graph **C.** Bar graph
B. Pictograph **D.** Line plot

12. Don bought 4 shirts. Three of them cost $14 each. The fourth shirt cost $18. Find the mean price.

F. $14 **H.** $16
G. $15 **J.** $18

Algebra and Functions

13. Which has the same value as $(8 \times 15) - (8 \times 12)$?

A. 16×3 **C.** 8×12
B. 8×3 **D.** 8×27

14. Which has the same value as $529 + 458$?

F. $530 + 459$ **H.** $527 + 460$
G. $530 + 460$ **J.** Not Here

15. Which does not have the same value as $22 + 45 + 8$?

A. $(22 + 8) + (45 + 8)$
B. $22 + 8 + 45$
C. $45 + 8 + 22$
D. $45 + 30$

16. A restaurant offers tuna, turkey, bologna, or peanut butter on a choice of white or whole wheat bread. Only one type of filling is used in each sandwich. How many different kinds of sandwiches do they offer? Explain.

CHAPTER 5 Number Theory and Fraction Concepts

Theme: Performing Arts

Use the Data

Top 10 Jukebox Singles of All Time in the United States

Song	Artist(s)	Year Recorded
1. Crazy	Patsy Cline	1962
2. Old Time Rock'n'Roll	Bob Seger	1979
3. Hound Dog/ Don't Be Cruel	Elvis Presley	1956
4. Mack the Knife	Bobby Darin	1959
5. Born to Be Wild	Steppenwolf	1968
6. New York, New York	Frank Sinatra	1980
7. Rock Around the Clock	Bill Haley and His Comets	1955
8. I Heard It Through the Grapevine	Marvin Gaye	1968
9. (Sittin' On) The Dock of the Bay	Otis Redding	1968
10. Light My Fire	The Doors	1967

Source: The Top Ten of Everything

- Of the top 10 jukebox singles, what fraction was recorded in the 1960s? What fraction was recorded after 1975?

What You Will Learn

In this chapter, you will learn how to

- identify prime and composite numbers.
- find common factors and common multiples.
- simplify fractions and mixed numbers.
- compare and order fractions and mixed numbers.
- use strategies to solve problems.

Objective: Use divisibility rules for 2, 3, 5, 6, 9, 10.

5•1 Divisibility

Learn

Math Word

divisible A whole number is divisible by another number when the first is divided by the second and the remainder is 0.

The 82 members of the singing group stand in rows as they perform. Can the singers stand in 3 equal rows?

There's more than one way!

You need to find if 82 is **divisible** by 3.

Method A

Divide and see if there is a remainder.

$$3\overline{)82} = 27 \text{ R1}$$

Method B

You can use a divisibility rule.

A whole number is divisible by			
2	if the last digit is 0, 2, 4, 6, 8.	6	if the number is divisible by both 2 and 3.
3	if the sum of its digits is divisible by 3.	9	if the sum of the digits is divisible by 9.
5	if the last digit is 5 or 0.	10	if the last digit is 0.

The digits of 82 are 8 and 2.
The sum of the digits is $8 + 2 = 10$.
10 is not divisible by 3 because $10 \div 3 = 3$ R1.
The remainder is not 0.

The singers cannot stand in 3 equal rows.

Try It

Of 2, 3, 5, 6, 9, and 10, list which numbers each number is divisible by.

1. 90 **2.** 126 **3.** 486 **4.** 765 **5.** 1,314

Why are divisibility rules helpful?

Practice **Of 2, 3, 5, 6, 9, and 10, list which numbers each number is divisible by.**

6. 91
7. 126
8. 203
9. 417
10. 818
11. 150
12. 212
13. 375
14. 513
15. 1,521
16. 2,350
17. 3,172
18. 5,004
19. 6,123
20. 10,915
21. 20,550
22. 40,680
★23. 80,127
★24. 120,128

Problem Solving

25. There are 54 members of a youth chorus. The conductor wants to arrange the chorus members into equal rows with no more than 10 members in each row. What is the greatest number of members he can place in each row with no members left?

26. **Compare:** How are the divisibility rules for 2, 5, and 10 alike? How are the divisibility rules for 3, 6, and 9 alike?

27. The members of the junior chorus stand on stage in 8 rows. Each row has 14 singers. How many children sing in the chorus?

Use data from *Did You Know?* for problem 28.

28. **What if** the conductor wants to arrange the brass players into rows of 3, 5, 6, 9, or 10 chairs? Which size rows can the conductor use without having players left over?

29. A chorus is making a recording of a song. In the first recording, the song lasts 180.08 seconds. In the second recording, the song lasts 180.80 seconds. Which recording is shorter?

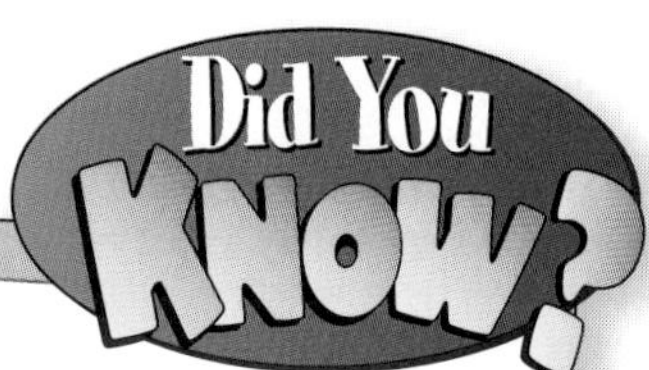

The Pittsburgh Symphony Youth Orchestra put on the world's largest orchestra performance in April 1998. The orchestra had 2,049 members, including 410 brass players.

Spiral Review and Test Prep

30. 10 − 5.2
31. 4.7 + 7.9
32. 3.46 − 0.92
33. 2.95 + 8.6

Choose the correct answer.

34. Armin made a list of the number of band members who came to the last 7 band rehearsals. What is the mode for the group of numbers?
39 41 42 43 44 44 48
A. 39
B. 42
C. 43
D. 44

35. An outdoor concert started at 11:35 A.M. and ended at 1:15 P.M. How long did the concert last?
F. 1 hour 15 minutes
G. 1 hour 40 minutes
H. 2 hours 40 minutes
J. 10 hours 20 minutes

Extra Practice, page 239

Objective: Determine whether a number is prime or composite. Express composite numbers as a product of primes.

5•2

Explore Primes and Composites

Math Words
- **prime number**
- **composite number**
- **prime factorization**
- **factor tree**

Learn

You can use counters to explore which numbers are prime and which are composite.

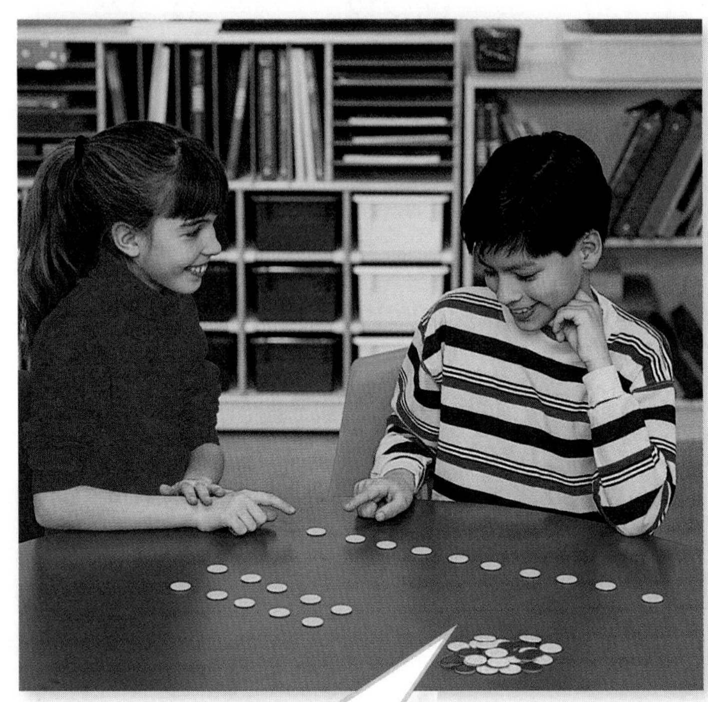

Work Together

You Will Need
- **counters**

- ▶ Use counters to model each number.
- ▶ Arrange the counters in as many ways as possible. Record the dimensions of each arrangement.
- ▶ Copy and complete the table.

Here are the arrangements for 12 counters.

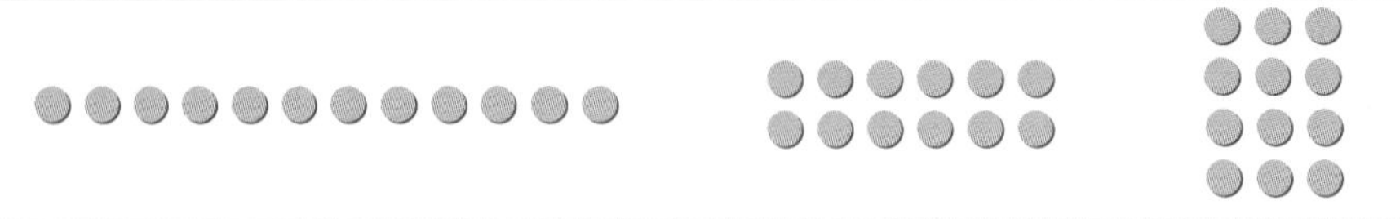

- ▶ Continue the activity for 2–11 counters.

Number of Counters	Dimension of Arrangements	Number of Counters	Dimension of Arrangements
2		7	
3		8	
4		9	
5		10	
6		11	

Make Connections

Using Models

1 × 7 = 7

7 is a prime number.

The factors of 7 are 1 and 7.
The numbers 2, 3, 5, 7 and 11 are **prime numbers**. They can be arranged in only one way. A prime number is defined as a number that is divisible only by itself and the number 1.

1 × 8 = 8
2 × 4 = 8

8 is a composite number.
The factors of 8 are 1, 2, 4, and 8.
The numbers 4, 6, 8, 9, 10 and 12 are **composite numbers**. They can be arranged in more than one way. A composite number is defined as a number that is divisible by more numbers than just itself and the number 1.

Using Paper and Pencil

Find the **prime factorization** of a composite number. Write the number as the product of prime numbers. Use a **factor tree**.

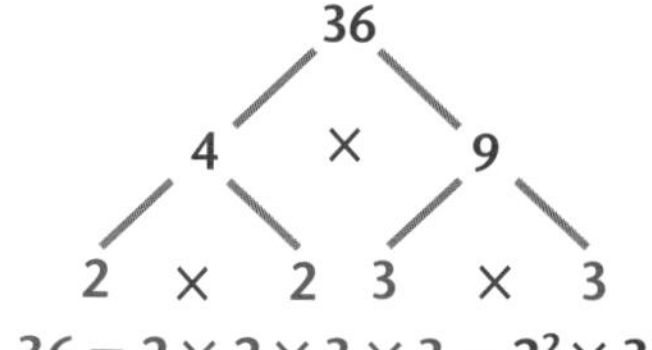

$36 = 2 \times 2 \times 3 \times 3 = 2^2 \times 3^2$

Remember:
An exponent is the number that tells how many times the base is used as a factor.

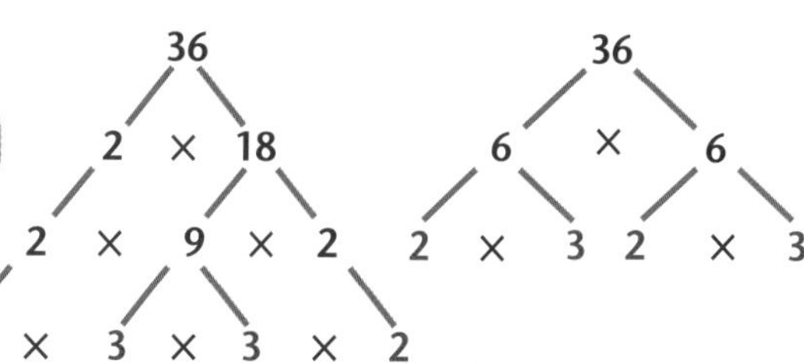

Try It For each number, tell whether it is prime or composite. Write a prime factorization for each composite number. Use exponents if you can.

1. 24
2. 17
3. 32
4. 48
5. 72

Explain why 13 is a prime number. Explain why 10 is a composite number.

Practice For each number, tell whether it is prime or composite. Write a prime factorization for each composite number. Use exponents if you can.

6. 21
7. 34
8. 37
9. 51
10. 75
11. **Explain** how to find the prime factorization of 54.

Objective: Find common factors and the greatest common factor for two numbers.

5•3

Common Factors and Greatest Common Factor

Math Words

common factor
a whole number that is a factor of two or more numbers

greatest common factor
(GCF) of two or more numbers, the greatest whole number that is a common factor of the numbers

Learn

A costume designer is going to attach the same number of each color button on each costume. What is the greatest number that can be put on each costume?

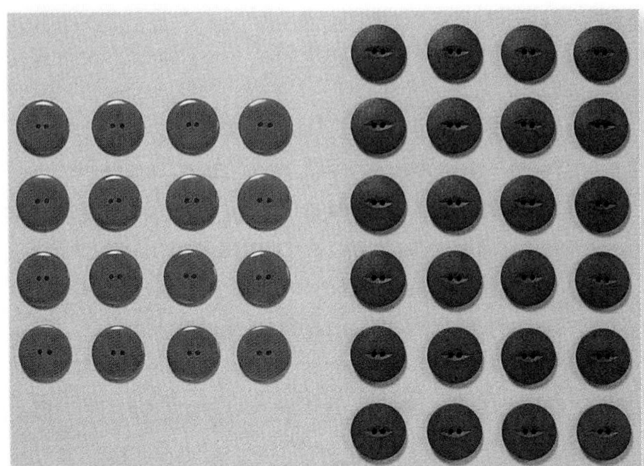

Example

Find the greatest common factor of 16 and 24 to solve the problem.

1 List all the factors of each number.

16: 1, 2, 4, 8, and 16 24: 1, 2, 3, 4, 6, 8, 12, and 24

2 Identify the **common factors**.

16: **1**, **2**, **4**, **8**, and 16 24: **1**, **2**, 3, **4**, 6, **8**, 12, and 24

1, 2, 4, 8 are the common factors.

3 Find the **greatest common factor** (GCF).

The greatest common factor of 16 and 24 is 8.

There can be 8 buttons of each color on a costume.

Try It

Find the greatest common factor (GCF) of the numbers.

1. 24 and 40
2. 30 and 48
3. 36 and 63
4. 24 and 27
5. 21 and 28
6. 16 and 60

Explain how to find the GCF of 12 and 30. What is the GCF of these two numbers?

Practice

Find the GCF of the numbers.

7. 12 and 30 **8.** 32 and 40 **9.** 22 and 55 **10.** 15 and 45 **11.** 14 and 28

12. 20 and 35 **13.** 18 and 45 **14.** 13 and 15 **15.** 8 and 24 **16.** 9 and 21

17. 26 and 12 **18.** 35 and 14 **19.** 30 and 24 **20.** 48 and 36 **21.** 23 and 3

★**22.** 6, 18, 39 ★**23.** 15, 25, 35 ★**24.** 8, 36, 52

★**25.** 14, 28, 35 ★**26.** 24, 48, 56 ★**27.** 25, 40, 100

Problem Solving

28. Twenty-five adults and 35 children attend a show. An equal number of adults and children will be seated in each row. What is the greatest number of children that can be seated in equal rows?

29. Mr. Olsen wants to arrange the boys and the girls in the Young Performers' Club into equal groups. There are 14 boys and 21 girls. What is the greatest number of children that can be in each group with no children left?

30. A show charges $12.50 for each ticket. If 120 people attend the show, how much will the ticket seller collect?

31. **Generalize:** Can the GCF of two numbers ever be 1? Explain your answer. Give an example.

32. How many common factors do the numbers 48 and 32 have? What is the greatest common factor of the two numbers?

33. **Summarize:** Can two numbers ever have more than one common factor? Can they ever have more than 1 GCF?

34. A 400-seat theater is divided into 5 sections. The 2 sections in the balcony have 50 seats each. The remaining sections have an equal number of seats. How many seats are in each of these sections?

★**35.** **Analyze:** Two numbers have a greatest common factor of 4. One of the numbers is 12. What might the other number be? Explain how you found out.

Spiral Review and Test Prep

Find the mean for each set of numbers.

36. 25, 28, 23, 27, 32 **37.** 90, 93, 88, 89 **38.** 15, 13, 17 **39.** 41, 43, 40, 47, 51, 48

Choose the correct answer.

40. Which decimal is equivalent to the number 0.08?

A. 0.80 **C.** 0.080
B. 8.00 **D.** 0.008

41. Which of the following numbers is less than 1.06?

F. 1.07 **H.** 1.061
G. 1.6 **J.** Not Here

Extra Practice, page 239

Objective: Draw and write a fraction to represent a part of a whole or a part of a group. Find equivalent fractions.

Fractions

Learn

A student ballet troupe plans to perform a dance from the ballet *Swan Lake*. Of the 8 students in the troupe, 3 have danced the ballet before. What fraction has this dance experience?

Lorena Feijoo, Principal Dancer for the San Francisco Ballet.

Math Words

fraction a number that names part of a whole or part of a group

numerator the number above the bar in a fraction

denominator the number below the bar in a fraction

equivalent fractions two different fractions that name the same number

Example 1

Find the **fraction** that shows the part of the troupe with *Swan Lake* experience.

Note: $\frac{3}{8}$ is another way of writing $3 \div 8$.

A fraction names parts of a whole or group.

3 ← **numerator** (number of dancers with experience)
8 ← **denominator** (number of dancers in the troupe)

So $\frac{3}{8}$ of the troupe have *Swan Lake* experience.

You can draw a model to represent fractions.

Example 2

Draw a model to show $\frac{3}{8}$.

3 shaded parts show the dancers with experience.

8 equal parts show all the dancers in the group.

What are some **equivalent fractions** of $\frac{3}{4}$?

There's more than one way!

Method A

- Show $\frac{3}{4}$ using fourths fraction strips.
- Put enough eighths fraction strips below the $\frac{3}{4}$ to make the models equal in length.
- Count the number of eighths strips needed and record your answer.
- Repeat with twelfths strips.

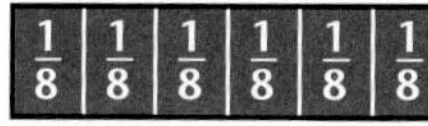

Method B

Multiply the numerator and denominator by the same nonzero number.

$\frac{3 \times 2}{4 \times 2} = \frac{6}{8}$ $\frac{3 \times 3}{4 \times 3} = \frac{9}{12}$

Multiplying both the numerator and the denominator by the same number is like multiplying the fraction by 1. The value of the fraction stays the same.

So $\frac{3}{4}$, $\frac{6}{8}$, and $\frac{9}{12}$ are equivalent fractions.

You can also find equivalent fractions by dividing.

Example 3

Divide the numerator and the denominator by a common factor.

$\frac{9 \div 3}{12 \div 3} = \frac{3}{4}$

$\frac{6 \div 2}{8 \div 2} = \frac{3}{4}$

Try It

Name each fraction shown.

1. 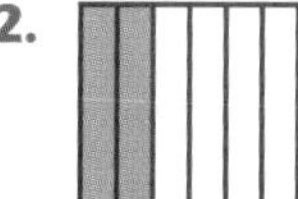

2. 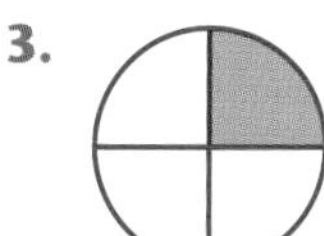

3. (circle with one of four parts shaded)

4. 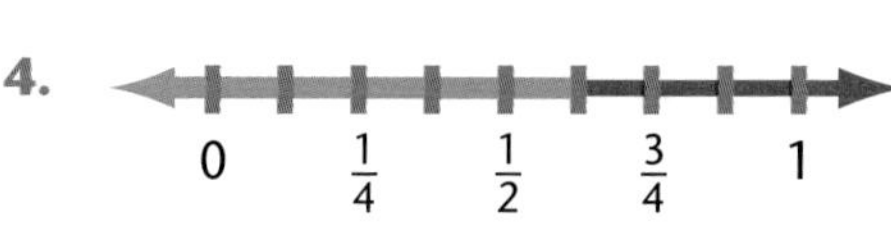

Write two equivalent fractions for each fraction. You may use fraction strips.

5. $\frac{2}{3}$

6. $\frac{1}{4}$

7. $\frac{1}{2}$

Show one way to find an equivalent fraction for $\frac{4}{5}$.

Practice Name each fraction shown.

8. 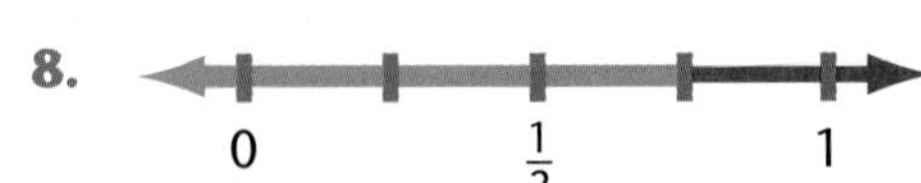

9. 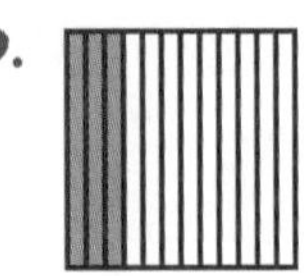

10. 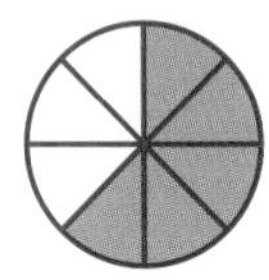

11. 

12. 0 $\frac{1}{4}$ $\frac{1}{2}$ $\frac{3}{4}$ 1

13. 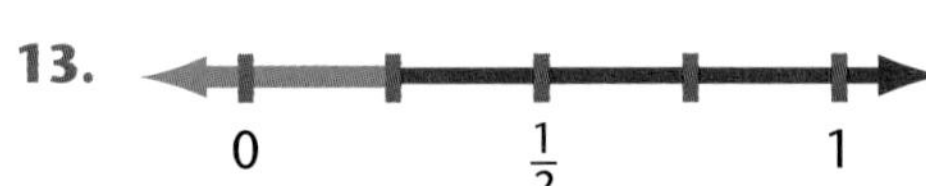

Draw a model to show each fraction.

14. $\frac{4}{7}$ 15. $\frac{9}{10}$ 16. $\frac{1}{6}$ 17. $\frac{3}{4}$ 18. $\frac{2}{2}$

Write two equivalent fractions for each fraction.

19. $\frac{5}{6}$ 20. $\frac{3}{8}$ 21. $\frac{2}{5}$ 22. $\frac{3}{4}$ 23. $\frac{6}{10}$ 24. $\frac{12}{12}$

25. $\frac{2}{4}$ 26. $\frac{1}{3}$ 27. $\frac{3}{6}$ 28. $\frac{2}{12}$ 29. $\frac{3}{5}$ ★30. $\frac{5}{8}$

Algebra & functions **Find each missing number.**

31. $\frac{1}{2} = \frac{n}{4}$ 32. $\frac{1}{3} = \frac{a}{9}$ 33. $\frac{1}{6} = \frac{b}{12}$ 34. $\frac{2}{5} = \frac{8}{a}$

35. $\frac{3}{9} = \frac{1}{c}$ 36. $\frac{6}{10} = \frac{3}{y}$ 37. $\frac{8}{16} = \frac{1}{p}$ 38. $\frac{5}{15} = \frac{1}{s}$

39. 

Here is how Marina found an equivalent fraction for $\frac{2}{3}$. Tell what mistake she made. Explain how to correct it.

Problem Solving

Use data from *Did You Know?* for problems 40–41.

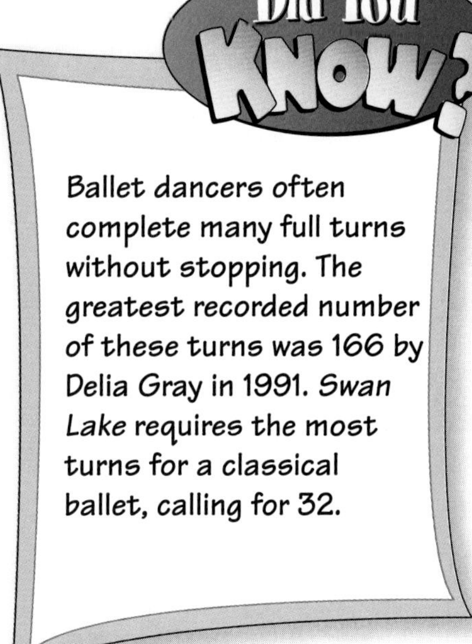

Did You Know?
Ballet dancers often complete many full turns without stopping. The greatest recorded number of these turns was 166 by Delia Gray in 1991. *Swan Lake* requires the most turns for a classical ballet, calling for 32.

40. How many more turns did Delia Gray complete than are required by *Swan Lake*?

41. What fraction of Delia Gray's record are the 32 turns of *Swan Lake*?

42. George is estimating the number of people in the audience at a ballet. He counted 12 seats in each row. He counted 20 rows. Each row had about 2 to 3 seats empty. About how many people were in the audience?

43. Peter uses 16 buttons to make a ballet costume. Four of them are red. Write 2 equivalent fractions that name the part of the buttons that are red.

44. Each dancer requires 3 pairs of toe shoes for a new ballet. There are 9 dancers. How many shoes are needed?

45. In one elementary school class, 5 of the 23 students take ballet lessons. What fraction is that?

46. An 8-foot piece of fabric is made into a ballet headpiece and tutu. Two feet of fabric are used for the headpiece. What fraction is needed for the tutu? How many feet is that?

★47. Roger needs 10 yards of ribbon to make costumes for a ballet. How many of each roll of ribbon shown should he buy? What would be the total cost?

Spiral Review and Test Prep

Find the median.

48. 19, 28, 59, 74, 78

49. 71, 73, 68

50. 83, 13, 54, 50

51. 34, 42, 45, 46, 53, 68

Choose the correct answer.

52. Which of these numbers is a prime number?

A. 4
B. 9
C. 11
D. 27

53. A bicycle path is 5.3 miles long. Margie rides 3.8 miles of the path. How many more miles does she have left to ride?

F. 0.15 mile
G. 1.5 miles
H. 2.5 miles
J. 9.1 miles

Objective: Identify extra or missing information.

5•5

Problem Solving: Reading for Math
Extra and Missing Information

Summer Arts Workshops Offered

Read What fraction of the students sign up for the dance workshop?

READING SKILL **Identify Important and Unimportant Information**
Some problems contain information that is not needed for the solution. If a problem is missing information you need, you may be able to find the missing information in a chart.

- **What do you know?** The total number of students; the number signed up for each workshop; the costs of the classes
- **What do you want to find?** The fraction of students that sign up for the dance workshop

Registration

Workshop	Sign-ups
Dance	24
Vocal Music	12
Theater Arts	15
Technical Theater	5
Writing	4

Registration begins May 25.
Fees: State Residents $50
Non-state Residents $125 per class, $500 maximum fee

MATH SKILL **Identify Extra and Find Missing Information**

- Think about what information you need to solve the problem. Do not be distracted by extra information. Identify missing information and find a way to get it.

Plan The important information is the number of dance students and the total number of students signed up for all of the workshops. All the other information is unimportant.

Solve
24 ← Number of dance students
60 ← Total number of students
Of the students, $\frac{24}{60}$ signed up for the dance workshop.

Look Back Is your answer reasonable?

What should you do with extra information in a problem? What should you do if a problem is missing information?

Solve. If there is not enough information, write *not enough information*.

1. Express as a fraction the number of students who sign up for vocal music.
2. How long will the dance workshop last?
3. Express as a fraction the number of students who sign up for the writing workshop.
4. Express as a fraction the number of students who are state residents.
5. Express as a fraction the number of students who do not sign up for dance or vocal music.
6. Judy is not a state resident. She wants to register for all five classes. What is her total fee?
7. Kevin is a state resident. He wants to register for the technical theater and writing classes. How much will he have to pay?
8. After attending the workshop, Betty decides to register for the regular dance class. How much will she have to pay?
9. After the workshops, 36 of the students decide to register for the regular classes. Express as a fraction the number of students who decide to register for the regular classes.
10. Suppose that of the 36 students who decide to register for the regular classes, 18 students will register for the dance class. What fraction is that?
11. Which workshop has the least registration?
12. When do classes begin?
13. Brandon wants to register for the dance class and the theater arts class. He is a state resident and he is 12 years old. He has $500 in his piggy bank. What fraction of the money does he need to take from the piggy bank to pay for the classes?
14. Last semester, 360 students attended the Performing Arts School. Of those, 120 attended the dance class. Eighty of the students in the dance class are state residents. Express as a fraction the number of dance class students who are state residents.

Spiral Review and Test Prep

Choose the correct answer.

There are 28 students in a dance class. Of the students, 21 students are girls. Of the girls, $\frac{2}{3}$ are state residents.

15. Which of the following statements is true?
    - **A.** $\frac{4}{3}$ of the students are girls.
    - **B.** All of the girls are state residents.
    - **C.** There are 7 boys in the class.
    - **D.** There are 28 state residents in the class.

16. If a problem has extra information, you should
    - **F.** find the missing information.
    - **G.** use the extra information to solve the problem.
    - **H.** not finish the problem.
    - **J.** ignore the extra information.

Problem Solving

Check Your Progress A

Of 2, 3, 5, 6, 9, and 10, list which numbers each number is divisible by. **(pages 200–201)**

1. 158
2. 306
3. 723
4. 980
5. 1,408
6. 2,610

Tell if each number is prime or composite. Write a prime factorization for each composite number. **(pages 202–203)**

7. 15
8. 19
9. 32
10. 49
11. 54
12. 59

Find the greatest common factor (GCF). **(pages 204–205)**

13. 15 and 25
14. 16 and 40
15. 12 and 48
16. 18 and 48

Name each fraction shown. Write two equivalent fractions. **(pages 206–209)**

17. 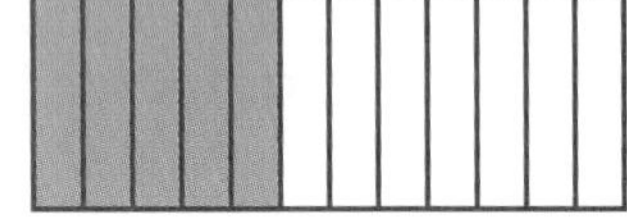

18. 

19. 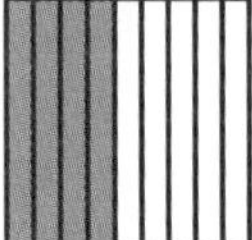

Solve. **(pages 200–209)**

20. Ms. Han wants to arrange 114 chorus members in equal rows. She wants to have fewer than 10 members in each row. What is the greatest number of members she can place in each row with no members left?

21. Mr. Parisi wants to arrange the 138 members of the marching band in equal rows. He wants no more than 10 members in each row. What is the greatest number of members he can place in each row with no members left?

22. Sandy is cutting yarn to make wigs for costumes. She has a piece 42 inches long and a piece 28 inches long. What is the longest length she can cut from the pieces and have all lengths the same?

23. Of the 36 members of the drama class, 8 have performed in a school play before. What fraction is that?

24. Of the 16 students in the drama class, 8 have been in a school play. Ten have also sung on stage in a chorus. What fraction have been in a school play?

25. **Analyze:** The GCF of two numbers is 5. The greater number is 15. What could the other number be?

Use Fraction Strips to Compare

Ryan studied for $\frac{3}{4}$ hour and Lisa studied for $\frac{5}{6}$ hour. Who studied longer?

You can model the number of hours using fraction strips.

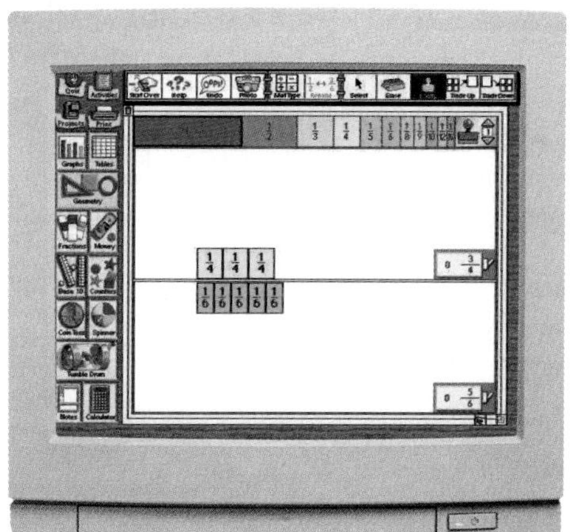

- Use a mat with two sections open.
- Stamp out three $\frac{1}{4}$ fraction strips in one section.
- Stamp out five $\frac{1}{6}$ fraction strips in the other section.
- The model shows that $\frac{5}{6} > \frac{3}{4}$.

Who studied longer?

Use the computer to model each pair of fractions. Then name the fraction that is greater.

1. $\frac{2}{3}$ and $\frac{3}{4}$ **2.** $\frac{2}{5}$ and $\frac{1}{4}$ **3.** $\frac{5}{8}$ and $\frac{7}{9}$ **4.** $\frac{11}{12}$ and $\frac{9}{10}$

Solve.

5. Mike lives $\frac{7}{10}$ mile from the park and Kim lives $\frac{3}{4}$ mile from the park. Who lives closer to the park?

6. Keith and Marissa are sharing a pizza. Keith ate $\frac{5}{12}$ of the pizza and Marissa ate $\frac{1}{3}$ of the pizza. Who ate more pizza?

7. Analyze: How do fraction strips help you compare fractions?

For more practice, use Math Traveler™.

Objective: Write fractions in simplest form.

5·6 Simplify Fractions

Learn

Math Word

simplest form A fraction is in simplest form when 1 is the only common factor of the numerator and denominator.

The instruments of an orchestra are divided into four groups. The groups are string, brass, percussion, and woodwind. Express as a fraction in simplest form the number of string instruments in the Youth Orchestra.

The Youth Orchestra

Category	Number of Players
Percussion	1
Woodwind	6
Brass	5
String	18

There's more than one way!

Find $\frac{18}{30}$ in **simplest form**.

Method A

1 Divide the numerator and denominator by a common factor.

$$\frac{18 \div 2}{30 \div 2} = \frac{9}{15}$$

2 Repeat until the fraction is in simplest form.

$$\frac{9 \div 3}{15 \div 3} = \frac{3}{5}$$

Think: Dividing the fraction by the GCF will give you a fraction in simplest form.

Method B

1 Write the numerator and denominator in prime factorization.

$$\frac{18}{30} = \frac{2 \times 3 \times 3}{2 \times 3 \times 5}$$

2 Cancel like terms.

$$\frac{18}{30} = \frac{\not{2} \times \not{3} \times 3}{\not{2} \times \not{3} \times 5}$$

Think: A 2 in the numerator cancels a 2 in the denominator.

3 Write the product of the remaining factors in the numerator as the numerator. Do the same for the denominator.

$$\frac{18}{30} = \frac{3}{5}$$

In the orchestra, $\frac{3}{5}$ of the instruments are string instruments.

Try It

Write each fraction in simplest form.

1. $\frac{12}{24}$
2. $\frac{21}{30}$
3. $\frac{18}{45}$
4. $\frac{6}{10}$
5. $\frac{4}{16}$
6. $\frac{25}{30}$

Explain how to find the simplest form of $\frac{12}{32}$.

Practice **Write each fraction in simplest form. Write *yes* if the fraction is already in simplest form.**

7. $\frac{9}{18}$ **8.** $\frac{10}{15}$ **9.** $\frac{21}{35}$ **10.** $\frac{3}{18}$ **11.** $\frac{18}{24}$ **12.** $\frac{5}{40}$

13. $\frac{6}{24}$ **14.** $\frac{8}{28}$ **15.** $\frac{36}{48}$ **16.** $\frac{16}{36}$ **17.** $\frac{12}{40}$ **18.** $\frac{49}{56}$

19. $\frac{3}{36}$ **20.** $\frac{8}{9}$ **21.** $\frac{35}{49}$ **22.** $\frac{9}{24}$ **23.** $\frac{4}{11}$ **24.** $\frac{3}{39}$

★25. $\frac{15}{100}$ **★26.** $\frac{21}{21}$ **★27.** $\frac{19}{105}$ **★28.** $\frac{61}{100}$ **★29.** $\frac{30}{102}$ **★30.** $\frac{104}{128}$

Algebra & functions **Find the missing number.**

31. $\frac{35}{42} = \frac{5}{\blacksquare}$ **32.** $\frac{35}{60} = \frac{\blacksquare}{12}$ **33.** $\frac{63}{70} = \frac{9}{\blacksquare}$ **34.** $\frac{6}{40} = \frac{3}{\blacksquare}$

35. $\frac{9}{42} = \frac{\blacksquare}{14}$ **36.** $\frac{44}{64} = \frac{11}{\blacksquare}$ **37.** $\frac{28}{56} = \frac{\blacksquare}{2}$ **38.** $\frac{26}{39} = \frac{2}{\blacksquare}$

Problem Solving

Use data from the table for problems 39–40.

Lakeville School Band	
Instrument	Number of Players
Clarinet	8
Drums	2
Saxophone	2
Trombone	2
Trumpet	3
Tuba	1

39. In simplest form, what fraction of the Lakeville School Band plays the trumpet?

40. **Create a problem** using the data from the table to write a problem about a fraction in simplest form. Solve it and give it to another student to solve.

41. **Generalize:** Can you simplify a fraction that has 1 as its numerator? Explain.

42. **Collect Data:** Survey your classmates. Ask how many of them play a musical instrument. Write a fraction in simplest form to show your result.

43. If a music concert ticket costs $19.50, how much will 4 tickets cost?

Spiral Review and Test Prep

Of 2, 3, 5, 6, 9, and 10, list the numbers that each number is divisible by.

44. 37 **45.** 96 **46.** 309 **47.** 972 **48.** 780 **49.** 623

Choose the correct answer.

50. Mrs. Montrose buys a CD for each of her 5 friends. Each CD costs $12.99. How much does she spend?

A. $12.99 C. $17.99
B. $25.98 D. $64.95

51. I am a number between 6 and 7. The sum of all my digits is 12. My thousandths digit is twice my hundredths digit. What number am I?

F. 6.24 H. 6.024
G. 6.42 J. 7.024

Objective: Find the least common multiple (LCM) and the least common denominator (LCD).

Least Common Multiple and Least Common Denominator

Math Words

least common multiple (LCM) of two or more whole numbers, the least whole number greater than 0 that is a multiple of each of the numbers

least common denominator (LCD) is the least common multiple of the denominators of two or more fractions

Learn

"Let's play a duet," said the trumpet player to the saxophone player. The trumpeter plays a note on the fourth beat and every 4 beats after that. The saxophonist plays a note on the sixth beat and every 6 beats after that. On which beat will the musicians play a note together?

Example 1

Find the **least common multiple (LCM)** of 4 and 6.

1 List multiples of 4 and 6.

4: 4, 8, 12, 16, 20, 24, 28, 32, 36, 40 **Think:** $1 \times 4 = 4$, $2 \times 4 = 8$, $3 \times 4 = 12$, and so on.

6: 6, 12, 18, 24, 30, 36, 42, 48, 54, 60 **Think:** $1 \times 6 = 6$, $2 \times 6 = 12$, $3 \times 6 = 18$, and so on.

2 Find the common multiples.

4: 4, 8, **12**, 16, 20, **24**, 28, 32, **36**, 40
6: 6, **12**, 18, **24**, 30, **36**, 42, 48, 54, 60

You can always find a common multiple by finding the product of the two numbers.

3 Some common multiples of 4 and 6 are 12, 24, and 36.
The least common multiple (LCM) of 4 and 6 is 12.

The musicians will first play a note together on the twelfth beat.

You can use a least common multiple to find the **least common denominator (LCD)** of two fractions.

Write equivalent fractions for $\frac{2}{3}$ and $\frac{3}{4}$ using the LCD.

Example 2

Rewrite the fractions $\frac{2}{3}$ and $\frac{3}{4}$ using the least common denominator (LCD).

1 First find the LCM of the denominators.

3: 3, 6, 9, **12**, 15, 18, 21, **24**, 27, 30, 33, **36**
4: 4, 8, **12**, 16, 20, **24**, 28, 32, **36**, 40

So 12 is the least common multiple of 3 and 4. The least common denominator of 3 and 4 is 12.

2 Write an equivalent fraction for each fraction using the LCD.

$\frac{2}{3} = \frac{2 \times 4}{3 \times 4} = \frac{8}{12} \leftarrow \text{LCD}$ $\qquad \frac{3}{4} = \frac{4 \times 3}{3 \times 3} = \frac{9}{12} \leftarrow \text{LCD}$

So $\frac{8}{12}$ and $\frac{9}{12}$ are equivalent fractions of $\frac{2}{3}$ and $\frac{3}{4}$ with the same denominator.

Example 3

The LCD can be the product of the two denominators or less than that product.

$\frac{1}{3}$ and $\frac{3}{4}$ have a LCD of 12. **Note:** 12 is the product of the two denominators.

$\frac{1}{2}$ and $\frac{3}{4}$ have a LCD of 4. **Note:** 4 is less than the product of the two denominators.
Think: The LCD cannot be less than the greater denominator.

Try It **Find the least common multiple (LCM) of the numbers.**

1. 5 and 6 **2.** 3 and 5 **3.** 6 and 8 **4.** 5 and 10 **5.** 3 and 8

Write equivalent fractions using the LCD.

6. $\frac{1}{5}$ and $\frac{1}{3}$ **7.** $\frac{1}{2}$ and $\frac{1}{6}$ **8.** $\frac{3}{4}$ and $\frac{7}{8}$ **9.** $\frac{2}{3}$ and $\frac{7}{10}$ **10.** $\frac{4}{5}$ and $\frac{5}{6}$

How are the LCM and LCD alike? How are they different?

Practice **Find the LCM of the numbers.**

11. 2 and 6
12. 6 and 10
13. 5 and 9
14. 6 and 8
15. 4 and 7
16. 3 and 11
17. 9 and 12
18. 4 and 14
19. 4 and 15
20. 6 and 16
★21. 2, 3, and 8
★22. 3, 9 and 15
★23. 2, 4 and 10
★24. 4, 6, and 12
★25. 3, 6, and 10
★26. 2, 4 and 7

Find the LCD for each pair of fractions.

27. $\frac{1}{2}$ and $\frac{3}{5}$
28. $\frac{2}{3}$ and $\frac{1}{4}$
29. $\frac{5}{6}$ and $\frac{4}{9}$
30. $\frac{2}{5}$ and $\frac{3}{4}$
31. $\frac{3}{10}$ and $\frac{1}{12}$
32. $\frac{7}{8}$ and $\frac{2}{3}$
33. $\frac{2}{7}$ and $\frac{1}{6}$
34. $\frac{11}{12}$ and $\frac{3}{8}$

Write equivalent fractions using the LCD.

35. $\frac{1}{2}$ and $\frac{1}{3}$
36. $\frac{1}{4}$ and $\frac{1}{6}$
37. $\frac{2}{5}$ and $\frac{3}{10}$
38. $\frac{1}{3}$ and $\frac{5}{9}$
39. $\frac{1}{3}$ and $\frac{5}{6}$
40. $\frac{1}{5}$ and $\frac{1}{4}$
41. $\frac{1}{2}$ and $\frac{3}{8}$
42. $\frac{2}{3}$ and $\frac{7}{12}$
43. $\frac{2}{3}$ and $\frac{4}{11}$
44. $\frac{2}{3}$ and $\frac{3}{4}$
45. $\frac{5}{7}$ and $\frac{4}{5}$
46. $\frac{1}{6}$ and $\frac{5}{10}$
47. $\frac{1}{3}$ and $\frac{5}{15}$
48. $\frac{2}{6}$ and $\frac{3}{7}$
49. $\frac{3}{4}$ and $\frac{5}{8}$
★50. $\frac{1}{5}$, $\frac{2}{3}$, and $\frac{4}{15}$
★51. $\frac{1}{4}$, $\frac{5}{8}$, and $\frac{3}{16}$
★52. $\frac{3}{4}$, $\frac{1}{5}$, and $\frac{7}{20}$
★53. $\frac{2}{3}$, $\frac{5}{9}$, and $\frac{7}{18}$
★54. $\frac{3}{5}$, $\frac{11}{12}$, and $\frac{18}{60}$

55.

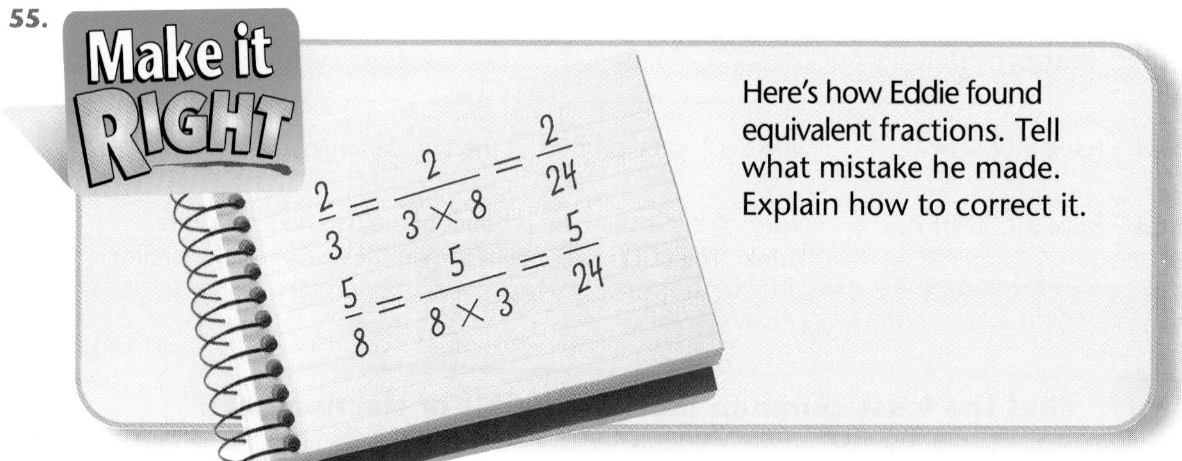

Make it RIGHT
$\frac{2}{3} = \frac{2}{3 \times 8} = \frac{2}{24}$
$\frac{5}{8} = \frac{5}{8 \times 3} = \frac{5}{24}$

Here's how Eddie found equivalent fractions. Tell what mistake he made. Explain how to correct it.

Problem Solving

56. Sarah and Marcus both collect music CDs. Of the CDs Sarah collects, $\frac{1}{2}$ are jazz music. Of the CDs Marcus collects, $\frac{3}{4}$ are jazz music. Rename the fractions with a common denominator.

57. Emil practiced the piano every other day during June, beginning on June 2. He had a piano lesson on June 7 and one every week after that. What was the first date on which he both practiced and had a lesson?

58. **Analyze:** Give an example of how two fractions with different denominators can be written as fractions with the same denominator in two different ways.

59. Bessie Smith was a popular singer of blues music. Her 1923 recording of "Down Hearted Blues" sold 780,000 copies in less than 6 months. Round this number to the nearest hundred thousand.

★60. To get ready for a Friday 9:00 P.M. performance, an opera singer warms up her voice for 25 minutes. It then takes 30 minutes to get into costume and 20 minutes to apply stage make up. What time should she start to get ready in order not to be late for her performance?

61. Philip can play three different instruments: violin, cello, and piano. His daily practice schedule is as follows: violin, $\frac{1}{2}$ hour; piano, $\frac{3}{4}$ hour; and cello, $\frac{3}{5}$ hour. Find the LCD for these fractions.

Use data from the table for problems 62–64.

62. **Time:** Make a calendar showing the practice schedule for each day of November. Show which part of the band is rehearsing on which date. Show when the whole band is rehearsing.

63. In a 2-week period, which instrument group practices the most?

64. List the dates on which more than one group has practice on the same date. Include the names of the groups each time.

Band Practice

Whole Band	Every 4th day
Drums	Every 7th day
Woodwinds	Every 3rd day
Strings	Every 6th day
Brass	Every 5th day

Spiral Review and Test Prep

65. $\begin{array}{r} 2.54 \\ \times\ 2.6 \\ \hline \end{array}$

66. $\begin{array}{r} 0.6 \\ \times\ 0.2 \\ \hline \end{array}$

67. $0.3\overline{)24}$

68. $17\overline{)3.4}$

Choose the correct answer.

69. If you multiply two even whole numbers, the product will be
   A. an odd number.
   B. a prime number.
   C. an even number.
   D. a negative number.

70. Which number makes this statement true?
   $(43.5 + 3.4) + 21.6 = \blacksquare + (21.6 + 3.4)$
   F. 43.5
   G. 21.6
   H. 3.4
   J. Not Here

Objective: Compare and order fractions.

5•8 Compare and Order Fractions

What You Need:

- Wood pieces, each 1 inch wide:
  - $\frac{3}{4}$ foot long
  - $\frac{2}{3}$ foot long
  - $\frac{7}{8}$ foot long
- Tacks
- String
- Foam ball
- Markers or paint
- Cotton stuffing

Learn

Some puppeteers make their own puppets. The materials for one puppet include three pieces of wood. Which piece is shortest?

There's more than one way!

Compare the fractions to solve the problem.

Method A

Use fraction strips.

1/8 | 1/8 | 1/8 | 1/8 | 1/8 | 1/8 | 1/8

Method B

Rewrite the fractions using the LCD.

$\frac{3}{4} = \frac{3 \times 6}{4 \times 6} = \frac{18}{24}$ $\frac{2}{3} = \frac{2 \times 8}{3 \times 8} = \frac{16}{24}$ $\frac{7}{8} = \frac{7 \times 3}{8 \times 3} = \frac{21}{24}$

Think: The LCM of 4, 3, and 8 is 24.

Compare and order the fractions by looking at the numerators.

$\frac{16}{24} < \frac{18}{24} < \frac{21}{24}$.

The shortest piece of wood is the $\frac{2}{3}$-foot-long piece.

Try It

Order from least to greatest.

1. $\frac{1}{4}, \frac{1}{3}, \frac{1}{8}$
2. $\frac{1}{4}, \frac{1}{2}, \frac{1}{6}$
3. $\frac{2}{3}, \frac{1}{2}, \frac{5}{8}$
4. $\frac{3}{8}, \frac{1}{2}, \frac{3}{4}$
5. $\frac{3}{4}, \frac{5}{6}, \frac{7}{10}$

Explain how to order the fractions $\frac{7}{10}$, $\frac{1}{2}$, and $\frac{3}{5}$ from least to greatest.

Practice

Compare. Write >, <, or =.

6. $\frac{1}{3}$ ● $\frac{1}{4}$
7. $\frac{1}{9}$ ● $\frac{1}{6}$
8. $\frac{2}{3}$ ● $\frac{6}{9}$
9. $\frac{3}{4}$ ● $\frac{3}{7}$
10. $\frac{5}{12}$ ● $\frac{3}{9}$
11. $\frac{3}{5}$ ● $\frac{5}{8}$
12. $\frac{1}{2}$ ● $\frac{4}{8}$
13. $\frac{2}{15}$ ● $\frac{1}{5}$
14. $\frac{4}{7}$ ● $\frac{3}{8}$
15. $\frac{3}{10}$ ● $\frac{9}{20}$

Order from least to greatest.

16. $\frac{1}{2}, \frac{1}{3}, \frac{3}{4}$
17. $\frac{1}{4}, \frac{1}{2}, \frac{1}{5}$
18. $\frac{1}{1}, \frac{4}{7}, \frac{2}{3}$
19. $\frac{7}{8}, \frac{2}{2}, \frac{3}{4}$
20. $\frac{2}{6}, \frac{2}{8}, \frac{2}{3}$
21. $\frac{3}{10}, \frac{1}{6}, \frac{4}{5}$
22. $\frac{5}{5}, \frac{2}{3}, \frac{5}{6}$
23. $\frac{1}{6}, \frac{3}{4}, \frac{7}{8}$
24. $\frac{1}{2}, \frac{4}{14}, \frac{5}{7}$
25. $\frac{3}{4}, \frac{1}{2}, \frac{6}{9}$
26. $\frac{1}{5}, \frac{3}{8}, \frac{1}{4}$
27. $\frac{1}{3}, \frac{3}{8}, \frac{2}{9}$
★28. $\frac{31}{100}, \frac{2}{5}, \frac{7}{25}$
★29. $\frac{37}{90}, \frac{8}{15}, \frac{13}{30}$
★30. $\frac{99}{200}, \frac{49}{100}, \frac{157}{300}$

Problem Solving

31. The seats in the theater for the puppet show are divided into three equal sections. On one night of the play, $\frac{4}{5}$ of the seats in Section A are filled, $\frac{2}{3}$ of Section B are filled, and $\frac{1}{2}$ of Section C is filled. Which section has the greatest number of seats filled?

32. **Social Studies:** The Taiwanese traditional puppet show is called Bo De Hi. Each puppet is about 1 foot tall. Ling's puppet is $\frac{11}{12}$ foot tall and Steve's is $\frac{3}{4}$ foot tall. Whose puppet is closer to the height of a Taiwanese puppet?

33. **Literature:** The puppet character in Bo De Hi often recites classical poetry. If there are 4 lines in a poem, how can you name the first 2 lines, using a fraction in simplest form?

34. **What if** a puppeteer makes puppets 6 days a week during February with no leap year? How many days does she work?

Spiral Review and Test Prep

35. 12×18.7
36. $25 \times 1{,}045$
37. $100 \times \$15.99$
38. $34\overline{)1{,}904}$

Choose the correct answer. Use data from the graph for problem 39.

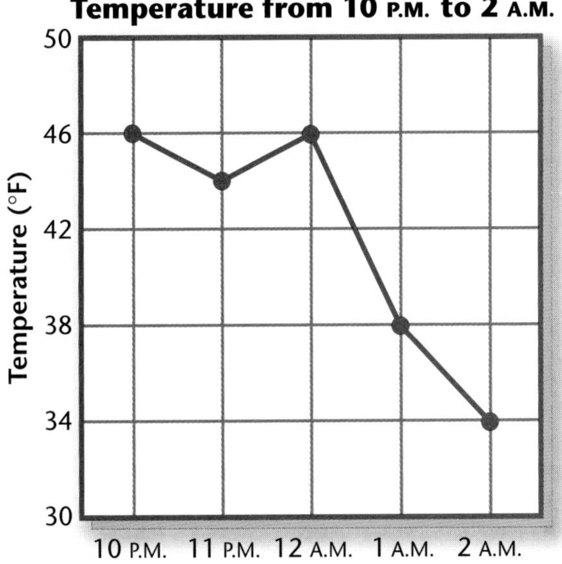

39. During what time of day was there an increase in temperature?
    A. Between 10 P.M. and 11 P.M.
    B. Between 11 P.M. and 12 A.M.
    C. Between 12 A.M. and 1 A.M.
    D. Between 1 A.M. and 2 A.M.

Extra Practice, page 240

Objective: Change decimals to fractions and fractions to decimals.

5•9 Relate Fractions and Decimals

Learn

The Double Pit Xylophone of Benin, Africa, is the largest of its type in the world. The longest keys can be up to $1\frac{4}{5}$ meters. A typical xylophone has keys as long as 0.75 meter, what is this decimal written as a fraction?

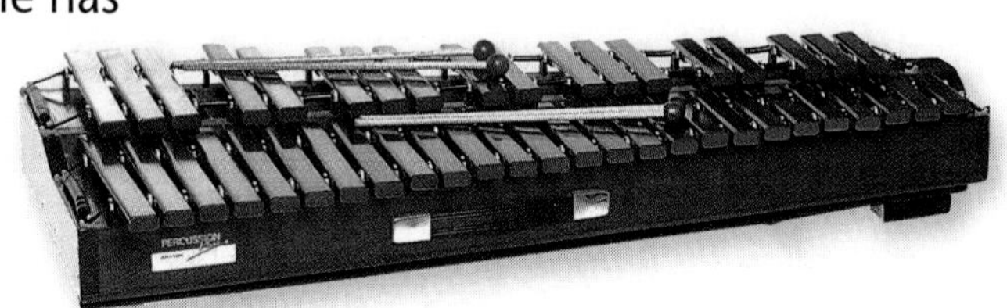

Example

Rename 0.75 as a fraction to solve the problem.

1 Write the decimal as a fraction with 100 as the denominator.

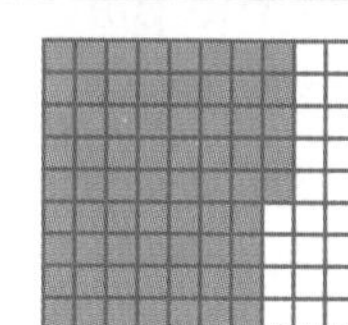

$0.75 = \frac{75}{100}$

2 Write the fraction in simplest form.

$\frac{75}{100} = \frac{75 \div 25}{100 \div 25} = \frac{3}{4}$

Think: The GCF of 75 and 100 is 25.

The smaller xylophone has keys as long as $\frac{3}{4}$ meter.

Another Example

Rename the fraction as a decimal by dividing the numerator by the denominator.

$4\overline{)3.00}$ = 0.75

Try It

Write each decimal as a fraction in simplest form.

1. 0.5
2. 0.55
3. 0.08
4. 0.7
5. 0.6

Write each fraction as a decimal.

6. $\frac{1}{4}$
7. $\frac{1}{10}$
8. $\frac{3}{8}$
9. $\frac{4}{5}$
10. $\frac{1}{2}$

Sum it Up Explain how to write 0.8 as a fraction.

Practice

Write each decimal as a fraction in simplest form.

11. 0.4 **12.** 0.2 **13.** 0.3 **14.** 0.9 **15.** 0.8

16. 0.5 **17.** 0.25 **18.** 0.15 **19.** 0.1 **20.** 0.02

★**21.** 0.08 ★**22.** 0.45 ★**23.** 0.56 ★**24.** 0.007 ★**25.** 0.005

Write each fraction as a decimal.

26. $\frac{1}{2}$ **27.** $\frac{2}{5}$ **28.** $\frac{2}{10}$ **29.** $\frac{1}{8}$ **30.** $\frac{3}{5}$

31. $\frac{1}{5}$ **32.** $\frac{9}{10}$ **33.** $\frac{7}{8}$ **34.** $\frac{7}{10}$ **35.** $\frac{5}{8}$

★**36.** $\frac{4}{100}$ ★**37.** $\frac{9}{50}$ ★**38.** $\frac{3}{25}$ ★**39.** $\frac{1}{40}$ ★**40.** $\frac{1}{80}$

Is each pair of numbers equivalent? Write *yes* or *no*.

41. $\frac{1}{4}$; 0.5 **42.** $\frac{2}{5}$; 0.4 **43.** $\frac{1}{8}$; 0.125 **44.** $\frac{7}{10}$; 0.07 **45.** $\frac{4}{5}$; 0.8

46. $\frac{3}{8}$; 0.375 **47.** $\frac{1}{20}$; 0.05 **48.** $\frac{6}{6}$; 6 **49.** $\frac{1}{5}$; 0.2 **50.** $\frac{1}{10}$; 0.01

Problem Solving

51. If the shortest key on a xylophone is 0.15 meter long, what is this length written as a fraction in simplest form?

52. A band has 30 instruments. Josie notices that $\frac{1}{2}$ of those instruments are string instruments and that $\frac{3}{8}$ are brass instruments. Does the band have more string or brass instruments?

★**53. Science:** In a water bottle xylophone, the less water there is in a bottle, the higher the pitch of a sound. Using the chart below, order the bottles from highest to lowest pitch.

Bottle	Amount of Water
A	0.5 liter
B	0.63 liter
C	0.25 liter
D	0.48 liter
E	0.3 liter

54. Explain how to write the fraction $\frac{3}{8}$ as a decimal.

Spiral Review and Test Prep

55. 1.4 × 2.3 **6.** 6 ÷ 1.5 **57.** 1.2 ÷ 0.4 **58.** 4.4 ÷ 4

Choose the correct answer.

59. Which number is the same as 2 million 7 thousand?

A. 207,000 **C.** 2,700,000
B. 2,007,000 **D.** 2,070,000

60. What is the median of the test scores?
74 74 75 77 80

F. 74 **H.** 76
G. 75 **J.** 80

Extra Practice, page 241

Objective: Solve problems by making a table.

Problem Solving: Strategy
Make a Table

Read

Read the problem carefully.

Rosalia writes the art reports for her school newspaper. She recorded the attendance for each day of a 12-day tour of a jazz band. What fraction of the days was attendance between 40–49? 50–59? 60–69?

Day	Number of People	Day	Number of People
1	64	7	62
2	60	8	50
3	58	9	69
4	49	10	51
5	61	11	68
6	43	12	56

- **What do you know?** How many people went to the concert each day
- **What are you asked to find?** The fraction of the days a certain number of people went to the concert

Plan

One way to help solve the problem is to make a table.

Range	Number of People	Number of Days
From 40 to 49	49, 43	2
From 50 to 59	58, 50, 51, 56	4
From 60 to 69	64, 60, 61, 62, 69, 68	6

Solve

Find the fraction for each range.

Range		Fraction
40 to 49 people	2 of the 12 days	$\frac{2}{12} = \frac{1}{6}$
50 to 59 people	4 of the 12 days	$\frac{4}{12} = \frac{1}{3}$
60 to 69 people	6 of the 12 days	$\frac{6}{12} = \frac{1}{2}$

Look Back

Does your answer seem reasonable?

How does making a table help you solve problems?

 **Use the make-a-table strategy to solve.**

A record store kept track of the number of jazz CDs it sold each week.

Number of Jazz CDs Sold

Week	Number	Week	Number	Week	Number
1	38	6	28	11	17
2	36	7	25	12	15
3	29	8	19	13	18
4	30	9	23	14	21
5	31	10	20	15	23

1. In what fraction of the weeks was the number of CDs sold in the range from 31 to 40? Write the fraction in simplest form.
2. In what fraction of the weeks was the number of CDs sold in the range from 21 to 30? Write the fraction in simplest form.
3. In what fraction of the weeks was the number of CDs sold 20 or less? Write the fraction in simplest form.
4. The store records an additional 5 weeks of data about the number of jazz CDs sold. The data is as follows:
   Week 16: 22 CDs
   Week 17: 45 CDs
   Week 18: 29 CDs
   Week 19: 18 CDs
   Week 20: 24 CDs

   In what fraction of the weeks was the number of CDs sold 20 or greater? Write the fraction in simplest form.

Mixed Strategy Review

5. The string orchestra has 14 more violin players than cello players. There are 38 violin and cello players in all. How many violin players are there? How many cello players are there?
6. One number is twice as great as another number. Can the greater number be an odd number? Explain.
7. A CD display has 128 boxes on the bottom row. Each row has half the number of boxes as the row below. If there is one box on top, how many rows are there?

CHOOSE A STRATEGY
- Find a Pattern
- Work-Backwards
- Use Logical Reasoning
- Write a Number Sentence
- Make a Table or List
- Guess and Check
- Make a Graph
- Solve Simpler Problem

Problem Solving

Extra Practice, page 241

Objective: Write mixed numbers as improper fractions and decimals and improper fractions and decimals as mixed numbers.

Mixed Numbers

Learn

The school play decorating committee hangs stars for a new show. They have hung all 6 gold and all 6 silver and 1 of 6 green stars. What part of the three groups of decorations have they already hung?

Math Words

mixed number a number that combines a whole number and a fraction

improper fraction a fraction that has a numerator greater than its denominator

Example 1

You can use a **mixed number** to name the whole groups and the part of another group.

1 Write the two whole groups as a whole number: 2

2 Write the one star of the third group as a fraction: $\frac{1}{6}$

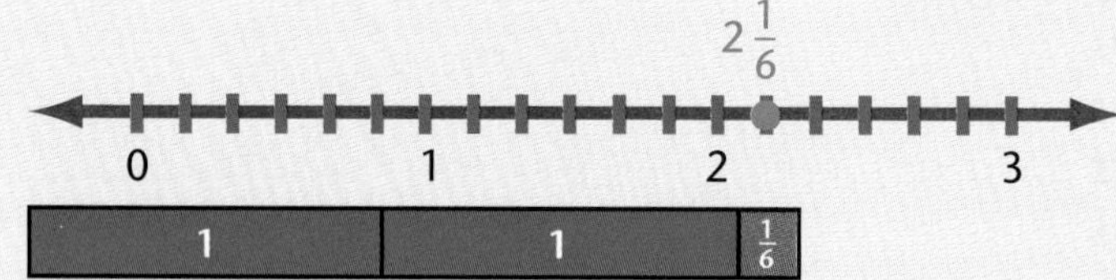

The mixed number $2\frac{1}{6}$ represents the stars that have been hung.

Example 2

Rename $2\frac{1}{6}$ as an **improper fraction**.

1 Multiply the whole number by the denominator.

$2\ \frac{1}{6}$ $\quad 2 \times 6 = 12$

2 Add the numerator.

$12 + 1 = 13$  $\frac{13}{6}$

The mixed number $2\frac{1}{6}$ is the same as the improper fraction $\frac{13}{6}$.

Another Example

Rename the improper fraction as a mixed number this way.
Divide the numerator by the denominator.

$$\begin{array}{r} 2 \text{ R1} \\ 6\overline{)13} \end{array} \qquad \frac{13}{6} = 2\frac{1}{6}$$

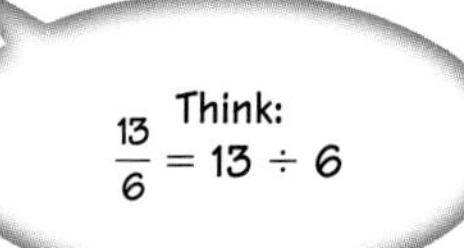

Example 3

Rename $4\frac{3}{5}$ as a decimal.

1

Divide the numerator of the fraction by the denominator.

$$\frac{3}{5} = 3 \div 5 \qquad \begin{array}{r} 0.6 \\ 5\overline{)3.0} \end{array}$$

2

Add the whole number to the decimal.

$$4 + 0.6 = 4.6$$

So $4\frac{3}{5} = 4.6$.

You can also rename a decimal as a mixed number.

Example 4

Rename 3.75 as a mixed number.

1

Rename the decimal part as a fraction in simplest form.

$$0.75 = \frac{75}{100} = \frac{3}{4}$$

2

Add the whole number.

$$3 + \frac{3}{4} = 3\frac{3}{4}$$

So $3.75 = 3\frac{3}{4}$.

Try It **Write each improper fraction as a mixed number, in simplest form.**

1. $\frac{10}{4}$ **2.** $\frac{18}{8}$ **3.** $\frac{22}{6}$ **4.** $\frac{12}{2}$ **5.** $\frac{39}{9}$ **6.** $\frac{36}{7}$

Write each mixed number as a decimal.

7. $3\frac{1}{4}$ **8.** $2\frac{1}{2}$ **9.** $4\frac{1}{5}$ **10.** $8\frac{3}{10}$ **11.** $9\frac{4}{5}$ **12.** $6\frac{3}{4}$

Explain how to write a mixed number as an improper fraction.

Practice **Write each mixed number as an improper fraction.**

13. $4\frac{1}{2}$ 14. $7\frac{4}{5}$ 15. $3\frac{5}{6}$ 16. $6\frac{1}{3}$ 17. $5\frac{3}{8}$ 18. $2\frac{7}{10}$

19. $3\frac{1}{3}$ 20. $1\frac{4}{5}$ 21. $2\frac{7}{8}$ 22. $6\frac{3}{4}$ 23. $5\frac{3}{10}$ ★24. $7\frac{7}{8}$

Write each improper fraction as a mixed number, in simplest form.

25. $\frac{10}{6}$ 26. $\frac{19}{5}$ 27. $\frac{29}{7}$ 28. $\frac{17}{3}$ 29. $\frac{72}{8}$ 30. $\frac{26}{4}$

31. $\frac{11}{10}$ 32. $\frac{21}{9}$ 33. $\frac{24}{12}$ 34. $\frac{62}{20}$ 35. $\frac{39}{15}$ ★36. $\frac{175}{100}$

Write each mixed number as a decimal.

37. $1\frac{2}{5}$ 38. $5\frac{9}{10}$ 39. $3\frac{2}{4}$ 40. $7\frac{3}{5}$ 41. $10\frac{4}{5}$ 42. $7\frac{7}{16}$

43. $2\frac{3}{4}$ 44. $4\frac{1}{5}$ 45. $3\frac{3}{10}$ 46. $5\frac{1}{2}$ 47. $1\frac{1}{8}$ ★48. $2\frac{1}{20}$

Write each decimal as a mixed number in simplest form.

49. 2.5 50. 5.2 51. 0.25 52. 7.8 53. 3.75 54. 0.625

55. 0.3 56. 1.7 57. 5.9 58. 12.5 59. 10.47 ★60. 4.1875

61. **Make it RIGHT**

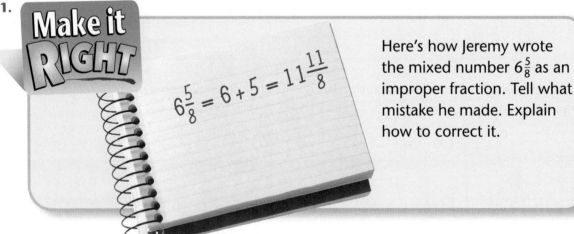

Here's how Jeremy wrote the mixed number $6\frac{5}{8}$ as an improper fraction. Tell what mistake he made. Explain how to correct it.

Problem Solving

62. In a ballet, 4 groups of dancers will perform together. There are 3 dancers in each group. Two dancers of the last group are on stage. The rest of the dancers are already on stage. How can you use a mixed number or an improper fraction to name the dancers on stage?

Use data from the sign for problems 63–64.

63. Stella buys 2 pairs of pants. What is the total cost of the pants?

64. Roberta buys 2 tops and 1 pair of shoes. What is the total cost of the tops and shoes?

The Dancer's Outlet
Clothing Sale!
Tops $15.39 each
Pants $24.19 each pair
Shoes $38.99 each pair

65. **Create a problem** about dancing that has a mixed number as an answer. Solve it and give it to another student to solve.

66. **Career:** Anna Pavlova (1882–1931) was a famous Russian ballerina. She gave 9 or 10 performances a week for more than 20 years. Over 20 years, about how many performances did she give?

67. **Health:** Dancing is good exercise. You use 160 calories for every 20 minutes of dancing. If you dance for 1 hour, how many calories do you use?

Use data from *Did You Know?* for problems 68–69.

68. What is the distance written as an improper fraction?

69. What is the distance written as a decimal?

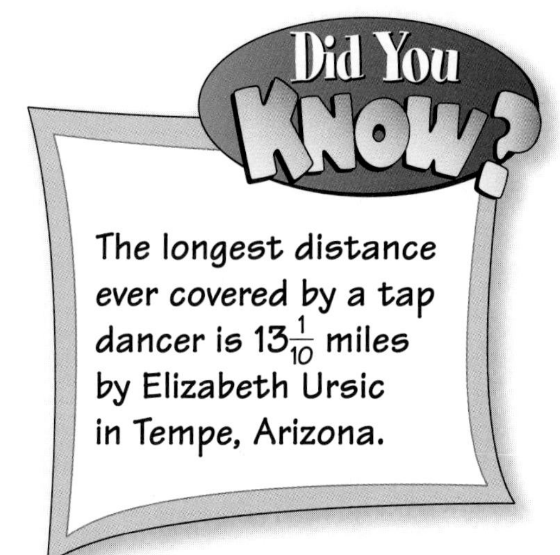

Did You Know?
The longest distance ever covered by a tap dancer is $13\frac{1}{10}$ miles by Elizabeth Ursic in Tempe, Arizona.

Spiral Review and Test Prep

70. 20 − 3.6

71. 13.1 − 4.9

72. 3.04 − 0.5

73. $9.00 − $5.89

Choose the correct answer.

74. In which range were most of the test scores for the class?
    - A. 60 to 69
    - B. 70 to 79
    - C. 80 to 89
    - D. 90 to 99

75. How many students had a test score of 84?
    - F. 1
    - G. 2
    - H. 3
    - J. Not Here

Test	Scores
6	9
7	6 8
8	4 4 5 7 9
9	4 4 4

Key: 2/9 = 29

5•12

Objective: Compare and order mixed numbers, whole numbers, decimals, and fractions.

Compare and Order Fractions, Mixed Numbers, and Decimals

Learn

A figure skater must choose music to accompany a performance. Which piece of music has the longest playing time?

Moonlight Sonata $5\frac{3}{10}$ minutes
The Music of the Night $3\frac{2}{3}$ minutes
A Midsummer Night's Dream: Nocturno $5\frac{1}{4}$ minutes

Example

Compare and order the mixed numbers to solve the problem.

1

Compare the whole numbers.

$$5\frac{3}{10} \quad 5\frac{1}{4} \quad 3\frac{2}{3}$$

The number with the greater whole number is the greater number.

So $5\frac{3}{10} > 3\frac{2}{3}$

and

$5\frac{1}{4} > 3\frac{2}{3}$

2

When two mixed numbers have the same whole numbers, compare the fractions.

Compare $5\frac{3}{10}$ and $5\frac{1}{4}$.

Rewrite the fractions with the same denominators.

$$\frac{3 \times 2}{10 \times 2} = \frac{6}{20}$$

$$\frac{1 \times 5}{4 \times 5} = \frac{5}{20}$$

$$\frac{6}{20} > \frac{5}{20}$$

So $5\frac{3}{10} > 5\frac{1}{4}$.

So $5\frac{3}{10} > 5\frac{1}{4} > 3\frac{2}{3}$.

The *Moonlight Sonata* has the longest playing time.

You can compare mixed numbers and decimals.

There's more than one way!

Compare 8.5 and $8\frac{5}{16}$.

Method A

Change the mixed number to a decimal.

$$16\overline{)5.0000} = 0.3125 \qquad 8\frac{5}{16} = 8.3125$$

Compare the decimals.

$8.5 > 8.3125$

Remember: To change a mixed number to a decimal, divide the numerator by the denominator and add the whole number.

Method B

Change the decimal to a mixed number.

$$8.5 = 8\frac{50}{100} = 8\frac{1}{2}$$

Compare the mixed numbers.

$8\frac{1}{2}$ ● $8\frac{5}{16}$

$8\frac{8}{16}$ ● $8\frac{5}{16}$

$8\frac{8}{16} > 8\frac{5}{16}$

So 8.5 is greater than $8\frac{5}{16}$.

Another Example

Order from least to greatest: 5.4, $5\frac{1}{2}$, 5.0

1. Change $5\frac{1}{2}$ to a decimal $\quad 5\frac{1}{2} = 5.5$
2. Order the decimals: $\quad 5.0 < 5.4 \quad 5.4 < 5.5$

So the answer is 5.0, 5.4, 5.5

Try It

Compare. Write >, <, or =.

1. $1\frac{3}{5}$ ● 2
2. $9\frac{3}{4}$ ● $9\frac{7}{10}$
3. $4\frac{1}{8}$ ● $4\frac{2}{5}$
4. $3\frac{3}{5}$ ● 3.6

Order from least to greatest.

5. $2\frac{1}{4}$, $2\frac{1}{2}$, 0.75
6. $\frac{7}{8}$, $1\frac{1}{5}$, 0.95
7. $5\frac{3}{4}$, $5\frac{1}{8}$, 6.02
8. $1\frac{3}{5}$, $\frac{2}{2}$, 2.1
9. $4\frac{1}{2}$, $4\frac{1}{10}$, 4.01

Sum it Up Explain how to compare $4\frac{1}{3}$ and 3.80.

Practice

Compare. Write >, <, or =.

10. $1\frac{1}{4}$ ● $1\frac{3}{10}$
11. $3\frac{1}{2}$ ● $3\frac{3}{5}$
12. 5 ● $4\frac{7}{8}$
13. $\frac{3}{4}$ ● $\frac{6}{8}$
14. $5\frac{1}{2}$ ● $5\frac{3}{4}$
15. $\frac{2}{10}$ ● $\frac{1}{5}$
16. $2\frac{5}{5}$ ● 3
17. $8\frac{10}{10}$ ● $8\frac{11}{11}$
18. $9\frac{3}{8}$ ● $9\frac{1}{5}$
19. $10\frac{3}{4}$ ● $9\frac{4}{5}$
20. $15\frac{9}{10}$ ● 17
21. $23\frac{3}{5}$ ● $23\frac{6}{10}$

Order from greatest to least.

22. $3\frac{1}{2}$, $3\frac{1}{4}$, 3.75
23. $\frac{5}{8}$, $1\frac{1}{5}$, 0.65
24. $4\frac{3}{4}$, $4\frac{1}{8}$, 4.02
25. $1\frac{3}{5}$, $\frac{3}{2}$, 1.75
26. $6\frac{1}{2}$, $6\frac{1}{10}$, 6.01
27. $2\frac{1}{8}$, $2\frac{1}{2}$, 1.75
28. $4\frac{7}{8}$, $4\frac{4}{5}$, 4.95
29. $8\frac{1}{4}$, $8\frac{1}{5}$, 8.05
30. $9\frac{3}{4}$, $\frac{20}{2}$, 10.1
31. $7\frac{2}{5}$, $7\frac{4}{8}$, 7.3
32. $5\frac{1}{2}$, $5\frac{4}{5}$, 5.75
33. $\frac{3}{4}$, $\frac{6}{4}$, 0.65

★34. $6\frac{3}{4}$, 6.1, $6\frac{9}{10}$, 5.9

★35. $10\frac{3}{5}$, 10.2, $\frac{30}{3}$, 12.3

★36. 14.4, $14\frac{1}{2}$, $\frac{41}{5}$, 14.55, $14\frac{1}{4}$

Write a number that makes each sentence true.

37. $4\frac{1}{5} >$ ■
38. $\frac{1}{3} >$ ■
39. $\frac{5}{6} =$ ■
40. $\frac{6}{8} <$ ■

41.

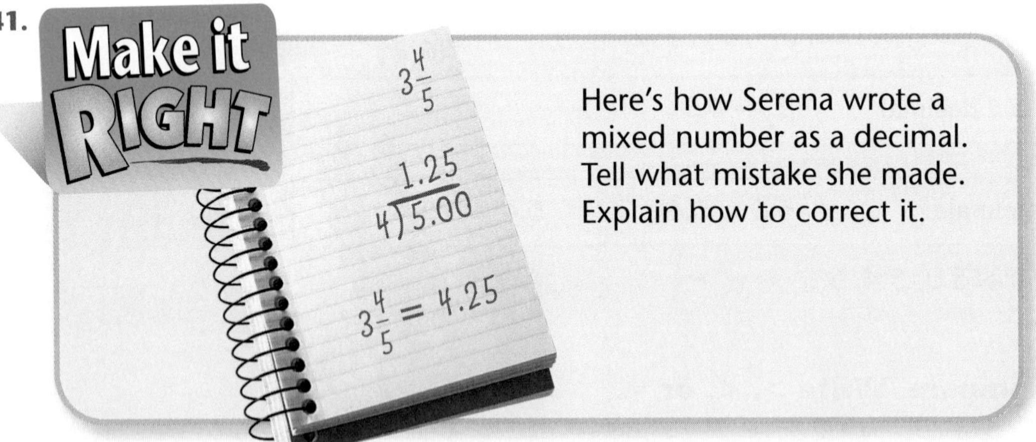

Here's how Serena wrote a mixed number as a decimal. Tell what mistake she made. Explain how to correct it.

Problem Solving

42. At the winter festival, the figure skating show lasts $1\frac{1}{2}$ hours and the Concert on the Ice lasts 1 hour and 20 minutes. Which show lasts longer? Explain.

43. **Compare:** How is comparing fractions like comparing whole numbers? How is it different?

Use data from the table for problems 44–47.

44. List the order of the playing times from least to greatest.

45. What is the playing time of *The Seasons: June* in decimal form?

46. Jimmy wants to choose background music that is less than 5.25 minutes. Which music could he choose?

★ 47. Which two pieces of music are closest in playing time?

Background Music for Figure Skating

Music	Playing Time
The Seasons: June	$4\frac{3}{4}$ minutes
Memory	$5\frac{5}{8}$ minutes
I Dreamed a Dream	$5\frac{1}{2}$ minutes
The Nutcracker; Scene No. 10	$4\frac{7}{10}$ minutes

48. At the 1998 U.S. Figure Skating Championships, Michelle Kwan earned 15 perfect scores out of a total of 36. Of the marks, what fraction were perfect scores? Write the fraction in simplest form.

49. **Time:** The 1999 World Figure Skating Championships was held in Helsinki, Finland. Helsinki's time zone is 10 hours ahead of Los Angeles' local time. If a competition were held at 8:30 P.M. in Helsinki, what would be the local time in Los Angeles?

★ 50. Mary rents practice time at an ice skating rink for $22 an hour. She practices from 8:45A.M. until 10:15A.M. How much does she owe?

Spiral Review and Test Prep

Write the value of the underlined digit in each number.

51. 10<u>3</u>,254,687 52. 16.58<u>4</u>2 53. <u>9</u>6,128 54. 0.<u>6</u>25 55. <u>5</u>1,074,932 56. 81.947<u>2</u>

Choose the correct answer.

57. Figure skating competitions are often judged this way: drop the highest and lowest scores and find the mean of the remaining scores. If a skater receives these scores from each judge, what is the final score?

5.7, 5.9, 5.6, 5.8, 5.7, 5.5

A. 5.5 C. 5.7
B. 5.6 D. 5.8

58. A skater spends $29 for each hour of practice time at the rink. What will it cost to practice for 4 hours?

F. $29 H. $58
G. $106 J. $116

Objective: Apply fractions to making decisions.

Problem Solving: Application
Decision Making

As the student director of the school orchestra, your job is to organize the annual concert. You need to include exactly 100 musicians. The piece of music must last at least 7 minutes.

Decide on the number of musicians for each instrument. Decide which piece will be played.

Group Number	Instrument	Range of Number of Musicians
1.	Violin	20–35
2.	Viola	10–15
3.	Cello	10–15
4.	Bass	5–10
5.	Flute	2–5
6.	Oboe	3–6
7.	Clarinet	3–6
8.	Bassoon	3–6
9.	Horns	4–8
10.	Trumpet	3–6
11.	Trombone	3–6
12.	Tuba	1–2
13.	Timpani and Percussion	2–4
14.	Piano	1–2

Symphony Choices and Times	
	Music Length in Minutes
Adagio for Strings by Barber	$7\frac{1}{4}$
Adagio in G Minor by Albinoni	$7\frac{3}{4}$
Andante Cantabile by Tchaikovsky	$6\frac{1}{8}$
Intermezzo from *Manon Lescaut* by Puccini	$6\frac{1}{2}$
Pavane by Fauré	$6\frac{1}{4}$
Pavane by Ravel	$6\frac{5}{8}$
Vocalise in F Major by Rachmaninoff	$7\frac{7}{8}$

Read for Understanding

1. What does the chart show?
2. What is the least and greatest number of musicians in the clarinet group that the guide shows?
3. How many musicians should be in your orchestra plan?
4. What is the fewest number of violins that could be in your plan?
5. What is the length of time for Pavane by Ravel?
6. What is the minimum length of time the music must last?

Problem Solving

Make Decisions

7. If you choose 30 violins, how would you write that as a fraction of 100 musicians, in simplest form?
8. If you choose 5 flutes, how would you write that as part of 100 musicians, in decimal form?
9. Which pieces of music last longer than 7 minutes?
10. Of the pieces that last longer than 7 minutes, what is their order from longest to shortest?
11. If you choose to include 2 tubas, what will the fraction of tubas be, written as a decimal?
12. What is the possible range of horns, written as a fraction in simplest form?
13. Which pieces of music cannot be used for the program?
14. What is the range of oboes that can be used, written as a fraction in simplest form?
15. If you use the maximum number of violins and violas, how many other instruments can you include?
16. If you use the maximum number of bassoons and the minimum number of horns, will there be more bassoons or horns?

Your Decision!

How many of each instrument will you use in your orchestra? Write the answer as a decimal and as a fraction of the whole orchestra. Order the numbers from greatest to least. Which musical program will you present?

Objective: Apply number theory and fraction concepts to investigate science concepts.

Problem Solving: Math and Science

What are the properties of matter?

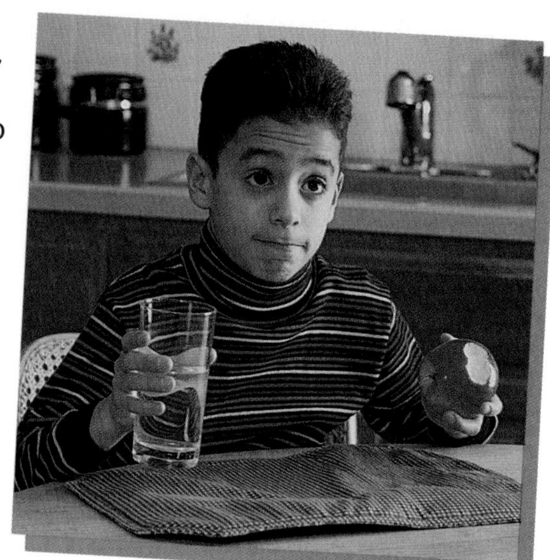

You breathe in, drink some water, and eat an apple. You have just put gases, liquids, and solids into your body. Nearly everything in the world can be classified as a gas, liquid, or solid.

You Will Need
- **assorted gases, liquids and solids**

In this activity, you will examine many objects and try to determine the properties of the three types of matter.

Hypothesize

Study each object given to you by your teacher. For each one, decide if you think it is a gas, liquid, or solid.

Procedure

1. Work in a group. Record your answers. Complete the table.
2. Separate the objects that hold their own shape. What fraction of all the objects is it?
3. Separate the objects that fill a container. What fraction of the total is it?
4. Separate the objects that will expand in a container. What fraction of the total is it?

Data

Copy and complete the chart to record your observations.

Object	State of Matter

Property	Fraction
Holds shape	
Fills a container	
Expands in a container	

Conclude and Apply

1. Use your data.
   - Which states of matter hold their shape?
   - Which states of matter fill a container?
   - Which states of matter expand in a container?
2. How well did you hypothesize?
3. Define gas, liquid, and solid.
4. Based on the fractions you found, would you conclude that most objects are solids, liquids, or gases?
5. Use data from *Did You Know?* to order gas, liquid, and solid from greatest density to least.

Did You Know?

The *density* of an object is how much stuff (matter) it packs into a given size (volume). You can get a rough idea of the density of an object by holding it and deciding whether it feels light or heavy for its size.

Going Further

1. Talk with a partner. How would you classify these objects—fire, clay, sawdust, ice, and clouds?
2. Place assorted objects in water and decide if they have a density greater or less than water.

Check Your Progress B

Simplify each fraction. **(pages 214–215)**

1. $\frac{4}{12}$ **2.** $\frac{5}{30}$ **3.** $\frac{14}{49}$ **4.** $\frac{36}{144}$ **5.** $\frac{4}{72}$ **6.** $\frac{12}{60}$

Find the LCM of the numbers. **(pages 216–219)**

7. 4, 6, 8 **8.** 2, 3, 7 **9.** 5, 6, 10 **10.** 3, 9, 12 **11.** 6, 9, 18

Use the LCD to rewrite the fractions. **(pages 216–219)**

12. $\frac{1}{2}, \frac{2}{5}, \frac{5}{8}$ **13.** $\frac{1}{2}, \frac{5}{6}, \frac{6}{7}$ **14.** $\frac{7}{9}, \frac{3}{4}, \frac{11}{18}$ **15.** $\frac{4}{5}, \frac{7}{10}, \frac{6}{15}$ **16.** $\frac{3}{4}, \frac{2}{7}, \frac{9}{14}$

Rewrite the fractions and mixed numbers as decimals. Order from least to greatest. **(pages 220–223, 226–229)**

17. $1.15, 1\frac{3}{8}, 1\frac{1}{5}$ **18.** $\frac{5}{2}, 2\frac{3}{4}, 2.3$ **19.** $3.04, 3\frac{2}{5}, 3\frac{1}{4}$ **20.** $5\frac{9}{10}, 5\frac{1}{2}, 5.89$ **21.** $\frac{7}{8}, 0.87, \frac{4}{5}$

Solve. **(pages 214–233)**

22. Lila made a chart to show the number of ticket sales for the play in the last 12 days. In what fraction of the days were the ticket sales in the range from 100 to 109? Write the fraction in simplest form.

23. In what fraction of the days were the ticket sales in the range from 110 to 119? Write the fraction in simplest form.

Ticket Sales in Last 12 Days

Day	Number	Day	Number
1	101	7	100
2	96	8	119
3	104	9	90
4	98	10	109
5	100	11	107
6	115	12	93

24. The Pine School band is rehearsing for a show. The diagram to the right shows the order of the songs the band will rehearse. What fraction of all the songs rehearsed will the song "Glow Worm" be?

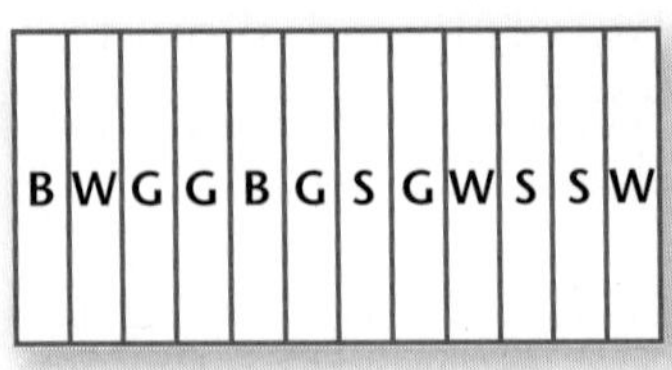

Key:
B–Blue Moon
G–Glow Worm
S–Star-Spangled Banner
W–What a Wonderful World

25. Compare: How are 3.9 and $3\frac{9}{10}$ alike and different?

Additional activities at
www.mhschool.com/math

Extra Practice

Divisibility (pages 200–201)

Of 2, 3, 5, 6, 9, and 10, list which numbers each number is divisible by.

1. 76
2. 93
3. 480
4. 735
5. 813
6. 524
7. 489
8. 1,931
9. 5,002
10. 12,006

Explore Primes and Composites (pages 202–203)

For each number, tell whether it is prime or composite. Write a prime factorization for each composite number.

1. 54
2. 18
3. 40
4. 15
5. 7
6. 43
7. 35
8. 120

Common Factors and Greatest Common Factor (pages 204–205)

Find the GCF of the numbers.

1. 8 and 20
2. 9 and 12
3. 6 and 10
4. 5 and 15
5. 16 and 24
6. 18 and 42
7. 42 and 56
8. 6 and 9

Fractions (pages 206–209)

Name each fraction shown.

1. 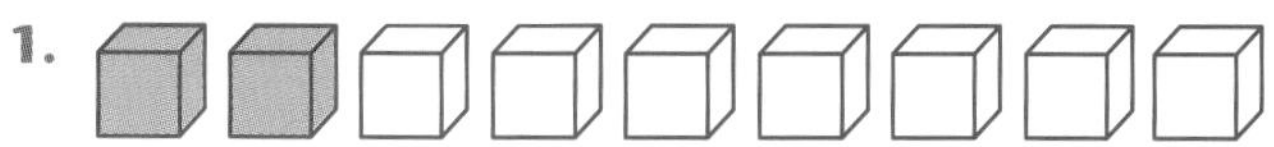
2. 
3. 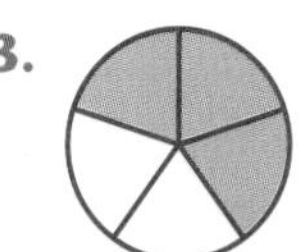

Write two equivalent fractions for each fraction.

4. 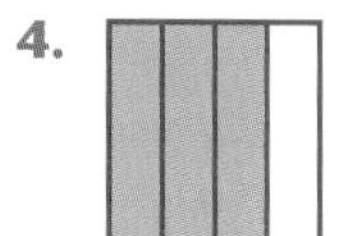
5. 
6. 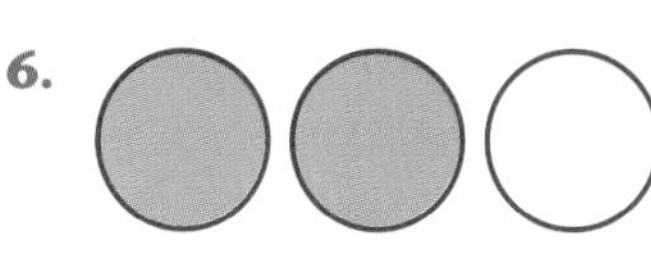

Solve.

7. The stage crew has 15 members and 6 of them are sixth graders. The rest are fifth graders. Express as a fraction the number of the crew who are fifth graders.

Extra Practice

Problem Solving: Reading for Math Extra and Missing Information (pages 210–211)

The Kettletown Marching Band is lining up for a song. The diagram below shows how the musicians will line up.

1. Express as a fraction the number of musicians in the Kettletown Marching Band who are drummers.
2. Express as a fraction the number musicians in the Kettletown Marching Band who are clarinet players.

D	D	Tu	Tu	D	D
D	Tr	Tr	Tr	Tr	D
D	C	C	C	F	F
C	C	C	F	F	F

Key:
C - Clarinet Tr - Trumpet
F - Flute Tu - Tuba
D - Drum

Simplify Fractions (pages 214–215)

Write each fraction in simplest form.

1. $\frac{12}{20}$ 2. $\frac{6}{32}$ 3. $\frac{18}{45}$ 4. $\frac{18}{60}$ 5. $\frac{70}{100}$

6. $\frac{8}{12}$ 7. $\frac{10}{18}$ 8. $\frac{20}{24}$ 9. $\frac{14}{72}$ 10. $\frac{32}{56}$

Least Common Multiple and Least Common Denominator (pages 216–219)

Find the LCM of the numbers.

1. 6 and 10 2. 4 and 8 3. 7 and 21 4. 3, 6, 10 5. 9, 5, 3

Use the LCD to write the fractions.

6. $\frac{3}{4}, \frac{4}{5}, \frac{5}{8}$ 7. $\frac{1}{2}, \frac{2}{3}, \frac{5}{6}$ 8. $\frac{1}{3}, \frac{2}{9}, \frac{1}{4}$ 9. $\frac{4}{7}, \frac{2}{9}$

Compare and Order Fractions (pages 220–221)

Compare. Order from least to greatest.

1. $\frac{1}{6}, \frac{1}{2}, \frac{1}{8}$ 2. $\frac{2}{3}, \frac{7}{10}, \frac{3}{5}$ 3. $\frac{2}{9}, \frac{1}{3}, \frac{4}{15}$ 4. $\frac{8}{9}, \frac{5}{6}, \frac{7}{12}, \frac{9}{10}$

Solve.

5. **Logical Reasoning:** Julio is using three equal pieces of cloth to make costumes. He has used $\frac{1}{2}$ of the red cloth, $\frac{5}{8}$ of the blue cloth, and $\frac{2}{3}$ of the yellow cloth. Which color cloth was used most?

Extra Practice

Relate Fractions and Decimals (pages 222–223)

Write each decimal as a fraction in simplest form.

1. 0.2
2. 0.5
3. 0.7
4. 0.8
5. 0.25

Write each fraction as a decimal.

6. $\frac{1}{8}$
7. $\frac{3}{5}$
8. $\frac{7}{8}$
9. $\frac{8}{10}$
10. $\frac{3}{16}$

Problem Solving Strategy: Make a Table (pages 224–225)

Solve.

1. In what fraction of the days were ticket sales in the range of 41 to 50?
2. In what fraction of the days were ticket sales in the range of 51 to 60? Write the fraction in simplest form.

Number of Tickets Sold in Last 15 Days

Day	Number	Day	Number	Day	Number
1	42	6	50	11	42
2	48	7	61	12	39
3	60	8	50	13	57
4	55	9	48	14	38
5	143	10	49	15	45

Mixed Numbers (pages 226–229)

Write each improper fraction as a mixed number, in simplest form.

1. $\frac{11}{2}$
2. $\frac{18}{4}$
3. $\frac{17}{5}$
4. $\frac{22}{3}$
5. $\frac{38}{6}$
6. $\frac{60}{9}$

Write each mixed number as a decimal.

7. $4\frac{3}{8}$
8. $3\frac{1}{4}$
9. $8\frac{2}{5}$
10. $7\frac{3}{4}$
11. $11\frac{9}{10}$
12. $12\frac{4}{5}$

Compare and Order Fractions and Mixed Numbers (pages 230–233)

Order from least to greatest.

1. $0.45, \frac{1}{4}, \frac{2}{5}$
2. $\frac{7}{2}, 3\frac{3}{4}, 3.55$
3. $5.3, 5\frac{1}{5}, \frac{5}{4}$
4. $6\frac{3}{8}, 6.3, 6\frac{3}{5}$

Solve.

5. Michael buys 2.2 yards of cloth to make a costume. The design calls for $2\frac{1}{4}$ yards. Did Michael buy enough cloth? Explain.

Chapter Study Guide

Language and Math

Complete. Use a word from the list.

1. A whole number greater than 1 that has exactly two factors, 1 and itself, is called a(n) ____.
2. The ____ of 4 and 10 is 20.
3. The ____ of 20 and 25 is 5.

Math Words

composite number
greatest common factor (GCF)
least common multiple (LCM)
least common denominator (LCD)
prime number
simplest form

Skills and Applications

Identify prime and composite numbers. (pages 202–203)

Example
Find the prime factorization of 24.

Solution
Use a factor tree.

$24 = 3 \times 2^3$

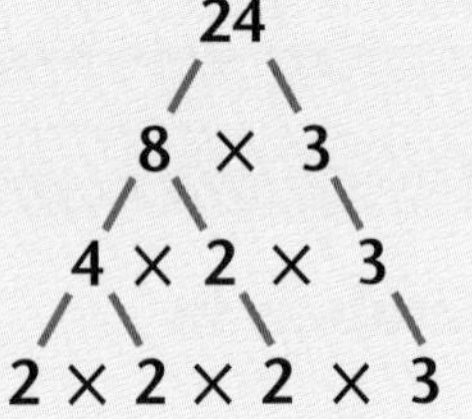

Tell if the number is prime or composite. Write a prime factorization for each composite number.

4. 18
5. 48
6. 23
7. 61
8. 34
9. 100

Find common factors and common multiples. (pages 204–205, 216–219)

Example
Find the greatest common factor of 18 and 45.

Solution
List all the factors of the two numbers.

18: 1, 2, 3, 6, 9, and 18
45: 1, 3, 5, 9, 15, and 45

Then find the greatest common factor: 9

Find the GCF.

10. 24 and 40
11. 12 and 30

Find the LCM.

12. 4 and 5
13. 2, 7, and 14

Write the fractions with a LCD.

14. $\frac{3}{5}, \frac{2}{3}, \frac{1}{2}$
15. $\frac{7}{8}, \frac{2}{3}, \frac{5}{6}$

Simplify fractions and mixed numbers. (pages 214–215, 226–229)

Example

Write the fraction $\frac{16}{24}$ in simplest form.

Solution

Write the prime factorization and cancel the terms.

$$\frac{16}{24} = \frac{\cancel{2} \times \cancel{2} \times \cancel{2} \times 2}{\cancel{2} \times \cancel{2} \times \cancel{2} \times 3} = \frac{2}{3}$$

Write each fraction in simplest form.

16. $\frac{24}{36}$
17. $\frac{13}{26}$
18. $\frac{9}{27}$
19. $\frac{20}{48}$
20. There are 60 members in the band, and 12 play the clarinet. Express as a fraction, in simplest form, the number of band members who play clarinet.

Compare and order fractions and mixed numbers. (pages 220–223, 226–233)

Example

Order from least to greatest:

$1\frac{4}{5}$, 1.45, and $\frac{7}{10}$.

Solution

Rename $1\frac{4}{5}$ and $\frac{7}{10}$ as decimals.

Compare. $0.7 < 1.45 < 1.8$

The order from least to greatest is

$\frac{7}{10}$; 1.45; $1\frac{4}{5}$.

Order from least to greatest.

21. $2\frac{1}{5}$, $\frac{9}{10}$, 2.85
22. $\frac{6}{3}$, 1.98, $1\frac{4}{5}$

Compare. Write >, <, or =.

23. $9\frac{10}{12}$ ● $9\frac{20}{24}$
24. $5\frac{1}{2}$ ● $5\frac{2}{5}$

Solve problems. (pages 210–211, 224–225)

Example

Temperature							
Day	1	2	3	4	5	6	7
Temperature, °F	54	65	58	60	68	48	64

In what fraction of the days did the temperature range from 51 to 60?

Solution

Make a table.

Range	Temperature, °F	Number of Days
From 41 to 50	48	1
From 51 to 60	54, 58, 60	3
From 61 to 70	65, 68, 64	3

$\frac{3}{7}$ of the days

Solve.

25. Chris charted the number of people who saw the school play.

Number of People at the School Play			
Day	Number of People	Day	Number of People
1	122	7	120
2	139	8	143
3	117	9	119
4	113	10	134
5	126	11	127
6	141	12	130

In what fraction of the days was the number of people in the range from 120 to 129? Write the fraction in simplest form.

Chapter Test

Tell if the number is prime or composite. Write a prime factorization for the composite numbers.

1. 99
2. 13
3. 38
4. 71

Find the GCF.

5. 18 and 30
6. 15 and 20
7. 32 and 8
8. 36 and 42

Find the LCM.

9. 4 and 12
10. 8 and 10
11. 3 and 7
12. 5, 6, and 15

Use the LCD to write equivalent fractions.

13. $\frac{3}{4}$ and $\frac{7}{10}$
14. $\frac{2}{3}$ and $\frac{7}{8}$
15. $\frac{5}{6}$ and $\frac{1}{4}$
16. $\frac{1}{2}, \frac{3}{4}, \frac{5}{8}$

Write each fraction in simplest form.

17. $\frac{27}{36}$
18. $\frac{16}{40}$
19. $\frac{12}{34}$
20. $\frac{22}{110}$

Write each improper fraction as a mixed number in simplest form.

21. $\frac{14}{4}$
22. $\frac{28}{3}$
23. $\frac{44}{7}$
24. $\frac{84}{9}$
25. $\frac{50}{6}$

Write these numbers as decimals in order from least to greatest.

26. $9\frac{1}{2}, 9\frac{1}{5}, 9.3$
27. $6\frac{7}{10}, \frac{35}{5}, 6.85$
28. $2\frac{4}{5}, 2\frac{7}{8}, 2.4$
29. $7\frac{3}{4}, \frac{15}{2}, 7.7$
30. $4\frac{5}{8}, 4\frac{3}{5}, 4\frac{1}{10}$

Use data from the chart for problems 31–32.

31. In what fraction of the days was the number of visitors from 50 to 59?
32. In what fraction of the days was the number of visitors from 60 to 69?
33. Which price is the least expensive? the most expensive? $\$119\frac{4}{5}$; $\$119\frac{9}{10}$; $\$119\frac{9}{20}$

Community Arts Center

Day	Number of Visitors	Day	Number of Visitors
1	53	7	70
2	57	8	53
3	68	9	55
4	59	10	67
5	48	11	51
6	60	12	49

Performance Assessment

You want to buy stock in a record company. The prices of stocks are given using fractions of a dollar.

1. List the companies and prices from least to greatest.
2. Stock prices will soon be given as decimals instead of fractions. Copy and complete the table below to show each stock price using a decimal.
3. Suppose you want to buy a stock that has a price of less than $8\frac{1}{2}$. Which companies' stocks can you buy?
4. Suppose you want to save \$315 to buy stocks. You want to save the same amount of money each week to get the exact amount of \$315. You are able to save up to \$10 each week. What amounts can you save each week so that you get the exact amount of \$315?

Record Company Stocks and Prices

Company	Price	Company	Price
ARC	8 3/4	MBR	8 3/8
CLM	9 1/2	SWD	9 3/8
GNV	7 5/8	WFI	7 9/16
JJT	7 1/4	ZEV	8 13/16

Record Company Stocks and Prices		
Company	Price in Fractions	Price in Decimals
ARC	$8\frac{3}{4}$	
CLM	$9\frac{1}{2}$	
GNV	$7\frac{5}{8}$	
JJT	$7\frac{1}{4}$	
MBR	$8\frac{3}{8}$	
SWD	$9\frac{3}{8}$	
WFI	$7\frac{9}{16}$	
ZEV	$8\frac{13}{16}$	

A Good Answer

- correctly orders the companies and prices from least to greatest.
- has a complete chart that shows the stock prices as decimals.
- correctly answers the questions about the stocks.

You may want to save this work in your portfolio.

Assessment

Enrichment

The Sieve of Eratosthenes

Eratosthenes (274–194 B.C.) was a Greek mathematician. He invented a "sieve" to find prime numbers. A sieve is a tool that helps separate one thing from another. The Sieve of Eratosthenes leaves only the prime numbers behind.

You will use the Sieve of Eratosthenes to find the prime numbers from 1–100.

▶ Write a chart like this one of the numbers from 1 to 100.

1	2	3	4	5	6	7	8	9	10	11	12	13	14	15	16	17	18	19	20
21	22	23	24	25	26	27	28	29	30	31	32	33	34	35	36	37	38	39	40
41	42	43	44	45	46	47	48	49	50	51	52	53	54	55	56	57	58	59	60
61	62	63	64	65	66	67	68	69	70	71	72	73	74	75	76	77	78	79	80
81	82	83	84	85	86	87	88	89	90	91	92	93	94	95	96	97	98	99	100

▶ Cross out the number 1 in the chart. It is not a prime number because it has only one factor, 1.

Think:
Multiples of any prime number must have more than two factors. Therefore, they are not prime.

▶ Circle the number 2. It is the first prime number. It has exactly two factors, 1 and itself. Then cross out every multiple of 2, for example 4, 6, 8, and so on, until you reach 100.

▶ Circle the number 3. It is the next prime number. Then cross out every multiple of 3. Some numbers which are multiples of 3 will already be crossed out because they are also multiples of 2.

▶ Circle the next number that is not crossed out, 5. Cross out every multiple of 5.

▶ Continue these steps until all the numbers have either been circled or crossed out. The numbers that are circled are all the prime numbers from 1 to 100.

Write whether each number is prime or composite.

1. 6 **2.** 7 **3.** 13 **4.** 43 **5.** 51 **6.** 91

7. How many prime numbers are there less than 100?

Test-Taking Tips

S.O.S.

When taking a multiple-choice test, you may find the information you need to solve a problem in a sign, picture, or chart. This method is called **finding needed information.**

Matt is buying paint to make scenery for the play. Four different sizes are on sale. Which brand comes in the largest-sized container?

A. True Color **C.** Rainbow Blend
B. Pearson Art **D.** Brilliant Shine

Paint Sale

Brand	Size
True Color	$2\frac{1}{2}$ quart
Pearson Art	$2\frac{5}{8}$ quart
Rainbow Blend	$1\frac{3}{4}$ quart
Brilliant Shine	$1\frac{1}{4}$ quart

Read the problem carefully.

You can find the sizes in the sign. Compare the numbers to decide which container is largest.

The correct answer is B.

Choose the correct answer.

1. Kim is painting a mural. What fraction of the mural does Kim still need to paint?

A. 2 **C.** $\frac{2}{5}$
B. $\frac{2}{3}$ **D.** $\frac{3}{5}$

2. Emilio chose the stock that had the lowest price. Which stock did he choose?

F. BWS
G. HTN
H. KRV
J. MZA

Company	Stock Price
BWS	$12\frac{3}{8}$
HTN	$12\frac{3}{4}$
KRV	$12\frac{7}{10}$
MZA	$12\frac{1}{2}$

Check for Success

Before turning in a test, go back one last time to check.

☑ I understood and answered the questions asked.
☑ I checked my work for errors.
☑ My answers make sense.

3. The Playhouse Theater is selling tickets for four shows. On which night has the least number of tickets been sold?

A. June 4 **C.** June 6
B. June 5 **D.** June 7

PLAYHOUSE THEATER
Romeo and Juliet

June 4th	$\frac{3}{4}$ of all tickets sold
June 5th	$\frac{7}{8}$ of all tickets sold
June 6th	$\frac{5}{6}$ of all tickets sold
June 7th	$\frac{2}{3}$ of all tickets sold

Test Prep

Spiral Review and Test Prep

Chapters 1–5

Choose the correct answer.

Number Sense

BICYCLE TRIPS

Trip 1 . . . . $6\frac{1}{3}$ miles

Trip 2 . . . . $5\frac{4}{5}$ miles

Trip 3 . . . . $6\frac{5}{8}$ miles

Trip 4 . . . . $6\frac{7}{10}$ miles

1. Which trip is the longest?
   - A. Trip 1
   - B. Trip 2
   - C. Trip 3
   - D. Trip 4

2. Write the length of Trip 2 as a decimal.
   - F. 5.45
   - G. 5.08
   - H. 5.8
   - J. 0.545

3. Which choice shows the order of the times from least to greatest?

Race Times for Four Trials

Trial Number	Time
1	20.53
2	21.06
3	20.89
4	20.72

   - A. 1, 2, 3, 4
   - B. 2, 3, 4, 1
   - C. 3, 4, 1, 2
   - D. 1, 4, 3, 2

4. The population of the United States in 1990 was about 248,710,000. Which digit is in the hundred millions place in the number?
   - F. 2
   - G. 4
   - H. 8
   - J. 7

Algebra and Functions

5. If the rule is add 5, which number goes in the blank to complete the pattern?

   6, 11, ____, 21, 26, 31
   - A. 12
   - B. 15
   - C. 16
   - D. 20

6. Which of the following values for n makes the expression true?

$$\frac{2}{6} = \frac{1}{n}$$

   - F. 2
   - G. 3
   - H. 4
   - J. 12

7. Which expression is equivalent to 20×33?
   - A. $33 \div 20$
   - B. $33 + 20$
   - C. 23×30
   - D. 33×20

8. Which number goes in the box to make the statement correct?

   $0.2 + \blacksquare = 0.7 + 0.5$
   - F. 0.10
   - G. 1
   - H. 10
   - J. 12

Statistics, Data Analysis, and Probability

Use data from the bar graph for problems 9–12.

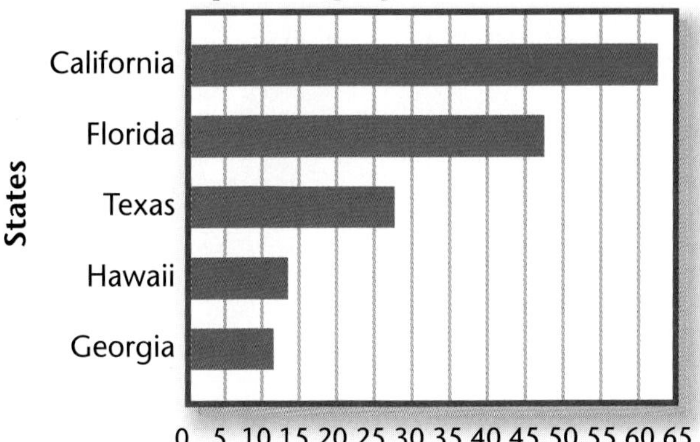

9. Which of these states had the greatest amount of tourist spending?
   - A. California
   - B. Florida
   - C. Georgia
   - D. Texas

10. Which state had $20 million less spending than Florida?
    - F. California
    - G. Georgia
    - H. Texas
    - J. Hawaii

11. Between which two states was there the greatest difference in spending?
    - A. California and Florida
    - B. California and Hawaii
    - C. Florida and Georgia
    - D. California and Georgia

12. Which state was closest in spending to Georgia?
    - F. California
    - G. Hawaii
    - H. Texas
    - J. Florida

Measurement and Geometry

A ribbon company uses 3 different package sizes.

Use data from the table for problems 13–14.

Ribbon Package Sizes	
Size	Length
Small	$1\frac{1}{2}$ yards
Medium	$2\frac{3}{4}$ yards
Large	$3\frac{1}{4}$ yards

13. How many yards are in a medium package, written as a decimal?
    - A. 1.5
    - B. 2.34
    - C. 2.75
    - D. 3.25

14. The company wants to design a smaller package than it has now. Which of these lengths is less than the other lengths?
    - F. $1\frac{3}{8}$ yards
    - G. $1\frac{4}{5}$ yards
    - H. $1\frac{2}{3}$ yards
    - J. $1\frac{7}{8}$ yards

15. Which kind of figure has exactly 3 sides?
    - A. Circle
    - B. Square
    - C. Triangle
    - D. Rectangle

16. Andy feeds his fish 2 scoops of fish food each day from Monday to Friday and 3 scoops for the whole weekend. How many scoops of food does he feed them each week? Explain.

CHAPTER 6 Add and Subtract Fractions

Theme: Careers

Use the Data

CAREERS OF MEN AND WOMEN

Career	Fraction of Women	Fraction of Men
Veterinarian	$\frac{1}{3}$	$\frac{2}{3}$
Artist	$\frac{1}{2}$	$\frac{1}{2}$
Bank Teller	$\frac{9}{10}$	$\frac{1}{10}$
Barber	$\frac{1}{4}$	$\frac{3}{4}$
Physical Therapist	$\frac{3}{5}$	$\frac{2}{5}$

- What fraction of artists are women? How much more is that fraction than the fraction of women who are barbers?

What You Will Learn

In this chapter you will learn how to
- add and subtract fractions and mixed numbers.
- use addition properties.
- estimate sums and differences of mixed numbers.
- use strategies to solve problems.

Objective: Add and subtract fractions and mixed numbers with like denominators.

6·1 Add and Subtract Fractions and Mixed Numbers with Like Denominators

Jay Liebowitz

Learn

Math Word

common denominator a denominator that is the same for two or more fractions

Jay Liebowitz was only 12 years old when he wrote his own computer software program. He sold it for $30,000 and invested his earnings. If Jay invested $\frac{1}{4}$ of his earnings in stocks and $\frac{1}{4}$ in bonds, what fraction of his earnings is invested in stocks and bonds?

There's more than one way!

Add $\frac{1}{4} + \frac{1}{4}$ to solve the problem.

You can use fraction strips to add fractions.

Method A

1. Model $\frac{1}{4}$ and $\frac{1}{4}$.

2. Count how many fourths there are in all.

$\frac{1}{4} + \frac{1}{4} = \frac{2}{4}$

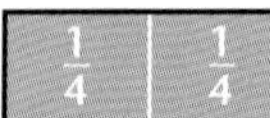

3. Simplify.

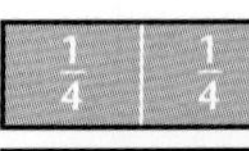

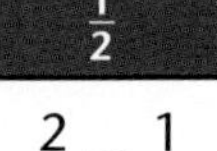

$\frac{2}{4} = \frac{1}{2}$

You can use paper and pencil to add fractions.

Method B

1. Add the numerators. Use the **common denominator**.

$\frac{1}{4} + \frac{1}{4} = \frac{1 + 1}{4} = \frac{2}{4}$

2. Simplify.

$\frac{2}{4} = \frac{1}{2}$

Jay would have invested $\frac{1}{2}$ of his money in stocks and bonds.

If Jay buys shares of stock for $5\frac{1}{4}$ dollars per share and sells each for $7\frac{3}{4}$ dollars, how much has each share gained?

Example

Find $7\frac{3}{4} - 5\frac{1}{4}$ to solve the problem.

1 Subtract the fractions.

$$\begin{array}{r} 7\frac{3}{4} \\ -5\frac{1}{4} \\ \hline \frac{2}{4} \end{array}$$

2 Subtract the whole numbers.

$$\begin{array}{r} 7\frac{3}{4} \\ -5\frac{1}{4} \\ \hline 2\frac{2}{4} \end{array}$$

3 Simplify.

$$2\frac{2}{4} = 2\frac{1}{2}$$

Each share gains $2\frac{1}{2}$ dollars.

More Examples

A

$$\begin{array}{r} 22\frac{3}{5} \\ +14\frac{4}{5} \\ \hline 36\frac{7}{5} \end{array} = 36 + 1\frac{2}{5} = 37\frac{2}{5}$$

B

$$\begin{array}{r} 8\frac{5}{8} \\ -2\frac{5}{8} \\ \hline 6 \end{array}$$

C

$$\begin{array}{r} 12\frac{5}{6} \\ +\ 6\frac{1}{6} \\ \hline 18\frac{6}{6} \end{array} = 18 + 1 = 19$$

D

$$\begin{array}{r} 5\frac{7}{10} \\ -5\frac{3}{10} \\ \hline \frac{4}{10} \end{array} = \frac{2}{5}$$

Try It **Add or subtract. Write your answer in simplest form.**

1. $\frac{2}{5} + \frac{1}{5}$

2. $1\frac{5}{8} + 2\frac{7}{8}$

3. $5\frac{5}{12} - 2\frac{1}{12}$

4. $5\frac{9}{10} - 5\frac{4}{10}$

Explain how you would add $2\frac{3}{8} + 1\frac{7}{8}$. Use the words *numerator* and *denominator* in your answer.

Practice Add or subtract. Write your answer in simplest form.

5. $\frac{1}{3} + \frac{1}{3}$
6. $\frac{5}{8} - \frac{3}{8}$
7. $\frac{13}{20} + \frac{17}{20}$
8. $\frac{9}{10} + \frac{9}{10}$
9. $\frac{11}{12} - \frac{1}{12}$
10. $\frac{7}{20} + \frac{17}{20}$
11. $\frac{4}{5} + \frac{4}{5}$
12. $\frac{15}{16} - \frac{7}{16}$
13. $\frac{3}{12} + \frac{10}{12}$
14. $\frac{5}{16} + \frac{7}{16}$
15. $\frac{15}{16} - \frac{7}{16}$
16. $\frac{5}{12} + \frac{11}{12}$

17. $5\frac{3}{5} + 7\frac{2}{5}$
18. $\frac{7}{10} - \frac{3}{10}$
19. $\frac{7}{8} - \frac{5}{8}$
20. $1\frac{7}{8} + 2\frac{1}{8}$
21. $9\frac{9}{10} + 7\frac{3}{10}$

22. $16\frac{5}{8} + 7\frac{3}{8}$
23. $41\frac{7}{12} - 22\frac{1}{12}$
24. $17\frac{7}{8} + 3\frac{5}{8}$
★25. $209\frac{3}{12} + 307\frac{7}{12}$
★26. $1\frac{3}{8} + 2\frac{5}{8} + 3\frac{5}{8}$

Algebra & functions Find each missing number.

27. $\frac{10}{12} - n = \frac{4}{12}$
28. $\frac{6}{8} + x = 1\frac{1}{8}$
29. $\frac{4}{5} + z = 2\frac{2}{5}$
30. $k - 2\frac{5}{20} = 10\frac{8}{20}$
31. $b + 3\frac{1}{5} = 3\frac{3}{5}$
32. $k - 11\frac{7}{16} = 6\frac{4}{16}$

Compare. Write >, <, or =.

33. $\frac{3}{8} + \frac{7}{8}$ ● $\frac{1}{10} + \frac{7}{10}$
34. $4\frac{2}{3} - \frac{2}{3}$ ● $\frac{4}{8} + 3\frac{2}{8}$
35. $\frac{7}{16} - \frac{3}{16}$ ● $\frac{7}{12} - \frac{5}{12}$
36. $\frac{7}{8} + \frac{7}{8}$ ● $\frac{13}{16} + \frac{15}{16}$
37. $2\frac{1}{2} + 3\frac{1}{2}$ ● $2\frac{3}{5} + 3\frac{4}{5}$
38. $12\frac{19}{20} + 10\frac{17}{20}$ ● $12\frac{2}{5} + 11\frac{1}{5}$
39. $\frac{1}{3} + \frac{4}{3}$ ● $1\frac{2}{3} - 0$
40. $1\frac{1}{4} - 1$ ● $\frac{1}{4} + \frac{1}{8}$
41. $3\frac{5}{12} + 1\frac{7}{12}$ ● $6\frac{1}{2} - 3$

42. 

Here is how Andy added $5\frac{1}{8}$ and $3\frac{5}{8}$. Tell what mistake he made. Explain how to correct it.

Problem Solving

43. A stock rises from $2\frac{1}{4}$ dollars per share to $3\frac{3}{4}$ dollars. What is the price gain?

44. A software program costs $35. How much will it cost to purchase 8 copies?

45. Rita discovers that three stocks cost $4\frac{1}{4}$, $4\frac{3}{4}$, and $3\frac{3}{4}$ dollars for each share. Order the price from least to greatest.

46. **Compare:** How are adding and subtracting mixed numbers with like denominators the same?

★ 47. Sandra puts $\frac{1}{4}$ of her money in stocks and $\frac{1}{4}$ in bonds. What fraction of her money does she have left to invest?

★ 48. Stock A rises from $3\frac{1}{2}$ to $4\frac{1}{2}$. Stock B rises from $2\frac{1}{4}$ to $3\frac{3}{4}$. Which stock shows the greater gain?

Use data from *Did You Know?* for problems 49–50.

49. How much money must a company have earned over the last three years to be listed on the NYSE?

50. If a company plans to offer one million shares valued at a total of $20,000,000, will it be able to list on the NYSE?

51. **Collect Data:** Choose a stock from the financial page of the newspaper. Check its price each day for one week. Graph the data to display the price.

52. **Analyze:** If you subtract two mixed numbers with like denominators, will the difference always be a mixed number? Give an example to support your answer.

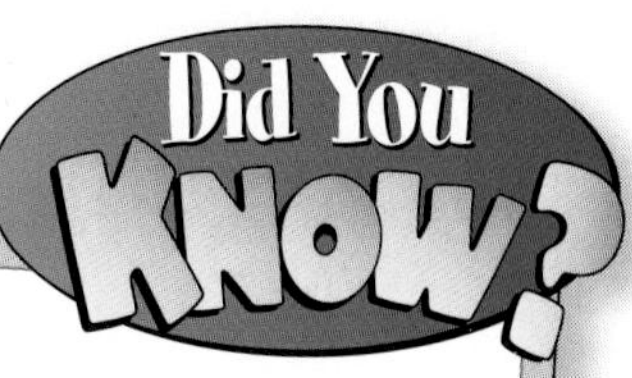

For a new company to be listed on the New York Stock Exchange (NYSE), it must meet at least these two requirements. The company must have earned at least $2,500,000 last year and at least $2,000,000 in each of the two years before that. It must offer a minimum of 1,100,000 shares of stock valued at a minimum of $18,000,000.

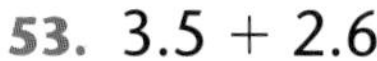

Spiral Review and Test Prep

53. $3.5 + 2.6$

54. $8.2 - 4.4$

55. $1.2 + 3.8$

56. $5.4 - 0.07$

Choose the correct answer.

57. Marian spends $2.50 more than Bill for comic books. Bill spends $4.75. How much does Marian spend?

A. $2.50
B. $4.75
C. $2.25
D. $7.25

58. The sum of two numbers is 18. Their product is 81. Which two numbers could they be?

F. 1 and 8
G. 9 and 2
H. 18 and 1
J. 9 and 9

Objective: Make a judgment to decide what operation is needed to solve a problem.

6•2

Problem Solving: Reading for Math

Choose an Operation

Beekeeper-A Sweet Job!

Read Beekeepers manage hives to produce honey and other products. In April and May, a hive made $14\frac{3}{4}$ pounds of honey. If $6\frac{1}{4}$ pounds were made in May, how much honey was made in April?

READING SKILL ▶ **Make a Judgment**

You make a judgment when you think about known facts and decide to take a certain action.

- **What do you know?** The amounts made in May, and in April and May together
- **What do you need to find?** The amount made in April

MATH SKILL ▶ **Choose the Operation**

Use key words and phrases to help choose the operation. Because words can be misleading, read the problem carefully.

Words and Phrases	Likely Operation
Total, altogether, in all, sum	Addition
How much more, how much less, increase, decrease, difference	Subtraction

Plan Subtract to find the difference between the total and the amount made in May.

Solve $14\frac{3}{4} - 6\frac{1}{4} = 8\frac{1}{2}$. The bees made $8\frac{1}{2}$ pounds of honey in April.

Look Back Is your answer reasonable?

Sum it Up Explain how you knew to subtract to solve this problem.

Practice Solve. Tell how you chose the operation.

1. During the first week of May, a hive of bees made $1\frac{1}{8}$ pounds of honey. During the second week of May, the bees made $2\frac{7}{8}$ pounds of honey. How much more honey did the bees make during the second week than the first week?

2. The greatest amount of honey Mrs. Canseco's bees ever made in one week was $6\frac{3}{4}$ pounds. The least amount of honey her bees ever made in one week was $2\frac{1}{4}$ pounds. What is the difference between the greatest and least amount of honey the bees made in a week?

Use data from the *Monthly Record* for problems 3–8.

3. What is the total amount of beeswax made in April and May?
4. What is the difference in the amount of honey the bees made in April and in June?
5. How much more beeswax did the bees make in July than in June?
6. How much honey did the bees make in May and July combined?
7. How much more honey did the bees make in April and May compared to June and July?
8. Estimate the total amount of honey the bees made during the four months listed on the monthly record.

Monthly Record of Bee Products

Month	Total Honey (in Pounds)	Total Beeswax (in Pounds)
April	$44\frac{3}{4}$	$6\frac{2}{3}$
May	$38\frac{5}{8}$	$8\frac{1}{3}$
June	$37\frac{1}{4}$	7
July	$40\frac{3}{8}$	$9\frac{1}{4}$

Spiral Review and Test Prep

Choose the correct answer.

A beekeeper shipped 3 jars of honey. Each jar contained $2\frac{1}{2}$ pounds of honey. The beekeeper shipped a total of $7\frac{1}{2}$ pounds of honey.

9. Which of the following statements is true?
   - A. Each jar held 3 pounds of honey.
   - B. Two jars contained 6 pounds of honey.
   - C. The beekeeper shipped 7 jars of honey.
   - D. Two jars contained 5 pounds of honey.

10. When you are deciding which operation to use, you should
    - F. try subtraction first.
    - G. look for clues in the problem.
    - H. take a good guess.
    - J. estimate the answer.

Problem Solving

Objective: Add fractions with unlike denominators.

6•3 Explore Adding Fractions with Unlike Denominators

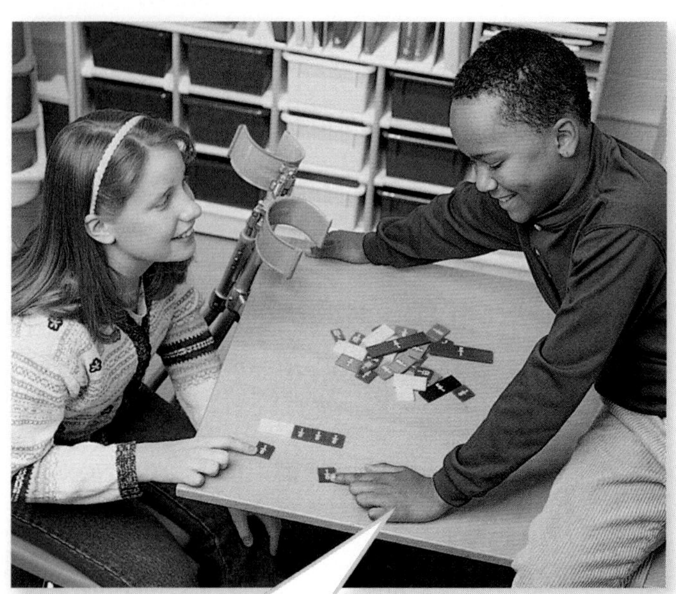

Learn

You can use fraction strips to explore adding fractions with unlike denominators.

Work Together

You Will Need
- **fraction strips**

► Use fraction strips to find $\frac{3}{8} + \frac{1}{4}$.

Model $\frac{3}{8} + \frac{1}{4}$.

$\frac{1}{8}$	$\frac{1}{8}$	$\frac{1}{8}$		$\frac{1}{4}$

$\frac{3}{8} + \frac{1}{4}$

Rename $\frac{1}{4}$ as $\frac{2}{8}$.

$\frac{1}{8}$	$\frac{1}{8}$	$\frac{1}{8}$		$\frac{1}{4}$	
$\frac{1}{8}$	$\frac{1}{8}$	$\frac{1}{8}$		$\frac{1}{8}$	$\frac{1}{8}$

Think: $\frac{1}{4}$ is the same as $\frac{2}{8}$.

Add $\frac{3}{8} + \frac{2}{8}$.

$\frac{1}{8}$	$\frac{1}{8}$	$\frac{1}{8}$		$\frac{1}{8}$	$\frac{1}{8}$

Record the addition sentence. $\frac{3}{8} + \frac{1}{4} = \frac{3}{8} + \frac{2}{8} = \frac{5}{8}$.

► Use fraction strips to solve.
Record each addition sentence.

$\frac{1}{2} + \frac{1}{4}$ $\frac{1}{3} + \frac{3}{4}$ $\frac{1}{6} + \frac{2}{3}$ $\frac{2}{3} + \frac{1}{4}$

Make Connections

You can use the LCD to add fractions with unlike denominators.

Remember: The least common denominator (LCD) is the least common multiple (LCM) of the denominators.

Find: $\frac{5}{6} + \frac{1}{4}$

	Using Models	Using Paper and Pencil
1 Show each addend.	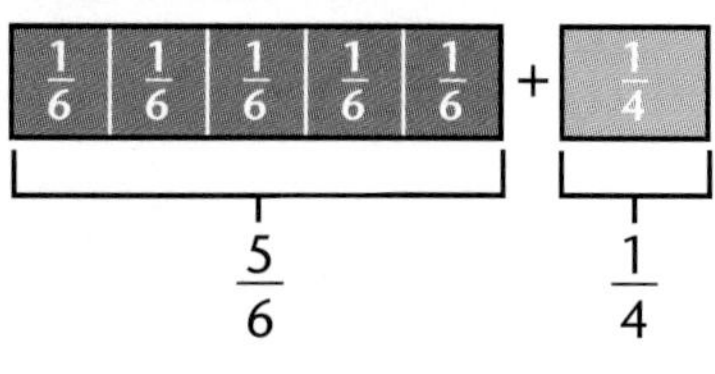	Find the LCM of 6 and 4. Multiples of 4: 4, 8, 12, 16, . . . Multiples of 6: 6, 12, 18, 24, . . . The LCM is 12.
2 Show $\frac{5}{6}$ and $\frac{1}{4}$ using 12 as a common denominator.	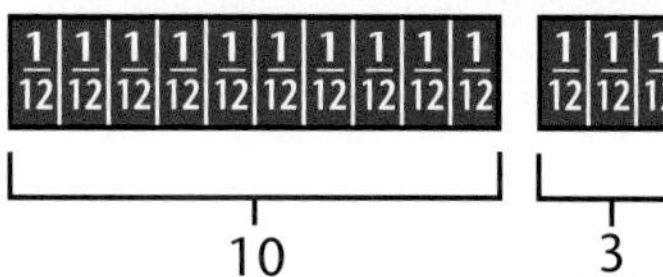	Rename $\frac{5}{6}$ and $\frac{1}{4}$ using the LCD 12: $\frac{5}{6} = \frac{10}{12}$ $\frac{1}{4} = \frac{3}{12}$
3 Combine strips to add.		Add. $\frac{5}{6} + \frac{1}{4} = \frac{10}{12} + \frac{3}{12} = \frac{13}{12}$
4 Simplify.	1	Simplify. $\frac{13}{12} = 1\frac{1}{12}$

Try It

Add. You may use fraction strips.

1. $\frac{2}{3} + \frac{1}{6}$
2. $\frac{1}{4} + \frac{5}{12}$
3. $\frac{2}{5} + \frac{1}{2}$
4. $\frac{1}{3} + \frac{1}{4}$

How is adding fractions with unlike denominators similar to adding fractions with like denominators? How is it different?

Practice

Add.

5. $\frac{5}{6} + \frac{1}{12}$
6. $\frac{3}{8} + \frac{5}{16}$
7. $\frac{1}{6} + \frac{3}{4}$
8. $\frac{2}{5} + \frac{3}{10}$
9. $\frac{2}{3} + \frac{3}{4}$
10. $\frac{5}{8} + \frac{1}{4}$
11. $\frac{1}{2} + \frac{1}{3}$
12. $\frac{2}{5} + \frac{3}{12}$
13. **Summarize** the steps to add $\frac{2}{5}$ and $\frac{1}{2}$.

Objective: Subtract fractions with unlike denominators.

6•4 Explore Subtracting Fractions with Unlike Denominators

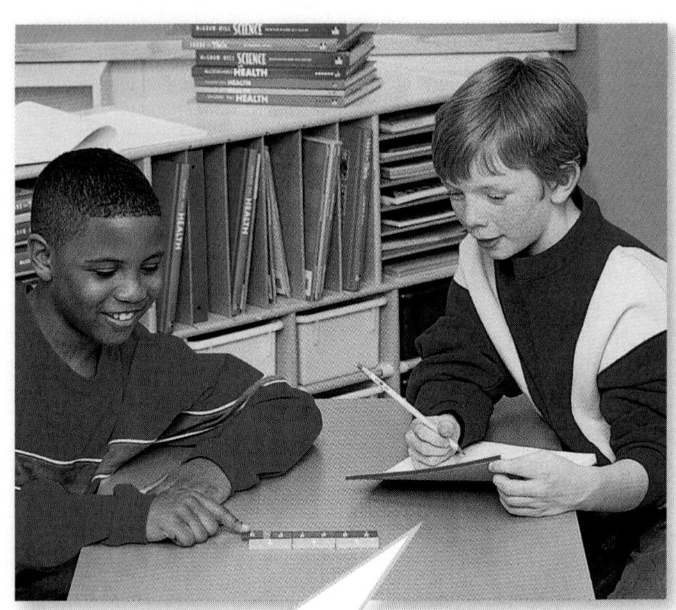

Learn

You can use fraction strips to explore subtracting fractions with unlike denominators.

Work Together

▶ Use fraction strips to find $\frac{3}{4} - \frac{1}{8}$.

You Will Need
- **fraction strips**

Model $\frac{3}{4}$.

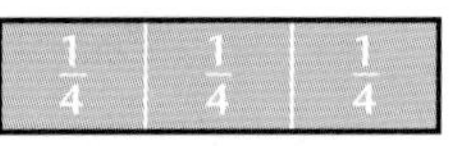

Find out how many eighths equal $\frac{3}{4}$.

$\frac{3}{4} = \frac{6}{8}$

Take away strips to subtract.

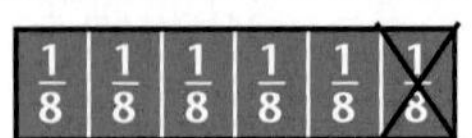

Record the subtraction sentence. $\frac{3}{4} - \frac{1}{8} = \frac{6}{8} - \frac{1}{8} = \frac{5}{8}$

▶ Use fraction strips to solve.

$\frac{4}{5} - \frac{7}{10}$ $\frac{2}{3} - \frac{7}{12}$ $\frac{1}{2} - \frac{2}{5}$ $\frac{2}{3} - \frac{1}{4}$

Make Connections

You can use the least common denominator (LCD) to subtract fractions with unlike denominators.

Find: $\frac{1}{2} - \frac{2}{5}$.

Think: You can find the LCD by writing multiples of each denominator and choosing the least multiple shared by both numbers.

Using Models / Using Paper and Pencil

1 Use fraction strips to show each number.

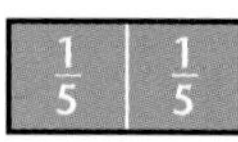

$\frac{1}{2}$ $\frac{2}{5}$

Find the LCD of $\frac{1}{2}$ and $\frac{2}{5}$.

Multiples of 2: 2, 4, 6, 8, 10 . . .

Multiples of 5: 5, 10, 15, 20, 25 . . .

The LCD is 10.

2 Show $\frac{1}{2}$ and $\frac{2}{5}$ using 10 as a denominator.

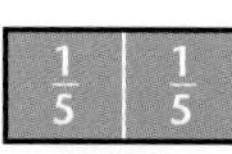

$\frac{1}{2} = \frac{5}{10}$ $\frac{2}{5} = \frac{4}{10}$

Rename $\frac{1}{2}$ and $\frac{2}{5}$ using the LCD 10:

$\frac{1}{2} = \frac{5}{10}$

$\frac{2}{5} = \frac{4}{10}$

3 Take away strips to subtract.

Subtract.

$\frac{5}{10} - \frac{4}{10} = \frac{1}{10}$

4 Simplify.

Try It

Subtract. You may use fraction strips.

1. $\frac{7}{8} - \frac{1}{4}$
2. $\frac{5}{6} - \frac{1}{2}$
3. $\frac{5}{6} - \frac{1}{4}$
4. $\frac{2}{3} - \frac{3}{10}$

Summarize the steps you would use to subtract $\frac{7}{8} - \frac{1}{4}$. What is the difference?

Practice

Subtract.

5. $\frac{5}{8} - \frac{1}{2}$
6. $\frac{3}{4} - \frac{5}{8}$
7. $\frac{1}{6} - \frac{1}{8}$
8. $\frac{13}{20} - \frac{2}{5}$
9. $\frac{1}{3} - \frac{1}{8}$
10. $\frac{5}{6} - \frac{1}{2}$
11. $\frac{4}{5} - \frac{3}{10}$
12. $\frac{7}{8} - \frac{1}{4}$
13. **Analyze:** What is the first thing you must do when subtracting fractions with unlike denominators?

Objective: Add and subtract fractions with unlike denominators.

6·5 Add and Subtract Fractions with Unlike Denominators

Learn

How do store owners learn about new products? A sales representative travels to stores and shows them. Some sales representatives record their mileage and report it as part of their expenses. One day a representative drives to his client and then to the office. How far does he drive?

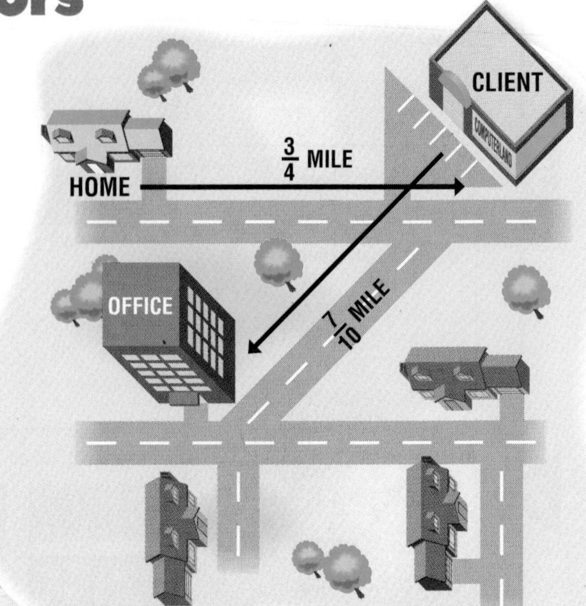

Example 1

Add: $\frac{3}{4} + \frac{7}{10}$ to solve the problem.

Think: You can find the LCD by writing multiples of each denominator and choosing the least multiple shared by both numbers.

1 Find the least common denominator (LCD).

Multiples of 4: 4, 8, 12, 16, 20...

Multiples of 10: 10, 20, 30...

The LCD is 20.

2 Rename each fraction using the LCD.

$\frac{3}{4} = \frac{15}{20} \qquad \frac{7}{10} = \frac{14}{20}$

3 Add. Simplify.

$\frac{15}{20} + \frac{14}{20} = \frac{29}{20} = 1\frac{9}{20}$

The representative drives $1\frac{9}{20}$ miles.

More Examples

A

Find: $\frac{2}{3} + \frac{5}{6}$

Think: The LCD is 6.

$\frac{2}{3} = \frac{4}{6}$

$\frac{4}{6} + \frac{5}{6} = \frac{9}{6} = 1\frac{3}{6} = 1\frac{1}{2}$

B

Find: $\frac{5}{6} + \frac{3}{4}$

Think: The LCD is 12.

$\frac{5}{6} = \frac{10}{12} \qquad \frac{3}{4} = \frac{9}{12}$

$\frac{10}{12} + \frac{9}{12} = \frac{19}{12} = 1\frac{7}{12}$

A representative drives $\frac{1}{3}$ mile to a client's store and $\frac{1}{4}$ mile to the office. How much farther is the store than the office?

Example 2

Find: $\frac{1}{3} - \frac{1}{4}$

Subtracting fractions with unlike denominators is similar to adding fractions with unlike denominators.

Step 1: Rename each fraction using the LCD. The LCD is 12.

$\frac{1}{3} = \frac{4}{12}$ $\frac{1}{4} = \frac{3}{12}$

Step 2: Subtract. Simplify.

Think: Keep the fractions in the proper order.

$\frac{4}{12} - \frac{3}{12} = \frac{1}{12}$

The store is $\frac{1}{12}$ mile farther than the office.

More Examples

A

Find: $\frac{4}{5} - \frac{1}{4}$

$\frac{4}{5} = \frac{16}{20}$

$\frac{1}{4} = \frac{5}{20}$

$\frac{16}{20} - \frac{5}{20} = \frac{11}{20}$

Think: The LCD is 20.

B

Find: $\frac{11}{12} - \frac{2}{3}$

$\frac{2}{3} = \frac{8}{12}$

$\frac{11}{12} - \frac{8}{12} = \frac{3}{12} = \frac{1}{4}$

Think: The LCD is 12.

Try It **Add or subtract. Write your answer in simplest form.**

1. $\frac{1}{2} + \frac{1}{3}$
2. $\frac{3}{4} + \frac{1}{2}$
3. $\frac{7}{8} - \frac{1}{6}$
4. $\frac{5}{6} - \frac{1}{4}$
5. $\frac{7}{8} + \frac{1}{12}$
6. $\frac{3}{4} + \frac{1}{8}$
7. $\frac{2}{3} + \frac{3}{4}$
8. $\frac{9}{10} - \frac{3}{5}$
9. $\frac{3}{4} - \frac{3}{10}$
10. $\frac{1}{3} + \frac{1}{2}$

Summarize the steps you use to subtract fractions with unlike denominators.

Practice **Add or subtract. Write your answer in simplest form.**

11. $\frac{3}{8} + \frac{3}{4}$

12. $\frac{1}{3} + \frac{1}{2}$

13. $\frac{3}{4} + \frac{7}{8}$

14. $\frac{4}{5} + \frac{9}{20}$

15. $\frac{4}{5} - \frac{9}{20}$

16. $\frac{5}{12} + \frac{2}{3}$

17. $\frac{5}{6} - \frac{5}{24}$

18. $\frac{1}{2} + \frac{4}{5}$

19. $\frac{3}{4} + \frac{7}{12}$

20. $\frac{2}{3} + \frac{1}{12}$

21. $\frac{7}{8} + \frac{1}{2}$

22. $\frac{11}{20} + \frac{1}{4}$

23. $\frac{5}{16} + \frac{3}{16}$

24. $\frac{2}{15} + \frac{9}{10}$

25. $\frac{1}{2} - \frac{1}{3}$

26. $\frac{3}{4} - \frac{1}{12}$

27. $\frac{5}{6} - \frac{1}{6}$

28. $\frac{3}{8} - \frac{5}{16}$

29. $\frac{4}{5} - \frac{1}{4}$

30. $\frac{9}{10} - \frac{3}{10}$

31. $\frac{4}{5} - \frac{3}{10}$

32. $\frac{7}{8} - \frac{5}{6}$

33. $\frac{9}{42} - \frac{1}{7}$

★**34.** $\frac{13}{64} - \frac{3}{16}$

★**35.** $\frac{15}{21} - \frac{7}{20}$

Use the fractions in the box to write an addition or subtraction sentence that gives the answer shown.

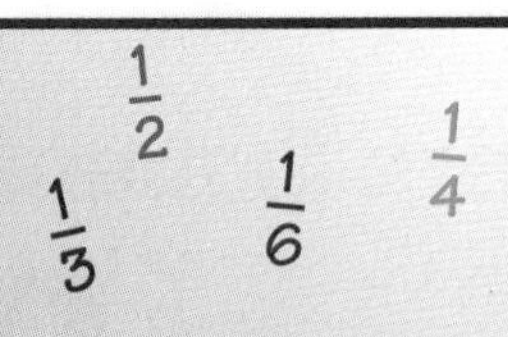

36. $\frac{5}{6}$

★ **37.** $\frac{1}{12}$

★ **38.** $\frac{2}{3}$

39. $1\frac{1}{4}$

Algebra & functions **Find the number that makes each sentence true.**

40. $n + \frac{3}{10} = \frac{3}{5}$

41. $x + \frac{5}{16} = \frac{11}{16}$

42. $\frac{3}{8} - \frac{1}{4} = t$

43. $\frac{19}{20} - y = \frac{7}{20}$

44. $\frac{5}{6} - \frac{7}{12} = d$

45. $g - \frac{1}{4} = \frac{1}{4}$

46. $\frac{9}{10} - \frac{3}{4} = b$

47. $r - \frac{1}{6} = \frac{7}{12}$

48. **Make it RIGHT**

Here is how Lisa added $\frac{3}{4} + \frac{9}{10}$. Tell what mistake she made. Explain how to correct it.

Problem Solving

49. Sales representatives sometimes give presentations to large groups of customers. If a presentation takes $\frac{1}{2}$ hour to prepare and $\frac{3}{4}$ hour to present, how much time does the presentation take altogether?

50. Some sales representatives offer free samples to new and old customers. If $\frac{1}{2}$ the samples go to one client and $\frac{1}{3}$ to another client, what fraction has been given away?

51. Ms. Fallow travels $\frac{7}{8}$ mile to her office. Mr. Reston travels $\frac{7}{10}$ mile. How much farther does Ms. Fallow travel than Mr. Reston?

52. Each trip a sales representative makes takes $\frac{3}{4}$ hour to drive to a client. Estimate how many hours it will take to make the trip 16 times.

Use data from the table for problems 53–55.

53. A representative travels from New York City to Boston by going through Hartford. How far does she travel in all?

54. **What if** during one year, a representative makes 17 trips from Atlanta to Cincinnati? How many miles does she travel?

★ 55. Mr. Chan traveled from Charlotte to Baltimore during week 1. During week 2 he traveled from Charlotte to Atlanta. During which week did he travel more? by how much?

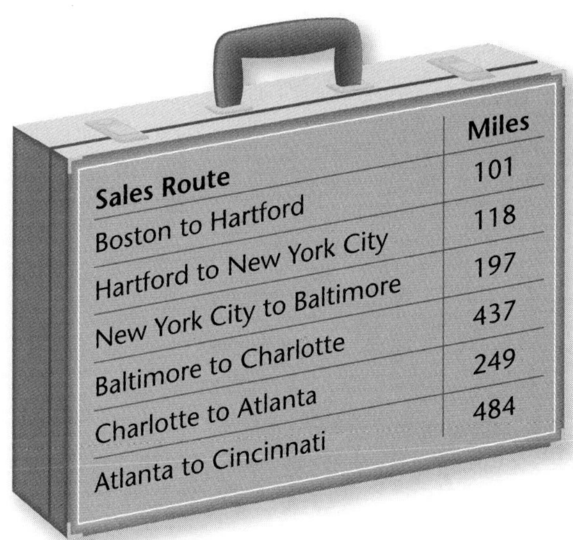

Sales Route	Miles
Boston to Hartford	101
Hartford to New York City	118
New York City to Baltimore	197
Baltimore to Charlotte	437
Charlotte to Atlanta	249
Atlanta to Cincinnati	484

★ 56. **Analyze:** When will the difference of two fractions be equal to zero?

57. **Create a problem** that must be solved by adding or subtracting fractions with unlike denominators. Solve it, then give it to another student to solve.

Spiral Review and Test Prep

Is each number prime or composite?

58. 43
59. 45
60. 17
61. 133

Choose the correct answer.

62. Which number is an equivalent decimal to 2.3?
A. 20.3
B. 2.03
C. 2.30
D. Not Here

63. What is the greatest common factor of 12 and 30?
F. 2
G. 4
H. 6
J. 12

Extra Practice, page 288

Check Your Progress A

Add or subtract. Write your answer in simplest form. **(pages 252–265)**

1. $\frac{3}{8} + \frac{7}{8}$

2. $\frac{5}{6} + \frac{2}{3}$

3. $\frac{7}{10} + \frac{1}{5}$

4. $\frac{4}{5} - \frac{3}{10}$

5. $4\frac{1}{4} + 7\frac{3}{4}$

6. $\frac{11}{12} - \frac{5}{6}$

7. $19\frac{5}{8} + 24\frac{7}{8}$

8. $36\frac{3}{10} + 45\frac{1}{2}$

9. $\frac{7}{8} - \frac{5}{8}$

10. $17\frac{5}{6} - 9\frac{1}{2}$

11. $\frac{13}{16} - \frac{9}{16}$

12. $\frac{11}{12} + \frac{11}{12}$

13. $12\frac{3}{4} - 4\frac{1}{4}$

14. $10\frac{1}{8} + 15\frac{1}{16}$

15. $64\frac{17}{20} - 39\frac{11}{20}$

16. $95\frac{1}{6} - 46\frac{1}{12}$

Solve. **(pages 252–265)**

17. A stock price falls from $\frac{3}{4}$ to $\frac{1}{4}$ for each share. How much does the stock fall?

18. You are given the amount of honey produced by a hive of bees for each of the last 3 months. You are asked to find how much honey was made during that time. Which operation will you choose? Explain.

19. Tim's bees make $\frac{3}{4}$ pound of honey on Tuesday. If they make $\frac{1}{2}$ pound more than that on Wednesday, how much do they make on Wednesday?

20. **Generalize:** If you add a fraction less than 1 with another fraction less than 1, will the answer always be less than one? Give an example to support your answer.

NS 2.3; MR 1.1, 2.3, 3.2

Use Fraction Strips to Add

Brent has $\frac{5}{6}$ yard of ribbon on one spool and $\frac{3}{4}$ yard on another spool. How many yards of ribbon does Brent have?

You can model the number of yards of ribbon using fraction strips.

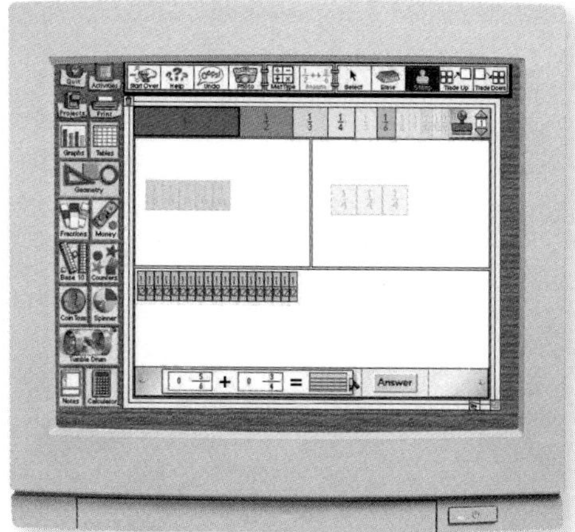

- Choose addition for the mat type.
- Stamp out five $\frac{1}{6}$ fraction strips in one section.
- Stamp out three $\frac{1}{4}$ fraction strips in the other section.
- Click on the Answer key.
- Rename up or down as necessary.

The number boxes show that you are finding $\frac{5}{6} + \frac{3}{4}$ and show how you trade.

How many yards of ribbon does Brent have?

Use the computer to model each addition. Then find each sum.

1. $\frac{1}{6} + \frac{2}{3}$ **2.** $\frac{1}{2} + \frac{5}{6}$ **3.** $\frac{2}{3} + \frac{3}{4}$ **4.** $\frac{1}{4} + \frac{5}{6}$

Solve. Write your answer in simplest form.

5. Mandi spent $\frac{3}{4}$ hour writing a report and $\frac{1}{2}$ hour proofreading it. How long did she work on her report?

6. Ms. Damron drove $\frac{2}{3}$ mile from her home to the grocery store and then drove $\frac{1}{2}$ mile from the grocery store to the gas station. How far did she drive?

7. **Analyze:** How do fraction strips help you add fractions?

For more practice, use Math Traveler™.

Objective: Add mixed numbers with unlike denominators.

Explore Adding Mixed Numbers with Unlike Denominators

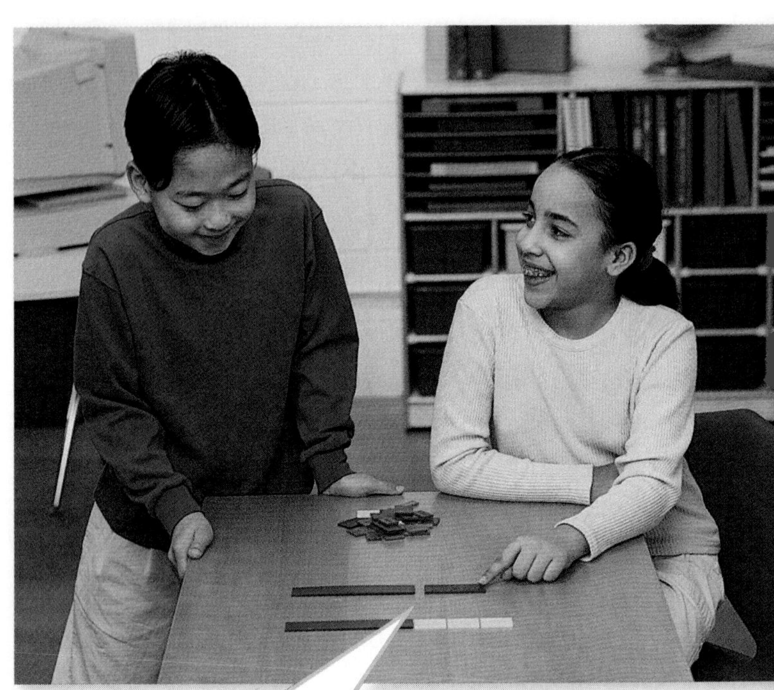

Learn

You can use fraction strips to explore adding mixed numbers with unlike denominators.

Work Together

You Will Need
- **fraction strips**

▶ Use fraction strips to find $1\frac{1}{2} + 1\frac{3}{4}$.

1 Model $1\frac{1}{2}$ and $1\frac{3}{4}$.

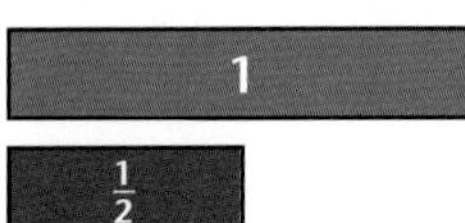

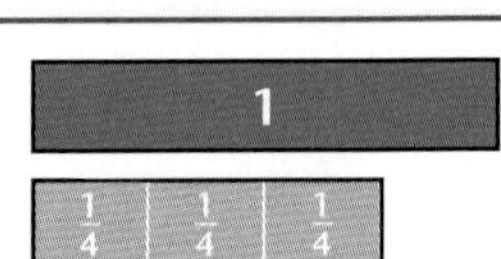

2 Join the whole strips.

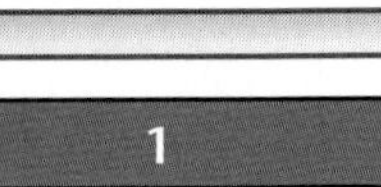

Join the fraction strips.

3 Simplify.

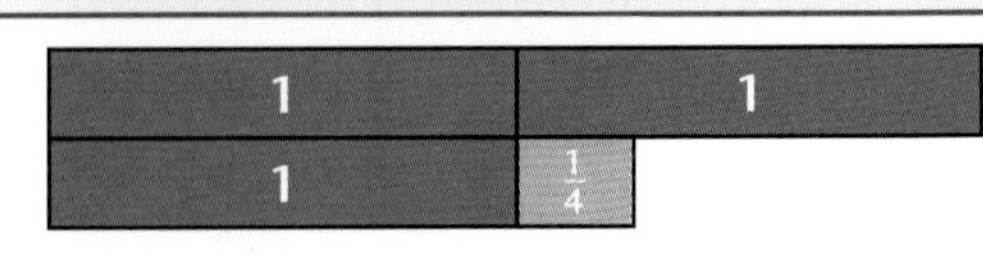

Simplify. Record the addition sentence.

▶ Use fraction strips to solve.
Record each addition sentence.

$1\frac{1}{5} + 1\frac{1}{10}$ $1\frac{1}{3} + 2\frac{1}{4}$ $1\frac{1}{3} + 1\frac{5}{6}$ $2\frac{1}{2} + 1\frac{2}{3}$

Make Connections

Find: $1\frac{5}{6} + 1\frac{3}{4}$

	Using Models	Using Paper and Pencil
1 Model $1\frac{5}{6}$ and $1\frac{3}{4}$.	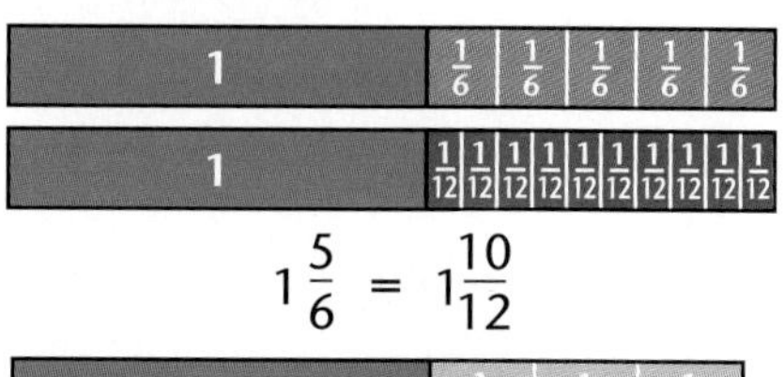	Find the LCD of $\frac{5}{6}$ and $\frac{3}{4}$. The LCD is 12.
2 Show $1\frac{5}{6}$ and $1\frac{3}{4}$ using 12 as a denominator.	$1\frac{5}{6} = 1\frac{10}{12}$ $1\frac{3}{4} = 1\frac{9}{12}$	Rename $1\frac{5}{6}$ and $1\frac{3}{4}$ using the LCD 12: $1\frac{5}{6} = 1\frac{10}{12}$ $1\frac{3}{4} = 1\frac{9}{12}$
3 Join the whole strips, then join the fraction strips. Simplify.	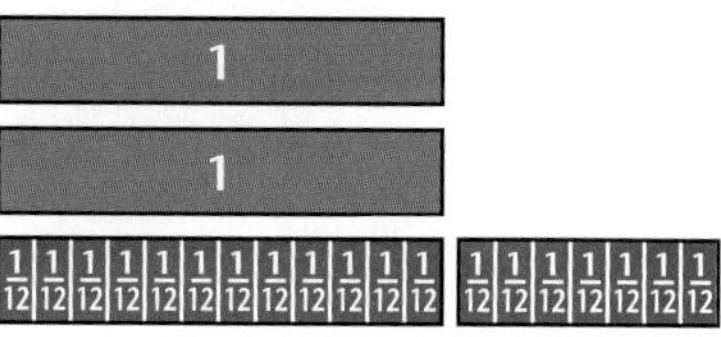	Add the whole numbers. Add the fractions. $1\frac{10}{12} + 1\frac{9}{12} = 2\frac{19}{12}$ Simplify. $2\frac{19}{12} = 2 + 1\frac{7}{12} = 3\frac{7}{12}$

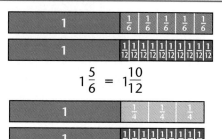

Try It Add. You may use fraction strips. Simplify.

1. $1\frac{1}{4} + 2\frac{3}{8}$
2. $2\frac{2}{3} + 3\frac{1}{6}$
3. $2\frac{3}{4} + 2\frac{5}{6}$
4. $1\frac{3}{10} + 1\frac{1}{2}$

Sum it Up Explain how you would add $1\frac{3}{4} + 2\frac{1}{2}$.

Practice Add. Write your answer in simplest form.

5. $2\frac{4}{5} + 1\frac{1}{10}$
6. $1\frac{1}{12} + 1\frac{1}{4}$
7. $3\frac{2}{3} + 4\frac{5}{6}$
8. $3\frac{1}{4} + 4\frac{5}{6}$
9. $1\frac{2}{5} + 1\frac{1}{2}$
10. $1\frac{1}{6} + 3\frac{1}{4}$
11. $2\frac{1}{3} + 2\frac{3}{5}$
12. $2\frac{1}{16} + 1\frac{5}{8}$
13. **Analyze:** How is adding mixed numbers with unlike denominators different from adding fractions with unlike denominators.

Objective: Add mixed numbers with unlike denominators.

6·7 Add Mixed Numbers with Unlike Denominators

Learn

Architects design buildings for homes, offices, and any place where people work, live, and play. An architect wants to put a shelf that measures $6\frac{3}{4}$ feet wide next to a $2\frac{1}{2}$ foot wide window. Will they fit along the wall?

Example

Find: $6\frac{3}{4} + 2\frac{1}{2}$

1 Rename the fractions using the LCD. The LCD is 4.

$$2\frac{1}{2} = 2\frac{2}{4}$$

$$6\frac{3}{4} = 6\frac{3}{4}$$

2 Add the whole numbers. Add the fractions.

$$\begin{array}{r} 2\frac{2}{4} \\ +6\frac{3}{4} \\ \hline 8\frac{5}{4} \end{array}$$

3 Simplify.

$$8\frac{5}{4} = 8 + 1\frac{1}{4} = 9\frac{1}{4}$$

Since $9\frac{1}{4} > 9$, the shelf and window will not fit along the wall.

Try It

Add. Write your answer in simplest form.

1. $5\frac{3}{8} + 14\frac{1}{4}$
2. $4\frac{2}{3} + 5\frac{5}{6}$
3. $25\frac{1}{2} + 41\frac{1}{3}$
4. $37\frac{3}{4} + 59\frac{5}{6}$

Compare and contrast adding mixed numbers with like and unlike denominators.

Practice

Add. Write your answer in simplest form.

5. $1\frac{3}{4} + 2\frac{2}{3}$
6. $11\frac{9}{10} + 17\frac{1}{4}$
7. $25\frac{4}{5} + 7\frac{1}{3}$
8. $6\frac{3}{4} + 11\frac{5}{8}$
9. $9\frac{3}{20} + 32\frac{1}{4}$
10. $87\frac{1}{3} + 53\frac{7}{24}$
11. $6\frac{4}{5} + 13\frac{2}{3}$
12. $\frac{1}{5} + 38\frac{3}{4}$
13. $10\frac{4}{5} + 15\frac{9}{10}$
14. $67\frac{9}{10} + 27\frac{5}{8}$
15. $85\frac{3}{10} + 57\frac{9}{20}$
16. $207\frac{5}{6} + 120\frac{11}{12}$
17. $108\frac{9}{20} + 1\frac{4}{30}$
18. $88\frac{5}{6} + \frac{1}{6}$
19. $\frac{7}{8} + 48\frac{5}{16}$
20. $\frac{2}{5} + 95\frac{1}{2}$

Algebra & functions **Find the number that makes each sentence true.**

21. $1\frac{7}{8} + 1\frac{3}{4} = \blacksquare\frac{5}{8}$
22. $6\frac{8}{35} + 1\frac{8}{21} = 7\frac{\blacksquare}{105}$
★23. $5\,\blacksquare + 4\frac{1}{6} = 9\frac{5}{12}$
★24. $\blacksquare + 5\frac{1}{4} + 7\frac{1}{6} = 13\frac{3}{4}$

Problem Solving

25. An architect wants to put double doors in an entryway. Each door measures $3\frac{1}{2}$ feet across. How wide is the double door?

26. A wall of windows extends 56 feet. Each window is 8 feet wide. If each window touches the one next to it, how many windows are on the wall?

27. **Language Arts:** The word *architect* comes from the Greek words *archi* + *tekton,* meaning "master builder." If an architect spends 10 months each year in school for 6 years, how many months does he or she spend in school?

28. Suppose an architect works $62\frac{1}{2}$ hours designing a home and $12\frac{3}{4}$ hours planning a garage. How many hours did it take to design the two buildings?

29. **Summarize** the steps you take to add mixed numbers with unlike denominators.

30. **Create a problem** about an architect that can be solved by adding mixed numbers with unlike denominators.

Spiral Review and Test Prep

31. 4.5×1.3
32. $4.5 \div 1.5$
33. 2.22×2
34. $15 \div 2.5$

Choose the correct answer.

35. Lonnie spends $2.25 for each comic book. He buys 8 comic books. How much does he spend?
   A. $2.25
   B. $8.00
   C. $16.25
   D. $18.00

36. Two people in a class of 23 wear the same color T-shirt. Write this number as a fraction.
   F. $\frac{2}{23}$
   G. $\frac{23}{2}$
   H. 46
   J. Not Here

Objective: Apply properties of addition to fractions and mixed numbers.

6·8 Properties of Addition

Algebra & functions

Learn

Math Words

Associative Property of Addition

Commutative Property of Addition

Identity Property of Addition

You can use the properties of addition to help add more than two fractions.

The properties you learned for adding whole numbers are also true for fractions and mixed numbers.

Commutative Property of Addition

When adding, the order of the addends does not change the sum.

$2\frac{1}{2} + 3\frac{1}{4} = 5\frac{3}{4}$ $\quad$ $3\frac{1}{4} + 2\frac{1}{2} = 5\frac{3}{4}$

Associative Property of Addition

When adding three addends, the grouping of the addends does not change the sum.

$(7\frac{1}{10} + 5\frac{9}{16}) + \frac{3}{8} = 7\frac{1}{10} + (5\frac{9}{16} + \frac{3}{8})$

Identity Property of Addition

When a number is added to 0, the sum is that number.

$\frac{5}{8} + 0 = \frac{5}{8}$ $\quad$ $0 + \frac{5}{8} = \frac{5}{8}$

Example

Think: Use the Associative Property.

Find: $1 + \frac{1}{4} + \frac{1}{4} + \frac{1}{2}$

$$1 + \left(\frac{1}{4} + \frac{1}{4}\right) + \frac{1}{2} \rightarrow 1 + \left(\frac{1}{2}\right) + \frac{1}{2} = 1 + \left(\frac{1}{2} + \frac{1}{2}\right) = 1 + 1 = 2$$

The sum is 2.

Try It

Find each missing number. Identify the property.

1. $85\frac{1}{3} + y = 85\frac{1}{3}$
2. $m + \frac{7}{10} = \frac{7}{10} + \frac{3}{5}$
3. $12\frac{3}{4} + \left(\frac{1}{2} + \frac{1}{3}\right) = \left(d + \frac{1}{2}\right) + \frac{1}{3}$
4. $\left(\frac{1}{6} + \frac{1}{4}\right) + \frac{1}{6} = \frac{1}{6} + \left(h + \frac{1}{6}\right)$

Explain how you would use the Associative Property to add $\frac{3}{4} + \frac{1}{2} + \frac{1}{4}$. What is the sum?

Practice

Find each missing number. Identify the property you used.

5. $\blacksquare + \frac{2}{3} = \frac{2}{3}$

6. $\blacksquare + 3\frac{9}{10} = 3\frac{9}{10} + 5\frac{7}{8}$

7. $\frac{7}{16} + \blacksquare = \frac{3}{5} + \frac{7}{16}$

8. $17\frac{9}{10} + \blacksquare = 17\frac{9}{10}$

9. $\frac{1}{8} + \left(\blacksquare + \frac{1}{12}\right) = \left(\frac{1}{8} + \frac{1}{10}\right) + \frac{1}{12}$

10. $\blacksquare + \left(\frac{1}{12} + \frac{1}{12}\right) = \left(\frac{1}{2} + \frac{1}{12}\right) + \frac{1}{12}$

Use the Associative Property to solve. Show your work.

11. $\frac{1}{12} + \left(\frac{1}{12} + \frac{1}{4}\right)$

12. $2\frac{1}{2} + \left(3\frac{1}{2} + \frac{7}{8}\right)$

13. $\frac{9}{10} + \left(\frac{3}{10} + \frac{21}{4}\right)$

14. $\left(\frac{1}{16} + \frac{3}{10}\right) + \frac{7}{10}$

15. $\left(\frac{3}{16} + 2\frac{1}{2}\right) + 3\frac{1}{2}$

16. $\left(3\frac{1}{3} + 5\frac{3}{4}\right) + 7\frac{3}{4}$

Algebra & functions **Copy and complete.**

17. $\frac{7}{8} + \frac{9}{20} = \frac{9}{20} + n$

18. $9\frac{3}{5} + s = 9\frac{3}{5}$

19. $0 + t = 75\frac{9}{16}$

20. $12\frac{3}{8} + 4\frac{9}{10} = g + 12\frac{3}{8}$

21. $\frac{1}{2} + \left(\frac{1}{3} + \frac{1}{4}\right) = \left(\frac{1}{2} + k\right) + \frac{1}{3}$

★ 22. $1\frac{2}{3} + \left(\frac{1}{3} + \frac{1}{4}\right) = \left(1\frac{2}{3} + \frac{1}{3}\right) + d$

Problem Solving

23. A songwriter combines 2 whole beats, 1 quarter beat, and an eighth beat. How many beats are there altogether?

24. **Analyze:** Chloe adds $\left(\frac{1}{2} + \frac{1}{3}\right) + \frac{1}{4}$. Joe adds $\left(\frac{1}{3} + \frac{1}{4}\right) + \frac{1}{2}$. Will they get the same answer? Explain.

25. Jeremy practices playing piano for $\frac{3}{4}$ hour on Monday, $1\frac{1}{2}$ hours on Tuesday, no hours on Wednesday and $\frac{1}{2}$ hour on Thursday. How many hours did he practice over the four days?

★ 26. **Number Sense:** A musician wants to make a rhythm using a half note, a quarter note, and an eighth note. How many different ways can these 3 notes be combined?

Spiral Review and Test Prep

27. $480 \div 5$

28. 27×6

29. $276 \div 12$

30. 46×3

Choose the correct answer.

31. Which number is 100 greater than 2,698,801?
   - A. 3,698,801
   - B. 2,798,801
   - C. 2,698,901
   - D. 2,698,811

32. What is the least common multiple (LCM) of the numbers 3 and 7?
   - F. 7
   - G. 14
   - H. 21
   - J. 28

Objective: Solve problems by writing an equation.

Problem Solving: Strategy
Write an Equation

Read

Read the problem carefully.

Professional bakers use so much flour, sugar, and butter that they buy their ingredients in large amounts. A baker buys a bag of flour. After a week, there are $4\frac{1}{2}$ pounds left. How much flour did he use?

- **What do you know?** The amount of flour in the bag before and after use
- **What are you asked to find?** How much flour has been used

Plan

You can write an equation to make it easier to solve the problem.

Solve

Write an equation to show the problem.

$4\frac{1}{2} + \blacksquare = 25$

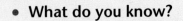

$4\frac{1}{2} + 20\frac{1}{2} = 24\frac{2}{2} = 25$

The baker used $20\frac{1}{2}$ pounds of flour.

Think: The number that makes the number sentence true is $20\frac{1}{2}$.

Look Back

Is your answer reasonable?

Explain how you use equations to solve problems.

Practice Write an equation, then solve.

1. A baker buys 20 pounds of butter. At the end of the week, there is only $1\frac{1}{4}$ pounds left. How much did she use?

2. A pie shop owner pays a cashier \$60 a day. After paying the employee, the owner has \$140 for the day. How much did the store earn during the day?

3. If $2\frac{1}{2}$ pounds of cookies are left in a cookie tin, how many pounds were there if $2\frac{1}{4}$ pounds have already been eaten?

4. **What if** a bag contains $7\frac{1}{2}$ cups of flour. There are $1\frac{3}{4}$ cups left in the bag. How many cups have been used?

Problem Solving

Mixed Strategy Review

CHOOSE A STRATEGY
- Logical Reasoning
- Draw a Diagram
- Make a Graph
- Make a Table or List
- Find a Pattern
- Guess and Check
- Write an Equation
- Work Backward
- Solve a Simpler Problem
- Conduct an Experiment

5. Ms. Miller is throwing a party. She expects 210 people to come, but 31 more people than expected show up. How many people come to the party?

6. Mr. Rivera plans the seating for a wedding. Sixteen people will sit at the head table. The other guests will sit at round tables that seat 8 people each. How many round tables does he need if a total of 64 guests attend the wedding?

7. Latisha makes ceramic mugs. She sells them for \$2.59 each. She pays \$7.50 to enter an arts festival. She sells 29 of her mugs at the arts festival. How much money does Latisha make after paying to enter the festival?

8. Leonard buys blue socks and white socks. Blue socks cost \$8 per pair and white socks cost \$5. He buys a total of 7 pairs and spends \$44. How many pairs of each color socks did he buy?

Use data in the table for problems 9–10.

Tunnels

Name	Country	Length in miles
St. Gotthard	Switzerland	10.2
Pinglin Highway	Taiwan	8.0
Trans-Tokyo Bay I and II	Japan	5.8
Mt. Blanc	Italy	7.5

9. What is the average length of these 4 tunnels? Round your answer to the nearest tenth.

10. How much longer is the St. Gotthard tunnel than the Mt. Blanc tunnel?

Extra Practice, page 289

Objective: Subtract mixed numbers with unlike denominators.

Explore Subtracting Mixed Numbers with Unlike Denominators

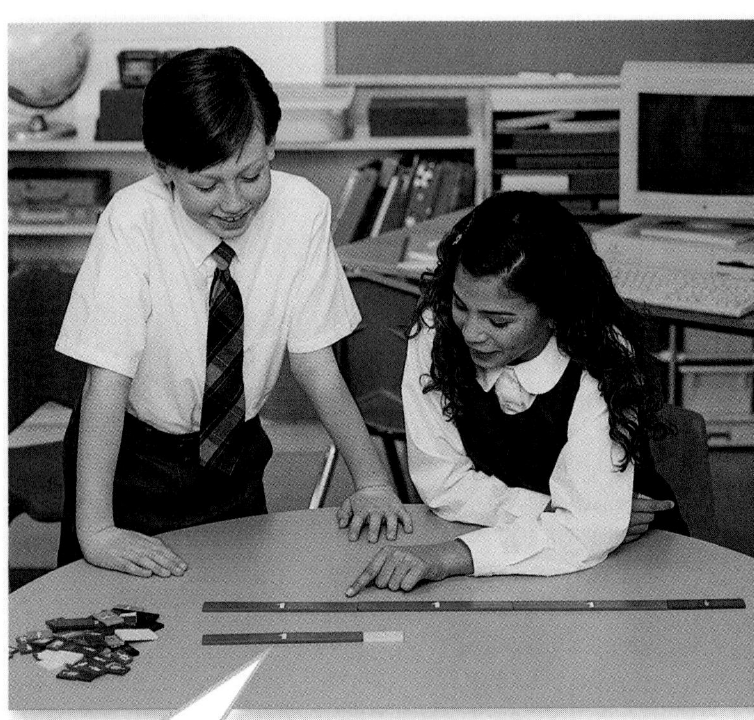

Learn

You can use fraction strips to explore subtracting mixed numbers with unlike denominators.

Work Together

You Will Need
- fraction strips

- Use fraction strips to find $3\frac{1}{2} - 1\frac{1}{4}$.

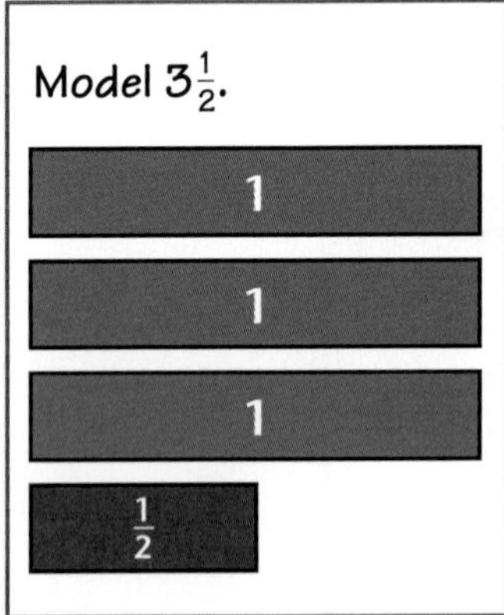

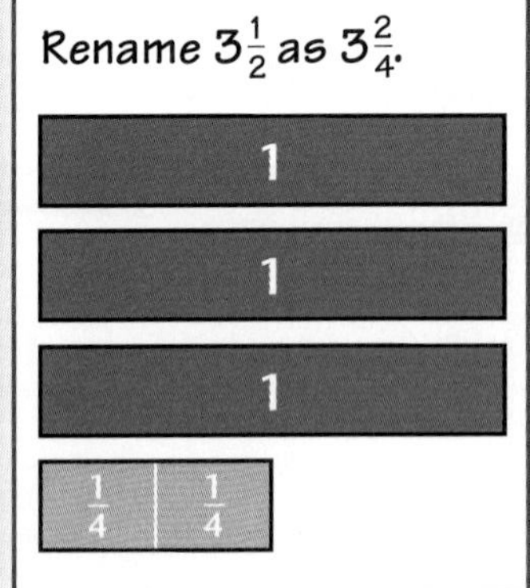

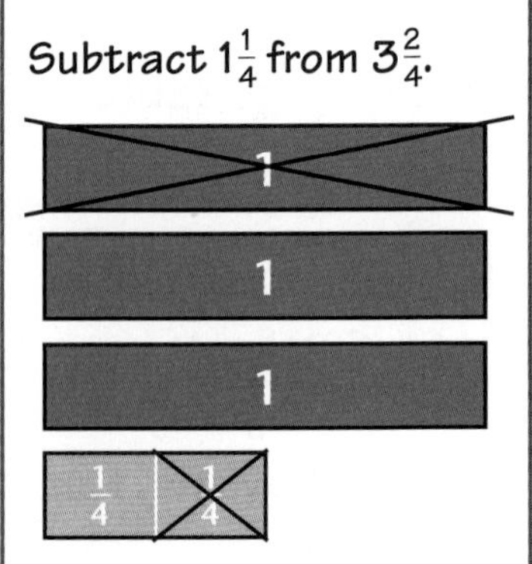

- Record the subtraction sentence.
- Use fraction strips to solve.

$3\frac{1}{2} - 1\frac{1}{2}$ $\quad$ $2\frac{2}{3} - 1\frac{1}{6}$ $\quad$ $4\frac{7}{10} - 1\frac{2}{5}$ $\quad$ $5\frac{1}{6} - 2\frac{1}{12}$

Make Connections

Find: $2\frac{1}{4} - 1\frac{2}{3}$

	Using Models	Using Paper and Pencil
1	Show each mixed number. 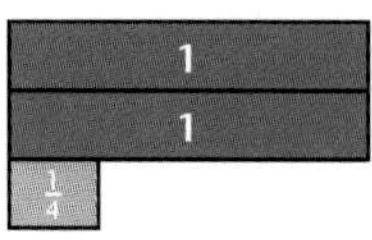 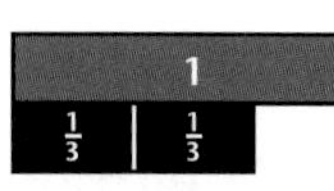	Find the LCD of $\frac{1}{4}$ and $\frac{2}{3}$. The LCM is 12.
2	Show $2\frac{1}{4}$ and $1\frac{2}{3}$ using 12 as a denominator. 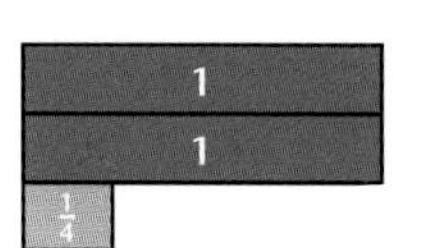 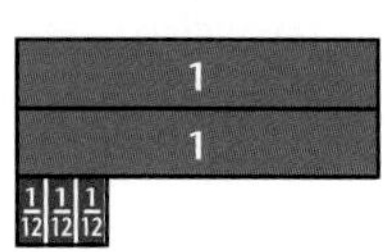	Rename $2\frac{1}{4}$ and $1\frac{2}{3}$ using the LCD 12: $2\frac{1}{4} = 2\frac{3}{12}$ $1\frac{2}{3} = 1\frac{8}{12}$
3	Regroup $2\frac{3}{12}$ to subtract $1\frac{8}{12}$. 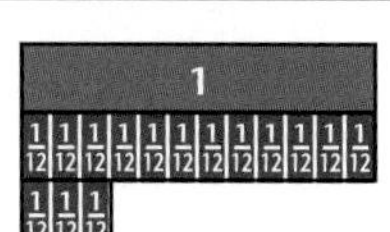	Since $\frac{3}{12} < \frac{8}{12}$, regroup $2\frac{3}{12}$. $2\frac{3}{12} = 1 + \frac{12}{12} + \frac{3}{12} = 1\frac{15}{12}$
4	Take strips away to subtract. Simplify. 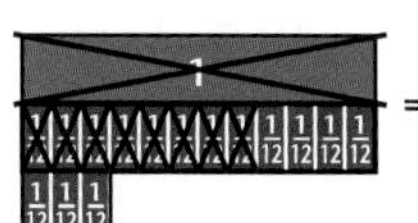	Subtract the fractions. Subtract the whole numbers. $1\frac{15}{12} - 1\frac{8}{12} = \frac{7}{12}$

So $2\frac{1}{4} - 1\frac{2}{3} = \frac{7}{12}$.

Try It

Subtract. You may use models. Write your answer in simplest form.

1. $4\frac{3}{4} - 2\frac{3}{8}$
2. $6\frac{5}{6} - 3\frac{2}{3}$
3. $5\frac{1}{4} - 2\frac{1}{3}$
4. $6\frac{1}{5} - 1\frac{1}{2}$

How would you subtract $3\frac{1}{2}$ from $4\frac{1}{4}$ using paper and pencil?

Practice

Subtract. Write your answer in simplest form.

5. $6\frac{3}{16} - 4\frac{1}{8}$
6. $4\frac{1}{3} - 2\frac{3}{4}$
7. $5\frac{1}{4} - 2\frac{5}{6}$
8. $6\frac{1}{8} - 1\frac{1}{2}$
9. $2\frac{1}{4} - 1\frac{5}{8}$
10. $8\frac{2}{3} - 2\frac{2}{3}$
11. $5 - 2\frac{1}{6}$
12. $6\frac{7}{8} - \frac{1}{2}$
13. **Analyze:** When you subtract mixed numbers, can you always start by subtracting the whole parts of each? Explain.

Objective: Subtract mixed numbers with unlike denominators.

6•11 Subtract Mixed Numbers

Learn

Local farmers often sell their fruit and vegetables at outdoor farmers' markets. A farmer sold $6\frac{9}{10}$ pounds of green beans on Wednesday. How many pounds of green beans are left?

Example

Find: $10\frac{1}{2} - 6\frac{9}{10}$

Note: You can use any common denominator to solve the problem, but the LCD will keep the numerators smaller.

1 Write equivalent fractions using the LCD.

$$\begin{array}{rcr} 10\frac{1}{2} & = & 10\frac{5}{10} \\ -\ 6\frac{9}{10} & = & 6\frac{9}{10} \\ \hline \end{array}$$

2 Rename if necessary.

$$\begin{array}{rcr} 10\frac{5}{10} & = & 9 + \frac{10}{10} + \frac{5}{10} = 9\frac{15}{10} \\ -\ 6\frac{9}{10} & = & 6\frac{9}{10} \\ \hline \end{array}$$

3 Subtract. Simplify.

$$\begin{array}{r} 9\frac{15}{10} \\ -6\frac{9}{10} \\ \hline 3\frac{6}{10} = 3\frac{3}{5} \end{array}$$

There are $3\frac{3}{5}$ pounds of green beans left.

More Examples

A

$5\frac{3}{5} - 2\frac{1}{3}$

$\downarrow \quad \downarrow$

$5\frac{9}{15} - 2\frac{5}{15} = 3\frac{4}{15}$

B

$4\frac{3}{4} - 2 = 2\frac{3}{4}$

C

$8 - 5\frac{5}{6}$

$\downarrow \quad \downarrow$

$7\frac{6}{6} - 5\frac{5}{6} = 2\frac{1}{6}$

Try It

Subtract. Write your answer in simplest form.

1. $5\frac{7}{8} - 2\frac{1}{2}$
2. $25 - 14\frac{7}{10}$
3. $19\frac{3}{4} - 5\frac{5}{6}$
4. $11\frac{1}{2} - 3\frac{2}{3}$

When is it necessary to rename when subtracting mixed numbers?

Practice Subtract. Write your answer in simplest form.

5. $8\frac{1}{8} - 2\frac{3}{4}$
6. $9\frac{2}{3} - \frac{5}{6}$
7. $15 - 7\frac{9}{42}$
8. $34\frac{5}{12} - 14\frac{1}{12}$

9. $45 - 27\frac{7}{8}$
10. $31\frac{3}{4} - 5\frac{5}{6}$
11. $17 - 11\frac{9}{10}$
12. $81\frac{1}{3} - 79\frac{9}{10}$
13. $8\frac{1}{3} - 7\frac{1}{10}$

14. $77\frac{3}{5} - 17\frac{1}{4}$
15. $49 - 17\frac{5}{6}$
16. $4\frac{3}{4} - 2\frac{1}{5}$
★17. $51\frac{7}{30} - 16\frac{2}{25}$
★18. $97\frac{1}{7} - 69\frac{8}{35}$

Algebra & functions Find the missing number.

19. $n - 2\frac{1}{2} = 6\frac{7}{10}$
20. $k - 7\frac{5}{8} = 3\frac{1}{4}$
21. $13\frac{1}{4} - t = 3\frac{5}{6}$
★22. $10\frac{1}{25} - g = 5\frac{49}{50}$

Problem Solving

Use data from the sign for problems 23–24.

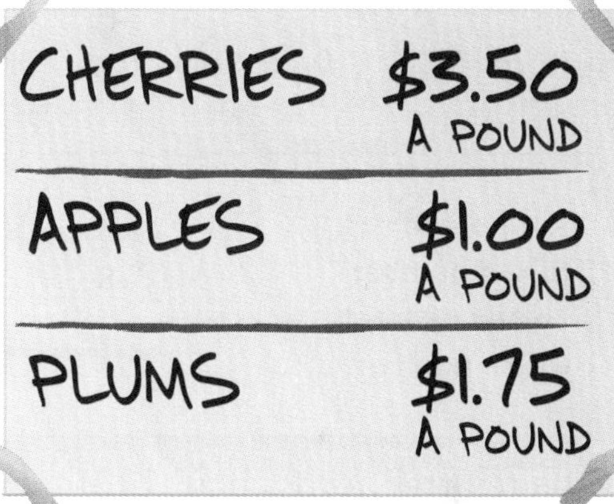

23. Phil buys $2\frac{1}{2}$ pounds of cherries, 5 pounds of apples, and $1\frac{3}{4}$ pounds of plums. How many pounds of fruit did he buy?

24. How much would it cost to buy 3 pounds of cherries and 2 pounds of plums?

29. A farmer sells $4\frac{1}{4}$ pounds of peaches from a 10 pound box. How many pounds are left?

30. **Compare:** How is subtracting mixed numbers with unlike denominators the same as subtracting mixed numbers with like denominators?

Spiral Review and Test Prep

Simplify each fraction.

31. $\frac{12}{20}$
32. $\frac{8}{16}$
33. $\frac{8}{36}$
34. $\frac{14}{70}$

Choose the correct answer.

35. There are 630 miles between St. Louis and Minneapolis. If you drive halfway, how many miles do you drive?
    - A. 125 miles
    - B. 150 miles
    - C. 300 miles
    - D. 315 miles

36. Sharon gives 87 cookies to the fifth-grade students. There are 29 fifth-grade students. How many cookies does each one get?
    - F. 7
    - G. 5
    - H. 3
    - J. Not Here

Objective: Estimate sums and differences of mixed numbers.

Estimate Sums and Differences of Mixed Numbers

Learn

An art restorer uses his or her knowledge of math and art history to return old or damaged pieces of art to their original condition. About how much more wood does the art restorer need to complete this frame?

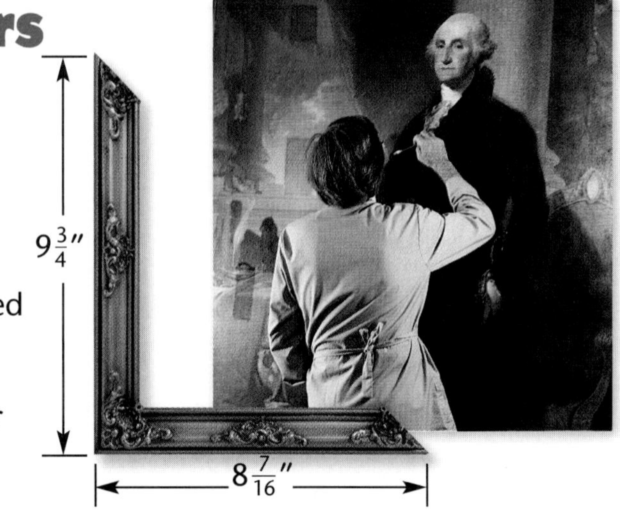

Example

Estimate $8\frac{7}{16} + 9\frac{3}{4}$ to solve the problem.

1 Round each mixed number to the nearest whole number.

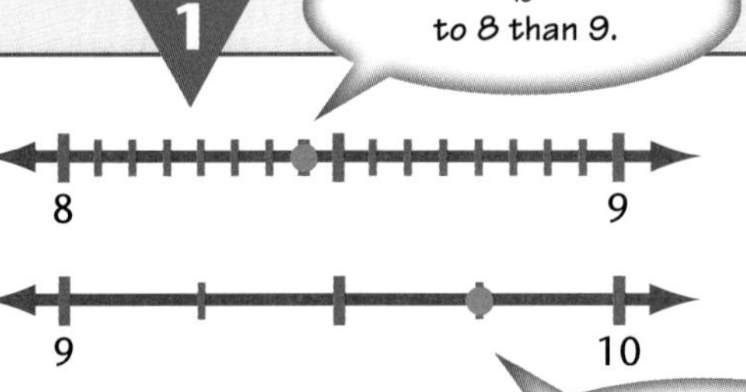

Think: $8\frac{7}{16}$ is closer to 8 than 9.

Think: $9\frac{3}{4}$ is closer to 10 than 9.

2 Add the rounded numbers.

$8 + 10 = 18$

The restorer needs about 18 inches of wood.

More Examples

A You can also estimate to find the difference.

Think: $\frac{1}{2}$ rounds up.

Estimate: $6\frac{7}{12} - 5\frac{1}{2}$

$7 - 6 = 1$

B With greater numbers you might round to the nearest ten.

Think: You can ignore the fraction when you round to the nearest 10.

Estimate: $44\frac{3}{8} + 26\frac{1}{4}$.

$40 + 30 = 70$

Try It

Estimate.

1. $2\frac{5}{16} + 3\frac{11}{12}$
2. $9\frac{11}{12} - 2\frac{1}{12}$
3. $16\frac{1}{3} + 12\frac{3}{4}$
4. $43\frac{5}{6} - 25\frac{1}{6}$

Sum it Up Explain how you would estimate $4\frac{1}{8} + 3\frac{9}{16}$.

Practice

Round to the nearest whole number.

5. $3\frac{2}{3}$ 6. $5\frac{2}{5}$ 7. $2\frac{1}{2}$ 8. $4\frac{5}{8}$ 9. $6\frac{3}{4}$

Estimate.

10. $3\frac{3}{5} + 8\frac{5}{8}$ 11. $7\frac{5}{12} + 2\frac{7}{10}$ 12. $8\frac{7}{10} - 6\frac{3}{8}$ 13. $8\frac{9}{20} - 4\frac{7}{16}$

14. $11\frac{4}{5} + 1\frac{1}{5}$ 15. $3\frac{1}{4} + 17\frac{9}{10}$ 16. $8\frac{4}{5} - 6\frac{7}{8}$ 17. $12\frac{1}{12} - 2\frac{3}{4}$

18. $25\frac{3}{8} + 83\frac{7}{12}$ 19. $66\frac{1}{5} - 17\frac{1}{8}$ ★20. $295\frac{9}{10} + 105\frac{3}{10}$ ★21. $315\frac{5}{8} - 180\frac{3}{10}$

Problem Solving

Use data from *Did You Know?* for problem 22.

22. **Art:** If a painting was created in 1486 and laboratory analysis suggests it was repainted 56 years later, when was the first restoration?

23. **Analyze:** Do $5\frac{7}{16}$ and $5\frac{7}{12}$ round to the same whole number? Explain.

24. A square painting measures $14\frac{1}{8}$ inches on each side. About how many inches of wood will be needed to frame it?

25. **What if** large canvases require $3\frac{1}{4}$ ounces of special fluid to clean them. Small canvases require $2\frac{1}{2}$ ounces. About how much fluid is needed to clean one large and one small canvas?

Some Renaissance paintings have been through several periods of restoration since they were first painted. Today, restorers can use Xrays and chemical analysis to date the original painting and the changes made to it.

★ 26. **Science:** A restorer is fixing a frame originally built in the late 1700s. She wants to use wood from the same era. She knows that a tree adds a new ring each year. If the wood she examines was cut in 1995 and has 216 rings, could she use it in the frame? Explain.

Spiral Review and Test Prep

Compare. Write >, <, or =.

27. 47.3 ● 4.73 28. 1.02 ● 1.20 29. 0.05 ● 0.050 30. $1\frac{1}{4}$ ● $\frac{5}{4}$

Choose the correct answer.

31. What is the GCF of 24 and 32?
A. 1 C. 4
B. 2 D. 8

32. What is the LCM of 6 and 9?
F. 9 H. 36
G. 18 J. Not Here

Objective: Apply fractions and mixed numbers to make decisions.

6•13 A Problem Solving: Application

Decision Making

Which pattern and which store should you choose?

An interior designer decorates homes and offices. Suppose you are an interior designer decorating a bedroom. You have $75 to spend on wallpaper border. There are 3 patterns from which to choose.

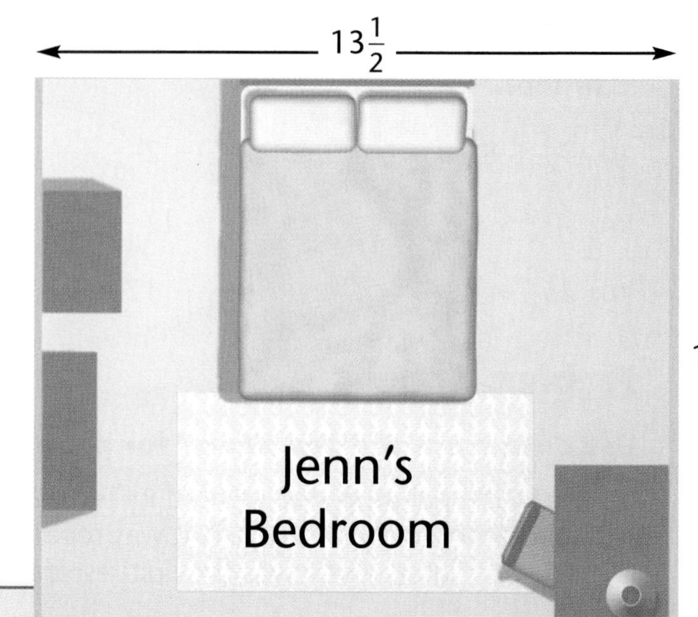

Option 1

Interior Décor Store
Get Your Wallpaper Border Here!
Flowered: 20-foot roll for $11
Plaid: 15-foot roll for $8
Striped: 10-foot roll for $6

Option 2

Wallpaper City's
WALLPAPER BORDER SALE!
Flowered: 10-foot roll for $5
Plaid: 20-foot roll for $8
Striped: 15-foot roll for $7

Read for Understanding

1. How much money do you have to spend?
2. Which store sells the longer roll of plaid border?
3. How much does a 10-foot roll of striped border cost at Interior Décor Store?
4. Which store sells rolls of flowered border for $11?

Make Decisions

5. If the wallpaper border runs along the length of each wall of the bedroom, how much border is needed?
6. How many 10-foot rolls of wallpaper border would you need to buy? how many 15-foot rolls? how many 20-foot rolls?
7. If you buy wallpaper border from Wallpaper City, how many rolls of flowered border are needed? how many rolls of plaid? how many rolls of striped?
8. If you buys wallpaper border from Interior Décor Store, how many rolls of flowered border are needed? how many rolls of plaid? how many rolls of striped?
9. Wallpaper paste costs $5 at Wallpaper City. How much would it cost to buy enough flowered wallpaper border and a container of paste at Wallpaper City?
10. How much would it cost to buy enough plaid wallpaper border and a container of paste at Wallpaper City?
11. How much would it cost to buy enough striped wallpaper border and a container of paste at Wallpaper City?
12. Wallpaper paste costs $3 at Interior Décor Store. How much would it cost to buy enough flowered wallpaper border and a container of paste at Interior Décor Store?
13. How much would it cost to buy enough plaid wallpaper border and a container of paste at Interior Décor Store?
14. How much would it cost to buy enough striped wallpaper border and a container of paste at Interior Décor Store?
15. Whichever pattern is used, there will be the same amount of border left over after the bedroom is finished. How much border will be left over?
16. Which pattern do you like best?

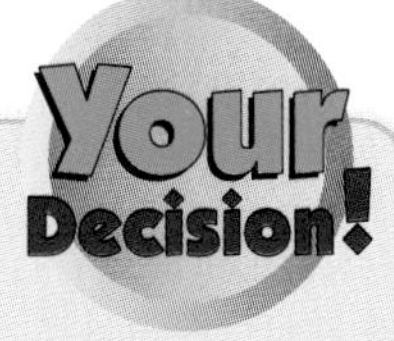

What pattern and store would you choose? Explain.

Problem Solving

Objective: Apply addition and subtraction of fractions and mixed numbers to investigate science concepts.

Problem Solving: Math and Science

How does the length of your arms, feet, and hands relate to your height?

You Will Need
- **ruler**
- **meterstick**

Have you ever noticed that very tall basketball players usually wear very large sneakers?

Your height generally relates to the size of your other body parts, such as your arms, feet, and hands. In this activity you will explore how the size of these body parts relates to your height.

Hypothesize

Estimate your height. Estimate what fraction the lengths of your feet, hands, and arm span are of your total height.

Procedure

1. Work with a partner. Round measurements to the nearest centimeter.
2. Measure your height.
3. Measure the length of your foot.
4. Measure the length of your hand.
5. Measure your arm span. With your arms spread out, measure from finger tip to finger tip.

Data

Copy and complete the chart to record your observations.

Height:		
Body Part	Length (in cm)	Fraction of height
Foot		
Hand		
Arm Span		

Conclude and Apply

- Calculate and record the fraction of height for each measurement.
- Are there any two fractions you can add that equal close to 1?
- Collect the data from the entire class. Do you see a pattern in the class data? Explain.
- How can you use your arms and feet to estimate the size of objects?

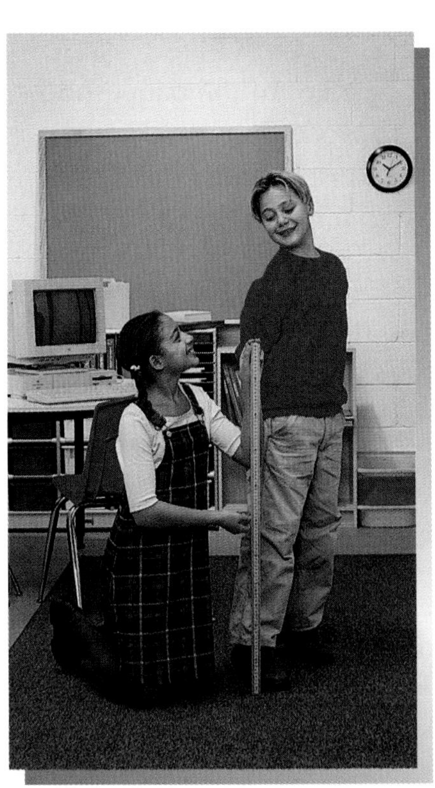

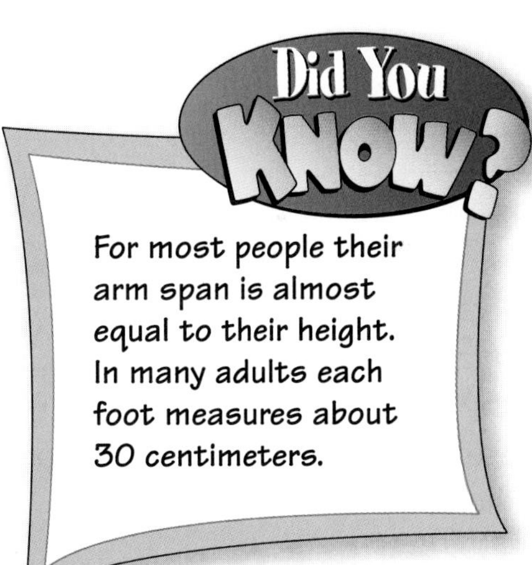

For most people their arm span is almost equal to their height. In many adults each foot measures about 30 centimeters.

Going Further

1. Design and complete an activity to find the fractions of foot, hand, and arm span for people of different ages. Are the fractions the same across different ages or not?
2. Design and complete an activity to relate the size of your head to your height.

Check Your Progress B

Add. Write your answer in simplest form. **(pages 268–271)**

1. $1\frac{5}{8} + \frac{7}{8}$
2. $\frac{3}{4} + \frac{5}{6}$
3. $\frac{2}{3} + 2\frac{3}{4}$
4. $\frac{5}{6} + 7\frac{5}{6}$
5. $\frac{3}{4} + 29\frac{2}{3}$
6. $75\frac{9}{16} + \frac{13}{16}$

Subtract. Write your answer in simplest form. **(pages 276–279)**

7. $\frac{15}{16} - \frac{7}{16}$
8. $\frac{11}{12} - \frac{2}{3}$
9. $\frac{15}{16} - \frac{3}{4}$
10. $19\frac{5}{6} - \frac{1}{6}$
11. $25\frac{1}{12} - \frac{7}{12}$
12. $82\frac{9}{16} - \frac{1}{4}$
13. $67\frac{1}{10} - 15\frac{4}{5}$
14. $50\frac{1}{8} - \frac{1}{2}$

Identify each property. **(pages 272–273)**

15. $\frac{1}{2} + \frac{1}{5} = \frac{1}{5} + \frac{1}{2}$
16. $0 + 124\frac{1}{8} = 124\frac{1}{8}$
17. $\frac{1}{2} + \left(\frac{1}{3} + \frac{1}{4}\right) = \left(\frac{1}{2} + \frac{1}{3}\right) + \frac{1}{4}$

Estimate. **(pages 280–281)**

18. $6\frac{9}{20} + 9\frac{13}{20}$
19. $7\frac{2}{5} + 8\frac{9}{16}$
20. $13\frac{7}{8} + 34\frac{1}{3}$
21. $9\frac{8}{12} - 5\frac{5}{16}$

Solve. **(pages 268–281)**

22. Richard maintains the grounds on the miniature golf course for $3\frac{3}{4}$ hours in the morning and for $4\frac{1}{2}$ hours in the afternoon. How many hours does Richard work on the grounds?

23. Terry drives $5\frac{3}{5}$ miles to the bagel shop on her way to work. Then she drives $\frac{9}{10}$ mile to work. How many miles does Terry drive?

24. Jerry buys a $1\frac{1}{2}$-pound bag of grass seed. There is only $\frac{1}{4}$ pound left in the bag. How much did he use? Write an equation and solve.

25. Explain the steps you would take to solve $27\frac{1}{2} - 19\frac{4}{5}$.

Additional activities at
www.mhschool.com/math

Extra Practice

Add and Subtract Fractions and Mixed Numbers with Like Denominators (pages 252–255)

Add. Write your answer in simplest form.

1. $\frac{11}{16} + \frac{7}{16}$
2. $\frac{5}{6} + 18\frac{1}{6}$
3. $58\frac{9}{10} + \frac{7}{10}$
4. $67\frac{11}{12} + 24\frac{11}{12}$
5. $1\frac{1}{4} + \frac{3}{4}$
6. $5\frac{3}{8} + \frac{3}{8}$
7. $4\frac{2}{3} + 2\frac{2}{3}$
8. $\frac{4}{5} + 6\frac{2}{5}$
9. $82\frac{3}{4} + 18\frac{3}{4}$
10. $\frac{7}{8} + \frac{1}{8}$
11. $\frac{3}{10} + 1\frac{1}{10}$
12. $9\frac{5}{12} + 3\frac{1}{12}$

Subtract. Write your answer in simplest form.

13. $\frac{5}{6} - \frac{1}{6}$
14. $21\frac{7}{12} - \frac{5}{12}$
15. $50\frac{3}{4} - 29\frac{1}{4}$
16. $35\frac{17}{20} - 17\frac{13}{20}$
17. $8\frac{1}{12} - 6$
18. $5\frac{15}{16} - 4\frac{7}{16}$
19. $5\frac{5}{8} - 3\frac{5}{8}$
20. $14\frac{7}{10} - 4\frac{1}{10}$
21. $1\frac{2}{3} - \frac{1}{3}$
22. $4\frac{4}{5} - 2\frac{2}{5}$
23. $44\frac{5}{8} - 32\frac{1}{8}$
24. $6\frac{13}{16} - 2\frac{7}{16}$

Solve.

25. Bill works $7\frac{3}{4}$ hours during the day. He works $1\frac{3}{4}$ hours at a second job at night. How many hours does he work in all?
26. A designer plants trees along $\frac{1}{4}$ mile of a path. The entire path runs $1\frac{3}{4}$ miles. How much of the path has no trees?
27. Mr. Jones spent $2\frac{1}{2}$ hours returning phone calls. Then he spent $1\frac{1}{2}$ hours calling new clients. How much time did he spend on the phone?
28. A forest ranger marked $\frac{1}{3}$ mile of a $\frac{2}{3}$ mile trail. How much still needs to be marked?

Problem Solving: Reading for Math Choose the Operation. (pages 256–257)

Solve.

1. A sales representative keeps a record of how many miles he drives each day of the week. He needs to give the weekly total to his boss. Which operation will he need to find this number?
2. A park ranger cleans $3\frac{1}{4}$ miles of trail on Saturday. The whole trail runs for $6\frac{1}{4}$ miles. How much more needs to be cleaned? Choose an operation and solve.

Extra Practice

Add and Subtract Fractions with Unlike Denominators (pages 262–265)

Add. Write your answer in simplest form.

1. $\frac{7}{8} + \frac{3}{4}$
2. $\frac{2}{3} + \frac{5}{6}$
3. $\frac{11}{16} + \frac{5}{8}$
4. $\frac{9}{10} + \frac{9}{20}$
5. $\frac{3}{4} + \frac{1}{3}$
6. $\frac{7}{10} + \frac{3}{4}$
7. $\frac{5}{6} + \frac{1}{4}$
8. $\frac{4}{5} + \frac{1}{2}$

Subtract. Write your answer in simplest form.

9. $\frac{9}{10} - \frac{2}{5}$
10. $\frac{3}{4} - \frac{1}{8}$
11. $\frac{5}{6} - \frac{1}{3}$
12. $\frac{9}{10} - \frac{3}{20}$
13. $\frac{1}{2} - \frac{1}{5}$
14. $\frac{3}{4} - \frac{2}{5}$
15. $\frac{5}{6} - \frac{1}{4}$
16. $\frac{2}{3} - \frac{1}{2}$

Find the missing number.

17. $\frac{1}{2} + b = \frac{5}{6}$
18. $\frac{3}{4} + x = 1\frac{1}{8}$
19. $t + \frac{4}{5} = 1\frac{11}{20}$
20. $d + \frac{1}{8} = \frac{7}{16}$
21. $\frac{17}{20} - y = \frac{3}{4}$
22. $\frac{7}{8} - n = \frac{1}{8}$
23. $z - \frac{3}{16} = \frac{9}{16}$
24. $m - \frac{1}{2} = \frac{1}{3}$

Add Mixed Numbers with Unlike Denominators (pages 270–271)

Add. Write your answer in simplest form.

1. $3\frac{2}{3} + 4\frac{1}{6}$
2. $9\frac{5}{8} + 5\frac{1}{4}$
3. $7\frac{1}{2} + 8\frac{2}{3}$
4. $6\frac{1}{4} + 9\frac{2}{3}$
5. $27\frac{5}{6} + 37\frac{7}{12}$
6. $12\frac{7}{10} + 19\frac{4}{5}$
7. $85\frac{1}{2} + 47\frac{3}{5}$
8. $56\frac{3}{4} + 59\frac{5}{6}$

Properties of Addition (pages 272–273)

Identify the property.

1. $98\frac{7}{10} + 0 = 98\frac{7}{10}$
2. $\left(\frac{3}{4} + \frac{5}{6}\right) + \frac{1}{2} = \frac{3}{4} + \left(\frac{5}{6} + \frac{1}{2}\right)$
3. $3\frac{1}{10} + \frac{7}{8} = \frac{7}{8} + 3\frac{1}{10}$

Use the Associative Property to solve.

4. $\left(\frac{1}{3} + \frac{1}{4}\right) + \frac{1}{4}$
5. $4\frac{1}{4} + \left(1\frac{1}{4} + 2\frac{1}{3}\right)$
6. $9\frac{5}{6} + \left(\frac{2}{6} + \frac{1}{4}\right)$

Find the missing number.

7. $\frac{2}{5} + \frac{3}{4} = \blacksquare + \frac{2}{5}$
8. $0 + \blacksquare = 45\frac{9}{10}$
9. $\frac{3}{10} + \left(\frac{1}{4} + \frac{1}{5}\right) = \left(\frac{3}{10} + \blacksquare\right) + \frac{1}{5}$

Extra Practice

Problem Solving: Strategy Write an Equation (pages 274–275)

Write an equation, then solve.

1. A 25-pound bag of sugar has only $3\frac{1}{2}$ pounds left. How much sugar has been used?

2. A pastry shop owner pays an employee \$35 to work the morning shift. The shop earns \$115 during the shift. How much does the owner make?

Subtract Mixed Numbers with Unlike Denominators (pages 278–279)

Subtract. Write your answer in simplest form.

1. $17\frac{15}{16} - 5\frac{3}{8}$
2. $14\frac{4}{5} - 7\frac{3}{20}$
3. $25\frac{3}{4} - 13\frac{1}{5}$
4. $19\frac{9}{10} - 10\frac{1}{4}$
5. $20\frac{1}{8} - 6\frac{1}{2}$
6. $31\frac{3}{10} - 8\frac{13}{20}$
7. $19\frac{1}{6} - 4\frac{3}{4}$
8. $18\frac{1}{2} - 8\frac{2}{3}$
9. $7\frac{2}{3} - 5\frac{1}{6}$
10. $8 - 4\frac{1}{4}$
11. $40\frac{1}{4} - 26\frac{7}{8}$
12. $36\frac{1}{4} - 20$

Estimate Sums and Differences of Mixed Numbers (pages 280–281)

Round to the nearest whole number.

1. $2\frac{1}{3}$
2. $5\frac{3}{4}$
3. $9\frac{1}{2}$
4. $7\frac{7}{16}$
5. $6\frac{5}{12}$
6. $16\frac{1}{3}$
7. $4\frac{8}{9}$
8. $22\frac{11}{22}$
9. $\frac{2}{3}$
10. $7\frac{2}{5}$

Estimate each sum or difference.

11. $19\frac{1}{4} + 4\frac{5}{6}$
12. $4\frac{1}{2} + 12\frac{1}{3}$
13. $6\frac{1}{8} - 3\frac{5}{6}$
14. $12\frac{15}{16} - 1\frac{7}{17}$
15. $7\frac{1}{8} - 6\frac{3}{4}$
16. $6\frac{1}{2} + 9\frac{1}{8}$
17. $5\frac{3}{10} + 5\frac{7}{8}$
18. $23\frac{5}{6} + 46\frac{1}{3}$
19. $35\frac{1}{12} + 58\frac{1}{10}$

Chapter Study Guide

Language and Math

Complete. Use a word from the list.

1. The equation $\frac{7}{16} + 0 = \frac{7}{16}$ is an example of the ____.
2. The same denominator shared by two or more fractions is called a ____.

Math Words

- Associative Property
- common denominator
- Commutative Property
- Identity Property

Skills and Applications

Add and subtract fractions and mixed numbers, with like and unlike denominators. (pages 252–255, 258–265, 268–274, 276–279)

Example

Add: $\frac{2}{5} + \frac{3}{10}$

Solution

Rename $\frac{2}{5}$ using the LCD of 10.

$$\frac{2}{5} = \frac{2 \times 2}{5 \times 2} = \frac{4}{10}$$

Add the fractions.

$$\frac{4}{10} + \frac{3}{10} = \frac{7}{10}$$

So $\frac{2}{5} + \frac{3}{10} = \frac{7}{10}$.

Add. Write your answer in simplest form.

3. $\frac{7}{8} + \frac{5}{8}$
4. $\frac{3}{5} + \frac{9}{10}$
5. $\frac{2}{3} + 47\frac{2}{3}$
6. $\frac{1}{2} + 16\frac{4}{5}$
7. $16\frac{9}{10} + \frac{7}{10}$
8. $9\frac{3}{5} + \frac{4}{5}$
9. $25\frac{5}{6} + \frac{5}{12}$
10. $17\frac{2}{3} + \frac{3}{4}$
11. $9\frac{5}{16} + 14\frac{7}{16}$
12. $31\frac{9}{20} + 19\frac{19}{20}$
13. $31\frac{3}{4} + 12\frac{5}{12}$
14. $28\frac{1}{2} + 7\frac{2}{3}$

Subtract fractions and mixed numbers with like and unlike denominators. (pages 252–255, 260–265, 276–279)

Example

Find: $1\frac{7}{8} - \frac{3}{4}$

Solution

Rename each fraction using the LCD.

$$\frac{3}{4} = \frac{6}{8}$$

Subtract the whole numbers. Subtract the fractions.

$$1\frac{7}{8} - \frac{6}{8} = 1\frac{1}{8}$$

Subtract. Write your answer in simplest form.

15. $\frac{5}{6} - \frac{1}{6}$
16. $\frac{1}{2} - \frac{1}{3}$
17. $\frac{9}{16} - \frac{1}{4}$
18. $15\frac{1}{3} - \frac{2}{3}$
19. $17\frac{3}{20} - \frac{4}{5}$
20. $35\frac{1}{3} - \frac{7}{12}$
21. $31 - 8\frac{7}{8}$
22. $90 - 7\frac{3}{10}$

Identify and use properties of addition. (pages 272–273)

Example

Identify the property.

$$\frac{3}{5} + \left(9 + \frac{3}{4}\right) = \left(\frac{3}{5} + 9\right) + \frac{3}{4}$$

Solution

Associative Property: When adding three addends, the grouping of the addends does not change the sum.

Identify each property.

23. $9\frac{4}{5} + 10\frac{7}{8} = 10\frac{7}{8} + 9\frac{4}{5}$

24. $\frac{13}{16} + \left(\frac{3}{4} + \frac{1}{8}\right) = \left(\frac{13}{16} + \frac{3}{4}\right) + \frac{1}{8}$

Use the Associative Property to solve.

25. $\frac{5}{16} + \left(\frac{7}{16} + \frac{1}{3}\right)$

26. $\left(\frac{4}{5} + \frac{3}{4}\right) + \frac{1}{2}$

27. $\left(\frac{1}{3} + \frac{9}{10}\right) + \frac{3}{5}$

Estimate sums and differences of mixed numbers. (pages 280–281)

Example

Estimate: $2\frac{1}{4} + 5\frac{7}{8}$

Solution

Round to the nearest whole number.

$2\frac{1}{4}$ rounds to 2. $5\frac{7}{8}$ rounds to 6.

$2 + 6 = 8.$

Estimate each sum or difference.

28. $5\frac{5}{6} + 4\frac{2}{3}$

29. $7\frac{3}{8} + 6\frac{7}{12}$

30. $9\frac{7}{16} - 3\frac{3}{10}$

31. $35\frac{1}{10} - 27\frac{1}{8}$

Solve problems. (pages 256–257, 274–275)

Example

Renee buys $3\frac{7}{8}$ yards of blue ribbon and $4\frac{1}{2}$ yards of red ribbon for the grand opening of a store. How much ribbon does Renee buy?

Solution

Add:

$$\begin{aligned} 3\frac{7}{8} &= 3\frac{7}{8} \\ +4\frac{1}{2} &= 4\frac{4}{8} \\ & \quad 7\frac{11}{8} = 8\frac{3}{8} \end{aligned}$$

Renee buys $8\frac{3}{8}$ yards of ribbon.

Solve.

32. Jack buys $5\frac{1}{2}$ yards of canvas. He uses $3\frac{3}{4}$ yards to cover the floor. How much canvas is not used? Choose an operation and solve.

33. A baker finds that $3\frac{1}{4}$ cups of cream are left after making cake icing. If the original container held 8 cups, how much cream was used?

Chapter Test

Add. Write your answer in simplest form.

1. $\frac{9}{20} + \frac{7}{20}$

2. $\frac{3}{10} + \frac{1}{4}$

3. $\frac{3}{5} + 14\frac{1}{2}$

4. $21\frac{2}{3} + \frac{3}{4}$

5. $19\frac{1}{2} + 54\frac{1}{3}$

6. $\frac{7}{8} + 59\frac{3}{4}$

7. $15\frac{5}{24} + 16\frac{1}{8}$

8. $3\frac{5}{12} + 16\frac{1}{8}$

Subtract. Write your answer in simplest form.

9. $\frac{7}{8} - \frac{1}{4}$

10. $7\frac{9}{10} - \frac{2}{5}$

11. $15\frac{1}{4} - \frac{2}{3}$

12. $21\frac{7}{8} - 13\frac{3}{16}$

13. $32\frac{1}{2} - 22\frac{4}{5}$

14. $73\frac{3}{8} - 14\frac{1}{6}$

15. $18\frac{4}{5} - 5\frac{1}{4}$

16. $6\frac{5}{6} - 3$

Find the missing number.

17. $\frac{5}{9} + \frac{7}{16} = n + \frac{5}{9}$

18. $\frac{7}{10} + \left(\frac{1}{5} + \frac{1}{2}\right) = \left(\frac{7}{10} + \frac{1}{5}\right) + x$

Estimate.

19. $3\frac{9}{10} + 9\frac{2}{5}$

20. $5\frac{5}{12} + 7\frac{9}{16}$

21. $8\frac{7}{12} - 4\frac{3}{10}$

22. $9\frac{9}{20} - 2\frac{7}{16}$

Solve.

23. A hive of bees makes $4\frac{1}{2}$ pounds of honey in May and $3\frac{1}{4}$ pounds in June. Which operation would you use to find the total amount of honey made in the two months? How much honey is it?

24. How much honey does a hive make in June if it makes $1\frac{1}{4}$ pounds more than May? It makes $7\frac{3}{4}$ pounds in May.

25. Elle has $\frac{3}{4}$ gallon of paint after she repaints her room. The full container held 10 gallons. Write an equation and solve for the gallons she uses.

Performance Assessment

You work as a park ranger. You are planning a hiking trip for a group of campers. They can hike between 5 and 6 miles. Which 2 trails can you direct them to?

Copy and complete the chart below. Use the chart to answer these questions:

- Which 2 trails together will cover between 5 and 6 miles?
- How many miles difference is there between the shortest and longest hike?

Trail 1	Trail 2	Total Trail Length
Easy Loop	Sage's Ravine	▮
Sage's Ravine	Summit	▮
Summit	Easy Loop	▮

A Good Answer

- has a complete chart that shows the combined lengths of the trails.
- shows which 2 trails combined are between 5 and 6 miles long.
- shows the difference between the shortest and longest trails.

You may want to save this work for your portfolio.

Assessment

Enrichment

Egyptian Fractions

The ancient Egyptians wrote numbers using different symbols than those we use today.

100 10 1

The ancient Egyptians wrote the number 215 like this:

A unit fraction has 1 as its numerator. Ancient Egyptians wrote all fractions as unit fractions. To show a fraction, they used the symbol for a mouth above the denominator.

The ancient Egyptians wrote $\frac{1}{12}$ like this:

Write each number as the ancient Egyptians would have.

1. 3 **2.** 17 **3.** 25 **4.** 132 **5.** 201

Write each fraction as the ancient Egyptians would have.

6. $\frac{1}{2}$ **7.** $\frac{1}{3}$ **8.** $\frac{1}{10}$ **9.** $\frac{1}{12}$ **10.** $\frac{1}{16}$

Write each Egyptian fraction as it would be written today.

11.  **12.** **13.** **14.**

15. Write a number sentence that shows two unit fractions being added together. Then rewrite your number sentence using Egyptian symbols.

16. Write a number sentence that shows two unit fractions being subtracted. Then rewrite your number sentence using Egyptian symbols.

Test-Taking Tips

When taking a multiple-choice test, some choices may be eliminated to make it easier to choose the correct answer. You can estimate to eliminate choices before you solve the problem.

Thomas drives $7\frac{3}{4}$ miles to the dentist. Then he drives $5\frac{1}{8}$ miles to work. How many miles in all does Thomas drive?

A. $2\frac{5}{8}$ miles C. $12\frac{7}{8}$ miles

B. $9\frac{5}{8}$ miles D. $20\frac{1}{8}$ miles

Estimate to eliminate choices:

- $7\frac{3}{4} + 5\frac{1}{8}$

  $\downarrow \quad \downarrow$

  $8 + 5 = 13$

- The answer is close to 13.

Look at the answer choices.

- You can eliminate choices A, B, and D; they are not close to the estimate of 13.
- The correct answer is C.

Check for Success

Before turning in a test, go back one last time to check.

☑ I understood and answered the questions asked.

☑ I checked my work for errors.

☑ My answers make sense.

Practice

Estimate to eliminate choices. Choose the correct answer.

1. There are $5\frac{3}{4}$ gallons of milk at the restaurant. They use $1\frac{1}{4}$ gallons of the milk. How much milk is left?

   A. $1\frac{1}{2}$ gallons C. 7 gallons

   B. $4\frac{1}{2}$ gallons D. $8\frac{1}{4}$ gallons

2. There are $9\frac{1}{8}$ pounds of ice in the cooler. Betty adds another $10\frac{3}{4}$ pounds. How many pounds of ice are there now?

   F. 2 pounds H. $15\frac{3}{8}$ pounds

   G. $11\frac{1}{4}$ pounds J. $19\frac{7}{8}$ pounds

3. Last week Mr. Lasko bought $11\frac{1}{4}$ gallons of gas. This week he bought $10\frac{3}{4}$ gallons. How much gas did he buy in all?

   A. 1 gallon C. 22 gallons

   B. 11 gallons D. 110 gallons

4. James bought 8 bags of potato chips for a party. After the party there were $1\frac{1}{4}$ bags left. How many bags were eaten?

   F. $9\frac{1}{4}$ bags H. 8 bags

   G. 5 bags J. $6\frac{3}{4}$ bags

Test Prep

Spiral Review and Test Prep

Chapters 1–6

Choose the correct answer.

Number Sense

1. What is 5,079,321 rounded to the nearest ten thousand?
   A. 5,100,000
   B. 5,080,000
   C. 5,079,300
   D. 5,079,320

2. Georgia sold 32 boxes of candles during a fundraiser for her local hospital. Each box contained 48 candles. Which of the following gives the best estimate of the number of candles Georgia sold?
   F. 30×40
   G. 30×50
   H. 40×40
   J. 40×50

3. Find the number that makes this equation true. $9\frac{7}{10} + 7\frac{3}{4} = n$
   A. $11\frac{9}{20}$
   B. $16\frac{9}{20}$
   C. $17\frac{9}{20}$
   D. Not Here

4. Which picture below models the fraction $\frac{1}{4}$?

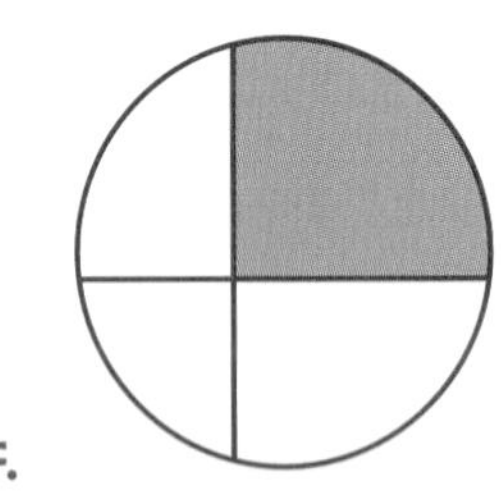
F.

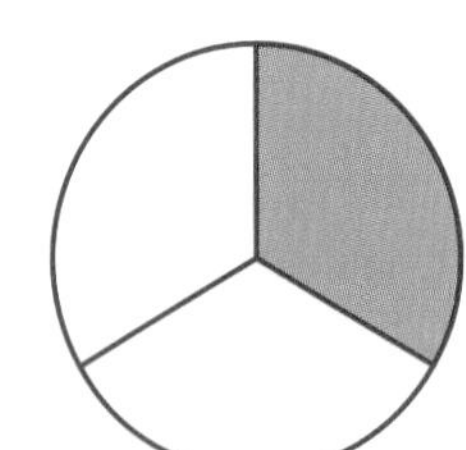
H.

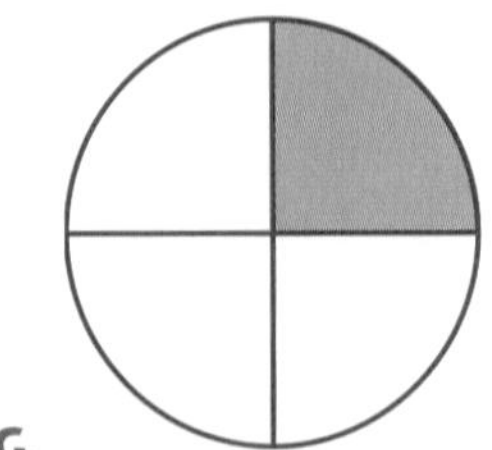
G.

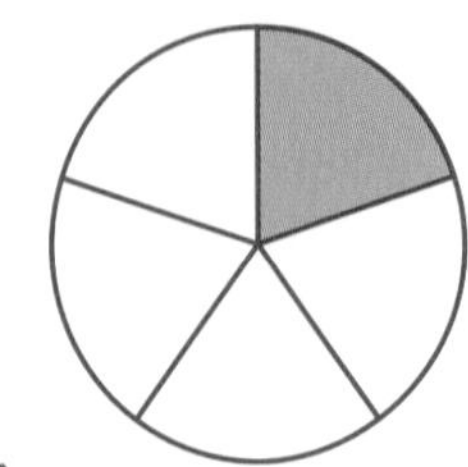
J.

Measurement and Geometry

5. Which unit can be used to measure the area of a rectangle?
   A. Inches
   B. Square inches
   C. Cubic inches
   D. Not Here

6. Which set of lines is parallel?

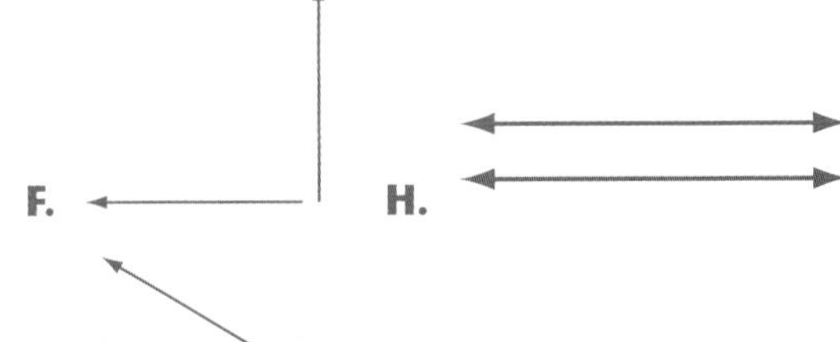

7. Which 3-dimensional figure is shown?

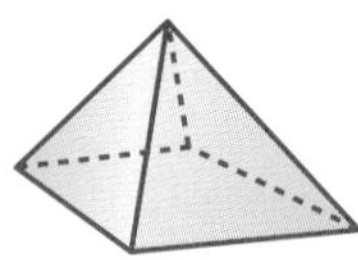

   A. Cone
   B. Cylinder
   C. Pyramid
   D. Sphere

8. What kind of angle is shown?

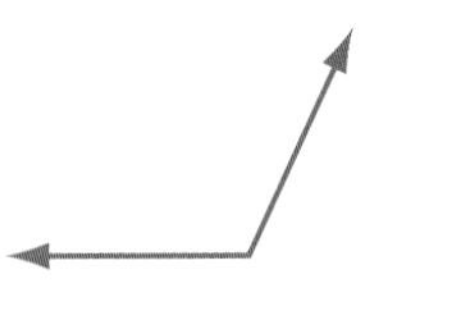

   F. Acute
   G. Right
   H. Obtuse
   J. Open

Statistics, Data Analysis, and Probability

Use data from the graph for problems 9–12.

Average Time for Cathy to Run 1 Mile

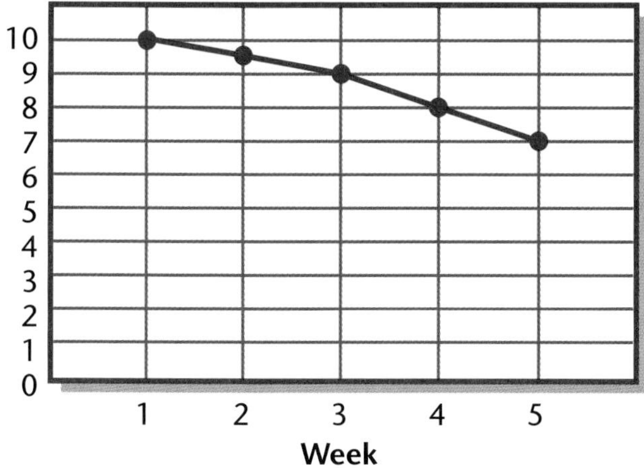

9. How much faster does Cathy run in Week 5 than in Week 1?
   A. 3 minutes   C. 5 minutes
   B. 4 minutes   D. 6 minutes

10. What is the average number of minutes it takes Cathy to run 1 mile in the 5 weeks?
   F. 7 minutes   H. 9.5 minutes
   G. 8.7 minutes   J. 10 minutes

11. If the trend shown continues, how many minutes might it take Cathy to run 1 mile in Week 6?
   A. 10 minutes   C. 9 minutes
   B. 8 minutes   D. 6 minutes

12. How long would it take Cathy to run 5 miles in Week 2?
   F. 9.5 minutes   H. 28.5 minutes
   G. 19 minutes   J. 47.5 minutes

Mathematical Reasoning

13. Carlos earns $5.25 each week delivering newspapers. How much does he earn in 36 weeks?
   A. $189.00   C. $47.25
   B. $186.70   D. $45.85

14. Selena works $5\frac{7}{8}$ hours in the morning. She works $3\frac{1}{4}$ hours in the afternoon. How many hours does Selena work in a day?
   F. $9\frac{1}{8}$ hours   H. $8\frac{2}{3}$ hours
   G. 9 hours   J. Not Here

15. Kevin works $9\frac{1}{4}$ hours on Monday. He works $8\frac{5}{6}$ hours on Tuesday. How much longer does Kevin work on Monday than on Tuesday?
   A. $18\frac{1}{12}$ hours   C. $1\frac{7}{12}$ hours
   B. $14\frac{3}{5}$ hours   D. $\frac{5}{12}$ hour

16. Two fractions have a common denominator of 8. Their sum is $\frac{3}{8}$. Which fractions are they?

Spiral Review and Test Prep

Multiply and Divide Fractions

Theme: Hobbies

Use the Data

Volunteers in 4-H by Age Group

Age Group	Fraction of Total Membership
K–3	$\frac{1}{3}$
4–6	$\frac{2}{5}$
7–9	$\frac{19}{100}$
10–12	$\frac{2}{25}$

- In 1998, $\frac{1}{3}$ of the 4-H participants lived in cities of 50,000 people or more. What fraction of all participants are in grades K–3 and live in large cities?

What You Will Learn

In this chapter you will learn how to
- multiply fractions and mixed numbers.
- estimate products of fractions and mixed numbers.
- use properties of multiplication.
- divide fractions.
- use strategies to solve problems.

Objective: Multiply a whole number by a fraction.

7·1 Multiply a Whole Number by a Fraction

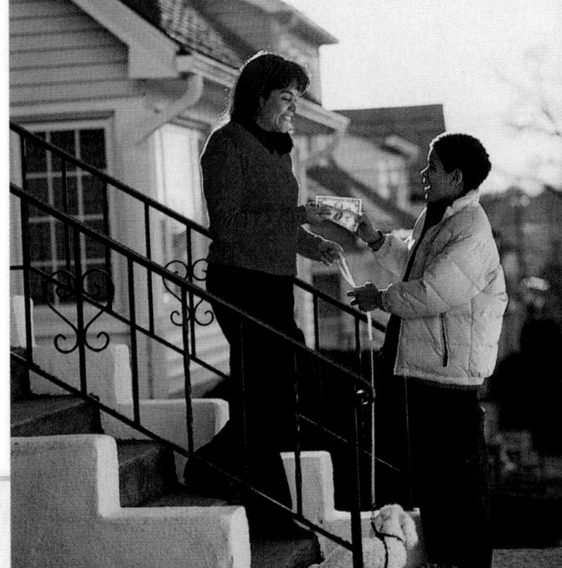

Learn

Pete loves to watch the sky on starry nights and wants to buy a telescope. To earn money, he walks the neighbor's dog for $15 each week. If he saves $\frac{2}{3}$ of his earnings each week, how much does he save?

Example

Find: $15 \times \frac{2}{3}$ to solve the problem

1 Divide the whole number by the denominator of the fraction.

$15 \div 3 = 5$

2 Multiply the quotient by the numerator of the fraction.

$2 \times 5 = 10$

Pete saves $10 each week.

More Examples

A

$\frac{1}{3}$ of $18 = \blacksquare$

Divide: $18 \div 3 = 6$
Multiply: $1 \times 6 = 6$

So $\frac{1}{3}$ of $18 = 6$.

Think: When the numerator is 1, you do not need to multiply the quotient.

B

$5 \times \frac{2}{5} = \blacksquare$

Divide: $5 \div 5 = 1$
Multiply: $1 \times 2 = 2$

So $5 \times \frac{2}{5} = 2$.

Try It

Multiply.

1. $15 \times \frac{1}{5}$ **2.** $24 \times \frac{1}{12}$ **3.** $48 \times \frac{3}{8}$ **4.** $\$60 \times \frac{2}{5}$ **5.** $54 \times \frac{5}{6}$

Sum it Up Explain how you would find $42 \times \frac{5}{6}$. What is the product?

Practice

Multiply.

6. $36 \times \frac{1}{3}$
7. $36 \times \frac{2}{3}$
8. $44 \times \frac{3}{4}$
9. $50 \times \frac{2}{5}$
10. $80 \times \frac{9}{10}$
11. $60 \times \frac{7}{12}$
★12. $120 \times \frac{5}{8}$
★13. $25 \times 10 \times \frac{3}{5}$

Algebra & functions **Copy and complete each table.**

Rule: Multiply by $\frac{1}{2}$.

	Input	Output
14.	12	■
15.	16	■
16.	20	■

Rule: Multiply by $\frac{7}{2}$.

	Input	Output
17.	24	■
18.	72	■
19.	84	■

Rule: Multiply by ■.

	Input	Output
20.	24	2
21.	72	■
22.	84	■

Problem Solving

Use data from *Did You Know?* for problem 23.

23. How many times wider is the Keck than the Hale telescope?

24. During the month of February, Pete watches the stars on $\frac{2}{7}$ of the nights. How many nights does he stargaze? It is not a leap year.

★25. **Science:** Jupiter has 16 moons. Mars has $\frac{1}{8}$ the number of moons as Jupiter. Neptune has 8 moons. How many more moons does Neptune have than Mars? Explain.

26. **Analyze:** Ben says that $96 \times \frac{3}{4} = 128$. Kelley says that Ben's answer is impossible. Why?

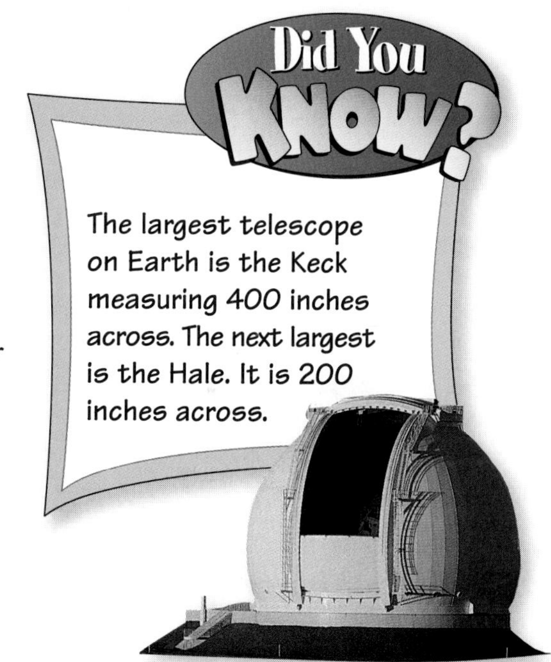

Did You Know?
The largest telescope on Earth is the Keck measuring 400 inches across. The next largest is the Hale. It is 200 inches across.

Spiral Review and Test Prep

Order from least to greatest.

27. 2.3, 3.3, 3
28. 0.05, 0.049, 0.5
29. 6.53, 4.44, 4.27
30. 1.001, 1.01, 1.1

Choose the correct answer.

31. Ashley is making punch with $\frac{3}{4}$ quart of pineapple, $1\frac{1}{2}$ quarts of orange, and $2\frac{3}{4}$ quarts of lemonade. How much punch is she making?
   - A. 4 quarts
   - B. 5 quarts
   - C. $4\frac{3}{4}$ quarts
   - D. $5\frac{1}{2}$ quarts

32. A string ensemble has 6 violas, 12 violins, and 9 cellos. In how many rows can the players sit and have the same number of instruments in each row?
   - F. 3 rows
   - G. 6 rows
   - H. 5 rows
   - J. 36 rows

Objective: Multiply a fraction by a fraction.

7·2 Multiply a Fraction by a Fraction

Learn

Gardening is one of the most popular hobbies in America. In this garden, $\frac{3}{4}$ of the flowers are tulips and $\frac{2}{3}$ of the tulips are red. What fraction of the flowers in the garden are red tulips?

Example 1

Remember: The expression "$\frac{2}{3}$ of" means "$\frac{2}{3}$ times."

Find: $\frac{2}{3}$ of $\frac{3}{4}$

1 Fold the paper in fourths one way. Shade 3 of the 4 sections blue.

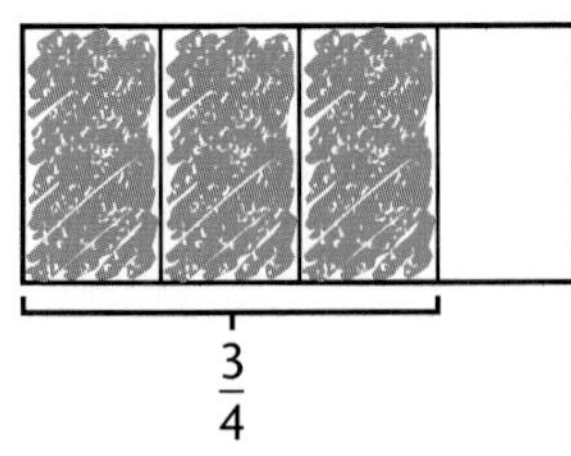

2 Fold the paper in thirds the other way. Shade two of the three sections of the paper red.

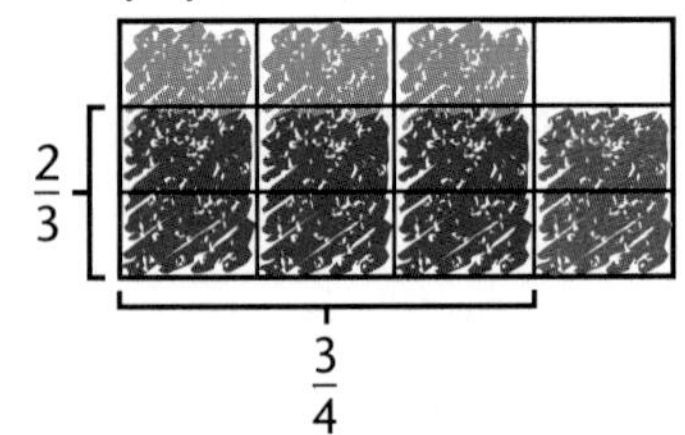

3 Count the total number of sections. Count the number of sections shaded with both colors.

$\frac{6}{12}$ ← number of sections with both colors / ← total number of sections

In the garden, $\frac{6}{12}$ or $\frac{1}{2}$ of the flowers are red tulips.

More Examples

A

Find: $\frac{1}{4}$ of $\frac{1}{4}$

$\frac{1}{16}$ is shaded with both colors.

So $\frac{1}{4}$ of $\frac{1}{4}$ is $\frac{1}{16}$.

$\frac{1}{4}$ $\frac{1}{4}$

B

Find: $\frac{3}{5}$ of $\frac{1}{2}$

$\frac{3}{10}$ is shaded with both colors.

So $\frac{3}{5}$ of $\frac{1}{2}$ is $\frac{3}{10}$.

$\frac{3}{5}$ $\frac{1}{2}$

A gardener plants $\frac{1}{4}$ of a vegetable garden with squash. One morning, he picks $\frac{2}{3}$ of the squash. What fraction of all of the vegetables does he pick?

There's more than one way!

Find: $\frac{2}{3} \times \frac{1}{4}$

Method A

1. Multiply the numerators. $2 \times 1 = 2$
2. Multiply the denominators. $3 \times 4 = 12$
3. Simplify. $\frac{2}{3} \times \frac{1}{4} = \frac{2 \times 1}{3 \times 4} = \frac{2}{12} = \frac{1}{6}$

Method B

When the numerator and denominator of either fraction have a common factor, you can simplify before you multiply.

$$\frac{2}{3} \times \frac{1}{4} = \frac{\overset{1}{\cancel{2}} \times 1}{3 \times \underset{2}{\cancel{4}}} = \frac{1 \times 1}{3 \times 2} = \frac{1}{6}$$

Think: Divide both the numerator and the denominator by 2.

The gardener picks $\frac{1}{6}$ of the vegetables.

More Examples

C

$$\frac{5}{6} \times \frac{3}{5} = \frac{5 \times 3}{6 \times 5} = \frac{15}{30} = \frac{1}{2}$$

D

$$\frac{3}{4} \times \frac{2}{9} = \frac{\overset{1}{\cancel{3}} \times \overset{1}{\cancel{2}}}{\underset{2}{\cancel{4}} \times \underset{3}{\cancel{9}}} = \frac{1}{6}$$

E

$$\frac{2}{3} \times \frac{3}{5} = \frac{2 \times \overset{1}{\cancel{3}}}{\underset{1}{\cancel{3}} \times 5} = \frac{2}{5}$$

F

$$\frac{3}{4} \times \frac{2}{3} \times \frac{2}{5} = \frac{\overset{1}{\cancel{3}} \times \overset{1}{\cancel{2}} \times 2}{\underset{2}{\cancel{4}} \times \underset{1}{\cancel{3}} \times 5} = \frac{1 \times 1 \times \overset{1}{\cancel{2}}}{\underset{1}{\cancel{2}} \times 1 \times 5} = \frac{1}{5}$$

Try It **Multiply. You may use models. Write each answer in simplest form.**

1. $\frac{1}{4} \times \frac{3}{4}$
2. $\frac{2}{5} \times \frac{1}{4}$
3. $\frac{2}{5} \times \frac{5}{8}$
4. $\frac{2}{3} \times \frac{5}{6}$
5. $\frac{2}{9} \times \frac{3}{8}$

Explain how you would multiply $\frac{5}{8} \times \frac{2}{5}$.

Practice

Multiply. Write each answer in simplest form.

6. $\frac{1}{4} \times \frac{1}{8}$
7. $\frac{1}{2} \times \frac{1}{4}$
8. $\frac{2}{3} \times \frac{2}{5}$
9. $\frac{3}{8} \times \frac{2}{3}$
10. $\frac{3}{4} \times \frac{3}{4}$
11. $\frac{4}{5} \times \frac{1}{4}$
12. $\frac{5}{6} \times \frac{2}{5}$
13. $\frac{1}{8} \times \frac{1}{2}$
14. $\frac{3}{5} \times \frac{5}{6}$
15. $\frac{4}{5} \times \frac{3}{8}$
16. $\frac{1}{6} \times \frac{3}{4}$
17. $\frac{2}{5} \times \frac{1}{2}$
18. $\frac{5}{12} \times \frac{2}{3}$
19. $\frac{3}{8} \times \frac{4}{9}$
20. $\frac{7}{10} \times \frac{4}{5}$
21. $\frac{3}{16} \times \frac{8}{9}$
22. $\frac{7}{20} \times \frac{5}{6}$
23. $\frac{7}{9} \times \frac{6}{7}$
24. $\frac{5}{6} \times \frac{3}{8}$
25. $\frac{3}{7} \times \frac{5}{9}$
26. $\frac{1}{3} \times \frac{5}{6}$
27. $\frac{3}{4} \times \frac{2}{5}$
28. $\frac{3}{8} \times \frac{3}{4}$
★29. $\frac{9}{20} \times \frac{2}{45}$
★30. $\frac{3}{40} \times \frac{4}{30}$

Algebra & functions

Find *n* so that each expression is true.

31. $\frac{2}{3} \times \frac{n}{5} = \frac{8}{15}$
32. $\frac{3}{4} \times \frac{n}{2} = \frac{3}{8}$
33. $\frac{2}{3} \times \frac{n}{4} = \frac{1}{6}$
34. $\frac{3}{4} \times \frac{n}{5} = \frac{3}{5}$

35.

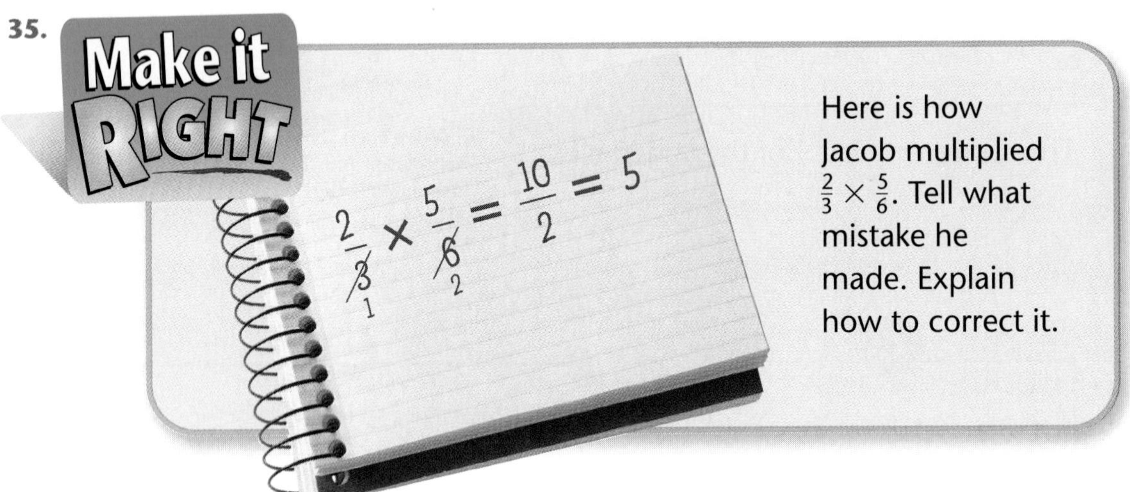

Here is how Jacob multiplied $\frac{2}{3} \times \frac{5}{6}$. Tell what mistake he made. Explain how to correct it.

Problem Solving

36. Cameron spends $\frac{2}{3}$ of an hour each day in his garden. When he is in his garden, he spends $\frac{1}{2}$ of the time watering the plants. How much time does Cameron spend watering the plants each day?

37. Fong's garden has 5 rows of berry bushes with 10 bushes in each row. If she picks about 20 berries from each plant, about how many berries will she have?

38. Joe wants to buy a CD-ROM on home garden landscaping. The CD-ROM costs $24.99. If Joe saves $2.50 each week, about how many weeks will pass before he saves enough money to buy the CD-ROM?

39. One fourth of the roses in Annie's garden are yellow. She gives $\frac{1}{3}$ of the yellow roses to Judy. What fraction of her roses does Annie give to Judy?

Use data from the table for problems 40–43.

40. Which of the plants is the tallest this week?

41. The tomato plant grew about $\frac{1}{3}$ of its height last week. How much did the tomato plant grow last week?

42. How much taller is the tomato plant than the broccoli plant?

43. How much taller is the tomato plant than the bean plant?

Plant Heights

Plant	Height
Tomato	$2\frac{1}{2}$ inches
Broccoli	$1\frac{3}{4}$ inches
Corn	2 inches
Bean	$2\frac{1}{4}$ inches

Use data from *Did You Know?* for problems 44 and 45.

44. **Social Studies:** During which century did the art of bonsai become popular in Japan?

45. Some bonsai live for hundreds of years. **What if** a bonsai was planted around the time when the practice of bonsai started in China? The plant lived for 256 years. About how many years ago did the plant die?

46. Rose buys a box of tulip bulbs for $24.60. The box has 12 bulbs. How much did each bulb cost?

★ 47. Andy buys 12 seed packets at a nursery. Each packet costs $0.35. He pays with a five-dollar bill. How much change does he receive?

★ 48. **Analyze:** How can you tell if the product of two fractions can be simplified?

Did You Know?

Bonsai is the ancient Asian art and science of growing miniature trees. The Japanese word bonsai means "growing in a pot." The practice began in China about 1,000 years ago. It has been popular in Japan for over 700 years.

Spiral Review and Test Prep

Estimate.

49. 22×42

50. 4.2×12.4

51. $149 \div 48$

52. $2,000 \div 465$

Choose the correct answer.

53. Marty usually pays $23.95 for a box of tulip bulbs. She finds them on sale for $19.99. How much does she save?

A. $4.99 C. $4.04
B. $4.94 D. $3.96

54. The instructions for a plant fertilizer state, "put 5 drops in the water." Artie puts twice as many in by mistake. How many more drops did he add than he should have?

F. 5 H. 10
G. 2.5 J. Not Here

Extra Practice, page 333

Objective: Make inferences to solve multistep problems.

7•3 Problem Solving: Reading for Math
Solve Multistep Problems

Students Build Furniture

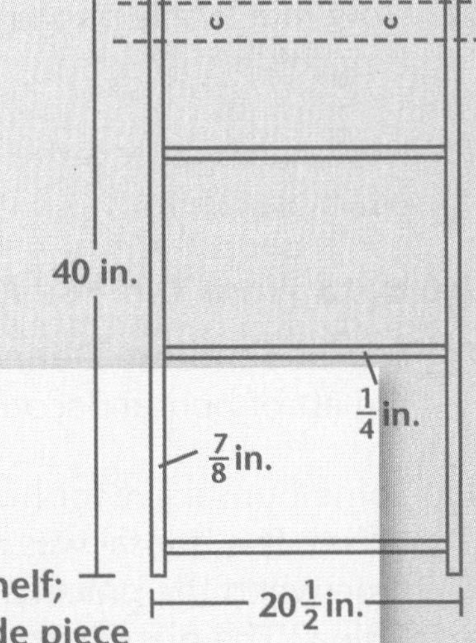

Read Many people make furniture as a hobby. Suppose you want to make the hanging bookshelf in the plans. What is the length of each shelf?

READING SKILL ▶ **Make an Inference**

When you make an inference, you draw a conclusion from suggested information.

- **What do you know?** Width of the hanging shelf; the thickness of each side piece
- **What can you infer?** Each shelf has the same length
- **What do you need to find?** The total length of each shelf

MATH SKILL ▶ **Solving Multistep Problems**

Solving a multistep problem involves more than one action.

Plan The length of each shelf is $20\frac{1}{2}$ inches minus the thickness of each side piece. First, multiply the thickness of the side boards times 2. Then, subtract the width of both side boards from $20\frac{1}{2}$ inches.

Solve Multiply: $\frac{\not{2}^{1}}{1} \times \frac{7}{\not{8}_{4}} = \frac{7}{4} = 1\frac{3}{4}$ The thickness of the two side boards is $1\frac{3}{4}$ inches.

Subtract: $20\frac{1}{2} - 1\frac{3}{4} = 18\frac{3}{4}$ Each shelf is $18\frac{3}{4}$ inches wide.

Look Back Is your answer reasonable?

Explain why making an inference was necessary to solve this problem.

Use data from the hanging bookshelf on page 306. Solve. Write the inference that you made.

1. How many inches of $\frac{7}{8}$-inch board are needed to make the sides of the hanging bookcase?
2. Arthur wants to make 2 shelves. How much $\frac{1}{4}$-inch lumber does Arthur need for both?
3. If one side of each shelf is fastened to the side boards with 2 screws, how many screws does Arthur need to attach the shelves?
4. How much thicker is the $\frac{7}{8}$-inch wood than the $\frac{1}{4}$-inch wood?

Use data from Arthur's supply list for problems 5–8.

5. If Arthur uses 4 ounces of varnish on each bookcase, how many bookcases can he varnish? Explain.
6. If Arthur makes a bookshelf half the size of the one on the plan on page 306, how much $\frac{7}{8}$-inch wood will he need?
7. How many total feet of wood does Arthur have?
8. How much thicker is the pine board than the oak board?
9. Suppose a woodworker cuts a 36-inch board in half and shaves $\frac{1}{4}$ inch from each side of the boards. How long will each board be?

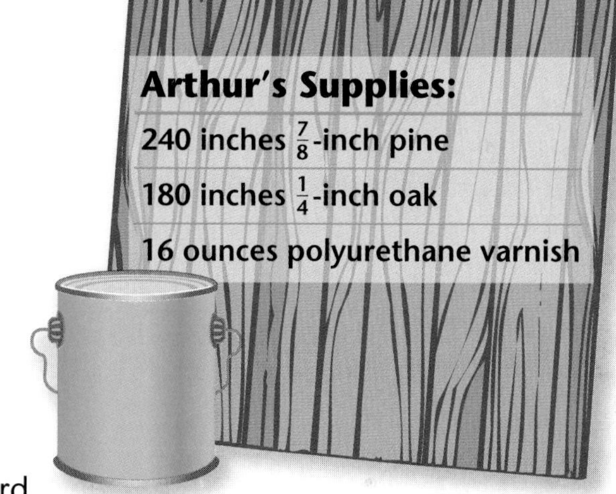

10. A board for a shelf is $27\frac{3}{8}$ inches long. Millie shaves the board to the nearest inch, then cuts it into 3 equal pieces. How long is each piece?

Spiral Review and Test Prep

Choose the correct answer.

Sue has $63\frac{7}{8}$ inches of wood. Since she uses equal amounts of wood to make 7 boxes, each box uses $9\frac{1}{8}$ inches of wood.

11. Which of following statements is true?
    - A. Sue uses $9\frac{1}{8}$ inches of wood.
    - B. Sue made 8 boxes.
    - C. Each box uses $9\frac{1}{8}$ inches of wood.
    - D. Each box uses $63\frac{7}{8}$ inches of wood.
12. When you solve a multistep problem, you
    - F. use only one operation.
    - G. simply guess at the answer.
    - H. never estimate an answer.
    - J. perform a series of actions.

Problem Solving

Check Your Progress A

Multiply. (pages 300–301)

1. $\frac{2}{5} \times 60$
2. $\frac{3}{8}$ of 56
3. $\frac{7}{12} \times 48$
4. $\frac{5}{6} \times 54$
5. $\frac{3}{4} \times 24$
6. $\frac{2}{3} \times 27$
7. $\frac{1}{2}$ of 50
8. $\frac{3}{10} \times 70$

Multiply. Write each answer in simplest form. (pages 300–305)

9. $\frac{3}{4} \times 10$
10. $\frac{2}{3} \times 25$
11. $38 \times \frac{5}{6}$
12. $32 \times \frac{2}{5}$
13. $\frac{4}{5} \times \frac{11}{20}$
14. $\frac{8}{9} \times \frac{15}{16}$
15. $\frac{7}{12} \times \frac{9}{10}$
16. $\frac{7}{8} \times \frac{2}{3}$
17. $\frac{1}{2} \times \frac{4}{5}$
18. $\frac{3}{10} \times \frac{5}{6}$
19. $\frac{1}{8} \times \frac{4}{5}$
20. $\frac{11}{12} \times \frac{6}{8}$

Find *n* to make each sentence true. (pages 300–305)

21. $\frac{2}{5} \times n = 2$
22. $3 \times n = 2$
23. $\frac{3}{5} \times \frac{5}{3} = n$
24. $\frac{2}{3} \times \frac{n}{5} = \frac{4}{15}$
25. $\frac{1}{3} \times \frac{1}{n} = \frac{1}{6}$
26. $\frac{3}{4} \times \frac{n}{6} = \frac{1}{2}$
27. $\frac{5}{8} \times \frac{4}{n} = \frac{5}{6}$
28. $\frac{5}{12} \times \frac{n}{10} = \frac{1}{8}$

Solve. (pages 300–307)

29. Arthur uses $\frac{3}{4}$ feet of wood to build a stool. How much wood does he need to build 3 stools?

30. Martine has $\frac{3}{4}$ of a roll of film left in her camera. Today she takes pictures using half of that amount. What fraction of a whole roll did she take today?

31. Arthur uses a $5\frac{3}{4}$ foot board for the top of a desk. If he shaves $\frac{1}{12}$ of a foot from each side of the board, how wide will the desk be?

32. Pete has 21 new baseball cards. Of these, $\frac{1}{3}$ are of the Red Sox. How many of Pete's new baseball cards are of the Red Sox?

33. Janell's model collection is $\frac{1}{3}$ airplanes. Of these, $\frac{3}{5}$ are models of airplanes designed before World War II. How many of Janell's models are airplanes that were designed before World War II?

Use the Internet

Aaron is gathering information about the planets for a science project. He needs to find data for three different planets that are smaller than Earth. He will use the data he collects to complete the following table. How can he use the Internet to gather the data?

Planet	Size of Planet (Diameter)	Fraction of the Size of Earth
Earth		

- Go to www.mhschool.com/math.
- Find the list of sites that provide science data. Click on a link.
- Find the data on the planets. Choose three planets for which data is given.
- Copy the table. Write the names of the planets you chose in your table.
- Find the size of Earth.
- Find the size of each planet.
- Record the fraction of the size of Earth for each in the table.

1. Which planet is the largest in comparison to the size of Earth? Which planet is the largest in size?

2. Which planet is the smallest in comparison to the size of Earth? Which planet is the smallest in size?

3. **Analyze:** Why does using the Internet make more sense than using another reference source to find the data needed to complete your table?

For more practice, use Math Traveler™.

Objective: Multiply with mixed numbers, fractions, and whole numbers.

7·4 Multiply Mixed Numbers

Model Boat Kit
450 pieces
Sailboat model $\frac{1}{5}$ original size

Learn

Some people like to build models of boats, cars, and buildings. If the real sailboat measures $17\frac{1}{2}$ feet, how long will the model in the box be when it is built?

Example 1

Find: $\frac{1}{5} \times 17\frac{1}{2}$ to solve the problem

1 Rename the mixed number as an improper fraction.

$$17\frac{1}{2} = \frac{(17 \times 2) + 1}{2} = \frac{35}{2}$$

2 Divide the numerator and denominator by common factors, then multiply.

$$\frac{1}{5} \times \frac{35}{2} = \frac{1 \times \overset{7}{\cancel{35}}}{\underset{1}{\cancel{5}} \times 2} = \frac{7}{2}$$

3 Simplify.

$$\frac{7}{2} = 3\frac{1}{2}$$

The model will be $3\frac{1}{2}$ feet long.

More Examples

A Find: $8\frac{5}{6} \times \frac{3}{8}$

$$8\frac{5}{6} \times \frac{3}{8} = \frac{53}{6} \times \frac{3}{8} = \frac{53 \times \overset{1}{\cancel{3}}}{\underset{2}{\cancel{6}} \times 8} = \frac{53}{16} = 3\frac{5}{16}$$

B Find: $2\frac{2}{3} \times 1\frac{1}{2}$

$$2\frac{2}{3} \times 1\frac{1}{2} = \frac{8}{3} \times \frac{3}{2} = \frac{\overset{4}{\cancel{8}} \times \overset{1}{\cancel{3}}}{\underset{1}{\cancel{3}} \times \underset{1}{\cancel{2}}} = 4$$

The sailboat model will be mounted on a rectangular board. The length of the board is $1\frac{1}{5}$ times as long as the width. The width of the board is $6\frac{7}{8}$ inches. What is the length of the board?

Example 2

Find: $1\frac{1}{5} \times 6\frac{7}{8}$

1 Rename the mixed number as an improper fraction.

$$1\frac{1}{5} \times 6\frac{7}{8}$$
$$\downarrow \quad \downarrow$$
$$\frac{6}{5} \times \frac{55}{8}$$

2 Divide by common factors, then multiply.

$$\frac{6}{5} \times \frac{55}{8} = \frac{\overset{3}{\cancel{6}}}{\underset{1}{\cancel{5}}} \times \frac{\overset{11}{\cancel{55}}}{\underset{4}{\cancel{8}}} = \frac{33}{4}$$

3 Simplify.

$$\frac{33}{4} = 8\frac{1}{4}$$

The length of the board is $8\frac{1}{4}$ inches.

More Examples

C $4\frac{3}{4} \times 4 = \frac{19}{4} \times \frac{4}{1} = 19$

D $1\frac{5}{8} \times 1\frac{5}{8} = \frac{13}{8} \times \frac{13}{8} = \frac{169}{64} = 2\frac{41}{64}$

E $4\frac{2}{5} \times 1\frac{3}{4} \times \frac{5}{11} = \frac{22}{5} \times \frac{7}{4} \times \frac{5}{11} = \frac{\overset{2}{\cancel{22}} \times 7 \times \overset{1}{\cancel{5}}}{\underset{1}{\cancel{5}} \times 4 \times \underset{1}{\cancel{11}}} = \frac{\overset{1}{\cancel{2}} \times 7 \times 1}{1 \times \underset{2}{\cancel{4}} \times 1} = \frac{7}{2} = 3\frac{1}{2}$

Try It **Multiply. Write each answer in simplest form.**

1. $\frac{2}{5} \times 4\frac{3}{8}$ **2.** $\frac{5}{6} \times 1\frac{1}{10}$ **3.** $12 \times 2\frac{1}{5}$ **4.** $6\frac{1}{2} \times 4\frac{3}{4}$ **5.** $\frac{2}{3} \times 6 \times 1\frac{1}{2}$

Sum it Up Explain how you would multiply $3\frac{1}{8} \times 2\frac{2}{3}$.

Practice **Multiply. Write each answer in simplest form.**

6. $\frac{1}{4} \times 3\frac{1}{3}$
7. $\frac{2}{5} \times 9\frac{1}{2}$
8. $4\frac{1}{4} \times \frac{5}{12}$
9. $3\frac{2}{3} \times \frac{7}{10}$
10. $\frac{1}{7} \times 4\frac{1}{5}$
11. $\frac{5}{6} \times 5\frac{3}{4}$
12. $\frac{1}{2} \times 7\frac{1}{12}$
13. $8\frac{4}{9} \times \frac{2}{3}$
14. $10\frac{1}{2} \times \frac{3}{4}$
15. $1\frac{1}{8} \times \frac{2}{3}$
16. $25 \times \frac{1}{2}$
17. $33 \times \frac{3}{4}$
18. $\frac{3}{10} \times 15$
19. $\frac{5}{16} \times 9$
20. $\frac{2}{15} \times 12$
21. $4\frac{4}{15} \times 3\frac{1}{2}$
22. $10\frac{1}{6} \times 3\frac{2}{9}$
23. $6\frac{5}{12} \times 13\frac{4}{5}$
24. $7\frac{3}{8} \times 8\frac{7}{10}$
25. $41\frac{5}{6} \times 9$
26. $1\frac{1}{3} \times \frac{3}{4}$
27. $6\frac{1}{8} \times \frac{2}{7}$
28. $4\frac{1}{6} \times 3\frac{1}{5}$
29. $2\frac{5}{8} \times 1\frac{1}{3}$
30. $4\frac{3}{5} \times 2\frac{1}{3}$
31. $7\frac{3}{20} \times 2\frac{5}{16}$
32. $4\frac{3}{14} \times 15\frac{5}{14}$
33. $5\frac{5}{8} \times \frac{1}{9} \times 2$
★34. $7\frac{1}{5} \times \frac{3}{8} \times 2\frac{2}{9}$

Algebra & functions **Find the missing number.**

35. $\frac{n}{6} \times 18 = 12$
36. $\frac{x}{4} \times 16 = 12$
37. $\frac{z}{3} \times 18 = 12$
38. $\frac{y}{6} \times 12 = 2$
39. $\frac{t}{9} \times 18 = 4$
40. $\frac{u}{3} \times 12 = 12$
41. $\frac{a}{5} \times 20 = 12$
42. $\frac{d}{8} \times 24 = 12$
43. $\frac{c}{5} \times 15 = 9$
44. $\frac{b}{2} \times 12 = 12$

45.

Here is how Mitchell multiplied $8\frac{1}{4} \times 1\frac{1}{4}$. Tell what mistake he made. Explain how to correct it.

Problem Solving

46. A model is $\frac{1}{16}$ the actual size of a car. The real car is 8 feet, or 96 inches long. How long is the model?

47. Each model train in a kit is $1\frac{1}{2}$ inches long. How long will a train made of 6 cars be?

48. Matt builds a model of a cable car. The model is 3 feet wide. It is $2\frac{1}{4}$ times as long as it is wide. How long is it?

49. Ann builds model trains. She makes a train with 7 cars. Each car measures $3\frac{1}{2}$ inches. How long is her model?

50. **Language Arts:** The phrase, *scale drawing*, means a reduced or enlarged drawing of an actual object. Derrick makes a $\frac{1}{4}$ scale drawing of a sculpture that is $5\frac{1}{3}$ feet high. How high is the sculpture in Derrick's drawing?

51. Jena likes to put together models of ships. She is making a model that has 325 pieces. If $\frac{3}{5}$ of the pieces go above the deck, how many pieces go below the deck?

52. Len is making a model airplane. The hobby store charges $15.50 for the model airplane kit, $7.99 for paint, and $2.00 for glue. What is Len's total cost?

53. Ted has completed 14 of the 42 steps needed to build a model. What fraction of the steps has he completed? Write your answer in simplest form.

54. A model kit has 52 pieces that must be painted before assembly. Four friends each paint an equal number of pieces. How many does each friend paint?

55. Grant builds a model train set. Three train cars complete the track in 4.5, 4 and 4.3 seconds. Order these numbers from least to greatest.

56. **Collect Data:** Find at least 3 landmarks in your city. Make a table of the length, width, and height of each landmark. Then find the length, width, and height of a model that would be $\frac{1}{10}$ the size of each.

★57. **Analyze:** Len is making 6 miniature models of bicycles and tricycles. He has a total of 16 wheels. How many tricycles can he make?

★58. Hank has used $\frac{2}{3}$ of the 51 pieces in his model kit. Vivian has used $\frac{1}{2}$ of the 72 pieces in her kit. Who has used more pieces?

Journal ★59. **Analyze:** If you multiply a mixed number by a mixed number, will your answer ever be a whole number? Explain.

Spiral Review and Test Prep

Tell whether or not the number is divisible by 3.

60. 193 61. 2,334 62. 465 63. 212 64. 153

Choose the correct answer.

65. Which is the best graph to display data that changes over time?

A. Pictograph
B. Line graph
C. Circle graph
D. Not Here

66. What is the least common multiple of 18 and 27?

F. 9
G. 27
H. 54
J. 972

Extra Practice, page 334

7•5

Objective: Estimate products with mixed numbers, whole numbers, and fractions.

Estimate Products

Cellist Han-Na Chang

Learn

Suppose Han-Na practices her cello $2\frac{3}{4}$ hours each day, 5 days a week. About how many hours would she practice each week?

Example 1

Estimate: $5 \times 2\frac{3}{4}$ to solve the problem

1 Round the mixed number to the nearest whole number.

$2\frac{3}{4}$ rounds to 3.

2 Multiply.

$5 \times 3 = 15$

Han-Na would practice about 15 hours each week.

More Examples

Remember: With larger numbers, round to the nearest ten.

A

Estimate: $4\frac{3}{8} \times 5\frac{7}{12}$

$4\frac{3}{8} \times 5\frac{7}{12}$

$\downarrow \quad \downarrow$

$4 \times 6 = 24$

So $4\frac{3}{8} \times 5\frac{7}{12}$ is about 24.

B

Estimate: $36\frac{1}{2} \times 53\frac{1}{4}$

$36\frac{1}{2} \times 53\frac{1}{4}$

$\downarrow \quad \downarrow$

$40 \times 50 = 2{,}000$

So $36\frac{1}{2} \times 53\frac{1}{4}$ is about 2,000.

Suppose Han-Na puts 43 of her photos in a photo album. About $\frac{3}{5}$ are from her concerts. About how many of the photographs are from concerts?

Example 2

Estimate: $\frac{3}{5} \times 43$

1 Use a compatible number for the whole number.

$$\frac{3}{5} \times 43$$
$$\downarrow \quad \downarrow$$
$$\frac{3}{5} \times 45$$

2 Multiply.

Because 5 divides evenly into 45, 45 and 5 are compatible numbers.

$$\frac{3}{5} \times 45 = 27$$

About 27 of the photographs would be from concerts.

More Examples

C

Estimate: $\frac{2}{3} \times 11\frac{1}{5}$

$\frac{2}{3} \times 11\frac{1}{5}$

$\downarrow \quad \downarrow$

$\frac{2}{3} \times 12$

Remember: Use compatible numbers to estimate.

$\frac{2}{3} \times 12 = 8$

So $\frac{2}{3} \times 11\frac{1}{5}$ is about 8.

D

Estimate: $\frac{3}{8} \times 23\frac{4}{5}$

$23\frac{4}{5}$ is close to 24. ← Round to a whole number.

$\frac{3}{8} \times 24 = 9$

So $\frac{3}{8} \times 23\frac{4}{5}$ is about 9.

Try It **Estimate.**

1. $2\frac{1}{2} \times 3\frac{2}{5}$
2. $52\frac{7}{8} \times 68\frac{1}{5}$
3. $\frac{2}{3} \times 20$
4. $43 \times \frac{4}{5}$
5. $10\frac{1}{8} \times 50\frac{1}{3}$

Explain how you would estimate $\frac{5}{6} \times 22\frac{3}{4}$.

Practice

Estimate.

6. $6 \times 3\frac{1}{3}$
7. $4\frac{3}{4} \times 7$
8. $12 \times 5\frac{3}{8}$
9. $6\frac{1}{2} \times 3\frac{2}{3}$
10. $8\frac{4}{5} \times 9\frac{3}{5}$
11. $10\frac{7}{10} \times 5\frac{1}{3}$
12. $49\frac{1}{3} \times 65\frac{1}{2}$
13. $28\frac{1}{4} \times 85\frac{1}{4}$
14. $72\frac{1}{5} \times 38\frac{3}{4}$
15. $21\frac{11}{12} \times \frac{6}{13}$
16. $16\frac{4}{9} \times \frac{5}{9}$
17. $58\frac{4}{7} \times \frac{6}{11}$
18. $\frac{3}{8} \times 35$
19. $\frac{7}{12} \times 51$
20. $27 \times \frac{2}{5}$
21. $46 \times \frac{5}{6}$
22. $\frac{3}{4} \times 13\frac{1}{3}$
23. $\frac{3}{7} \times 36\frac{1}{2}$
24. $59\frac{3}{5} \times \frac{2}{9}$
25. $33\frac{1}{3} \times \frac{4}{9}$
26. $78\frac{3}{4} \times 92\frac{1}{9}$
27. $\frac{3}{5} \times 5\frac{2}{3}$
28. $\frac{5}{8} \times 23\frac{3}{4}$
29. $\frac{4}{7} \times 18\frac{1}{3}$
30. $\frac{5}{11} \times 17\frac{9}{10}$
★31. $545\frac{5}{8} \times 334\frac{7}{8}$
★32. $250\frac{1}{12} \times 705\frac{7}{12}$
★33. $608\frac{1}{2} \times \frac{5}{6}$
★34. $479\frac{3}{4} \times \frac{3}{8}$
★35. $179\frac{1}{3} \times \frac{9}{20}$

Estimate to compare. Write >, <, or =.

36. $8 \times 4\frac{2}{3}$ ● $6 \times 5\frac{1}{4}$
37. $\frac{5}{6} \times 51$ ● $\frac{3}{4} \times 30$
38. $6\frac{3}{10} \times 4$ ● $7\frac{1}{2} \times 4$
39. $38 \times \frac{4}{5}$ ● $6\frac{2}{5} \times 7\frac{1}{3}$
40. $18\frac{1}{2} \times \frac{4}{5}$ ● $21\frac{7}{9} \times \frac{3}{8}$
41. $42\frac{1}{3} \times 31\frac{5}{8}$ ● $27\frac{1}{2} \times 66\frac{1}{9}$

42.

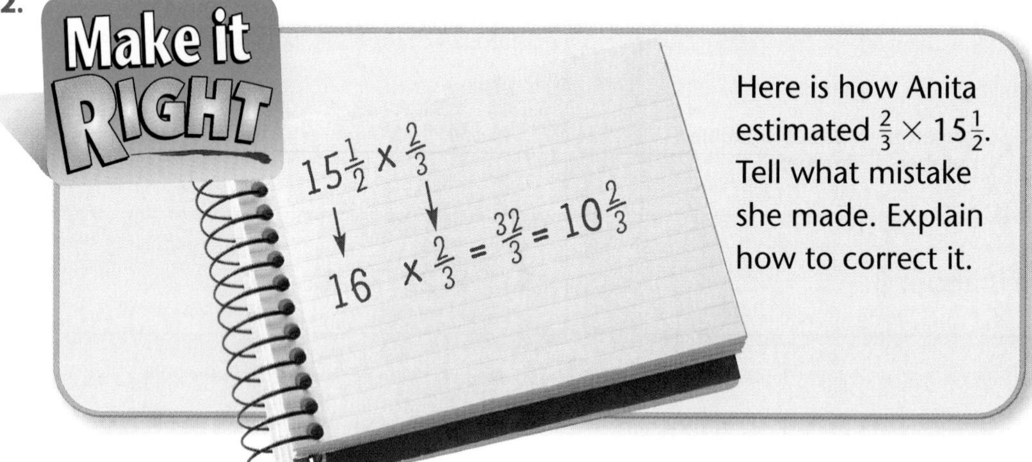

Here is how Anita estimated $\frac{2}{3} \times 15\frac{1}{2}$. Tell what mistake she made. Explain how to correct it.

Problem Solving

43. **Health:** A musician swims for exercise. She swims 6 days each week. She swims $2\frac{1}{8}$ miles each day. About how far does she swim in a week?

44. A young musician gives 99 concerts one year. About $\frac{1}{4}$ of these concerts are given at his school. About how many concerts are at school?

45. *Young Musicians* magazine costs \$3.25 at a newsstand. The annual subscription fee for the magazine is \$24.95 for 12 issues. How much do you save each year by subscribing rather than buying the magazine at the newsstand every month?

46. **Social Studies:** Suppose Han-Na learns in school that the Caspian Sea is actually the largest lake in the world. It is 143,244 square miles. Lake Superior is 31,700 square miles. How much larger is the Caspian Sea than Lake Superior?

Use data from the graph for problems 47–50.

47. Which type of music has the greatest number of votes?

48. What fraction of the readers surveyed voted for jazz?

49. What fraction of the readers surveyed voted for either opera or classical?

★ **50.** **Analyze:** Suppose the graph showed that 10 people voted for jazz, but nothing else was changed. Would that mean that $\frac{1}{10}$ of those surveyed voted for jazz? Why or why not?

Favorite Types of Music

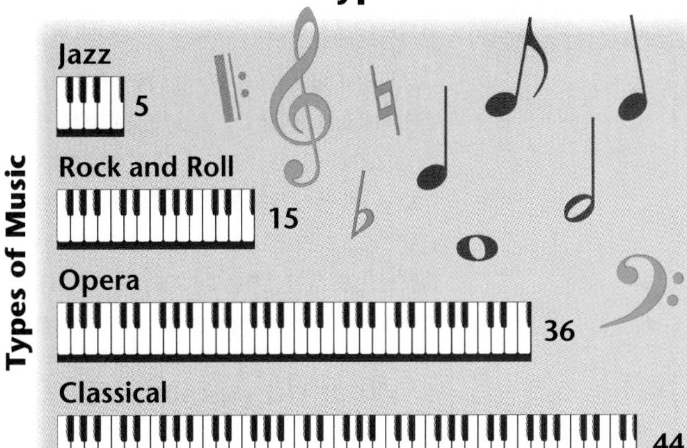

51. Nara puts her best concert photos in an album. Each photo album has 45 pages. Each page holds 6 pictures. She has 5 albums filled. How many photos does Nara have?

★ **52.** Maria has 18 concert photographs. She frames $\frac{2}{3}$ of them and gives $\frac{1}{2}$ of the remainder to her friends. How many photographs does she give to her friends?

53. **Create a problem** that can be solved by estimating the product of a mixed number and a fraction. Solve it and give it to another student to solve.

54. **Explain** when the estimate of a number times a whole number could be greater than the whole number.

Spiral Review and Test Prep

Round each number to the underlined place.

55. $2\underline{3}.54$ **56.** $4.62\underline{5}7$ **57.** $0.0\underline{0}76$ **58.** $5.3\underline{9}60$ **59.** $\underline{0}.8048$

Choose the correct answer.

60. Which of these numbers is a prime number?

A. 1 **C.** 13
B. 12 **D.** 15

61. Which choice orders the numbers from least to greatest? $\frac{1}{2}$, 0.4, $\frac{1}{5}$, 0.24

F. $\frac{1}{2}$, 0.24, $\frac{1}{5}$, 0.4 **H.** $\frac{1}{5}$, $\frac{1}{2}$, 0.24, 0.4
G. 0.4, $\frac{1}{2}$, 0.24, $\frac{1}{5}$ **J.** Not Here

Objective: Solve problems by making an organized list.

Problem Solving: Strategy
Make an Organized List

Read

Read the problem carefully.

Christina likes to invent and play games. One of the games she created is called *Fractionmania*. To play the game, a player spins the two spinners shown and finds the product of the two fractions. What products can the player make?

- **What do you know?** Spinner A is marked $\frac{1}{2}$, $\frac{1}{4}$, and $\frac{1}{3}$; Spinner B is marked $1\frac{1}{2}$ and $2\frac{1}{6}$.
- **What do you need to find?** What products a player can make

Remember:
A product is the answer in a multiplication problem.

Plan

You can make an organized list of the products that the player can make.

Solve

Make a list of all the possible spinner products. Find each product.

The player can make these products: $\frac{3}{4}$, $1\frac{1}{12}$, $\frac{3}{8}$, $\frac{13}{24}$, $\frac{1}{2}$, $\frac{13}{18}$.

Spinner A		Spinner B		Product
$\frac{1}{2}$	$\times$	$1\frac{1}{2}$	$=$	$\frac{3}{4}$
$\frac{1}{2}$	$\times$	$2\frac{1}{6}$	$=$	$1\frac{1}{12}$
$\frac{1}{4}$	$\times$	$1\frac{1}{2}$	$=$	$\frac{3}{8}$
$\frac{1}{4}$	$\times$	$2\frac{1}{6}$	$=$	$\frac{13}{24}$
$\frac{1}{3}$	$\times$	$1\frac{1}{2}$	$=$	$\frac{1}{2}$
$\frac{1}{3}$	$\times$	$2\frac{1}{6}$	$=$	$\frac{13}{18}$

Look Back

How can you check your answer?

Describe how an organized list helped you solve this problem.

Practice Make an organized list to solve.

1. Kendra plays this spinner game. She spins both spinners and finds the product of the mixed numbers. What products can Kendra make?

2. Otto plays this spinner game. He spins both spinners and finds the product of the fractions. What products can Otto make?

3. There are two sets of chips in Ashley's new board game. One set contains a red, a blue, a yellow, and a green chip. The other set contains a purple, a white, a black, and a brown chip. If Ashley takes one chip from each set, how many combinations of chips are possible?

4. Mrs. Key has two sets of math shapes. One set has a square and a triangle. The other set has a circle, a rectangle, and a pentagon. If she chooses one shape from each set, how many combinations of shapes can she have?

Problem Solving

Mixed Strategy Review

CHOOSE A STRATEGY

- Logical Reasoning
- Draw a Diagram
- Make a Graph
- Make a Table or List
- Find a Pattern
- Guess and Check
- Write an Equation
- Work Backward
- Solve a Simpler Problem
- Conduct an Experiment

5. Betty, Doug, Jill, and April are about to begin a chess tournament. Each player shakes hands with each of the other players once. How many handshakes are there in all?

6. Six friends sit at a round table to play a board game. Olive sits at Sue's right. Sue sits across from Pete. Ben does not sit next to Pete, but he does sit next to Ann. Mark sits between Olive and Pete. Which of the friends sits at Pete's right?

7. Fred sends letters and postcards to friends. A letter costs \$0.33 to mail and a postcard costs \$0.20. He spends \$2.12 in all and sends a total of 8 letters and postcards. How many of each kind did he send?

8. Juan has 12 card games and 14 board games. Liz has $1\frac{1}{2}$ as many board games and $\frac{1}{3}$ as many card games. How many games does Liz have?

9. Eduardo wants to order a game that costs \$39.95 plus \$4.45 for shipping. He has 150 quarters in his bank. Does he have enough money?

10. Lin opens a $4\frac{1}{2}$-ounce jar of metallic paint to cover a model. When he finishes, there are $1\frac{3}{4}$ ounces left. How much paint was used?

Extra Practice, page 335

7·7

Objective: Apply properties of multiplication to fractions, mixed numbers, and whole numbers.

Properties of Multiplication

Algebra & functions

Learn

You can use the properties of multiplication with fractions and mixed numbers.

Math Words

Properties of Multiplication

- Associative
- Commutative
- Distributive
- Identity
- Zero

Associative Property

The way factors are grouped does not change the product.

$$\left(\frac{3}{4} \times \frac{1}{2}\right) \times 2 = \frac{3}{4} \times \left(\frac{1}{2} \times 2\right)$$

Distributive Property

To multiply a sum by a number, you can multiply each addend by the number and add the products.

$$\left(\frac{1}{2} + \frac{3}{4}\right) \times 2 = \left(\frac{1}{2} \times 2\right) + \left(\frac{3}{4} \times 2\right)$$

Commutative Property

The order of the factors does not change the product.

Identity Property

The product of any factor and 1 equals the factor.

$$1\frac{2}{3} \times 1 = 1\frac{2}{3}$$

Zero Property

The product of any factor and zero equals zero.

$$\frac{7}{8} \times 0 = 0$$

Example

Simplify: $\left(\frac{1}{2} \times 22\frac{7}{12}\right) \times 2$

Think: It is easier to mulitply $\frac{1}{2} \times 2$ first

$$\left(22\frac{7}{12} \times \frac{1}{2}\right) \times 2 = 22\frac{7}{12} \times \left(\frac{1}{2} \times 2\right) = 22\frac{7}{12} \times 1 = 22\frac{7}{12}$$

So $\left(\frac{1}{2} \times 22\frac{7}{12}\right) \times 2 = 22\frac{7}{12}$.

Try It

Identify each property of multiplication.

1. $\frac{2}{11} \times 1 = \frac{2}{11}$
2. $\frac{2}{3} \times \left(5\frac{1}{2} \times 7\right) = \left(\frac{2}{3} \times 5\frac{1}{2}\right) \times 7$
3. $\frac{3}{4} \times \frac{2}{5} = \frac{2}{5} \times \frac{3}{4}$

Explain why $\left(3\frac{1}{3} + 2\right) \times \frac{1}{2}$ is equal to $\left(\frac{1}{2} \times 3\frac{1}{3}\right) + \left(2 \times \frac{1}{2}\right)$.

Practice

Identify each property of multiplication.

4. $0 \times 13\frac{1}{5} = 0$
5. $\frac{7}{9} \times \frac{3}{4} = \frac{3}{4} \times \frac{7}{9}$
6. $7\frac{1}{8} \times 5 = (7 \times 5) + \left(\frac{1}{8} \times 5\right)$
7. $9 \times \frac{3}{10} = \frac{3}{10} \times 9$
8. $1 \times 38\frac{7}{15} = 38\frac{7}{15}$
9. $\frac{5}{12} \times \left(4\frac{1}{2} \times 3\right) = \left(\frac{5}{12} \times 4\frac{1}{2}\right) \times 3$

Simplify.

10. $6 \times \left(\frac{2}{3} \times \frac{3}{5}\right)$
11. $\left(7\frac{1}{2} \times 1\frac{3}{4}\right) \times 4$
12. $4\frac{2}{3} \times 0$
13. $1\frac{1}{2} \times 3 \times \frac{1}{3}$
14. $5\frac{1}{4} \times 1$
15. $3\frac{2}{9} \times 18$
16. $12 \times 4\frac{5}{6}$
17. $\frac{7}{12} \times 6\frac{1}{3}$

Algebra & functions **Find the number that makes each sentence true.**

18. $5 \times 48 = 5 \times (40 + n)$
19. $3 \times 21 \times 2 = 21 \times f \times 2$
20. $\left(\frac{3}{4} \times \frac{1}{2}\right) \times \frac{3}{8} = d \times \left(\frac{1}{2} \times \frac{3}{8}\right)$

Problem Solving

21. Jenny practices piano $5\frac{2}{3}$ hours on Saturday. On Sunday she practices $\frac{3}{4}$ of the time she practices on Saturday. How much time does Jenny practice on Sunday?

22. **Compare:** Would you use the Commutative Property or the Distributive Property to solve $2\frac{4}{9} \times 27$ mentally? Tell why and solve.

23. Carmen says that $4\frac{5}{8} \times 1 = 0$ by the Identify Property of Multiplication. Is she correct? Explain.

24. **Music:** J. S. Bach wrote the Goldberg Variations, which are 30 variations on a theme. Every 2 variations are followed by a canon. How many canons are in the Goldberg Variations?

★25. In a band, $\frac{1}{3}$ of the horns are trombones and $\frac{1}{4}$ of the band is horns. If there are 24 people in the band, how many play trombone?

26. **Create a problem** that can be solved using the Distributive Property of Multiplication. Solve it and give it to another student to solve.

Spiral Review and Test Prep

Write each fraction in simplest form.

27. $\frac{4}{32}$
28. $\frac{7}{70}$
29. $\frac{15}{330}$
30. $\frac{140}{180}$
31. $\frac{96}{240}$

Choose the correct answer.

32. What is the greatest common factor of 56 and 72?
    A. 1 B. 2 C. 4 D. 8

33. What is the median of the numbers 23, 38, 38, 19, 23, 67, 39, 23, 39?
    F. 19 G. 23 H. 38 J. 39

Objective: Divide fractions.

7•8 Explore Dividing Fractions

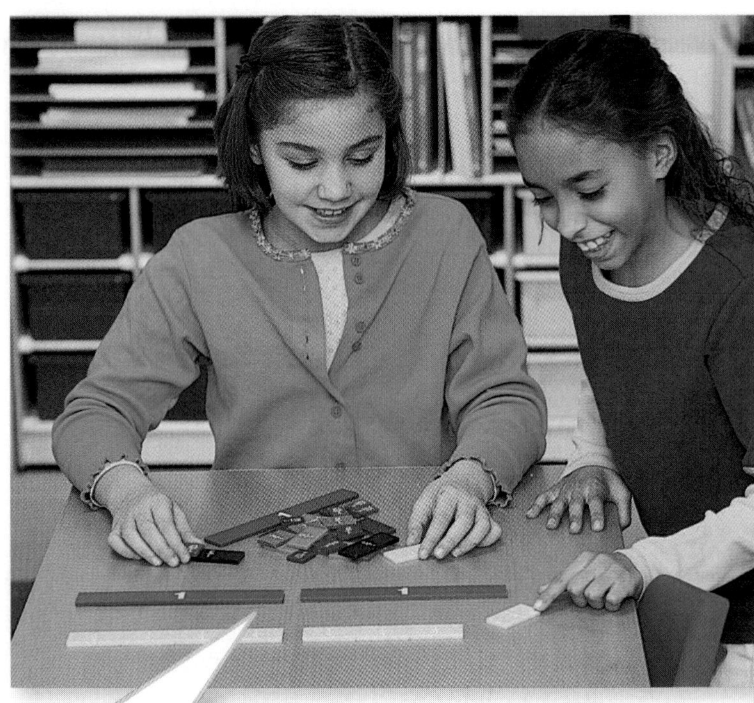

Learn

You can use fraction strips to explore dividing fractions.

Work Together

Find: $2 \div \frac{1}{4}$

You Will Need
- **fraction strips**

▶ Use fraction strips to find how many $\frac{1}{4}$s are in 2.

- Use whole fraction strips to model 2.

1	1

- Place $\frac{1}{4}$ fraction strips below the whole fraction strips. Count how many one-fourth strips equal the length of the 2 whole strips.

1				1			
$\frac{1}{4}$	$\frac{1}{4}$	$\frac{1}{4}$	$\frac{1}{4}$	$\frac{1}{4}$	$\frac{1}{4}$	$\frac{1}{4}$	$\frac{1}{4}$

Record your work.

▶ Use fraction strips to find these quotients.

$3 \div \frac{1}{3}$ $2 \div \frac{1}{5}$ $1 \div \frac{1}{4}$ $2 \div \frac{1}{8}$

Make Connections

Division and multiplication are related operations. You can use this fact to think about dividing with fractions.

Using Models

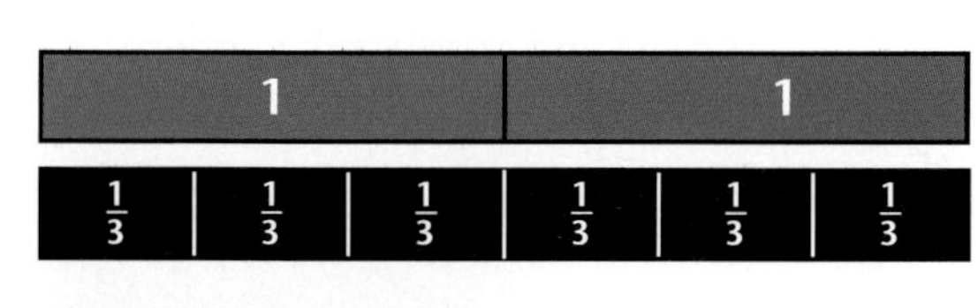

1

1/2 1/2

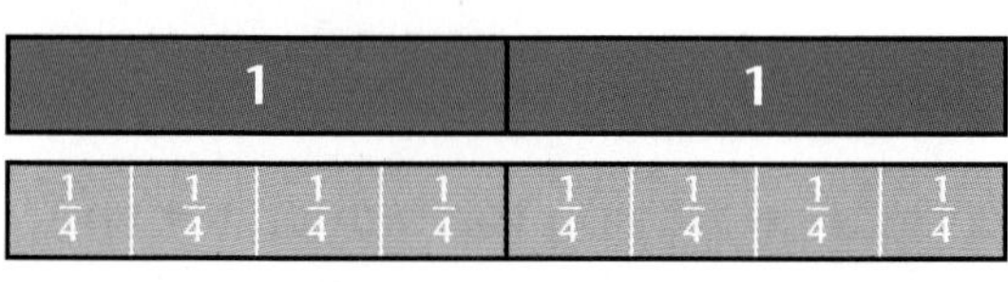

Using Paper and Pencil

Division	Multiplication
$2 \div \frac{1}{3} = 6$	$2 \times \frac{3}{1} = 6$
$1 \div \frac{1}{2} = 2$	$1 \times \frac{2}{1} = 2$
$2 \div \frac{1}{4} = 8$	$2 \times \frac{4}{1} = 8$

Look at the division and multiplication columns. What relationship do you see?

When you divide a number by a fraction, you get the same answer as when you multiply the first number by the fraction turned upside down.

Try It **Divide. You may use fraction strips.**

1. $1 \div \frac{1}{5}$ **2.** $2 \div \frac{1}{2}$ **3.** $3 \div \frac{1}{4}$ **4.** $1 \div \frac{1}{6}$ **5.** $2 \div \frac{1}{3}$

Explain how you could find $1 \div \frac{1}{4}$. What is the answer?

Practice **Divide.**

6. $1 \div \frac{1}{4}$ **7.** $2 \div \frac{1}{5}$ **8.** $1 \div \frac{1}{3}$ **9.** $3 \div \frac{1}{2}$ **10.** $2 \div \frac{1}{3}$

11. $1 \div \frac{1}{8}$ **12.** $2 \div \frac{1}{6}$ **13.** $1 \div \frac{1}{12}$ **14.** $3 \div \frac{1}{4}$ **15.** $4 \div \frac{1}{2}$

16. **Analyze:** Does $2 \div \frac{1}{4}$ equal 2×4? Explain.

Extra Practice, page 335

Objective: Find reciprocals and divide fractions.

7·9 Divide Fractions

Learn

Many people enjoy cooking and baking for fun. Julia is making this recipe for lasagna. She needs to measure the Parmesan cheese, but only has a $\frac{1}{8}$ measuring cup. How many $\frac{1}{8}$ cups should she use?

Mama's Lasagna

- $\frac{1}{2}$ pound lasagna noodles
- 4 cups homemade spaghetti sauce
- 1 pound ricotta cheese
- 1 pound mozzarella cheese
- 1 egg
- $\frac{3}{4}$ cup Parmesan cheese

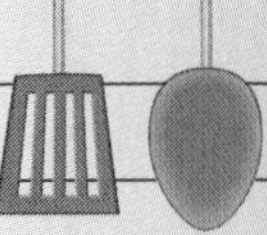

Math Words

reciprocals two numbers whose product is 1

divisor the number by which a dividend is divided

Example

Dividing is the same as multiplying by the **reciprocal** of the divisor. Reciprocals are 2 numbers whose product is 1. For example, $\frac{2}{3} \times \frac{3}{2} = 1$, so $\frac{3}{2}$ is the reciprocal of $\frac{2}{3}$.

Find the reciprocal of a fraction by switching the numerator and denominator. To find the reciprocal of a mixed number, first rename it as an improper fraction and then invert the fraction.

Divide $\frac{3}{4} \div \frac{1}{8}$ to solve this problem.

1 Find the reciprocal of the divisor.

$\frac{1}{8} \rightarrow \frac{8}{1}$

The reciprocal of $\frac{1}{8}$ is $\frac{8}{1}$.

2 Multiply by the reciprocal of the divisor.

$\frac{3}{4} \div \frac{1}{8} = \frac{3}{4} \times \frac{8}{1}$

3 Simplify.

$\frac{3}{\not{4}_1} \times \frac{\not{8}^2}{1} = \frac{3}{1} \times \frac{2}{1} = \frac{6}{1} = 6$

Julia should use six $\frac{1}{8}$ cups of Parmesan cheese.

Try It

Write the reciprocal of each number.

1. $\frac{2}{5}$
2. $\frac{7}{8}$
3. 3
4. $1\frac{1}{4}$
5. $\frac{1}{6}$

Divide. Write each answer in simplest form.

6. $\frac{4}{9} \div \frac{2}{3}$
7. $2 \div \frac{1}{6}$
8. $\frac{3}{4} \div \frac{1}{2}$
9. $\frac{1}{4} \div 3$
10. $\frac{1}{4} \div \frac{2}{3}$

Sum it Up Explain how you use a reciprocal to divide fractions.

Practice

Write the reciprocal of each number.

11. $\frac{5}{6}$
12. 8
13. $\frac{12}{5}$
14. $\frac{1}{4}$
15. $\frac{7}{12}$

Divide. Write each answer in simplest form.

16. $\frac{4}{9} \div \frac{1}{3}$
17. $\frac{5}{12} \div 15$
18. $\frac{3}{4} \div \frac{3}{8}$
19. $\frac{5}{6} \div 2\frac{7}{10}$
20. $\frac{1}{2} \div \frac{1}{2}$

Write × or ÷ to make each number sentence true.

21. $\frac{5}{6} \bullet \frac{7}{8} = \frac{35}{48}$
22. $\frac{3}{4} \bullet \frac{5}{12} = 1\frac{4}{5}$
23. $\frac{9}{16} \bullet \frac{6}{7} = \frac{21}{32}$
24. $\frac{1}{4} \bullet \frac{4}{7} = \frac{1}{7}$

Solve. Find the number that makes the sentence true.

25. $\frac{2}{3} \div n = 1$
26. $\frac{2}{3} \div t = \frac{1}{6}$
★27. $z \div 2\frac{1}{5} = \frac{1}{11}$
★28. $b \div 1\frac{1}{4} = \frac{8}{25}$

Problem Solving

29. Ronnie must measure $\frac{1}{2}$ cup of cocoa using a $\frac{1}{4}$-cup measuring cup. How many $\frac{1}{4}$ cups should he use?

Journal

30. **Analyze:** If you divide a fraction by a fraction, do you always get a fraction as an answer? Explain.

Use data from *Did You Know?* for problems 31–32.

31. A baker bakes a cake 110 feet high, but it shrinks to $\frac{9}{10}$ its size when it cools. Does he set a new record?

32. **What if** each layer of the tallest cake ever baked was 6 inches tall. How many layers would the cake have?

33. **Science:** Baking soda helps cakes rise by making tiny gas bubbles in the batter. If a 2-inch layer of batter doubles during baking, how tall is the cake?

34. **Create a problem** about cooking or baking that can be solved by dividing a whole number by a fraction. Solve it and give it to another student to solve.

Did You
KNOW?
The tallest cake ever made was 105 feet tall. It was made in Faisalabad, Pakistan.

Spiral Review and Test Prep

35. 0.321 − 0.29
36. 4.75 + 23.092
37. 8.01 − 3.12
38. 4.5 + 0.09

Choose the correct answer.

39. Which number does *not* divide evenly into 48?
 A. 4
 B. 5
 C. 8
 D. 12

40. Students sit in 25 rows with 22 seats in each row. Eighteen leave for band practice. How many are left?
 F. 450
 G. 532
 H. 550
 J. 568

Extra Practice, page 335

Objective: Divide fractions and mixed numbers.

7•10 Divide Mixed Numbers

Learn

The Bird-watchers Club uses seeds to attract more birds to their area. Suppose they divide the seeds in this bag into 3 different feeders. How many pounds of seed go in each feeder?

Example

Find: $4\frac{1}{2} \div 3$ to solve this problem

1 Write both numbers as fractions.

$4\frac{1}{2} \div 3 = \frac{9}{2} \div \frac{3}{1}$

2 Multiply the dividend by the reciprocal of the divisor.

$4\frac{1}{2} \div 3 = \frac{9}{2} \times \frac{1}{3} = \frac{9}{6}$

3 Simplify.

$\frac{9}{6} = \frac{3}{2} = 1\frac{1}{2}$

Each feeder will have $1\frac{1}{2}$ pounds of seed.

More Examples

A

$2\frac{1}{4} \div 1\frac{1}{2} = \frac{9}{4} \div \frac{3}{2}$

$\frac{9}{4} \times \frac{2}{3} = \frac{3}{2} = 1\frac{1}{2}$

B

$3 \div 3\frac{2}{3} = \frac{3}{1} \div \frac{11}{3}$

$\frac{3}{1} \div \frac{11}{3} = \frac{3}{1} \times \frac{3}{11} = \frac{9}{11}$

Try It

Divide. Write each answer in simplest form.

1. $1\frac{2}{3} \div \frac{2}{3}$ **2.** $2\frac{1}{2} \div \frac{1}{4}$ **3.** $1\frac{3}{4} \div 1\frac{1}{2}$ **4.** $1\frac{5}{6} \div 2$ **5.** $2\frac{5}{6} \div \frac{2}{3}$

Sum it Up Explain how you would divide $3\frac{1}{3}$ by $\frac{1}{3}$.

Practice

Divide. Write each answer in simplest form.

6. $1\frac{1}{3} \div \frac{1}{3}$
7. $5\frac{1}{12} \div \frac{5}{6}$
8. $\frac{3}{4} \div 1\frac{3}{8}$
9. $2\frac{7}{10} \div 1\frac{4}{5}$
10. $1\frac{1}{2} \div 1\frac{1}{6}$
11. $5 \div 1\frac{5}{6}$
12. $1\frac{3}{8} \div \frac{5}{8}$
13. $2\frac{2}{10} \div \frac{2}{5}$
14. $3\frac{1}{3} \div \frac{5}{6}$
15. $1\frac{3}{5} \div 2$
16. $1 \div \frac{2}{5}$
17. $1\frac{11}{12} \div \frac{1}{2}$

★18. $1\frac{7}{12} \div \frac{1}{12}$

★19. $7\frac{7}{8} \div 2\frac{1}{6}$

★20. $\frac{3}{5} \div 5$

Solve.

21. $1\frac{1}{2} \div n = 3$
22. $2\frac{2}{3} \div t = 1\frac{1}{3}$

★23. $z \div 2\frac{5}{6} = \frac{15}{17}$

★24. $b \div 6 = 1\frac{3}{5}$

Problem Solving

25. A $6\frac{1}{2}$-pound bag of bird seed is divided evenly between two feeders. How many pounds of seed go in each?
26. **Compare:** How is dividing a mixed number like dividing a fraction? How is it different?
27. Harry watches birds for $1\frac{1}{2}$ hours each day, four days each week. How many hours does he spend watching birds?
28. Mrs. Villardo starts watching birds at 3:15 P.M. She must leave by 4:50 P.M. What is the most time she can spend bird-watching?
29. An 8-cup bird feeder is full in the morning. By evening there are $2\frac{1}{4}$ cups left. How much seed did the birds eat during the day?
30. A bird-watcher wants to add $3\frac{1}{2}$ cups of bird seed to a feeder. She only has a $\frac{1}{4}$ cup measure. How many scoops will she need to add?

★31. **Science:** Many birds migrate from cold climates in the fall and back again in the spring. If a flock of birds migrates 800 miles each season, how many miles do they cover in 5 years?

32. **Create a problem** about bird-watching that can be solved by dividing a mixed number by a fraction. Solve it and give it to another student to solve.

Spiral Review and Test Prep

Find the LCM for each pair of numbers.

33. 8 and 12
34. 10 and 25
35. 4 and 16
36. 12 and 16

Choose the correct answer.

37. Which of the following fractions is not equivalent to $\frac{6}{4}$?

A. $\frac{3}{2}$ C. $\frac{12}{8}$

B. $\frac{4}{6}$ D. $1\frac{1}{2}$

38. Buffy ate $\frac{3}{4}$ of a bunch of grapes. If there were 40 grapes on the bunch, how many did she eat?

F. 20 H. 40

G. 30 J. 50

Extra Practice, page 335

Objective: Apply multiplying and dividing fractions to analyze data and make decisions.

Problem Solving: Application

Decision Making

Should Brandon bring Chicken Pasta Salad or German Potato Salad to the picnic?

Brandon can't wait for the family "pot-luck" dinner. He is making one of his favorite recipes and needs to make enough for 24 people. Brandon already has some of the ingredients for each recipe.

FOOD MARKET
EGGS....... $1.19 per dozen
MAYONNAISE.... $1.99
Prices good for 3 days only
POTATOES.................. $0.59 per pound
ARTICHOKES.... $2.39 per 6-ounce jar
PASTA SHELLS............. $1.29 per pound
CHICKEN... $5.00 per pound
VINEGAR... $1.79

Option 1

Need to buy:
- Pasta
- Mayonnaise
- Chicken
- Artichokes

Recipe: Chicken Pasta Salad Serves 8

1 pound pasta shells
2 tablespoons oil
$1\frac{1}{2}$ cups mayonnaise
3 tablespoons lemon juice
3 tablespoons parsley
$\frac{3}{4}$ pound diced cooked chicken
6-ounce jar artichokes

Option 2

Need to buy:
- Potatoes
- Vinegar
- Eggs

SALADS

German Potato Salad
Serves 8

2 pounds potatoes
$\frac{1}{2}$ onion, chopped
2 tablespoons flour
2 tablespoons sugar
$1\frac{1}{2}$ teaspoons salt
1 tablespoon celery seed
1 cup water
$\frac{1}{2}$ cup vinegar
4 hard-boiled eggs

Read for Understanding

1. How many people will be eating at the dinner?
2. How many people does each recipe serve?
3. By what number will Brandon have to multiply the ingredients in each recipe to have enough servings? Explain.
4. How many pounds of potatoes are needed for one recipe of potato salad?
5. How many cups of mayonnaise are needed in one recipe of the pasta salad?
6. Does Brandon need to buy pasta if he makes chicken pasta salad?
7. Does Brandon need to buy celery seed?
8. How much do potatoes cost?

Problem Solving

Make Decisions

9. If Brandon makes German Potato Salad for 24 people, how many onions will he need? how much salt? how much vinegar?
10. How many hard-boiled eggs will Brandon need to make German Potato Salad for 24 people?
11. Suppose Brandon decides to make the Chicken Pasta Salad. How much will it cost to buy enough pasta? artichokes? a jar of mayonnaise?
12. How much will it cost to buy enough chicken to make the Chicken Pasta Salad? (Hint: $\frac{1}{4}$ of 1 dollar = $0.25.)
13. Suppose Brandon decides to make German Potato Salad. How much will it cost to buy enough potatoes? eggs?
14. A bottle of vinegar holds 4 cups. How many bottles of vinegar will Brandon need if he makes German Potato Salad? How much will that cost?
15. Eggs come in containers that hold one dozen. How many packages will Brandon need to buy if he makes German Potato Salad? How much will that cost?
16. How much in all would it cost Brandon to make the Chicken Pasta Salad?
17. How much in all would it cost Brandon to make the German Potato Salad?
18. **What if** Brandon doesn't put artichokes in the Chicken Pasta Salad? How much would it cost?

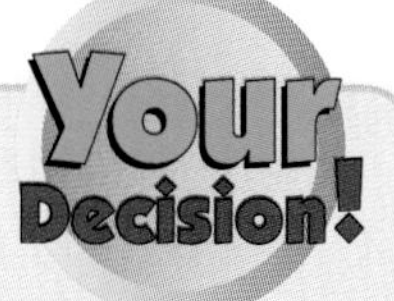

What is your recommendation for Brandon? Explain.

Apply multiplying and dividing fractions to investigate science concepts.

Problem Solving: Math and Science
What is GLOP?

Objects can usually be sorted as solids, liquids, or gases. Some unusual things, however, act like both solids and liquids.

In this activity, you will make GLOP. Then you will observe it and decide whether it is a solid or a liquid.

You Will Need
- **white glue**
- **water**
- **borax**
- **2 large cups or bowls**
- **measuring cups**
- **measuring spoons**
- **food coloring or poster paint (optional)**

Safety

Do not eat GLOP.

Hypothesize

An object is thick and smooth. It will take the shape of a cup, but can sit in your hand without spilling over. Is it a solid or liquid? Explain.

Procedure

1. Work with a group. Look at the recipe for GLOP.
2. Multiply each ingredient so that the recipe will make 4 times as much.
3. Follow the recipe.
4. Record your observations.
5. Clean up!

Recipe for GLOP!

In a cup, mix together $\frac{1}{4}$ cup of water and $\frac{1}{4}$ cup of white glue until the glue dissolves. You can add a few drops of food coloring or poster paint.

In another cup, mix $\frac{1}{4}$ cup of warm water with $\frac{3}{8}$ teaspoon of borax powder until the powder dissolves.

Mix the liquids together. Stir for 2 minutes. Knead with your hands for one minute.

Your GLOP is ready.

Data

Copy and complete the chart.

Recipe	Recipe Times 4
$\frac{1}{4}$ cup water	
$\frac{1}{4}$ cup glue	
$\frac{1}{4}$ cup water	
$\frac{3}{8}$ teaspoon borax	

Record your observations of GLOP. (Hint: Think about color, shape, sound, texture, and smell. Throw GLOP up in the air and catch it. Drop it on a table. Put it in a cup. Lay it on a table. Squeeze it. You can save GLOP in an air-tight container or let it dry.)

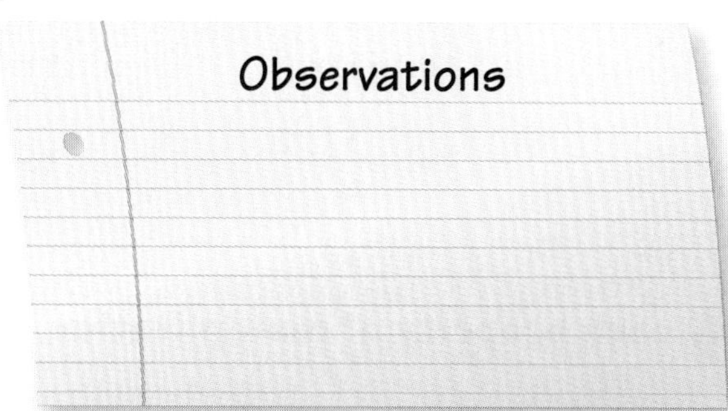

Conclude and Apply

- Is GLOP a solid or a liquid? Justify your answer.
- Suppose your whole school wants to make GLOP.
  - Estimate how many times you will need to multiply the original recipe.
  - How many cups of glue will you need? How much borax will you need?
  - If borax costs $0.50 for a teaspoon, how much will it cost to supply the whole school?
- Use data from *Did You Know?* to explain why it is dangerous to eat GLOP.

Borax can be used as a cleaner, disinfectant and water softener. It can be found in antifreeze, and is used in the production of fertilizers, Pyrex glass, and some medicines. It is poisonous if swallowed in anything but small amounts.

Going Further

1. Make a small amount of GLOP but use no borax. How did the GLOP turn out differently?

Journal

2. Write a story about an ocean that is made of GLOP instead of salt water.

Problem Solving

Check Your Progress B

Multiply. Write each answer in simplest form. **(pages 310–313)**

1. $\frac{5}{9} \times 1\frac{2}{3}$
2. $\frac{7}{10} \times 2$
3. $1\frac{1}{2} \times \frac{5}{6}$
4. $\frac{3}{20} \times 40$
5. $3\frac{6}{7} \times \frac{1}{9}$
6. $3\frac{1}{2} \times 2\frac{1}{5}$
7. $\frac{5}{8} \times 2\frac{2}{5}$
8. $3\frac{3}{4} \times 5\frac{3}{8}$

Estimate. **(pages 314–317)**

9. $35 \times \frac{5}{6}$
10. $52 \times \frac{3}{7}$
11. $\frac{7}{9}$ of 100
12. $\frac{11}{12}$ of 139
13. $2\frac{1}{8} \times 3\frac{5}{8}$
14. $5\frac{5}{6} \times \frac{2}{3}$
15. $10\frac{2}{3} \times 5\frac{1}{8}$
16. $100\frac{5}{6} \times \frac{2}{5}$

Identify each property of multiplication. **(pages 320–321)**

17. $\frac{1}{2} \times 3 = 3 \times \frac{1}{2}$
18. $\left(\frac{1}{2} \times \frac{1}{4}\right) \times \frac{1}{8} = \frac{1}{2} \times \left(\frac{1}{4} \times \frac{1}{8}\right)$
19. $\frac{5}{12} \times 1 = \frac{5}{12}$

Divide. Write each answer in simplest form. **(pages 322–327)**

20. $\frac{4}{7} \div \frac{2}{3}$
21. $\frac{3}{5} \div \frac{9}{20}$
22. $7\frac{5}{12} \div \frac{5}{6}$

Solve. **(pages 310–327)**

23. Carol plays a spinner game with 2 spinners. She spins both spinners and finds the product of the two fractions. What products can Carol find?

24. Susan collects stamps. She has $10\frac{1}{2}$ albums filled with stamps. Some are foreign stamps, and $\frac{2}{3}$ are United States stamps. How many albums are filled with stamps from the United States?

25. Marta's hobby is baking. She baked 6 pies for a party and left $\frac{1}{3}$ of them home for her family. How many pies will the family have?

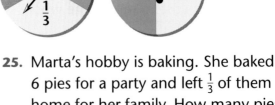

Additional activities at www.mhschool.com/math

Extra Practice

Multiply a Whole Number by a Fraction (pages 300–301)

Multiply.

1. $\frac{2}{3}$ of 9
2. $\frac{4}{5}$ of 30
3. $\frac{3}{8} \times 32$
4. $\frac{5}{12} \times 48$

Copy and complete each table.

Rule: Multiply by $\frac{1}{2}$.

	Input	Output
5.	8	▒
6.	10	▒
7.	14	▒
8.	22	▒

Rule: Multiply by $\frac{2}{5}$.

	Input	Output
9.	10	▒
10.	35	▒
11.	45	▒
12.	60	▒

Rule: Multiply by $\frac{3}{4}$.

	Input	Output
13.	16	▒
14.	28	▒
15.	36	▒
16.	48	▒

Multiply a Fraction by a Fraction (pages 302–305)

Multiply. Write each answer in simplest form.

1. $\frac{1}{2} \times \frac{4}{5}$
2. $\frac{3}{8} \times \frac{2}{9}$
3. $\frac{2}{3} \times \frac{5}{6}$
4. $\frac{5}{7} \times \frac{3}{4}$
5. $\frac{5}{12} \times \frac{7}{10}$
6. $\frac{6}{11} \times \frac{11}{20}$
7. $\frac{5}{16} \times \frac{6}{15}$
8. $\frac{8}{9} \times \frac{1}{2}$
9. $\frac{3}{10} \times \frac{7}{12}$
10. $\frac{4}{7} \times \frac{14}{15}$
11. $\frac{5}{13} \times \frac{1}{10}$
12. $\frac{7}{8} \times \frac{5}{14}$
13. $\frac{8}{11} \times \frac{33}{40}$
14. $\frac{3}{4} \times \frac{1}{12}$
15. $\frac{14}{15} \times \frac{6}{7}$
16. $\frac{5}{12} \times \frac{7}{10}$
17. Mario multiplies $\frac{1}{2}$ by $\frac{1}{5}$. He finds that the product is $\frac{1}{7}$. Is he correct? Explain.
18. Find the product of $\frac{3}{4}$ and $\frac{2}{9}$ in simplest form.

Problem Solving: Reading for Math Solve Multistep Problems (pages 306–307)

1. Amanda is building a 3-D puzzle of a castle. There are 650 pieces in the puzzle. If she puts together $\frac{3}{5}$ of the pieces, how many more pieces will she need to put together?
2. Andy likes to build furniture. He has a 36-inch board to cut into 3 shelves. After cutting the board, he shaves $\frac{3}{8}$ of an inch off each shelf. How long is each shelf?
3. Leon makes bookshelves. Of the 48 bookshelves he built, $\frac{5}{6}$ are for sale. How many bookshelves are not for sale?

Extra Practice

Multiply Mixed Numbers (pages 310–313)

Multiply. Write each answer in simplest form.

1. $\frac{2}{3} \times 3\frac{1}{8}$
2. $\frac{4}{9} \times 10\frac{3}{4}$
3. $15 \times 8\frac{3}{5}$
4. $12 \times 7\frac{3}{11}$
5. $20 \times 8\frac{5}{6}$
6. $\frac{3}{7} \times 14$
7. $\frac{7}{12} \times 10$
8. $\frac{2}{9} \times 1\frac{1}{2}$
9. $19 \times \frac{5}{8}$
10. $\frac{2}{3} \times \frac{15}{16}$
11. $3\frac{2}{5} \times 7$
12. $11\frac{2}{3} \times 9$
13. $30\frac{3}{10} \times 1\frac{2}{3}$
14. $22 \times 8\frac{3}{4}$
15. $\frac{1}{6} \times \frac{3}{7}$
16. $\frac{2}{3} \times \frac{3}{4}$
17. $7\frac{9}{10} \times 10\frac{5}{14}$
18. $6\frac{2}{3} \times 6\frac{3}{5}$

Find the missing number.

19. $1\frac{1}{2} \times \frac{3}{4} = 1\frac{1}{n}$
20. $n \times 1\frac{1}{3} = 2\frac{2}{3}$
21. $2\frac{1}{4} \times n = 1\frac{1}{8}$
22. One half of a 5-foot model is already painted. How many feet are painted?
23. Kay builds a $\frac{1}{6}$-scale model of a train. The actual train is $42\frac{1}{2}$ feet. How long is the model?

Estimate Products (pages 314–317)

Estimate.

1. $7 \times 11\frac{2}{5}$
2. $6\frac{3}{8} \times 7\frac{7}{10}$
3. $58\frac{6}{7} \times 92\frac{3}{4}$
4. $468\frac{1}{4} \times 419\frac{2}{3}$
5. $\frac{2}{3} \times 32$
6. $75 \times \frac{5}{12}$
7. $\frac{5}{8} \times 53\frac{2}{9}$
8. $19 \times \frac{4}{11}$
9. $\frac{4}{7} \times 12\frac{1}{4}$
10. $9\frac{8}{9} \times \frac{5}{11}$
11. $\frac{5}{12} \times 23\frac{2}{3}$
12. $18\frac{1}{3} \times \frac{2}{3}$

Estimate. Write >, <, or =.

13. $15 \times \frac{3}{4}$ ● $\frac{2}{3} \times 17$
14. $\frac{1}{8} \times 21$ ● $\frac{5}{12} \times 20$
15. $\frac{3}{4} \times 27$ ● $\frac{9}{11} \times 20$
16. $37 \times \frac{3}{7}$ ● $\frac{3}{10} \times 52$

Extra Practice

Problem Solving: Strategy Make an Organized List (pages 318–318)

Solve.

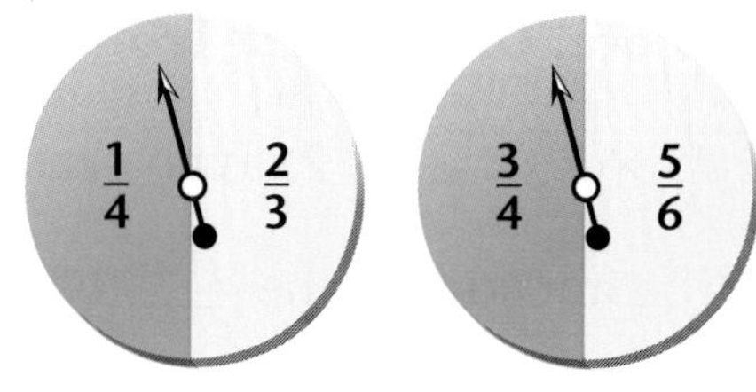

1. Eric collects antique games. He uses the spinners from two games to play a spinner game. He spins both spinners and finds the product of the two fractions. What products can Eric find?
2. Wendy makes dolls. She can make a doll with black, brown, or blonde hair. The doll can wear pants or a skirt. In how many ways can Wendy make a doll?
3. Charlie makes tuna, turkey, and peanut butter sandwiches on either wheat, white, or rye bread. How many different kinds of sandwiches can he make?

Properties of Multiplication (pages 320–321)

Identify each property of multiplication.

1. $12 \times 3\frac{1}{4} = (12 \times 3) + \left(12 \times \frac{1}{4}\right)$
2. $\frac{5}{12} \times \frac{7}{8} = \frac{7}{8} \times \frac{5}{12}$
3. $45\frac{3}{10} \times 0 = 0$

Solve.

4. $\frac{1}{8} \times \left(16 \times 2\frac{1}{3}\right)$
5. $\left(\frac{2}{9} \times \frac{5}{7}\right) \times \frac{7}{10}$
6. $\left(3\frac{2}{7} \times \frac{5}{12}\right) \times 4\frac{4}{5}$
7. $15 \times 4\frac{2}{3}$
8. $2\frac{11}{12} \times 48$
9. $16\frac{5}{8} \times 24$
10. $3\frac{1}{2} \times 0$
11. $\frac{1}{2} \times 4\frac{1}{4} \times 1$
12. $3\frac{1}{8} \times 4\frac{1}{4} \times 0 \times 2\frac{1}{2}$

Divide Fractions (pages 322–327)

Divide. Write each answer in simplest form.

1. $\frac{2}{3} \div \frac{6}{7}$
2. $\frac{5}{8} \div \frac{4}{5}$
3. $18 \div \frac{9}{20}$
4. $\frac{3}{16} \div 9$
5. $2\frac{7}{18} \div \frac{7}{9}$
6. $\frac{3}{4} \div \frac{1}{2}$
7. $1\frac{7}{12} \div 3\frac{1}{6}$
8. $\frac{7}{10} \div 4\frac{3}{20}$
9. $\frac{5}{6} \div \frac{5}{6}$
10. $2 \div \frac{1}{4}$
11. $\frac{5}{8} \div \frac{1}{4}$
12. $2\frac{1}{4} \div 3$

Chapter Study Guide

Language and Math

Math Words

Associative Property
compatible numbers
Commutative Property
Distributive Property
Identity Property
reciprocal
simplest form
Zero Property

Complete. Use a word from the list.

1. $25 \times 2\frac{1}{5} = 2\frac{1}{5} \times 25$ is an example of the ____.
2. The fraction $\frac{3}{2}$ is the ____ of the fraction $\frac{2}{3}$.
3. $\frac{2}{3} \times \left(\frac{4}{5} \times \frac{3}{8}\right) = \left(\frac{2}{3} \times \frac{4}{5}\right) \times \frac{3}{8}$ is an example of the ____.

Multiply fractions and mixed numbers. (pages 300–305, 310–313)

Example

Find the product $\frac{5}{6} \times 4\frac{4}{5}$.

Solution

Rename $4\frac{4}{5}$ as an improper fraction.

$4\frac{4}{5} = 4 \times 5 + \frac{4}{5} = \frac{24}{5}$

Multiply: $\frac{5}{6} \times \frac{24}{5}$

Remember to divide by common factors.

$\frac{\cancel{5}^{1} \times 24}{6 \times \cancel{5}_{1}} = \frac{1 \times \cancel{24}^{4}}{\cancel{6}_{1} \times 1} = \frac{4}{1} \times 1 = \frac{4}{1} = 4$

Multiply. Write your answer in simplest form.

4. $\frac{3}{4} \times 16$
5. $\frac{2}{9} \times \frac{3}{10}$
6. $4\frac{5}{8} \times \frac{2}{9}$
7. $18 \times \frac{2}{5}$
8. $24 \times 3\frac{5}{6}$
9. $7\frac{5}{12} \times 12\frac{3}{16}$

Estimate products of fractions and mixed numbers. (pages 314–317)

Example

Estimate: $\frac{3}{8} \times 35$

Solution

Use compatible numbers.

$\frac{3}{8} \times 35$

↓

$\frac{3}{8} \times 32 = 12$

So $\frac{3}{8} \times 35$ is about 12.

Estimate.

10. $\frac{3}{4} \times 23$
11. $5\frac{9}{11} \times 60\frac{1}{4}$
12. $40\frac{1}{8} \times \frac{3}{7}$

Use properties of multiplication. (pages 320–321)

Example

Identify the property of multiplication.

$\left(\frac{3}{4} \times \frac{1}{8}\right) \times 8 = \frac{3}{4} \times \left(\frac{1}{8} \times 8\right)$

Solution

The way factors are grouped does not change the product.

Associative Property of Multiplication

Identify each property of multiplication.

13. $239\frac{3}{8} \times 1 = 239\frac{3}{8}$
14. $12 \times 45\frac{1}{3} = 45\frac{1}{3} \times 12$
15. $16 \times 39\frac{1}{2} = (16 \times 39) + \left(16 \times \frac{1}{2}\right)$

Divide fractions. (pages 322–327)

Example

Find: $\frac{5}{9} \div \frac{5}{12}$

Solution

Remember to use a reciprocal to divide fractions.

$\frac{5}{9} \div \frac{5}{12} = \frac{5}{9} \times \frac{12}{5}$

$\frac{\cancel{5}^{1} \times \cancel{12}^{4}}{\cancel{9}_{3} \times \cancel{5}_{1}} = \frac{1}{3} \times \frac{4}{1} = \frac{4}{3}$

Write in simplest form: $\frac{4}{3} = 1\frac{1}{3}$

Divide. Write your answer in simplest form.

16. $\frac{4}{5} \div \frac{7}{8}$
17. $\frac{6}{11} \div \frac{7}{22}$
18. $12 \div \frac{2}{5}$
19. $\frac{8}{9} \div 4$
20. $5\frac{1}{2} \div \frac{6}{7}$
21. $14\frac{5}{6} \div 2\frac{2}{3}$
22. $45\frac{1}{3} \div 4\frac{2}{9}$
23. $7\frac{3}{4} \div 5\frac{5}{6}$

Solve problems. (pages 306–307, 318–319)

Example

Carlos shaves $\frac{5}{8}$ of an inch off both ends of a 10 inch board. Then he cuts the board in half. How long is each board?

Solution

Multiply: $2 \times \frac{5}{8} = \frac{5}{4}$

Subtract: $10 - 1\frac{1}{4} = 8\frac{3}{4}$

Divide: $8\frac{3}{4} \div 2 = 4\frac{3}{8}$

Each board is $4\frac{3}{8}$ inches long.

Solve.

24. Kim uses $\frac{5}{8}$ of 192 parts to build the rigging for a model ship. How many parts does she use for the rigging?
25. Andrew can use his old or new skateboard. He can skateboard in the park, at the school track, or along the path by the seashore. How many different ways can Andrew use his skateboard?

Chapter Test

Estimate.

1. $4\frac{3}{8} \times 6\frac{5}{9}$
2. $57 \times \frac{2}{7}$
3. $\frac{7}{12} \times 113$

Multiply. Write each answer in simplest form.

4. $\frac{9}{10} \times \frac{4}{5}$
5. $\frac{7}{8} \times 9\frac{2}{7}$
6. $8\frac{3}{8} \times 12\frac{5}{12}$
7. $17\frac{1}{4} \times 32$
8. $\frac{9}{10} \times \frac{2}{3}$
9. $1\frac{1}{8} \times \frac{2}{3}$
10. $5\frac{3}{4} \times 7\frac{1}{3}$
11. $\frac{2}{9} \times \frac{3}{10}$
12. $\frac{1}{2} \times 3$
13. $\frac{3}{4} \times 1\frac{1}{3}$
14. $1\frac{1}{2} \times 1\frac{1}{2}$
15. $\frac{3}{8} \times \frac{2}{3}$

Divide. Write each answer in simplest form.

16. $\frac{4}{7} \div \frac{3}{6}$
17. $\frac{9}{16} \div 21$
18. $\frac{9}{20} \div 2\frac{9}{10}$
19. $15\frac{2}{3} \div \frac{8}{9}$
20. $\frac{3}{4} \div \frac{1}{8}$
21. $10 \div \frac{2}{3}$
22. $\frac{7}{8} \div 1\frac{1}{2}$
23. $7\frac{5}{12} \div \frac{4}{5}$
24. $\frac{2}{3} \div \frac{2}{3}$
25. $\frac{2}{5} \div \frac{3}{10}$
26. $1\frac{1}{2} \div \frac{1}{2}$
27. $2 \div \frac{1}{8}$

Use the Distributive Property to solve.

28. $13\frac{3}{4} \times 16$
29. $100 \times 12\frac{7}{10}$
30. $28 \times 12\frac{5}{8}$

Solve.

31. Jolene helps her sister paper the walls of a dollhouse. If the paper is 45 inches long, and she uses $\frac{3}{5}$ of it to paper the downstairs, how many inches does she use?

32. Martin measures out $2\frac{3}{4}$ cups of flour using a $\frac{1}{4}$-cup measure. How many $\frac{1}{4}$ cups does he need?

33. Michele can spin $\frac{1}{2}$, $\frac{1}{3}$, or $\frac{1}{4}$ on one spinner. She can spin $2\frac{1}{2}$ or $3\frac{5}{8}$ on the other spinner. She spins both spinners and finds the product. What products can Michele find?

Performance Assessment

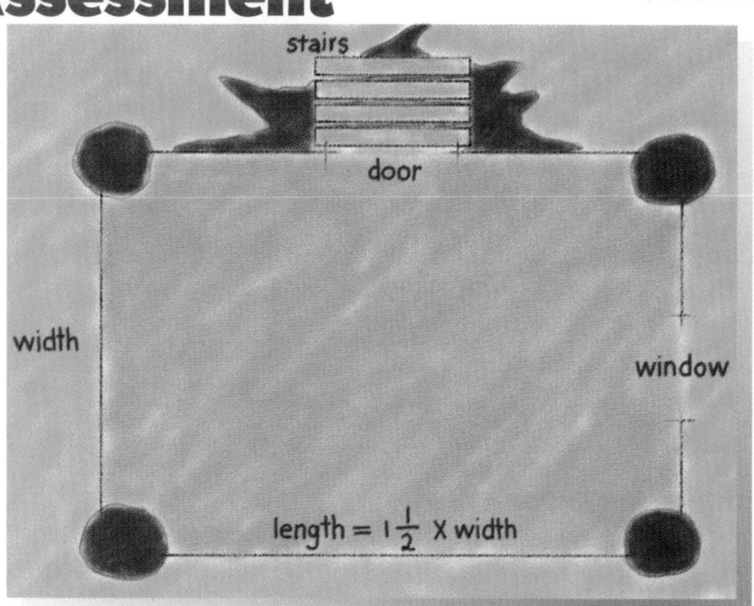

You and your friends are building a tree house. First you plan it on paper to decide how big to make it. You want it to be $1\frac{1}{2}$ times as long as it is wide. You also want the steps to be $2\frac{1}{4}$ feet wide.

Copy and complete the charts below. Use the charts to answer these questions:

- How much longer will the tree house be if you make it 8 feet wide instead of 5 feet wide?
- Which board lengths can be cut into a whole number of steps without any wood left over?

Floors	
Possible Width (in Feet)	Length (in Feet)
5	▮
6	▮
7	▮
8	▮

Steps	
Length of Board (in Feet)	Number of Steps That Can Be Cut
$4\frac{1}{2}$	▮
$7\frac{7}{8}$	▮
11	▮
$13\frac{1}{2}$	▮

A Good Answer

- has a complete chart that shows floor lengths.
- shows the number of steps that can be cut from each length of board.
- tells how much longer an 8-foot wide tree house will be than a 5-foot wide one.
- tells which board lengths can be cut into a whole number of steps.

You may want to save this work for your portfolio.

Assessment

Enrichment

Another Way to Multiply

A group of 8 students repairs a hiking trail. Each student cleans a different $\frac{3}{10}$-mile long section. Then the group divides the entire section of cleaned trail into $\frac{3}{10}$-mile sections and marks each one. How many marked sections will there be?

There's more than one way!

Multiply $\frac{3}{10} \times 8$, then divide by $\frac{3}{10}$. Find: $\left(\frac{3}{10} \times 8\right) \div \left(\frac{3}{10}\right)$

Method A

You can solve this problem by following the order of operations.

$$\frac{3}{10} \times 8 = \frac{24}{10} = \frac{12}{5} \qquad \frac{12}{5} \div \frac{3}{10} = \frac{12}{5} \times \frac{10}{3} = 8$$

Method B

You can solve this problem using Properties of Multiplication.

$$\left(\frac{3}{10} \times 8\right) \div \frac{3}{10} = \left(\frac{3}{10} \times 8\right) \times \frac{10}{3} = \left(\frac{3}{10} \times \frac{10}{3}\right) \times 8 = 1 \times 8 = 8$$

Think: Use the Associative and Commutative Properties of Multiplication.

Method C

You can solve this problem mentally. When you divide a number by itself, the quotient equals 1. Look for a number divided by itself in a problem.

$$\left(\frac{3}{10} \times 8\right) \div \left(\frac{3}{10}\right) = \left(\frac{3}{10} \div \frac{3}{10}\right) \times 8 = 1 \times 8 = 8$$

There will be 8 marked sections.

More Examples

A

$$\left(\frac{4{,}534}{5{,}295} \times \frac{3}{5}\right) \div \left(\frac{4{,}534}{5{,}295}\right) = \frac{3}{5}$$

B

$$\left(\frac{42}{2{,}705} \times \frac{376}{9}\right) \div \frac{376}{2{,}705} = \frac{42}{9}$$

Simplify.

1. $\left(\frac{2}{9} \times \frac{3}{16}\right) \div \frac{2}{9}$
2. $\frac{766}{2{,}587} \times \frac{45}{938} \div \frac{766}{2{,}587}$
3. $\frac{21{,}576}{32} \div \frac{21{,}576}{32} \times \frac{2}{3}$
4. $7\frac{1}{5} \times 8\frac{1}{8} \div 7\frac{1}{5}$
5. $45\frac{9}{11} \times \frac{121}{504} \div \frac{121}{504}$
6. $\frac{114}{3} \times \frac{1}{47} \div \frac{1}{3}$
7. $\frac{4}{998} \times \frac{997}{5} \div \frac{997}{998}$
8. $\frac{5{,}280}{1{,}760} \times \frac{1}{8} \times \frac{1{,}760}{5{,}280}$

Test-Taking Tips

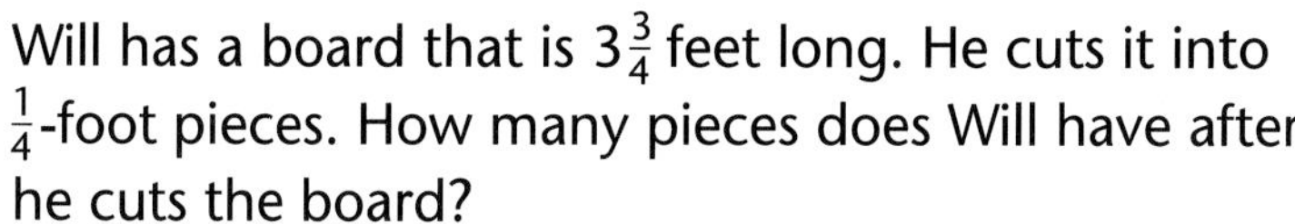

When taking a multiple-choice test, you need to read problems carefully. Before you solve the problem, you may need to **choose an operation** to solve the problem.

Will has a board that is $3\frac{3}{4}$ feet long. He cuts it into $\frac{1}{4}$-foot pieces. How many pieces does Will have after he cuts the board?

A. 15 pieces
B. 10 pieces
C. 5 pieces
D. 3 pieces

Look at the information given in the problem.

- **What do you know?** The length of the board; the size of the pieces
- **What do you need to find?** The number of pieces

You are taking a large piece of board and dividing it into smaller pieces. The context of the problem tells you to divide.

Solve the problem.

$3\frac{3}{4} \div \frac{1}{4} = 15$

The correct answer is A.

Check for Success

Before turning in a test, go back one last time to check.

- ☑ I understood and answered the questions asked.
- ☑ I checked my work for errors.
- ☑ My answers make sense.

Practice

1. There are 22 cookies in each batch. Miriam bakes $4\frac{1}{2}$ batches. How many cookies are there in all?

   A. 33
   B. 44
   C. 88
   D. 99

2. Anita has $48\frac{1}{2}$ pages left to read in a book. She has 4 days left to read it. How many pages on average should she read each day in order to finish?

   F. 4
   G. $12\frac{1}{8}$
   H. $44\frac{1}{2}$
   J. $52\frac{1}{2}$

3. Monya's club collected $80\frac{1}{4}$ pounds to recycle, and Jim's club collected 40 pounds. How many pounds did they collect together?

   A. $39\frac{1}{2}$ pounds
   B. 80 pounds
   C. $120\frac{1}{4}$ pounds
   D. 3,210 pounds

4. The steps on Karen's tree house are $24\frac{1}{8}$ inches wide. The steps on Mo's are $23\frac{7}{8}$ inches wide. How much wider are Karen's steps?

   F. $\frac{1}{4}$ inch
   G. $\frac{3}{4}$ inch
   H. $1\frac{1}{4}$ inches
   J. Not Here

Spiral Review and Test Prep

Chapters 1–7

Choose the correct answer.

Number Sense

1. Which sign makes this statement true?
   3,486 ▮ 3,592
   A. $<$ C. $=$
   B. $>$ D. $+$

2. What place is the 4 in 57.342?
   F. Tens H. Tenths
   G. Ones J. Hundredths

3. Multiply: $\frac{2}{9} \times \frac{5}{6}$
   A. $\frac{5}{27}$ C. $\frac{7}{15}$
   B. $\frac{4}{15}$ D. Not Here

4. Divide: $3\frac{1}{6} \div 2\frac{1}{9}$
   F. $6\frac{37}{54}$ H. $1\frac{1}{2}$
   G. $2\frac{2}{9}$ J. $1\frac{1}{4}$

Measurement and Geometry

5. What is the perimeter?

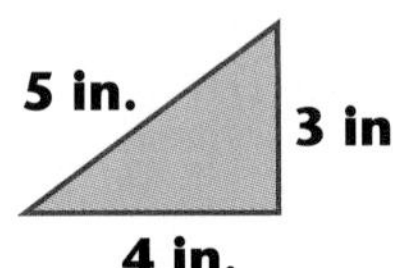

   A. 12 inches C. 16 inches
   B. 14 inches D. 18 inches

6. What is the best name for the figure?

   F. Triangle H. Rectangle
   G. Rhombus J. Trapezoid

7. What kind of triangle is shown?

   A. Isosceles C. Scalene
   B. Equilateral D. Not Here

8. What three-dimensional figure is shown?

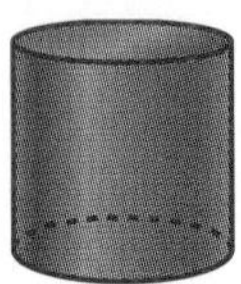

   F. Sphere H. Rectangular prism
   G. Pyramid J. Cylinder

Algebra and Functions

9. $21 + n = 91.2$

A. $n = 70.2$
B. $n = 0.8$
C. $n = 112.2$
D. Not Here

10. $4.5n = 27.9$

F. $n = 0.2$
G. $n = 6.2$
H. $n = 32.4$
J. $n = 125.55$

11. $n - 5\frac{3}{8} = 2\frac{7}{8}$

A. $n = 8\frac{1}{4}$
B. $n = 8\frac{1}{8}$
C. $n = 2\frac{1}{4}$
D. Not Here

12. If the rule for a pattern us to divide by one half, which number comes next in this sequence? $\frac{1}{16}, \frac{1}{8}, \frac{1}{4} \ldots$

F. $\frac{1}{8}$
G. $\frac{1}{4}$
H. $\frac{1}{2}$
J. 1

Mathematical Reasoning

13. Bill has a board that is $6\frac{2}{3}$ feet long. He cuts it into 12 equal pieces. How long is each piece?

A. 80 feet
B. 8 feet
C. $\frac{2}{5}$ foot
D. $\frac{5}{9}$ foot

14. CDs cost \$10.99 each. José buys 3 CDs. How much does José spend?

F. \$43.32
G. \$35.97
H. \$32.97
J. \$30.77

15. Cynthia has \$135.98 in her savings account. She deposits \$15.75 more. How much money is in Cynthia's savings account now?

A. \$293.48
B. \$151.73
C. \$140.63
D. \$120.23

16. Becky divides a fraction by a fraction. The quotient is 2. What might the fractions be? Write two possible division sentences to show your answer.

CHAPTER

8 Measurement

Theme: Communication

Use the Data

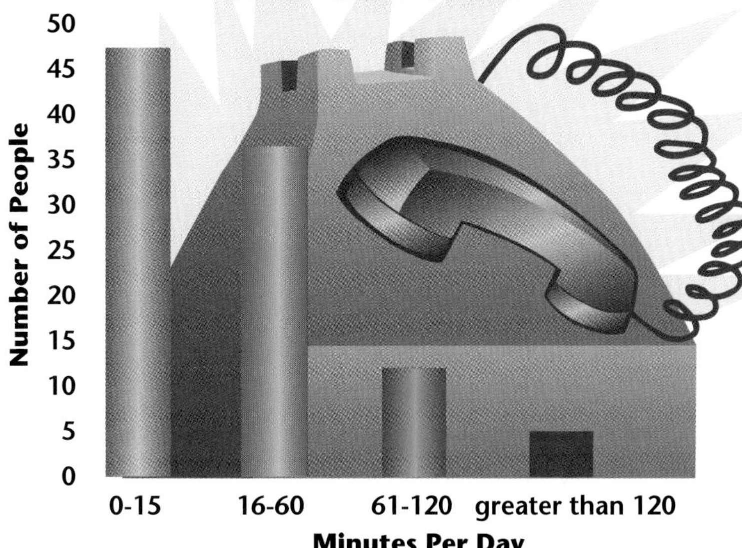

- How many minutes do most people spend at home talking on their phones each day? Do more people talk for 16 to 60 minutes or 61 to 120 minutes?

What You Will Learn

In this chapter you will learn how to

- change units of time and find elapsed time.
- estimate length, volume, weight, mass, and temperature.
- measure length.
- change from one unit to another.
- use strategies to solve problems.

Objective: Choose an appropriate unit for measuring a length of time; find elapsed time; change units of time.

8·1

Time

Learn

Math Word

elapsed time the amount of time that passes from the start of an activity to the end of the activity

Jasmine is allowed to talk on the phone a total of 2 hours each week. How many minutes of phone time does she have left this week?

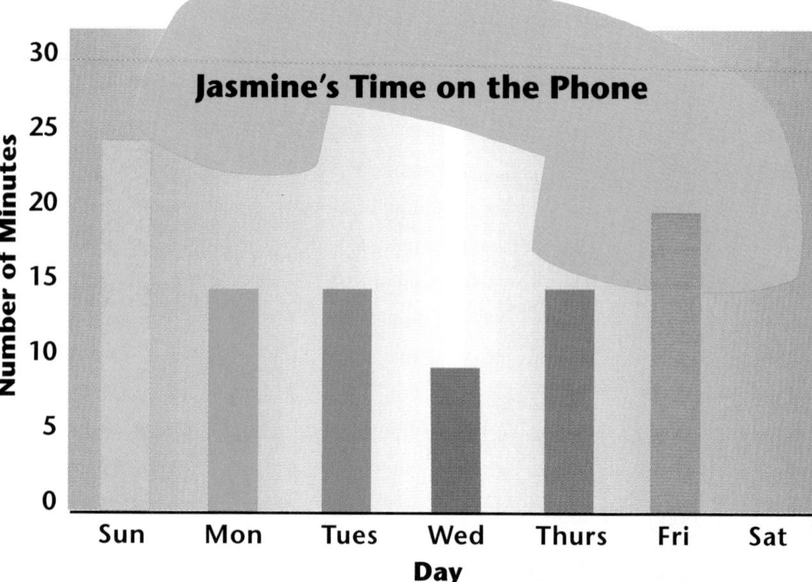

Units of Time			
1 minute (min)	= 60 seconds (s)	1 hour (h)	= 60 min
1 day (d)	= 24 h	1 week (wk)	= 7 d
1 month (mo)	is about 4 wk	1 year (y)	= 12 mo
1 year (y)	is about 52 wk	1 year (y)	= 365 d
1 leap year	= 366 d	1 decade	= 10 y
1 century	= 100 y		

Example 1

Change 2 hours to minutes to solve the problem.

Multiply to change from a larger unit to a smaller unit.

Think: 1 hour = 60 minutes

1 Multiply to change hours to minutes.

2 hours = ■ minutes

$2 \times 60 = 120$

So 2 hours = 120 minutes.

2 Add the minutes talked on the phone so far this week.

$25 + 15 + 15 + 10 + 15 + 20 = 100$ minutes

3 Subtract.

$$\begin{array}{r} 120 \\ -\ 100 \\ \hline 20 \end{array}$$

Jasmine has 20 minutes of phone time left this week.

Jill calls a friend at 5:55 P.M. to talk about a book report. She finishes talking at 7:30 P.M. How long does Jill spend on the phone?

Example 2

You can add using mental math to find the **elapsed time** from 5:55 P.M. to 7:30 P.M.

Think: From 5:55 to 6:00 is 5 minutes.
From 6:00 to 7:00 is 1 hour.
From 7:00 to 7:30 is 30 minutes.

5 minutes + 1 hour + 30 minutes = 1 hour 35 minutes

Note: when the elapsed time crosses from a.m. to p.m. or P.M. to A.M., find the elapsed time in each part of the day separately and then add them together.

So Jill spends 1 hour 35 minutes on the phone.

More Examples

A

Multiply to change from a larger unit to a smaller unit.

3 minutes = ▮ seconds

$3 \times 60 = 180$

1 minute = 60 seconds

So 3 minutes = 180 seconds.

B

Divide to change from a smaller unit to a larger unit.

36 hours = ▮ day ▮ hours

$36 \div 24 = 1$ R12

1 day = 24 hours

So 36 hours = 1 day 12 hours.

C

  4 h 15 min 20 s
+3 h 55 min 12 s
  7 h 70 min 32 s
= 8 hours 10 minutes 32 seconds

Try It

Copy and complete.

1. 5 h = ▮ min
2. 420 s = ▮ min
3. 7 d = ▮ h
4. 42 mo = ▮ y ▮ mo

Find each elapsed time.

5. 4:00 A.M. to 10:23 A.M.
6. 6:05 A.M. to 4:43 P.M.
7. 8:15 P.M. to 1:11 A.M.

Would you multiply or divide to find the number of seconds in 3 minutes? Explain.

Practice Copy and complete.

8. 72 h = ■ d
9. 500 y = ■ centuries
10. 1,095 d = ■ y
11. 12 min = ■ s
12. 12 wk = ■ d
13. 24 h = ■ min
14. 90 y = ■ decades
15. 90 min = ■ h
16. 8 centuries = ■ y
17. 84 h = ■ d ■ h
18. 270 s = ■ min ■ s
19. 252 d = ■ wk
20. 585 min = ■ h ■ min
21. 6 decades = ■ y
22. 8 d 15 h = ■ h
23. 15 min 24 s = ■ s
24. 65 mo = ■ y ■ mo
25. 50 d = ■ wk ■ d
26. 366 d = 1 ■
★27. 1 d = ■ s
★28. 604,800 s = ■ d

Find each elapsed time.

29. 3:15 A.M. to 11:00 A.M.
30. 9:20 A.M. to 11:58 A.M.
31. 7:45 A.M. to 9:31 A.M.
32. 1:27 P.M. to 5:30 P.M.
33. 6:19 P.M. to 10:05 P.M.
34. 12:57 P.M. to 3:12 P.M.
35. 4:11 A.M. to 6:21 P.M.
36. 1:37 A.M. to 1:14 P.M.
37. 10:58 A.M. to 5:29 P.M.
38. 11:07 P.M. to 6:54 A.M.
39. 4:14 P.M. to 3:09 A.M.
40. 9:23 P.M. to 11:39 A.M.

Find each time.

41. 2 h 30 min after 1:00 P.M.
42. 4 h 27 min after 5:49 A.M.
43. 5 h 49 min after 1:56 A.M.
44. 3 h 24 min after 11:30 A.M.
45. 6 h 58 min after 9:59 A.M.
46. 11 h 12 min after 6:23 P.M.

Choose the most reasonable unit. Write *s, min, h, d, wk, mo,* or *y*.

47. It takes Bob 6 ■ to dial his phone number.
48. The local TV news show lasts for 30 ■ each day.
49. It takes 2 ■ to read the Sunday newspaper.
50. We go to school for 6 ■ every day.
51. A high school fall soccer season lasts 8 ■.
52. The president of the United States is elected for 4 ■.

53.

Here is how Anita found the elapsed time. Tell what mistake she made. Explain how to correct it.

Problem Solving

54. Brendan reads Braille. It takes him 42 days to read the *Chronicles of Narnia* by C. S. Lewis. How many weeks does it take?

55. Alicia makes a telephone call that lasts 90 minutes. How many hours is she on the phone?

Use data from the graph for problems 56–58.

56. What is the average number of e-mail messages Clare receives each day?

57. What is the median for the number of e-mail messages received?

58. **What if** Clare receives the same number of e-mail messages each week for 4 weeks? How many messages would that be?

59. Jose starts talking on the phone at 6:29 P.M. He finishes 1 hour 55 minutes later. When does he finish?

★**60.** **Science:** Atomic clocks can record times with great precision. An atomic timer starts timing on Monday at 6:53 and 29 seconds A.M. and runs for 4 days, 7 hours, 19 minutes, and 33 seconds. On what day and time does the timer stop?

61. **Create a problem** that can be solved by finding elapsed time. Solve it and give it to another student to solve.

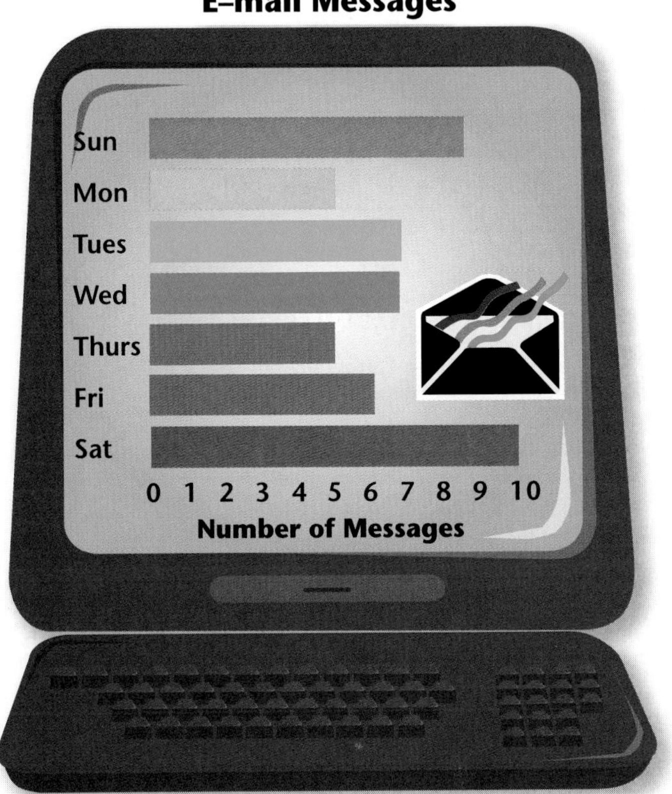

62. **Compare:** How would you find the elapsed time from 8:30 A.M. to 11:30 A.M. and from 10:30 P.M. to 1:30 A.M.?

Spiral Review and Test Prep

63. 3.10 + 9.8 **64.** 91.4 − 1.27 **65.** 7 + 5.8 **66.** 22.4 − 19.1 **67.** 2.4 − 1.8

Choose the correct answer.

68. What number does 1|3 represent in a stem-and-leaf plot?

A. 113
B. 3
C. 13
D. $\frac{1}{3}$

69. Write the number 81 using a base and exponent.

F. $3 \times 3 \times 3 \times 3$
G. 3^3
H. 4^3
J. 3^4

Objective: Estimate and measure length in customary units; choose an appropriate unit for measuring length; change between units of length.

8•2 Customary Length

Learn

How many inches long is the cellular phone?

Customary Units of Length
1 foot (ft) = 12 inches (in.)
1 yard (yd) = 36 in.
1 yard (yd) = 3 ft
1 mile (mi) = 5,280 ft
1 mile (mi) = 1,760 yd

Example

The cellular phone is:

- 5 inches to the nearest inch.
- 5 inches to the nearest half inch.
- $5\frac{1}{4}$ inches to the nearest quarter inch.
- $5\frac{3}{8}$ inches, to the nearest eighth inch.
- $5\frac{5}{16}$ inches to the nearest sixteenth inch.

A foot is about the length of a 3-ring binder.

1 foot

Use feet to measure distances like the height of a mailbox.

A yard is about the length of a baseball bat.

1 yard

Use yards to measure distances like the length of a delivery truck.

A mile is the distance 4 times around a $\frac{1}{4}$-mile-track.

$\frac{1}{4}$ mile

Use miles to measure distances like the distance from Earth to a satellite.

Linda's mailbox is 16 inches long. She gets a package that is 2 feet long. Will the package fit in Linda's mailbox?

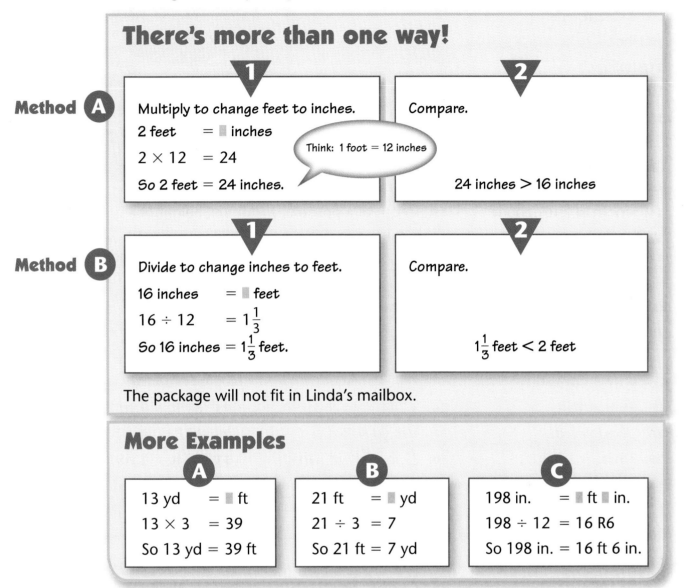

There's more than one way!

Method A

1 Multiply to change feet to inches.

2 feet = ▮ inches

$2 \times 12 = 24$

So 2 feet = 24 inches.

Think: 1 foot = 12 inches

2 Compare.

24 inches > 16 inches

Method B

1 Divide to change inches to feet.

16 inches = ▮ feet

$16 \div 12 = 1\frac{1}{3}$

So 16 inches = $1\frac{1}{3}$ feet.

2 Compare.

$1\frac{1}{3}$ feet < 2 feet

The package will not fit in Linda's mailbox.

More Examples

A	B	C
13 yd = ▮ ft	21 ft = ▮ yd	198 in. = ▮ ft ▮ in.
$13 \times 3 = 39$	$21 \div 3 = 7$	$198 \div 12 = 16$ R6
So 13 yd = 39 ft	So 21 ft = 7 yd	So 198 in. = 16 ft 6 in.

Try It **Measure the length of the pen to the nearest:**

1. inch
2. half inch
3. quarter inch
4. eighth inch

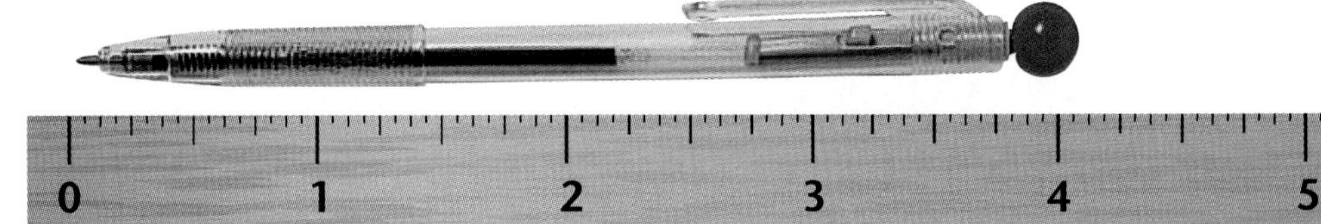

Copy and complete.

5. 54 ft = ▮ yd
6. 50 yd = ▮ ft
7. 4 ft = ▮ in.
8. 45 in. = ▮ yd ▮ in.

Explain how to change units from feet to inches.

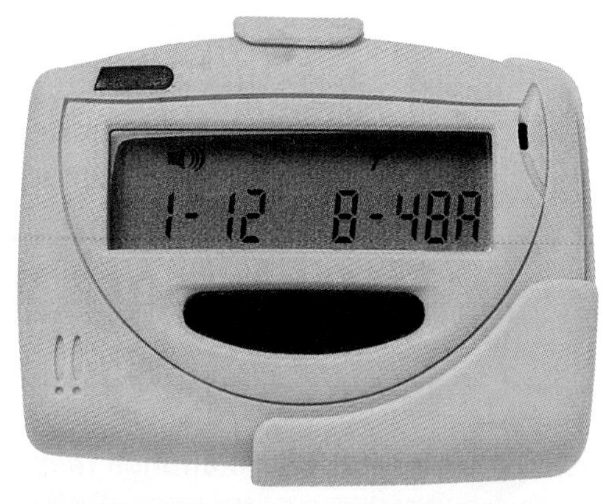

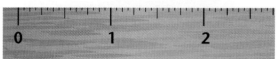

Practice

Measure the length of the pager to the nearest:

9. sixteenth inch
10. inch
11. half inch
12. quarter inch
13. eighth inch

0 1 2

Choose an appropriate unit to measure the length of each. Write *in., ft, yd,* or *mi.*

14. length of a telephone
15. length of a post office
16. height of a computer
17. distance an airplane flies to deliver packages
18. height of a televison set
19. distance between two telephone poles

Estimate. Then use a ruler to measure exactly.

20. length of the chalkboard
21. height of your desk
22. length of your math book

Copy and complete.

23. 29 ft = ■ in.
24. 3,744 in. = ■ yd
25. 81 ft = ■ yd
26. 19 yd = ■ in.
27. 108 yd = ■ ft
28. 132 in. = ■ ft
29. 75 in. = ■ ft ■ in.
30. 79 in. = ■ yd ■ in.
31. 22 ft = ■ yd ■ ft

★32. 133 in. = ■ yd ■ ft ■ in.

★33. 12,320 yd = ■ mi

★34. 26,400 ft = ■ mi

Compare. Write >, <, or =.

35. 100 ft ● 30 yd
36. 9 yd ● 324 in.
37. 11,000 ft ● 2 mi
38. 12 ft ● 145 in.
39. 75 yd ● 220 ft
40. 1,740 in. ● 145 ft
41. 900 in. ● 26 yd
42. 654 ft ● 218 yd
43. 950 ft ● 11,412 in.

44.

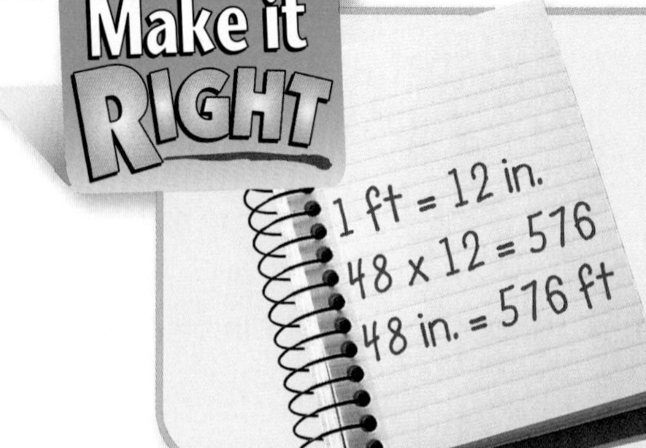

Here is how Sam changed 48 inches to feet. Tell what mistake he made. Explain how to correct it.

Problem Solving

45. Carla's fax machine is $1\frac{1}{2}$ feet wide. The width of the paper it uses is $8\frac{1}{2}$ inches. How much wider is Carla's fax machine than the paper width?

46. Ken wants to know how long his cell phone is. Which customary unit of length is the most reasonable for measuring it?

Use data from *Did You Know?* for problems 47–48.

47. How long ago was the first marathon?

★ 48. If your school has a 100-yard dash, about how many times shorter is that than the first marathon?

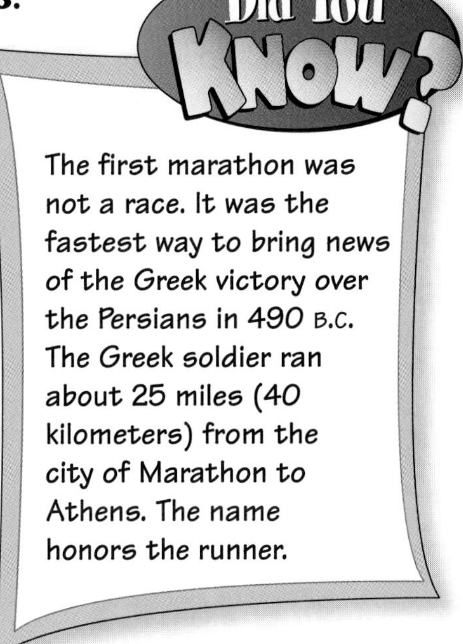

Did You
KNOW?
The first marathon was not a race. It was the fastest way to bring news of the Greek victory over the Persians in 490 B.C. The Greek soldier ran about 25 miles (40 kilometers) from the city of Marathon to Athens. The name honors the runner.

49. **Science:** Samuel Morse invented the telegraph in 1844. Morse lived from 1791 to 1872. About how old was he when the first telegraph message was sent?

50. **Social Studies:** Prehistoric people used cave drawings to tell stories about what happened to them. If there are 115 drawings in each of 9 caves, how many drawings is that?

51. Al puts a 1-foot-wide computer tower next to a 16-inch-wide monitor. Will they fit on a desk that is 30 inches wide? Explain.

52. **Create a problem** that compares the length of 2 objects that you use for communicating in your home. Solve it and give it to another student to solve.

53. **Summarize:** How do you change between larger and smaller units?

Spiral Review and Test Prep

54. 212×45

55. 3.9×5.8

56. 48×9.6

57. 15.3×4.5

Choose the correct answer.

58. Jon and Paulo are biking $15\frac{1}{2}$ miles to the beach. They have gone $9\frac{3}{4}$ miles. How many more miles do they need to go?

A. $5\frac{3}{4}$ mi

C. $24\frac{1}{4}$ mi

B. $6\frac{1}{2}$ mi

D. $25\frac{1}{2}$ mi

59. Manna counts the number of birds that visit a bird feeder each day. Find the mean of the numbers.
29 33 28 21 19 27 25

F. 14

H. 27

G. 26

J. Not Here

Extra Practice, page 381

Objective: Estimate, choose an appropriate unit for, and change between units of capacity and weight.

8•3 Customary Capacity and Weight

Learn

Math Words

volume the amount of space that an object occupies

capacity the volume of a container, given in units of liquid measure

The students who run the school radio station are making posters to advertise their sports bottle give-away. How many fluid ounces of paint did they use?

The customary units for measuring capacity are the fluid ounce (fl oz), cup (c), pint (pt), quart (qt), and gallon (gal).

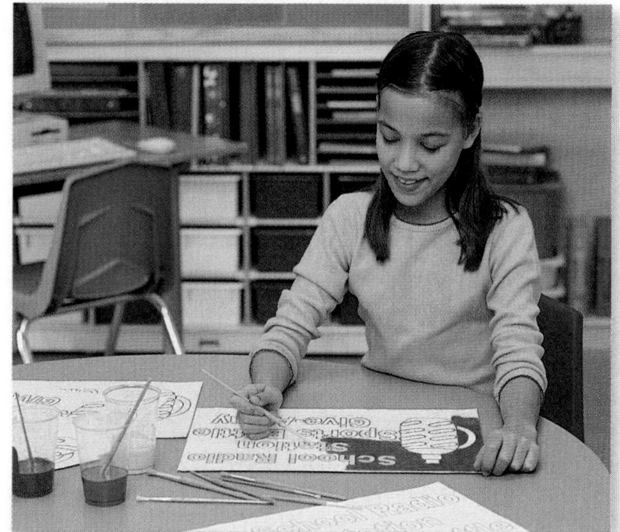

3 cups of paint

Customary Units of capacity

1 fluid ounce, 1 cup,

1 pint,

1 quart,

1 gallon

Customary Units of Capacity
1 cup (c) = 8 fluid ounces (fl oz)
1 pint (pt) = 2 c = 16 fl oz
1 quart (qt) = 2 pt = 32 fl oz
1 gallon (gal) = 4 qt

Example 1

Change 3 cups to fluid ounces to solve the problem. Multiply to change from a larger unit to a smaller unit.

3 cups = ▮ fluid ounces $3 \times 8 = 24$ 3 cups = 24 fluid ounces

Think: 1 cup = 8 fluid ounces

The students used 24 fluid ounces of paint.

More Examples

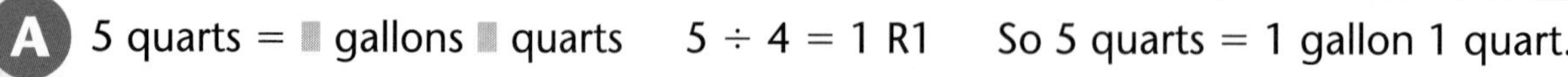

A 5 quarts = ▮ gallons ▮ quarts $5 \div 4 = 1$ R1   So 5 quarts = 1 gallon 1 quart.

B 49 cups = ▮ gallons ▮ quarts ▮ cups

Change cups to quarts. $49 \div 4 = 12$ R1   So 49 cups = 12 quarts 1 cup.

Change quarts to gallons. $12 \div 4 = 3$ So 49 cups = 3 gallons 1 cup.

A marker weighs about 1 ounce (oz).

A telephone weighs about 1 pound (lb).

A small car weighs about 1 ton (T).

Paco's printer weighs 32 ounces. How many pounds is that?

Example 2

Change 32 ounces to pounds to solve the problem.

Customary Units of Weight
1 pound (lb) = 16 ounces (oz)
1 ton (T) = 2,000 lb

Note: An ounce is a unit of weight and a fluid ounce is a unit of capacity.

32 ounces = ▮ pounds	32 ÷ 16 oz = 2	32 ounces = 2 pounds.

Divide to change a smaller unit to a larger unit.

Think: 1 pound = 16 ounces

The printer weighs 2 pounds.

More Examples

C	4 tons = ▮ pounds	4 × 2,000 = 8,000	So 4 T = 8,000 lb.
D	64 ounces = ▮ pounds	64 ÷ 16 = 4	So 64 oz = 4 lb.
E	15,000 pounds = ▮ tons	15,000 ÷ 2,000 = $7\frac{1}{2}$	So 15,000 lb = $7\frac{1}{2}$ T.

Try It **Choose an appropriate unit to measure the capacity of each. Write *fl oz, c, pt, qt,* or *gal.***

1. swimming pool
2. soup spoon
3. coffee pot

Choose an appropriate unit to measure the weight of each. Write *oz, lb,* or *T.*

4. computer mouse
5. mail delivery truck
6. computer printer

Copy and complete.

7. 3 c = ▮ fl oz
8. 4 qt = ▮ c
9. 80 oz = ▮ lb
10. 17 fl oz = ▮ c ▮ fl oz

Explain how to change from fluid ounces to pints.

Practice

Choose an appropriate unit to measure the capacity of each. Write *fl oz, c, pt, qt,* or *gal*.

11. coffee mug
12. bathtub
13. water bottle
14. fish tank
15. baby bottle
16. trash can
17. glass of milk
18. swimming pool
19. flower vase

Choose an appropriate unit to measure the weight of each. Write *oz, lb,* or *T*.

20. bag of potatoes
21. elephant
22. fork
23. tube of toothpaste
24. fifth-grade student
25. bed sheet
26. car
27. textbook
28. dog

Copy and complete.

29. 5 c = ■ fl oz
30. 18 pt = ■ qt
31. 50 gal = ■ qt
32. 28 c = ■ pt
33. 16 pt = ■ c
34. 96 fl oz = ■ c
35. 25 fl oz = ■ c ■ fl oz
36. 19 qt = ■ gal ■ qt
37. 2 gal = ■ fl oz
38. 80 oz = ■ lb
39. 50 oz = ■ lb ■ oz
40. 3,000 lb = ■ T
41. $3\frac{1}{2}$ T = ■ lb
42. 104 oz = ■ lb
43. $14\frac{1}{4}$ lb = ■ oz
★ **44.** 10,000 T = ■ lb
★ **45.** 9,512 lb = ■ T ■ lb
★ **46.** 2 T = ■ oz

Compare. Write >, <, or =.

47. 3 c ● 25 fl oz
48. 165 pt ● 82 c
49. 25 pt ● 10 qt
50. 24 gal ● 96 qt
51. 110 fl oz ● 14 c
52. 75 qt ● 35 pt
53. 396 qt ● 99 gal
54. 39 c ● 312 fl oz
55. 147 fl oz ● 19 c
56. 15 c 7 fl oz ● 130 fl oz
57. 12 gal 2 qt ● 50 qt
58. 135 fl oz ● 16 c 6 fl oz
59. 16 lb ● 246 oz
60. 7,500 lb ● 4 T
61. 1,200 oz ● 75 lb
62. 195 lb ● 3,120 oz
63. 7 T 500 lb ● 7,300 oz
64. 17 lb 11 oz ● 282 oz

65.

Here is how Jan changed pounds to ounces. Tell what mistake she made. Explain how to correct it.

Problem Solving

66. Lisa is shopping for a cell phone. What customary unit of weight should she use to measure how heavy the cell phones are?

67. Communications satellites work best orbiting at an altitude of 22,300 miles above the equator. How do you write 22,300 in expanded form?

Use data from *Did You Know?* for problems 68–69.

68. **Social Studies:** How many times faster was the telegraph than the Pony Express?

69. How long ago did the Pony Express end?

70. Mrs. Forsyth's fifth-grade students are painting posters advertising their class's fair. Mrs. Forsyth buys seven 16-ounce jars of paint, a 1-gallon jar, and three 8-ounce jars. How many ounces of paint does she buy in all?

71. **Health:** It is a good idea to drink 8 cups of water each day. Sonya drinks 6 ounces of water while reading e-mail. She drinks 1 cup of water at lunch and 20 ounces of water the rest of the day. How much more water should she drink today?

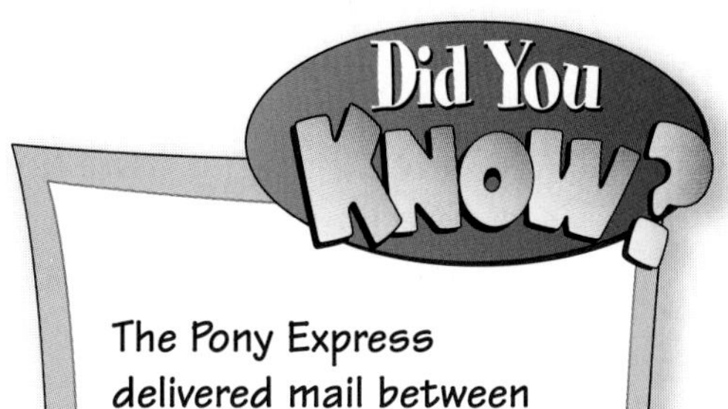

The Pony Express delivered mail between Sacramento, California, and St. Joseph, Missouri, in 10 days. The service ended in 1861 when the first transcontinental telegraph line was completed. It delivered a message in 5 minutes.

72. **Science:** Sound travels through air at about 1,000 feet per second. A boat sounds a distress signal that is heard by a fishing boat $1\frac{1}{2}$ minutes later. About how many miles away is the fishing boat?

73. **Analyze:** Pierre and Louise are shipping language tapes to schools overseas. One box weighs 9 pounds 8 ounces and the other box weighs 152 ounces. Which box weighs more?

Spiral Review and Test Prep

Find the LCD for each pair of numbers.

74. $\frac{1}{4}$ and $\frac{1}{3}$

75. $\frac{3}{5}$ and $\frac{7}{8}$

76. $\frac{3}{4}$ and $\frac{1}{10}$

77. $\frac{1}{2}$ and $\frac{5}{6}$

Choose the correct answer.

78. What is the value of 9 in 798,351,602?
    A. 900,000,000
    B. 90,000,000
    C. 900,000
    D. Not Here

79. 6.21×4.11 rounded to the nearest tenth is
    F. 25.6
    G. 24.1
    H. 25.5
    J. 25.51

Extra Practice, page 381

Objective: Check for reasonableness.

8•4 Problem Solving: Reading for Math

Check for Reasonableness

School Gets Internet Access

Read

A technician is installing a computer modem in a classroom. The length of the room the cable must cross is 36 feet. He estimates he will need 100 yards of cable to wire the room. Is his estimate reasonable?

READING SKILL ▶

Compare and Contrast

When you compare and contrast, you look for things that are alike and different.

- **What do you know?** How much cable is needed
- **What do you need to find?** Whether the estimate is reasonable

MATH SKILL ▶

Check for Reasonableness

An answer is reasonable if it makes sense and agrees with what you know about the world.

Plan

You want to compare the length of a classroom to something you know is about 100 yards long.

Solve

The length of a football field is 100 yards long. It is much longer than the length of a classroom. Therefore, the answer is not reasonable.

The technician multiplied to change a smaller unit to a larger unit. He should have divided.

$36 \div 3 = 12$ ← **Remember: 3 feet = 1 yard**

The technician's estimate is not reasonable. He will need 12 yards of cable.

Look Back

How else could you check to see if the technician's estimate was reasonable?

Why is checking for reasonableness a good idea?

Practice Is each estimate reasonable? Explain.

1. A telephone pole weighs about 350 pounds. Tamara says that equals about 21,000 ounces.

2. A telephone pole is buried 96 inches underground. How many feet is 96 inches? Chris says 1,152 feet.

3. There are 12 yards of cable between phone poles. How many feet is this? Marie says 4 feet. Is her answer reasonable?

4. When the installer brings new cable, she carries 854 ounces of cable from the utility truck. How many pounds does she carry? Beth says she carries 1,708 pounds. Is her answer reasonable?

5. A telephone pole left a hole in the ground when it was removed. It rained, and $1\frac{1}{2}$ cups of rainwater collected in the hole. Rick says that 64 fluid ounces is $1\frac{1}{2}$ cups. Is his estimate reasonable?

6. Mrs. Gregg is setting up telephones made of paper cups and string in her class. Each pair of students gets 2 paper cups and 4 feet of string. Mrs. Gregg estimates that for her 24 students she will need about 16 yards of string. Is her estimate reasonable?

7. Carmen estimates that a sports bottle holds up to 100 cups of water. Is this estimate reasonable?

8. Hannah estimates that she will need a 3-foot ladder to reach the roof of a house. Is her estimate reasonable?

9. Amanda estimates that she must walk 5,280 miles to the post office. Is her estimate reasonable?

10. Joshua estimates that his bicycle weighs 15 ounces. Is his estimate reasonable?

Spiral Review and Test Prep

Choose the correct answer.

Karl cuts off a section of wire 1 foot long. He says that the wire is 3 yards long.

11. Which of the following statements is true?
   - A. The wire is 1 foot long.
   - B. The wire is 3 feet long.
   - C. The wire is 1 yard long.
   - D. The wire is 3 yards long.

12. When you check the reasonableness of an answer, you
   - F. compare the answer with what you know.
   - G. do all calculations twice.
   - H. make a good guess.
   - J. always multiply.

Problem Solving

Check Your Progress A

Find each elapsed time. **(pages 346–349)**

1. 6:29 A.M. to 4:47 P.M.
2. 10:16 P.M. to 9:55 A.M.

Copy and complete. **(pages 346–357)**

3. 15 min = ■ s
4. 52 wk = ■ d
5. 144 h = ■ d
6. 670 min = ■ h ■ min
7. 3,456 in. = ■ yd
8. 309 ft = ■ in.
9. 10 mi = ■ yd
10. 500 in. = ■ ft ■ in.
11. 19 c = ■ fl oz
12. 50 c = ■ pt
13. 25 gal = ■ qt
14. 75 fl oz = ■ c ■ fl oz

Choose an appropriate unit to measure the length of each. **(pages 350–353)**

15. a hearing aid
16. a football field
17. a computer keyboard

Choose an appropriate unit to measure the capacity of each. **(pages 354–357)**

18. car transmission fluid
19. water tower
20. glass of orange juice

Choose an appropriate unit to measure the weight of each. **(pages 354–357)**

21. a cell phone
22. a newborn baby
23. a compact disc

Solve. **(pages 358–359)**

24. Joy wants to send a 15-inch-long poster to a friend. She can choose an envelope that is $1\frac{1}{2}$ feet long or $1\frac{1}{2}$ yards long. Which is a reasonable choice? Explain.

25. **Analyze:** When do you use multiplication to change one unit to another?

Additional activities at www.mhschool.com/math

Use the Internet

Kaylin is gathering data on the lengths of rivers or coastlines of different countries of the world. She needs to find data for four different rivers or countries. She will use the data she collects to complete the following table. How can she use the Internet to gather the data?

Country or River	Length of River or Coastline	Converted Length
	km	m
	km	m
	mi	ft
	mi	ft

- Go to www.mhschool.com/math.
- Find the list of sites that provide geography data. Click on a link.
- Find the data on the length of rivers or the length of the coastline of countries. Choose four rivers or countries for which data is given.
- Copy the table. Write the names of the rivers or countries you chose in your table.
- Record the length of each river or coastline in the table. Be sure two of the lengths are in kilometers and two are in miles.
- Convert kilometers to meters and miles to feet.

1. Is it better to give the lengths of the rivers or coastlines in the larger or the smaller units? Explain.

2. **Analyze:** Why does using the Internet make more sense than using another reference source to find the data needed to complete your table?

For more practice, use Math Traveler™.

Objective: Estimate and measure length in metric units; choose an appropriate metric unit for measuring length.

Explore Metric Length

Learn

You can use a centimeter ruler to explore metric length.

Work Together

You Will Need
- **centimeter ruler**
- **meterstick**

▶ Use a centimeter ruler to measure the two-way radio.

The two-way radio is
- exactly 107 millimeters long.
- 11 centimeters to the nearest centimeter.

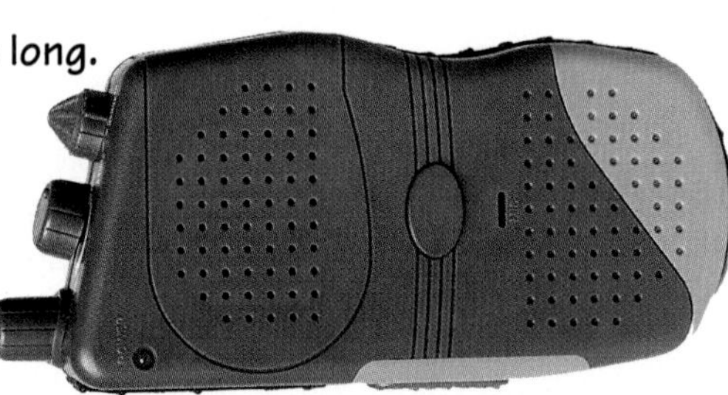

The millimeter (mm), centimeter (cm), meter (m), and kilometer (km) are common metric units of length.

▶ Find 5 items in your classroom to measure. First estimate, and then measure with a centimeter ruler or a meterstick. Copy the chart and record your measurements.

Object	Length		Width		Depth	
	Estimate	Exact	Estimate	Exact	Estimate	Exact

Make Connections

You can use the size of known objects to help you estimate the length of other objects. You can use a ruler or meterstick to make exact calculations.

Metric Units of Length
1 centimeter (cm) = 10 millimeters (mm)
1 meter (m) = 100 cm = 1,000 mm
1 kilometer (km) = 1,000 m

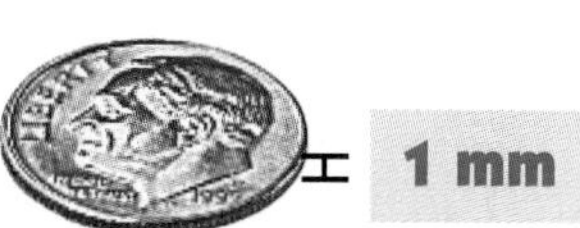

1 mm

1 millimeter is about the thickness of a dime.

1 cm

1 centimeter is about the width of your pencil.

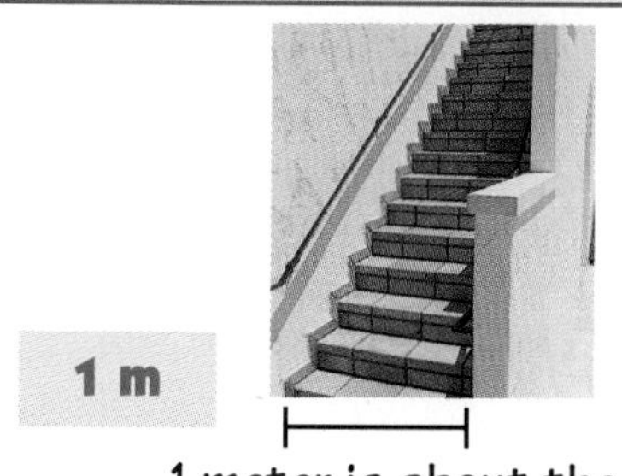

1 m

1 meter is about the width of a stairway.

1 kilometer is about how far you can walk in 10 minutes.

Try It **Measure to the nearest centimeter and millimeter.**

1. ├────────────┤

2. ├────────────────────┤

Sum it Up

Name something you would measure in millimeters, in centimeters, and in kilometers.

Practice **Measure to the nearest centimeter and millimeter.**

3. ├──┤

4. ├────────────────────────────────────┤

Choose an appropriate unit. Write *mm, cm, m,* or *km*.

5. length of a pencil
6. width of a door
7. thickness of a telephone cord
8. thickness of this math book
9. thickness of pencil lead
10. distance from Earth to a satellite
11. **Analyze:** Would you measure the distance between Los Angeles and New York City in millimeters? Explain.

Objective: Measure capacity and mass in metric units; choose an appropriate unit for measuring capacity and mass.

Metric Capacity and Mass

Math Word

mass the amount of matter in an object

Learn

The students who work at the school's radio station are giving away free sports bottles to promote the station. Do the bottles hold 1 milliliter, 1 centiliter, or 1 liter of liquid?

Metric Units of Volume
1 centiliter (cL) = 10 milliliters (mL)
1 metric cup (c) = 250 mL
1 liter (L) = 1,000 mL= 100cL

Example 1

1 milliliter (mL)

1 centiliter (cL)

1 liter (L)

The sports bottle holds 1 liter.

You can use metric units to measure the **mass** of an object.

Metric Units of Mass
1 centigram (cg) = 10 milligrams (mg)
1 gram (g) = 1,000 milligrams (mg)
1 kilogram (kg) = 1,000 (g)

Example 2

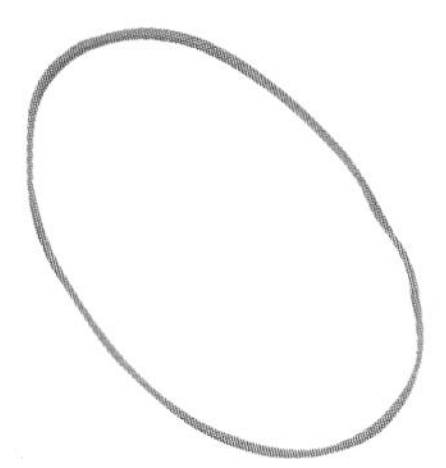

A rubber band has a mass of about 1 milligram (mg).

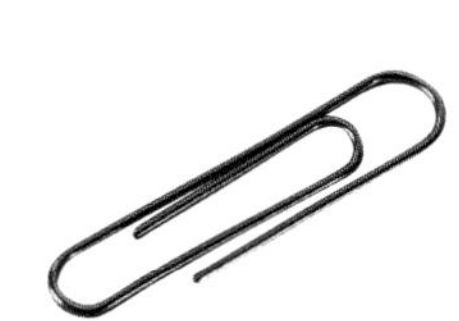

A large paper clip has a mass of about 1 gram (g).

A camera has a mass of about 1 kilogram (kg).

Note: Sometimes small objects have more mass than large ones. For example stone has more mass than a balloon.

Example 3

The units of volume and mass are related for water.

One milliliter of water has a mass of 1 gram.

One liter of water has a mass of 1 kilogram.

Try It **Choose an appropriate unit to measure the volume of each. Write *mL, cL,* or *L*.**

1. spoonful of honey
2. waterbed
3. large pot of soup
4. glass of milk

Choose an appropriate unit to measure the mass of each. Write *mg, g,* or *kg*.

5. yourself
6. tissue
7. pager
8. fax machine

Which unit would you use to measure the mass of a magazine? Explain.

Practice

Choose an appropriate unit of capacity to measure each. Write *mL* or *L*.

9. thermos
10. carton of milk
11. gasoline tank
12. soup bowl
13. salt shaker
14. juice box
15. swimming pool
16. cup of tea
17. toothpaste
18. glass of water
19. fishtank
20. bathroom sink

Choose an appropriate unit of mass to measure each. Write *mg*, *g*, or *kg*.

21. crayon
22. television
23. index card
24. cell phone
25. dog
26. ant
27. compact disc
28. laserdisc player
29. pen
30. person
31. grain of rice
32. notebook

Choose an appropriate estimate for each.

33. trash can
A. 2 milliliters **C.** 2 liters
B. 20 milliliters **D.** 20 liters

34. toothpaste tube
A. 2 milliliters **C.** 2 liters
B. 250 milliliters **D.** 250 liters

35. paint bucket
A. 2 milliliters **C.** 2 liters
B. 20 milliliters **D.** 20 liters

36. yogurt cup
A. 12 milliliters **C.** 12 liters
B. 120 milliliters **D.** 120 liters

37. telephone handset
A. 90 milligrams **C.** 90 grams
B. 900 milligrams **D.** 900 grams

38. crayon
A. 5 milligrams **C.** 50 grams
B. 5 grams **D.** 5 kilograms

39. sheet of paper
A. 4 milligrams **C.** 10 grams
B. 450 kilograms **D.** 450 grams

40. computer disk
A. 20 milligrams **C.** 20 grams
B. 200 milligrams **D.** 200 grams

41. a cat
A. 5 grams **C.** 5 kilograms
B. 50 grams **D.** 50 kilograms

★**42.** bathtub
A. 20 liters **C.** 200 liters
B. 40 liters **D.** 4,000 liters

43.

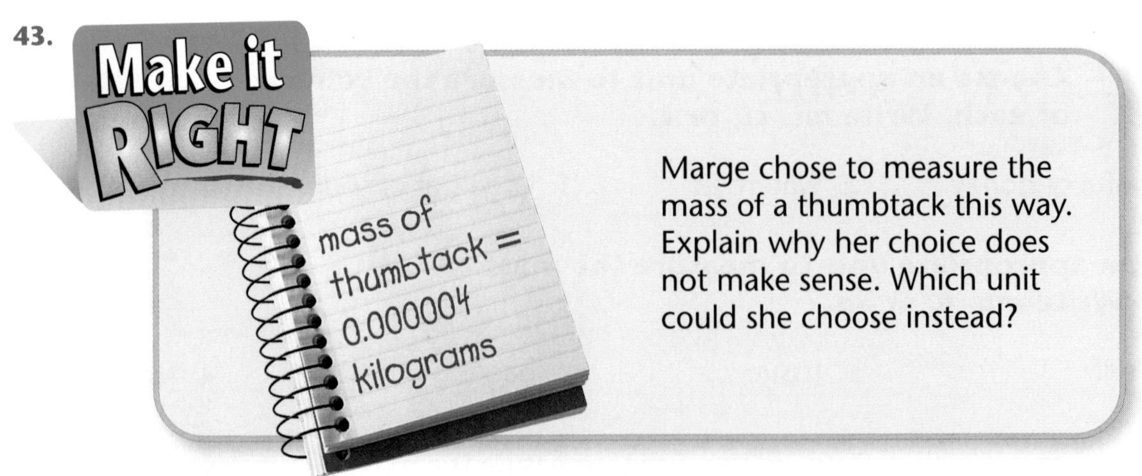

Marge chose to measure the mass of a thumbtack this way. Explain why her choice does not make sense. Which unit could she choose instead?

Problem Solving

44. Carolyn brings drinks for the Debate Club meeting. Does she bring 8 mL, 8 cL, or 8 L of drinks?

45. **What if** a cellular phone tower can transmit across a large town? What metric unit would be used to measure this distance?

46. Dale is going to Los Angeles to give a speech. What metric unit of mass does he use to measure his suitcase?

47. **Summarize:** Is it possible to measure the mass of a truck in milligrams? Is it the best choice? Explain.

48. Ian's cell phone weighs 41.3 grams without its battery. The battery weighs 61.5 grams. How much do the cell phone and battery weigh together?

49. The school radio club has a $400 budget for the school year. They spend $\frac{1}{2}$ of their money. How much do they spend?

50. The school radio news team meets in a room that has square tables that seat one person on each side. How many tables must be put together to seat the entire 8-person team?

51. The radio news team mails a 1-page newsletter to each student's home. To find the correct postage, they weigh one copy. About how much would it weigh?

52. **Language Arts:** There are 874,000,000 native speakers of Mandarin and 341,000,000 native speakers of English in the world. How many more native speakers of Mandarin than English are there?

★53. The school radio news team broadcasts from 9:05 until 9:15 in the morning. They spend an hour each afternoon writing the news for the next day. How many more times do they spend writing the news than broadcasting it?

Spiral Review and Test Prep

Write each fraction in simplest form.

54. $\frac{43}{15}$ 55. $\frac{25}{105}$ 56. $\frac{665}{90}$ 57. $\frac{40}{160}$

58. $\frac{55}{110}$ 59. $\frac{18}{81}$ 60. $\frac{24}{60}$ 61. $\frac{11}{121}$

Choose the correct answer.

62. What is 459,207 rounded to the nearest ten thousand?
A. 500,000 C. 459,000
B. 460,000 D. Not Here

63. Which of these numbers is not divisible by 9?
F. 1,026 H. 594
G. 882 J. 499

Extra Practice, page 382

Objective: Change from one metric unit to another.

8·7 Metric Conversions

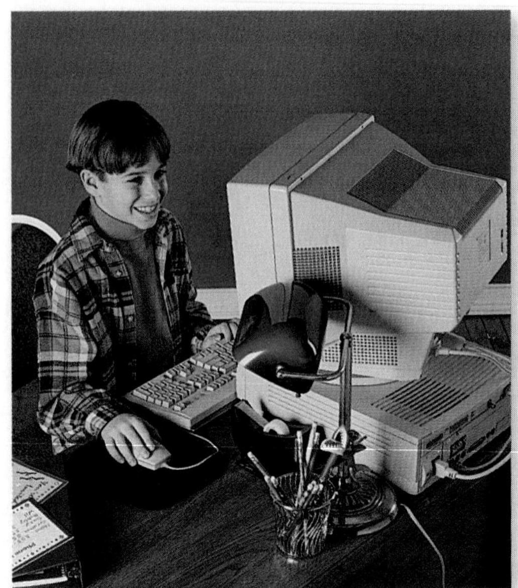

Learn

Franco wants to buy a printer for his desk. The area on his desk for the printer is 15 centimeters wide. Will a printer that is 132 millimeters wide fit?

Example 1

Change 132 millimeters to centimeters to solve the problem.

Divide to change from a smaller unit to a larger unit.

To change between metric units, you multiply or divide by powers of ten.

Remember: A power of ten is the number 10 raised to an exponent.

1

132 millimeters = ▮ centimeters

Think: 10 millimeters = 1 centimeter

$132 \div 10 = 13.2$

132 millimeters = 13.2 centimeters

2

Compare.

$13.2 < 15$

The printer will fit.

More Examples

A

2.51 km = ▮ m

$2.51 \times 1{,}000 = 2{,}510$

So 2.51 kilometers = 2,510 meters.

B

90.5 cm = ▮ m

$90.5 \div 100 = 0.905$

So 90.5 centimeters = 0.905 meters.

C

97.8 mg = ▮ g

$97.8 \div 1{,}000 = 0.0978$

So 97.8 milligrams = 0.0978 grams.

Mona puts a 19-centimeter fax machine on an 8-centimeter stack of paper. The fax and paper sit on a desk that is 0.75 meter tall. Will these items fit below a shelf that is 95 centimeters off the ground?

Example 2

Add 19 cm, 8 cm and 0.75 m and then compare to 95 cm to solve the problem.

1

Change the numbers so they have the same units.

0.75 meter = ▮ centimeters

Think: 1 meter = 100 centimeters

$0.75 \times 100 = 75$

0.75 meter = 75 centimeters

2

Add.

$$\begin{array}{r} 8 \text{ cm} \\ 75 \text{ cm} \\ +19 \text{ cm} \\ \hline 102 \text{ cm} \end{array}$$

3

Compare.

$102 > 95$

The items will not fit below the shelf.

More Examples

D

13 cm + 8.5 m + 7.12 m = ▮ m

13 cm = ▮ m

$13 \div 100 = 0.13$

13 cm = 0.13 m

$0.13 + 8.5 + 7.12 =$

15.75

So 13 cm + 8.5 m + 7.12 m = 15.75 m

E

420 mL + 8.5 L + 6.7 L = ▮ L

420 mL = ▮ L

$420 \div 1{,}000 = 0.420$

420 mL = 0.42 L

$0.42 + 8.5 + 6.7 =$

15.62

So 420 mL + 8.5 L + 6.7 L = 15.62 L

Try It **Copy and complete.**

1. 35 cm = ▮ m
2. 1.75 kg = ▮ g
3. 6.25 L = ▮ mL
4. 58 mm = ▮ cm
5. 3.8 m + 15 cm + 2.8 m = ▮ m
6. 3.4 kg + 34 g + 29 g = ▮ g

Explain how to change units from grams to kilograms.

Practice Copy and complete.

7. 255 m = ■ km
8. 809 cm = ■ m
9. 15 cm = ■ mm
10. 5 km = ■ m
11. 3 mm = ■ cm
12. 2.5 m = ■ cm
13. 0.75 km = ■ m
14. 25 cm = ■ m
15. 875 mL = ■ L
16. 9.01 L = ■ mL
17. 16 cL = ■ mL
18. 32 cL = ■ L
19. 15 mL = ■ cL
20. 51 L = ■ cL
21. 4.14 mL = ■ L
22. 18.2 L = ■ mL
23. 15 g = ■ kg
24. 85 mg = ■ g
25. 145.2 mg = ■ g
26. 78.3 g = ■ kg
27. 15 kg = ■ g
28. 90 g = ■ mg
★29. 7.125 kg = ■ g
★30. 400 mg = ■ kg

Find each sum.

31. 35 cm + 23 mm + 19 cm = ■ cm
32. 85 cm + 9.8 m + 4.9 m = ■ m
33. 1.9 m + 24 cm + 38 cm = ■ cm
34. 5.7 km + 20 m + 54 m = ■ m
35. 6.7 km + 12 m + 20 km = ■ km
36. 5 m + 7.25 m + 75 cm = ■ m
37. 2.6 L + 48 mL + 7 mL = ■ mL
38. 9.7 L + 808 mL + 12.4 L = ■ L
39. 54 cL + 10 mL + 85 mL = ■ mL
40. 3.8 cL + 89 mL + 26.3 cL = ■ cL
41. 55.2 g + 19.1 g + 214 mg = ■ g
42. 965 g + 5.4 kg + 40 kg = ■ kg
★43. 9.34 kg + 140 g + 64 g = ■ g
★44. 1 mg + 1 g + 1 kg = ■ g

Compare. Write >, <, or =.

45. 5.6 km ● 560 m
46. 84.7 cm ● 8.47 m
47. 10.55 m ● 0.1055 km
48. 4,024 mm ● 40.24 cm
49. 504 cm ● 5.04 m
50. 514.5 cm ● 5,145 mm
51. 58.5 L ● 585 mL
52. 834 mL ● 8.34 L
53. 15 cL ● 1,500 mL
54. 27.8 cL ● 278 mL
55. 4,016 mL ● 0.4016 L
56. 8.125 L ● 8,125 mL
57. 0.65 kg ● 6,500 g
58. 814 g ● 8.14 kg
59. 9,458 mg ● 9.458 g
60. 0.87 g ● 87 mg
61. 0.621 kg ● 621 g
62. 5.02 g ● 0.0502 kg
63.

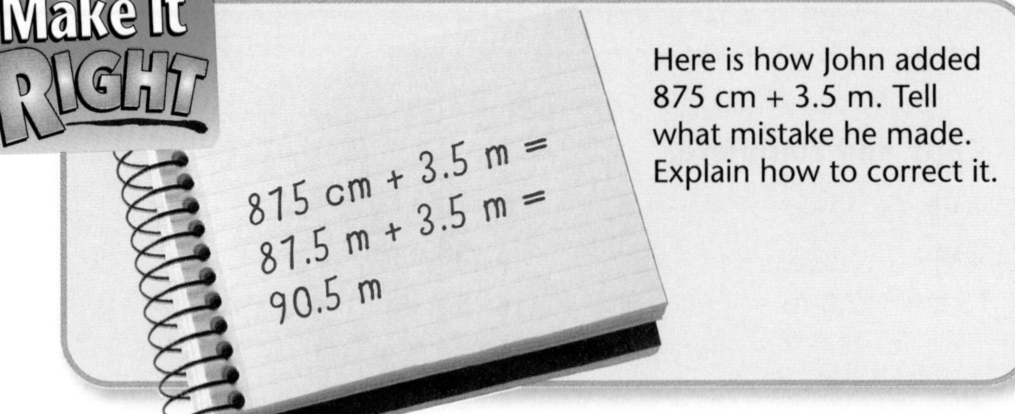

Here is how John added 875 cm + 3.5 m. Tell what mistake he made. Explain how to correct it.

Problem Solving

64. The phone company installs 5 kilometers of wire from the main computer to your street, 75 meters from your street to your house, and 95 centimeters to your phone jack inside. To the nearest tenth, how many kilometers of wire do they install?

65. **Science:** The cellular phone was invented in 1947, but it did not become popular until the 1990s. About how long was the cellular phone around before it became popular?

Use data from *Did You Know?* for problems 66–68.

66. About how many copies of *Time* are sold each year?

67. Many people receive their information about the world by reading magazines. About how many copies of *Time* are sold each month?

68. How many years has *Time* been in publication?

69. **Logical Reasoning:** Maria's cell phone is 105 millimeters long. Her purse is 15 centimeters long. Will the cell phone fit inside the purse? Explain.

70. **Summarize:** Why do you multiply when changing from larger units to smaller units and divide when changing from smaller units to larger units?

Time magazine was first published in 1923. More people buy *Time* than any other news magazine in the world. There are 4,150,000 copies of it sold each week.

Spiral Review and Test Prep

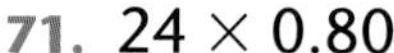

71. 24×0.80

72. 5.1×7

73. 60×0.03

74. 0.4×90

Choose the correct answer.

75. Find the mean of the number of calls made from different pay phones in a given hour. 24, 32, 36, 31, 27
    - A. 26
    - B. 28
    - C. 30
    - D. Not Here

76. Suppose phone service costs \$4.95 each month plus \$0.10 for each minute. If a caller uses the phone a total of 250 minutes during the month, how much will the bill be?
    - F. \$4.95
    - G. \$24.95
    - H. \$25.00
    - J. \$29.95

Extra Practice, page 383

Objective: Solve problems by drawing a diagram.

8·8 Problem Solving: Strategy
Draw a Diagram

Math in ACTION

Read

Read the problem carefully.

Suppose an auditorium is being prepared for Ayinde Jean-Baptiste to speak. The sound system uses speakers every 10 meters around the walls and no speakers at the corners. The auditorium is 70 meters by 100 meters. How many wall speakers does the auditorium have?

motivational speaker
Ayinde Jean-Baptiste

- **What do you know?** Auditorium is 70 meters by 100 meters; speaker every 10 meters; no speaker at corners
- **What are you being asked to find?** How many wall speakers the auditorium has

Plan

You can draw a diagram to solve the problem.

Draw a rectangle on graph paper. Draw and label dots to represent the speakers every 10 meters.

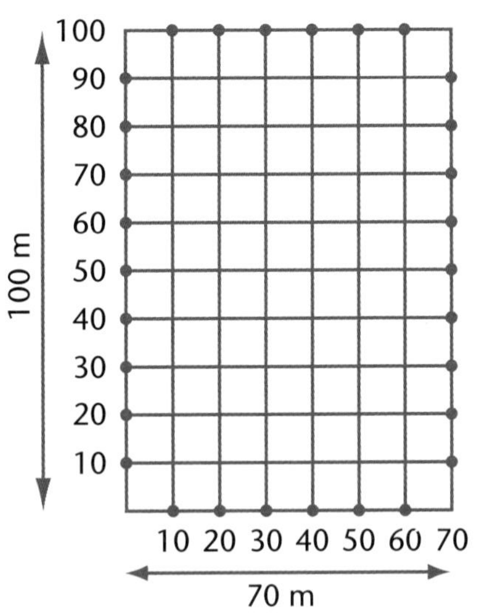

Solve

There are 30 dots.
The auditorium has 30 wall speakers.

Look Back

How can you tell if your answer is reasonable?

How does drawing a diagram help you solve the problem?

Practice Draw a diagram to solve.

1. Mark builds a telephone stand. He nails a square piece of wood that is 35 centimeters on each side to a pole. Mark puts a nail every 7 centimeters, including at the corners. How many nails does Mark use?

2. Cellular phone towers are evenly spaced in a circle with Tower 3 opposite Tower 9. How many cellular phone towers are in the circle?

3. A table 4 feet wide and 12 feet long has microphones on each side every foot and one at each corner. How many microphones are there on the table?

4. Erika makes a 5-by-5 grid. She writes the numbers 1 through 25 in order on the grid, starting with the top left square. What are the three inside numbers in the middle column of the grid?

5. A 1-mile-long scenic route has signposts every $\frac{1}{10}$ of a mile. There are signposts at the beginning and end of the mile. How many signposts are there?

6. An auditorium has special box seats. Each box is 6 feet by 4 feet. Each chair requires a space 2 feet by 3 feet. What is the maximum number of seats that can fit into a box?

Mixed Strategy Review

CHOOSE A STRATEGY

- Logical Reasoning
- Draw a Diagram
- Make a Graph
- Make a Table or List
- Find a Pattern
- Guess and Check
- Write an Equation
- Work Backward
- Solve a Simpler Problem
- Conduct an Experiment

7. Bill tells Randy to choose a number, add 5, and multiply by 8. Randy tells Bill that he found the number 64. What number did Randy choose?

8. Sue has 6 walkie-talkies and Jen has 4. They put all their walkie-talkies together and sell them at 2 walkie-talkies for $5.25. How much money do they earn if they sell all of the walkie-talkies?

9. Sam helped his father place a 31-letter ad in the newspaper. If the first five letters are free, and every other letter is $1.35, how much did it cost to place the ad?

10. Linda receives 15 faxes on Monday. This is 5 more than twice the number of faxes she receives on Tuesday. How many faxes does Linda receive on Tuesday?

11. Toby has a phone interview at 10:35 A.M. The interview lasts 35 minutes. He goes to lunch for 1 hour 15 minutes, then sends e-mail for 1 hour 45 minutes. Then he returns phone calls for 55 minutes. At what time does Toby finish returning phone calls?

12. The sound engineer installs speakers around a square auditorium. He places 8 speakers on each side and one at the corners. How many speakers does he install?

Extra Practice, page 383

Objective: Estimate measurement in degrees Fahrenheit, given the Celsius temperature.

Temperature

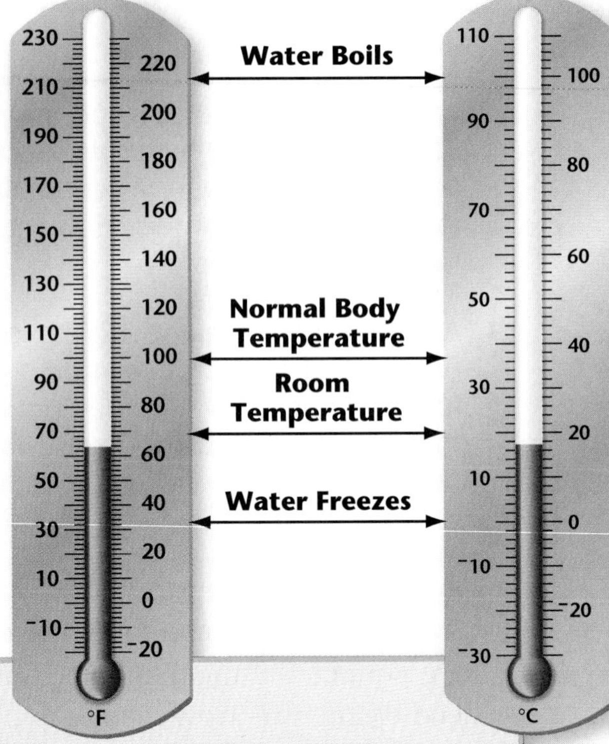

Learn

Suppose that the temperature in the library is 15°C. You want to know the temperature in °F. The temperature scales are related by this equation: $°F = \frac{9}{5}°C + 32$. In many situations, it is enough to estimate the temperature in °F from the known temperature in °C. What is the approximate temperature in the library in °F?

Math Words

degree (°) a unit used to measure temperature

Fahrenheit a temperature scale in which water freezes at 32°F and boils at 212°F

Celsius a temperature scale in which water freezes at 0°C and boils at 100 °C

Example

Temperature can be measured in **degrees Fahrenheit (°F)** or **degrees Celsius (°C)**.

If you know a temperature in degrees Celsius, you can estimate the temperature in degrees Fahrenheit.

Double the Celsius temperature and add 30.

15°C is about ■°F.
2 × 15 = 30   30 + 30 = 60
15°C is about 60°F.

Here is what Celsius temperatures feel like:

0°C is cold
10°C is cool
20°C is warm
30°C is hot

The temperature in the room is about 60°F.

Try It

Estimate each temperature in °F and °C.

1. person with a fever
2. a snowy day
3. a glass of milk

Estimate each Fahrenheit temperature.

4. 5°C = ■°F
5. 15°C = ■°F
6. 50°C = ■°F
7. 42°C = ■°F

What Fahrenheit and Celsius temperatures would you expect it to be outside on a cool day?

Practice

Estimate each temperature in °F and °C.

8. room temperature
9. glass of ice water
10. bowl of warm soup
11. hot apple pie
12. hot summer day
13. inside a refrigerator
14. warm bath
15. swimming pool in summer
16. snowy day
17. cool day
18. boiling water
19. warm day

Estimate each Fahrenheit temperature.

20. 16°C = ■°F
21. 2°C = ■°F
22. 45°C = ■°F
23. 24°C = ■°F
24. 8°C = ■°F
25. 100°C = ■°F
26. 75°C = ■°F
27. 38°C = ■°F
28. 12°C = ■°F
29. 19°C = ■°F
30. 17°C = ■°F
31. 29°C = ■°F
32. 31°C = ■°F
33. 25°C = ■°F
34. 95°C = ■°F

★35. 38.25°C = ■°F

Problem Solving

36. Suppose today's forecast says it will be 10°C. Could it snow today? Explain.
37. The temperature is 12 degrees Celsius. What is it in degrees Fahrenheit?
38. **Create a problem** that relates degrees Fahrenheit and degrees Celsius. Solve it. Then have another student solve it.
39. A new thermometer costs $29.95 including tax. Mrs. Roberts pays with two twenty-dollar bills. How much change does she receive?
40. The library thermometer reads 19 degrees Celsius. Approximate this temperature in degrees Fahrenheit. Is it cold, cool, warm, or hot?
41. There are 294 new books to be shelved in the rare books room. If each shelf holds a maximum of 15 books, how many shelves are needed? Explain.
42. When Mrs. Camden left for work the temperature was 9°C. When she returned home the temperature was 0°C. How many degrees did the temperature fall?

★43. Pat's closet holds her clothes for all 4 seasons. One third of Pat's closet has summer clothes, $\frac{1}{4}$ has winter clothes, and $\frac{1}{4}$ has spring clothes. What fraction of the closet has fall clothes?

Spiral Review and Test Prep

44. $3\frac{3}{10} \times 1\frac{1}{2}$
45. $2\frac{5}{8} \div 7$
46. $6\frac{3}{4} \times 4\frac{2}{3}$
47. $9\frac{7}{12} \div 3\frac{2}{3}$

Choose the correct answer.

48. A crew has 10 liters of water. They drink 3 in the morning, 2 at lunch, buy another 1 liter, and drink 4 in the afternoon. How many liters are left?
   - A. 5 liters
   - B. 4 liters
   - C. 3 liters
   - D. 2 liters
49. What is the sum of 1.796 and 5.854?
   - F. 7.65
   - G. 6.54
   - H. 4.058
   - J. Not Here

Extra Practice, page 383

Objective: Apply measurement to analyze data and make decisions.

8·10 A

Problem Solving: Application

Decision Making

Adela is choosing an Internet service provider so she can do research for school papers. She also wants to e-mail her friends and her brother who is in college.

E-Mail Pals	
Tracey	Howard
Elizabeth	Miguel
Brandi	Chen
Elena	Jeff
Lisa	Ricky

You Decide!

Which Internet service provider should Adela choose?

Option 1
World Wide Web
ADELPHI
An Internet Service Provider
$19.95 per month
500 minutes per month
250 e-mail messages per month
Sign up today!

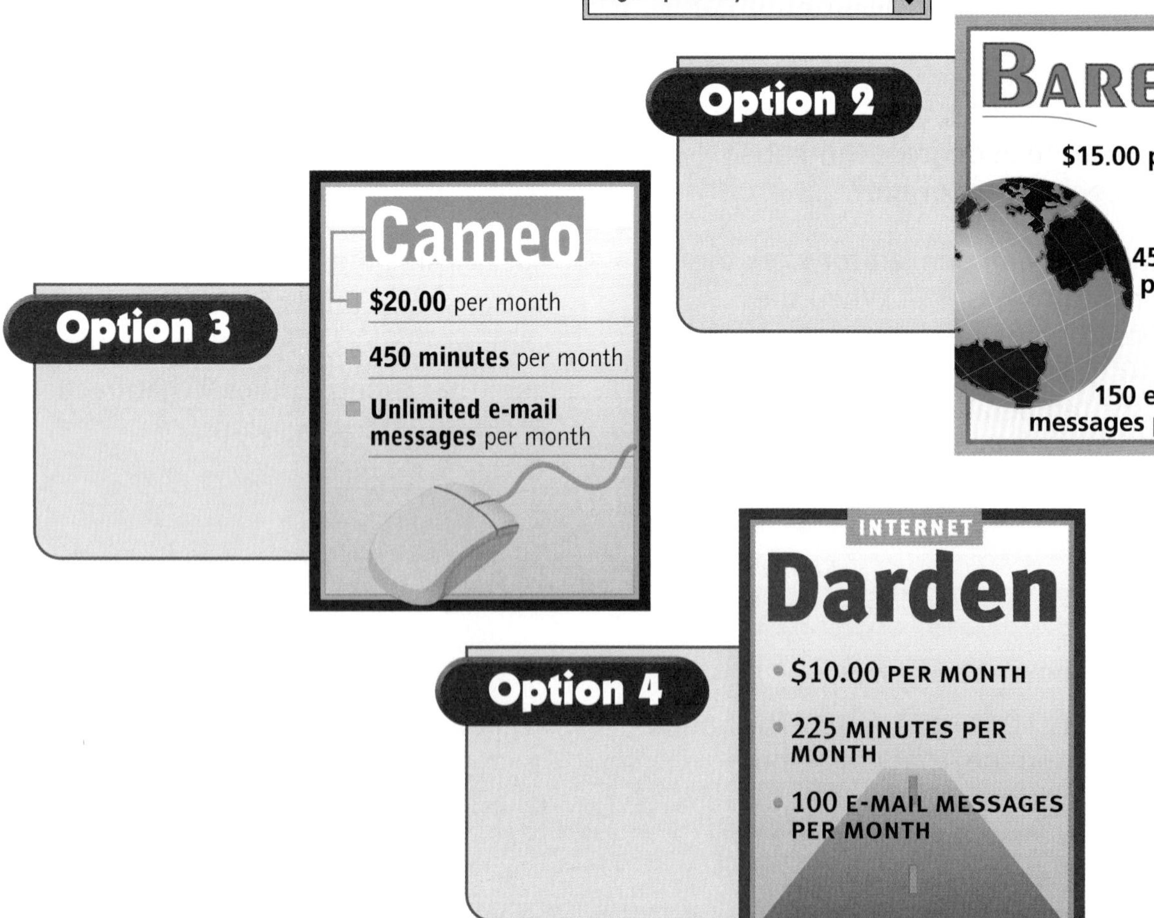

Option 2
BARETTA
$15.00 per month
450 minutes per month
150 e-mail messages per month
Option 3
Cameo
$20.00 per month
450 minutes per month
Unlimited e-mail messages per month
Option 4
INTERNET
Darden
$10.00 PER MONTH
225 MINUTES PER MONTH
100 E-MAIL MESSAGES PER MONTH

Read for Understanding

1. How many hours each month does Adelphi allow? Beretta? Cameo? Darden?

2. To the nearest cent, what is the cost for each minute for Adelphi? Beretta? Cameo? Darden?

3. About how many e-mail messages a day does Adelphi allow?

4. About how many e-mail messages each day do Beretta and Darden allow?

Problem Solving

Make Decisions

5. What is the range in minutes a month?

6. What is the median number of minutes a month?

7. Suppose Adela sends 8 messages to each friend each month. How many messages does she send?

8. Suppose Adela receives 7 messages from each friend each month. How many messages does she receive?

9. About how many minutes each day does each company allow?

10. Suppose Adela spends 300 minutes each month doing research. Which company will she definitely not choose?

11. Suppose Adela spends 200 minutes each month doing research. How many minutes does she have left to e-mail her friends and her brother if she uses Darden?

12. If Adela spends 200 minutes each month doing research, how many minutes does she have left to e-mail her friends and her brother if she uses Adelphi?

13. What are some advantages of choosing Adelphi?

14. What are some advantages of choosing Beretta?

15. What are some advantages of choosing Cameo?

16. What are some advantages of choosing Darden?

17. What are some disadvantages of choosing Adelphi?

18. What are some disadvantages of choosing Beretta?

19. What are some disadvantages of choosing Cameo?

20. What are some disadvantages of choosing Darden?

What is your recommendation for Adela? Explain.

Objective: Apply measurement to investigate science concepts.

Problem Solving: Math and Science

How does temperature affect how fast salt dissolves?

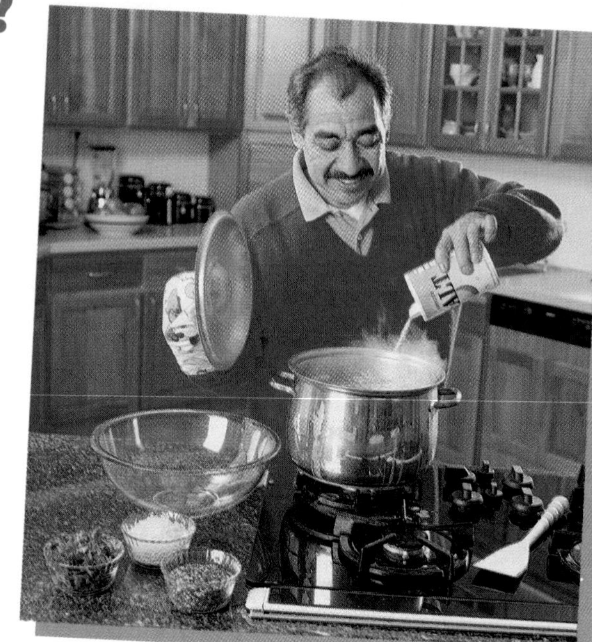

Have you ever seen someone add salt to a pot of boiling water? You may have noticed how quickly the salt dissolves. You may also have noticed how long it takes to dissolve sugar in a cold glass of iced tea.

In this activity, you will explore how quickly salt will dissolve in different temperatures of water.

You Will Need

- **four bowls**
- **measuring cup**
- **measuring spoon**
- **stirrer**
- **water (cold, cool, warm, and hot)**
- **salt**
- **timer or clock**
- **thermometer**
- **goggles**

Hypothesize

Order cold, cool, warm, and hot water in terms of which will dissolve salt fastest.

Safety

Be careful when working with hot water.

Procedure

1. Put on goggles. Pour $\frac{1}{4}$ liter (1 cup) of cold water into a bowl.
2. Measure the temperature of the water.
3. Add 5 ml (1 teaspoon) of salt to the cold water. Stir until the salt dissolves.
4. Time how long it takes for the salt to dissolve.
5. Repeat with cool water.
6. Repeat with warm water.
7. Repeat with hot water.

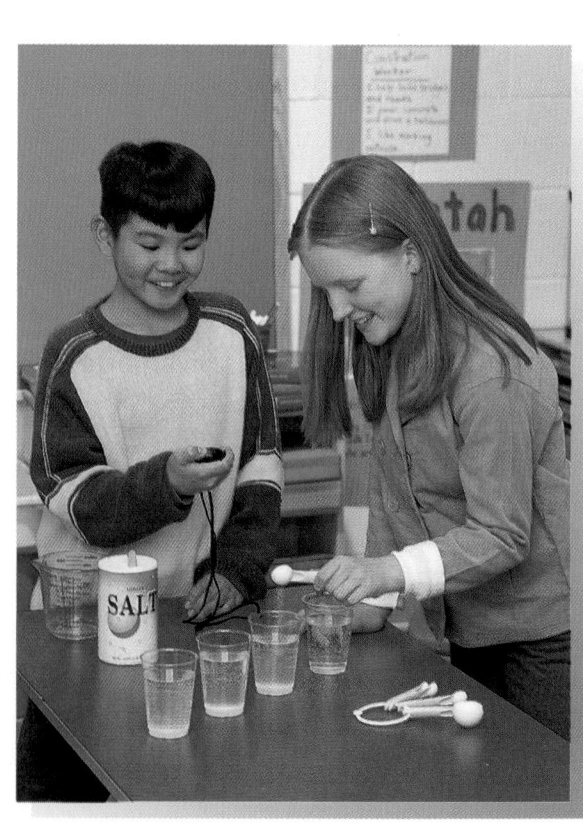

Data

Copy and complete the chart to record your observations.

Water	Temperature	Time to Dissolve
Cold		
Cool		
Warm		
Hot		

Did You Know?

An object that can dissolve in something else is said to be soluble. An insoluble object cannot be dissolved. A pencil, for example, is insoluble in cool water.

Conclude and Apply

- In which temperature of water did the salt dissolve the fastest? the slowest?
- Do you notice a pattern in the data? If so, explain what it is.
- If you want to graph your data, what kind of graph would be best? Make that graph and show your data to another group.
- Use data from *Did You Know?* to determine whether salt is **soluble** or **insoluble** in hot water? Explain.

Going Further

1. Choose 3 substances like salt. Determine if they are soluble or insoluble in room temperature water.
2. Do a research project to find out why we salt icy roads in the winter.

Check Your Progress B

Choose the most reasonable unit of length to measure. Write *mm, cm, m,* or *km.* **(pages 362–363)**

1. pager
2. length of a hiking trail
3. thickness of a paper clip

Choose the most reasonable unit of capacity to measure. Write *mL* or *L.* **(pages 364–367)**

4. rainfall in one day
5. a carton of juice
6. amount of soap to wash the dishes

Choose the most reasonable unit of mass to measure. Write *mg, g,* or *kg.* **(pages 364–367)**

7. ink pen
8. sheet of paper
9. bus

Copy and complete. **(pages 362–367)**

10. 48 cm = ▮ m
11. 0.45 L = ▮ mL
12. 250 g = ▮ kg

Add. **(pages 364–367)**

13. 458 cm + 47 m + 55 cm = ▮ cm
14. 10.7 kg + 85.9 kg + 850 g = ▮ kg

Estimate each Fahrenheit temperature. **(pages 374–375)**

15. 52°C = ▮°F
16. 9°C = ▮°F
17. 18°C = ▮°F

Solve. **(pages 362–375)**

18. Plants communicate that they need water by wilting or turning brown. Kevin gives his plant 30 milliliters each day, and it wilts. Should he give the plant 300 milliliters, 300 centiliters, or 300 liters?

19. Phillip is comparing cell phones. He finds one that has a mass of 48.9 grams. He finds another that has a mass of 0.05 kilograms. Which phone weighs less?

Journal

20. **Explain** how to change 4.5 kilometers to meters.

Additional activities at
www.mhschool.com/math

Extra Practice

Time (pages 346–349)

Copy and complete.

1. 96 h = ▮ d
2. 45 d = ▮ w ▮ d
3. 500 min = ▮ h ▮ min

Find each elapsed time.

4. 7:53 A.M. to 11:39 A.M.
5. 9:25 A.M. to 3:48 P.M.
6. 10:19 P.M. to 5:27 A.M.

Find each time.

7. 6 hr 13 min after 3:45 P.M.
8. 10 hr 55 min after 4:12 A.M.

Choose the most reasonable unit. Write *s, min, h, d, wk, mo,* or *y*.

9. Jane writes a letter in 15 ▮.
10. Luke goes on vacation for 1 ▮.

Customary Length (pages 350–353)

Measure the length of the line to

1. the nearest inch.
2. the nearest $\frac{1}{4}$ inch.
3. the nearest $\frac{1}{16}$ inch.

Choose the most reasonable unit for measuring. Write *in., ft, yd,* or *mi*.

4. height of a telephone pole
5. distance from New York to California

Copy and complete.

6. 19 ft = ▮ in.
7. 100 ft = ▮ yd ▮ ft
8. 95 in. = ▮ ft ▮ in.

Customary Capacity and Weight (pages 354–357)

Choose the most reasonable unit of capacity to measure. Write *fl oz, c, pt, qt,* or *gal*.

1. swimming pool
2. bowl of soup
3. fishbowl

Choose the most reasonable unit of weight. Write *oz, lb,* or *T*.

4. couch
5. magazine
6. space shuttle
7. envelope

Copy and complete.

8. 36 fl oz = ▮ c
9. 50 oz = ▮ lb ▮ oz
10. 4.24 T = ▮ lb

Compare. Write >, <, or =.

11. 17 gal ● 70 qt
12. 78 fl oz ● 9 c 6 fl oz
13. 85 lb ● 1,350 oz

Extra Practice

Problem Solving: Reading for Math Check for Reasonableness (pages 358–359)

Solve.

1. The hole left when a telephone pole was removed filled with $1\frac{1}{2}$ gallons of water after it rained. Does this equal 6 quarts or $\frac{3}{8}$ of a quart? Explain.
2. When Tamara disconnects the phone wires, she carries 864 ounces of wire to the utility truck. How many pounds does she carry?

Metric Length (pages 362–363)

Measure the length of the line to

1. the nearest centimeter.
2. the nearest millimeter.

Metric Capacity and Mass (pages 364–367)

Choose the most reasonable unit of capacity to measure. Write *mL* or *L*.

1. fish tank
2. eyedropper
3. raindrop
4. bathtub

Choose the most reasonable unit of mass to measure. Write *mg, g,* or *kg*.

5. portable CD player
6. empty soup can
7. bicycle
8. grain of rice

Choose the most reasonable estimate.

		A.	B.	C.	D.
9.	water bottle	A. 0.5 milliliter	B. 5 milliliters	C. 0.5 liter	D. 5 liters
10.	yogurt cup	A. 12.5 milliliters	B. 125 milliliters	C. 1.25 liters	D. 125 liters
11.	bottle of salad dressing	A. 237 milliliters	B. 2.37 liters	C. 23.7 liters	D. 237 liters
12.	fish tank	A. 10 milliliters	B. 100 milliliters	C. 10 liters	D. 100 liters
13.	flower vase	A. 80 milliliters	B. 800 milliliters	C. 8 liters	D. 80 liters
14.	stapler	A. 2 milligrams	B. 2 grams	C. 20 grams	D. 2 kilograms
15.	sheet of paper	A. 5 milligrams	B. 50 milligrams	C. 5 grams	D. 50 grams
16.	paper clip	A. 1 gram	B. 10 grams	C. 1 kilogram	D. 10 kilograms
17.	dog	A. 18 milligrams	B. 1.8 grams	C. 18 grams	D. 18 kilograms

Extra Practice

Metric Conversion (pages 368–371)

Copy and complete.

1. 408 m = ■ km
2. 6.7 m = ■ cm
3. 75 mm = ■ cm
4. 2.125 kg = ■ g
5. 640 g = ■ kg
6. 87.9 g = ■ mg
7. 355 mL = ■ L
8. 9.01 L = ■ mL

Add.

9. 16 cm + 98 mm + 81 cm = ■ cm
10. 56 cm + 8.5 m + 7.8 m = ■ m
11. 60 cL + 4.7 L + 5.25 L = ■ L
12. 699 g + 744 g + 4.509 kg = ■ g

Compare. Write >, <, or =.

13. 755 cm ● 7.55 m
14. 650 mm ● 6,500 cm
15. 1.8 L ● 180 mL
16. 981 mL ● 9.81 cL
17. 4,587 mg ● 45.87 g
18. 4.3 kg ● 430 g

Problem Solving: Strategy Draw a Diagram (pages 372–373)

Draw a diagram to solve.

1. Telephones are placed every 12 meters on the walls of a warehouse that is 48 meters long and 36 meters wide. There is also a phone at each corner. How many phones are there?
2. Speakers are installed around the outside of a circular arena. If speaker 6 is directly across from speaker 13, how many speakers are there?
3. Speaker towers are installed evenly around a circular room. Tower 2 is directly opposite tower 6. How many towers are there?
4. A cafeteria serves sandwiches during the lunch break of a lecture. They serve tuna, turkey, peanut butter, and ham on either white or wheat bread. How many sandwich combinations are available?

Temperature (pages 374–375)

Estimate each temperature in °F and °C.

1. cup of tea
2. a day to go ice skating
3. inside your house

Estimate each Fahrenheit temperature.

4. 8°C = ■°F
5. 105°C = ■°F
6. 23°C = ■°F
7. 11°C = ■°F
8. 31°C = ■°F
9. 1°C = ■°F
10. 54°C = ■°F
11. 61°C = ■°F
12. 14°C = ■°F
13. 29°C = ■°F
14. 20°C = ■°F
15. 48°C = ■°F

Chapter Study Guide

Language and Math

Math Words

capacity
degree Celsius (°C)
degree Fahrenheit (°F)
elapsed time
mass

Complete. Use a word from the list.

1. The ____ of a container is the amount of liquid that the container can hold.
2. The amount of matter in an object is its ____.

Skills and Applications

Change units of time and find elapsed time. (pages 346–349)

Example

48 hours = ▮ days

Solution

48 ÷ 24 = 2

Think: 1 day = 24 hours

So 48 hours = 2 days.

Copy and complete.

3. 1,260 min = ▮ h
4. 360 h = ▮ d

Find each time.

5. 7 h 29 min after 10:57 A.M.
6. 5 h 48 min after 7:48 P.M.

Find each elapsed time.

7. 8:36 A.M. to 11:24 A.M.
8. 10:21 A.M. to 2:35 P.M.

Estimate length, capacity, weight, mass, and temperature. (pages 350–357, 36 2–367, 374–375)

Example

Choose the most reasonable metric unit for measuring the width of your hand.

Solution

Think:

1 millimeter is about the thickness of a dime.

1 centimeter is about the width of a pencil.

1 meter is about the width of a stairway.

The most reasonable unit is centimeter.

Choose the most reasonable unit for measuring: Write *in., ft, yd,* or *mi.*

9. height of television

Write *mm, cm, m,* or *km.*

10. thickness of a mousepad

Write *fl oz, c, pt, qt,* or *gal.*

11. sip of juice

Write *oz, lb,* or *T.*

12. bag of apples

Estimate in degrees Fahrenheit.

13. 37 degrees Celsius

Measure length. (pages 362–363)

Example

Measure to the nearest centimeter and millimeter.

Solution

The line is 4 cm to the nearest centimeter and 41 mm to the nearest millimeter.

Measure the line.

14. to the nearest centimeter
15. to the nearest millimeter

Change from one unit to another. (pages 350–357, 362–373)

Example

Copy and complete.

5 meters = ▯ centimeters

Solution

Multiply to change from a larger unit to a smaller unit. $5 \times 100 = 500$

Think: 1 meter = 100 centimeters

So 5 meters = 500 centimeters.

Copy and complete.

16. 72 in. = ▯ ft
17. 7,590 m = ▯ km
18. 504 mg = ▯ g

Solve problems. (pages 358–359, 372–373)

Example

Jen's printing press uses 1 liter of ink in the morning and 957 milliliters of ink in the afternoon. How many liters of ink does it use in all?

Solution

Divide to change from a smaller unit to a larger unit.

957 milliliters = ▯ liters

Think: 1,000 milliliters = 1 liter

$957 \div 1{,}000 = 0.957$

$1 + 0.957 = 1.957$

Jen's printing press uses 1.957 liters of ink.

Solve.

19. Cameron's desk is 72 centimeters tall. On the desk he puts a 45-centimeter computer monitor on top of a 155-millimeter CPU. He wants to add a shelf above the computer monitor. How far off the ground must the shelf be?

20. Sixteen speakers are arranged evenly around a square arena for a concert. If one speaker is placed in each corner, how many will go on each side?

Chapter Test

Copy and complete.

1. 8 d = ▮ h
2. 78 yd = ▮ ft
3. 15 gal = ▮ qt
4. 25 lb = ▮ oz
5. 90 cm = ▮ mm
6. 406 mL = ▮ L
7. 3.1 kg = ▮ g

Find each time.

8. 9 h 25 min after 10:57 A.M.
9. 5 h 45 min after 8:38 P.M.

Choose the most reasonable unit for measuring.
Write *in., ft, yd,* or *mi.*

10. height of a lamp
11. length of a cat's tail

Choose the most reasonable unit for measuring.
Write *mm, cm, m,* or *km.*

12. width of a computer disk
13. length of a soccer field

Choose the most reasonable unit for measuring.
Write *fl oz, c, pt, qt,* or *gal.*

14. watering can
15. amount of liquid you can hold in your mouth

Choose the most reasonable unit for measuring.
Write *oz, lb,* or *T.*

16. stick of butter
17. whale

Choose the most reasonable estimate.

18. sip of juice **A.** 1.7 mL **B.** 17 mL **C.** 1.7 L **D.** 17 L
19. sheet of paper **A.** 4 mg **B.** 40 mg **C.** 400 mg **D.** 4 g

Measure the line to the nearest:

20. centimeter
21. millimeter

Solve.

22. Michele leaves for school at 7:50 A.M. She gets home at 4:10 P.M. How many hours is Michele gone?
23. It is 8°C. What is the approximate temperature in degrees Fahrenheit? Is it cold, cool, warm, or hot?
24. Jonathan puts a telephone that is 148 millimeters wide next to an answering machine that is 9 centimeters wide. Will they fit in a space that is 23 centimeters wide? Explain.
25. A city arena is 90 meters long and 60 meters wide. Large speakers are in each corner and every 15 meters around the outside of the arena. How many speakers are there?

Performance Assessment

People have used newspapers to communicate and stay informed for hundreds of years. You will need a copy of a daily newspaper, a ruler, and a scale.

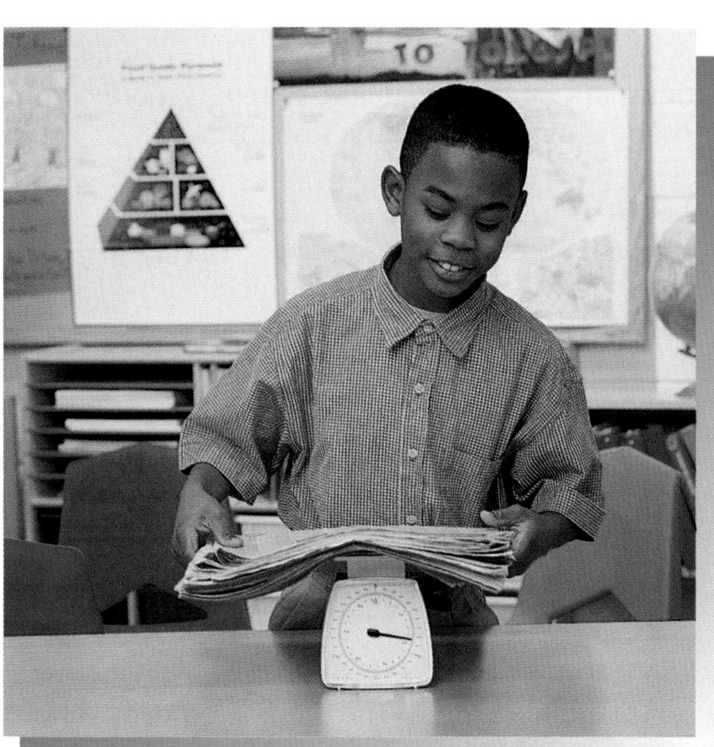

Answer each question below using your copy of the newspaper.

1. Find a Celsius temperature reported in the newspaper. Show how to estimate this temperature in degrees Fahrenheit.

2. Measure and record the length and width of your newspaper's front page. Then measure and record the height of the largest letter on the front page. Use an appropriate unit for each measurement.

3. Weigh and record the weight of your newspaper. Based on your measurement, estimate the weight of a single sheet of your newspaper. Explain the method you used to estimate that weight.

A Good Answer

- includes accurate measurements and reasonable estimates.
- shows all calculations.
- describes steps you took to find each measurement.

You may want to save this work in your portfolio.

Enrichment

Change Units Between Systems

In the United States, measurements are usually made in customary units. In Canada, the metric system is more common. You can change units between the systems.

Length

1 inch is about 2.5 centimeters.
1 yard is a little shorter than 1 meter.
1 mile is about 1.5 kilometers.

1 centimeter is a little less than $\frac{1}{2}$ inch.
1 meter is a little longer than 1 yard.
1 kilometer is just over 0.5 mile.

Capacity

1 quart is a little less than 1 liter.

1 liter is a little more than 1 quart.

Weight/Mass

1 ounce is about 28 grams.
1 pound is a little less than 0.5 kilogram.

1 kilogram is a little more than 2 pounds.

You can change units between systems the same way you change units within a system. The symbol ≈ means "about equal to."

Examples

10 inches is about ■ centimeters.

Think: 1 inch ≈ 2.5 centimeters

$10 \times 2.5 = 25$

So 10 inches is about 25 centimeters.

B

3 miles is about ■ kilometers.

Think: 1 mile ≈ 1.5 kilometers

$3 \times 1.5 = 4.5$

So 3 miles is about 4.5 kilometers.

C

10 kilometers is about ■ miles.

Think: 1 kilometer ≈ 0.5 mile

$10 \times 0.5 = 5$

So 10 kilometers is about 5 miles.

Copy and complete.

1. 7 inches is about ■ centimeters.
2. 20 inches is about ■ centimeters.
3. 15 meters is about ■ yards.
4. 100 yards is about ■ meters.
5. 26 miles is about ■ kilometers.
6. 6 kilometers is about ■ miles.
7. 2.5 quarts is about ■ liters.
8. 17 liters is about ■ quarts.
9. 4 ounces is about ■ grams.
10. 16 ounces is about ■ grams.
11. 120 pounds is about ■ kilograms.
12. 100 kilograms is about ■ pounds.

Test-Taking Tips

When taking a multiple-choice test, you may need more than one step to solve a problem.

Compare. Choose the correct answer.

7 c 10 fl oz ● 70 fl oz

A. $<$ **C.** $>$
B. $=$ **D.** Not Here

Look at the measurements given in the problem:

- 7 c 10 fl oz
- 70 fl oz

Think:
1 cup = 8 fluid ounces

Work step-by-step to solve the problem:

Step 1 7 c = ■ fl oz
7 c = 56 fl oz

Step 2 7 c 10 fl oz = 56 fl oz + 10 fl oz = 66 fl oz
7 c 10 fl oz = 66 fl oz

Now look at the original problem.

Step 3 7 c 10 fl oz ● 70 fl oz
66 fl oz $<$ 70 fl oz
7 c 10 fl oz $<$ 70 fl oz

The correct answer choice is A.

Check for Success

Before turning in a test, go back one last time to check.

- ☑ I understood and answered the questions asked.
- ☑ I checked my work for errors.
- ☑ My answers make sense.

Choose the correct answer.

1. 12 c 6 fl oz ● 102 fl oz

A. $<$ **C.** $>$
B. $=$ **D.** Not Here

2. 12 ft 9 in. ● 150 in.

F. $<$ **H.** $>$
G. $=$ **J.** Not Here

3. 184 oz ● 11 lb 13 oz

A. $<$ **C.** $>$
B. $=$ **D.** Not Here

4. 19 cm 3 mm ● 195 mm

F. $<$ **H.** $>$
G. $=$ **J.** Not Here

5. 29 yd 1 ft ● 88 ft

A. $<$ **C.** $>$
B. $=$ **D.** Not Here

6. 2 mi 25 yd ● 3,600 yd

F. $<$ **H.** $>$
G. $=$ **J.** Not Here

Spiral Review and Test Prep

Chapters 1–8

Choose the correct answer.

Number Sense

1. 621 cm ● 62.1 m
   A. $>$　　C. $<$
   B. $=$　　D. Not Here

2. Estimate $31{,}074 \times 692$.
   F. 438,968　　H. 21,400,000
   G. 527,918　　J. 21,700,000

3. Write $3 \times 3 \times 3 \times 3$ using exponents.
   A. 3333　　C. 3^4
   B. 3×4　　D. 4

4. A political speech was $1\frac{1}{2}$ hours long. Halfway through the speech the sound system broke. How many minutes was the speaker without a sound system?
   F. 180 minutes　　H. 75 minutes
   G. 90 minutes　　J. 45 minutes

Measurement and Geometry

5. How long is the line, to the nearest centimeter?
   A. 5 centimeters　　C. 56 centimeters
   B. 6 centimeters　　D. 57 centimeters

6. How long is the line, to the nearest $\frac{1}{4}$ inch?
   F. 2 inches　　H. $2\frac{2}{4}$ inches
   G. $2\frac{1}{4}$ inches　　J. $2\frac{3}{4}$ inches

7. What is the perimeter of the rectangle?

   A. 184 centimeters　　C. 92 centimeters
   B. 138 centimeters　　D. Not Here

8. Which figure is a triangle?

F. 　　H. 

G. 　　J. 

Statistics, Data Analysis, and Probability

Use data from the graph for problems 9–12.

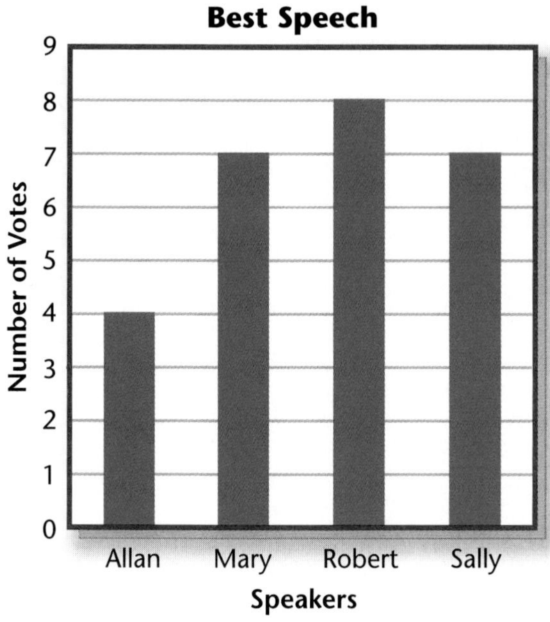

9. What type of graph is shown?
   - A. Histogram
   - B. Line graph
   - C. Bar graph
   - D. Double bar graph

10. What is the range of votes?
    - F. 8
    - G. 7
    - H. 6.5
    - J. 4

11. What is the median number of votes?
    - A. 4
    - B. 6.5
    - C. 7
    - D. 8

12. Who received the greatest number of votes?
    - F. Alan
    - G. Mary
    - H. Robert
    - J. Sally

Mathematical Reasoning

13. Alison measures 17 cups 4 fluid ounces of water. Kendra measures 138 fluid ounces of water. Does Kendra measure more, less, or the same amount of water as Alison?
    - A. More
    - B. Less
    - C. Same
    - D. Not Here

14. Roland fences in a 20-foot by 25-foot section of his yard for his dog to play in. He puts fence posts every 5 feet and at the corner. How many posts are there?
    - F. 20 posts
    - G. 18 posts
    - H. 15 posts
    - J. 10 posts

15. Kay buys school supplies. She buys 3 notebooks at $0.79 each, a binder for $3.25, and 2 packs of pencils at $1.29 each. How much money in all does Kay spend?
    - A. $4.13
    - B. $5.33
    - C. $7.00
    - D. $8.20

16. Jane is 6 years older than her brother. She is 3 times as old as her brother. How old are Jane and her brother?

CHAPTER 9 Integers

Theme: Science

Use the Data

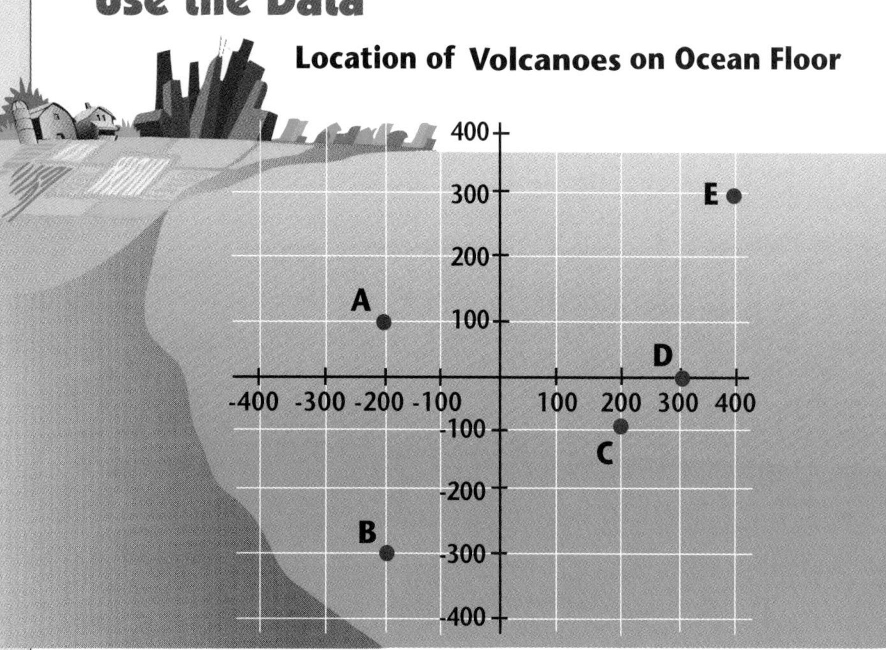

- If each point marks an underwater volcano, what is the location of point A? How can you find a volcano that is 300 miles east and 200 miles south of the center?

What You Will Learn

In this chapter you will learn how to

- compare and order integers.
- add integers and subtract integers.
- use strategies to solve problems.

Objective: Use integers to represent situations. Represent integers on a number line. Find the opposite of an integer. Compare and order integers.

9·1 Integers and the Number Line: Comparing and Ordering Integers

Learn

Math Words

integer a whole number or its opposite

positive integer an integer greater than zero

negative integer an integer less than zero

opposite integers integers with the same number, but different signs

Meteorologists have identified four air masses that control weather in the United States. The coldest is the continental polar air mass. It leaves Alaska in January with temperatures between $^-20$°F and $^-40$°F. What do the numbers $^-20$ and $^-40$ mean?

Dr. Peter Ray

Example 1

Numbers such as $^-20$, $^-40$, 0, 22, and 47 are called **integers**. The set of integers includes the **positive integers**, the **negative integers**, and zero

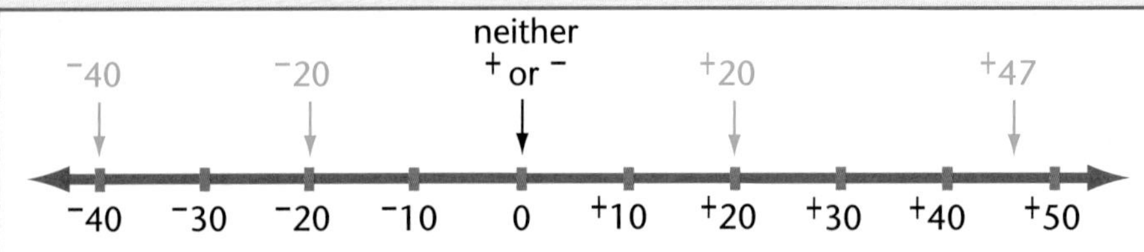

A negative integer, such as 220, is read "negative 20."
A positive integer, such as 122, is read "positive 22."

Note: You can write $^+22$ as 22.

Each integer has an **opposite integer**.
The opposite of $^-20$ is 20, and the opposite of 20 is $^-20$.
Zero is its own opposite.

Note: Opposites are the same distance from 0 on a number line, but on opposite sides of it.

The numbers $^-20$°F and $^-40$°F represent temperatures that are 20 and 40 degrees colder than 0°F.

Compare $^-8$°F and $^-15$°F.

Example 2

You can use a number line to compare and order integers.

Of any two numbers on a number line, the number to the left is less than the number to the right.

Locate the values on the number line.

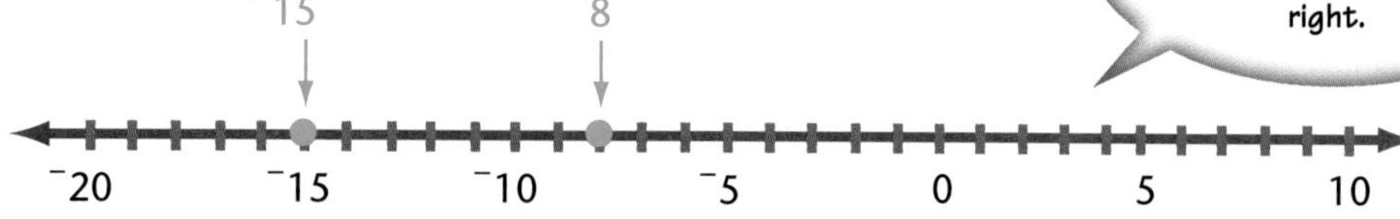

So $^-15°F < {}^-8°F$ or $^-8°F > {}^-15°F$.

Example 3

Order the numbers $^-10$, 8, 2, $^-5$, and 0 from least to greatest.

Locate the values on the number line.

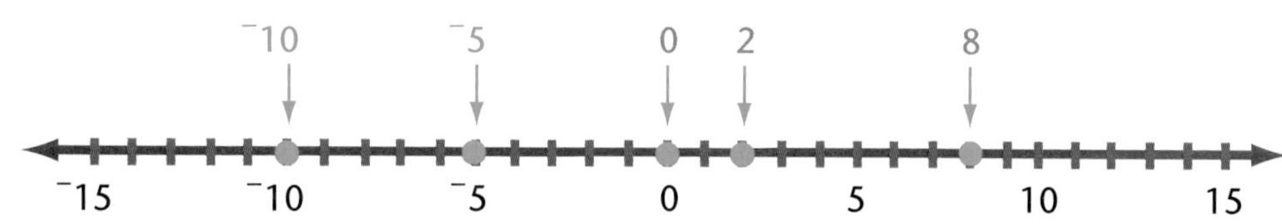

List the numbers in order on the number line from left to right.

So $^-10$, $^-5$, 0, 2, and 8 are in order from least to greatest.

More Examples

A Compare: 9 and $^-4$

Think: 9 is to the right of $^-4$, so 9 is larger than $^-4$.

$9 > {}^-4$

B Compare: $^-4$ and $^-7$

Think: $^-4$ is to the right of $^-7$, so $^-4$ is larger than $^-7$.

$^-4 > {}^-7$

C Compare: 0 and $^-2$

Think: 0 is to the right of $^-2$, so 0 is larger than $^-2$.

$0 > {}^-2$

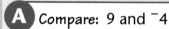

Write an integer to represent each situation. Give the opposite of each.

1. 27°C below zero
2. 16 degrees Fahrenheit above zero
3. weight loss of 7 pounds

Compare. Write $>$ or $<$. You may use a number line to help.

4. 2 ● $^-8$
5. $^-5$ ● 10
6. 6 ● $^-6$
7. $^-3$ ● $^-7$
8. $^-1$ ● 0

What is an integer? How can you find its opposite?

Practice

Write an integer to represent each situation.

9. 4-yard loss in football
10. 250 feet below sea level
11. 10 miles below the surface
12. 12 feet above sea level
13. $35 loss
14. profit of $68

Describe a situation that can be represented by the integer.

15. $^-12$
16. $^+7$
17. $^-675$
18. $^-\$99$
19. 0

Compare. Write > or <. You may use a number line.

20. 7 ● $^-2$
21. $^-3$ ● 1
22. 8 ● 10
23. $^-4$ ● 4
24. 6 ● 0
25. $^-5$ ● $^-8$
26. $^-10$ ● 9
27. $^-100$ ● 1
28. $^-8$ ● $^-4$
29. $^-1$ ● $^-2$
30. $^-12$ ● $^-10$
31. $^-7$ ● $^-4$
32. $^-14$ ● $^-20$
★33. $^-48$ ● $^-47$
★34. $^-1,205$ ● $^-1,211$

Order the integers from least to greatest.

35. 2, $^-3$, 0
36. $^-2$, 3, $^-4$
37. $^-7$, $^-1$, 5
★38. $^-37$, 14, $^-56$, $^-63$, 22

Copy and complete the number line.

39.
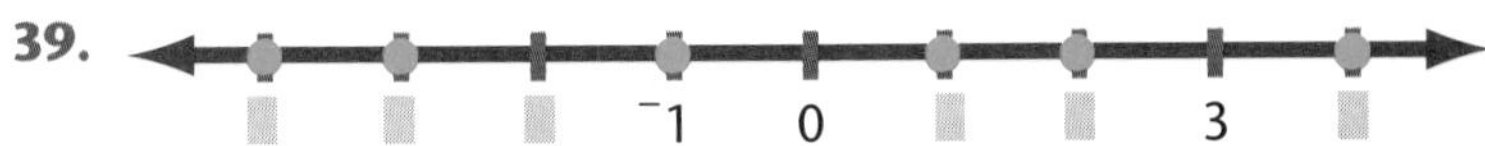

40.
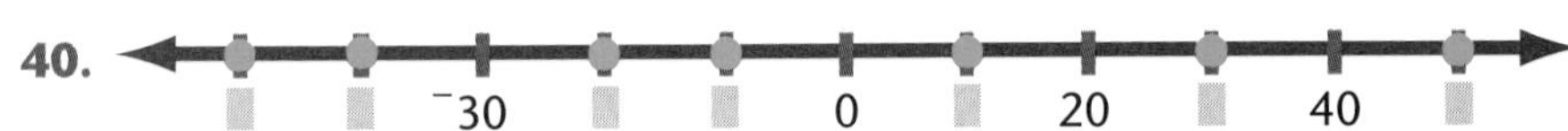

41.
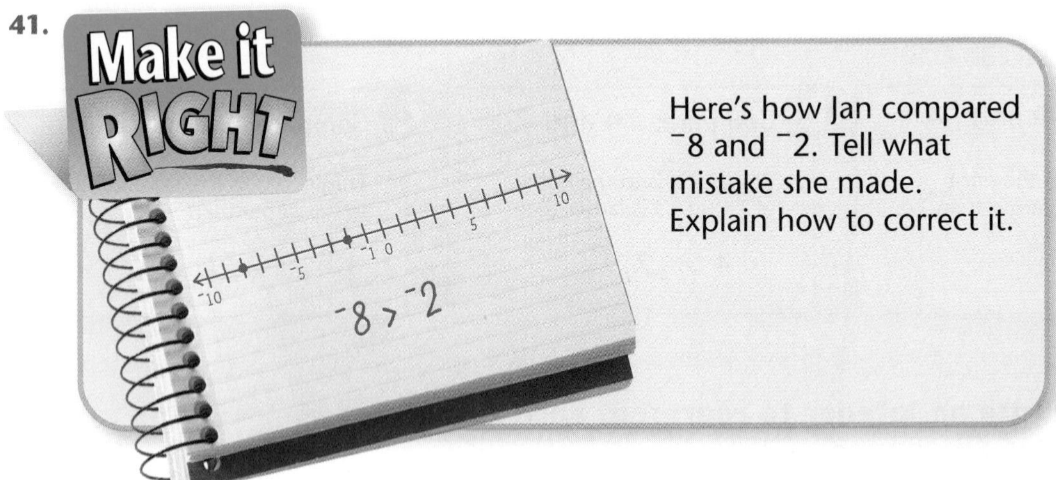

Here's how Jan compared $^-8$ and $^-2$. Tell what mistake she made. Explain how to correct it.

Problem Solving

42. At 4:00 A.M. the temperature reads $^-23$°F. By 2:00 P.M., the temperature has risen to the opposite of that temperature. What is the temperature at 2:00 P.M.?

43. Bill records the low temperature for a week: 23°, 34°, 19°, 20°, 22°, 30°, 20°. What is the mean low temperature for the week?

Use data from *Did You Know?* for problems 44–45.

44. What is the opposite of ⁻80°F?

45. The coldest temperature ever recorded in Russia is ⁻90°F. Is that higher or lower than the coldest temperature ever recorded in the United States?

46. **Create a problem** about temperature that can be solved by comparing two integers. Solve it and ask others to solve it.

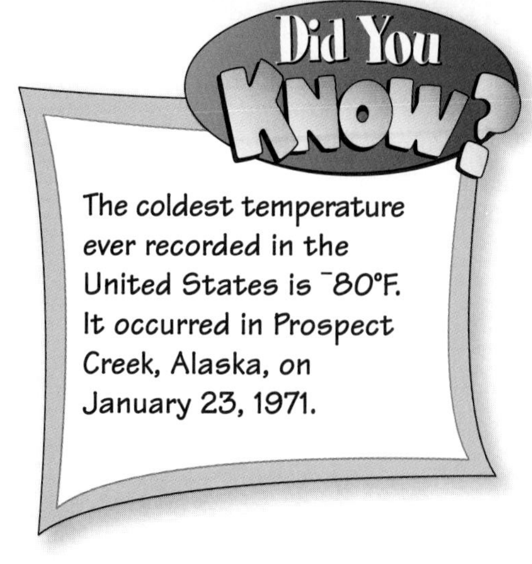

The coldest temperature ever recorded in the United States is ⁻80°F. It occurred in Prospect Creek, Alaska, on January 23, 1971.

Use data from the table for problems 47–49.

47. **Science:** What is the coldest temperature given? the hottest?

48. Which two temperatures besides water freezing are closest to 0°C?

49. A thermometer reads ⁻5°F. Would a person need to wear a coat outside? Explain.

50. **Time:** A weather balloon rises 100 feet each minute. If it takes off at 5:05 p.m., how high will it be at 5:17 p.m.?

Physical Conditions

Condition	Temperature (°C)
Water boils	100
Water freezes	0
Human body	37
Mercury freezes	⁻38.8
Daytime on the moon	120
Nighttime on the moon	⁻180
Dry ice	⁻160

51. Gordon descended 350 feet straight down into a cave to make temperature readings. Alma descended 290 feet down. Who descended the farthest?

52. **Compare** the numbers 12 and ⁻12. How are they alike and different?

★53. **Analyze:** Is a positive integer always greater than a negative integer? Explain.

Spiral Review and Test Prep

Find the GCF for each set of numbers.

54. 8 and 20 55. 14 and 42 56. 6 and 43 57. 3, 6, and 9 58. 4, 18, and 20

Choose the correct answer.

59. Todd's stopwatch reads 240 seconds. How many minutes is this?
   - A. 2 minutes
   - B. 4 minutes
   - C. 24 minutes
   - D. 40 minutes

60. Which number is not divisible by 6?
   - F. 42
   - G. 126
   - H. 138
   - J. 166

Extra Practice, page 421

Objective: Add integers.

Explore Adding Integers

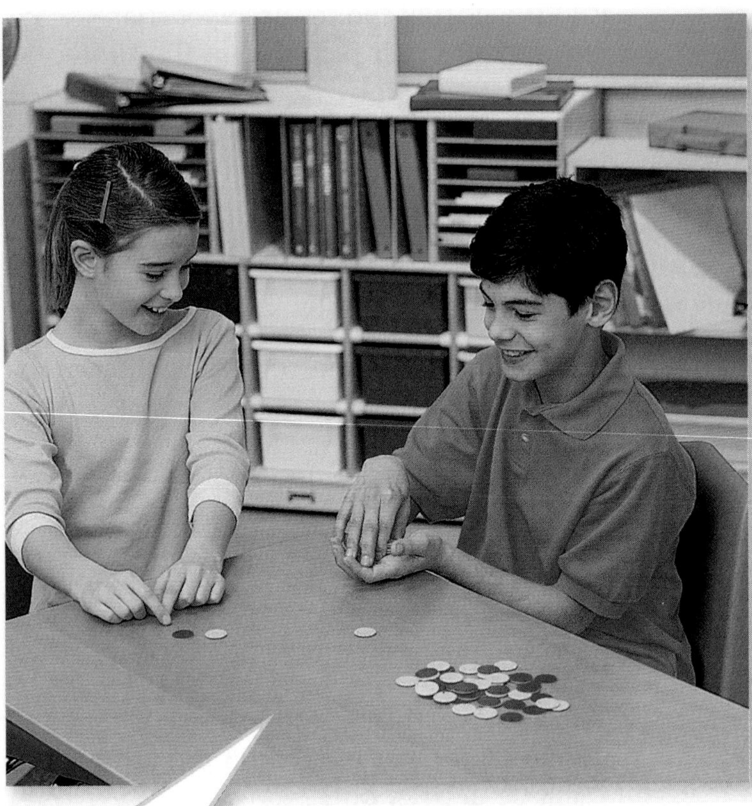

Learn

You can use two-color counters to explore adding integers.

Work Together

- **two-color counters**

▶ Find: ${}^{+}2 + {}^{-}1$

- Use yellow counters to represent positive integers and red counters to represent negative integers.
- Show ${}^{+}2$ with two yellow counters. Show ${}^{-}1$ with one red counter.
- Each pair of positive and negative counters combines to make 0.

Note:
A pair that has a total of zero is called a "zero pair."

 +  = 0

- Count the unpaired positives or negatives. These counters represent the total.
- Record your work.

▶ Use counters to find each total. Record your work.

4 positive and 5 negative

2 positive and 2 negative

1 positive and 3 negative

2 positive and 3 negative

Make Connections

	Using Models	Using Paper and Pencil
Find: $3 + 5$		$3 + 5 = 8$
Find: $^{-}3 + 4$	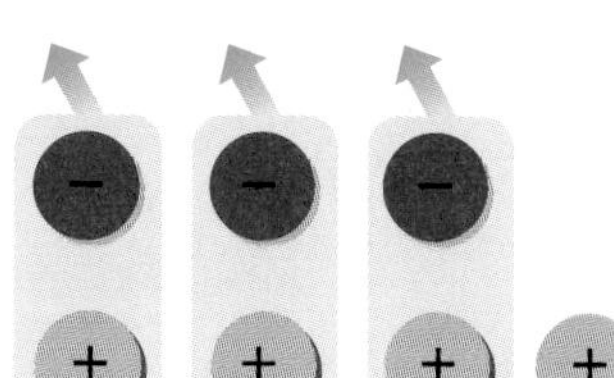	$^{-}3 + 4 = 1$
Find: $5 + {}^{-}5$	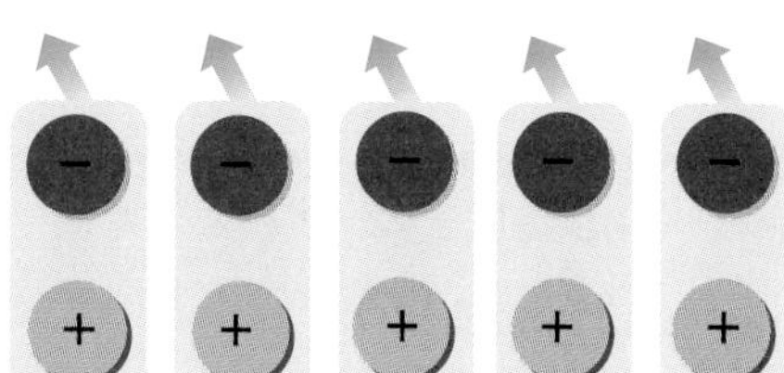	$^{-}5 + 5 = 0$
Find: $^{-}5 + {}^{-}4$		$^{-}5 + {}^{-}4 = {}^{-}9$

Try It **Add. You may use counters.**

1. $3 + 5$
2. $^{-}4 + {}^{-}7$
3. $12 + {}^{-}8$
4. $^{-}9 + 2$

Sum it Up Explain how you could use models to find $^{-}4 + {}^{-}3$.

Practice **Add.**

5. $6 + {}^{-}4$
6. $^{-}5 + 8$
7. $^{-}10 + {}^{-}8$
8. $10 + 18$
9. $^{-}12 + 2 + 4$
10. $9 + {}^{-}9$
11. $^{-}8 + 4 + 7$
12. $^{-}7 + {}^{-}7$
13. **Analyze:** When will the sum of a positive integer and a negative integer be 0?

Objective: Add integers.

9•3 Add Integers

Learn

An underwater volcano creates islands that are both below and above sea level. The volcano Mauna Loa rises 10 kilometers from the sea floor. How many kilometers of the volcano appear above sea level?

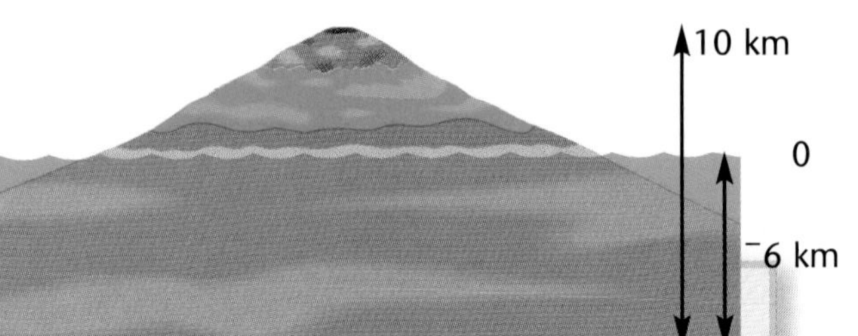

Example 1

Find: $^{-}6 + 10$

You can use a number line to add integers.

- When you add a positive integer, you move to the right.
- When you add a negative integer, you move to the left.

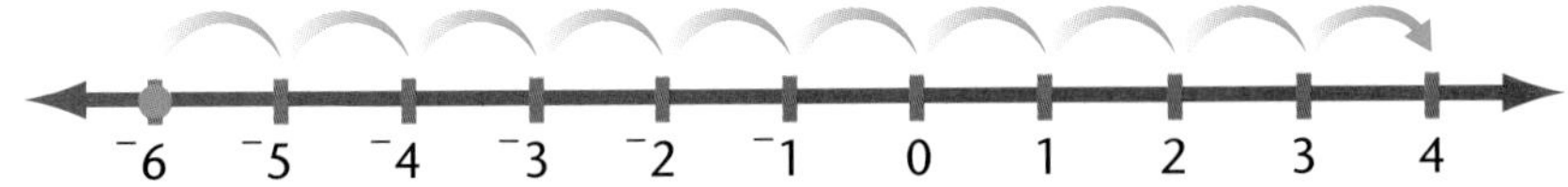

Start at $^{-}6$. Move 10 spaces to the right to add 10.

The volcano rises 4 kilometers above sea level.

More Examples

A

Find: $^{-}7 + 3$

$^{-}7$ $^{-}6$ $^{-}5$ $^{-}4$ $^{-}3$ $^{-}2$ $^{-}1$ 0

$^{-}7 + 3 = {}^{-}4$

B

Find: $2 + {}^{-}4$

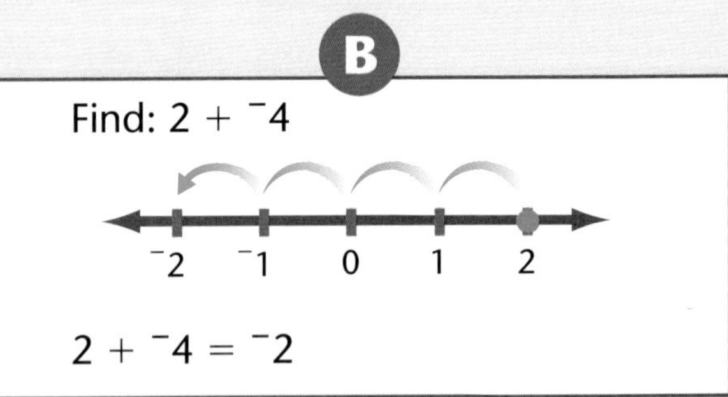

$2 + {}^{-}4 = {}^{-}2$

C

Find: $^{-}2 + {}^{-}5$

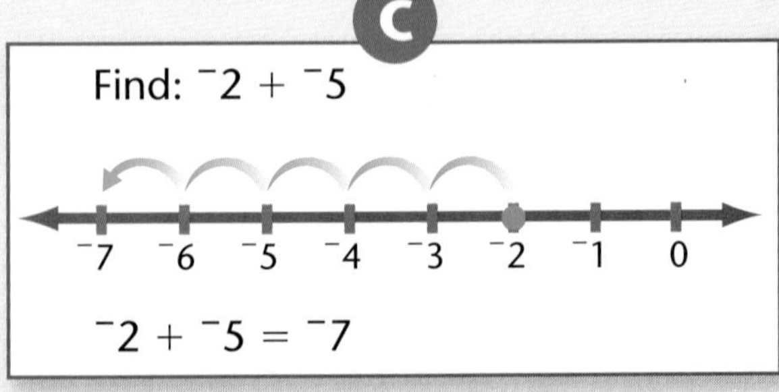

$^{-}2 + {}^{-}5 = {}^{-}7$

D

Find: $5 + {}^{-}3$

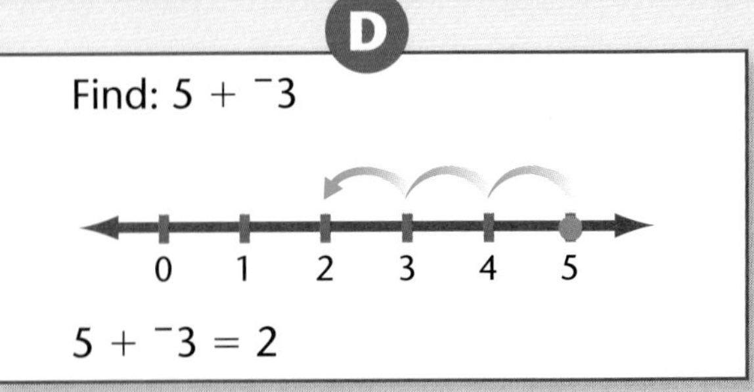

$5 + {}^{-}3 = 2$

The total height of a volcano model is 22 inches.
It will be submerged in a tank of water 16 inches high.
Will it rise above the water?

Find whether the sum of $^{-}16$ and 22 is positive or negative.

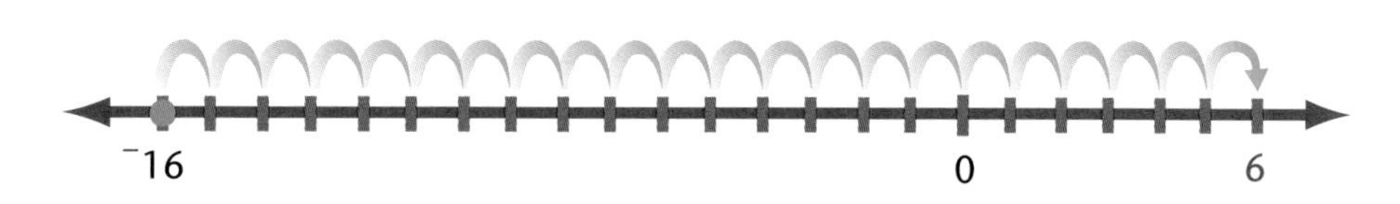

The volcano will rise above the water in the tank.

More Examples

You can follow these guidelines when using a number line to add integers.

E Find: $3 + 4$ — $3 + 4 = 7$

The sum of two positive integers is always positive.

Think: Both integers are positive, so the sum is positive.

F Find: $^{-}2 + {^{-}3}$ — $^{-}2 + {^{-}3} = {^{-}5}$

The sum of two negative integers is always negative.

Think: Both addends are negative integers, so the sum is negative.

G Find: $^{-}5 + 3$ — $^{-}5 + 3 = {^{-}2}$

If the signs of the addends are different, the sum could be positive or negative.

Think: $^{-}5$ is farther from 0 than 2, so the sum is negative.

H Find: $^{-}4 + 6$ — $^{-}4 + 6 = 2$

If the signs of the addends are different, the sum could be positive or negative.

Think: 6 is farther from 0 than $^{-}4$, so the sum is positive.

Find: $^{-}5 + 5$ — $^{-}5 + 5 = 0$

If the addends are opposites, the sum is 0.

Think: $^{-}5$ and 5 are opposite integers, so their sum is zero.

Try It **Add. You may use a number line.**

1. $6 + {^{-}5}$
2. $^{-}7 + {^{-}3}$
3. $9 + {^{-}9}$
4. $^{-}15 + 8$
5. $22 + {^{-}20}$

Explain how to add $^{-}6 + 5$. How do you know if the sum will be negative or positive?

Practice **Add.**

6. $3 + {}^{-}8$
7. ${}^{-}5 + 7$
8. $5 + 8$
9. $25 + {}^{-}15$
10. ${}^{-}10 + {}^{-}2$
11. ${}^{-}4 + {}^{-}2$
12. $8 + {}^{-}3$
13. $10 + {}^{-}6$
14. ${}^{-}9 + 9$
15. ${}^{-}1 + 11$
16. $7 + {}^{-}6$
17. ${}^{-}9 + 3$
18. ${}^{-}6 + {}^{-}8$
19. ${}^{-}31 + {}^{-}10$
20. $15 + {}^{-}6$
21. ${}^{-}8 + 15$
22. ${}^{-}11 + 3$
23. ${}^{-}5 + 3 + {}^{-}3$

★24. $11 + {}^{-}12 + 3$

★25. $5 + {}^{-}7 + {}^{-}17$

Complete the function tables.

	$y = x + {}^{-}6$	
	x	y
26.	${}^{-}3$	
27.	${}^{-}1$	
28.	0	
29.	2	
30.	6	

	$y = x + 4$	
	x	y
31.	${}^{-}7$	
32.	${}^{-}6$	
33.	${}^{-}4$	
34.	0	
35.	2	

	$y = 2x + {}^{-}2$	
	x	y
★36.		${}^{-}2$
★37.	1	
★38.		2
★39.	3	
★40.		14

41. 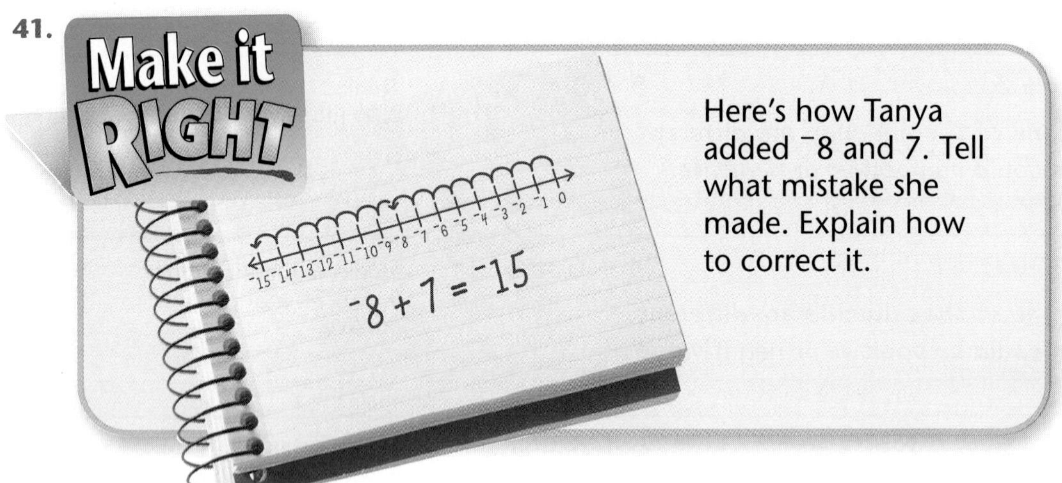

Here's how Tanya added ${}^{-}8$ and 7. Tell what mistake she made. Explain how to correct it.

Problem Solving

42. For a certain volcano, magma travels 19.1 miles from beneath the crust up to the volcano opening. It starts 17.5 miles below Earth's surface. How high above ground is the mouth of the volcano?

43. An underwater volcano rises from the ocean floor. Below sea level there are 2.6 kilometers. Above sea level there are 3.4 kilometers. What is the total height of the volcano?

44. **What if** you have 3 red counters with minus signs and 4 yellow counters with plus signs? List all the different integers you can represent using the counters.

45. **Analyze:** Will the sum of 37, $^{-}15$, and $^{-}17$ be positive, negative, or zero? Explain.

Use data from *Did You Know?* for problems 46–47.

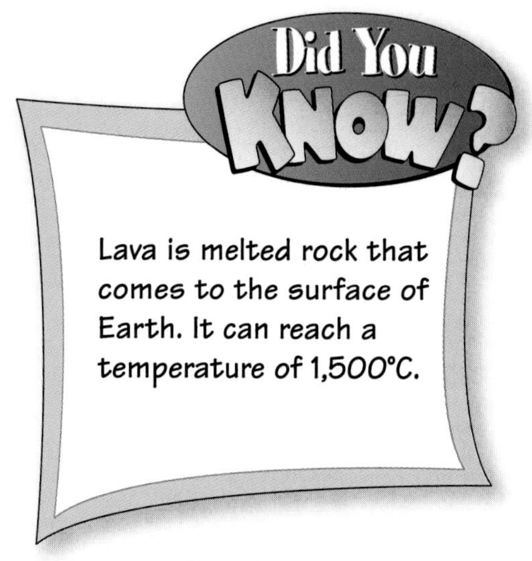

Did You Know?
Lava is melted rock that comes to the surface of Earth. It can reach a temperature of 1,500°C.

46. You can approximate temperatures in degrees Fahrenheit by doubling the temperature given in degrees Celsius. Approximate the maximum temperature of lava in degrees Fahrenheit.

47. How many degrees Celsius above the freezing point of water is the maximum temperature of lava?

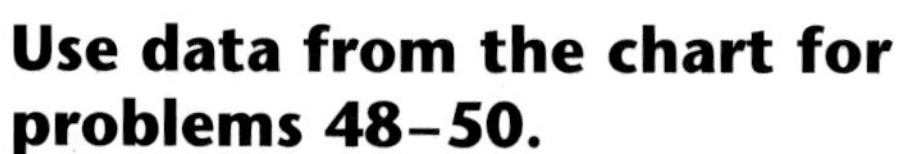

Use data from the chart for problems 48–50.

Volcano	Height (in feet)
Ruiz	17,716
Purace	15,600
Lascar	18,346
Kilimanjaro	19,340
Sangray	16,736

48. Which volcano is the tallest of the 5 listed in the chart?

49. Which two volcanoes are closest in height?

50. What is the difference in height between the highest and the lowest volcano?

★ 51. An iceberg is a chunk of ice floating in the ocean. The total height of an iceberg is 2,000 feet. The lower 1,500 feet of the iceberg are submerged. What fraction of the iceberg rises above sea level?

52. **Collect Data:** Survey other students to see how many have heard of the following volcanoes: Vesuvius, Mount St. Helens, Mount Rainier, Aniakchak, and Mount Lassen. Record your results in a table and a graph.

Spiral Review and Test Prep

Add or subtract. Write your answer in simplest form.

53. $4\frac{1}{2} + 2\frac{1}{8}$

54. $\frac{5}{6} + 3\frac{1}{3}$

55. $5\frac{3}{4} - 4\frac{3}{8}$

56. $4 - 2\frac{1}{6}$

Choose the correct answer.

57. Dr. Merton spends $3.90 for six test tubes. How much did each one cost?
A. $0.65
B. $2.34
C. $23.40
D. Not Here

58. If Mary places two equally sized squares next to each other, what shape will she make?
F. Square
G. Triangle
H. Rectangle
J. Rhombus

Extra Practice, page 422

Objective: Compare and contrast information.

9·4

Problem Solving: Reading for Math

Check the Reasonableness of an Answer

Student Conducts Science Experiment

Read

Alma does an experiment to see the effect of salt on the freezing point of water. She knows that the sample gets colder during the day. Her log reads:

9 A.M.: 5°C 12 noon: $^{-}5$°C 3 P.M.: $^{-}1$°C

Which entry may not be correct?

READING SKILL ▶ **Compare and Contrast**

When you compare and contrast, you determine how items are alike and different.

- **What do you know?** The temperature at each time; the sample gets colder during the day
- **What do you need to find?** Which entry is not reasonable

MATH SKILL ▶ **Check for Reasonableness**

When you check the reasonableness of an answer, you see if it makes sense. You compare the answer with known facts.

Plan

Check to see if the sample gets colder during the day.

You need to compare each entry with the one before it.

Solve

Compare → The 9 A.M. entry with the 12 noon entry. $5 > {}^{-}5$
The 12 noon entry with the 3 P.M. entry. ${}^{-}5 < {}^{-}1$
The 9 A.M. entry with the 3 P.M. entry. $5 > {}^{-}1$

If Alma entered an incorrect entry, the noon temperature is not reasonable.

Think:
The entries show that the temperature rose from 12 noon to 3 P.M.

Look Back

How could you check your answer?

What would be a reasonable noontime entry? Explain.

Practice

1. At 3 P.M. the temperature of another sample was $^{-}1$°C. Log entries show that the temperature at 9 A.M. was 2°C, and the noon temperature was 0°C. Are these entries reasonable?

2. The morning temperature of a third liquid was $^{-}1$°F. By noon, the temperature of this sample had dropped 2 degrees. Alma recorded that temperature as 1°F. Is her calculation reasonable?

Use data from the table for problems 3–8.

Sample A	
Time	Temperature
7 A.M.	0°F
9 A.M.	2°F
11 A.M.	-21°F

Sample B	
Time	Temperature
7 A.M.	-3°F
9 A.M.	0°F
11 A.M.	4°F

3. The table shows temperature readings taken from two samples. Do all the entries seem reasonable? Explain why.

4. Alma wrote that between 9 A.M. and 11 A.M. the temperature of Sample B rose 4 degrees. Is her statement reasonable?

5. Alma also wrote that between 7 A.M. and 9 A.M. the temperature of Sample B fell 3 degrees. Is her statement reasonable?

6. Alma wrote that at 11 a.m., Sample B had the greatest temperature of all the samples. Is her statement reasonable?

7. Alma predicts that the 1 P.M. reading for Sample B will be about 7°F. Is her prediction reasonable? Explain why.

Spiral Review and Test Prep

Choose the correct answer.

The air temperature at 12 midnight was $^{-}5$°F. By 12 noon the temperature had risen 9 degrees. The noon temperature was 4°F.

8. Which of the following statements is true?
   - A. The air temperature dropped between 12 midnight and 12 noon.
   - B. At 12 midnight the air temperature was $^{-}4$°F.
   - C. At 12 noon the air temperature was 9°F.
   - D. The air temperature rose between 12 midnight and 12 noon.

9. When you check the reasonableness of an answer, you
   - F. solve the problem two different ways.
   - G. do all calculations twice.
   - H. take a good guess at the answer.
   - J. think about what you know.

Problem Solving

Extra Practice, page 242

Check Your Progress A

Write an integer to represent each situation. **(pages 394–397)**

1. 8,235 feet below the surface
2. a $680 loss
3. a 12-yard gain in football
4. 2,896 feet above sea level

Compare. Write > or <. You may use a number line. **(pages 394–397)**

5. $^{-}8$ ● $^{-}2$ 6. 13 ● $^{-}14$ 7. $^{-}6$ ● 10 8. $^{-}23$ ● 23 9. $^{-}1$ ● 0

Order the integers from least to greatest. **(pages 394–397)**

10. 8, $^{-}7$, $^{-}2$ 11. $^{-}3$, 4, 1 12. 16, $^{-}17$, 18 13. 3, $^{-}3$, 4, 0

Add. **(pages 398–403)**

14. $^{-}6 + 3$ 15. $7 + {}^{-}6$ 16. $5 + {}^{-}5$ 17. $0 + {}^{-}23$
18. $8 + 5$ 19. $^{-}6 + 9$ 20. $^{-}13 + 9$ 21. $7 + 10 + {}^{-}18$
22. $^{-}8 + 6$ 23. $^{-}2 + {}^{-}7$ 24. $6 + {}^{-}2$ 25. $^{-}5 + 10$
26. $0 + {}^{-}2$ 27. $8 + {}^{-}7$ 28. $^{-}9 + 8$ 29. $^{-}10 + {}^{-}3$

Solve. **(pages 394–405)**

30. Earth's mantle begins about 25 miles below Earth's surface. If there is a pool of magma, or melted rock, at a depth of 46.8 miles below the upper boundary of the mantle, how far below the surface does it lie?
31. A weather report said that the temperature was 18 degrees below zero. Write an integer to express this value.
32. Scientists locate 2 epicenters of earthquakes from a seismograph recording. Epicenter A is 4,612 feet below the surface; epicenter B is 4,968 feet below the surface. Which epicenter is farther below the surface?
33. The morning temperature of a water sample is $^{-}8$°F. At 12 noon the temperature of the sample increases by 3 degrees. That evening, the temperature of the sample is 2°F. Between which two readings did the water sample show the greatest increase in temperature?

Additional activities at
www.mhschool.com/math

Use Tables to Add Integers

Mr. Weibel's class gathered data on the change in temperature each day for four days. They recorded the starting temperature and the change in temperature, but forgot to record the final temperature. On Monday the temperature started at 6°F and fell 10°F. On Tuesday it started at 12°F and fell 9°F. On Wednesday it started at $^-2$°F and rose 7°F. On Thursday, it started at $^-4$°F and fell 8°F. What were the final temperatures?

You can use a spreadsheet table to add.

- Click on the Table key.
- Label the columns *Day, Starting Temperature, Change in Temperature,* and *Final Temperature.*
- In the column labeled *Day,* enter the days.
- In the column labeled *Starting Temperature,* enter the starting temperatures.
- In the column labeled *Change in Temperature,* enter the amount the temperature fell or rose as an integer.
- In the column labeled *Final Temperature,* enter a formula to add Starting Temperature and Change in Temperature.

What were the final temperatures?

Use the computer to create a table to find each set of sums. Then use your table to complete each number sentence.

1. $^-6 + {}^-4 = t$
   $^-7 + {}^-5 = w$
   $^-8 + {}^-6 = f$
2. $12 + {}^-8 = u$
   $14 + {}^-6 = g$
   $16 + {}^-4 = n$
3. $^-16 + 6 = s$
   $^-15 + 7 = h$
   $^-14 + 8 = k$

Solve.

4. Four scuba divers were 3 feet below the surface of the water. One diver dove 2 feet deeper, another 4 feet deeper, another 1 foot deeper, and another 3 feet deeper. How deep was each diver?

For more practice, use Math Traveler™.

Objective: Subtract integers.

9·5 Explore Subtracting Integers

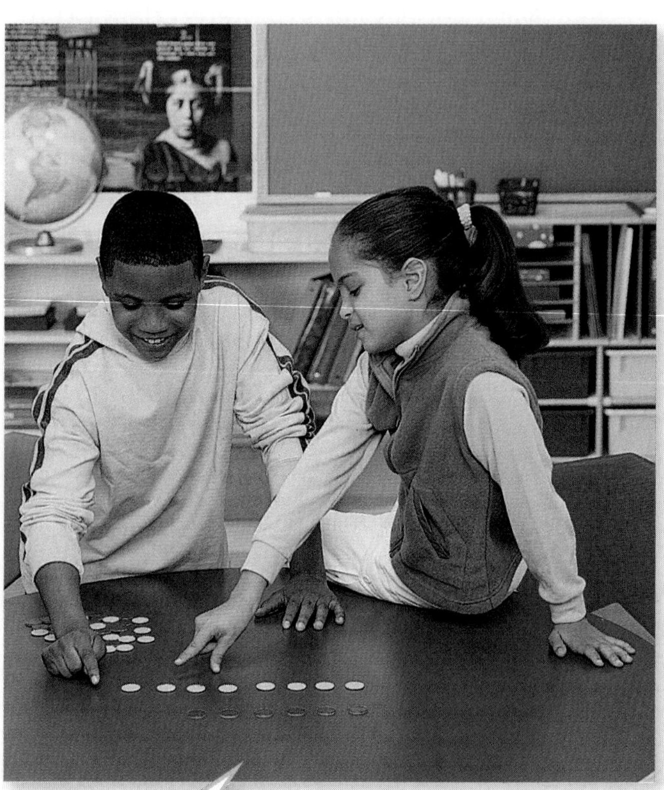

Learn

You can use two-color counters to explore subtracting integers.

Work Together

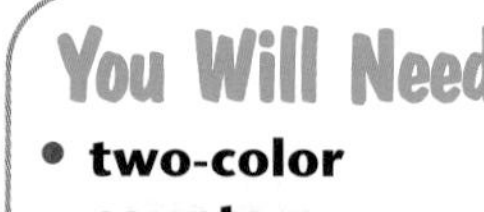

You Will Need
- **two-color counters**

▶ Use two-color counters to find $8 - {}^{-}6$.
- Show the positive number with 8 yellow counters.
- Show the negative number with 6 red counters.
- Replace each red counter with a yellow counter.
- Count the yellow counters to find the answer.

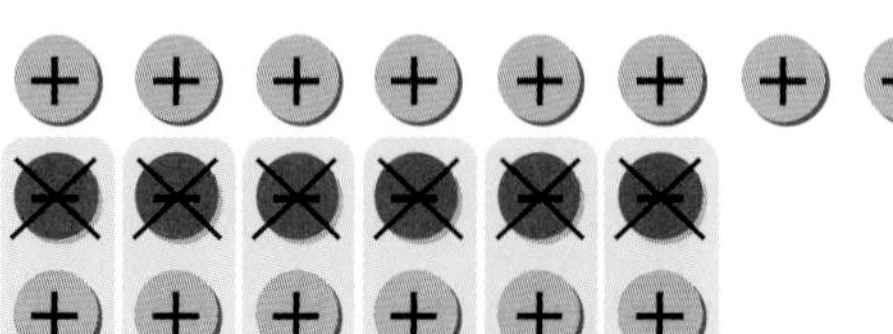

Note:
Subtracting a negative number is like adding its opposite.

▶ Use counters to find each difference. Record your work.

$5 - {}^{-}3$ $\quad {}^{-}4 - 3$ $\quad {}^{-}3 - {}^{-}5$ $\quad 2 - 6$

Make Connections

Using Models | **Using Paper and Pencil**

Find: $3 - 7$

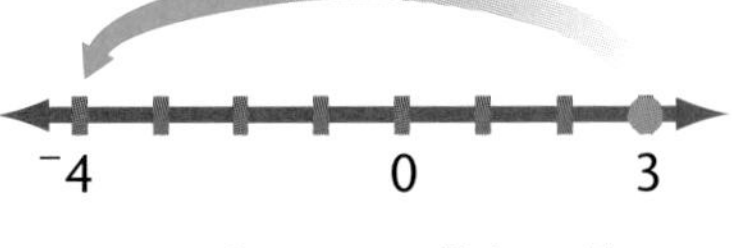

$3 - 7 = 3 + {}^{-}7 = {}^{-}4$

Find: $2 - {}^{-}1$

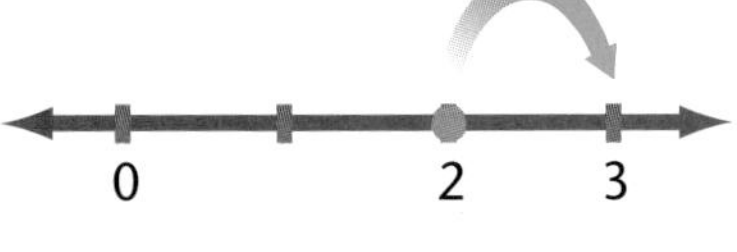

$2 - {}^{-}1 = 2 + 1 = 3$

Find: ${}^{-}5 - 2$

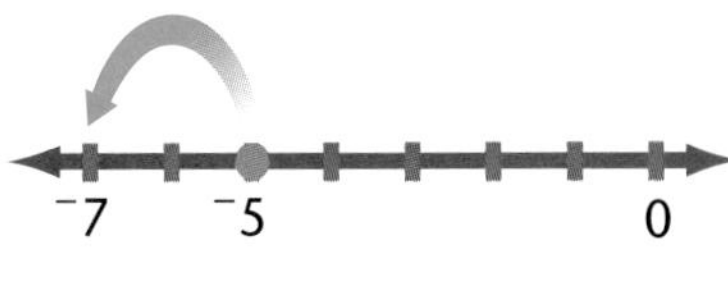

${}^{-}5 - 2 = {}^{-}5 + {}^{-}2 = {}^{-}7$

Find: ${}^{-}2 - {}^{-}5$

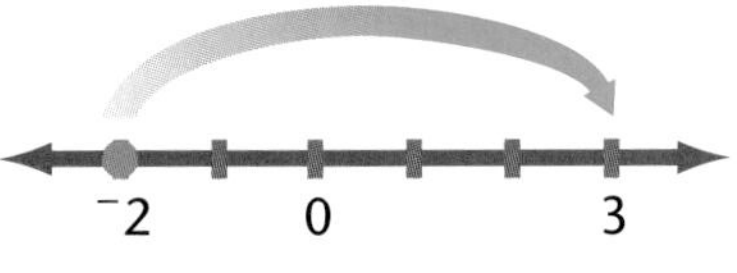

${}^{-}2 - {}^{-}5 = {}^{-}2 + 5 = 3$

Try It **Subtract. You may use counters.**

1. ${}^{-}5 - 3$
2. ${}^{-}6 - {}^{-}3$
3. $8 - {}^{-}2$
4. $3 - 6$

Sum it Up How can you find ${}^{-}2 - 7$?

Practice **Subtract.**

5. ${}^{-}2 - 1$
6. ${}^{-}3 - 5$
7. ${}^{-}2 - {}^{-}5$
8. $6 - 7$
9. ${}^{-}3 - {}^{-}2$
10. ${}^{-}8 - 2$
11. $3 - 9$
12. ${}^{-}4 - {}^{-}4$
13. **Analyze:** Write a subtraction sentence where the difference of two negative numbers is positive.

Objective: Subtract integers.

9·6 Subtract Integers

Learn

Satellite towers transmit radio waves around the world. Suppose a tower is being installed on a hilltop. The supports for the tower must go 64 feet underground. What is the difference in height between the top of the tower and the underground supports?

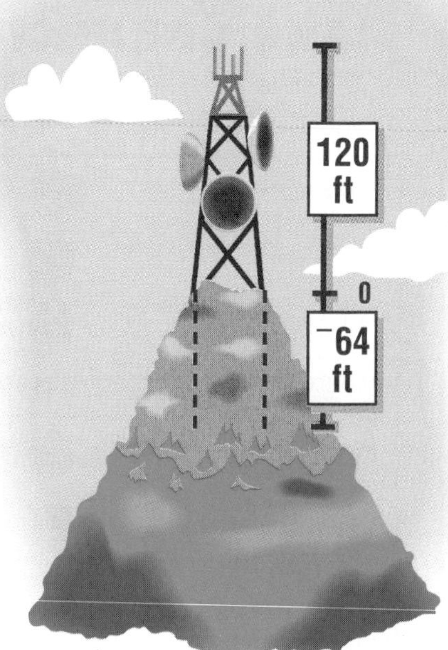

There's more than one way!

Find: 120 − ⁻64

Method A

You can use a number line.

- Let 0 represent the top of the mountain.
- Mark the point 120 units to the right.
- Mark the point 64 units to the left.
- Count the number of units between the two marks.

⁻64 0 120

There are 184 units between ⁻64 and 120.

So 120 − ⁻64 = 184.

Method B

You can add the opposite of the negative number.

120 − ⁻64 = 120 + 64 = 184

Think: 64 is the opposite of ⁻64.

The difference is 184 feet.

More Examples

A
23 − ⁻4 =
23 + 4 = 27

B
⁻5 − ⁻2 =
⁻5 + 2 = ⁻3

C
4 − 5 =
4 + ⁻5 = ⁻1

To build the satellite tower, workers need to pound a steel pole into the ground. At 38 feet below the surface, they discover loose soil and they find bedrock at 87 feet below the surface. What is the difference in feet between the depth of the loose soil and the depth of the bedrock?

Example 1

Find : $^{-}38 - {}^{-}87$.

$^{-}38 - {}^{-}87 =$
$^{-}38 + 87 =$
49

The difference between the depth of the loose soil and the bedrock is 49 feet.

Example 2

The difference between two negative numbers can also be negative.

Find: $^{-}4 - {}^{-}2$

$^{-}4 - {}^{-}2 =$
$^{-}4 + 2 =$
$^{-}2$

So $^{-}4 - {}^{-}2$ is $^{-}2$.

More Examples

A $^{-}13 - 6 =$
$^{-}13 + {}^{-}6 = {}^{-}19$

B $14 - 20 =$
$14 + {}^{-}20 = {}^{-}6$

C $^{-}32 - {}^{-}16 =$
$^{-}32 + 16 = {}^{-}16$

Try It **Subtract. Rewrite each question as an addition equation.**

1. $2 - 3$
2. $^{-}4 - 9$
3. $8 - {}^{-}3$
4. $^{-}8 - {}^{-}8$
5. $4 - {}^{-}6$
6. $12 - 34$
7. $^{-}30 - 27$
8. $105 - 108$

How can you change a subtraction problem involving integers to an addition problem?

Practice

Subtract.

9. $4 - 1$
10. $^-5 - {}^-2$
11. $8 - 10$
12. $^-7 - 14$
13. $14 - {}^-6$
14. $^-21 - 21$
15. $^-9 - {}^-9$
16. $11 - 13$
17. $^-51 - {}^-50$
18. $97 - {}^-52$
19. $^-45 - 32$
20. $100 - 201$

★21. $^-3 - 8.2$

★22. $4.5 - 10$

★23. $^-4 - 2 + 5$

★24. $^-5 - 2.5$

Copy and complete.

25. $8 - {}^-4 = 8 + ■ = ■$
26. $^-9 - 5 = {}^-9 + ■ = ■$
27. $^-10 - {}^-8 = {}^-10 + ■ = ■$
28. $^-3 - {}^-6 = {}^-3 + ■ = ■$
29. $2 - ■ = 2 + {}^-7 = ■$
30. $11 - ■ = 11 + {}^-3 = ■$
31. $18 - ■ = 18 + 5 = ■$

★32. $■ - 3 = ■ + {}^-3 = {}^-14$

★33. $■ - {}^-6 = ■ + 6 = {}^-18$

Compare. Write >, <, or =.

34. $3 - 1$ ● $^-3 + 5$
35. $2 - 3$ ● $^-1 + 1$
36. 4 ● $^-2 - {}^-7$
37. $^-1 + 2$ ● $^-1 - 2$
38. $3 + 3$ ● $^-3 + 3$
39. $8 - 5$ ● $^-3$
40. $^-2 - {}^-3$ ● $3 - 2$
41. $^-5 + 2$ ● $^-2 + 5$
42. $4 - 6$ ● $3 - 6$

★43. $4.5 - 3$ ● $^-1.5 + 3$

★44. $^-2 + 1\frac{1}{2}$ ● $3 - 3$

★45. $^-4 - 2.5$ ● $^-3 - {}^-2$

46.

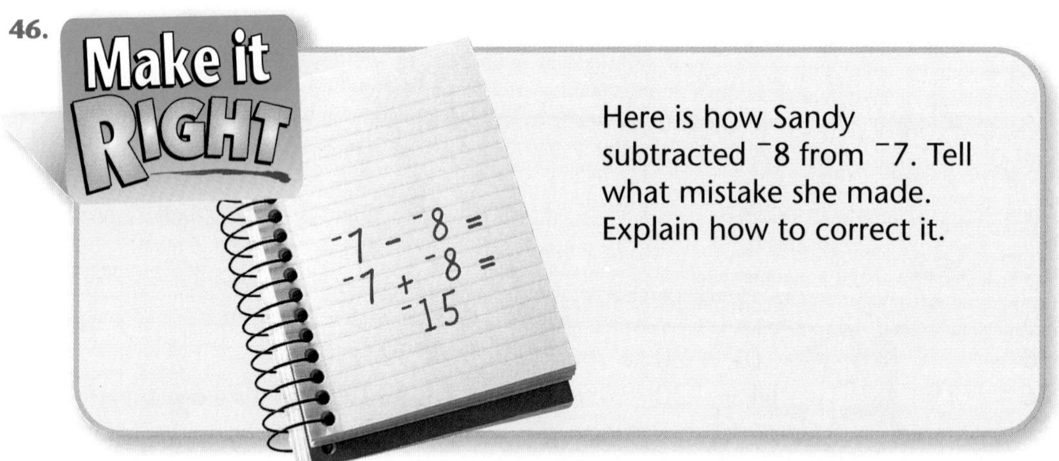

Here is how Sandy subtracted $^-8$ from $^-7$. Tell what mistake she made. Explain how to correct it.

Problem Solving

47. What is the difference when you subtract $^-2$ from 3?

48. Which of these numbers would appear farthest to the left on a number line: $^-4$, $^-2$, or $^-5$? Explain.

49. **Analyze:** When will a subtraction sentence with two negative integers have a difference of zero?

50. Explain how the number sentences $3 - {}^-2$ and $3 + 2$ are alike.

51. Geologists drill 123 feet into the ground. They find a band of gold 34 feet above where they stopped. How deep is the gold band?

52. A 230-foot radio tower is built on top of a 1,230-foot mountain. How far above the base of the mountain is the top of the tower?

53. A satellite tower extends underground $^{-}275$ feet. A radio tower extends to a depth of $^{-}192$ feet. Which tower extends farther below the surface? How much farther?

54. Two identical radio towers are as far apart from each other as they are in total height. Each tower structure is 567 feet above the surface and extends 189 feet below the surface. How far apart are the towers?

55. **Art:** Jackie wants to change a photograph of electricity-generating windmills. The width of the orginal photo is 4 inches. The length is 6 inches. If she increases the width by $8\frac{1}{2}$ inches and decreases the length by $1\frac{1}{4}$ inches, what are the new dimensions of the photo?

56. **Social Studies:** Satellite towers send and receive signals from satellites orbiting Earth. The Soviet Union launched Sputnik 1, the world's first artificial satellite, on October 4, 1957. It remained in orbit until January 4, 1958. How many days was Sputnik 1 in orbit?

57. **Compare** the expressions $39 - 52$ and $39 + {}^{-}52$. How are they different?

58. **Create a problem** about satellite towers that involves adding or subtracting integers. Solve it and give it to another student to solve.

★ 59. Ron tells Wendy that he subtracted $^{-}2$ from $^{-}3$ and that the answer is $^{+}1$. Wendy says that Ron has made an error and that his answer is incorrect. Which student do you agree with? If you agree with Wendy, what should the answer be?

★ 60. Jon collects weather data during a very cold part of the winter. He collected these temperatures in degrees Celsius: $^{-}1, 0, 4, 3, {}^{-}3, {}^{-}1, {}^{-}2, 0, 2$. Find the median of these temperatures.

Spiral Review and Test Prep

Multiply or divide. Write your answer in simplest form.

61. $4\frac{1}{2} \times 2$

62. $\frac{5}{6} \times \frac{3}{5}$

63. $3 \div \frac{1}{3}$

64. $\frac{3}{8} \div \frac{1}{4}$

Choose the correct answer.

65. Fred adds 4 quarts of water to a new fish tank. He used a 1-cup measure. How many cups did he need to fill the tank?

A. 4
B. 8
C. 12
D. 16

66. What is the probability of tossing a 1 to 6 number cube and getting a number greater than 5?

F. $\frac{1}{6}$
G. $\frac{1}{5}$
H. $\frac{1}{4}$
J. $\frac{1}{2}$

Objective: Solve problems using more than one method.

Problem Solving: Strategy
Alternate Solution Methods

Read

Read the problem carefully.

A certain ceramic material is being cooled at a regular rate to create the proper structure. The ceramic starts at a temperature of 2,825°F. If it cools at an average rate of 240°F a day, about how long will it take to cool to 65°F?

- **What do you know?** The temperature of the ceramic; the rate of cooling
- **What are you asked to find?** How long it will take to cool

Plan

Some problems can be solved using more than one strategy. This problem can be solved by writing an equation or by making a table. Use one method to solve the problem. Use the other method to check your work.

Solve

Method A

Make a Table

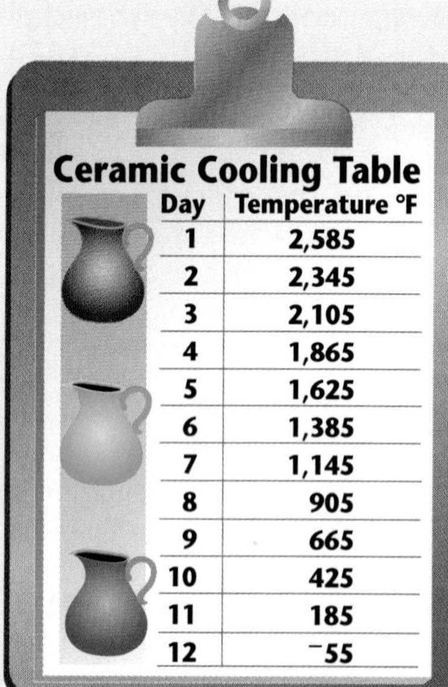

Ceramic Cooling Table

Day	Temperature °F
1	2,585
2	2,345
3	2,105
4	1,865
5	1,625
6	1,385
7	1,145
8	905
9	665
10	425
11	185
12	⁻55

Method B

Write an Equation

$2{,}825 - 65 = 2{,}760$
$2{,}760 \div 240 = 11.5$

The ceramic will cool to a temperature of 65°F on the eleventh day.

Look Back

How did using alternative strategies help you solve the problem?

Why is it useful to have alternate strategies to solve problems?

Solve using two different methods. Tell which methods you used.

1. Leah buys 164 apples. Her brother Les buys half as many. How many do they buy in all?

2. Simone has $\frac{3}{4}$ of a pie. She divides it evenly among her 6 guests. How much of the entire pie does each guest get?

3. Donna has $4\frac{3}{4}$ cups of flour. She plans to make muffins that take $1\frac{2}{3}$ cups of flour per batch. If she makes 2 batches of muffins, how much flour will she have left over?

4. Riley paints the ceilings in his house. He uses 2 gallons of paint to cover 330 square feet. How many gallons of paint does he use to cover 825 square feet?

Mixed Strategy Review

5. **Spatial Reasoning:** Len has 4 boards of equal length. He estimates that the boards will measure about 7 feet if he lays them end to end. About how long is each board?

6. **Literature:** *Moby Dick* is an adventure story about Captain Ahab's hunt to catch a fierce white whale. The book was written by Herman Melville, who lived from 1819 to 1891. About how old was Melville when he died?

7. Scientists worked two days on an experiment. They worked a total of 295 minutes. If they worked 145 minutes longer on the first day, how long did they work each day?

8. **Music:** A certain symphony orchestra has 22 violins, 8 cellos, 8 double basses, 1 piano, and 2 harps. These instruments, together with the violas, total 50 string instruments. How many violas are in the symphony?

CHOOSE A STRATEGY

- Logical Reasoning
- Draw a Diagram
- Make a Graph
- Make a Table or List
- Find a Pattern
- Guess and Check
- Write an Equation
- Work Backward
- Solve a Simpler Problem
- Conduct an Experiment

Use data from the line graph for problems 9–10.

9. Which month had the highest number of video rentals? Describe it with an ordered pair.

10. How many more movie rentals did June have than April?

11. During which months did the number of rentals stay the same?

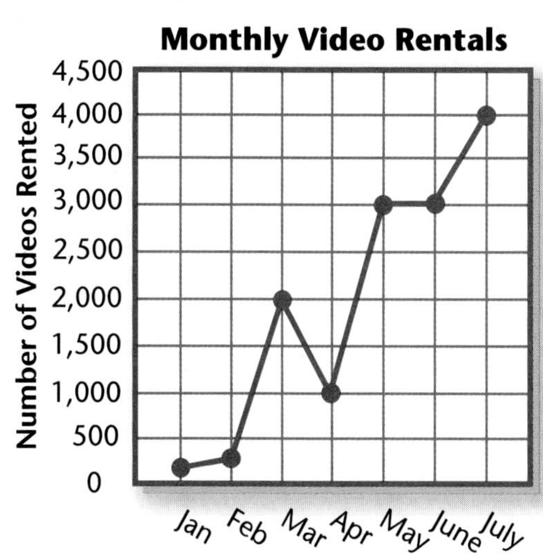

Extra Practice, page 423

Objective: Apply integers to analyze data and make decisions.

9·8 A Problem Solving: Application
Decision Making

The Science Club is making a budget for next year. They receive and spend money each semester and these numbers must balance for the year.

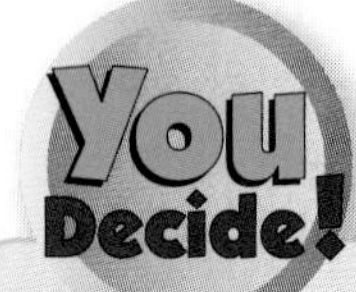

How can the Science Club balance the budget so that the expenses are less than the income?

Science Club Annual Budget

	Type of Expense	Amount of Expense	Type of Income	Amount of Income
First Semester	Science Club newsletter	$12.00	Science Club dues	$175.00
	Club T-shirts	$60.00	School activities fund	$60.00
	Science Fair materials	$27.00	Science Fair fundraiser	$120.00
	Meeting snacks	$13.00		
	Field trip to Science Museum	$55.00		
Second Semester	Science Club newsletter	$12.00	School activities fund	$55.00
	Science fair entry fee	$25.00		
	Science fair materials	$23.00		
	Bus for state science fair team	$175.00		
	Hotel for state science fair team	$136.00		
	Meeting snacks	$13.00		

STATE SCIENCE FAIR

Second weekend in May
Entry fee: $25.00

No team is allowed to spend more than $50.00 on materials for their science project.

Read for Understanding

1. How many types of expenses does the club have in the second semester?
2. How much is spent on snacks for the club meetings each semester?
3. Does the Science Club get more money from club dues, the fundraiser, or from the school activities fund?
4. How much money does the club get from the school activities fund each semester?
5. What is the greatest expense for the Science Club this year?
6. How much does the club spend on T-shirts the first semester?
7. What is the maximum total expense for the entry fee and materials for the state science fair?
8. How many different sources of income does the Science Club have?

Problem Solving

Make Decisions

9. Estimate the total amount of expenses for the first semester.
10. Find the exact amount of the expenses for the first semester.
11. Estimate the total amount of expenses for the second semester.
12. Find the exact amount of expenses for the second semester.
13. What is the total amount of expenses for the Science Club for the year?
14. What is the total income of the Science Club for the year?
15. Which is greater, the expenses or the income? Will the Science Club balance the budget as it is now?
16. How much more or less are expenses than income?
17. If the members of the Science Club were to bring their own snacks for the year, make their own club T-shirts, and give up the field trip, will they have enough money for the year?
18. Suppose the Science Club holds a fundraiser in the second semester that earns $150.00. Will they have enough money for the year?
19. If the Science Club members stay with friends and relatives instead of in a hotel for the state science fair and they bring their own snacks for meetings for the year, how much can they save? Will they have enough money for the year?
20. Suppose the Science Club finds car rides to the state science fair instead of taking the bus. Will they have enough money for the year?

Your Decision!

What is your recommendation for how the Science Club can balance its budget so that the club takes in more than it spends? Explain.

Objective: Apply integers to investigate science concepts.

Problem Solving: Math and Science

Is it easier to memorize positive or negative numbers?

You Will Need
- **number sequences**

Quick! What is your phone number? Phone numbers, TV channels, and addresses are all represented by positive numbers. What would the world be like if we used negative numbers instead?

In this activity you will decide if it is easier to memorize positive or negative numbers—or neither.

Hypothesize

Do you think it will be easier to memorize negative or positive numbers (or neither)?

Procedure

1. Work with a partner. Take turns.
2. Study the first number sequence until you think you have it memorized.
3. Cover the sequence and recite it to your partner.
4. Record whether you knew the sequence perfectly or not.
5. Switch. Let your partner memorize the next sequence.
6. Continue taking turns until you complete all of the sequences.

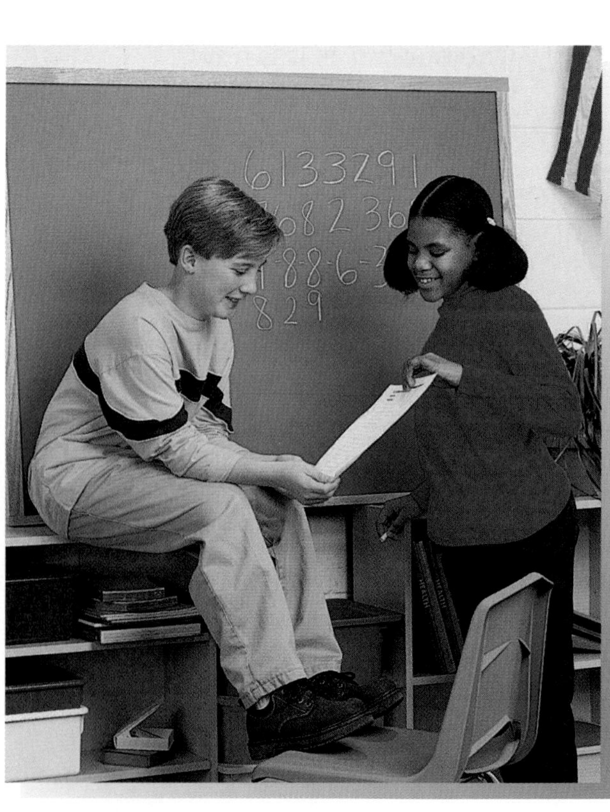

Data

Copy and complete the chart to record your observations.

Sequence	Positive or Negative?	Perfect (yes or no)?
1		
2		
3		
4		
5		
6		

Conclude and Apply

- What fraction of the positive sequences did you memorize perfectly?
- What fraction of the negative sequences did you memorize perfectly?
- Was it easier to memorize positive or negative numbers (or neither)?
- Use data from *Did You Know?* to explain how chunking makes long sequences of numbers easier to memorize and remember.

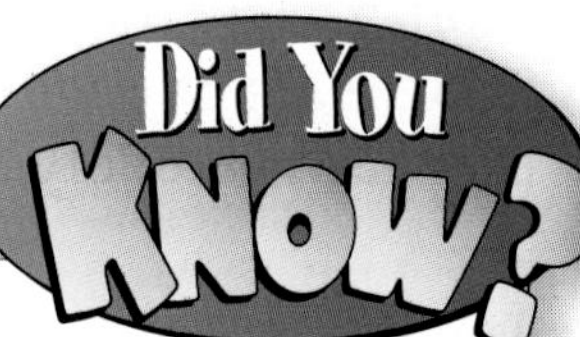

You can memorize long chains of numbers more easily by chunking (grouping) them in meaningful ways. Look for birthdays, addresses, area codes, or ages hidden in the sequences.

Going Further

1. Continue testing patterns of negative numbers, positive numbers and a mix of both. How difficult is it to memorize patterns with both types of numbers?
2. Design and complete an activity to determine the maximum number of digits you can memorize.

Check Your Progress B

Subtract. **(pages 408–413)**

1. $7 - 6$
2. $4 - 9$
3. $^{-}4 - 2$
4. $9 - {}^{-}9$
5. $6 - 6$
6. $^{-}7 - 4$
7. $8 - 10$
8. $^{-}4 - {}^{-}8$
9. $5 - {}^{-}8$
10. $^{-}4 - {}^{-}4$
11. $8 - 12$
12. $^{-}12 - 2$
13. $^{-}2 - {}^{-}5$
14. $^{-}1 - {}^{-}1$
15. $4 - {}^{-}4$
16. $0 - 4$
17. $3 - 6$
18. $^{-}4 - {}^{-}5$
19. $^{-}2 - {}^{-}3$
20. $4 - 6$

Solve. **(pages 408–415)**

21. The Science Cub is holding a cooking contest to raise money. How many entries are in each of 3 categories if there are 186 entries, and the same number of entries is in each category?

22. The Whole Grain Bakery donated 36 loaves of bread to a bake sale for the Science Club. Half the loaves are rye, 12 are multigrain and the rest are whole wheat. How many loaves of whole wheat bread did the bakery donate?

23. The temperature at breakfast time is 6 degrees celsius below zero. By lunch it drops another 3 degrees celsius. What is the temperature at lunch?

24. A drill begins to dig at 5 feet above sea level. It drills to 18 feet below sea level. How far did it drill?

25. A scientist climbs 14 feet below Earth's surface into a cave to collect water samples. The next day she climbs 6 feet deeper than the day before. How far below the surface does she go on the second day? Write your answer as a negative integer.

Additional activities at
www.mhschool.com/math

Extra Practice

Integers and the Number Line: Comparing and Ordering Integers (pages 394–397)

Write an integer to represent the situation.

1. a weight loss of 3 pounds
2. 12° below zero
3. 15 meters above sea level
4. 120 ft below the surface
5. 32° above zero
6. a weight gain of 4 pounds

Use an integer to represent each situation.

7. An air mass leaving Alaska is 10°F below zero. Write the temperature using an integer.
8. On Monday the high temperature for the day was 2°F. On Tuesday the high temperature was the opposite of Monday's high temperature. What was the high temperature on Tuesday?

Compare. Write > or <.

9. $^-7$ ● $^-8$
10. 0 ● $^-5$
11. 4 ● 7
12. $^-6$ ● 6
13. 0 ● 3
14. $^-10$ ● $^-15$
15. $^-3$ ● $^-2$
16. $^-4$ ● 3
17. 0 ● 1
18. $^-20$ ● $^-22$

Order these numbers from least to greatest.

19. 3, $^-3$, 0
20. $^-2$, 4, $^-3$
21. 1, 5, $^-5$
22. $^-3$, $^-5$, $^-2$
23. 0, $^-1$, $^-2$
24. 1, $^-2$, 3
25. $^-13$, $^-6$, $^-4$, $^-8$
26. $^-11$, $^-23$, $^-4$

Solve.

27. Jolene's notes from science class say that Earth's inner core begins 3,180 miles below the surface, and the outer core begins 1,800 miles below the surface. Which core is farther below the surface?
28. If the Cretaceous period began 136 million years ago, and the Jurassic period began 190 million years ago, which period began first?
29. Would $^-10$, $^-5$, or $^-15$ appear farthest to the left on a number line? Explain
30. Write a list of 5 positive integers and their opposites. Put the numbers, and the number zero, in order from least to greatest.

Extra Practice

Add Integers (pages 398–403)

1. $4 + {}^-5$
2. ${}^-3 + 2$
3. $6 + 3$
4. ${}^-5 + {}^-7$
5. $14 + {}^-6$
6. ${}^-9 + 9$
7. $0 + {}^-5$
8. ${}^-9 + 11$
9. $4 + {}^-3$
10. ${}^-7 + 0$
11. ${}^-3 + {}^-2$
12. ${}^-3 + 5$
13. ${}^-1 + 1$
14. ${}^-2 + 1$
15. ${}^-2 + {}^-2 + {}^-2$
16. ${}^-4 + 3 + 2$
17. $2 + 0 + {}^-1$
18. $4 + 3 + {}^-3$
19. ${}^-1 + {}^-3 + {}^-2$
20. $3 + {}^-1 + 2 + {}^-2$

Solve.

21. The total height of an iceberg is 345 feet. The lower 150 feet of the iceberg are submerged below sea level. How many feet of the iceberg rise above sea level?

22. Without solving the problem, how would you know if the sum of ${}^-3$ and ${}^-2$ is a positive or negative number? Explain.

23. Suppose a research scientist collects samples from a cave 12 feet below the surface. Then she climbs up 6 feet to collect more samples. How many feet below the surface will she be?

Problem Solving: Reading for Math
Check the Reasonableness of an Answer (pages 404–405)

Solve.

1. At the noon the temperature of a water sample is 7°F. The next morning the temperature of the sample is 10°F lower. A lab worker records the temperature as 3°F. Is this calculation reasonable?

2. The morning temperature of a liquid sample is ${}^-2$°F. By noon, the temperature of the sample rises 4°F. The record shows the temperature as 2°F. Is this record reasonable?

3. Mr. Fargus hears on the radio that it is 30°C outside. He puts on a heavy coat and walks to work. Is his action reasonable? Explain.

Extra Practice

Subtract Integers (pages 408–413)

Copy and complete.

1. $^-9 - 5 = {}^-9 + ■ = ■$
2. $5 - {}^-4 = 5 + ■ = ■$
3. $^-8 - {}^-2 = {}^-8 + ■ = ■$
4. $7 - 8 = 7 + ■ = ■$
5. $6 - 10 = 6 + ■ = ■$
6. $^-11 - {}^-3 = {}^-11 + ■ = ■$

Subtract.

7. $7 - 4$
8. $^-3 - {}^-1$
9. $^-9 - {}^-9$
10. $^-4 - 8$
11. $^-5 - 6$
12. $7 - {}^-3$
13. $^-13 - 5$
14. $6 - {}^-6$
15. $^-7 - {}^-6$
16. $^-8 - {}^-3$
17. $^-9 - 3$
18. $12 - 5$
19. $4 - 5$
20. $^-3 - {}^-2$
21. $0 - 4$
22. $^-3 - 0$

Solve.

23. A communication tower is built on top of a hill that is 850 feet above sea level. The top of the tower is 927 feet above sea level. What is the height of the tower?
24. A mine is drilled to 15 feet below the surface. The next day, it is drilled 6 feet deeper. How far below the surface does the mine reach?
25. Do these two number sentences have the same answer: $3 - 4$ and $3 + {}^-4$? Explain.

Problem Solving: Strategy Alternate Solution Methods (pages 414–415)

Solve using more than one method.
Tell what methods you used.

1. If 75 earthquake relief volunteers raised $19,875, what is the average amount of money raised by each volunteer?
2. Each time a volcano erupts, its height increases. If a 2,050-foot volcanic mountain grows an average of 3 inches a year, how high will the mountain be in 20 years?
3. A ceramic sample cools from 1,350°F to 75° in 25 days. How many degrees does it cool each day?

Chapter Study Guide

Language and Math

Complete. Use words from the list.

1. Whole numbers and their opposites are called ____.
2. The numbers 4 and $^{-}4$ are called ____.
3. An integer that is less than zero is a ____.
4. The opposite of $^{-}19$ is a ____.

Math Words

integer
negative integer
positive integer
opposite integers

Skills and Applications

Compare and order integers. (pages 394–397)

Example

Compare $^{-}2$ and 4.

Solution

Use a number line.

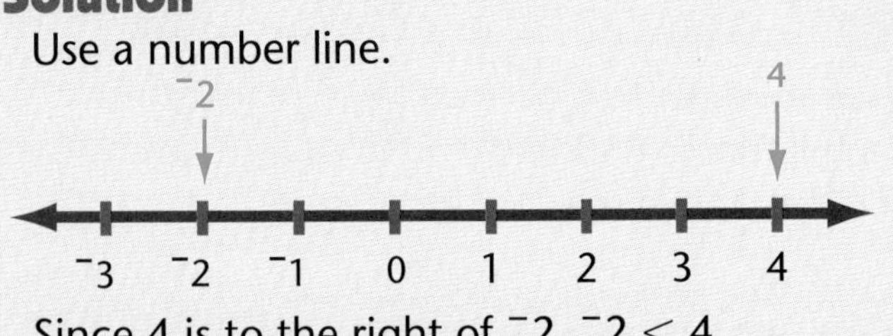

Since 4 is to the right of $^{-}2$, $^{-}2 < 4$.

Compare. Write $>$ or $<$.

5. 7 ● $^{-}8$
6. $^{-}4$ ● $^{-}3$
7. 0 ● 6
8. $^{-}2$ ● $^{-}6$

Order from least to greatest.

9. 2, $^{-}1$, 0
10. 3, $^{-}3$, $^{-}4$
11. $^{-}2$, $^{-}1$, $^{-}4$
12. 2, 1, $^{-}1$

Add integers. (pages 398–403)

Example

Find: $^{-}3 + 5$

Solution

Start at $^{-}3$. Move 5 places to the right.

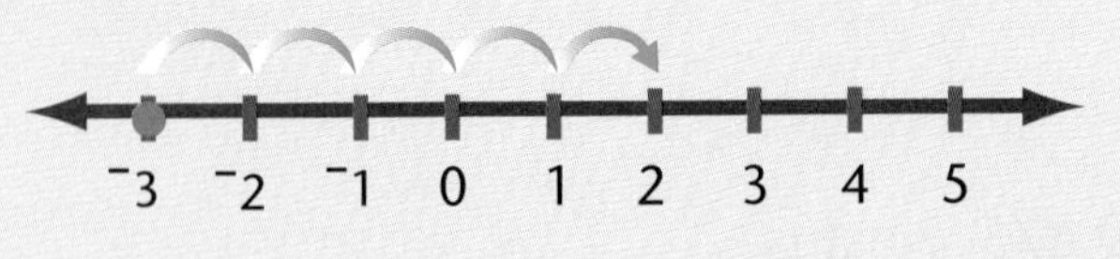

Add.

13. $6 + 8$
14. $^{-}3 + 2$
15. $^{-}9 + 12$
16. $^{-}8 + {}^{-}2$
17. $6 + {}^{-}4$
18. $^{-}5 + {}^{-}4$
19. $7 + {}^{-}11$
20. $^{-}15 + 15$
21. A cave explorer climbs down 6 feet below the surface into a cave. Then she climbs another 3 feet deeper. How far below the surface is she?

Subtract integers. (pages 408–413)

Example

Simplify: $^-8 - 6$

Solution

Change to an addition expression by adding the opposite.

$^-8 - 6 = {^-8} + {^-6} = {^-14}$

Subtract.

22. $^-5 - 6$
23. $7 - 4$
24. $^-8 - {^-2}$
25. $^-1 - {^-1}$
26. $6 - 11$
27. $^-9 - 3$
28. $0 - {^-12}$
29. $^-4 - {^-1}$
30. On Friday the high tide at Sunset Beach was 123 feet and the low tide was $^-86$ feet. What is the difference in feet between high and low tide?

Solve problems. (pages 404–405, 414–415)

Example

Tickets to a planetarium sky show cost \$8. If the show earns \$376, how many tickets were sold?

Solution

Many problems can be solved in more than one way. You can solve problems in two ways to check your answers.

Method 

Write an equation.

Let n = the number of tickets sold.

$n \times 8 = 376$

$(n \times 8) \div 8 = 376 \div 8 = 47$

Method 

Guess and check.

Guess: 50 tickets
Check: $50 \times 8 = 400$ ← too high

Guess: 45 tickets
Check: $45 \times 8 = 360$ ← too low

Guess: 47 tickets
Check: $47 \times 8 = 376$

31. Lava flows from 2 volcanoes meet and build up 144 inches of lava each year. If one lava flow contributes twice as much lava as the other flow, how much does each flow contribute?
32. A lava flow is traveling at a speed of 36 miles per hour. If the ocean is 99 miles from the volcano, how long will it take for the lava flow to reach the ocean?
33. A pyramid has 5 rows. The top row is made of 1 square. Each row has 2 more squares than the row above it. How many squares make up the bottom row?

Chapter Test

Compare. Write > *or* <.

1. $^-5$ ● 4
2. 10 ● $^-6$
3. $^-9$ ● $^-8$
4. $^-14$ ● 11
5. $^-46$ ● $^-51$

Order from least to greatest.

6. $^-1$, 3, 2
7. 0, $^-4$, $^-2$
8. $^-3$, $^-1$, $^-4$
9. 4, 2, $^-5$
10. $^-3$, 2, $^-4$
11. $^-3$, $^-5$, $^-1$
12. 3, $^-3$, 0
13. 0, $^-2$, 4
14. $^-4$, 5, $^-7$
15. $^-10$, $^-12$, $^-8$

Add.

16. $^-9 + 4$
17. $3 + {}^-7$
18. $^-5 + {}^-3$
19. $7 + {}^-7$
20. $6 + {}^-4$
21. $4 + {}^-4$
22. $^-2 + 3$
23. $^-3 + {}^-1$
24. $^-6 + 0$
25. $2 + {}^-4$
26. $^-3 + 0$
27. $^-3 + {}^-3$
28. $^-4 + 2$
29. $2 + {}^-1$
30. $^-6 + {}^-4$

Subtract.

31. $8 - 10$
32. $^-5 - 9$
33. $^-2 - {}^-8$
34. $^-9 - {}^-9$
35. $7 - {}^-3$
36. $3 - 6$
37. $^-2 - {}^-5$
38. $^-3 - 2$
39. $4 - {}^-2$
40. $^-2 - {}^-2$
41. $5 - {}^-3$
42. $0 - 4$
43. $^-2 - 2$
44. $^-3 - 0$
45. $4 - 7$

Solve.

46. Two wells are drilled. One is 134 feet deep. The other is 153 feet deep. Which well is deeper?
47. At 4.34 A.M. the tide was up 87 feet. By 2:30 P.M. it had dropped to $^-43$ feet. What is the difference in feet between high and low tide?
48. Myles saves \$1 every 2 days. How much will he save during September?
49. Can the sum of a positive integer and a negative integer be a positive integer? Give an example.
50. Judy solves the problem $2 - 4$ and Eric solves the problem $2 + {}^-4$. Will they get the same answer? Explain. What is the answer?

Performance Assessment

You keep track of the weather for one day each month of the school year so that your science class can track weather patterns.

You record this data:

Date	Temperature
Sept. 1	65°F
Oct. 1	59°F
Nov. 1	46°F
Dec. 1	32°F
Jan. 1	⁻5°F
Feb. 1	⁻12°F
Mar. 1	5°F
Apr. 1	36°F
May 1	59°F
June 1	70°F

Place your data on a number line and use it to answer these questions:

- What is the difference in temperature between February 1 and September 1?
- What is the difference in temperature between January 1 and June 1?
- Which months have temperatures that are opposite integers?
- Which day is the warmest? the coolest? What is the difference in temperature between them?

A Good Answer

- has a complete number line.
- shows a complete answer to each question.
- shows the steps used to find the months with the greatest temperature variation.

You may want to save this work in your portfolio.

Enrichment

Multiplying Integers

You can also multiply integers.

Note: These rules hold for division too.

Examples

A 4×3

Rule:
positive × positive = positive

Start at zero and count 4 groups of 3 on the number line.

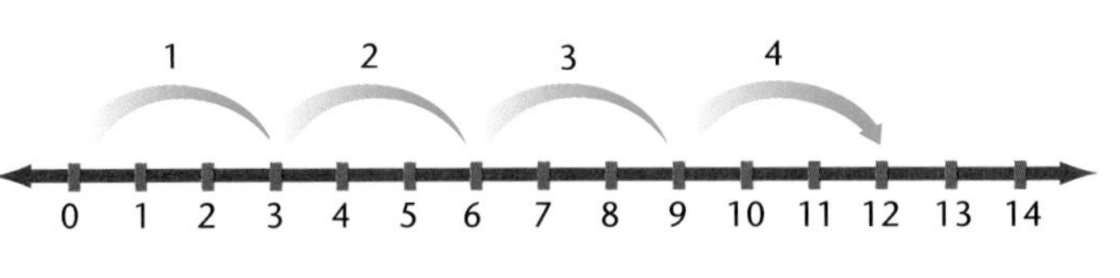

B $^{-}4 \times 3$

Rule:
negative × positive = negative
So $^{-}4 \times 3 = {}^{-}12$.

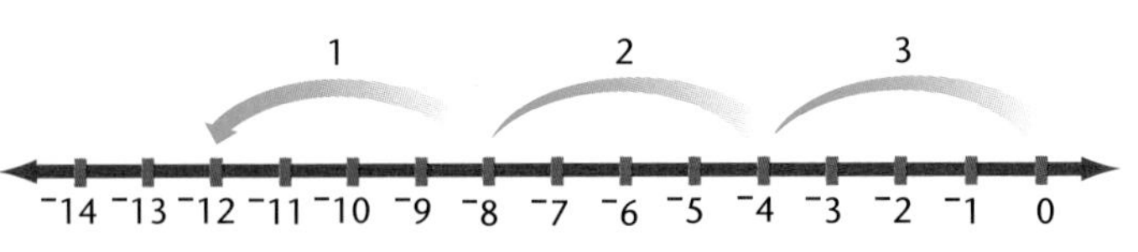

C $4 \times {}^{-}3$

Rule:
positive × negative = negative
So $^{-}3 \times 4 = {}^{-}12$.

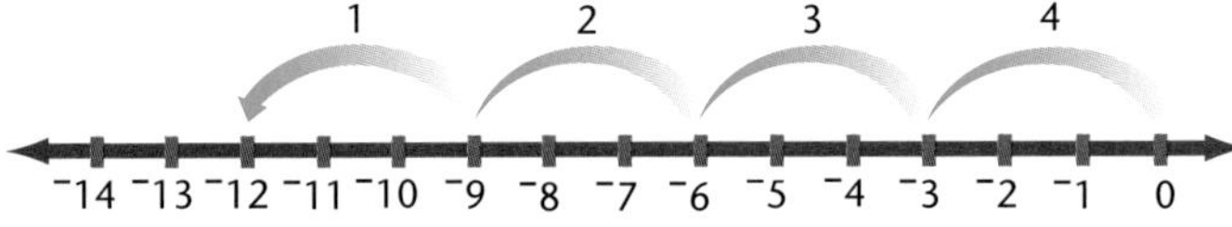

D $^{-}3 \times {}^{-}4$

Rule: negative × negative = positive

This example cannot be shown on the number line. The product is 12
So, $^{-}3 \times {}^{-}4 = 12$

You can remember the rules this way:

- If the signs are the same, the answer is positive: $3 \times 4 = 12$ and $^{-}3 \times {}^{-}4 = 12$.
- If the signs are different, the answer is negative: $^{-}3 \times 4 = {}^{-}12$ and $3 \times {}^{-}4 = {}^{-}12$.

Try It **Multiply.**

1. 5×4
2. $^{-}6 \times 3$
3. $7 \times {}^{-}4$
4. $^{-}6 \times {}^{-}8$
5. $12 \times {}^{-}3$
6. $^{-}9 \times {}^{-}2$
7. 10×6
8. $8 \times {}^{-}8$
9. $^{-}4^2$
10. $2 \times 3 \times {}^{-}4$
11. $^{-}1 \times {}^{-}4 \times 5$
12. $^{-}3 \times {}^{-}3 \times {}^{-}1$

Test-Taking Tips

When taking a multiple-choice test, you may not always be sure of the correct answer. Sometimes it is useful to **guess at the correct answer and then check** to see if it is correct.

The sum of two numbers is 20. Their product is 96. What are the two numbers?

A. 7 and 13
B. 11 and 12
C. 8 and 12
D. 6 and 16

Look at the choices carefully.

- You can guess answer A or C because their sums equal 20. You can reject B and D.
- Now check the product of 7 and 13. The product of 7 and 13 is 91, not 96.
- Check the product of 8 and 12. It is 96.

$$\begin{array}{r} 12 \\ \times\ 8 \\ \hline 96 \end{array}$$

The correct answer is C.

Check for Success

Before turning in a test, go back one last time to check.

☑ I understood and answered the questions asked.

☑ I checked my work for errors.

☑ My answers make sense.

Practice

Choose the correct answer.

1. The sum of two integers is 3. When the smaller integer is subtracted from the larger integer, the difference is 7. What are the two integers?

   A. 4 and 3
   B. 2 and 9
   C. $^-5$ and 8
   D. $^-2$ and 5

2. The sum of 3 numbers is 22. Their product is 320. What are the 3 numbers?

   F. 5, 7, 10
   G. 4, 5, 16
   H. 4, 8, 10
   J. 1, 2, 19

3. The Science Museum charges an entrance fee of $1.50 for children and $2.00 for adults. In one hour the museum collects $138.00 from 82 people. How many children and adults came to the Science Museum?

   A. 40 children, 42 adults
   B. 47 children, 35 adults
   C. 52 children, 30 adults
   D. 60 children, 30 adults

4. There are 8 more dolphins than whales at the aquarium. Altogether there are 36 dolphins and whales. How many are there of each?

   F. 30 dolphins, 5 whales
   G. 22 whales, 14 dolphins
   H. 20 dolphins, 20 whales
   J. 14 whales, 22 dolphins

Spiral Review and Test Prep

Chapters 1–9

Choose the correct answer.

Number Sense

1. Compare: $^{-}4$ ● $^{-}8$

   A. $<$
   B. $-$
   C. $>$
   D. $+$

2. What is another way to write 30×27?

   F. $30 \times 20 + 7$
   G. $(30 \times 20) + (30 \times 7)$
   H. 607
   J. $30 \times 20 \times 7$

3. Find the number that makes this sentence true.
   $42.23 = 42.20 +$ ■

   A. 0.03
   B. 0.23
   C. 0.3
   D. 3

4. What is the best estimate of 789×5?

   F. 3,000
   G. 4,000
   H. 35,000
   J. 40,000

Algebra and Functions

5. What is the opposite of $^{-}6$?

   A. $^{-}6$
   B. 6
   C. 0
   D. 16

6. If the rule of a function table is "multiply by 4," what would be the number that goes with 5?

   F. 4
   G. 5
   H. 10
   J. 20

7. What number added to 5 gives 8?

   A. 3
   B. 5
   C. 8
   D. 11

8. Ming's brother is 3 years older than he is. If m = Ming's age, which expression represents the brother's age?

   F. m
   G. 3
   H. $m + 3$
   J. $m - 3$

Measurement and Geometry

9. Which unit of capacity would you use to measure a glass of milk?

   A. Cup　　C. Quart
   B. Inch　　D. Gallon

10. What kind of triangle is *ABC*?

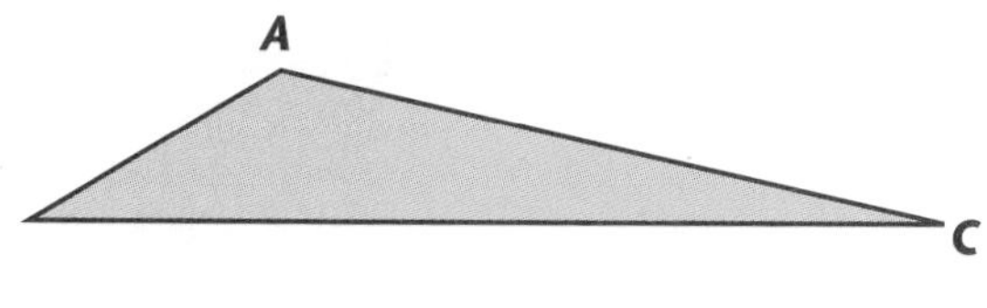

   F. Right　　H. Equilateral
   G. Acute　　J. Scalene

11. How many quarts are in $2\frac{1}{2}$ gallons?

   A. 6　　C. 10
   B. 8　　D. 12

12. A polygon has 4 vertices. It has 2 pairs of congruent sides but the 4 sides are not all equal. The vertices are right angles. What shape is it?

   F. Rectangle　　H. Triangle
   G. Square　　J. Circle

Mathematical Reasoning

13. Charlie has 6 quarters and 2 dimes. He spends $0.60. How much money does he have left?

   A. $0.80　　C. $1.50
   B. $1.10　　D. $1.70

14. A number increased by 8 is $^{-}4$. What is the number?

   F. $^{-}12$　　H. 12
   G. 4　　J. 16

15. The perimeter of a sandbox is 32 feet. The width is 6 feet. What is the length?

   A. 8 feet　　C. 12 feet
   B. 10 feet　　D. 20 feet

16. The sum of 2 integers is 7. When you subtract the smaller integer from the larger integer, the difference is 1. What are the two integers?

Algebra: Expressions and Equations

Theme: Our Environment

Use the Data

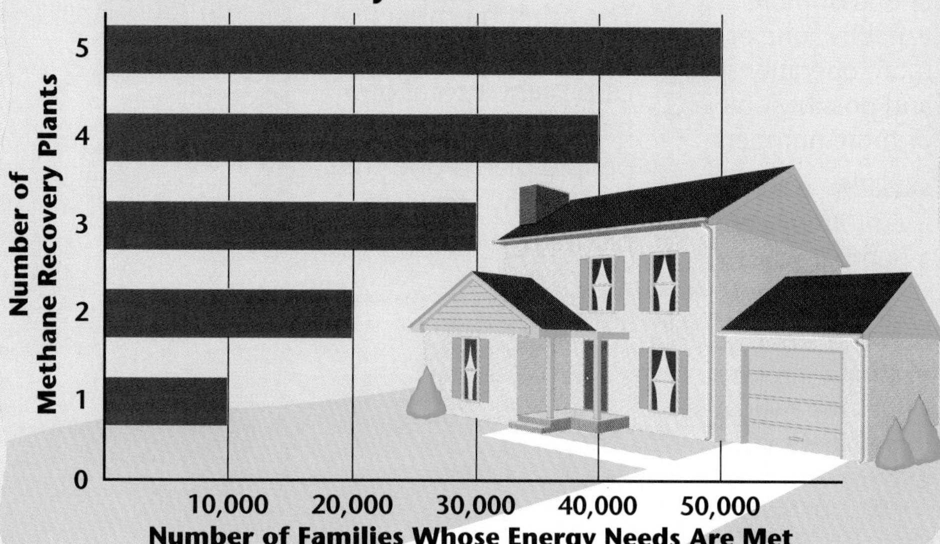

- If there are 120 methane recovery plants operating in the United States, how many families can use this energy? How can you use the graph and its equation to find the answer?

What You Will Learn

In this chapter you will learn how to
- write and evaluate algebraic expressions.
- use the order of operations.
- solve problems using graphs and equations.
- solve one- and two-step equations.
- use strategies to solve problems.

Objective: Write and evaluate addition and subtraction expressions.

10•1

Explore Addition and Subtraction Expressions

Algebra & functions

Learn

Math Words

algebraic expression a variable or a combination of one or more variables, one or more operations, and possibly one or more numbers

variable a symbol used to represent a number whose value we do not yet know

evaluate replace values for a variable in an algebraic expression

You can use tens models to explore this problem:

The adult members of an a environmental club plant a total of 5 trees. Each of 8 young people plants one tree. How many trees are planted?

Work Together

You Will Need
- **tens models**

- Use tens models to show the number of trees. Each ten represents 1 tree.

  Show how many trees are planted.

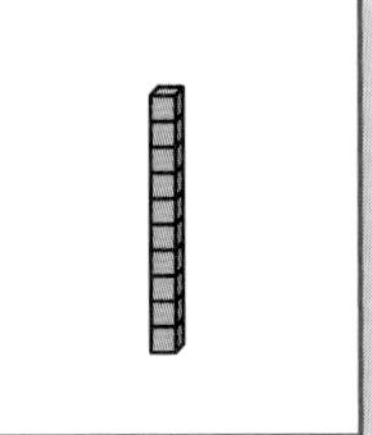
Adults

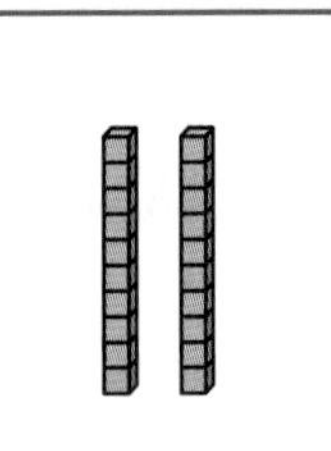
Adults plus one young person

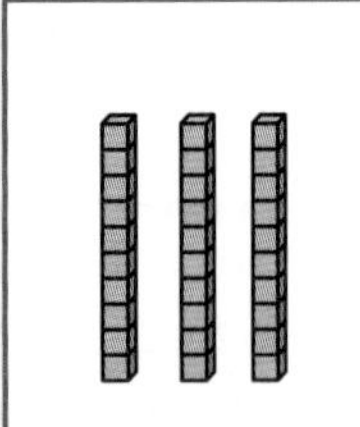
Adults plus two young people

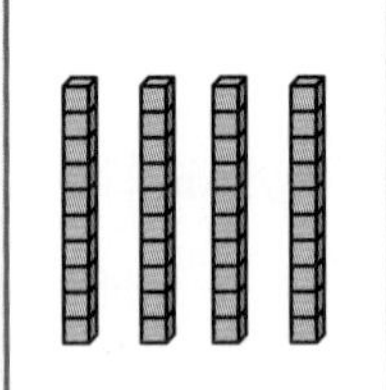
Adults plus three young people

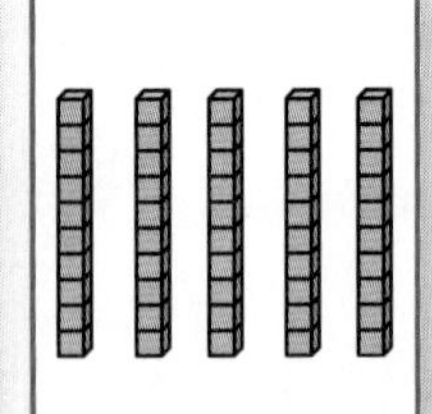
Adults plus four young people

Use tens models to show the number of trees planted by 8 young people. Record your work.

- Use tens models to show the number of trees planted if the following number of young people help.

  4 young people   7 young people   10 young people

The club plants 13 trees.

Make Connections

Using Models

Each ten represents one tree.

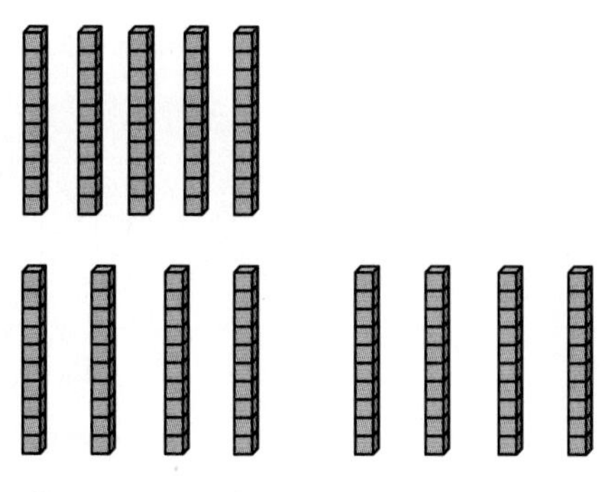

The group of adults plants 5 trees.

Each young person plants 1 tree.

The club plants 13 trees.

Using Paper and Pencil

Number of young people	0	1	2	3
Number of trees	5	6	7	8

- Look for a relationship. The number of trees is 5 more than the number of young people.
- Write an **algebraic expression** for this relationship.

  Use the **variable**, p, to represent the number of young people.
- The relationship is described by $t = 5 + p$, where the t is the total number of trees and p is the number of young people.
- You can **evaluate** the expression for $p = 8$.

  $t = 5 + p \quad t = 5 + 8 = 13$

Try It **Write an expression for each situation.**

1. Syd planted 3 more trees than Juan. How many trees did Syd plant?
2. Jody cut 6 flowers from a bush. How many flowers are left on the bush?

Explain how you would evaluate the expression $x + 6$ for $x = 3.3$.

Practice **Write an expression for each situation.**

3. Suzanne bought 7 trees. Wu bought t more trees than Suzanne. How many trees did Wu buy?
4. Jim planted 6 more trees than Shawn. Shawn planted p trees. How many trees did Jim plant?
5. On Monday a rose bush had r blooms on it. Deborah cut 8 roses off the bush to put in a vase. How many roses are left on the rose bush?
6. Emilio planted a tree h feet tall. The next day he trimmed $\frac{1}{2}$ foot off the top. How tall is Emilio's tree now?

Evaluate each expression for the value given.

7. $t + 14$ for $t = 10$
8. $n - 6$ for $n = 10.8$
9. $6\frac{1}{2} + x$ for $x = 20$
10. $b - 4.5$ for $b = 45$
11. **Analyze:** Write a situation about trees that might be described by the expression $m - 6$.

Objective: Write and evaluate multiplication and division expressions.

10•2

Explore Multiplication and Division Expressions

Algebra & functions

Learn

You can use counters to explore how to solve this problem:

A town will purchase 4 acres of land every year. How many acres of land will the town have purchased after each of the first four years?

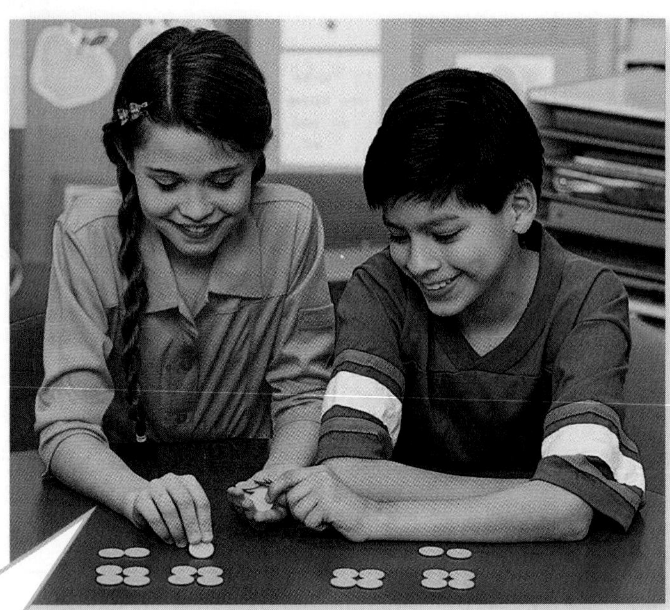

Work Together

You Will Need
- **counters**

▶ Use counters to model the number of acres. Show how many acres they have after 4 years.

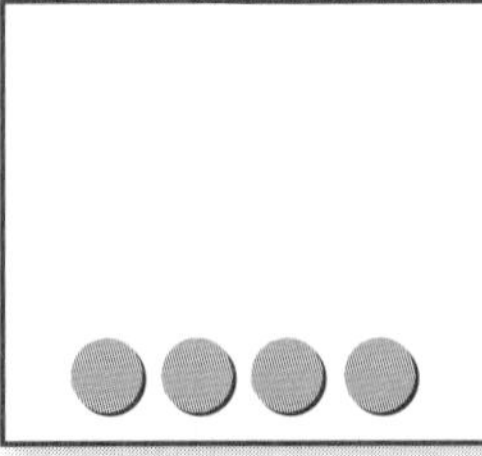

Number of acres after 1 year

Number of acres after 2 years

Number of acres after 3 years

Number of acres after 4 years

- Organize the data and look for the relationship between the number of acres and the number of years.

Number of years	1	2	3	4
Number of acres	4	8	12	16

The number of acres is 4 times the number of years.

- Write a multiplication expression to describe the relationship.

▶ Use counters to model each situation. Then write a multiplication expression.

The number of acres the town will own if they buy 2 acres each year

The number of acres the town will own if they buy 5 acres each year

Make Connections

You can also write division expressions.

If the town preserves half of its total number of acres as wetlands, how many acres of wetlands will it have?

Using Models

Total number of acres

Number of acres preserved as wetlands.

Using Paper and Pencil

Use the variable *a* to represent the total number of acres.

Write an expression for half the total:

$a \div 2$ or $\frac{a}{2}$

Note: $\frac{a}{2}$ is the same as $a \div 2$.

Evaluate the expression if the town has 40 total acres.

$a \div 2,$

$a = 40$

$40 \div 2 = 20$

The town will have 20 acres of wetlands.

Try It **Write an expression for each situation.**

1. The city uses $\frac{1}{4}$ of its total number of acres, *a*, for a fox habitat. How many acres are used as a fox habitat?
2. There are *g* geese in each acre in a preserve. The preserve is 100 acres. How many geese live on the preserve?

Evaluate each expression for the value given.

3. $6 \times b$ for $b = 7$
4. $12 \times g$ for $g = 3.3$
5. $\frac{p}{4}$ for $p = 2\frac{1}{2}$
6. $\frac{39}{c}$ for $c = 13$

Explain how the expressions $n \times 4$ and $\frac{n}{4}$ are alike and different.

Practice **Write an expression for each situation.**

7. There are *x* geese in the preserve. Each winter $\frac{1}{4}$ of them fly south. How many geese fly south?
8. Each year volunteers plant 10 trees in the preserve. How many trees will they plant in *y* years?

Evaluate each expression for the value given.

9. $6 \times b$ for $b = 17$
10. $\frac{d}{4}$ for $d = 200$
11. $8 \times y$ for $y = 17$
12. $\frac{2}{3} \times q$ for $q = 18$
13. $9 \times x$ for $x = 3$
14. $\frac{a}{4}$ for $a = 24$
15. $8 \times x$ for $x = 7$
16. $\frac{7}{8} \times z$ for $z = 16$
17. **Compare:** How are the expressions $5x$ and $5 + x$ alike? different?

Extra Practice, page 473

Objective: Evaluate expressions using the order of operations rule.

10·3 Order of Operations

Curtis Malovidov of St. Paul, Alaska, helps protect threatened animals by cleaning the environment

Learn

Math Word

order of operations the agreed-upon order for doing operations

Plants and animals become extinct when the last of the species dies. The dodo bird is an example of an extinct species. You can solve this expression to find the last year a dodo was seen alive.

$125 - (8 + 9) + 11^2 \times 13 = \blacksquare$

Example

Some expressions have more than one operation. Depending on the order you follow, you can get different answers. Mathematicians agree on a certain order so that everyone will get the same answer.

Operations must be performed in this order:

1. Perform the operations in the parentheses.
2. Evaluate terms with exponents.
3. Multiply and divide in order from left to right.
4. Add and subtract in order from left to right.

Use this phrase to remember the order:

"Please	Excuse	My Dear	Aunt Sally"
↓	↓	↓	↓
parentheses	exponents	multiply/ divide	add/ subtract

$$125 - (8 + 9) + 11^2 \times 13$$
$$125 - 17 + 11^2 \times 13$$
$$125 - 17 + 121 \times 13$$
$$125 - 17 + 1{,}573$$
$$108 + 1{,}573 = 1{,}681$$

The dodo bird became extinct in 1681.

More Examples

A Evaluate $x^2 + 12 \div 2$ for $x = 3$.

$3^2 + 12 \div 2 = 15$

B Simplify.

$(^{-}3 + 6) \times 2 + 3^2 = 15$

Try It **Evaluate each expression.**

1. $6 \times (3 + 2) - 4 \times 5$
2. $6 - 18 \div 6 + (4 \times 5)$
3. $4 + 52 \times (3 \times 2) - 1$

Sum it Up! Explain how to evaluate the expression $5 + (7 \times 9) - 4$. What is the value of the expression?

Practice

Simplify. Use the order of operations.

4. $60 - 4 \times 10$
5. $(60 - 4) \times 10$
6. $64.2 - (25.4 + 19)$
7. $100 + 45 \times 20 - 10$
8. $55 - 8 \times 2 + 38 \div 2$
9. $(2 + 4.4) \times 8$
10. $12 \times 4.5 + 8 \div 2$
11. $(16 - 8) \div 4 + 6$
12. $75 - 25 \div 25 + 10$

Evaluate the expression for the value given.

13. $125 - x + 13$ for $x = 43$
14. $200 + 32 \times a$ for $a = 20$
15. $28 + 3a - 2$ for $a = 6$
16. $19\frac{1}{4} - (a - 4)$ for $a = 8$
17. $4x \div 2 + 9$ for $x = 5$
18. $3.4 + (5x - 1.7)$ for $x = 2.2$

Place parentheses to make the sentence true.

★19. $6 \times 4 + 2 = 36$
★20. $15 + 9 \times 2 = 48$
★21. $76 - 40 \div 4 = 9$

Problem Solving

22. **Analyze:** Two students were asked to evaluate $82 + 4 \times 6$. One student got 106 and the other got 516. Which answer is correct? How do you know?

23. **Science:** The tail of one of the world's largest parrots, the macaw, can reach 3 feet in length. About how long is the macaw's tail in meters?

24. Use each of the numbers 2, 3, 4, and 5 exactly once to write an expression that equals 5.

★25. Write an expression that equals 3 using only the number 3 and each of the symbols +, −, ×, and ÷ exactly once.

Use data from the chart for problems 26–27.

26. Write an expression for the cost of 32 jars of ladybugs and 25 crates of bees, then evaluate.

★27. Anna buys 30 jars of ladybugs and 30 cases of beetles. If $\frac{1}{5}$ of these insects die, how many insects are still alive?

Cost of Insects

Item	Quantity	Price
Ladybugs	400 per jar	$10.50
Beetles	100 per case	$5.00
Bees	300 per crate	$12.75

Spiral Review and Test Prep

28. $\frac{4}{5} \times \frac{1}{3}$
29. $\frac{2}{3} \div \frac{1}{3}$
30. $\frac{3}{4} \times \frac{11}{2}$
31. $\frac{7}{8} \div 2$

Choose the correct answer.

32. Mike has written 7 pages of a 12-page report. What fraction of the report does he have left to write?

A. $\frac{1}{12}$
B. $\frac{5}{12}$
C. $\frac{7}{12}$
D. Not Here

33. Callie measured the length of her room with a yardstick. She measured 4 full yardsticks. What is the length of her room in feet?

F. 4 feet
G. 8 feet
H. 12 feet
J. 16 feet

Extra Practice, page 473

Objective: Represent situations and patterns with tables, words, and equations.

Functions

Algebra & functions

Learn

Math Words

function a relationship in which one quantity depends on another quantity

equation a mathematical statement with an equal sign in it

A fifth-grade student helps reduce trash by recycling. Each week she collects 10 pounds of newspaper from her family. Each neighbor gives her an additional 3 pounds of newspaper each week. What is the relationship between the amount of newspaper she collects and the number of neighbors she collects from?

Example

You can make a table to show the relationship.

Number of neighbors	0	1	2	3	4	5
Pounds of newspaper collected	10	13	16	19	22	25

- The amount of newspaper collected is equal to 10 plus 3 times the number of neighbors. This relationship is an example of a **function**.
- You can represent a function with an **equation**.
  let n = pounds of newspaper collected
  let c = number of neighbors
  Then $n = 3c + 10$ is an equation that represents the function.

Think: $3c$ is the same as $3 \times c$.

- Evaluate this equation if 5 neighbors give newspapers.
  Evaluate $n = 3c + 10$ for $c = 5$
  $n = 3 \times 5 + 10$
  $n = 15 + 10$
  $n = 25$

Think: Follow the order of operations.

Write an equation to describe each situation. Tell what each variable represents.

1. Ellie's family recycles 20 pounds of newspaper each week. Each neighbor recycles 5 pounds.
2. It costs $2.00 to dispose of recycling materials plus $0.25 a pound.

Explain what an equation is and how it is used.

Practice

Write an equation to describe each situation. Tell what each variable represents.

3. Joe collects cans for recycling. The recycling center pays him $5.00 for each trip to the center plus $0.05 a can.

4. Bill rents a truck to carry bottles to the recycling center. It costs $20.00 for the day plus $0.50 for each mile.

Complete the table. Write an equation to describe each situation.

★ 5.

Time Spent Collecting Recyclables					
Number of Neighbors	1	2	3	4	5
Total Time Spent Collecting Materials	15 min	25 min	35 min	■	■

★ 6.

Recycling Costs: Fee for Each Load—$5.00					
Pounds	10	15	20	25	30
Cost of One Load	$10.00	$12.50	$15.00	■	■

Problem Solving

Use data from the information below for problems 7–9.

It takes Ellie 15 minutes to collect her family's recycling materials and 5 minutes to collect materials from each neighbor.

7. How long will it take to collect materials from her family and 10 neighbors? Write an equation and solve the problem.

8. How long will it take Ellie to collect recycling materials from her family and 30 neighbors?

9. One week it took Ellie 25 minutes to collect her family's recycling material instead of 15 minutes. Write an equation to describe this new function.

10. **Art:** A sculptor makes art from recycled materials. With 4 wire hangers, she can make a mobile. How many wire hangers are needed to make a dozen mobiles?

11. Recycling bins cost $4.50 each. How much do five bins cost?

12. **Summarize:** How can writing an equation help you solve a problem?

Spiral Review and Test Prep

13. $\frac{5}{6} + \frac{2}{3}$

14. $4\frac{1}{2} - 2\frac{5}{6}$

15. $1\frac{7}{16} + \frac{1}{8}$

16. $8 - 4\frac{1}{3}$

Choose the correct answer.

17. Which number would you remove so that the range will be less than 60?

25, 16, 90, 70, 75, 38, 41, 17

A. 16 B. 90 C. 25 D. 17

18. Which number makes the sentence true?

$(0.4 + 2) + 3 = (6.2 - ■) + 5.2$

F. 6.2 G. 5 H. 6 J. 3

Extra Practice, page 473

Objective: Plot ordered pairs on a graph and graph linear equations.

10•5 Graphing a Function

Algebra & functions **Learn**

Math Words

ordered pair a pair of numbers that gives the location of a point on a graph, map, or grid

origin the point on a graph where the vertical axis meets the horizontal axis

coordinate one of two numbers in an ordered pair

axis (plural: axes) a reference number line on a graph

Environmental scientists sometimes look for possible sources of ground water pollution. To organize the data, they might map the sites on a grid. How can the location of the largest source of pollution be described?

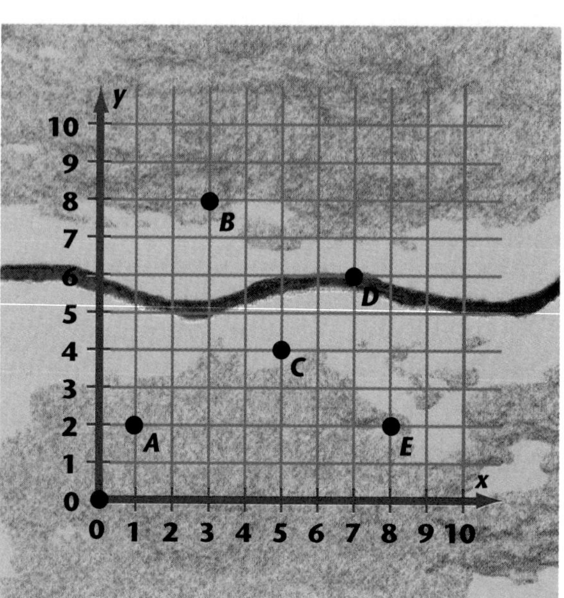

Example

You can write the location of a point on the graph using an **ordered pair**.

Start at the **origin**.

The location of the origin is described by the ordered pair (0, 0).

The following coordinates describe the point that is 7 miles to the right and 6 miles above base camp.

(7, 6)
↑ ↑

The first **coordinate** indicates units to the right of the origin. Count along the horizontal axis.

The second coordinate indicates units above the origin. Count along the vertical axis.

The location of the largest source of pollution is at (7, 6).

A scientist carries 8 pounds of equipment as she looks for sources of pollution. Each water sample she collects weighs 2 pounds. If she collects 5 samples, how much weight will she carry back to camp?

There's more than one way!

The relationship between the number of samples collected and the total weight carried is a function. You can represent a function using an equation, a table, or a graph.

Method A

You can represent the function using an equation.

Let w = total weight carried.

Let s = number of samples collected.

$w = 2s + 8$

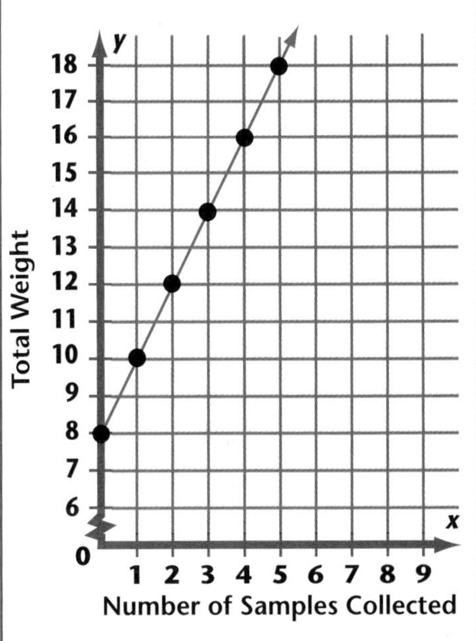

Method B

You can represent the function using a table to make a graph.

$w = 2s + 8$

s	w	Ordered Pairs
0	8	(0, 8)
1	10	(1, 10)
2	12	(2, 12)
3	14	(3, 14)
4	16	(4, 16)
5	18	(5, 18)

Plot the ordered pairs on the graph. Connect the points with a line.

The scientist will carry 18 pounds back to base camp.

Try It **Write the coordinates for each point.**

1. A
2. C
3. D
4. F
5. G

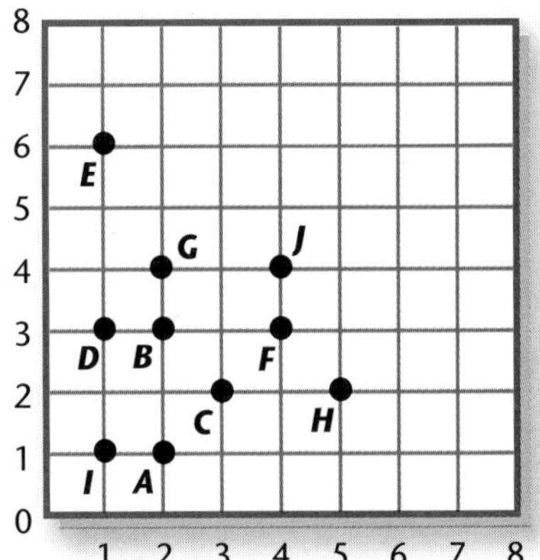

Name the point for the ordered pair.

6. (2, 3)
7. (1, 6)
8. (5, 2)
9. (1, 1)
10. (4, 4)

Sum it Up Describe how you would graph the equation $y = 3x + 4$.

Practice Write the coordinates for each point.

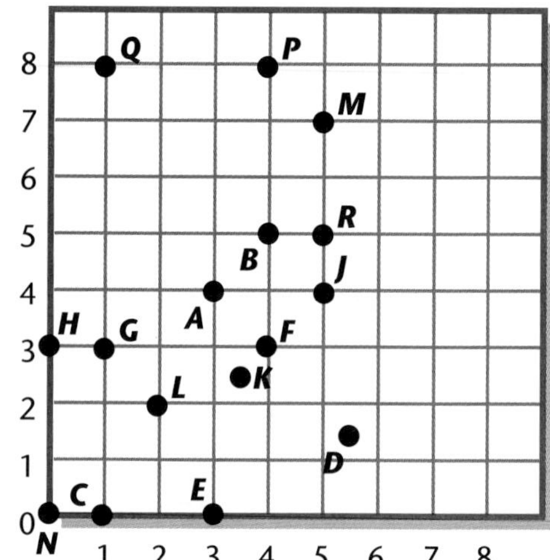

11. A **12.** C **13.** F **14.** H **15.** J

16. N **17.** R **18.** M **19.** P **20.** Q

Name the point for the ordered pair.

21. (3, 0) **22.** (4, 5) **23.** (1, 3)

24. (2, 2) ★**25.** (3.5, 2.5) ★**26.** (5.5, 1.5)

Complete the table then graph the function.

27. $d = 4t$

t	d
0	0
1	4
2	
3	

28. $a = b + 4$

b	a
0	4
1	5
2	
3	

29. $s = 3v - 2$

s	v
1	1
2	
3	7
4	

30. $y = 2x + 3$

x	y
0	
1	
2	7
3	

31. $c = 5w$

w	c
0	
1	5
2	
3	

32. $f = 4g + {}^{-}3$

f	g
1	1
2	5
3	
4	

33.

Here is how Ben plotted the ordered pair (5, 1) as point A. Tell what he mistake he made. Explain how to correct it.

Problem Solving

A group of students is helping the Salisbury Nature Center collect water samples. Each student collects 5 samples of water, and the park ranger collects 3 samples.

34. Write an expression that describes the relationship between the number of samples collected, *s*, and the number of students, *n*, that help collect them.

35. Make a table and graph the data.

36. How many samples will be collected if 8 students help?

★37. If 28 samples are collected, how many students helped to collect samples?

Use data from *Did You Know?* for problems 38–39.

38. If you use the average amount of water each day, how much is used in a week?

39. How many complete loads of clothes can be washed with 362 gallons of water?

40. **Summarize:** How do you locate a point on a graph using ordered pairs?

41. **Health:** It is healthy for a human to consume about $2\frac{1}{2}$ quarts of water each day. If Anna drinks eight 8-ounce glasses of water and gets 20 ounces from other sources, will she be consuming a healthy amount?

★42. **What if** the equation $d = 0.24t$ gives the distance d in miles that Parker can paddle a canoe in t minutes? How far can Parker canoe in 10 minutes?

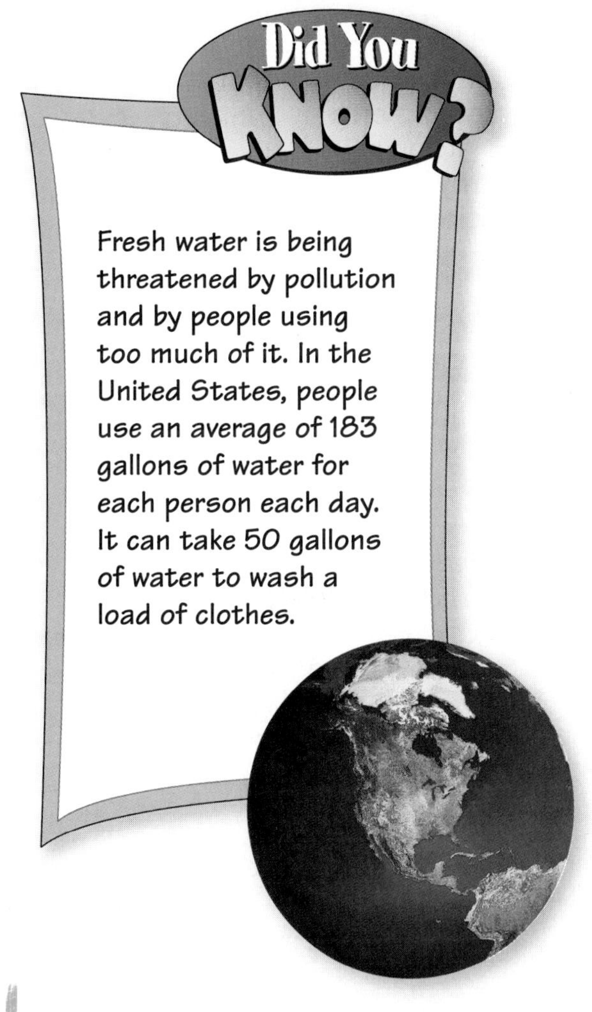

Did You Know?
Fresh water is being threatened by pollution and by people using too much of it. In the United States, people use an average of 183 gallons of water for each person each day. It can take 50 gallons of water to wash a load of clothes.

Spiral Review and Test Prep

Find each missing number.

43. $\frac{5}{6} = \frac{■}{12}$ 44. $\frac{5}{4} = 1\frac{■}{4}$ 45. $\frac{■}{8} = \frac{1}{2}$ 46. $\frac{2}{3} = \frac{8}{■}$ 47. $\frac{■}{16} = \frac{1}{4}$

Choose the correct answer.

48. How much would you pay for 2 books that cost $4.49 each?

A. $9.00 C. $8.98
B. $9.14 D. Not Here

49. Which of these numbers does not divide evenly into 324?

F. 2 H. 4
G. 3 J. 8

Objective: Graph points and functions in all four quadrants and use the graphs to solve problems.

10·6

Graph in Four Quadrants and Solve Problems Using Graphs

Algebra & functions

Learn

Math Word

quadrant one of the 4 sections on a coordinate graph formed by the x- and y-axes

Meteorologists map the positions of storms on graphs. This grid shows several storms that surround Charlotte, North Carolina, which is located at point (0, 0). The storms located around Charlotte can have positive or negative numbers showing their locations. Where is the center of storm A located?

Example 1

By using integers, you can also graph with negative numbers.

1

Draw a coordinate grid. Label the **quadrants**.

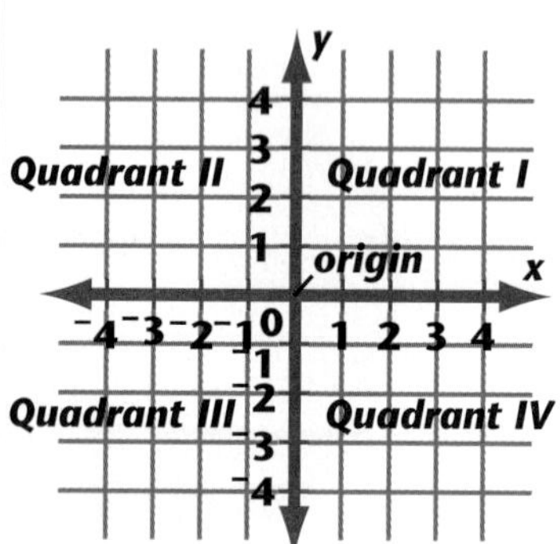

Remember: The point at which the axes intersect, point (0, 0), is called the origin.

2

Find the ordered pair that describes the location of point A, the center of the storm.

3

Count the units to the right or left of the origin first. Then count the units above or below the origin.

First coordinate: distance to the right or left of O

Think:
Moving up or right is positive.
Moving down or left is negative.

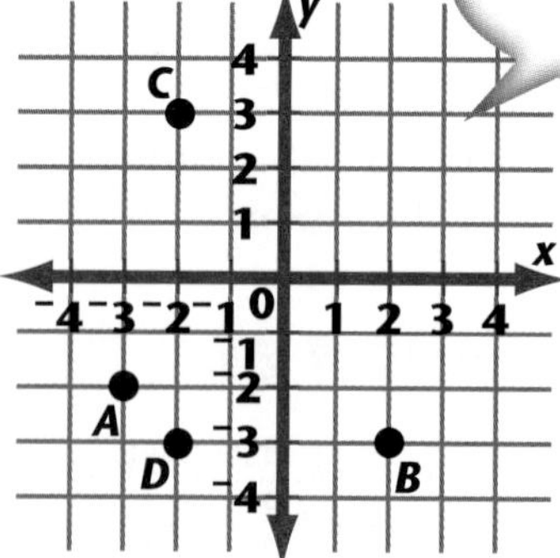

Second coordinate: distance above or below O

The point is ($^-3$, $^-2$).

The center of storm A is located at the point ($^-3$, $^-2$).

Meteorologists can use radar to track tornadoes. The radar tracking site sits at the origin on the graph. You can use the equation $y = x + 1$ to describe the path of a certain tornado. Will it hit Greenville, South Carolina at (⁻3, ⁻2)?

Example 2

Use the equation to graph the path of the storm.

1

Make a function table by substituting different values for x in the equation and calculating y each time.

y = x + 1		
x	y	Ordered Pairs
⁻3	⁻2	(⁻3, ⁻2)
⁻1	0	(⁻1, 0)
1	2	(1, 2)
3	4	(3, 4)

2

Plot each ordered pair. Then connect the points with a line that extends in both directions.

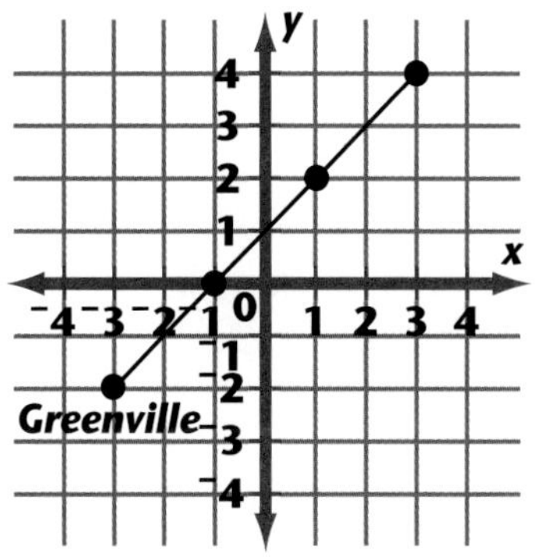

Greenville lies in the path of the tornado.

Try It **Write the ordered pair for the point described.**

1. 2 units to the right of the origin; 3 units below the origin
2. 3 units to the left of the origin; 1 unit above the origin
3. 2 units above the origin; 4 units to the right of the origin
4. 2 units below the origin; 1 units to the left of the origin
5. 1 unit to the left of the origin; 3 units below the origin
6. 3 units to the right of the origin

Use the graph above to find if the locations described are in the path of the tornado.

7. (2, 3)
8. (⁻4, 2)
9. (0, 0)
10. (⁻2, ⁻1)
11. (0, 3)

Explain how you would graph $y = x - 3$.

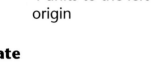

Practice Write the ordered pair for each point described.

12. 4 units to the left of the origin; 3 units below the origin

13. 4 units above the origin, 4 units to the left of the origin

14. 5 units below the origin

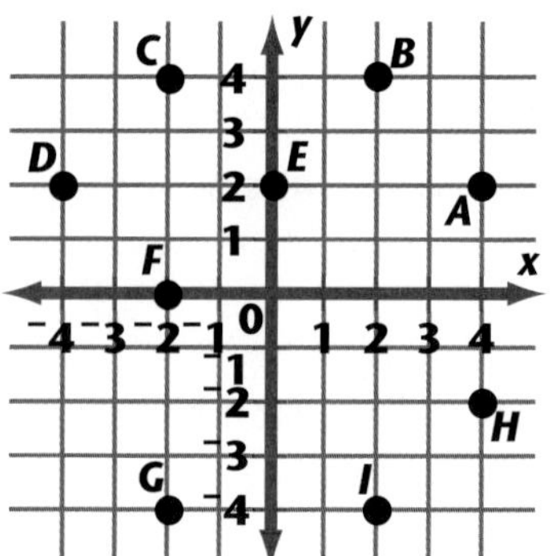

Use data from the coordinate graph for problems 15–24.

Give the coordinates of the point.

15. A
16. C
17. G
18. F
19. E

Name the point for the ordered pair.

20. $(^-2, 4)$
21. $(2, 4)$
22. $(4, ^-2)$
23. $(^-4, 2)$
24. $(2, ^-4)$

Copy and complete the tables. Then graph the function.

25.

$y = x + 2$	
x	y
$^-4$	▪
$^-2$	▪
0	▪
2	▪

26.

$y = x - 3$	
x	y
$^-1$	▪
0	▪
1	▪
2	▪

27.

$y = 4 - x$	
x	y
$^-2$	▪
0	▪
2	▪
4	▪

★28.

$y = 2x + 1$	
x	y
$^-2$	▪
$^-1$	▪
0	▪
2	▪

29.

This is how Bill plotted the point (2, 1). Tell what mistake he made. Explain how to correct it.

Problem Solving

Use data from the graph for problems 30–31.

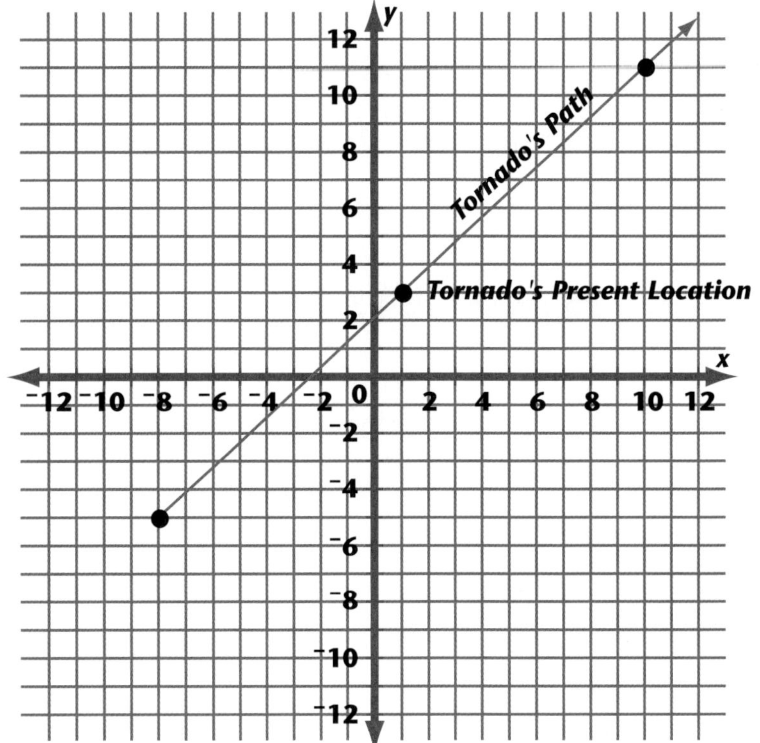

30. The location of a large city is described by the ordered pair (10, 11). Does this city lie in the path of the tornado?

★31. A town located at (3, 2) is concerned about being hit by the tornado. If each unit on the graph represents 100 miles, how far to the right of the tornado is the town? how far below?

Use data from the table for problems 32–33.

32. **Social Studies:** Which state has the greatest difference between its coldest and hottest recorded temperatures? What is the difference?

33. Which state has the least difference between its coldest and hottest recorded temperatures? What is the difference?

34. **Create a problem** that involves an equation. Trade equations with another student. Complete a function table and graph the equation.

Temperature Records

State	Lowest Temperature (in °F)	Highest Temperature (in °F)
Alaska	⁻80	100
Florida	⁻2	109
Georgia	⁻17	112
New York	⁻52	108
Wisconsin	⁻54	114

Spiral Review and Test Prep

35. $4\frac{1}{2} \times \frac{1}{4}$

36. $\frac{5}{6} \div 1\frac{1}{6}$

37. $1\frac{1}{8} \times 1\frac{1}{3}$

38. $2\frac{1}{2} \div 1\frac{1}{4}$

Choose the correct answer.

39. Find an equivalent number to 1.25.

A. $\frac{1}{25}$
B. $1\frac{1}{4}$
C. $1\frac{2}{5}$
D. $12\frac{1}{2}$

40. A figure has 3 sides and 3 angles. What is the figure?

F. Square
G. Triangle
H. Rectangle
J. Not Here

Extra Practice, page 474

Objective: Use graphs to solve problems.

Problem Solving: Reading for Math
Use Graphs to Identify Relationships

Heat Wave Hits Bedford

Read How would you use the graph to describe the relationship between time and temperature?

READING SKILL ▶

Use Illustrations

A graph relates two quantities.

- **What do you know?**
  Data about temperature and time
- **What do you need to find?**
  How temperature and time of day are related

MATH SKILL ▶

Use Graphs to Identify Relationships

- The line of a graph shows how a change in one quantity affects the other.
- If the line is rising, the second quantity is increasing as the first one increases.
- If the line is declining, the second quantity is decreasing as the first one increases. The steeper the slant of the line, the greater the change.
- If the line is horizontal, the quantity is not changing.

Plan Look at the line to identify the relationship.

Solve The line goes up from left to right. The graph shows that the temperature increased with every passing hour.

Look Back Is your answer reasonable?

What would a straight horizontal line tell you about the relationship between time and temperature?

Practice Solve.

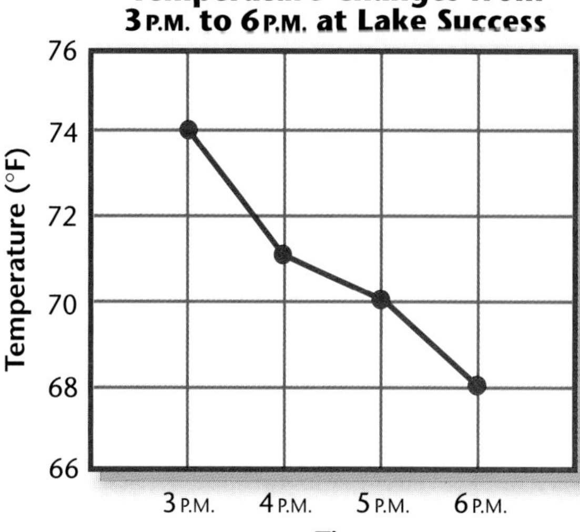

1. The graph shows air temperature at Lake Success from 3 P.M. to 6 P.M. How would you describe the relationship between time and air temperature as shown in this graph?

2. On Tuesday the air temperature in Fairfield was 51°F at 9 A.M. At 10 A.M. it was 52°F. At 11 A.M. it was 54°F, and at noon 55°F. Draw a graph and describe the relationship between time and air temperature.

Use data from the graph for problems 3–5.

Average Monthly Temperatures In San Francisco, California

Temperature (°F)

64
62
60
58
56
54
52
50
48
46

January February March April September October November December

Month

3. What change occurred in the monthly temperature between January and February? between February and March? between March and April?

4. Are there any months that show no change in temperature?

5. What change occurred in the average monthly temperature between September and October? between October and November? between November and December?

Spiral Review and Test Prep

Choose the correct answer.

During a four-week period, the water temperature of a pond increased 2 degrees each week. At the beginning of the time period the temperature of the pond was 49°F. At the end the temperature was 57°F.

6. Which of the following is true?
   - A. At the end of the time period, the water temperature was 49°F.
   - B. The water temperature increased as time passed.
   - C. The temperature of the water decreased as time passed.
   - D. The air temperature was 49°F.

7. What does the title of a graph tell you?
   - F. Who made the graph
   - G. The relationship shown
   - H. When the graph was created
   - J. If the line shows an increase or decrease

Extra Practice, page 474

Check Your Progress A

Write an expression for each situation. **(pages 434–437)**

1. Anne recycles p pounds of glass on Wednesday and 30 pounds on Friday, how much is that?
2. A grocer saves $1.45 a day using cloth instead of paper towels. How much will he save in x days?

Solve. Use the order of operations. **(pages 438–439)**

3. $8 \times 2 + (15 - 6) \div 3$
4. $12 + 27 \div 3 + 6^3$
5. $500 - 20 \times 5 + x^4$, if $x = 10$
6. $900 \times (2 + 1) \div 30$
7. $5^5 + 12 \times 7 - 36$
8. $9k + 150 \div 3 \div 300$, if $k = 50$

Write an expression to describe each situation. Tell what each variable represents. **(pages 440–441)**

9. Each homeroom class at Cora's school saved 30 paper bags a day by using lunch boxes instead of lunch bags.
10. For each truckload of newspaper that Eric collects, his school receives $0.35 a pound. The science department also contributes $10.00 for each truckload to cover expenses.

Use data from the graph for problems 11–16. Name the coordinates of the point. **(pages 442–449)**

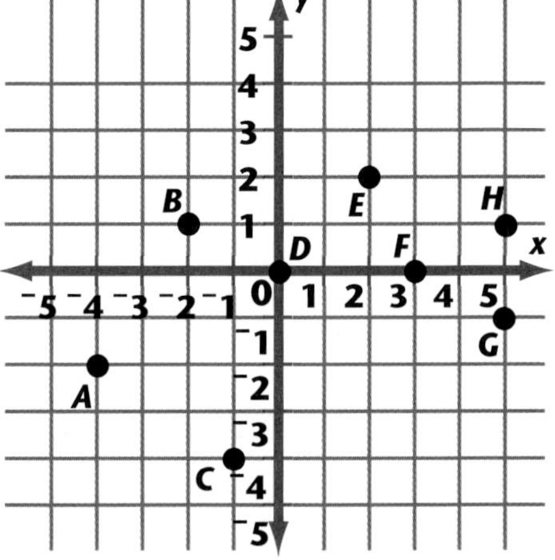

11. E
12. C
13. D

Name the point for each ordered pair.

14. (⁻4, ⁻2)
15. (5, ⁻1)
16. (5, 1)

Write the ordered pair for each point described. **(pages 446–449)**

17. 2 units to the left of the origin; 3 units above the origin
18. 4 units below the origin

Solve. **(pages 434–451)**

19. Graph the equation $y = 2x + 2$.

20. The path of a storm is described by the equation $y = x - 1$. Name three locations on a coordinate graph that the storm will pass through.

Use Coordinate Graphs

Eduardo wants to save $10 by saving $2 a week. He owes his brother $6 and must pay that back first. This situation is described by the equation $y = 2x - 6$, where x represents the number of weeks and y represents the amount Eduardo has saved. Graph this equation. In how many weeks will Eduardo pay his brother back? In how many weeks will Eduardo have saved $10?

You can use a computer program to graph the equation.

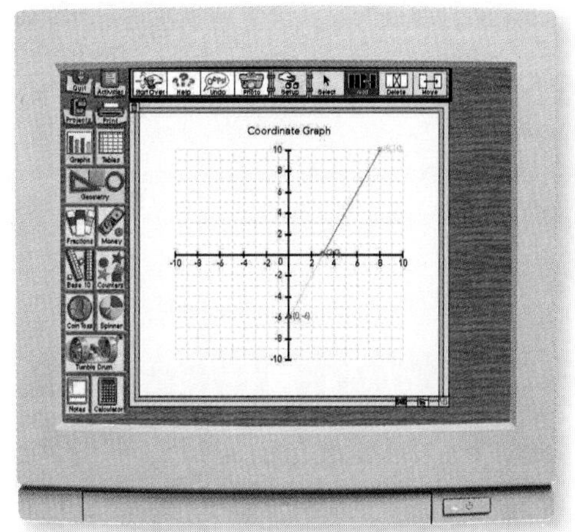

- Choose Coordinate Graph.
- Click on Setup. Choose the graph that goes from $^{-}10$ to 10 on both axes. Click on Show Ordered Pairs and Connect Points.
- Click on the point where $y = 0$.
- Click twice on the point where $x = 0$.
- Click on Select. Drag the point where $x = 0$ to extend the line.
- When will Eduardo pay his brother back?
- When will Eduardo have saved $10?

Use the computer to graph each equation. Then give the coordinates of three points on the line.

1. $y = x - 2$
2. $y = 2x + 1$
3. $y = 3x - 1$

Solve.

4. Misty is saving $1 a week to pay a bill of $4. In how many weeks will she have saved $4?
5. Kimbra is paying her sister $3 a day. In how many days will she have paid her sister $9?
6. **Analyze:** How does using the computer help you find coordinates of points on the graph of an equation?

For more practice, use Math Traveler™.

Objective: Solve addition equations.

10·8 Explore Addition Equations

Algebra & functions

Learn

You can use counters and cups to explore this problem:

If the number of seals needing to be freed from fish nets is $d + 9 = 24$ seals, how many seals need to be freed?

Work Together

You Will Need
- counters
- cups

▶ You can use counters and cups to find *d*, the number of seals still needing help.
- Use a sheet of paper to represent each side of the equation.
- Use counters to represent the numbers and a cup to stand for the variable, *d*.

seals still needing help seals already helped		total number of seals
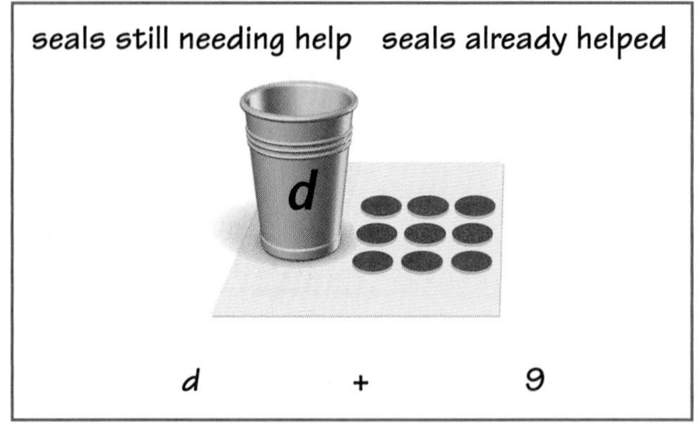		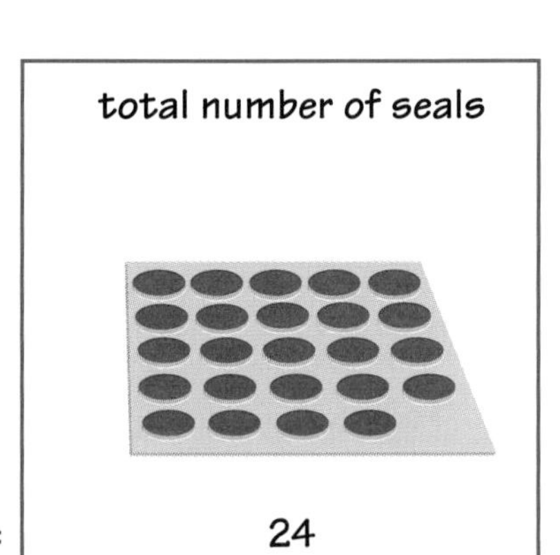
$d \quad + \quad 9$	=	24

- Take 9 counters away from each side of the equation.

Note: If you add or subtract the same number from both sides of an equation, the equation will still be true.

- The variable *d* is the same as the number of counters on the right side of the equal sign.
- Record your work.

▶ Use counters and cups to solve each equation. Record your work.

$9 + x = 23$ $3 + t = 12$ $y + 9 = 14$ $t + 7 = 19$

Make Connections

Here is how you solve $x + 6 = 9$.

Using Models

Make a model to show $x + 6 = 9$.

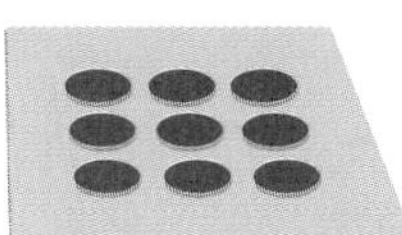

$x + 6 \quad = \quad 9$

Remove the same number of counters from each side of the equation.

=
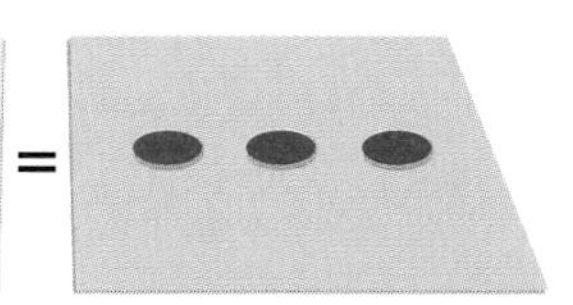

Using Paper and Pencil

Write an equation.

$$x + 6 = 9$$

Subtract 6 from both sides of the equation.

$$x + 6 - 6 = 9 - 6$$

Simplify.

$$x = 3$$

The solution of $x + 6 = 9$ is $x = 3$.

Try It **Solve. You may use models.**

1. $s + 14 = 23$
2. $8 + r = 18$
3. $b + 10 = 21$
4. $m + 5 = 20$

Explain how to use paper and pencil to solve $x + 2 = 5$. What is the answer?

Practice **Solve.**

5. $n + 4 = 12$
6. $e + 6 = 17$
7. $y + 5 = 23$
8. $m + 8 + 20$
9. $7 + a = 15$
10. $9 + h = 24$
11. $23 + k = 40$
12. $10 + d = 15$
13. $12 = b + 6$
14. $7 = p + 3$
15. $14 = 8 + f$
16. $20 = t + 10$
17. $5 + c = 13$
18. $z + 14 = 18$
19. $21 = g + 4$
20. $9 = r + 5$
21. **Explain** why you can subtract the same number from both sides of an equation.

Objective: Write and solve addition and subtraction equations.

10·9 Addition and Subtraction Equations

Algebra & functions **Learn**

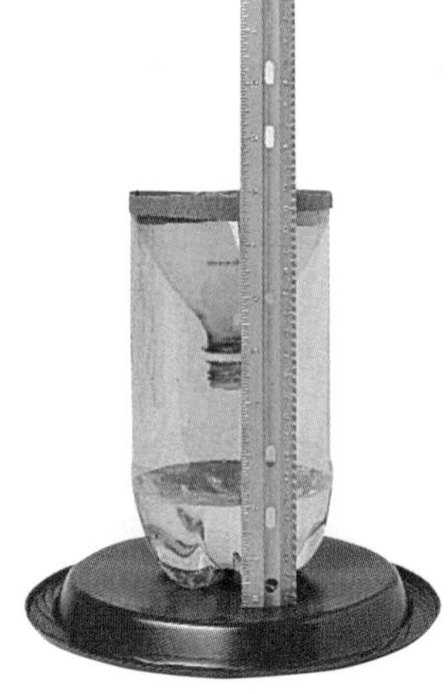

Rain in Seattle

> **Math Word**
> **inverse operations**
> Operations that "undo" each other; for example, adding 3 and subtracting 3 undo each other.

A science class is analyzing weather conditions in Seattle. Suppose the weather service reports that Seattle received 2 inches of rain on Sunday. Seattle got a total of 12 inches of rain on Saturday and Sunday. How many inches of rain fell on Saturday?

Example 1

You can use an addition equation to solve the problem.

Let r represent the number of inches of rainfall on Saturday.

Then $r + 2 = 12$

$r + 2 - 2 = 12 - 2$

$r = 10$

Think: adding and subtracting the same number are **inverse operations**—they undo each other.

Note: If you add to or subtract the same number from both sides of an equation, the equation will still be true.

Check your answer by substituting 10 for r.

$r + 2 = 12$

$10 + 2 = 12$

$12 = 12$ ✓

Seattle received 10 inches of rain on Saturday.

> Remember:
> The = sign means that the expression on the left is equal to, or balances the expression on the right.

More Examples

A

$6 + p = 17.5$

$6 + p - 6 = 17.5 - 6$

$p = 11.5$

Check: $6 + 11.5 = 17.5$

$17.5 = 17.5$ ✓

B

$x + 4 = 10\frac{1}{4}$

$x + 4 - 4 = 10\frac{1}{4} - 4$

$x = 6\frac{1}{4}$

Check: $6\frac{1}{4} + 4 = 10\frac{1}{4}$

$10\frac{1}{4} = 10\frac{1}{4}$ ✓

C

$y + 3 = {}^-5$

$y + 3 - 3 = {}^-5 - 3$

$y = {}^-8$

Check: ${}^-8 + 3 = {}^-5$

${}^-5 = {}^-5$ ✓

The science class finds data showing that Mount Sharon received 2.5 inches less snow than Mount Riga. If Mount Sharon received 18 inches of snow, how much did Mount Riga receive?

Example 2

You can use a subtraction equation to solve the problem.

Let y represent the number of inches of snow that Mount Riga received.

Then $y - 2.5 = 18$.

To find the value of y, undo the subtraction by adding 2.5 to each side of the equation.

$$y - 2.5 + 2.5 = 18 + 2.5$$
$$y = 20.5$$

Think: An equation stays equal if you add or subtract the same quantity on both sides.

Check:
$$y - 2.5 = 18$$
$$20.5 - 2.5 = 18$$
$$18 = 18 \checkmark$$

Mount Riga received 20.5 inches of snow.

More Examples

D

$$m - 15 = 3.6$$

Think: Add 15 to both sides.

$$m - 15 + 15 = 3.6 + 15$$
$$m = 18.6$$

Check: $18.6 - 15 = 3.6$

$$3.6 = 3.6 \checkmark$$

E

$$g - 2\frac{1}{4} = 10\frac{3}{4}$$

Think: Add $2\frac{1}{4}$ to both sides.

$$g - 2\frac{1}{4} + 2\frac{1}{4} = 10\frac{3}{4} + 2\frac{1}{4}$$
$$g = 13$$

Check: $13 - 2\frac{1}{4} = 10\frac{3}{4}$

$$10\frac{3}{4} = 10\frac{3}{4} \checkmark$$

F

$$t - 2 = {}^{-}4$$

Think: Add 2 to both sides.

$$t - 2 + 2 = {}^{-}4 + 2$$
$$y = {}^{-}2$$

Check: ${}^{-}2 - 2 = {}^{-}4$

$${}^{-}4 = {}^{-}4 \checkmark$$

Try It **Solve each equation. Check your answer.**

1. $x + 4 = 9$
2. $4 + p = 12$
3. $w - 7 = 20$
4. $t - 7.2 = 28$

Explain how to solve $y - 8 = 15$. What is the solution?

Practice Solve each equation. Check your answer.

5. $x + 7 = 12$ 6. $r + 4 = 13$ 7. $v - 9 = 8$ 8. $a - 6.6 = 10.1$

9. $n - 8 = 3$ 10. $m + 2.7 = 14.9$ 11. $c - 32 = 71$ 12. $d + 21.5 = 32.6$

13. $h + 200 = 470$ 14. $e + 1 = 1$ 15. $147 = f - 238$ 16. $b - 26.7 = 102.4$

17. $s - \frac{1}{2} = 16$ 18. $g - \frac{3}{5} = 21$ 19. $k + 6.8 = 58.3$ 20. $122.2 - q = 122$

21. $u - 8 = 12$ 22. $j - 13 = 7$ 23. $17 = y + 8$ 24. $14 = l - 2$

★25. $w + 6 = 1$ ★26. $120 + z = 225$ ★27. $t + {}^{-}4 = {}^{-}4$ ★28. $p - 3 = {}^{-}5$

Without solving each equation, tell whether the solution is greater than 38, less than 38, or equal to 38.

29. $x + 6 = 38$ 30. $n - 12 = 38$ 31. $38 = d + 11$

★32. $38 = p - 0$ ★33. $r - 38 = 38$ ★34. $38 - x = 0$

35.

Here is how Donna solved $x + 6 = 10$. Tell what mistake she made. Explain how to correct it.

Problem Solving

36. If it snowed 12 inches in February and 19 inches in March and February combined, how much did it snow in March? Write an equation and solve it.

37. During a heavy rainstorm, 4.8 inches of rain fell in 3 hours. What is the average amount of rain an hour?

38. **Explain:** When solving an equation such as $x + 8 = 10$, how is an inverse operation used to keep the equation balanced?

39. **Explain** why you can subtract 6 from both sides of the equation $d + 6 = 14$.

40. **Science:** A hurricane is a very powerful storm with winds of 73 miles an hour or greater. A tropical storm can have wind speeds as low as 39 miles an hour. Write an addition equation to represent the difference, d, between the lowest speeds of hurricane winds and tropical storm winds.

★41. There is a rainstorm in Seattle, 1,134 miles away from Los Angeles. The storm is headed for Los Angeles and traveling at 54 miles an hour. If it is 2:00 A.M. in Los Angeles, at about what time will the storm reach Los Angeles?

Use data from the chart for problems 42–44.

42. What is the average high temperature difference between January and July in Los Angeles?

43. Which city has the greatest temperature difference between January and July? Show how you found the answer.

44. The temperature difference between January and July in Gunnison is 66 degrees. Write a subtraction equation to describe the temperature, t, in July. Solve for t.

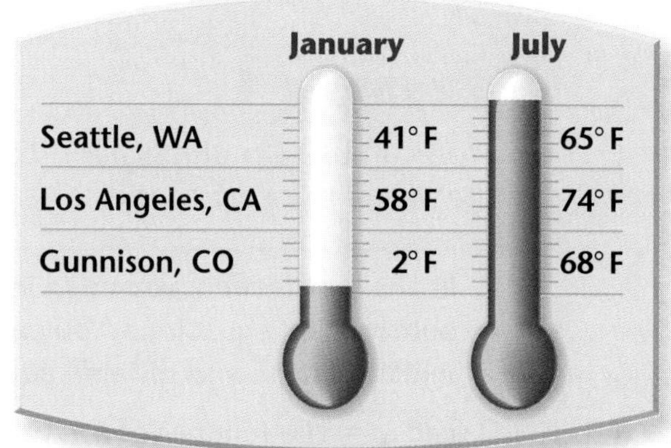

January
July
Seattle, WA
41° F
65° F
Los Angeles, CA
58° F
74° F
Gunnison, CO
2° F
68° F

45. **Create a problem** about weather that can be solved using the equation $m + 34 = 52$.

46. Write a situation that could be described by expression $x - 3$.

Spiral Review and Test Prep

47. 7,920 ft = ■ mi

48. 3.48 gal = ■ qt

49. 3.5 h = ■ min

50. 2.5 lb = ■ oz

Choose the correct answer.

51. The environmental science class collects rainwater samples each day for a week. If they collect the following amount in inches each day, how much rain fell from Monday to Friday?

0.05, 0.3, 0, 0, 0.1

A. 0.09
B. 0.3
C. 0.45
D. Not Here

52. A science class spends $45.98 for a rain gauge. The company charges $4.95 for shipping. How much does the class spend?

F. $4.95
G. $45.98
H. $41.03
J. $50.93

Extra Practice, page 474

Objective: Write and solve multiplication and division equations.

Multiplication and Division Equations

Learn

Solar cells convert energy from the sun into usable electricity without polluting the environment. The amount of electricity provided by the cell is measured in units called watts. What size unit could you buy for $600?

Example 1

You can use a multiplication equation to represent the relationship between the cost of the solar cell and the size of the unit.

In the last lesson, you used inverse operations to solve addition and subtraction equations. You can also use inverse operations to solve multiplication and division equations.

Let w = the number of watts you could buy.

$$(5 \times w) = 600$$
$$(5 \times w) \div 5 = 600 \div 5$$
$$w = 120$$

Note: If you multiply or divide the same number to both sides of an equation, the equation will still be true.

To check your answer, substitute 120 for w:

$$5 \times w = 600$$
$$5 \times 120 = 600$$
$$600 = 600 \checkmark$$

You could buy a 120-watt unit with $600.

More Examples

A

$4m = 24.5$

$4m \div 4 = 24.5 \div 4$

$m = 6.125$

Remember: $4m$ is the same as $4 \times m$.

B

$\frac{1}{2}x = 40$

$\frac{1}{2}x \div \frac{1}{2} = 40 \div \frac{1}{2}$

$x = 80$

A home-builder wants a new house to have 15 solar cells installed on the roof. Suppose each cell requires 9 square feet of space. How big must the roof be to fit all of the cells?

Example 2

You can use a division equation to solve the problem.

Remember: $\frac{r}{9}$ is the same as $r \div 9$.

Let r = the size of the roof.

$$\frac{r}{9} = 15$$
$$9 \times \frac{r}{9} = 9 \times 15$$
$$r = 9 \times 15$$
$$r = 135$$

To check your answer, substitute 135 for r.

$$\frac{r}{9} = 15$$
$$135 \div 9 = 15$$
$$15 = 15 \checkmark$$

The roof must be at least 135 square feet.

More Examples

C

$y \div 2.5 = 5$

$y \div 2.5 \times 2.5 = 5 \times 2.5$

$y = 12.5$

D

$\frac{x}{5} = \frac{2}{3}$

$\frac{x}{5} \times 5 = \frac{2}{3} \times 5$

$x = \frac{2}{3} \times 5$

$x = \frac{10}{3} = 3\frac{1}{3}$

Try It **For each equation, decide if you should multiply or divide both sides to solve.**

1. $4y = 48$
2. $n \times 7 = 63$
3. $n \div 5 = 9$
4. $6y = 6$
5. $\frac{a}{6} = 2.5$

Solve each equation. Check your answer.

6. $4y = 48$
7. $n \times 7 = 63$
8. $n \div 5 = 9$
9. $6y = 6$
10. $\frac{a}{6} = 2.5$

Explain how inverse operations are used to solve $7x = 35$. What is the solution?

Practice **For each equation, decide if you should multiply or divide both sides to solve.**

11. $t \div 5 = 4$ **12.** $6n = 12$ **13.** $w \div 3 = 4$ **14.** $\frac{d}{2} = 30$

15. $12h = 144$ **16.** $1.7x = 17$ **17.** $z \div 7 = 14$ **18.** $q \div 6 = \frac{1}{2}$

Solve each equation. Check your answer.

19. $\frac{t}{4} = 4$ **20.** $z \times 9 = 81$ **21.** $n \times 2.5 = 45$ **22.** $29f = 58$

23. $78 = 6w$ **24.** $\frac{s}{59} = 3$ **25.** $b \div 8.11 = 5$ **26.** $8x = 800.8$

27. $v \div 5 = 3$ **28.** $\frac{p}{2} = 10$ **29.** $12g = 24$ **30.** $5c = 15$

31. $6h = 44.4$ **32.** $5.4q = 10.8$ **33.** $\frac{a}{9} = 5$ **34.** $5m = 15$

35. $8k = 88$ **36.** $\frac{d}{13} = 3$ **37.** $5e = 65$ **38.** $17u = 34$

39. $\frac{j}{4.2} = 2$ **40.** $5.5l = 44$ **41.** $r \div 3 = 4$ **42.** $\frac{y}{3} = 3$

43. $13g = 39$ **44.** $7x = 35$ ★**45.** $44 \div m = 4$ ★**46.** $6{,}000 \div q = 1{,}000$

Choose the equation for which the value of *n* is a solution.

47. $n = 3$
- **A.** $4n = 7$
- **B.** $n + 4 = 7$
- **C.** $\frac{n}{4} = 7$

48. $n = \frac{1}{2}$
- **F.** $n - \frac{1}{2} = \frac{1}{2}$
- **G.** $\frac{n}{2} = 1$
- **H.** $4n = 2$

49. $n = 10$
- **A.** $4 + n = 10$
- **B.** $4 \times n = 13$
- **C.** $n - 108 = 98$

50. $n = 6$
- **F.** $\frac{36}{n} = 6$
- **G.** $3n = 2$
- **H.** $n + 6 = 6$

51. $n = 3.7$
- **A.** $\frac{n}{33.6}$
- **B.** $n + 12 = 15.7$
- **C.** $10 - n = 7.3$

52. $n = 1.3$
- **F.** $\frac{3.9}{n} = 3$
- **G.** $3.9n = 3$
- **H.** $3.9 + n = 3$

53.

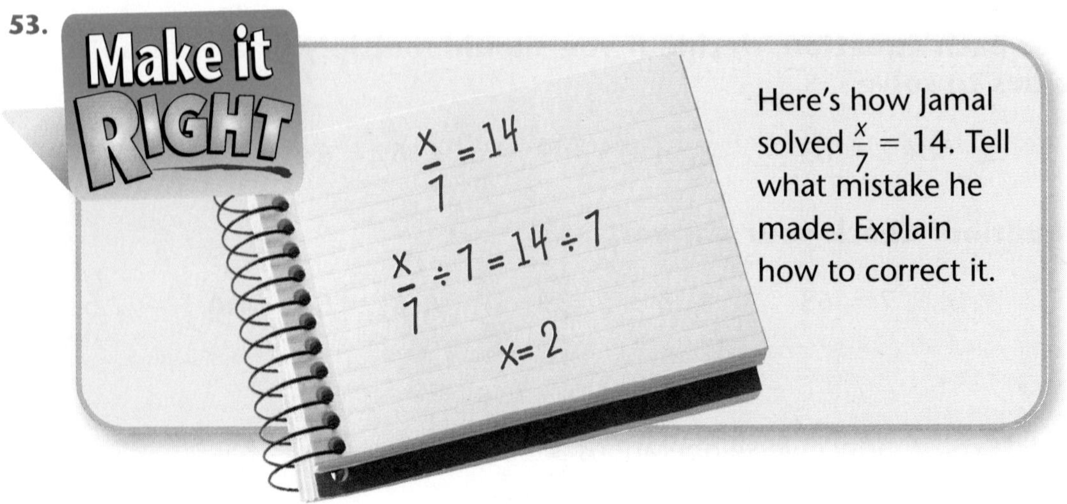

Here's how Jamal solved $\frac{x}{7} = 14$. Tell what mistake he made. Explain how to correct it.

Problem Solving

Use data from the chart for problems 54–56.

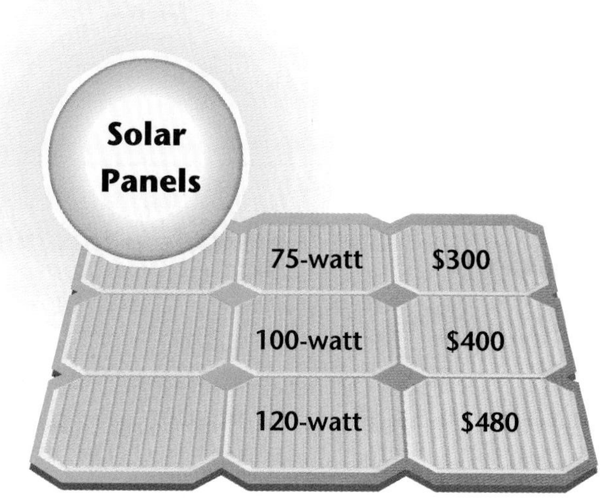

54. Write an equation that relates the cost of the solar cell to the number of watts.

55. If the price equation works for any size unit, how much will a 200-watt solar cell cost?

★56. If an apartment building buys four 120-watt units and splits the cost evenly among 6 families, how much would each family pay?

57. Nolan says that to solve $x \div 8 = 8$, you must divide both sides by 8. Is he correct? Explain.

58. Analyze: How are inverse operations used to solve multiplication and division problems? Give an example.

59. If the sun rises one day at 5:23 A.M. and sets at 7:31 P.M., how many hours of sunlight are there?

60. Suppose that on a cloudy day, the sun shines for only about 26 minutes each hour. If the day lasts $8\frac{1}{2}$ hours, how many minutes of sunlight will there be?

61. The amount of solar energy that reaches a certain place on earth depends on the number of hours of sunlight that day. What if two thousand kilowatts strike a certain area during each sunlight hour? Write an equation to find the total watts during a day.

62. Create a problem about solar panels that can be solved by writing and solving a multiplication problem. Solve it and give it to another student to solve.

Spiral Review and Test Prep

63. 0.5×2.5 **64.** $5{,}207.24 \div 777.2$ **65.** 3.4×7.9 **66.** $3.12 \div 0.3$

Choose the correct answer.

67. Which of these decimals is 9.5 when rounded to the nearest tenth?

A. 9.44 **C.** 9.55
B. 9.49 **D.** 9.6

68. The local temperature is 3.5 degrees above normal. If the normal temperature is 55°F, what is the temperature?

F. 51.5°F **H.** 57.5°F
G. 52.5°F **J.** 58.5°F

Extra Practice, page 475

Objective: Make graphs to solve problems.

10•11 Problem Solving: Strategy
Make a Graph

Read

Read the problem carefully.

The climate of a planet or a region describes the long-term patterns of temperature and weather. The average surface temperature of Earth is 59˚F. What is this temperature in degrees Celsius?

- **What do you know?** The Earth's temperature in °F
- **What are you asked to find?** The Earth's temperature in °C

The Earth and its atmosphere

Plan

You can use the equation $F = 1.8C + 32$.

You can also graph the function and use the graph to find a solution.

Solve

Make a table and graph the results.

To find the Celsius equivalent of 59°F:

- Find 59° on the vertical axis.
- Move across to the graphed line.
- Move down to find the value on the horizontal axis.

So 59°F is equal to 15°C.

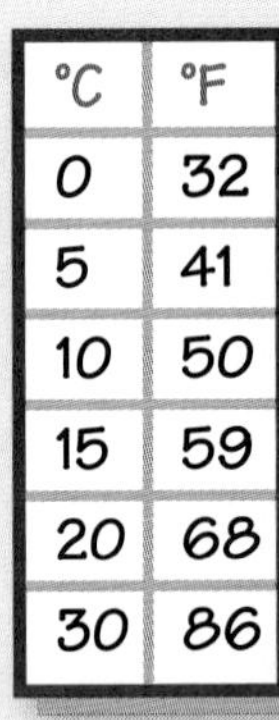

°C	°F
0	32
5	41
10	50
15	59
20	68
30	86

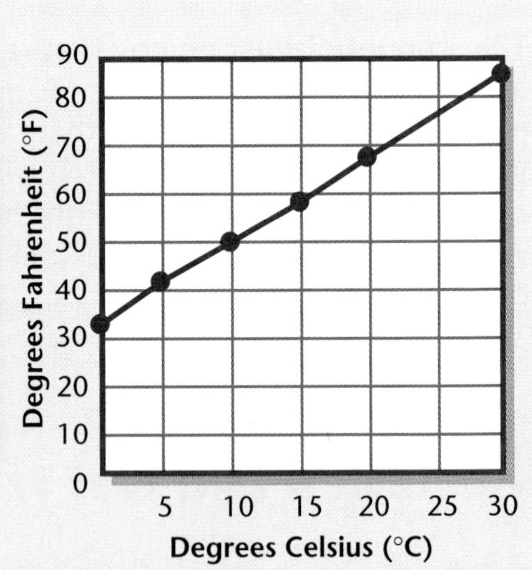

Look Back

Is your answer reasonable? How could you solve this problem another way?

Explain how you would use the graph to find the Fahrenheit equivalent of 5°C.

Practice

Solve. Use the graph on page 464 for problems 1–4.

1. If the average temperature of Earth rises to 62°F, about what is the new temperature in degrees Celsius?

2. If your backyard thermometer reads 30°C, what is the temperature in degrees Fahrenheit?

3. Shannon learned that the average temperature in some places on Earth has risen by as much as 15°F over the last 20 years. What is the average temperature in these places in degrees Celsius?

4. Temperatures in California's Death Valley can read as high as 120°F. Use the graph to find this temperature in degrees Celsius.

5. A scientist finds that the temperature increase in a valley is related to the number of hours of sunlight by the equation $y = 4x + 2$. Graph this equation.

6. If y is measured to be 22, what is the value of x? Use the graph from problem 5 to solve.

7. If x is measured to be 8, what is the value of y? Use the graph from problem 5 to solve.

8. **Create a problem** that can be solved using the graph from problem 5. Solve it and give it to another student to solve.

Problem Solving

Mixed Strategy Review

9. If you have 8 pairs of pants and 6 shirts, how many different outfits can you put together?

10. Together, 2 vans hold 21 people. One van holds twice as many people as the other. How many people can each van hold?

11. Elgin spends a total of $110 at the science store. Posters of Earth cost $5, and packages of notecards cost $25. If he bought exactly six items, how many of each did he buy?

12. How many triangles are in the figure?

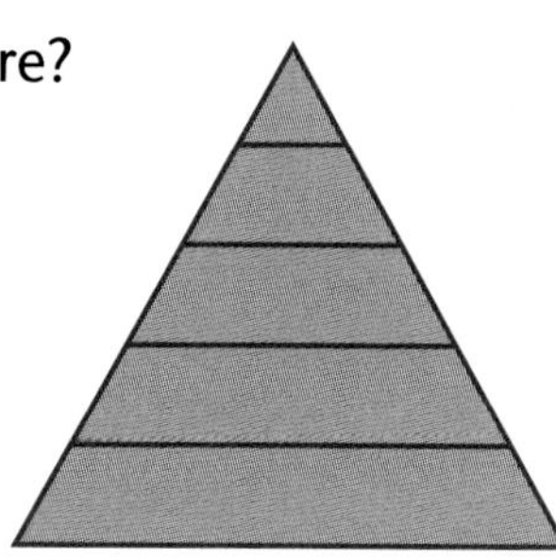

CHOOSE A STRATEGY
- Logical Reasoning
- Draw a Diagram
- Make a Graph
- Make a Table or List
- Find a Pattern
- Guess and Check
- Write an Equation
- Work Backward
- Solve a Simpler Problem
- Conduct an Experiment

Objective: Write and solve two-step equations.

10-12 Two-Step Equations

Algebra & functions

Learn

This camp area already has some camp sites around the lake. Now the park wants to add an equal number of sites to each of 30 acres. They want a total of 291 campsites. How many campsites will be on each acre?

Example

Write an equation to solve the problem: $30p + 21 = 291$.

Solve: $30p + 21 = 291$

1 First, undo the addition.

$30p + 21 = 291$
$30p + 21 - \mathbf{21} = 291 - \mathbf{21}$
$30p = 270$

2 Then undo the multiplication.

$30p = 270$
$30p \div \mathbf{30} = 270 \div \mathbf{30}$
$p = 9$

3 Check your answer by substituting 9 for p.

$30p + 21 = 291$
$30 \times 9 + 21 = 291$
$270 + 21 = 291$
$291 = 291$ ✓

There will be 9 campsites on each acre.

More Examples

A

$$\frac{t}{2} + 6 = 14$$
$$\frac{t}{2} + 6 - 6 = 14 - 6$$
$$\frac{t}{2} = 8$$
$$\frac{t}{2} \times 2 = 8 \times 2$$
$$t = 16$$

B

$$5m - 0.5 = 7$$
$$5m - 0.5 + 0.5 = 7 + 0.5$$
$$5m = 7.5$$
$$5m \div 5 = 7.5 \div 5$$
$$m = 1.5$$

C

$$3y - 5 = {}^{-}2$$
$$3y - 5 + 5 = {}^{-}2 + 5$$
$$3y = 3$$
$$3y \div 3 = 3 \div 3$$
$$y = 1$$

Try It

Solve.

1. $3y + 6 = 15$ **2.** $2f - 4 = 4$ **3.** $\frac{x}{3} + 1 = 2$ **4.** $\frac{z}{2} - 3 = 2$

Sum it Up Explain the steps involved in solving the equation $2x - 7 = 13$.

Practice

Solve.

5. $3f + 6 = 9$
6. $4z + 5 = 9$
7. $2 = 5s - 13$
8. $6b + 9 = 15$
9. $4h - 27 = 1$
10. $4 = 2a + 2$
11. $6t + 3 = 15$
12. $99 = 13d - 5$
13. $\frac{m}{2} - 3 = 7$
14. $\frac{v}{4} - 8 = 3$
15. $3 = \frac{w}{3} - 7$
16. $6.1 = 1.3 + 1.6r$
17. $7 + a = 18.4$
18. $12 - b = 3.6$
19. $c + 15 = 81$
20. $c + 15 - 3 = 75$
21. $2k - \frac{3}{4} = 7\frac{1}{4}$
22. $\frac{c}{2} - \frac{3}{8} = \frac{1}{8}$
★23. $2x + 4 = {}^{-}6$
★24. ${}^{-}1 = 4q - 5$

Problem Solving

25. It costs \$7 a night for a campsite. It also costs \$4 for each car. Carla and her friends have \$53 to spend on a campsite. If they have 1 car, what is the most number of nights they can camp?

26. A tent costs \$89.95. If Gerry buys two tents and pays with two one-hundred dollar bills, how much change should he receive?

27. The Lakeville Camp will provide 2 drinking fountains for every 5 campsites, plus 6 more by the boat launch. If there are 290 campsites, how many drinking fountains will there be?

28. **Music:** The song *Taps* is one of America's original camping songs. It was written by the Union Army during the Civil War in 1862. Write an expression to represent how long ago *Taps* was written. Tell what the variable represents.

29. **Create a problem** about camping that can be solved using the equation $12x + 4 = 100$.

★30. **Analyze:** Why wouldn't you divide first when solving $3x + 5 = 29$?

Spiral Review and Test Prep

Find the GCF for each pair of numbers.

31. 16 and 44
32. 10 and 30
33. 144 and 24
34. 8 and 11

Choose the correct answer.

35. During the first year that a campground opens, 200 people visit. If the number of visitors grows by 50 people each year, how many people will use the campground in the third year?
    - A. 200
    - B. 250
    - C. 300
    - D. 350

36. What is the value of the underlined digit? 4$\underline{6}$3,906,561
    - F. 60
    - G. 6,000,000
    - H. 60,000,000
    - J. Not Here

Objective: Apply algebra to analyze data and make decisions.

Problem Solving: Application

Decision Making

Which 2 projects should they do this spring?

The fifth-grade Save the Earth Committee is planning spring projects. They have a budget of $86.28. Together they have about 12 hours to devote to projects. The committee thought of four ideas.

Save the Earth Ideas

Option 1 **Tanya's Idea**

Buy and install 3 bird feeders.

Time: 4 hours to research, and 0.75 hours to install each bird feeder

RIVERS
RECYCLING CO.
Fee for Pick-Up of Recycled Paper:
$35.00
Bin Price
$5.00

Option 2 **Andrew's Idea**

Install paper-recycling containers.

Time: 7 hours to buy containers and place them in classrooms

Option 3 **Steve's Idea**

Encourage fifth-grade students to bring reusable lunch boxes instead of paper bags.

Time: 2 hours to buy lunch boxes and 6 hours to distribute them

Option 4 **Dena's Idea**

Encourage students to carpool to school.

Time: 2 hours to purchase materials, and 20 minutes to make one poster

Read for Understanding

1. How many bird feeders does Tanya want to install?
2. How much does one poster board cost?
3. What is the cost of a bird feeder?
4. How long will it take to complete Steve's project?
5. What is the cost to pick up recycling?
6. How long will it take to buy recycling containers and place them in classrooms?

Problem Solving

Make Decisions

7. How many bird feeders can Tanya buy and stay within the budget?
8. If the committee chooses Dena's and Andrew's projects, how much time will they take?
9. If there are 5 classrooms in the fifth grade, can Andrew complete his project within the budget?
10. What does Steve need to know before he can figure out how much money he needs to complete his project?
11. If all but $\frac{1}{10}$ of the 120 fifth-grade students use lunch boxes already, then how many lunch boxes will Steve need to buy?
12. Does Steve have enough money in the budget to buy a lunch box for every student who does not have one? How close to budget is he?
13. How much time will Dena's project take if they need to make 6 posters?
14. Dena decides to buy 12 sheets of posterboard. How much money will Dena need for her project?
15. Which 2 projects use nearly all the money?
16. How much would it cost for 6 poster boards and 3 bird feeders?
17. Does the committee have enough time to complete Andrew's and Steve's ideas?
18. Can the committee choose Steve and Tanya's ideas? Explain.
19. How many hours will it take to complete Tanya's project? Write an expression and solve it using the greatest number of bird feeders she can buy while staying within budget.
20. If the committee chooses Andrew's idea, will they have enough time and money for another project? If so, which one?

Your Decision!

What is your recommendation for which two projects the Save the Earth Committee should do this spring? Explain.

Objective: Apply algebra to investigate science concepts.

Problem Solving: Math and Science

How long can you make a string phone?

Have you ever tried listening to instructions from a person who is very far away? It can be very difficult to hear at such great distances.

In this activity you will build string phones and determine how long the phone can be and still send clear messages.

You Will Need

- **string**
- **scissors**
- **2 paper cups**
- **tape**
- **meterstick or tape measure**
- **candle or waxy crayon**

Hypothesize

Will it be easier to hear through a string phone that is 3 meters long or 15 meters long?

Safety

Be careful when handling scissors.

Procedure

1. Work with a partner.
2. Construct a string phone with a 15-meter piece of string. Poke a small hole in the bottom of each cup. Push the ends of the string through each hole and tape on the inside. Rub the candle or crayon down the length of the string.
3. Take turns sending your partner a message. Could you understand each other? Rate the sound quality (1 = perfect, 2 = good, 3 = OK, 4 = fair, 5 = terrible).
4. Rebuild the phone with 12 meters of string and send new messages.
5. Keep rebuilding the phone with a string that is 3 meters shorter each time.

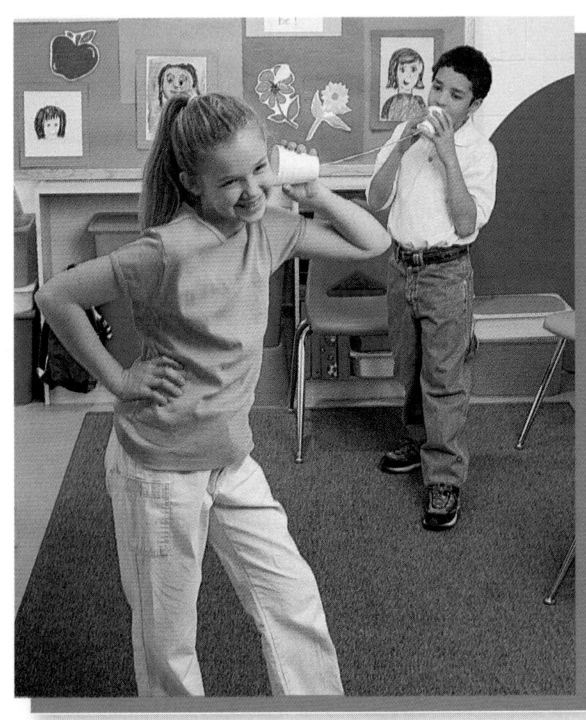

Data

Copy and complete the chart to record your observations.

Distance	Sound Quality
15 meters	
12 meters	
9 meters	
6 meters	
3 meters	

Conclude and Apply

- At what distance does the phone stop working?
- Was your hypothesis correct?
- Create a bar graph that compares string length and sound quality. Talk about how the graph looks and how it reflects the data.
- Let the center of the phone string represent the origin (0) of a number line. Draw the position of you and your partner for each phone.
- Use data from *Did You Know?* to explain the activity in terms of sound waves.

Did You Know?

Sound travels in waves shaped like a slinky. Any solid, liquid, or gas can carry the wave. In fact, sounds move faster as the material gets denser. In other words, sound moves faster through water than through air, and through rock faster than through water.

Going Further

1. Design and complete an activity that investigates which materials make the most useful string phones.
2. Design and complete an activity to discover which words can be best understood through a string phone.

Check Your Progress B

Solve. **(pages 454–463)**

1. $x + 8 = 12$
2. $d - 9 = 4$
3. $6 + g = 9$
4. $h + 4 = 6$
5. $5 - c = 3$
6. $z - 8 = 10$
7. $8 + b = 16$
8. $3 - w = 1$
9. $3m = 21$
10. $6 \times a = 42$
11. $12v = 96$
12. $f \div 4 = 22$
13. $12 \times t = 36$
14. $\frac{q}{5} = 7$
15. $k + 4 = 8$
16. $5r = 25$

Solve. **(pages 466–467)**

17. $8x + 9 = 25$
18. $2k - 9 = 5$
19. $13 = 6d + 1$
20. $\frac{q}{4} - 3 = 5$
21. $w + 0.8 = 2.1$
22. $a - 6.7 = 1.3$
23. $16.7 - f = 13.82$
24. $b + 14 = 32$
25. $t + 4 = 57$
26. $7 + c = 9.4$
27. $y - 1.2 = 7$
28. $22.16 - c = 12.32$

Solve. **(pages 454–467)**

29. The Boy Scouts are planting trees in an empty lot in the city. They have \$129.50. White oak trees cost \$25.90 each. How many trees can they buy? Write an equation and solve.

30. Admission to a campsite costs \$5 for each car plus \$3 for each person in the car. Write an equation and evaluate if there are 4 people in the car.
31. It rained 12.3 inches in January. It rained a total of 23.1 inches in January and February. How much did it rain in February? Write an equation and solve.
32. **Compare:** How are the processes used to solve the equations $5 + p = 100$ and $5q = 100$ alike? How are they different?
33. Explain how you can use a graph showing the relationship between Celsius and Fahrenheit temperatures to convert Fahrenheit temperatures to Celsius.

Additional activities at
www.mhschool.com/math

Extra Practice

Addition and Subtraction Expressions (pages 434–435)

Write an expression for each situation.

1. Andrea planted 8 more trees than Will. Will planted t trees. How many trees did Andrea plant?
2. Adam planted x maple trees to build a windbreak. They were too close together so he had to pull out 15 trees. How many trees are left?

Multiplication and Division Expressions (pages 436–437)

Evaluate each expression for the value given.

1. $3x$ for $x = 4$
2. $\frac{d}{7}$ for $d = 21$
3. $\frac{2}{3}m$ for $m = 18$
4. $3.5t$ for $t = 7$

Order of Operations (pages 438–439)

Simplify. Use the order of operations.

1. $30 - 3 \times 10$
2. $(25 + 8) \div 11$
3. $54 - 18 \div 3 + 10$
4. $(5^2 + 2) \div 9 - 2$
5. $(42 \div 7) + 2^3 \times 3$
6. $9.3 + (4 - 1^5) - 3.2$

Functions (pages 440–441)

Write an equation to describe each situation. Tell what each variable represents.

1. The cost to rent a recycling truck is \$30 plus \$15 per hour.
2. The time it takes to complete a recycling run is 1 hour to deliver the load plus 0.25 hour to collect from each house.

Graphing a Function (pages 442–445)

Write the coordinates for each point.

1. A
2. B
3. D
4. F
5. K
6. N

Name the point for the ordered pair.

7. (2, 1)
8. (6, 2)
9. (7, 5)
10. (9, 1)
11. (4, 3.5)
12. (11, 9)
13. A scientist walks from base camp at a rate of 2 miles per hour. Make a graph showing the relationship between the distance he has walked and the time he has walked.

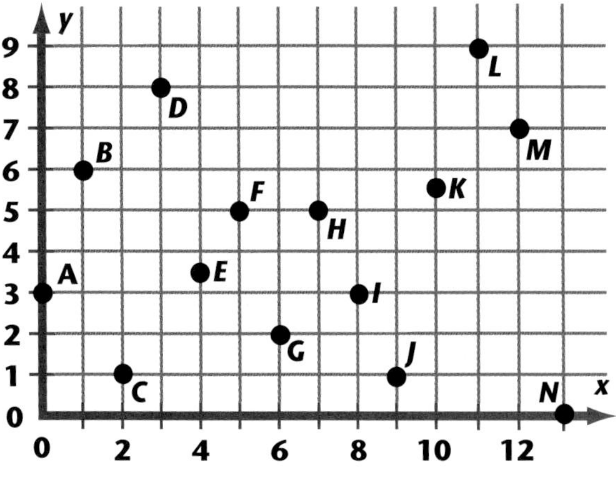

Extra Practice

Graph in Four Quadrants and Solve Problems (pages 446–449)

Give the coordinates of each point.

1. C 2. D 3. F 4. G 5. K

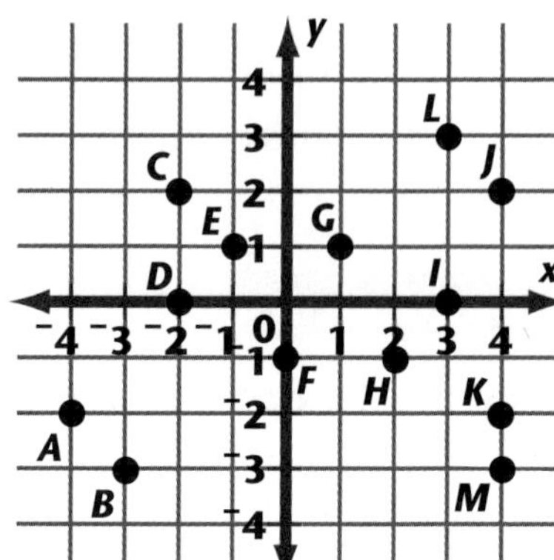

Name the point for each ordered pair.

6. $(4, 2)$ 7. $(^-4, ^-2)$ 8. $(^-1, 1)$ 9. $(2, ^-1)$ 10. $(^-3, ^-3)$

Solve.

11. The center of a storm is located at $(4, ^-3)$. What letter identifies this point?
12. Another storm is spotted at the point 3 units above point I. What are the coordinates of this point?
13. A storm's path can be described by the equation $y = x - 7$. Use the equation to graph the storm's path.

Problem Solving: Reading for Math Use Graphs to Identify Relationships (pages 450–451)

1. Tell a story about walking to the different places you are representing on the graph.

Distance at 5 mph

Distance in Miles

Time in Hours

Addition and Subtraction Equations (pages 456–459)

Solve. Check your answer.

1. $x + 7 = 19$
2. $t - 6 = 18$
3. $34 = k - 8$
4. $m + 1.6 = 4.8$
5. $z - 4\frac{2}{3} = 6\frac{1}{2}$
6. $a + 1\frac{1}{2} = 16$

Solve.

7. The annual rainfall in Atlanta is 48.61 inches. The annual rainfall in Los Angeles is 12.08 inches. How many more inches of rain are there each year in Atlanta than in Los Angeles? Write an equation and solve.
8. Mount Shasta received several inches of snow. The next day 6.7 inches of snow melted. By nightfall, there were 28.4 inches of snow. How much snow fell?

Extra Practice

Multiplication and Division Equations (pages 460–463)

Solve. Check each answer.

1. $5x = 20$
2. $7z = 21$
3. $w \div 4 = 8$
4. $2c = 108$
5. $t \div \frac{1}{2} = 36$
6. $12c = 120$
7. $\frac{b}{4} = 20$
8. $f \div 0.2 = 100$
9. A group of scientists will go out and collect insect specimens from 2,000 acres of rain forest. Each scientist can collect insects from 8 acres a day. How many scientists are needed to collect specimens from all 2,000 acres in one day?
10. It costs $62 a day for food and supplies for the scientists who are studying a redwood forest. How many days can the scientists stay in the rain forest if they have $500 to spend on food and supplies? Explain.

Problem Solving: Strategy Make a Graph (pages 464–465)

Solve

1. The relationship between the speed of travel and the distance traveled can be described by the equation $d = rt$, where d = distance traveled in miles, r = speed (or rate) of travel in miles an hour, and t = time traveled in hours. Graph this function when the speed of travel, r, is 40 miles per hour.
2. How far can you travel in 4 hours?
3. How long will it take to travel 120 miles?
4. Would you use the graph or the equation to find the distance traveled in 16.75 hours? Explain.

Two-Step Equations (pages 466–467)

Solve.

1. $2x + 7 = 25$
2. $4m - 3 = 29$
3. $15t + 18 = 123$
4. $5k - 2 = 93$
5. $\frac{s}{8} + 3 = 10$
6. $\frac{r}{9} - 6 = 12$
7. $45 = n \div 1.5 + 6$
8. $\frac{p}{4} - 18 = 25$
9. When 8 is added to three times a number the answer is 26. Find the number.
10. When 18 is subtracted from six times some number, the result is 24. Find the number.

Chapter Study Guide

Language and Math

Math Words

axis
coordinates
equation
evaluate
algebraic expression
function
inverse operations
ordered pair
origin
variable

Complete. Use a word from the list.

1. The pair of numbers that gives the location of a point on a graph is called a(n) ____ .
2. Mathematical operations that "undo" each other are ____.
3. The point on a graph where the vertical axis meets the horizontal axis is the ____.
4. A symbol used to represent a number is a(n) ____.
5. One of the two reference lines on a graph is a(n) ____.
6. A(n) ____ is a mathematical statement containing an equal sign.
7. A relationship in which one quantity depends on another is a(n) ____.

Skills and Applications

Use the order of operations. (pages 438–439)

Example

Evaluate $400 + (96 - 42) \times 10^3 \div (48 \div 12)$

Solution

$400 + 54 \times 10^3 \div 4 =$
$400 + 54 \times 1{,}000 \div 4 =$
$400 + 54{,}000 \div 4 =$
$400 + 13{,}500 =$
$13{,}900$

Evaluate.

8. $(8 \times 4) + 6^2 \div 4 - 40$
9. $4.3 \times 10^3 - (57 \div 3)$
10. $9.6 \times (4 + 2) - 12 \div 3$
11. $(448 - 387) \times (16 \div 4) + 3^6$

Solve problems with graphs and equations. (pages 440–441, 442–449)

Example

Patty discovered that only 7 kinds of plants in her garden are edible. How many plants in her garden are not edible?

Solution

$p - 7 = n$ where
p = plants growing in garden
n = plants not edible

Write an expression.

12. If the Sierra Club receives $65 per year from each member, how much money does it collect from members each year?
13. Danny sent 15 fewer letters by United States mail than by e-mail. If he sent 45 letters altogether, how many did he send by e-mail?

Graph points and functions in four quadrants. (pages 446–449)

Example

Find the ordered pair that describes the location of point A.

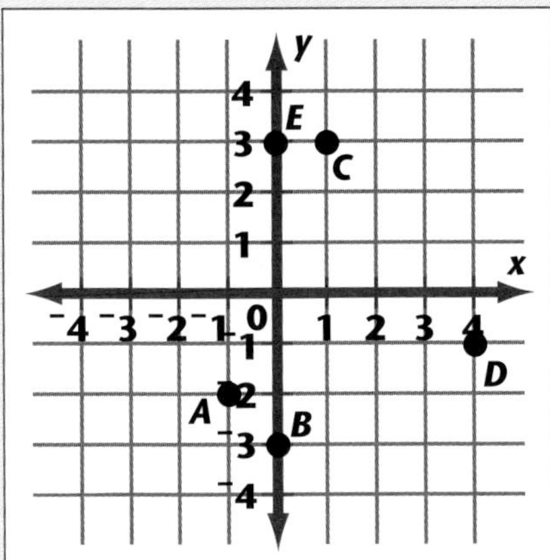

Solution

Point A is 1 unit to the left of the origin and 2 units below the origin. The ordered pair that describes point A is ($^-1$,$^-2$).

Solve.

14. Give the coordinates of point D.
15. Name the point for the ordered pair (0, $^-3$).
16. Graph the function $y = x + 2$.

Solve one and two step equations. (pages 454–463, 466–477)

Example

Solve: $x + 5 = 17$

Solution

$x + 5 - 5 = 17 - 5$

$x = 12$

Solve.

17. Hana and Michael planted 29 new trees in the park. Michael planted 14. How many trees did Hana plant? Write an equation and solve.

Solve each equation.

18. $x + 7 = 9$
19. $x - 7 = 15$

Example

Solve: $130b = 39{,}000$

Solution

$130b \div 130 = 39{,}000 \div 130$

$b = 300$

20. $q \div 9 = 5$
21. $19x = 76$
22. $3x + 14 = 20$
23. $4y - 10 = 6$
24. Cindy grew 21 pumpkins which turned out to be 3 times less than Dan's yield in his organic patch. How many pumpkins did Dan grow?
25. $5x = 15$

Study Guide

Chapter Test

Use the order of operations.

1. $6 + 7 \times 2$
2. $40 - (3 + 2^3) \times 2$
3. $4 + 15 \div 5 - 2$
4. $3^2 + 4 \times 6$

Write an expression for each situation.

5. Jana planted t tomato plants. She planted 6 more bean plants than tomato plants. How many bean plants did she plant?
6. Three times a number n, increased by 8.
7. Ahmad writes 3 pages of his essay in 1 hour. At the same rate, how many pages can he write in x hours?

Evaluate each expression for the value given.

8. $8 - 2x \div 2$ for $x = 4$
9. $1 + 4a$ for $a = 3$
10. $m + 12 \div 3$ for $m = 5$

Solve each equation.

11. $3 + x = 12$
12. $y - 7 = 15$
13. $2\frac{1}{2} + p = 5\frac{1}{2}$
14. $k - 6.5 = 8.5$
15. $2a = 14$
16. $m \div 3 = 9$
17. $3.5h = 7$
18. $\frac{r}{2} = 4$
19. $4b - 6 = 18$
20. $\frac{t}{2} + 8 = 10$
21. $150 = 4f - 10$
22. $2.5c - 7 = 3$

Use data from the graph for problems 23–25.

23. How much would you earn if you worked 8 hours?
24. If you earned $25.50, how many hours did you work?
25. About how many hours would you have to work to earn $35?

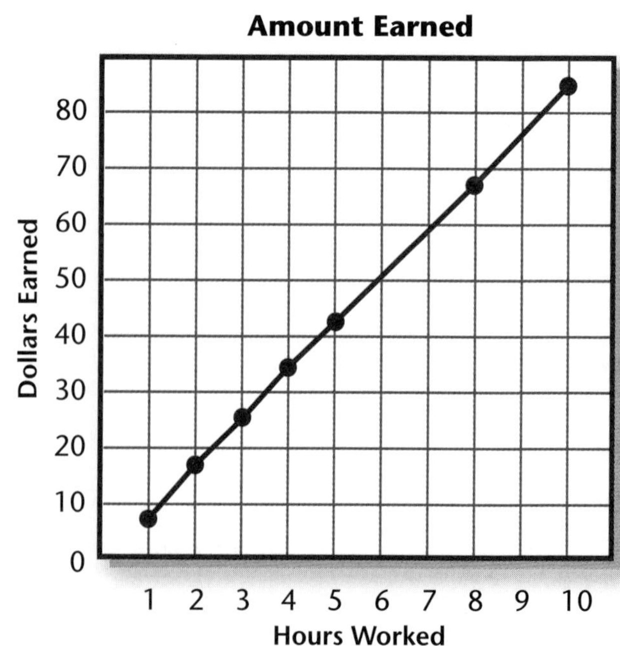

Performance Assessment

You are in charge of organizing the carpool to drive your group of 5 students to the Nature Center. You need to decide in what order to pick them up. You must stay on the road and not cut across the squares.

Name	Blocks East	Blocks North
Travis	1	2
Brent	5	7
Kari	2.5	4
Mary	6	9
Cameron	4	6

Plot and label the homes of the 5 students on a graph. Place your house at the origin.

Use data from the graph to complete the table.

Name	Location	Number of Blocks from Your House
Travis		
Brent		
Kari		
Mary		
Cameron		

In what order would you pick up the students, starting with the student who lives closest to you? Explain your reasoning.

A Good Answer

- has a complete and accurate graph.
- gives the name of the person and the ordered pair from the graph in order from closest to farthest from your house.
- shows your thinking in choosing an order.

You may want to save this work in your portfolio.

Assessment

Enrichment

Using the Distributive Property

The Distributive Property says that for all numbers a, b, and c, $a(b + c) = ab + ac$ and $(b + c)a = ba + ca$.

Example 1

If 4 members of the Earth Day committee each recruit x other students plus 1 of their teachers to join the committee, how many members of the committee will there be?

You can write this as:	Use the Distributive Property.
$4(x + 1)$, where x represents the number of students recruited	$4(x + 1) = 4x + (4 \times 1) = 4x + 4$

Example 2

Three fifth-grade students and 4 fourth-grade students each recruited the same number of members for the Earth Day committee. If they signed up 84 people, how many people did each person recruit?

You could express this as: $3x + 4x = 84$, where x represents the number of members each student recruited

Simplify using the distributive property.

$3x + 4x = 84$

$(3 + 4)x = 84$

$7x = 84$

2

Divide to solve.

$7x \div 7 = 84 \div 7$

$x = 12$

Check:
$3x + 4x = 84$
$3 \times 12 + 4 \times 12 = 84$
$36 + 48 = 84$
$84 = 84$

Solve. Show your work.

1. $(6 + 6)x = 60$
2. $(201 + 58)x = 1{,}036$
3. $9x + 5x = 42$
4. $29x + 2x = 341$
5. $75x + 2x = 5{,}929$
6. $40x + 10x = 10{,}040$
7. Ruby, Laura, Patty, and Tala each volunteer to clean up their neighborhood park several times each year. Jacy, Max, and Patrick also each volunteer for the same number of clean-ups. If the park is cleaned 42 times, how many times does each one clean the park?

Test-Taking Tips

When taking standarized tests, there may be problems where you must *create* your own solution instead of *choosing* the correct one.

Vinnie paid $24.55 for two new games and a CD. He knows that the CD cost $11.95, but he lost the receipt for the games. How much did each one cost? Write an equation and solve.

A good solution shows that you have understood the question and answered it fully. Show your work step by step.

- **What to do you know?** The total cost; the cost of the CD; the number of games.
- **What do you need to find?** The cost of each game.

Write an equation.

Let g = the cost of the games.
So, $2g + 11.95 = 24.55$

Solve.

$2g + 11.95 = 24.55$

$2g + 11.95 - 11.95 = 24.55 - 11.95$

$2g = 12.6$

$2g \div 2 = 12.6 \div 2$

$g = 6.3$

Each game cost $6.30.

Check for Success

Before turning in a test, go back one last time to check.

☑ I understood and answered the questions asked.

☑ I checked my work for errors.

☑ My answers make sense.

Practice

Write an equation and solve.

1. A receipt shows that Mary spent $6.62 at the supermarket. She knows that she bought pasta sauce for $3.65 and 3 boxes of pasta. How much did each box of pasta cost?

2. A group of friends divided 18 cookies. They gave their teacher 3 cookies and each student ate five cookies. How many friends were there?

3. Jane reads 42 pages of a 93-page book over the weekend. She reads an equal number of pages during the remaining 3 days before the book must be finished. How many pages does she read each day?

4. Four less than 3 times a number is 17. What is the number?

Spiral Review and Test Prep

Chapters 1–10

Choose the correct answer.

Number Sense

1. Compare.

   20.963 ● 20.0963

   A. <   C. >

   B. =   D. +

2. By how much is the value of 39,285 decreased if the 9 is changed to a 6?

   F. 3   H. 3,000

   G. 30   J. 6,000

3. Complete.

   $\frac{1}{4} = \frac{\blacksquare}{20}$

   A. 4   C. 12

   B. 5   D. 20

4. Write these fractions using the least common denominator. $\frac{1}{4}, \frac{5}{6}$

   F. $\frac{2}{6}, \frac{5}{6}$ H. $\frac{3}{12}, \frac{10}{12}$

   G. $\frac{5}{4}, \frac{6}{4}$ J. Not Here

Algebra and Functions

5. What is the value of s if $s - 10 = 14$?

   A. 4   C. 20

   B. 16   D. 24

6. Name the point for (3, 2).

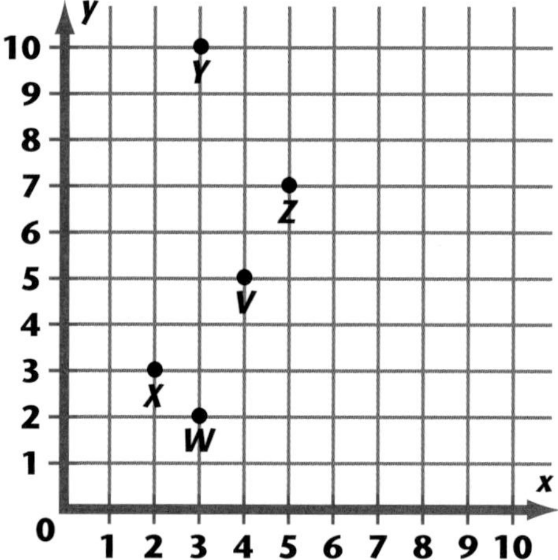

   F. W   H. Z

   G. X   J. Y

7. What is the value of t if $3t - 7 = 5$?

   A. $\frac{2}{3}$ C. 4

   B. $\frac{3}{2}$ D. 12

8. Kathy needs $60.49 to buy a skateboard. She has $23.00. If m represents how much more money she needs, which equation could you use to find the correct value of m?

   F. $23 + m = 60.49$

   G. $m + 60.49 = 23$

   H. $23 - m = 60.49$

   J. $60.49 + 23 = m$

Statistics, Data Analysis, and Probability

9. What is the range of the following numbers?

3, 17, 6, 19, 2, 21, 5, 17

A. 19 **C.** 16
B. 17 **D.** 2

10. How many students went to the movies and to the state fair?

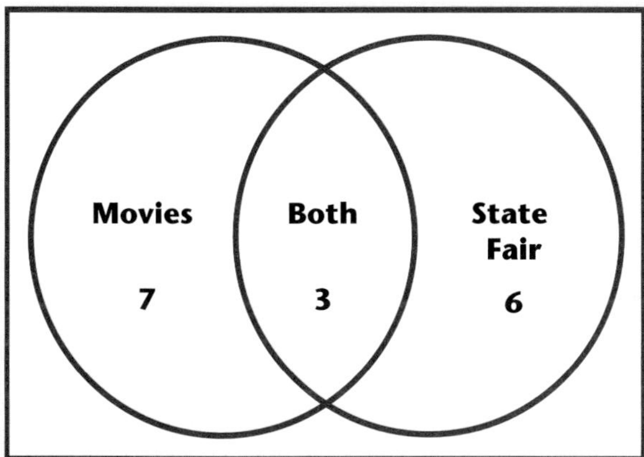

F. 10 **H.** 7
G. 9 **J.** 3

11. What is the mode of the following numbers?

3, 7, 8, 3, 9, 10, 3, 8, 7, 11, 3, 7, 8, 12

A. 3 **C.** 8
B. 7 **D.** Not Here

12. Tanya's times in her last 3 races are 7.1 minutes, 8.2 minutes, and 7.8 minutes. What is her mean time for the 3 races?

F. 7.1 minutes **H.** 7.7 minutes
G. 7.175 minutes **J.** 7.8 minutes

Mathematical Reasoning

13. Garrett has saved $125 to go to soccer camp. He will save $12 more each week. How much will he have saved at the end of 8 weeks?

A. $221 **C.** $333
B. $296 **D.** Not Here

14. Lena worked 20 hours last week. She makes $6 an hour. If x represents how much money she earned last week, which equation represents how much she earned?

F. $20 \times x = 6$ **H.** $\frac{6}{x} = 20$
G. $20 \times 6 = x$ **J.** $6 + x = 20$

15. Use the graph to find the approximate distance traveled in 9 hours.

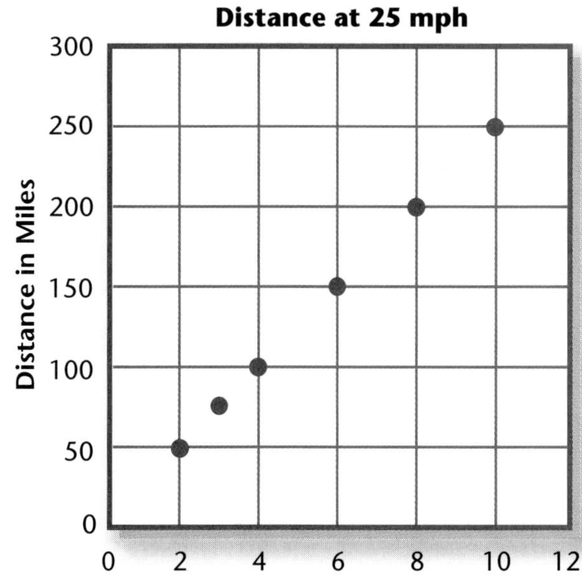

A. 20 miles **C.** 225 miles
B. 90 miles **D.** 250 miles

16. Sophia has 2 measuring cups – 1 cup and $\frac{3}{4}$ cup. How can she measure exactly $\frac{1}{4}$ cup of water using the measuring cups she has? Explain.

Spiral Review and Test Prep

CHAPTER 11 Geometry

Theme: Art and Design

- French painter Auguste Herbin made this oil painting, *Composition on the Word "Vie," 2,* in 1950. What kinds of lines, angles, and geometric figures did Herbin include in the painting?

What You Will Learn

In this chapter you will learn how to
- measure, draw, and classify angles.
- name and describe geometric figures.
- identify similar figures and transformations.
- find the unknown angles of a figure.
- use strategies to solve problems.

Additional activities at
www.mhschool.com/math

Objective: Describe and name points, lines, line segments, endpoints, and rays. Classify polygons.

Basic Geometric Ideas

Learn

Math Words
- **point**
- **line segment**
- **endpoint**
- **line**
- **ray**
- **open figure**
- **closed figure**
- **polygon**

Kenneth Snelson built this sculpture, *Free Ride Home,* with aluminum and steel. The wires that hold the structure together are line segments pushing out in different directions. Many geometric shapes and designs can be created by placing line segments at specific points in space.

Example 1

A B C

A **point** is an exact location in space. A, B, and C are points.

A **line segment** is a part of a line that connects two **endpoints**. $\overline{AC}$ is a line segment with endpoints A and C.

A **line** is a set of points made into a straight path that goes forever in both directions. $\overleftrightarrow{AB}$ is a line. The arrows indicate that it extends in both directions without end.

A **ray** is a part of a line that has one endpoint and continues in one direction without end. $\overrightarrow{BA}$ is a ray with an endpoint at B. The arrow indicates which end of the ray goes on.

Example 2

A vertical line runs straight up and down. A horizontal line runs straight across. Congruent line segments have the same length.

These figures are open. They start and stop in different places.

These figures are closed. They start and stop in the same place.

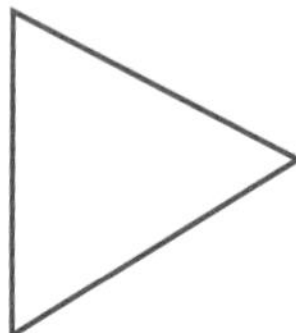

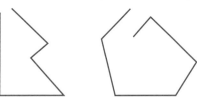

Example 3

A **polygon** is a closed figure made up of line segments that do not cross each other. It can be drawn without lifting up your pencil.

The point where two sides meet is a vertex. The plural of vertex is vertices.

Polygons are classified by the number of sides and vertices they have.

3 sides and 3 vertices	4 sides and 4 vertices	5 sides and 5 vertices	6 sides and 6 vertices	8 sides and 8 vertices
	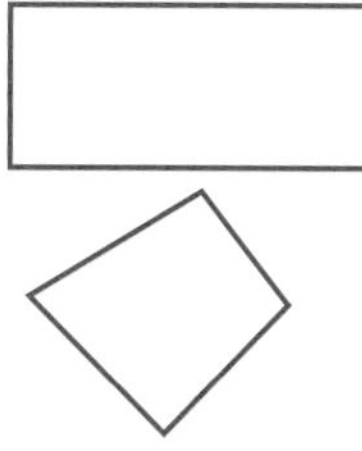	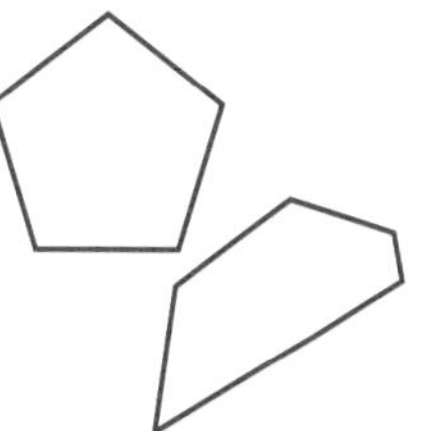	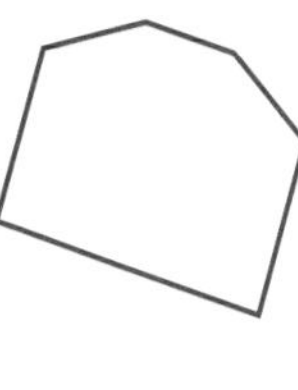	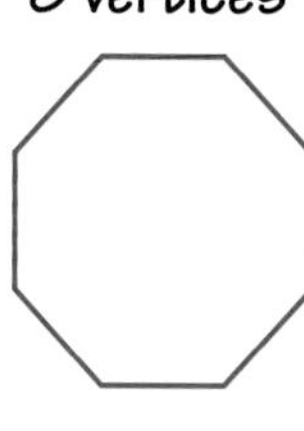
triangles	quadrilaterals	pentagons	hexagon	octagon

These are not polygons.

Example 4

A diagonal of a polygon is a special kind of line segment.

It is not a side of the figure, but connects two of the vertices of the polygon.

quadrilateral	pentagon	hexagon	octagon
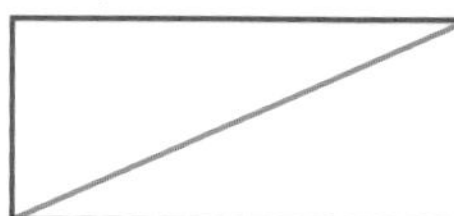	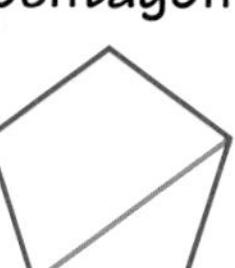	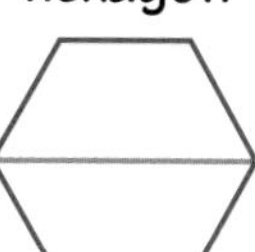	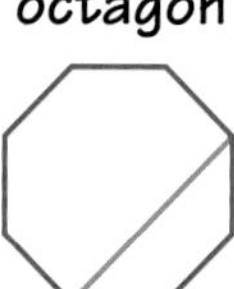

Try It **Identify the figure. Then name it using symbols.**

1. P
2. E F
3. Y Z
4. A B

How are lines, rays, and line segments alike? How are they different?

Practice

Identify the figure. Then name it using symbols.

5. A B

6. E F

7. Q

8. X Y

Use data from the diagram for problems 9–12.

9. Name all the points.
10. Name a ray with endpoint O.
11. Name a line segment.
12. Name a line.

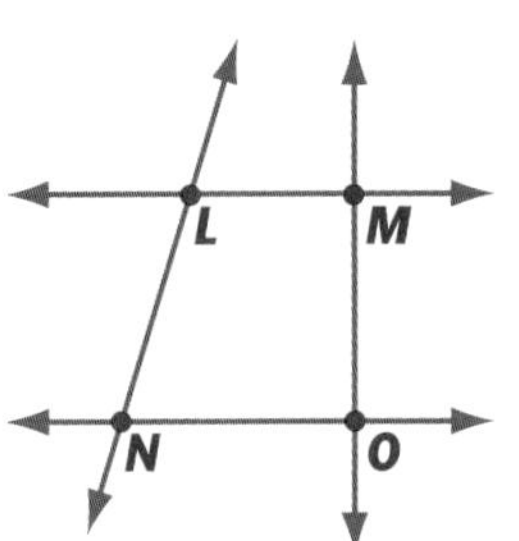

Tell whether or not line segments are congruent. Use a ruler to measure.

13.

14.

15.

Write whether or not the figure is a polygon. If not, explain why.

16. 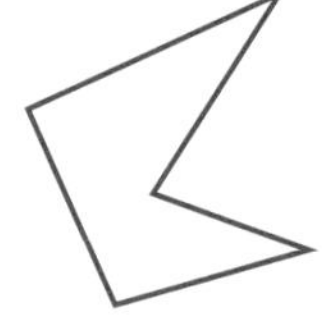

17. 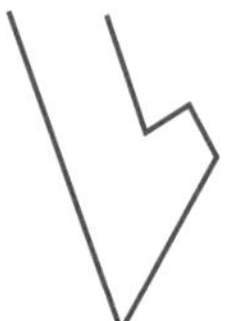

18. 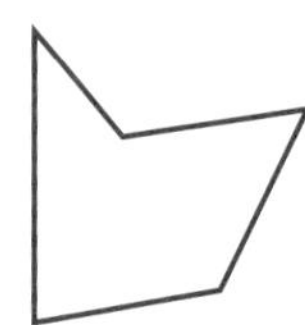

19. 

Draw and name the polygons.

20. 3 sides

21. 5 vertices

22. 4 sides

23. 6 vertices

Describe the similarities and differences between the figures.

★ 24. 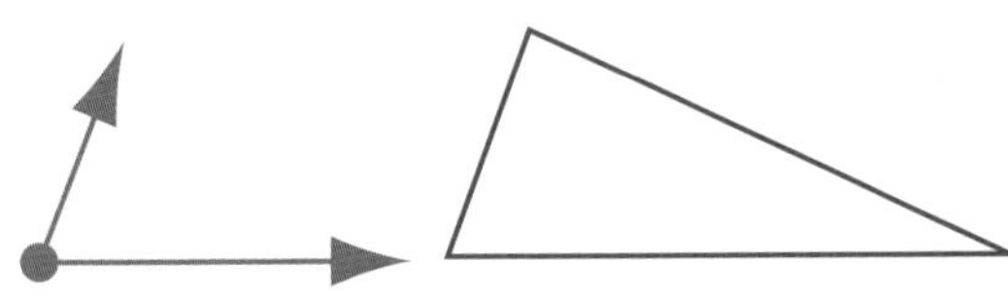

★ 25.  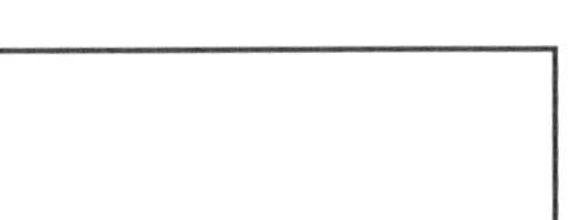

26. 

Here's how Conner drew a hexagon. Tell what mistake he made. Explain how to correct it.

Problem Solving

Use Pablo Picasso's *The Studio* for problems 27–29.

27. Sketch an open figure and a closed figure that can be found in the painting.

28. How many triangles are there?

29. The actual painting measures 231.2 cm across. A reprint measures 8 cm across. How many times greater is the actual length in the painting than in the reprint?

Use the picture of the stained glass window for problems 30–33.

30. **Social Studies:** The oldest glass objects were found in Egypt and Mesopotamia. They date from around 2000 B.C. Name the types of polygons found in the glass window.

31. What fraction of the window panes are triangles?

32. There are 31 panes of glass in the window. How many panes of glass are needed to make 10 of these windows?

33. **Create a problem** based on the stained glass window.

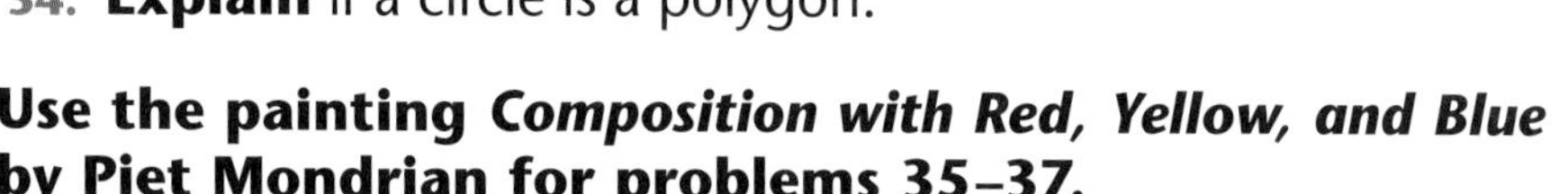

34. **Explain** if a circle is a polygon.

Use the painting *Composition with Red, Yellow, and Blue* by Piet Mondrian for problems 35–37.

35. Are there any congruent line segments in the painting? Use a ruler to measure.

36. This painting has a length of 92.4 cm and a width of 73.7 cm. What is the perimeter?

37. Mondrian was born in 1872 and made this painting in 1929. How old was he when he created this work of art?

★ 38. **Social Studies:** Look at a map of the United States. Are there any states with borders made entirely of line segments? Which ones?

Spiral Review and Test Prep

Solve for x.

39. $x + 8 = 10$ 40. $x \div 4 = 4$ 41. $31 + 4x = 39$ 42. $3x - 7 = 8$

Choose the correct answer.

43. Two prime numbers total 7. What numbers are they?
   A. 1 and 7
   B. 2 and 5
   C. 3 and 4
   D. Not Here

44. How many minutes is 450 seconds?
   F. 6 minutes
   G. $6\frac{1}{2}$ minutes
   H. 7 minutes
   J. $7\frac{1}{2}$ minutes

Objective: Measure and classify angles.

11·2 Measure and Classify Angles

Learn

This abstract painting called *Victory Over the Sun* by Russian painter El Lissitzky has many angles. Some look narrow and others look wide. How can you measure and classify the angles in this painting?

Math Words

angle a figure formed by two rays or line segments with the same endpoint

side the part of an angle formed by a ray

vertex the common point of the two rays of an angle

degree the unit for measuring angles

intersecting lines lines that meet or cross at a common point

perpendicular lines intersecting lines that cross each other at right angles

parallel lines lines (in the same plane) that never intersect

plane a flat surface that extends forever

Example 1

Name an **angle** by its **sides** or by its **vertex**.

This angle is called $\angle Q$ or $\angle PQR$ or $\angle RQP$. Notice that the vertex is always written in the middle.

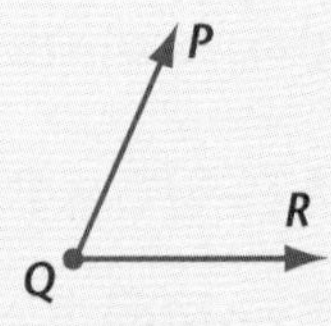

You can measure an angle by using a protractor, a tool used to measure and draw angles. Angles are measured in **degrees** (°).

1. Put the hole of the protractor on the vertex of the angle.
2. Align the 0-degree mark with one side of the angle.
3. Read the measure by counting from 0 to the other side of the angle.

The measure of $\angle Q$ is 65 degrees.

Example 2

You can classify any angle by its measure.

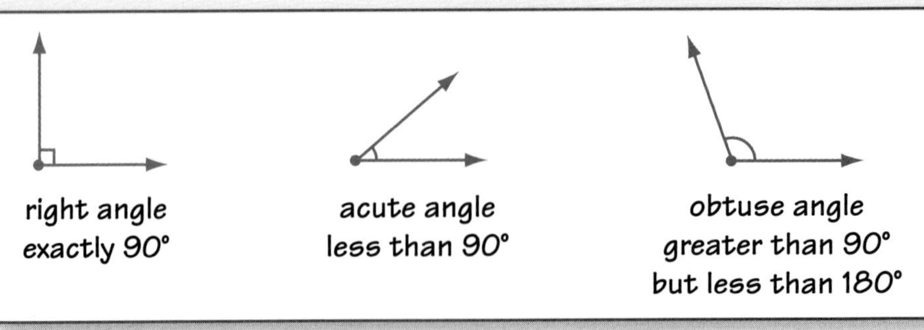

Since the measure of $\angle Q$ is 65 degrees, it is an acute angle.

William Johnson painted *Jitterbugs (IV)* to show people doing that popular dance. The angles in the painting help show this movement. How can you draw a copy of the 120-degree angle formed by the green and yellow shapes on the left side of the picture?

Example 3

You can use a straightedge and a protractor to draw angles of any measure.

Draw a 120-degree angle.

Use the straightedge to draw a line segment and label it *AB*.

Put the protractor so that the center rests on top of point *B*.

Mark a point at 120 degrees. Label it *C*.

Draw the line segment BC.

Example 4

Lines can be classified by how or whether they cross each other.

Intersecting lines cross each other.

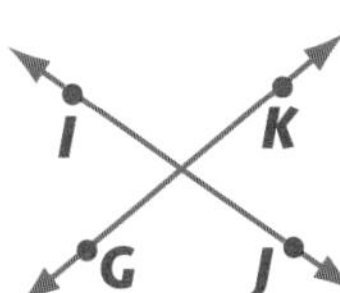

Read: $\overleftrightarrow{GK}$ intersects $\overleftrightarrow{IJ}$

Perpendicular lines cross at right angles.

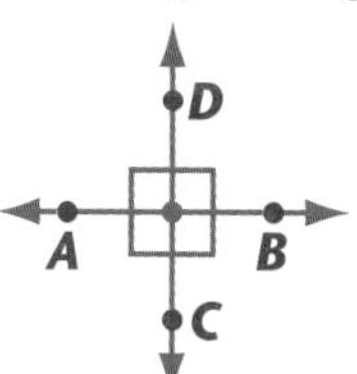

Read: $\overleftrightarrow{AB}$ is perpendicular to $\overleftrightarrow{CD}$

Write: $\overleftrightarrow{AB} \perp \overleftrightarrow{CD}$

Parallel lines are lines in the same plane that never intersect.

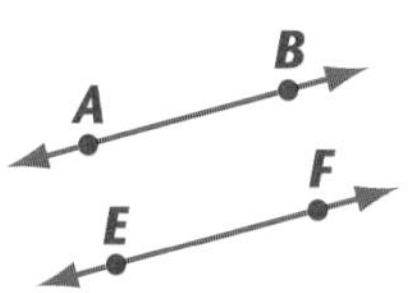

Read: $\overleftrightarrow{AB}$ is parallel to $\overleftrightarrow{EF}$

Write: $\overleftrightarrow{AB} \parallel \overleftrightarrow{EF}$

Try It **Use a protractor to measure each angle. Classify the angle as acute, right, or obtuse.**

1. 

2.

3. 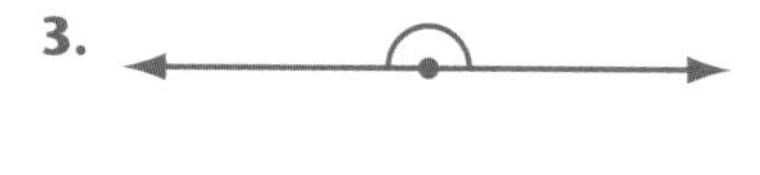

4. 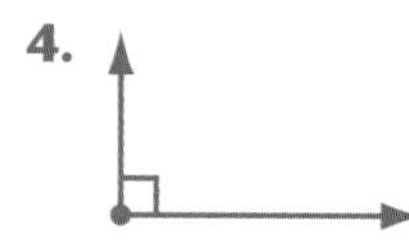

Define acute, right, and obtuse angle. How are they alike? How are they different?

Practice

Use a protractor to measure each angle. Classify the angle as acute, right, or obtuse.

5.
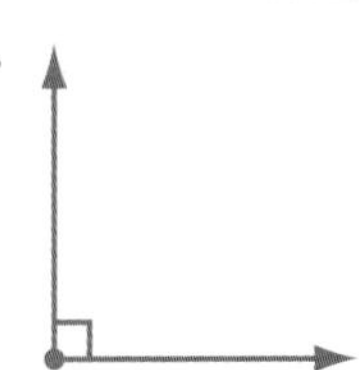

6.
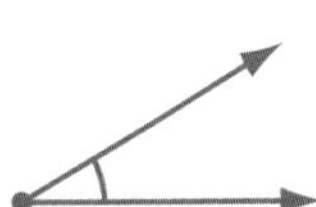

7.
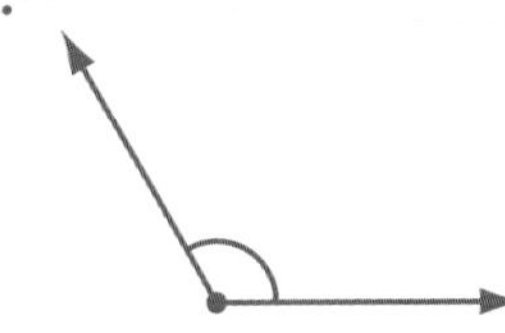

8.
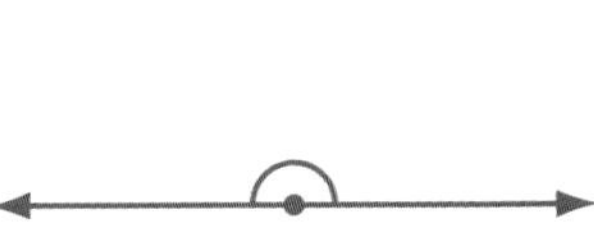

Name the pair of lines as intersecting, parallel, or perpendicular.

9.

10.

11.
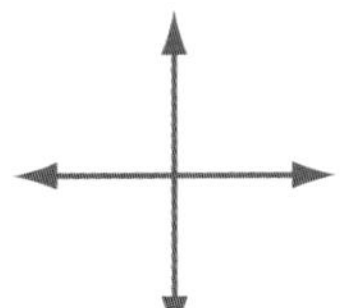

12.
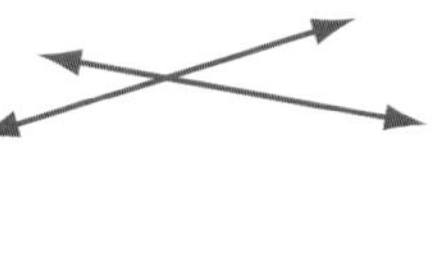

Find the measure of each angle in the diagram. Classify it as acute, right, or obtuse.

13. $\angle TUV$ **14.** $\angle XYV$ **15.** $\angle VYZ$

16. $\angle TUX$ **17.** $\angle UTV$

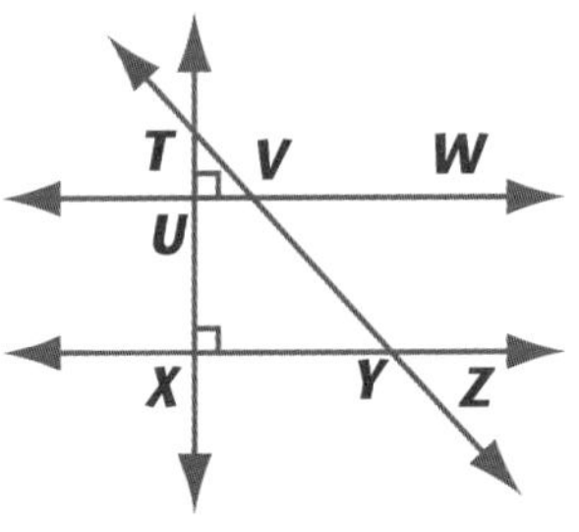

Use a protractor to draw an angle with the given measure.

18. 60 degrees **19.** 45 degrees **20.** 130 degrees **21.** 90 degrees **22.** 10 degrees

Draw the figure.

23. right angle XYZ **24.** obtuse angle JKL **25.** acute angle ABC

26. $\overleftrightarrow{RT} \perp \overleftrightarrow{MQ}$ **27.** $\overleftrightarrow{UV} \parallel \overleftrightarrow{XY}$ **28.** $\overleftrightarrow{CD}$ intersecting $\overleftrightarrow{FG}$

29.

Here's how Emma drew a 30-degree angle. Tell what mistake she made. Explain how to correct it.

Problem Solving

30. Many old clocks have been carved by artists. When these clocks read 2 o'clock, an acute angle of 60 degrees is formed. Name at least one other time of day when the hands form this angle.

31. **Analyze:** Can two obtuse angles be placed together to form a 179-degree angle? Why or why not?

Use the painting *Covenant* by Barnett Newman for problems 32–34.

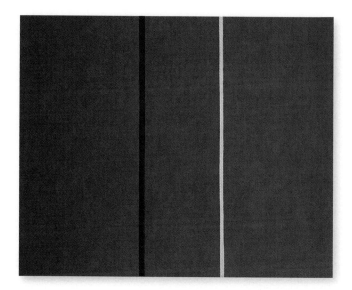

32. Describe the lines in the painting. Use words like perpendicular, parallel, horizontal, and vertical.

33. Describe the line segments that form the outside edges of the painting.

★34. The painting measures 152.4 centimeters across. If the center section takes up about $\frac{1}{4}$ of the painting, about how wide is it?

Use data from *Did You Know?* for problems 35–36.

35. Classify the angle formed by the escalator and the floor below it.

36. What is the measure of the angle formed by the escalator and the floor in front of the escalator?

★37. **Collect Data:** Examine different pieces of furniture. Collect data on the number and kind of angles you find in each piece. What generalizations can you draw about which kind of angles are used most?

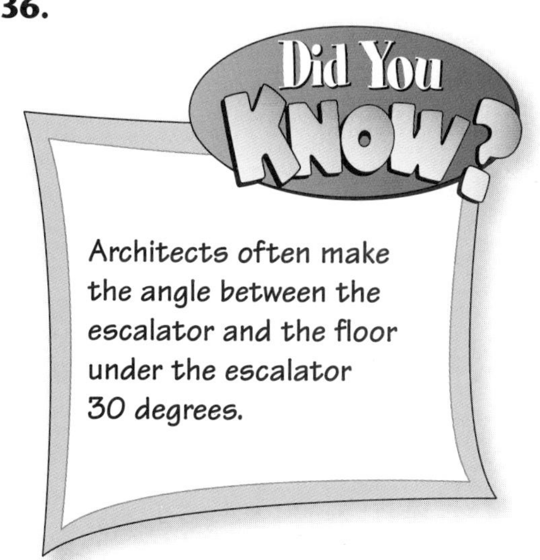

Spiral Review and Test Prep

38. 5,034 × 42
39. 79 × 547
40. 731 ÷ 43
41. 225 ÷ 15

Choose the correct answer.

42. Bob collects information on his friends' favorite colors and shapes. Which graph would best display the data?
    A. Line graph
    B. Pictograph
    C. Histogram
    D. Double bar graph

43. Find the missing number.
    30 × 87 = (30 × 80) + (30 × ■)
    F. 87
    G. 70
    H. 30
    J. 7

Extra Practice, page 527

Objective: Classify triangles. Use the fact that the sum of the measures of the angles of a triangle is 180 degrees to solve problems.

Triangles

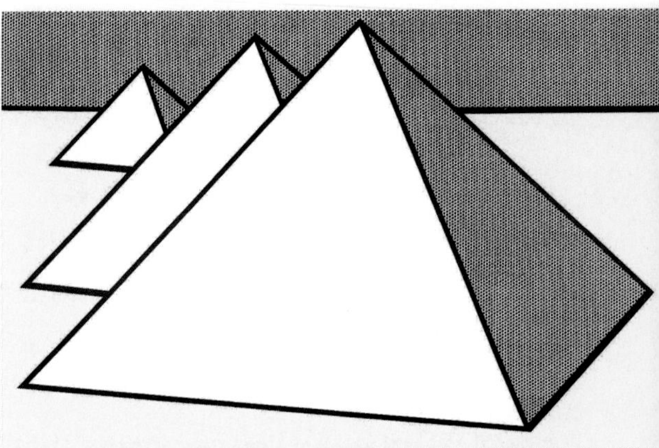

Learn

Pop artist Roy Lichtenstein created the pyramids in his 1969 artwork, *The Great Pyramid,* with 3-sided polygons called triangles. What kind of triangle is the largest one in the front of the painting?

Math Words

equilateral triangle a triangle with 3 congruent sides

isosceles triangle a triangle with at least 2 sides the same length

scalene triangle a triangle with no congruent sides

right triangle a triangle with 1 right angle

acute triangle a triangle with 3 acute angles

obtuse triangle a triangle with 1 obtuse angle

Example 1

You can identify triangles by the lengths of their sides.

equilateral triangle

3 sides the same length

isosceles triangle

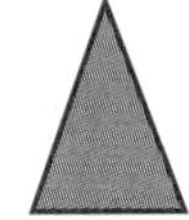

at least 2 sides the same length

scalene triangle

no sides the same length

You can also classify triangles by the number and kind of angles.

right triangle

1 right angle

acute triangle

3 acute angles

obtuse triangle

1 obtuse angle

It is an acute, scalene triangle.

More Examples

A triangle can be classified by both the lengths of the sides and the angles.

A

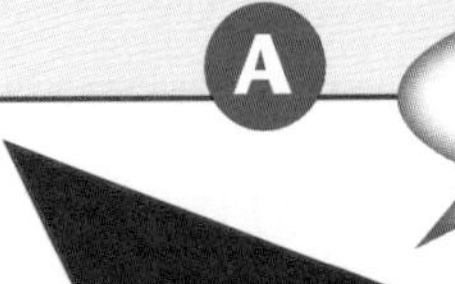

Think: This triangle has no congruent sides and 1 obtuse angle.

an obtuse scalene triangle

B

Think: This triangle has 2 congruent sides and 1 right angle.

an isosceles right triangle

Auguste Herbin's *Impasse* contains 11 triangles (can you find them all?). What is the sum of the measures of the angles of a triangle? Does changing the size or shape of a triangle change the sum of its angles?

Example 2

1. Use ruler, protractor, paper, and scissors to cut an acute, right, and obtuse triangle.

2. Measure the angles of the right triangle. Add them together. What is the sum?

3. Repeat with the acute and isosceles triangles. Is the sum of the measures of the angles the same?

The sum of the measures of the angles of any triangle is always 180 degrees, no matter what the shape or size.

If one angle of a triangle is 30 degrees and another angle is 100 degrees, what is the measure of the unknown angle?

Example 3

You can use the fact that all triangles have 180 degrees to find the measure of an unknown angle.

$$\begin{aligned} 30^\circ + 100^\circ + n &= 180^\circ \\ 130^\circ + n &= 180^\circ \\ 130^\circ - 130^\circ + n &= 180^\circ - 130^\circ \\ n &= 50^\circ \end{aligned}$$

The unknown angle measures 50 degrees.

Try It **Classify each triangle as equilateral, isosceles, or scalene and right, acute, or obtuse. Write the sum of the measures of the angles for each one.**

1. 

2. 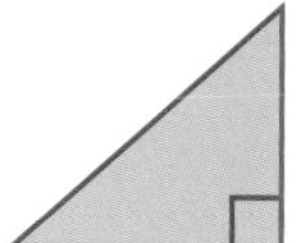

3. 

4. 

Sum it Up! Explain how you can identify and classify a triangle.

Practice

Classify each triangle as equilateral, isosceles, or scalene and right, acute, or obtuse.

5. 

6. 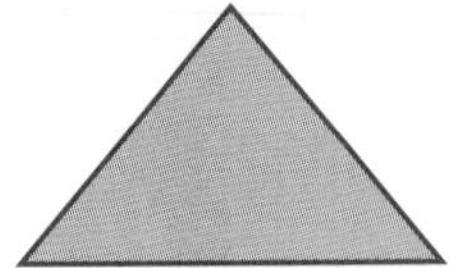

7. 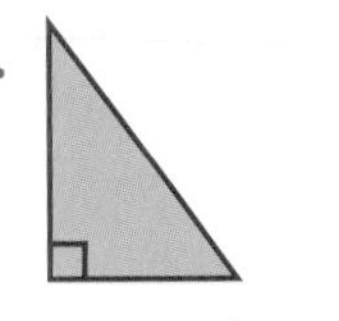

8. 

9. 

10. 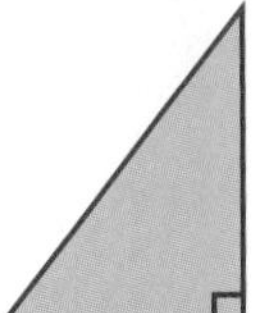

11. 

12. 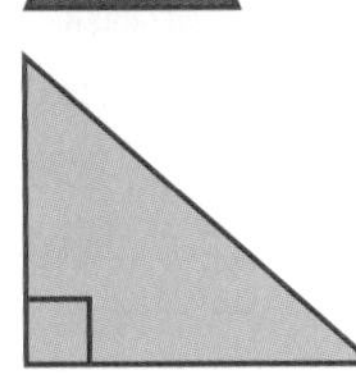

Use a protractor to draw a triangle with the given measure. Then classify the triangle.

13. all angles less than 90 degrees, no congruent sides
14. one right angle, two sides congruent
15. all sides congruent and all angles equal
16. one right angle, no sides congruent
17. one angle greater than 90 degrees, two sides congruent
18. one 90 degree angle, two sides congruent

Name the type of triangle described in each statement.

★19. One angle is greater than 90 degrees and two of the sides are congruent.

★20. All the sides are congruent.

★21. One angle is 90 degrees and none of the sides are congruent.

Find the measure of the unknown angle.

22. 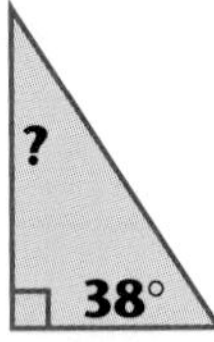

23. 20° 73° ?

24. 

25. 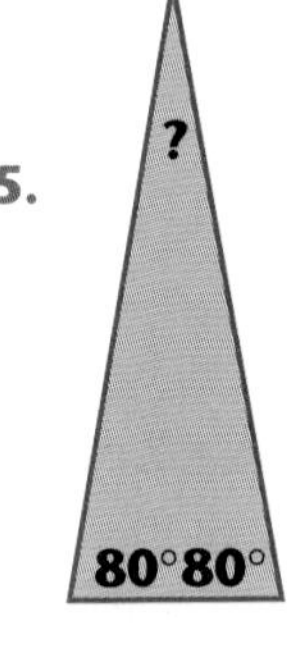

26. 

Here's how Bobbi-Jo drew an acute isosceles triangle. Tell what mistake she made. Explain how to correct it.

Problem Solving

Use the painting *Sailboats* by Lyonel Feininger for problems 27–28.

27. Find the black triangle labeled *X 54.* Classify this triangle.

28. Choose three other triangles in the painting and classify them.

29. **Analyze:** Are all equilateral triangles isosceles triangles? Explain.

30. What is the sum of the acute angles in a right triangle?

31. **Logical Reasoning:** Can a triangle be both right and obtuse? Explain why or why not.

32. A student says, "The sum of the measure of the angles of large triangles is greater than that of small ones." Did the student make an error? Explain.

Use data from the chart for problems 33–35.

PYRAMID
Π-ΡΑΜΙΔ

33. **Language Arts:** The English alphabet developed from the ancient Greek alphabet. Many of our letters, therefore, look similar to classical Greek ones. Look at the word *pyramid* written with Greek letters. Which letters include a triangle?

34. Is the Greek letter *A* a polygon? Is the letter *D*? Explain.

35. Which Greek letters are made from parallel and perpendicular lines?

Spiral Review and Test Prep

Find the GCF for each pair of numbers.

36. 8 and 32
37. 25 and 105
38. 14 and 42
39. 24 and 60

Choose the correct answer.

40. Find the mean of these numbers: 34, 21, 18, and 18.
    - A. 18
    - B. 91
    - C. 21
    - D. Not Here

41. What is the value of 5 quarters, 3 dimes, and 3 nickels?
    - F. \$5.33
    - G. \$4.55
    - H. \$1.70
    - J. \$0.56

Extra Practice, page 527

Objective: Classify quadrilaterals. Use the fact that the sum of the measures of the angles of a quadrilateral is 360 degrees to solve problems.

Quadrilaterals

Learn

Jean Leppien created this painting by including 4-sided shapes of various sizes and color. What types of quadrilaterals can be found in this work of art?

Math Words

parallelogram a quadrilateral with opposite sides that are parallel

trapezoid a quadrilateral with exactly one pair of parallel sides

rectangle a parallelogram with four right angles

rhombus a parallelogram with four congruent sides

square a rectangle with four congruent sides

Example 1

A quadrilateral is a 4-sided polygon.

Quadrilaterals

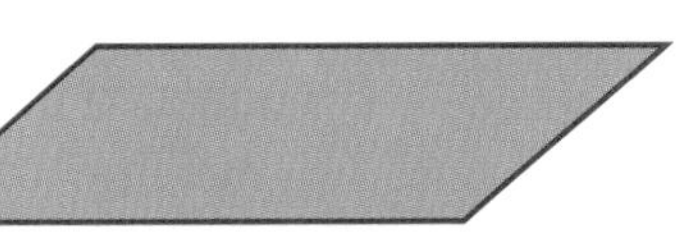

parallelogram
A quadrilateral with opposite sides that are congruent and opposite sides that are parallel

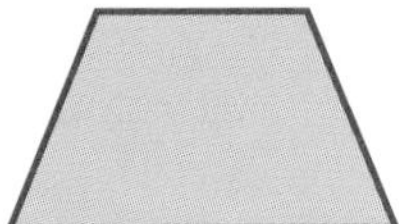

trapezoid
A quadrilateral with exactly 1 pair of parallel sides

rectangle
A parallelogram with four right angles

rhombus
A parallelogram with all sides the same length

square
A rectangle with all sides the same length

Every rhombus, rectangle, and square is a parallelogram. Every square is a rectangle.

The Leppien painting includes trapezoids, parallelograms, and rhombuses.

In Vincent Van Gogh's painting *The Artist's Bedroom,* the shape of the bed and the small table in the corner are both quadrilaterals. What is the sum of the measures of the angles of each quadrilateral?

Example 2

Find the sum of the measures of the angles of a quadrilateral.

1. Use a ruler to draw a rectangle.
2. Draw a diagonal. You now have 2 triangles.
3. Repeat with a square, trapezoid, and parallelogram.

Since two triangles are formed when you divide any quadrilateral, the sum of the measures of the angles is $180° + 180° = 360°$.

The sum of the measures of the angles of any quadrilateral is always 360 degrees, no matter what the shape or size.

Example 3

You can use the fact that all quadrilaterals have 360 degrees to find the measure of an unknown angle.

Find the measure of the unknown angle if the known angles are 70°, 120°, and 90°.

$$
\begin{aligned}
70° + 120° + 90° + n &= 360° \\
280° + n &= 360° \\
280° - 280° + n &= 360° - 280° \\
n &= 80°
\end{aligned}
$$

The unknown angle measures 80 degrees.

Classify each quadrilateral as many ways as possible. Write the sum of the measures of the angles for each one.

1. 

2. 

3. 

4. 

Sum it Up Explain why a trapezoid is not a parallelogram.

Practice

Classify each quadrilateral as many ways as possible. Write the sum of the measures of the angles for each one.

5. 

6.

7. 

8.

Algebra & functions

Find the measure of the unknown angle.

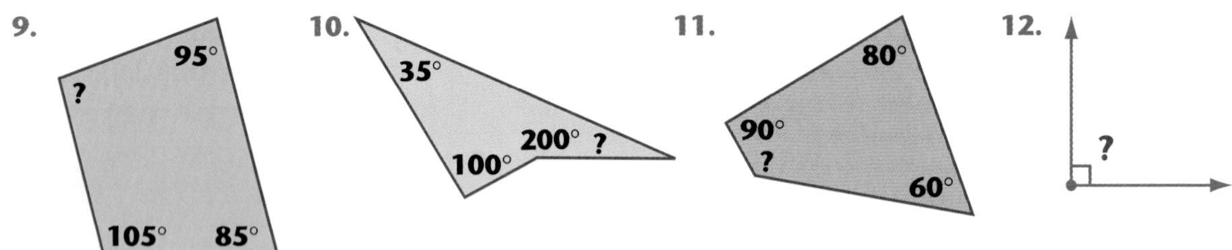

Write *true* or *false*.

13. A trapezoid may have two right angles.

14. All parallelograms are rhombuses.

15. All squares are rectangles.

16. All trapezoids are parallelograms.

17. All quadrilaterals have opposite sides that are parallel.

18. All rectangles are squares.

Draw each quadrilateral with a ruler and protractor. Tell what kind of quadrilateral you drew.

★19. 4 right angles

★20. a parallelogram with 4 congruent sides

★21. at least 2 sides are parallel

22.

Here's how Brittany found the measure of the unknown angle in a trapezoid. Tell what mistake she made. Explain how to correct it.

Problem Solving

Use the Yves Klein painting *Blue Sponge Relief* for problems 23–24.

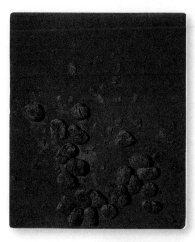

23. Use a ruler to measure the lengths of the sides of the painting. Name the quadrilateral in as many ways as you can. Write the sum of the measure of the angles.

★24. Without measuring, calculate the measure of each angle in the painting.

Use Theo van Doesburg's *Simultaneous Counter-Composition* for problems 25–26.

25. Identify all of the quadrilaterals in this painting.

26. **Create a problem** based on the van Doesburg painting. Give the problem to another student to solve.

★27. **Analyze:** When you draw two diagonals in a pentagon from the same vertex, 3 triangles are formed. What does this suggest about the sum of the measure of the angles in a pentagon?

Use the picture for problems 28–29.

28. **Health:** The Food Guide Pyramid is a visual way to show how to build a healthy diet. How many polygons make up the pyramid? how many quadrilaterals?

29. Which food group is not in a quadrilateral?

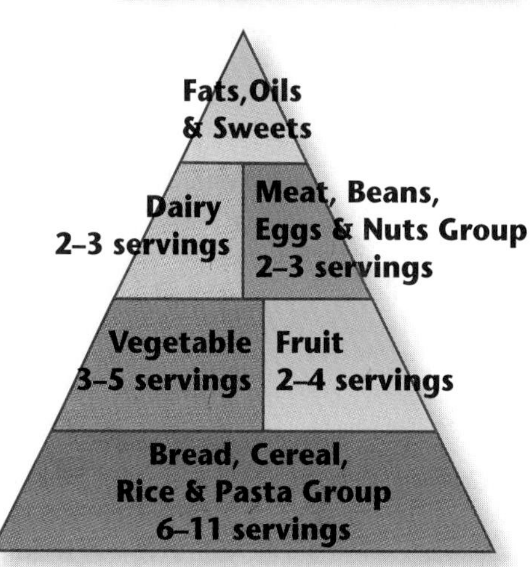

Food Guide Pyramid:
A Guide to Daily Food Choices

Spiral Review and Test Prep

Add or subtract. Write your answer in simplest form.

30. $\frac{4}{5} + \frac{1}{2}$ 31. $\frac{7}{8} - \frac{3}{4}$ 32. $\frac{2}{3} + 1\frac{1}{4}$ 33. $4 - 1\frac{5}{6}$

Choose the correct answer.

34. Evaluate the expression for the value given: $2m + 6$; $m = 7$.
    - A. 20
    - B. 18
    - C. 15
    - D. Not Here

35. Ellen has 3 CDs fewer than Janice. Janice has x CDs. Find an expression for the number of CDs Ellen has.
    - F. $3 - x$
    - G. $3x$
    - H. $x - 3$
    - J. $3 + x$

Extra Practice, page 528

Objective: Use illustrations to solve problems.

11•5 Problem Solving: Reading for Math

Draw a Diagram

National Art Contest

Read

An art student models a new artwork on Ellsworth Kelly's *Yellow with Red Triangle.* She paints two separate pieces of wood. The pieces are a rectangle 30 centimeters by 70 centimeters and an isosceles triangle 60 centimeters on the base and 50 centimeters on each side. She stacks the triangle on top of the rectangle for shipment. What is the smallest rectangular box she can use?

READING SKILL ▶

Read for Details

When you read a problem, you must look for the important details.

- **What do you know?** The size of the pieces; how they are going to be packaged
- **What do you need to find?** The smallest box possible

MATH SKILL ▶

Draw a Diagram

A diagram is a kind of illustration. It helps you see how different items can be combined. Drawing a diagram will help you solve problems that involve shapes and sizes.

Plan

You can draw a diagram to show what the art pieces will look like when they are stacked. Then you can draw a rectangle around the shapes to see how big the box must be.

Solve

Draw → Use the chalkboard and a yardstick or graph paper. Draw the shapes to take up the least amount of space. Draw and measure a rectangle that will enclose the shapes.

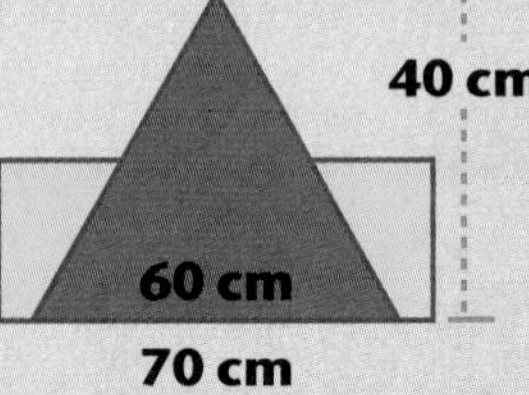

The smallest box would be 70 centimeters by 40 centimeters.

Look Back

Is your answer reasonable?

How did drawing a diagram help you solve this problem?

Practice

Draw a diagram to solve each problem.

1. Melvin's artwork for the contest is shaped like the trapezoid shown here. What is the smallest size rectangular box he can use to ship his painting?

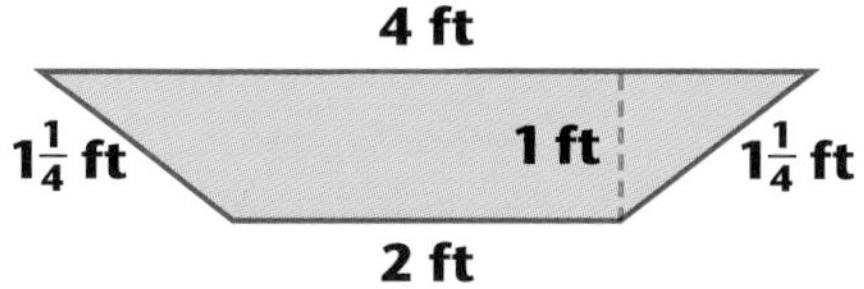

2. Vanya sends a rectangular canvas 2 feet by 3 feet to the contest. The shipping store only sells square boxes. What size must Vanya buy?

3. Marisa makes her artwork in two pieces. She stacks a 40-centimeter square on top of a 20-centimeter by 60-centimeter rectangle. What size and shape box does she need?

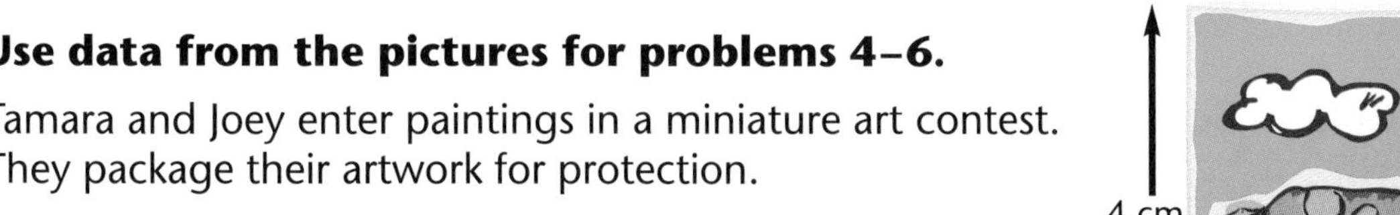

Use data from the pictures for problems 4–6.

Tamara and Joey enter paintings in a miniature art contest. They package their artwork for protection.

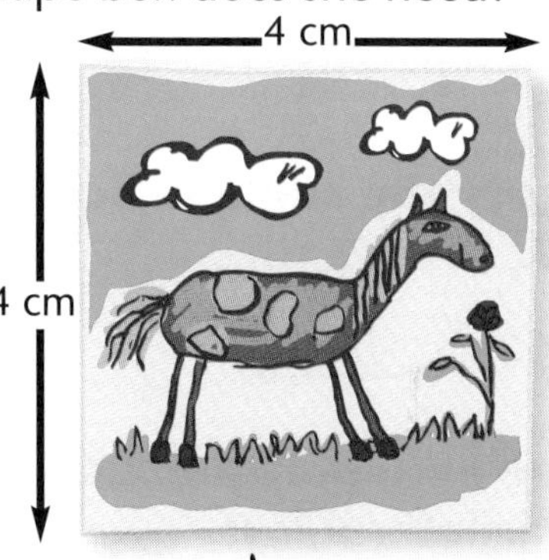

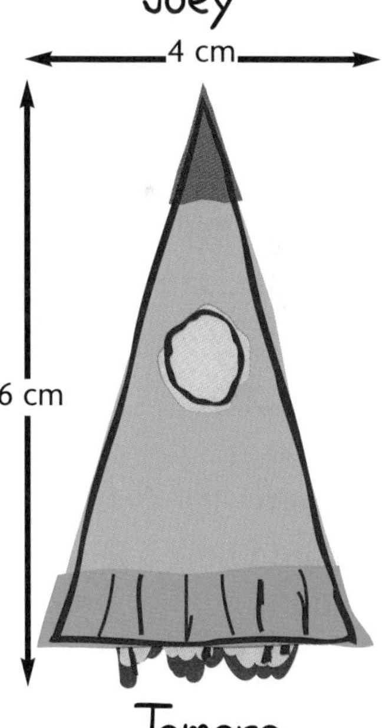

4. Which paintings could fit into a 4-centimeter square box?

5. Joey finds a box that measures 4 centimeters by 5 centimeters. Which paintings would fit inside? Explain your answer.

6. If the students can only find square boxes, what size will each of them need? What do you notice about the relationship between the size of the painting and the square box?

7. Jaime builds a tall, flat sculpture that looks like a stop sign. He sends the sculpture in two pieces. The octagon measures 16 inches across and the pole is 5-feet high. What size box does he need to send his artwork?

Spiral Review and Test Prep

Choose the correct answer.

Ellen has a piece of wood that is 1 inch wide and 1 foot long. She cuts the wood into four 3-inch strips.

8. Which of the following statements is true?
   - A. The strips are rectangles.
   - B. Each strip is 12 inches long.
   - C. The strips can be used to form a scalene triangle.
   - D. The total length of the strips is less than 1 foot.

9. A diagram shows
   - F. how long it will take to find a solution.
   - G. how a situation can be represented by a picture.
   - H. why you need to solve a problem.
   - J. the operation needed to find a solution.

Extra Practice, page 528

Check Your Progress A

Identify the figure. Then name it using symbols. (pages 486–489)

1. A B

2. C D

3. X Y

Name the pair of lines as intersecting, parallel, or perpendicular. (pages 490–493)

4.

5. 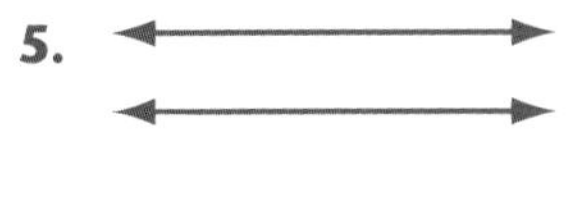

6. 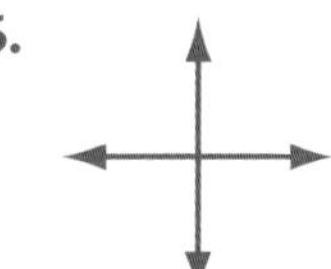

Classify the angle as acute, right, obtuse, or neither. (pages 494–497)

7. 

8. 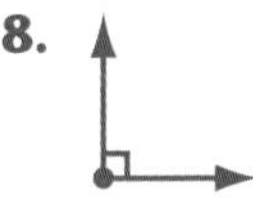

9. 

Name each polygon. Classify what type of triangle or quadrilateral it is. (pages 486–489, 494–501)

10. 

11. 

12. 

13. 

Find the measure of the unknown angle. (pages 494–501)

14. 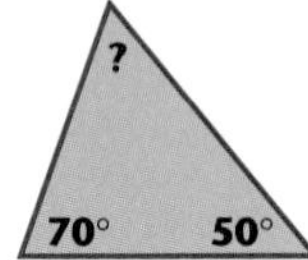

15. 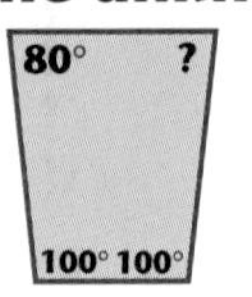

16. 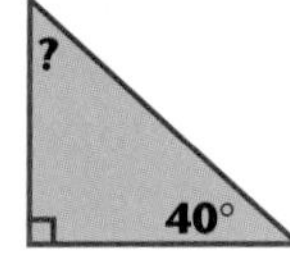

17. 150° 30° 30° ?

Solve. (pages 486–503)

18. Eduardo built a fence around his new painting studio. Two of the sides are parallel, and two are not. What type of quadrilateral is the fence?

19. Jodi paints a rectangular painting that is 30 cm by 40 cm. She also paints a square canvas 20 cm on each side. What is the smallest square box she can use to package both paintings?

20. **Summarize** the different ways that quadrilaterals can be classified.

Draw and Identify a Triangle

Brianna is designing a garden. She needs to draw an obtuse scalene triangle in her sketch of the garden. Draw an obtuse scalene triangle. How do you know that the triangle is obtuse and scalene?

You can use a drawing program with geometry tools to draw triangles.

- Click on the geometry tools.
- Click on Setup. Choose Show Labels.
- Choose the freeform polygon tool. Draw an obtuse scalene triangle.
- Use the measurement tool to find the measure of each angle and the length of each side.

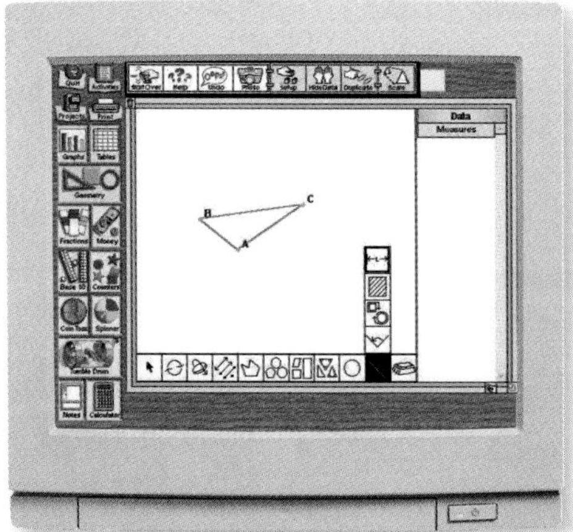

How do you know the triangle is obtuse and scalene?

Use the computer to draw each triangle. Explain how you know your triangle is correct.

1. Acute scalene triangle
2. Right isosceles triangle
3. Right scalene triangle

Solve.

4. Darrick is remodeling a room in his house. He wants to draw an equilateral triangle to show the shape of one of the windows in the room. Draw an equilateral triangle.
5. A company wants its logo to be in the shape of an acute isosceles triangle. Draw an acute isosceles triangle. Explain how you know that your triangle is correct.
6. **Analyze:** How do the geometry and measurement tools help you draw correct triangles?

For more practice, use Math Traveler™.

Objective: Describe and draw congruent and similar figures.

11•6 Congruence and Similarity

Learn

American artist Jasper Johns painted *Three Flags.* The three flags have the same rectangular shape but different sizes. These flags, therefore, are similar rectangles. The stars within each flag are exactly the same size and shape. They are congruent shapes.

Math Words

congruent figures
figures that have the same shape and size

similar figures
figures that have the same shape but not necessarily the same size

corresponding parts
matching parts of congruent or similar figures

Example 1

Look at triangle *ABC.* Draw a **congruent** triangle.

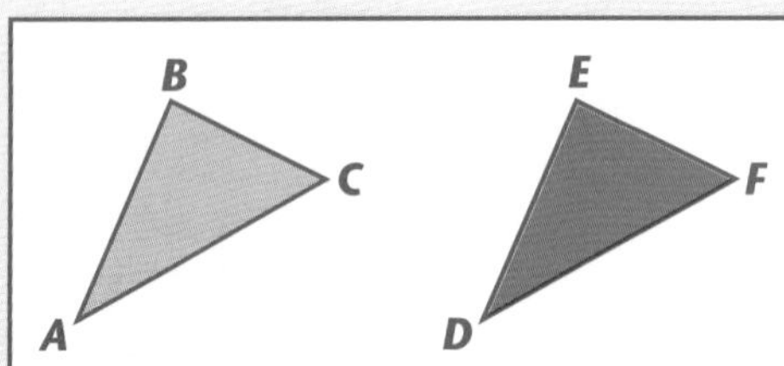

Copy the triangle, or draw a triangle with the same angle measures and side lengths.

Read: Triangle *ABC* is congruent to triangle *DEF.* **Write:** $\Delta ABC \cong \Delta DEF$

Read: $\overline{AB}$ is congruent to $\overline{DE}$. **Write:** $\overline{AB} \cong \overline{DE}$

Read: $\angle C$ is congruent to $\angle F$. **Write:** $\angle C \cong \angle F$

Example 2

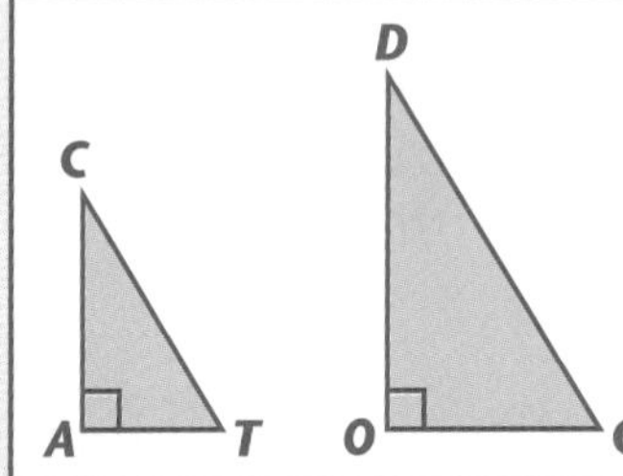

*Triangle CAT is **similar** to triangle DOG. The **corresponding** angles, such as C and D, are congruent.*

Note: Congruent figures are always also similar.

Try It

Tell whether the figures are congruent, similar, or neither.

1. 

2. 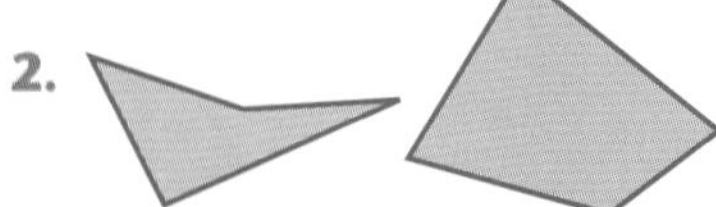

3. 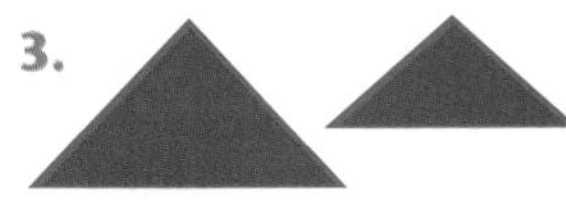

Sum it Up! How can you tell if two figures are similar?

Practice **Tell whether the figures are congruent, similar, or neither.**

4. 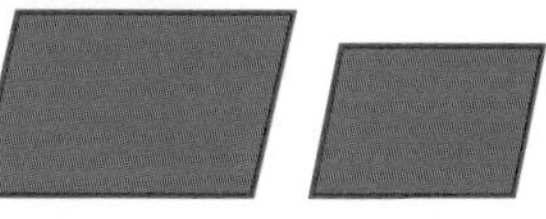

5. 

6. 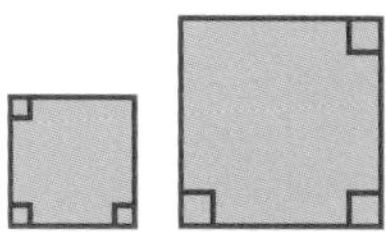

7. 

8. 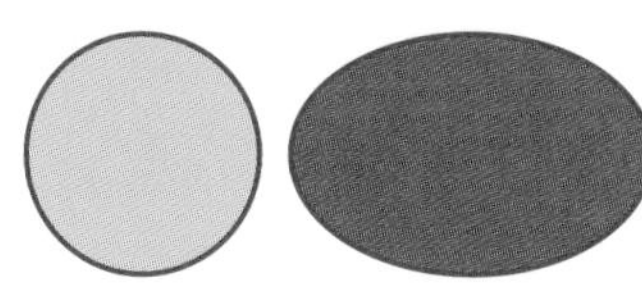

9. 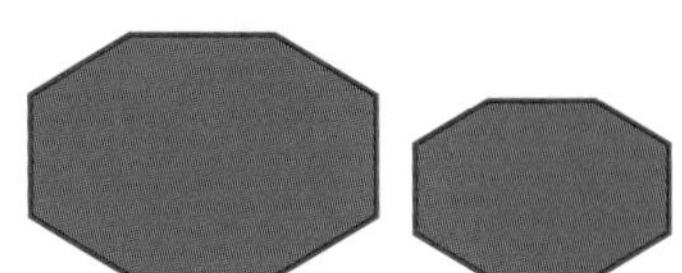

Find the measure of the missing angle in each pair of similar figures.

10. 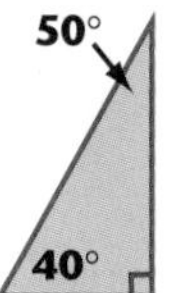

11. 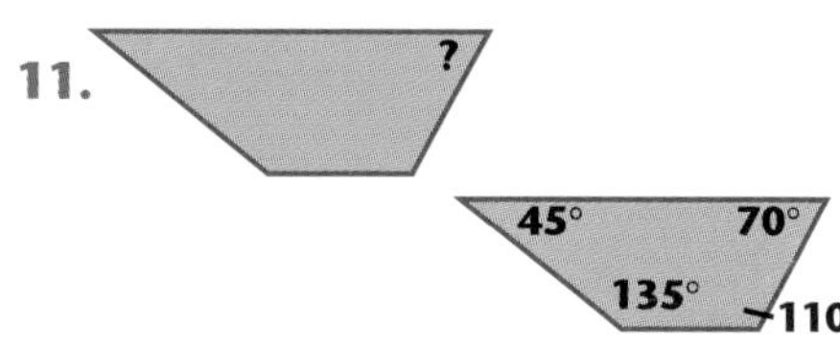

12. 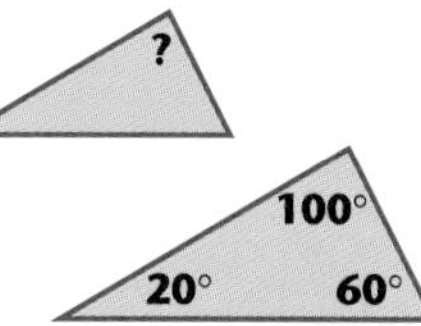

Identify the corresponding side or angle.

13. $\overline{AB}$
14. $\overline{ED}$
15. $\overline{QU}$
16. $\angle B$
17. $\angle T$
18. $\angle S$

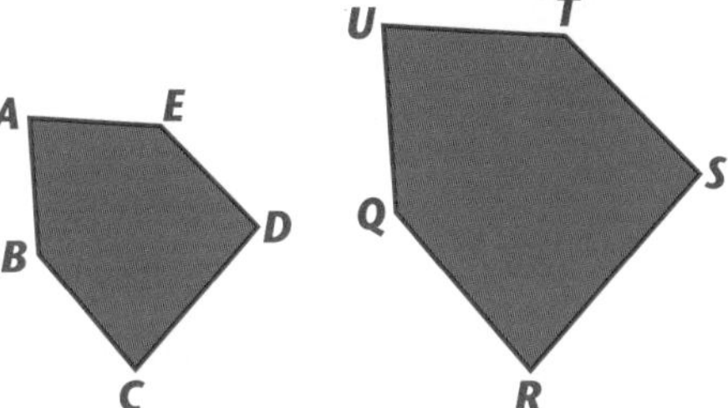

Problem Solving

Use the painting *Three Flags* for problems 19–21.

19. How many congruent rectangles are in the painting?

20. How many similar rectangles are in the painting?

21. **Explain** how the artist might have drawn the smallest flag using the largest one.

★22. **Generalize:** Are all squares similar? Explain why or why not.

23. **Literature:** In E. L. Konigsburg's book, *From the Mixed Up Files of Mrs. Basil E. Frankweiler,* two children spend the night in the Metropolitan Museum of Art. If the museum opens at 10 A.M. and stays open for $7\frac{1}{2}$ hours, what time does it close?

Spiral Review and Test Prep

24. $\frac{1}{4} \times \frac{4}{5}$
25. $8 \times \frac{3}{4}$
26. $2\frac{1}{2} \times \frac{2}{3}$
27. $2\frac{1}{4} \times 1\frac{1}{3}$

Choose the correct answer.

28. If Bill sells 5 comic books for $2.25 each, how much does he earn?
   A. $2.25
   C. $11.25
   B. $0.45
   D. $10.25

29. What is $\frac{16}{100}$ written in simplest form?
   F. $\frac{8}{50}$
   H. $\frac{4}{25}$
   G. $\frac{100}{16}$
   J. Not Here

Objective: Identify translations, reflections, and rotations.

11·7 Transformations

Math Words

transformation a change of position of a geometric figure

translation a figure that is moved horizontally, vertically, or diagonally

reflection the mirror image of a figure about a line

rotation a figure that is rotated around a point

glide reflection a transformation that is a combination of a reflection and a translation

Learn

Artistic quilt patterns often include shapes that have been turned, flipped or moved. What kind of transformations can be seen in the pattern seen here?

Example 1

You can transform figures by using **translations**, **reflections**, or **rotations**.

A translation moves a figure horizontally, vertically, or diagonally.

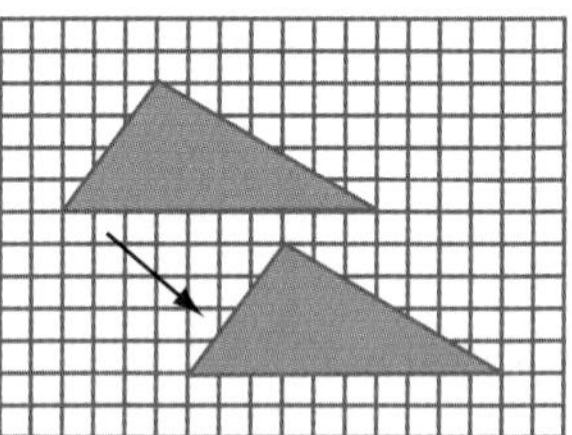

A reflection flips a figure over a real or imaginary line, creating a mirror image of the figure.

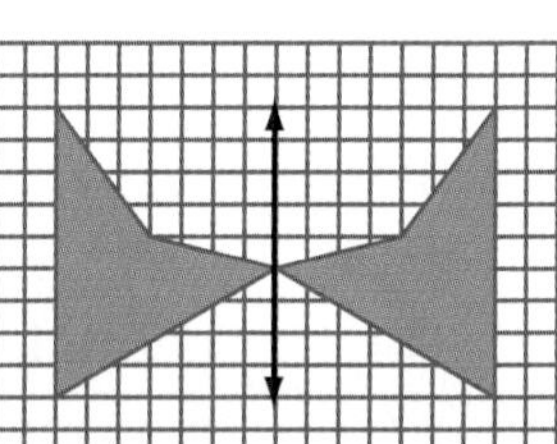

A rotation moves a figure by rotating it around a point on the figure.

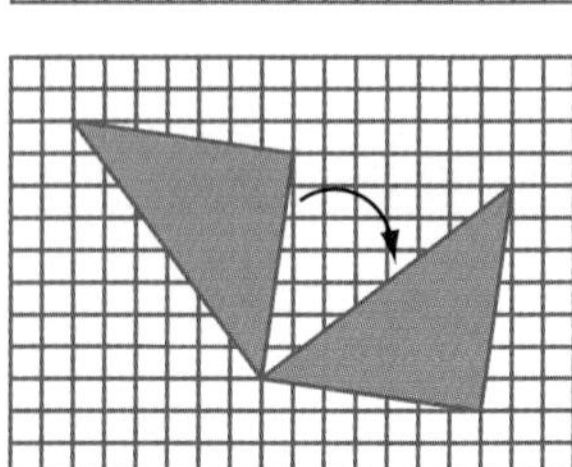

Note: When one figure is a translation, reflection, or rotation of another figure, the two figures are congruent.

The quilt pattern includes translations, reflections and rotations.

Example 2

You can transform figures by using translations, reflections, or rotations.

You can transform a figure by rotating it first, and then reflecting it. Triangle 2 is obtained from triangle 1 by rotation. Triangle 3 is obtained from triangle 2 by reflection.

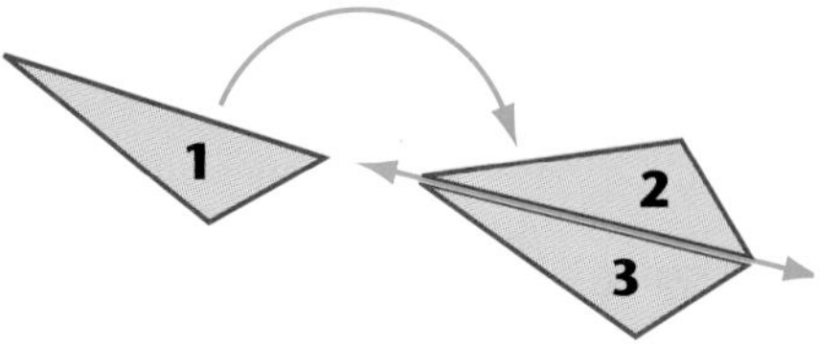

You can also use a combination of a translation and a rotation to transform a figure. Triangle 2 is obtained from Triangle 1 by translation. Triangle 3 is obtained from Triangle 2 by rotation.

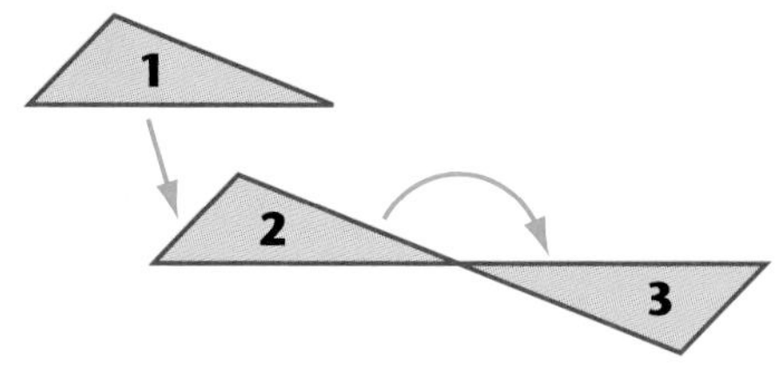

When you transform a figure by combining a reflection and a translation, it is called a **glide reflection**. Triangle 2 is obtained from Triangle 1 by translation. Triangle 3 is obtained from Triangle 2 by reflection.

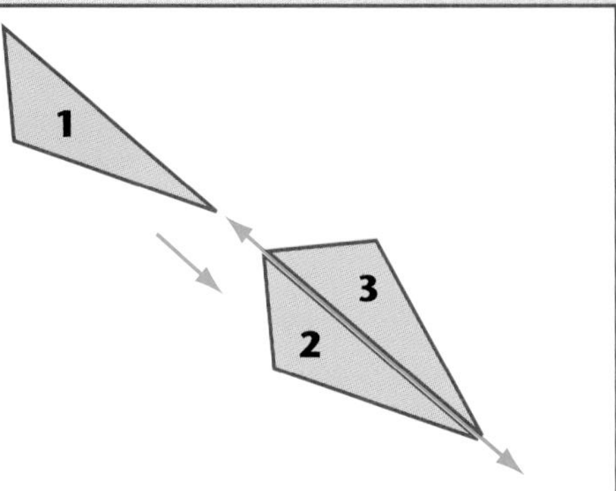

Try It **Write whether a translation, reflection, or rotation was made.**

1. 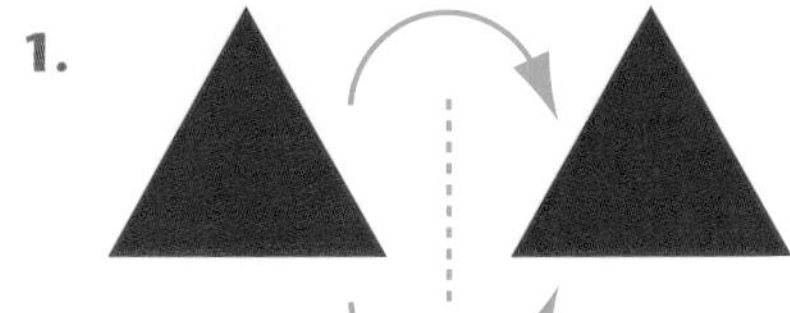

2. 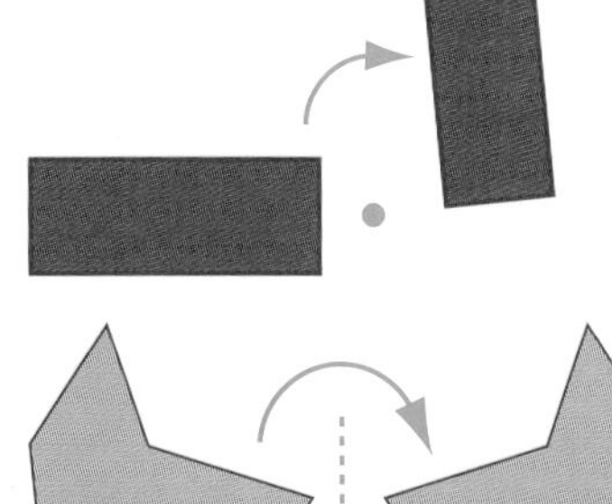

3. 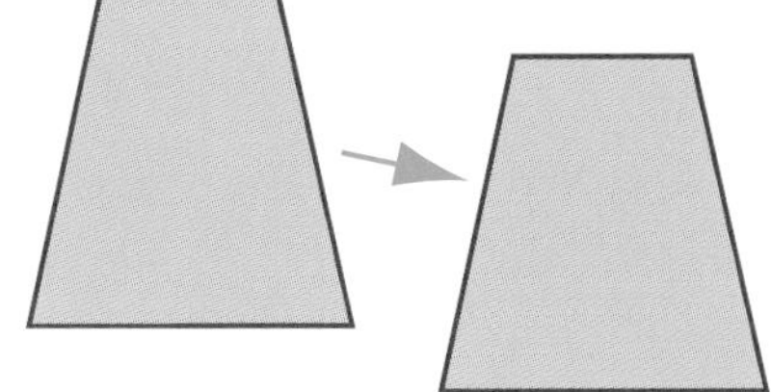

4. 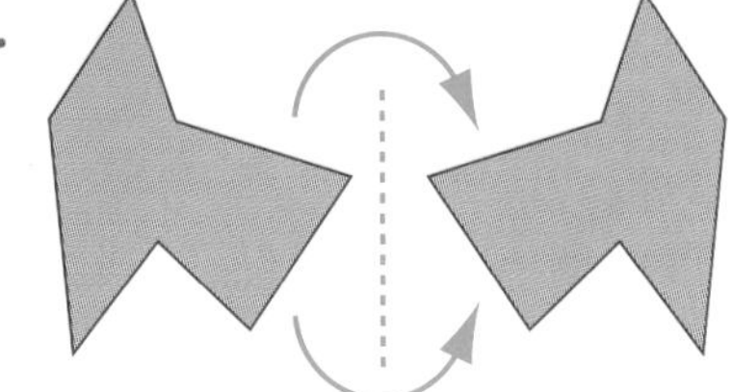

Compare and contrast translation, reflection, and rotation.

Practice **Write whether a translation, reflection, or rotation was made.**

5. 

6. 

7. 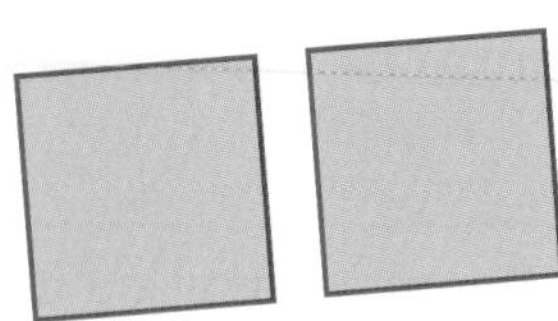

8. 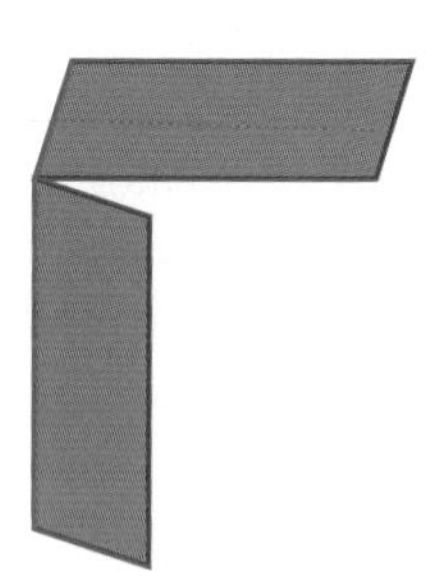

Write the combination of transformations used.

9. 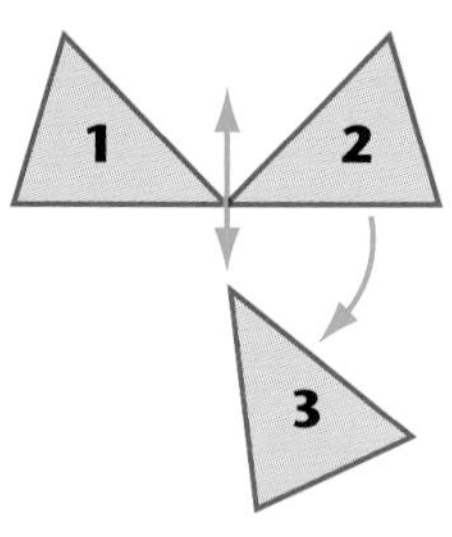

10. 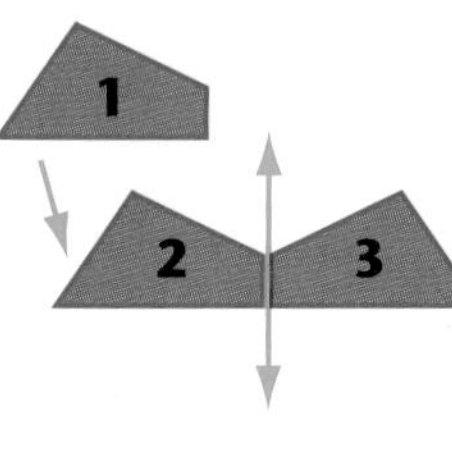

11. 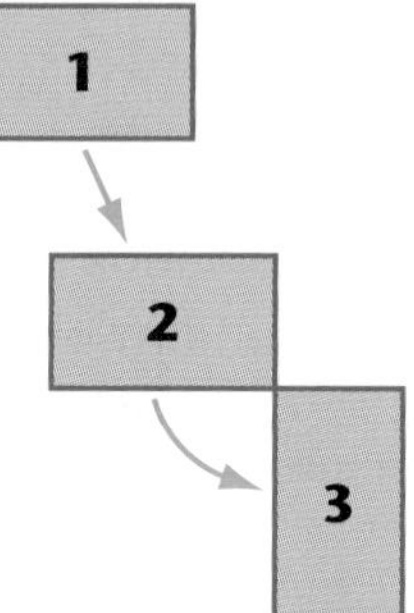

12. 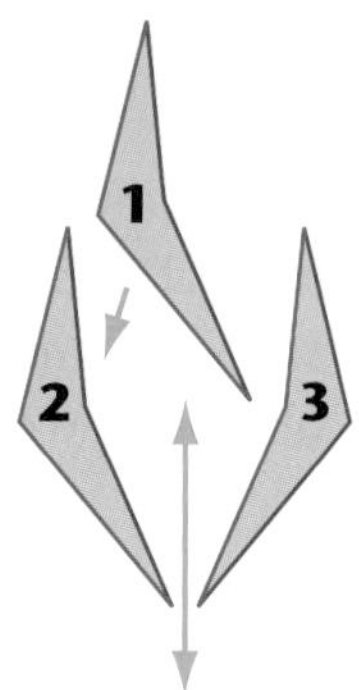

Choose the figure that is made by the transformation described.

13. Reflection

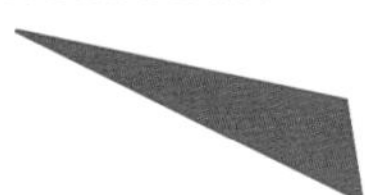

A. 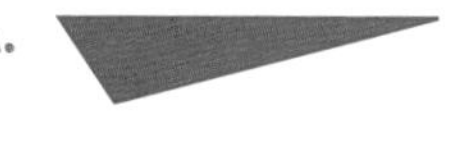

B. 

C. 

14. Translation

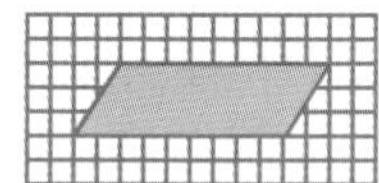

A. 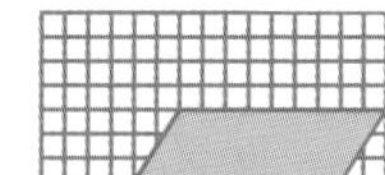

B. 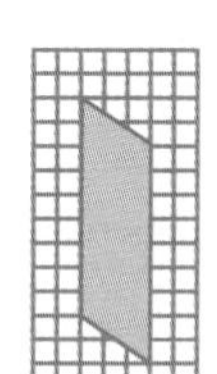

C. 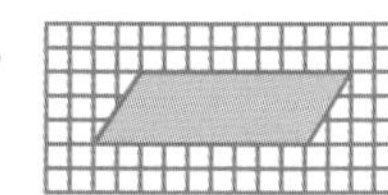

15. Rotation

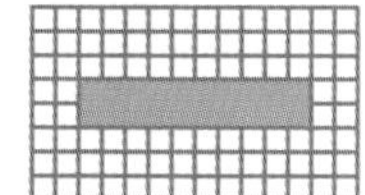

A. 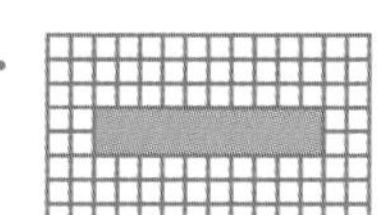

B. 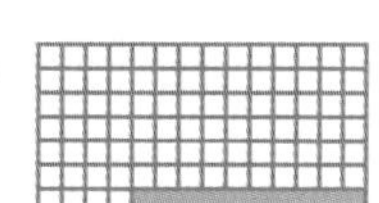

C. 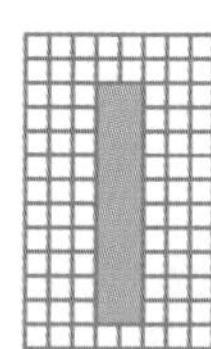

16. 

Here's how Vinnie reflected a triangle across a vertical line. Tell what mistake he made. Explain how to correct it.

Problem Solving

17. **Language Arts:** Find 4 upper-case letters that look the same after being reflected.

18. Find 2 lower-case letters that are transformations of the letter *b*.

★ 19. If Anne wants to move an easel in her studio from the north wall to the east wall, what combination of transformations can she use?

★ 20. Anne wants to move a right-triangular table from one corner to another. If both corners have 90-degree angles, will the translated figure fit in the new corner? Explain.

Use Diego Rivera's painting, *Cactus on the Plains*, for problems 21–22.

21. What kind of transformation was needed to copy the cactus on the front left to the back of the painting?

22. What kind of transformation was needed to create the cactus in the front right of the picture from the front left?

23. **Generalize:** How many different types of transformations are needed to make a glide reflection?

24. Jenny draws two identical triangles. Their only difference is that triangle *A* is higher up on the page than triangle *B*. Has Jenny made a translation or rotation?

25. **Analyze:** How does a translation differ from a rotation?

Spiral Review and Test Prep

Simplify each expression.

26. $(7 + 3) - 4 \times 2$

27. $4 \times 4 \div 8 - 2$

28. $23 \times 4 + 7$

29. $3 + 4^2 \times 2 \div 8$

Choose the correct answer.

30. The sum of two numbers is 11. Their product is 30. Find the two numbers.
    A. 4 and 7
    B. 5 and 6
    C. 2 and 15
    D. 8 and 3

31. A number decreased by 18 is 47. Find the number.
    F. 29
    G. 34
    H. 65
    J. Not Here

Extra Practice, page 529

Objective: Draw shapes with lines of symmetry and draw all the lines of symmetry in a figure.

Symmetry

Learn

Although Navajo rug weavings include many fine details, the overall patterns are often symmetric about a line. Where are the lines of symmetry in this pattern?

Math Words

symmetric about a line a figure that can be folded along a line so that the two halves match exactly, or are congruent

line of symmetry lines that divide a figure into two parts that match, or are congruent

Note: Figures that are symmetric across a line of symmetry are "symmetric about a line." Figures can also be symmetric about a point.

Example

The rug weaving is **symmetric about these lines**. These lines are the **lines of symmetry**.

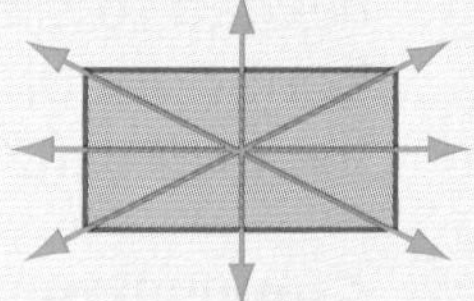

More Examples

Polygons can have 0, 1, or more lines of symmetry.

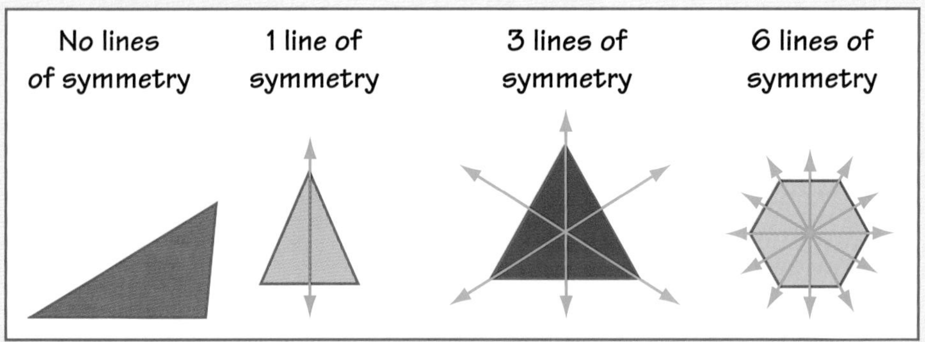

Try It

Tell which figures are symmetric about a line.

1. 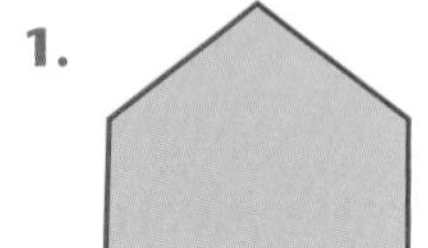
2. 
3. 
4. 

How can you tell if a figure is symmetric?

Practice

Tell which figures are symmetric about a line.

5. 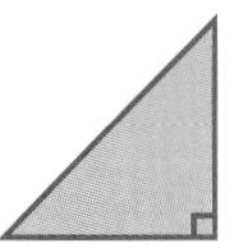

6. 

7. 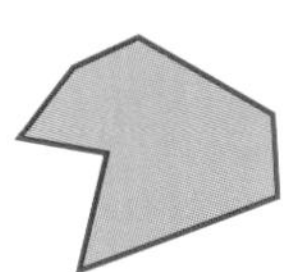

8. 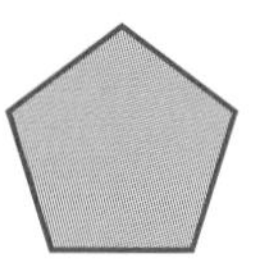

9. 

10. 

11. 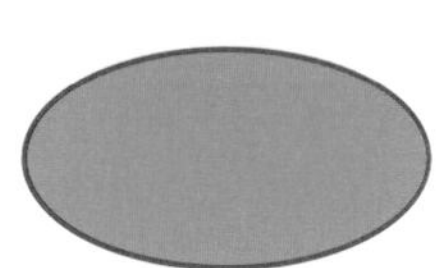

12. 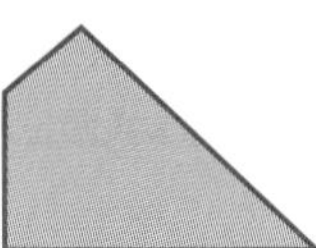

Trace the figure. Draw all its lines of symmetry.

13. 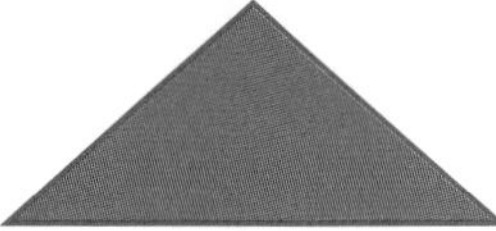

14. 

15. 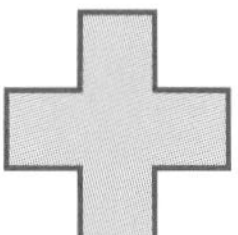

16. 

Problem Solving

17. Draw a four-sided figure with at least 2 lines of symmetry. Show all lines of symmetry.

18. **Analyze:** How many lines of symmetry does a rhombus have? a rectangle?

19. **Music:** Most of the string instruments in an orchestra, such as the violins or cellos, are symmetric about a line. Can you name a string orchestra instrument that is not symmetric about a line?

20. **Social Studies:** The five points of the star in the national flag of Somalia represent a claim to the five territories in which the Somalis live. How many lines of symmetry can be drawn?

Use *Two Panels: Yellow, Black* for problems 21–22.

21. Sketch this painting. Draw all lines of symmetry. How many are there?

22. Name the shape of this painting in as many ways as possible. Use a ruler to measure.

Spiral Review and Test Prep

Find the LCD.

23. 4 and 10

24. 8 and 12

25. 2 and 16

26. 5, 10 and 15

Choose the correct answer.

27. Which of the following numbers is not a multiple of 12?
   - A. 0
   - B. 12
   - C. 24
   - D. 36

28. Which number makes $v - 8 = 17$ true?
   - F. 8
   - G. 9
   - H. 17
   - J. 25

Extra Practice, page 529

Objective: Find a pattern in a geometric sequence and extend the sequence.

Problem Solving: Strategy
Find a Pattern

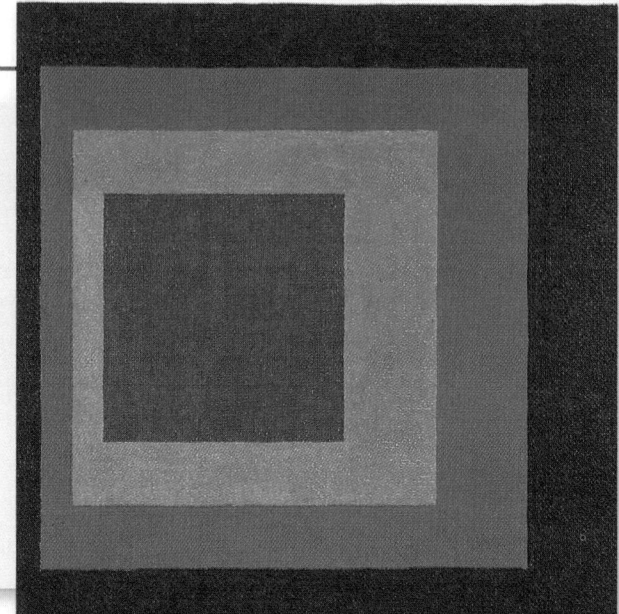

Read

This painting by Josef Albers is called *Study for Homage to the Square.* If you measure the length of the sides of the 4 squares in the painting, you will see a pattern. What is it? If the pattern continues, what would be the length of the side of the next square?

- **What do you know?** The lengths of the sides of the squares
- **What do you need to know?** The pattern; the length of the side of the next square

Plan

Find the pattern and extend it. Measure the side of each square in millimeters. Record the data in a table to help see a pattern.

Solve

Square color	Length (mm)	Difference between the length and next largest square
Red	38	—
Pink	56	18
Blue	74	18
Brown	92	18

Each square is 18 millimeters longer than the one before. The length of the side of the next square would be $92 + 18 = 110$ millimeters.

Look Back

Is your answer reasonable? How can you check your answer?

Explain how making a table and looking for a pattern made it easier to solve this problem.

Use *Arithmetic Composition* by Theo van Doesburg and a ruler for problems 1–2.

1. Measure the length of the sides of the four squares in the painting. If you were going to add another square after the largest one, what would the length of the side be?

2. What is the pattern for the size of the squares?

3. For his art project, Christian is making an abstract drawing using a pattern that repeats 4 symbols as shown. If he continues the pattern, what will the sixth figure look like?

4. A pattern is made by rotating the rectangle at the right 90 degrees for each new figure in the pattern. Will the twelfth rectangle in the pattern be horizontal or vertical?

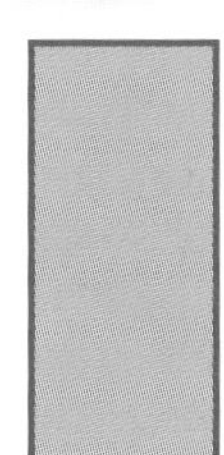

Problem Solving

Mixed Strategy Review

5. Jackson is arranging rows of chairs in an amphitheater. There are 68 chairs in the first row, 72 chairs in the second row, 76 chairs in the third row, and 80 chairs in the fourth row. If this pattern continues, how many chairs will be in the tenth row? State the pattern you followed.

6. Jamie took a square piece of paper and folded it along all lines of symmetry. How many triangles were formed by the fold lines? What kind of triangles were formed?

CHOOSE A STRATEGY

- Logical Reasoning
- Draw a Diagram
- Make a Graph
- Make a Table or List
- Find a Pattern
- Guess and Check
- Write an Equation
- Work Backward
- Solve a Simpler Problem
- Conduct an Experiment

Use the picture for problems 7–8.

7. To count her money, Stacey arranged it as shown. If she had 6 more quarters, 8 more dimes, and 4 more nickels, how many more times can she repeat the pattern?

8. If Stacey makes exactly 6 complete patterns using all of her money, how much money will she have?

Extra Practice, page 529

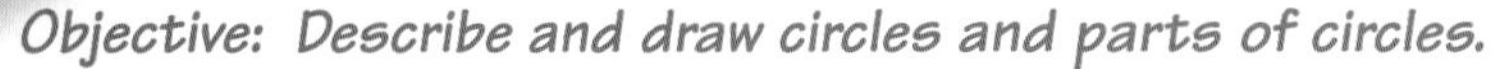

Objective: Describe and draw circles and parts of circles.

Circles

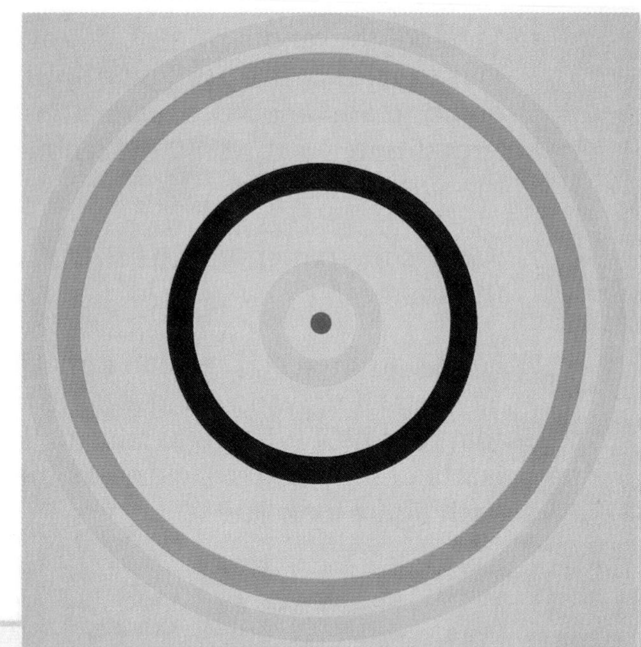

Learn

Math Words
- circle
- center
- chord
- diameter
- central angle
- radius (plural: radii)

Kenneth Noland's painting *Turnstole* has many circles on the canvas. How are a circle and its parts defined?

Example 1

A **circle** is a closed, 2-dimensional figure that has all of its points the same distance from the center.

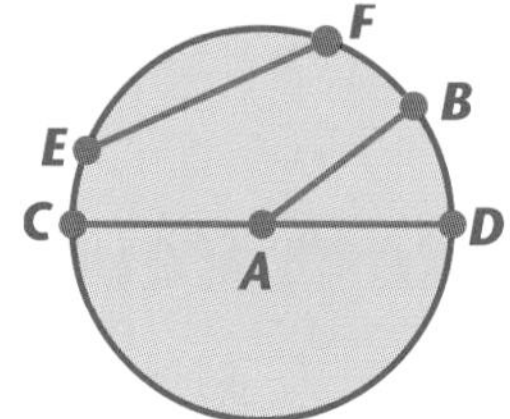

A circle can be named by its **center**. — This circle is called circle A. Center: A

A **chord** is a line segment that connects any two points on the circle. — $\overline{EF}$ is a chord of circle A. Chord: $\overline{EF}$

A special chord, called a **diameter**, passes through the center of the circle. — $\overline{CD}$ is a diameter of circle A. Diameter: $\overline{CD}$

A **radius** is a line segment that connects the center to a point on the circle. — $\overline{AB}$ is a radius of circle A. Radius: $\overline{AB}$

A **central angle** is an angle formed between two radii. $\angle CFA$, $\angle DFB$, and $\angle BFC$ are central angles in circle F. The sum of the measures of the central angles of a circle is always 360 degrees.

You can confirm this fact by looking at the four right angles formed by two perpendicular diameters. The sum of the measure of those angles is $4 \times 90° = 360°$.

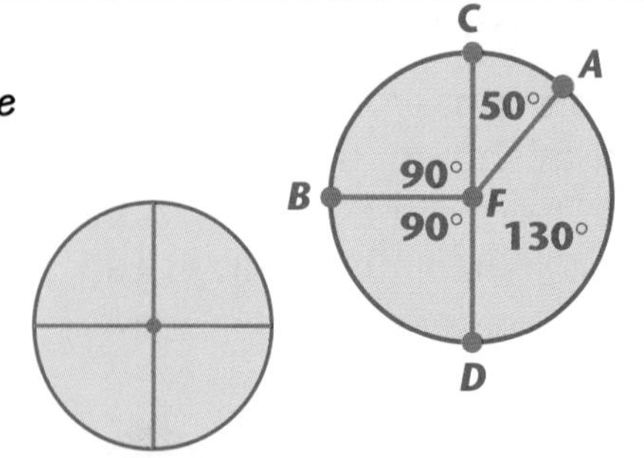

What if you wanted to make your own drawing with circles? How do you draw a circle?

Example 2

Draw a circle with a one-inch radius. Label it circle *A*.

If you know the radius of a circle, you can draw it using a Triman compass.

Draw a point. Center the blue circle over the point you use as the center.

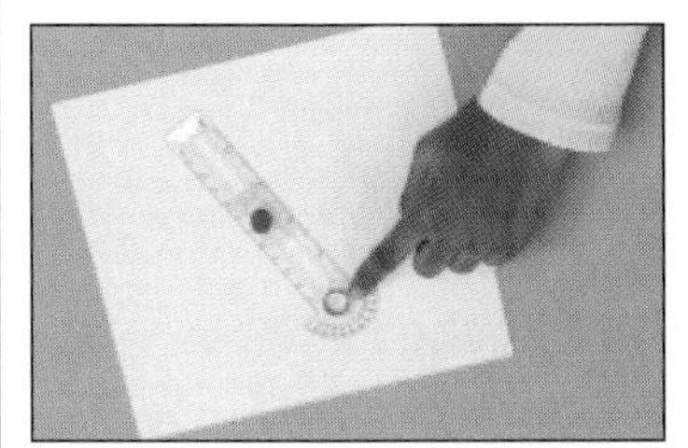

Slide the center of the compass to the length you choose as a radius. Secure it.

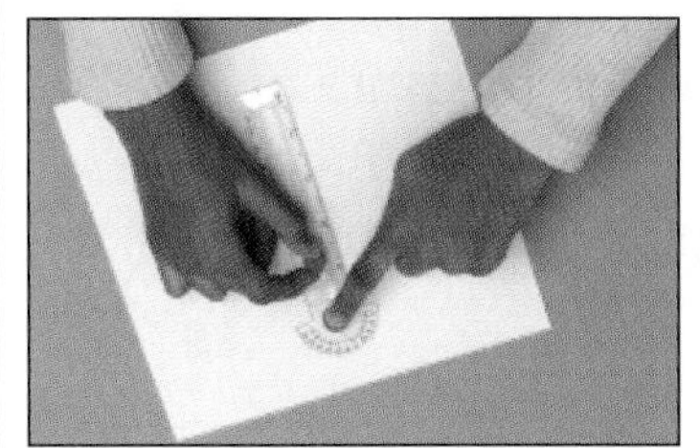

3

Place your finger on the blue circle and your pencil in the hole. Move the compass to make a circle.

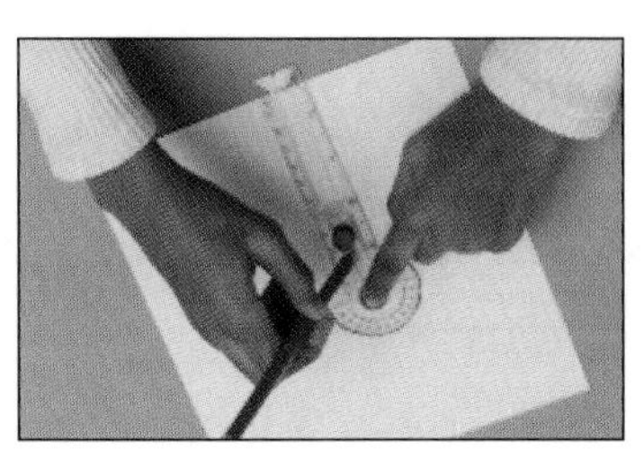

More Examples

A

Draw a circle with a diameter of 4 inches.

Find the radius by dividing the diameter in half. Then follow the steps for drawing a circle.

Draw a circle with a chord of 3 inches.

You cannot find the radius of a circle from the length of the chord. You cannot draw a circle from this information.

Draw a circle with a central angle of 60°.

You cannot find the radius of a circle from a central angle. You cannot draw a circle from this information.

Try It **Identify the parts of circle *M*.**

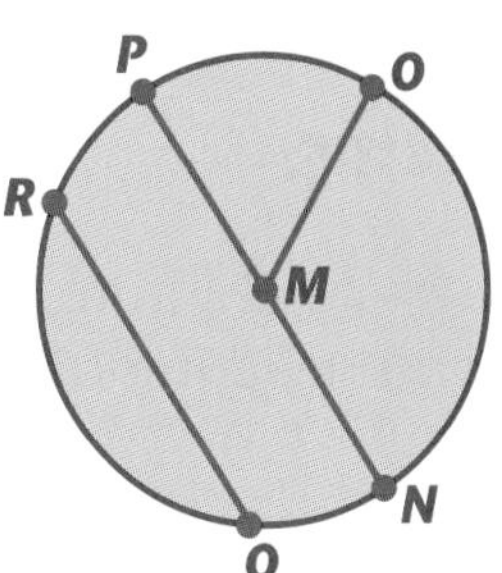

1. Center
2. Diameter
3. Radii
4. Chords
5. Central angles
6. Points on the circle

Identify and describe the three kinds of line segments you can draw in a circle.

Practice

Identify the parts of circle *P*.

7. Center
8. Diameters
9. Radii
10. Chords
11. Points on the circle
★12. Central angles

Solve. Use circle *P*.

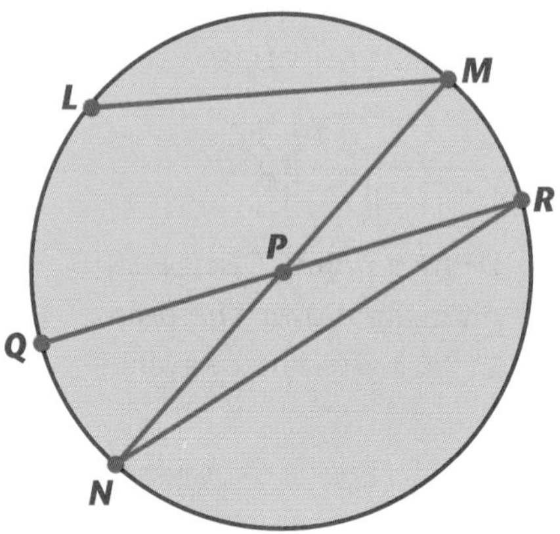

13. If $\overline{PQ} = 2$ feet, how long is $\overline{PR}$?
14. If $\overline{NP} = 4$ inches, how long is $\overline{NM}$?
15. If $\angle NPR = 150$ degrees, what is the sum of the measures of $\angle PNR$ and $\angle PRN$?
16. If $\overline{QR} = 6$ meters, how long is $\overline{QP}$?
17. If $\overline{NM} = 8$ inches, how long is $\overline{PQ}$?
18. If the sum of the measures of $\angle QPN$, $\angle NPR$, and $\angle RPM = 220$ degrees, what is the measure of $\angle QPM$?

Draw circles with the given measurements.

19. radius = 1 inch
20. diameter = 6 inches
21. diameter = 3 inches
22. radius = 3 inches

23.

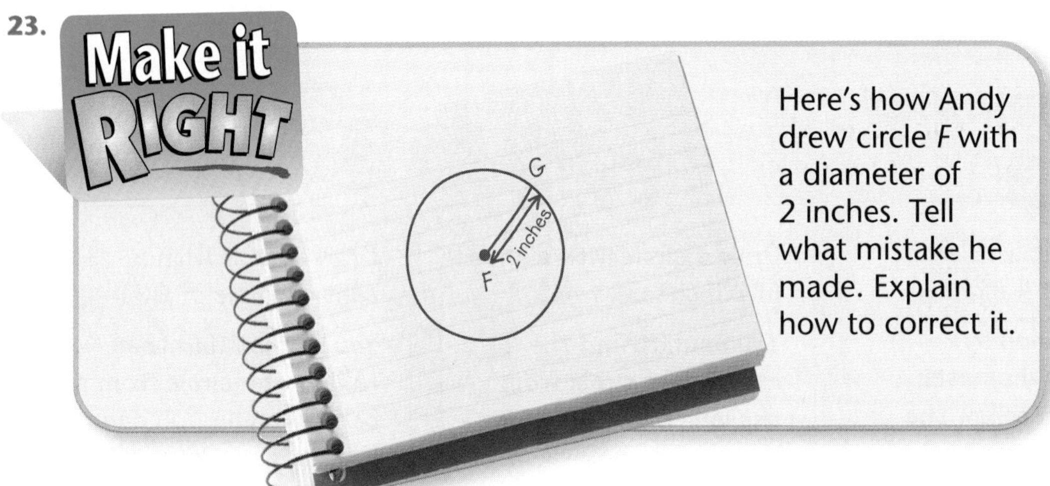

Here's how Andy drew circle *F* with a diameter of 2 inches. Tell what mistake he made. Explain how to correct it.

Problem Solving

24. **Summarize:** What information about a circle do you need in order to draw it?
25. At 3 P.M., what is the measure of the central angle of the hands on a clock?
26. A central angle of a circle is 75 degrees. What is the measure of the remaining central angle?
★27. **Generalize:** What happens to the radius of a circle when the diameter doubles? triples? What about when the diameter is reduced by half?

Use data about Guiseppe's Pizza for problems 28–30.

28. Yolanda and three friends each eat two slices of pizza when they go to Guiseppe's. Would it be less expensive to buy a whole pizza or individual slices?

29. **Create a problem** using the data about Guiseppe's Pizza. Solve it and give it to another student to solve.

30. If each piece is exactly the same size, what would be the measure of the central angle of a single slice?

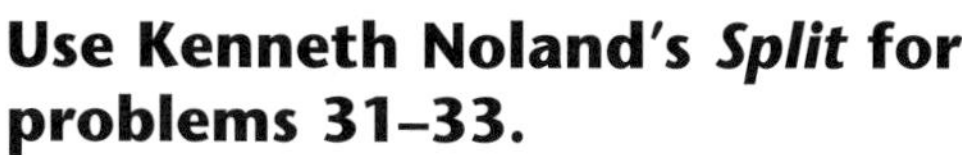

Use Kenneth Noland's *Split* for problems 31–33.

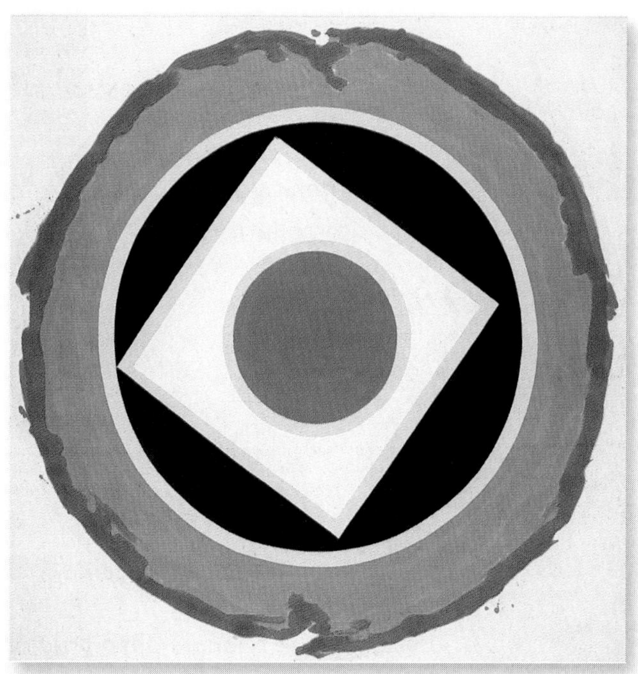

31. Measure the diameter of the smallest circle. Without measuring, calculate the radius of that circle.

★32. Measure the diameter of the circle on the canvas. About how many times larger is the diameter of the largest circle than the smallest circle?

33. **Explain** how Noland could have used a Triman compass to draw the circles in his painting.

Spiral Review and Test Prep

Identify each property.

34. (1,832 + 1,906) + 44 = 1,832 + (1,906 + 44)

35. 456 × 1 = 1

36. 20 × 28 = (20 × 30) − (20 × 2)

37. 3,517,584,694 × 0 = 0

Choose the correct answer.

38. A museum curator has 42 new paintings to catalog. Of the 42, $\frac{1}{2}$ are from the 1900s. Of those paintings, $\frac{1}{3}$ need to be reframed. How many paintings need to be reframed?
    - A. 21
    - B. 14
    - C. 7
    - D. 5

39. If it takes 45 minutes for a museum carpenter to make a stand for a sculpture, how many hours does it take to make 8 stands?
    - F. 6
    - G. 8
    - H. 10
    - J. 12

Objective: Describe and draw tessellations.

11·11 Explore Tessellations

Math Word

tessellation an arrangement of shapes that covers an area without any gaps or overlaps

Learn

You can use different shapes to explore tessellations.

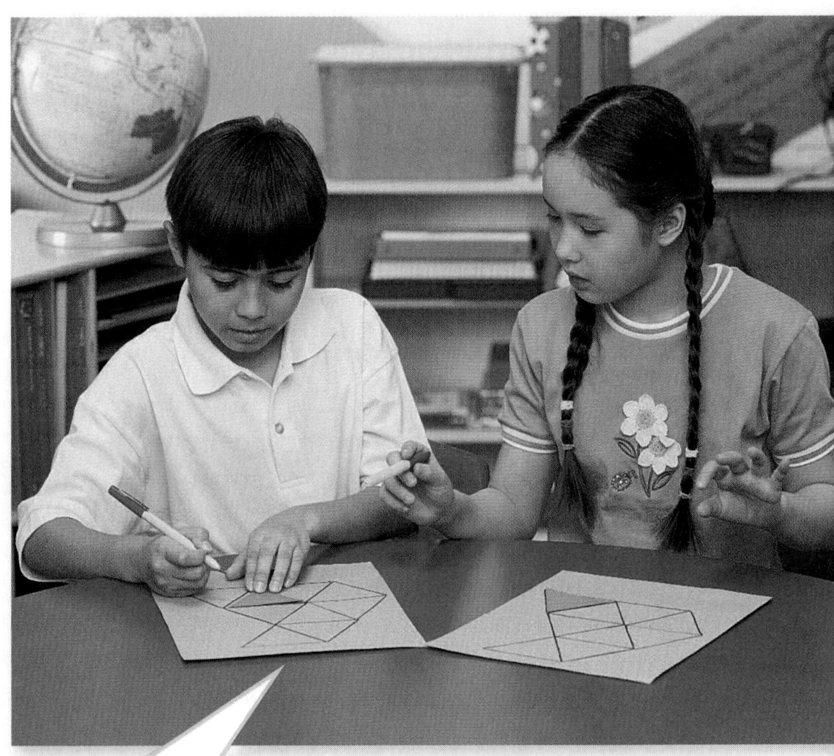

Work Together

You Will Need
- **tracing paper**

- Use tracing paper to decide if this triangle **tessellates**.
  - Copy the triangle onto tracing paper.
  - Copy it again. Match one of the sides with a side of the first triangle.
  - Continue to trace new triangles until you have surrounded the original triangle.
  - Record your work. Does the triangle tessellate?

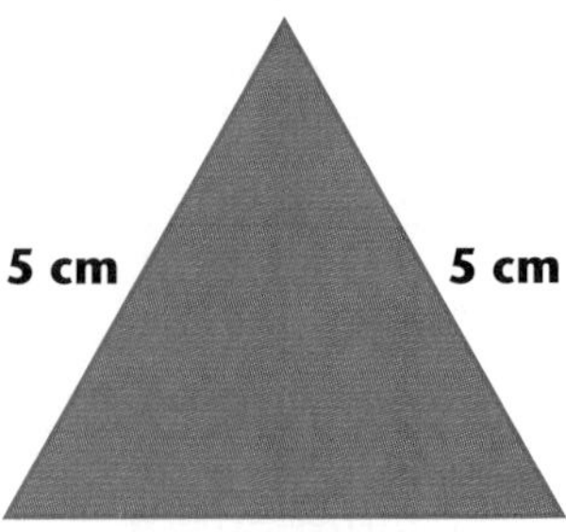

- Repeat the steps above for the other figures shown.

Make Connections

Using Models	Using Paper and Pencil
	Some figures, such as a square or a hexagon, tessellate.
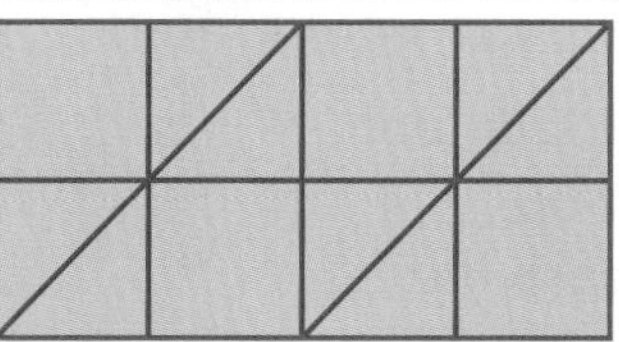	Other figures, such as circles, do not.
	Sometimes, two or more shapes together will tessellate.

Not every shape tessellates, but many shapes and combinations of shapes do.

Try It **Tell whether the shapes tessellate. Record your work.**

1. 
2. 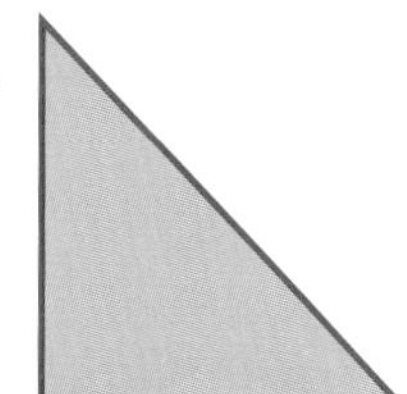
3. 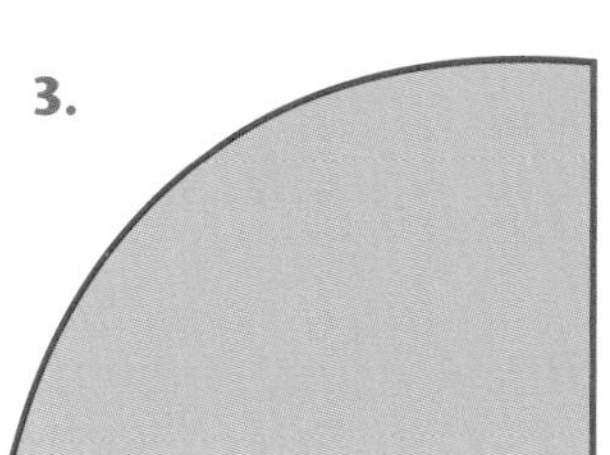
4. 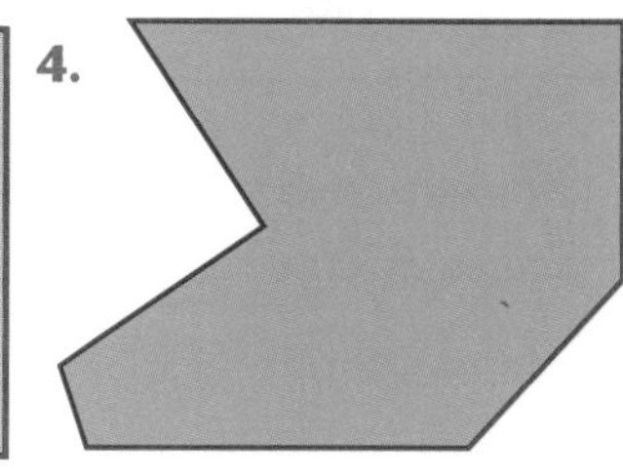

Sum it Up Explain how you know if a shape tessellates.

Practice **Tell whether the shapes tessellate. Record your work.**

5. 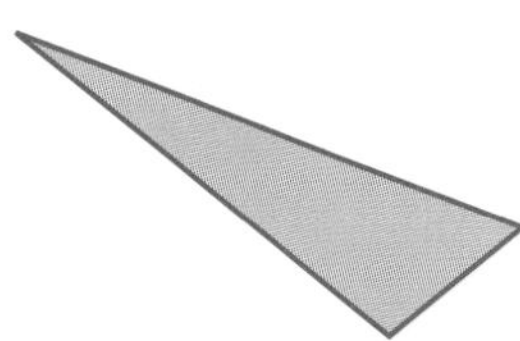
6. 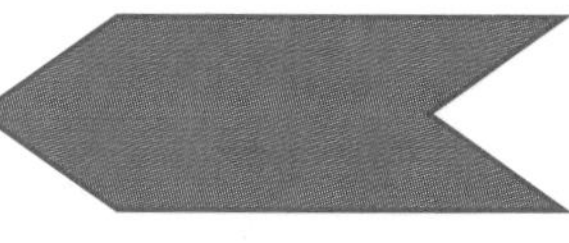
7. 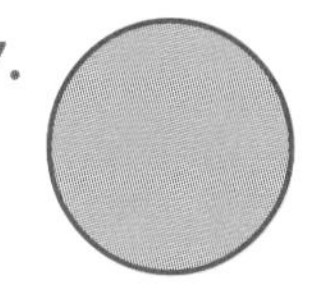
8. 

9. **Analyze:** Does a circle tessellate? Provide a drawing and explain why or why not.

Extra Practice, page 529

Objective: Apply geometry to analyze data and make decisions.

Problem Solving: Application

Decision Making

Which tiles should you choose for the mosaic?

You have won a design competition to design the 10-foot by 10-foot mosaic at the school entrance. Your group must choose the tiles. The tiles must cover the entire space without any gaps and form an even edge along the outer border. You can spend up to $60 for tiles.

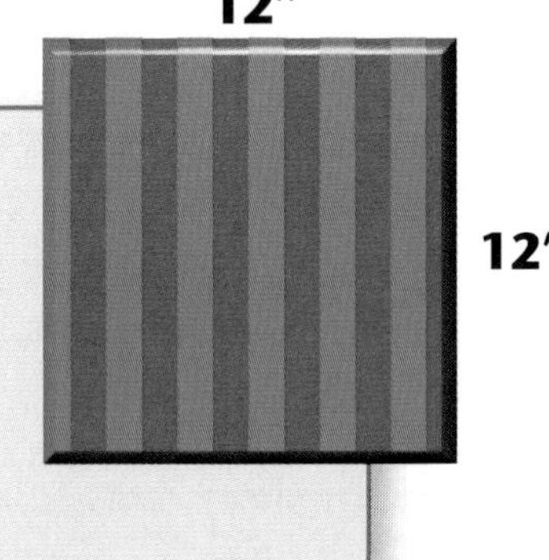

Option 1

1 tile covers 1 square foot
Sold in boxes of 50
Price: $30 for each box
If you buy 3 or more boxes, the price is $25.

Option 2

4 tiles cover 1 square foot
Sold in boxes of 50
Price: $7 for each box

4″

4″

Option 3

9 tiles cover 1 square foot
Sold in boxes of 150
Price: $10 for each box

Option 4

1 tile covers 1 square foot
Sold in boxes of 30
Price: $12.50 for each box

You also need one box of filler tiles for every 100 tiles to complete the border.
Price: $8 for each box

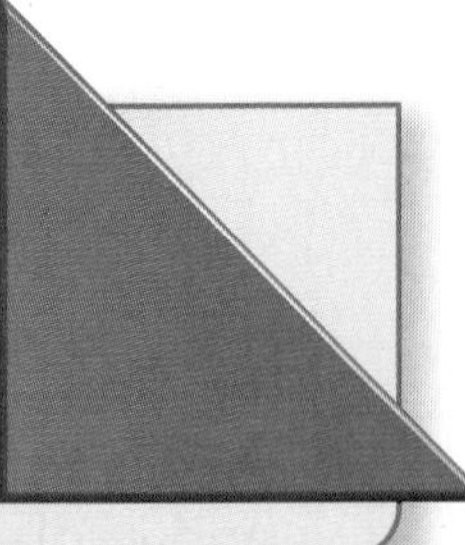

Option 5

2 tiles cover 1 square foot
Sold in boxes of 100
Price: $27.50 for each box

Read For Understanding

1. How many square feet do you need to cover to make the mosaic?
2. How much money can you spend?
3. How many 12-by-12 tiles come in a box?
4. How many 6-by-6 tiles do you need to cover 1 square foot?
5. How many 4-by-4 tiles can you buy for $10?
6. How many boxes of filler tiles would you need if you used 100 hexagon tiles?
7. How many triangle tiles do you need to cover 1 square foot?
8. What is the minimum number of triangle tiles you can buy?

Problem Solving

Make Decisions

9. How many 12-by-12 tiles would you need to make the mosaic? how many boxes?
10. How many 6-by-6 tiles would you need to make the mosaic? how many boxes?
11. How many 4-by-4 tiles would you need to make the mosaic? how many boxes?
12. How many hexagon tiles would you need to make the mosaic? how many boxes?
13. How many hexagon tiles would be left over if you bought 4 boxes and used 100 of them?
14. How many boxes of filler tiles would you need if you use hexagon tiles?
15. How many triangle tiles would you need to make the mosaic? how many boxes?
16. Calculate how much it will cost to use 12-by-12 square tiles.
17. How much will it cost to use the 6-by-6 square tiles?
18. How much will it cost to use the 4-by-4 square tiles?
19. How much will it cost to use the hexagon tiles?
20. How much will it cost to use the right triangle tiles?
21. Are there any tiles you cannot afford to use?
22. Are there any shapes that will not tessellate?
23. Which shape do you think will make the most interesting design?
24. Which shape do you think will be the easiest to install?

Your Decision!

Which tile would you choose? Explain your decision.

Objective: Apply geometry to investigate science concepts.

Problem Solving: Math and Science
What shape holds the most weight?

If you have ever performed on a stage or seen a performance, you may have noticed that the platform must hold a lot of weight.

In this activity you will attempt to design and build a platform that can hold as much weight as possible.

You Will Need
- **sheets of paper**
- **textbooks**
- **tape**
- **scissors**
- **ruler**

Hypothesize

What is the greatest number of math textbooks a paper structure can hold?

Safety

Be careful when working with scissors.

Procedure

1. Build a platform that holds as many books as possible.

   You can:

   - fold, bend or tape the paper any way you want
   - cut the paper
   - try as many different shapes as you want

   You cannot:

   - use any extra materials

2. Build your first platform. Count how many books you can lay across it.

3. Try again.

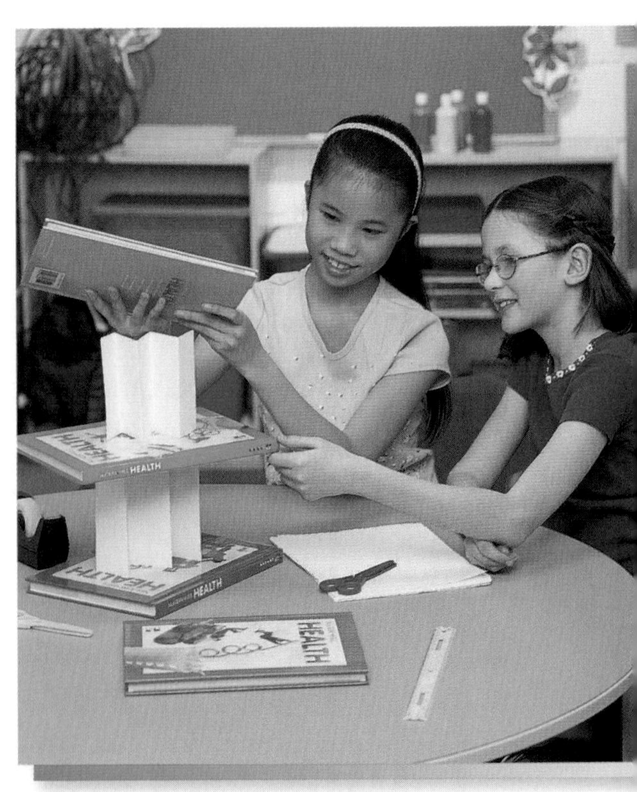

Data

Copy and complete the chart to record your observations. Sketch or describe each platform you built. Record how many books it held.

Shape	Number of Books

Problem Solving

Conclude and Apply

- Which structure held the most weight? Why was it so strong?
- Explain the strategies you used to improve your design.
- Record the maximum number of books each group's platform could hold. Make a bar graph to display the data.

- Explain how you worked like a **design engineer** during this activity.

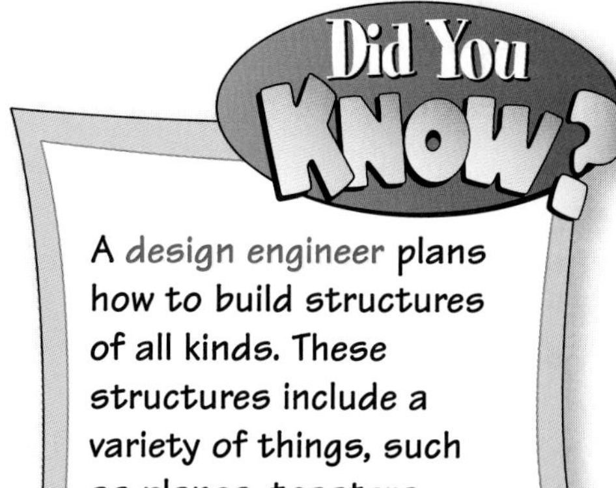

A design engineer plans how to build structures of all kinds. These structures include a variety of things, such as planes, toasters, bridges, and engines.

Going Further

1. Build the smallest possible structure that will hold at least one textbook.
2. Design a bridge that will let a toy car cross it.

Check Your Progress B

Tell whether the figures are congruent, similar, or neither. **(pages 506–507)**

1. 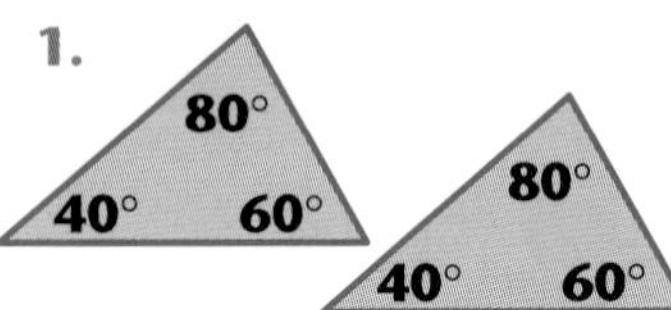

2. 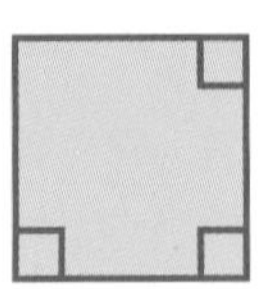

3. 130° 150° 50° 30° / 130° 150° 50° 30°

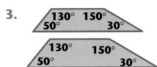

4. 

Write whether a translation, reflection, or rotation was made. **(pages 508–511)**

5. 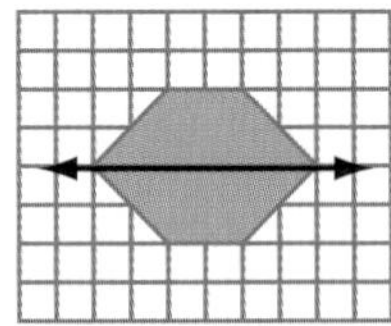

6. 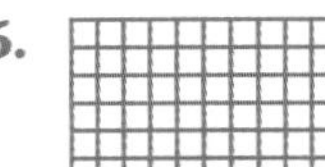 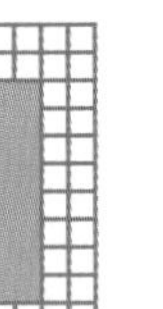

7. 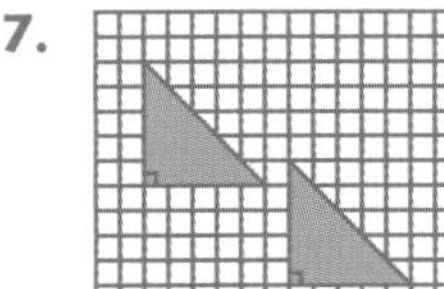

8. 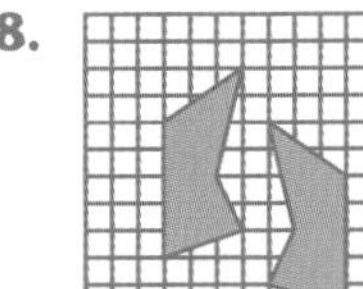

Draw all the lines of symmetry. **(pages 512–513)**

9. 

10. 

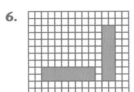

11. 

12. 

Identify the parts of circle *X*. **(pages 516–519)**

13. Center
14. Radius
15. Diameter
16. Chord

Solve. Use circle *X*. **(pages 516–519)**

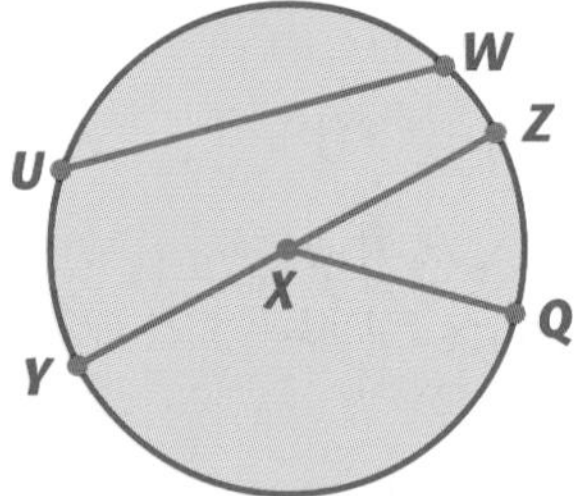

17. If the length of $\overline{YZ}$ is 8 feet, how long is $\overline{XQ}$?

Solve. **(pages 506–521)**

18. Emmanuel looks at a painting and says, "I see a quadrilateral with four congruent sides but no right angles." What shape does he see?

19. A sculpture is made of boxes holding metal balls. The number of balls in each consecutive box is 8, 11, 14, 17, 20. Explain what the pattern could be. Tell how many balls would be next.

20. **Explain** how to use a Triman compass to draw a circle with a diameter of 4 centimeters.

Additional activities at
www.mhschool.com/math

Extra Practice

Basic Geometric Ideas (pages 486–489)

Identify the figure. Then name it using symbols.

1. A B
2. •P
3. R S
4. C D

Name the polygons.

5. 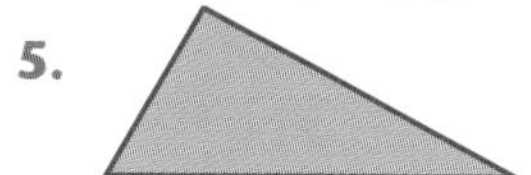
6. 
7. 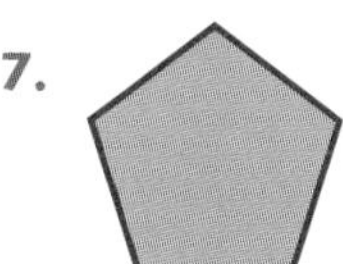
8. 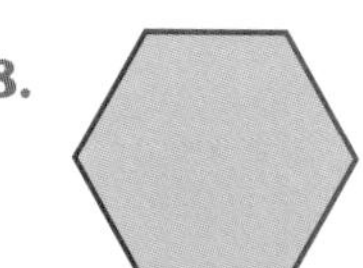

Solve.

9. Order the following polygons from greatest to least number of vertices—pentagon, octagon, triangle.
10. Is an oval a polygon? Explain.

Measure and Classify Angles (pages 490–493)

Use a protractor to measure each angle. Classify the angle as acute, right, or obtuse.

1. 
2. 
3. 
4. 

Name the pair of lines as intersecting, parallel, or perpendicular.

5. 
6. 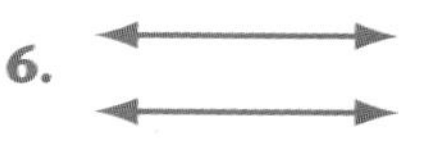
7. 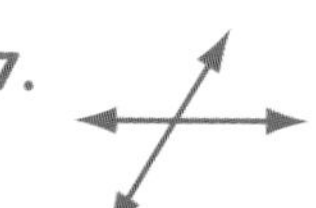
8. 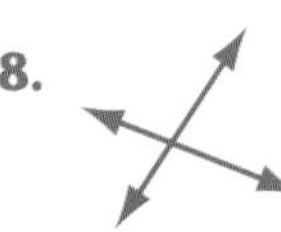

Triangles (pages 494–497)

Classify each triangle as equilateral, isosceles, or scalene and right, acute, or obtuse.

1.
2. 
3. 
4. 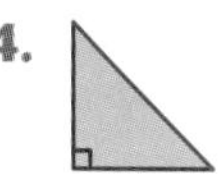

Find the measure of the unknown angle.

5. 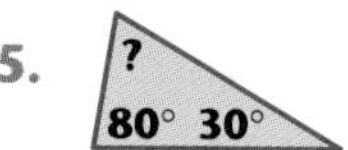

6. 

7. 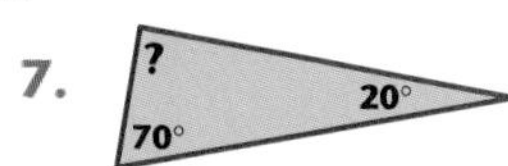

8. 

Solve.

9. A right triangle has a 60 degree angle. Find the measure of the third angle.
10. Can an obtuse triangle be an isosceles? Explain.

Extra Practice

Quadrilaterals (pages 498–501)

Classify the quadrilateral. Then find the measure of the unknown angle.

1. ?

2. 100° ? 80° 80°

3. 150° 30° ? 150°

Problem Solving: Reading for Math Draw a Diagram (pages 502–503)

1. Bill stacks a 5-centimeter square on top of a 2-centimeter by 20-centimeter rectangle. What is the smallest rectangular box he can use to pack them together?

2. Carmen ships a 30-inch by 20-inch painting in a square box. What is the smallest size box she can use?

Congruence and Similarity (pages 506–507)

Identify the corresponding side or angle.

1. $\overline{HA}$

2. $\angle CUP$

3. $\overline{CP}$

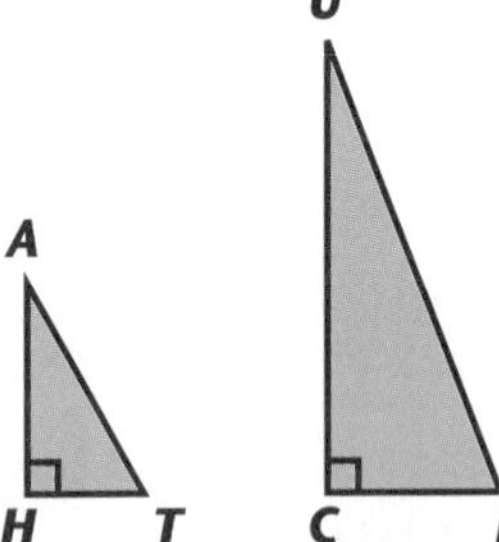

Transformations (pages 508–511)

Write whether a translation, reflection, or rotation was made.

1.

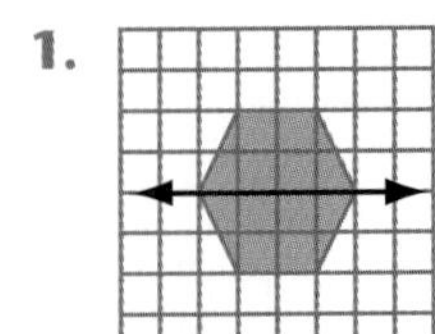

2.

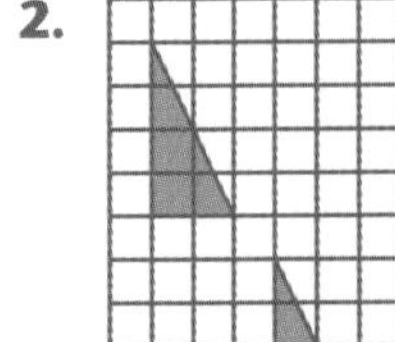

3.

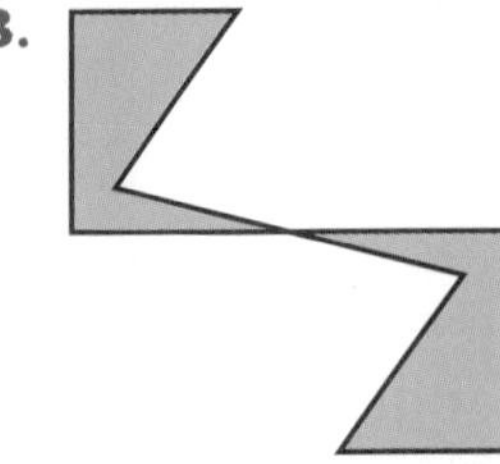

4. Jana is rearranging her bedroom furniture. She wants to move an art poster from under the window to the right of the window along the same wall. What kind of transformation will this move require?

Extra Practice

Symmetry (pages 512–513)

Tell which figures are symmetric about a line.

1. 
2. 
3. 
4. 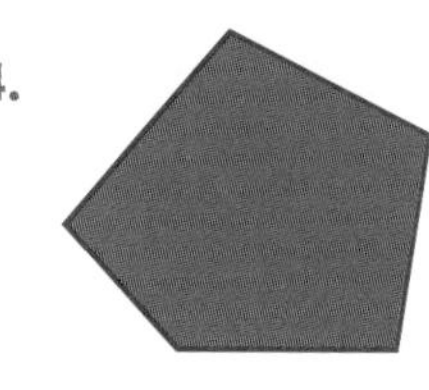

Trace the figure. Draw all the lines of symmetry.

5. 
6. 
7. 
8. 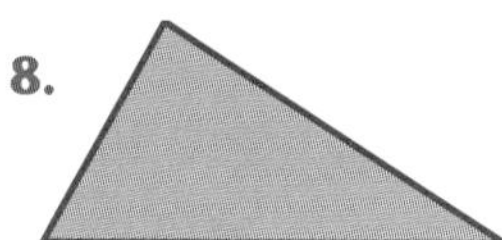

Problem Solving: Strategy Find a Pattern (pages 514–515)

1. Ming takes a 4-week painting class. He makes one painting the first week. After that he makes three more paintings each week than the week before. How many paintings will he make in the last week of the class?
2. For a drawing class, Nestor uses one pencil the first week, and twice as many pencils each week as the week before. How many pencils does he need the sixth week?

Circles (pages 516–519)

Identify the parts of circle Q.

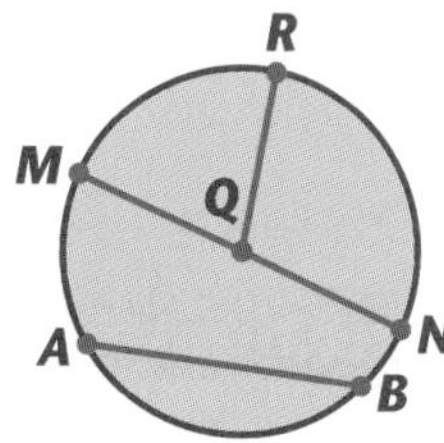

1. Center
2. Chord
3. Diameter
4. Central angle

Solve.

5. Explain how Laura can draw a circle with a 6-centimeter diameter using a Triman compass.

Tessellations (pages 520–521)

Tell whether the shape tessellates.

1. Square
2. Hexagon
3. Circle
4. Right triangle

Solve.

5. Explain how you know that a shape tessellates.

Chapter Study Guide

Language and Math

Complete. Use words from the list.

1. A straight path that goes in two directions without end is a(n) ____.
2. A three-sided polygon whose angle measures are all less than 90 degrees is called a(n) ____.
3. A line segment drawn from one point on a circle to another point and passing through the center is called a(n) ____.
4. Two figures that have the same shape but are different sizes are called ____.
5. When you make a transformation of a figure by moving it to a new location it is called a(n) ____.

Math Words

acute triangle
corresponding parts
diameter
line
parallelogram
radius
ray
similar figures
tessellation
translation

Skills and Applications

Measure, draw, and classify angles. (pages 490–493)

Example

Classify each angle as right, acute, or obtuse.

Solution

Use a protractor to find the measure of the angle.

$\angle ABC$ measures 120 degrees.

So $\angle ABC$ is an obtuse angle.

Classify each angle as right, acute, or obtuse.

6. 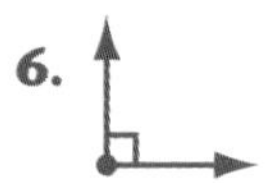

7. 

8. Can an obtuse and an acute angle ever total 180 degrees? Give an example to justify your answer.

Name and describe geometric figures. (pages 486–489, 494–501)

Example

Classify each polygon.

Solution

The figure has 4 sides. So it is a quadrilateral.

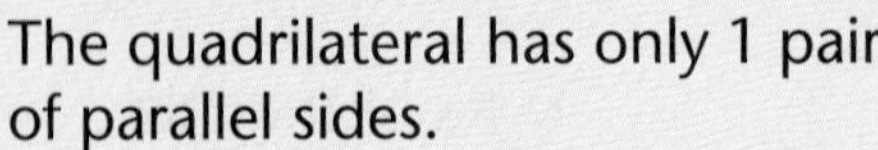

The quadrilateral has only 1 pair of parallel sides.

The figure is a trapezoid.

Write the name that best describes each polygon.

9. 

10. 

11. Mark is making a stained glass window. The window has 4 congruent sides, the opposite sides are parallel, and there are no right angles. What is the shape of Mark's window?

Identify similar figures and transformations. (pages 506–511)

Example

Tell what kind of transformation was made.

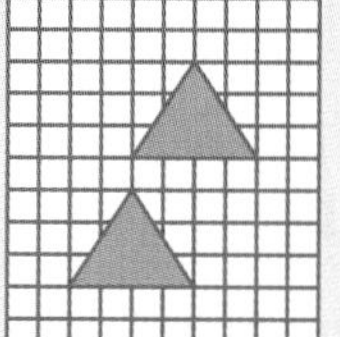

Solution

The original shape has been moved to a new location on the grid.

A translation was made.

Tell the kind of transformation.

12. 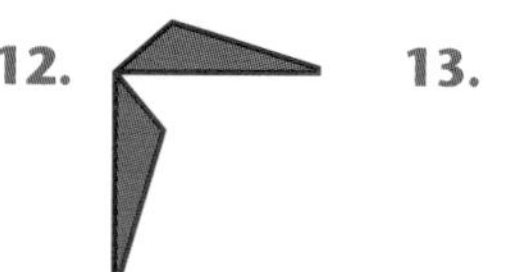

13. 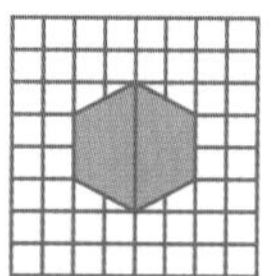

Identify the corresponding side or angle.

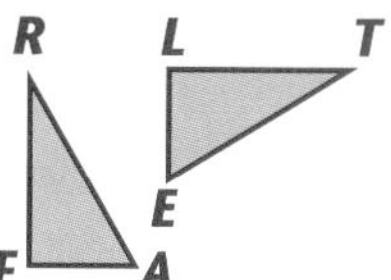

14. $\overline{AF}$

15. *LET*

16. Angelica draws a triangle, makes a mirror image of it, and slides it across the page. What kind of transformation did she make?

Find the unknown angle of a figure. (pages 494–501)

Example

Find the measure of the missing angle.

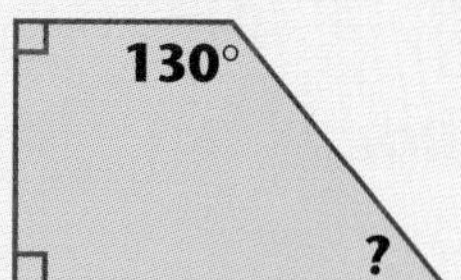

Solution

The sum of the measures of the angles in a quadrilateral is 360 degrees.

$90° + 90° + 130° + n = 360°$
$n = 50°$

The measure of the missing angle is 50 degrees.

Find the measure of the missing angle.

17. 18.

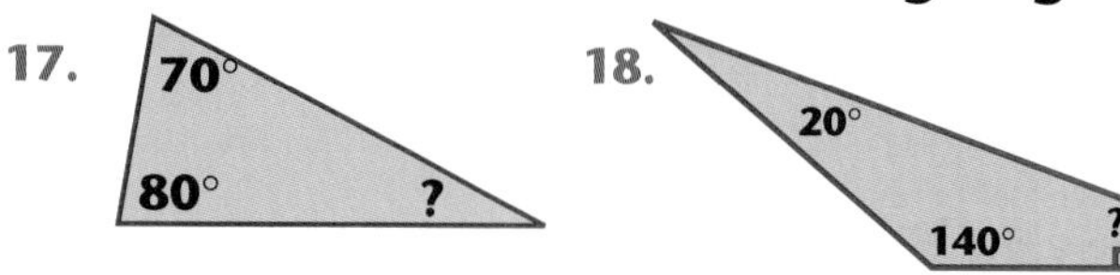

Solve.

19. **Explain:** Jonah has a 4-sided figure. He finds that the sum of the measures of 3 of the angles is 275 degrees. Is the missing angle a right angle?

Use strategies to solve problems. (pages 514–515)

Example

Max can finish 2 paintings in 3 weeks, 3 paintings in 4 weeks, 4 in 5 weeks, and 7 in 8 weeks. How long will it take Max to finish 10 paintings?

Solution

Organize the information.

Paintings	1	2	3	4	7
Weeks	2	3	4	5	8

The number of weeks is 1 more than the number of paintings.
It will take Max 11 weeks.

Solve.

20. Hector paints two paintings during his first week of art class. He paints one more painting each week than the week before. How many paintings does he make in the fourth week?

Chapter Test

Classify the triangles as right, acute, or obtuse.

1.

2.

3.

Classify each polygon. Classify any triangle as scalene, isosceles, or equilateral.

4.

5.

6.

Tell what kind of transformation was made.

7. 

8.

9.

Identify the congruent parts.

10. $\overline{AL}$ 11. $\angle LAM$

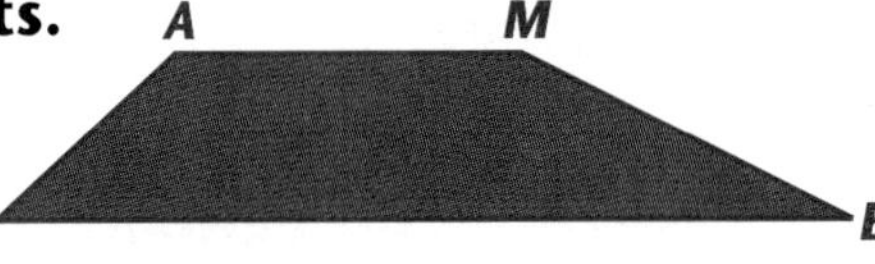

Identify the parts of the circle *O*.

12. Diameter 13. Center 14. Central angle

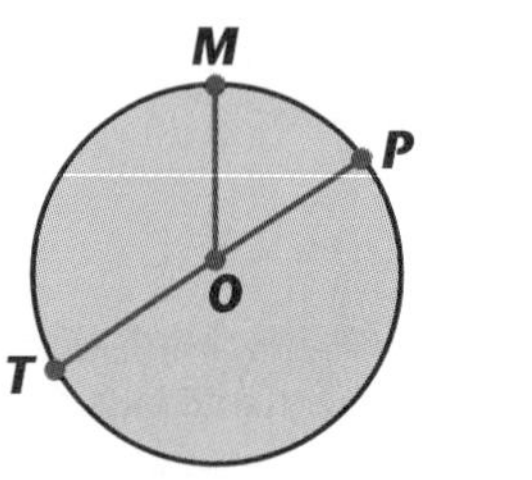

Find the measure of the missing angle.

15. 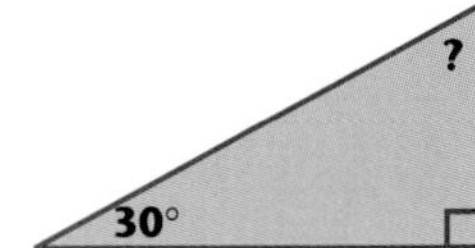

16. 

17. 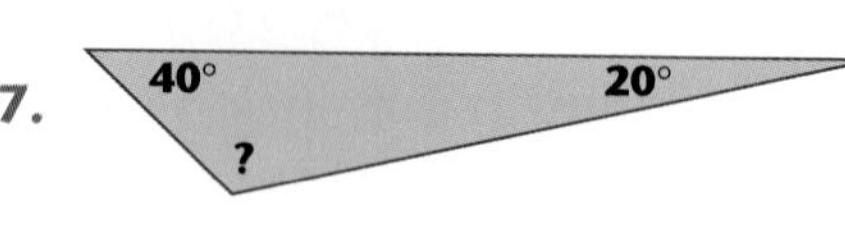

Solve.

18. A sculpture has a trapezoid-shaped base. The sum of the measures of two of the angles is 160 degrees. What is the sum of the measures of the other 2 angles?

19. August paints twice as many pictures each week as the week before. If he paints two pictures during the first week, how many does he paint during the third week?

20. Chris cuts a square along one of its diagonals. What 2 figures does he make?

Performance Assessment

One of your responsibilities working at a museum might be to catalog paintings. Suppose your museum acquires the Auguste Herbin painting you saw at the beginning of the chapter. You are responsible for writing a general description of the painting and answering the questions below.

- Are there any congruent or similar shapes in the painting? Explain.
- Are there any transformations in the painting? Explain.
- Are there any symmetric shapes in the painting? Explain.
- Are there any tessellations in the painting? Explain.

A Good Answer

- has a general description of the painting.
- answers the questions

You may want to save this work in your portfolio.

Enrichment

Networks

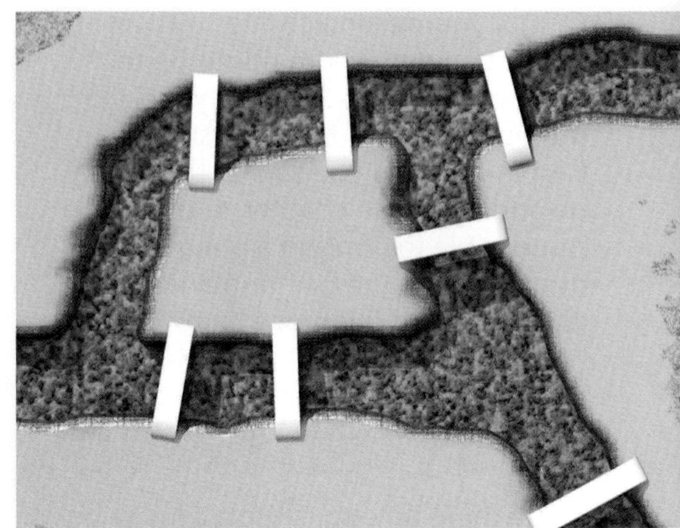

The city of Königsberg in Eastern Prussia sits on the banks of the Pregel River. The river passes a small island before forking into two paths. To connect the sides of the city, seven bridges span the river, as seen in the drawing on the right.

The citizens of Königsberg once tried to find a path around the city that would cross each bridge exactly once. No one could do it. Then, in 1736, the Swiss mathematician Leonhard Euler attacked the problem.

Instead of using a map, Euler used capital letters to stand for the land masses and small letters to stand for the bridges. Today, we build on Euler's approach, using **vertices** to stand for the land masses and **edges** to stand for the bridges. This combination of vertices and edges is called a **network.**

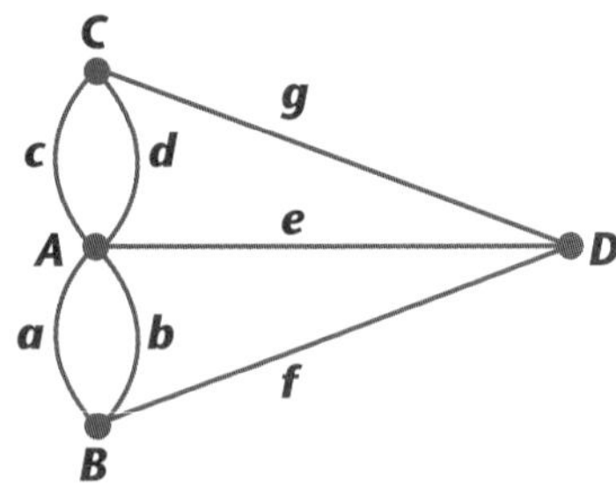

Look at the network carefully. All four of its vertices meet either 3 or 5 edges. Euler proved that such a network cannot have a path along it that crosses each bridge exactly once. The reason may seem surprising: it is the fact that all four vertices meet an odd number of edges. **In order for a path crossing all edges exactly once to be possible, there must be 0 or 2 vertices meeting an odd number of edges.**

Practice

1. Add 1 new edge to the network shown for Königsberg. Then find a path that would please the citizens of Königsberg.

Determine whether a path can be drawn in which each edge is crossed exactly once. If one can be, find and trace it. If it cannot, explain why not.

2. 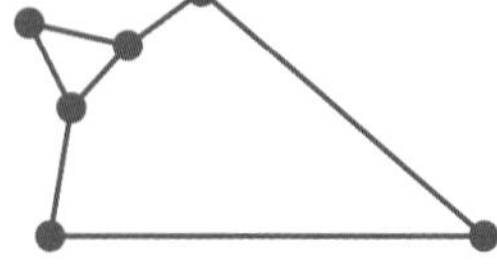

3. 

4. 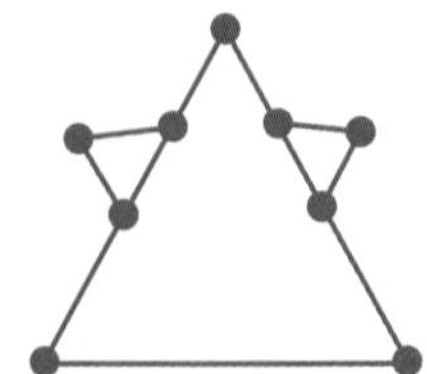

5. 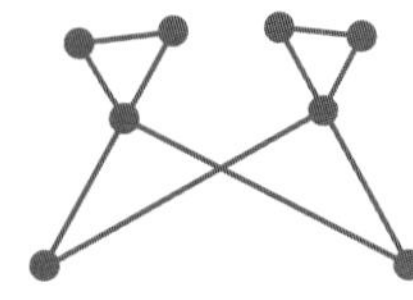

Test-Taking Tips

Sometimes when you are taking a test, it is helpful to **draw a diagram.** Read the problem carefully, then use the information in the problem to draw a diagram that represents the problem situation. Use your diagram to help find the solution.

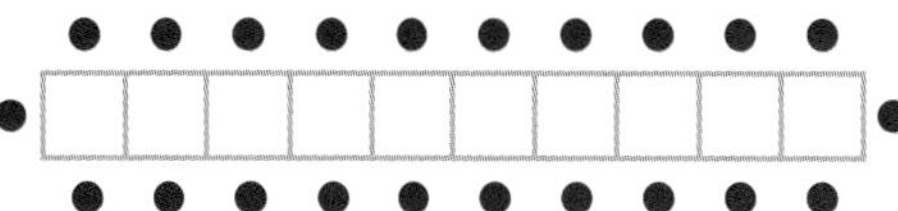

Four students can sit at one square table with one student on each side. How many students can sit at 10 tables placed together to form a row?

A. 24 C. 12

B. 22 D. Not Here

Draw a diagram.

Draw ten squares next to each other in a row. Draw a dot for each seat.

You can see from your diagram that there are 22 places for students to sit.

The correct choice is B.

Check for Success

Before turning in a test, go back one last time to check.

- ☑ I understood and answered the questions asked.
- ☑ I checked my work for errors.
- ☑ My answers make sense.

Practice **Draw a diagram to solve.**

1. Michael, Brittany, and Shawn are running in a race. Shawn finishes right ahead of Michael, but Michael does not finish last. In what order did they finish the race?
   A. Michael, Shawn, Brittany
   B. Shawn, Michael, Brittany
   C. Britanny, Michael, Shawn
   D. Michael, Brittany, Shawn

2. Amy is drilling holes in two 3-foot boards that she will use as a frame for a woven hammock. She drills a hole every 4 inches, beginning and ending 2 inches from the ends of the board. How many holes does Amy drill?
   F. 12 H. 9
   G. 10 J. 4

3. A closed figure has straight sides and no right angles. Exactly two of its sides are parallel, but not congruent. The figure has fewer sides than a pentagon. What is the figure?
   A. A square C. A rhombus
   B. A rectangle D. A trapezoid

4. Tim is decorating a picture frame that is 36 inches by 36 inches. He paints a star every 6 inches along the edge, including one in each corner. How many stars are on the frame?
   F. 216 H. 36
   G. 180 J. 24

Test Prep

Spiral Review and Test Prep

Chapters 1–11

Choose the correct answer.

Number Sense

1. Find the number that is equal to 40,000 + 3,000 + 600 + 9.
   A. 40,369 C. 43,619
   B. 43,609 D. 43,690

2. Find an equivalent decimal for 87.06.
   F. 87.00 H. 87.60
   G. 87.060 J. 870.6

3. Find the greatest common factor of 8, 12, and 24.
   A. 2 C. 24
   B. 4 D. 48

4. What is the best estimate of 23.7×97?
   F. 23,700 H. 2,037
   G. 2,400 J. 237

Algebra and Functions

5. Evaluate the expression: $3(x + 9)$ when $x = 7$.
   A. 50 C. 30
   B. 48 D. 19

6. Find the ordered pair for D.

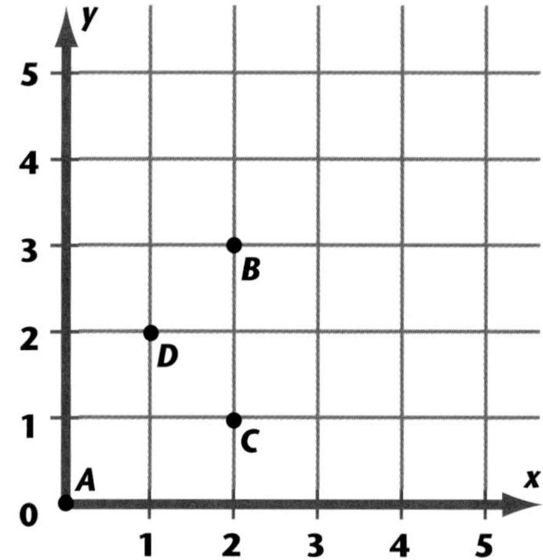

   F. (2, 1) H. (1, 2)
   G. (1, 1) J. (2, 2)

7. Solve for x: $3x + 2 = 17$.
   A. 19 C. 5
   B. $6\frac{1}{3}$ D. 3

8. Joe has 4 times as many quarters as nickels. If n = the number of nickels he has, which expression represents the number of quarters?
   F. $25n$ H. $4 + n$
   G. $4n$ J. Not Here

Measurement and Geometry

9. The sum of the measures of the angles in a triangle is

A. 90 degrees.
B. 180 degrees.
C. 210 degrees.
D. 360 degrees.

10. What kind of triangle is $\angle ABC$?

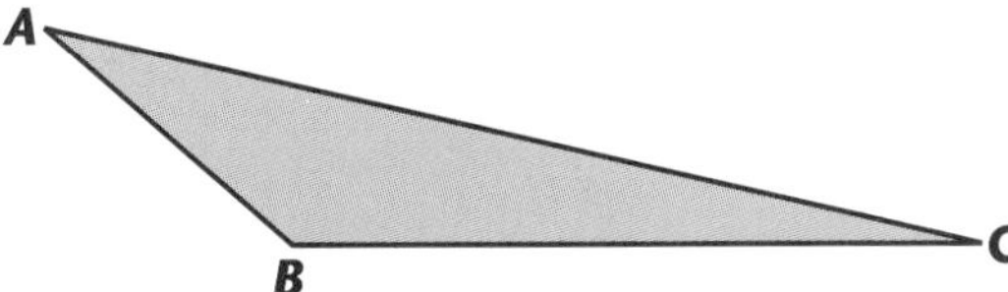

F. Acute isosceles
G. Equilateral
H. Acute right
J. Scalene obtuse

11. If the diameter of a circle is 12 feet, what is the length of the radius?

A. 6 feet
B. 12 feet
C. 4 feet
D. Not Here

12. What kind of transformation was made?

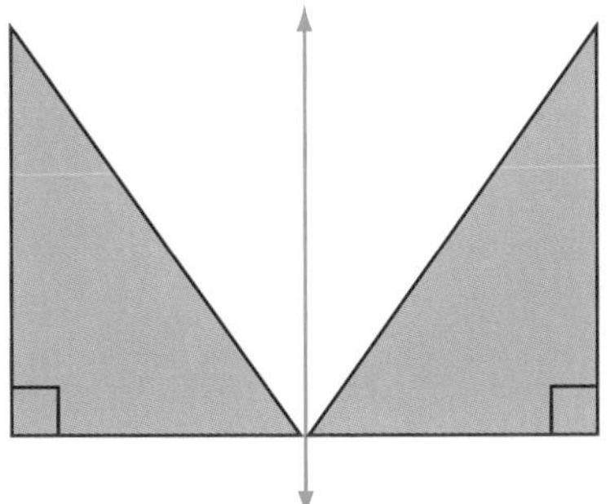

F. Reflection
G. Translation
H. Rotation
J. Glide reflection

Mathematical Reasoning

13. Mario bought a new watch set that includes 3 watch faces and 5 colored bands. How many different watches can he make?

A. 1
B. 8
C. 12
D. 15

14. A 45-pound bag of dog food weighs 3 times as much as a bag of cat food. How much does a bag of cat food weigh?

F. 42 pounds
G. 30 pounds
H. 10 pounds
J. Not Here

15. The sum of two numbers is 12. When you subtract the smaller number from the larger number, the difference is 10. What are the two numbers?

A. 8 and 4
B. 10 and 2
C. 11 and 1
D. 16 and 6

16. Use the numbers 3, 3, 4, 6 and any operations to write an expression that equals 3.

CHAPTER 12

Perimeter, Area, and Volume

Theme: Architecture

Use the Data

Building	Dimensions
Coliseum (indoor seating area)	Diameter: 51 meters Height: 49 meters
The Great Pyramid	Length: 229 meters Width: 229 meters Height: 145.75 meters
Parthenon	Length: 69 meters Width: 31 meters Height: 18 meters

- What is the distance around the Coliseum? How much land does The Great Pyramid cover? How much space is inside the Parthenon?

What You Will Learn

In this chapter, you will learn how to

- find perimeter.
- find area.
- find the surface area of rectangular prisms and cubes.
- find the volume of rectangular prisms.
- use strategies to solve problems.

Additional activities at
www.mhschool.com/math

Objective: Find the perimeter of a polygon.

12•1 Perimeter of Polygons

Learn

Math Words

perimeter the distance around a closed figure

formula an equation with at least two variables, showing how one variable depends on the other variable or variables

The Place de la Concorde is a public square in Paris, France, built between 1754 and 1763. If you walked around the outside of the square, how far would you walk?

285 m (top), 285 m (left), 285 m (right), 285 m (bottom)

This fountain is in the Place de la Concorde square. The square is 285 m on each side.

There's more than one way!

Find the **perimeter** of the square.

Method A

You can add the length of the sides.

285 m + 285 m + 285 m + 285 m = 1,140 m

Method B

You can use a **formula**.

Formula for perimeter (P) of a square:
Let s be the length of a side.

$P = s + s + s + s = 4 \times s = 4s$

Note: This formula is true because a square has four equal length sides.

Formula for perimeter (P) of a rectangle:

P = length + width + length + width
$P = \ell + w + \ell + w$

$P = (2 \times \ell) + (2 \times w)$ or $P = 2\ell + 2w$

Remember: 2ℓ means $2 \times \ell$, and $2w$ means $2 \times w$.

The Place de la Concorde has a perimeter of 1,140 meters.

Try It

Find the perimeter of each figure.

1. $18\frac{1}{2}$ ft, 12 ft, 12 ft, $18\frac{1}{2}$ ft
2. 6 m, 6 m, 9 m, 9 m, 10.5 m
3. 9 in., 4 in.
4. 15.4 cm, 15.4 cm

Describe two ways to find the perimeter of a rectangle.

Practice

Find the perimeter of each figure.

5. $4\frac{1}{2}$ ft, $4\frac{1}{2}$ ft

6. 13.8 m, 6.04 m

7. 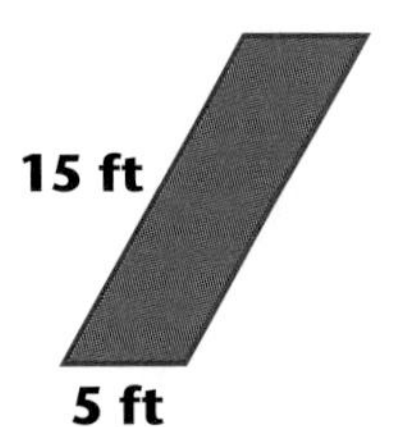

8. 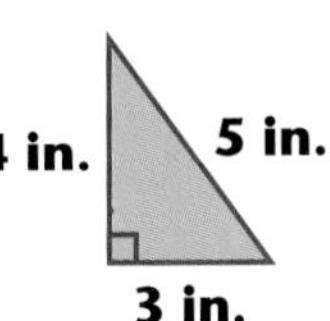

Algebra & functions **Find each missing measurement.**

9. $P = 28.2$ ft
$t = \blacksquare$

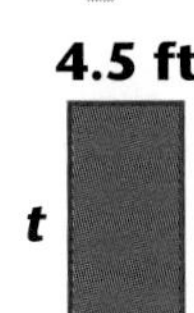

10. $P = 60$ cm
$s = \blacksquare$

11. $P = 24$ in.
$a = \blacksquare$

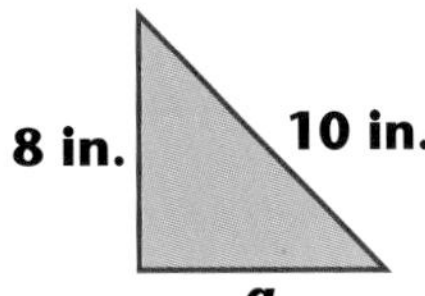

12. $P = 30$ cm
$b = \blacksquare$

b, 5 m, 5 m, 5 m, 5 m, 5 m

Problem Solving

13. A plaza measures 32 feet in length and 14 feet in width. How many feet of fencing are needed to enclose the plaza?

14. A garden in a public square is 15 feet on each side. What is the perimeter?

15. A new public space is going to have a width of 65 feet and a length of 135 feet. How many feet is it around the entire space?

16. **What if** the length of your stride is 2 feet? How many steps does it take to walk the perimeter of the new public space in problem 15?

17. **Analyze:** Give an example of two different rectangles that have the same perimeter.

18. Fourteen students help install tiles in an outdoor plaza. If each student installs 5 boxes with 30 tiles in each, how many tiles do they install?

19. **Collect Data:** Choose spaces in your home or school. Measure their lengths and widths. Find the perimeters. Make a table to show the spaces and their lengths, width, and perimeters.

★20. **Spatial Reasoning:** You have 24 feet of fencing material for a public space. Draw 4 different figures that can be enclosed by the fencing. Label their side lengths.

Spiral Review and Test Prep

21. 4×5.3

22. 0.28×4

23. $3.27 \div 1.09$

24. $10.76 \div 4$

Choose the correct answer.

25. What is the measurement of the missing angle of the triangle?

B, 60°, ?, 80°, A, C

A. 20°
C. 40°
B. 30°
D. 220°

26. Which word describes the lines below?

F. Intersecting
H. Parallel
G. Perpendicular
J. Angular

Objective: Find the area of rectangles and squares.

12·2 Area of Rectangles

Learn

Math Word

area the number of square units needed to cover a region or figure

The Parthenon of ancient Greece was built between 447 and 438 B.C. Its rectangular shape measures 69 meters long and 31 meters wide. How much area does the building cover?

There's more than one way!

You need to find the **area** of the rectangular bottom.

Method A

One way to find the area of a rectangle is to count the squares.

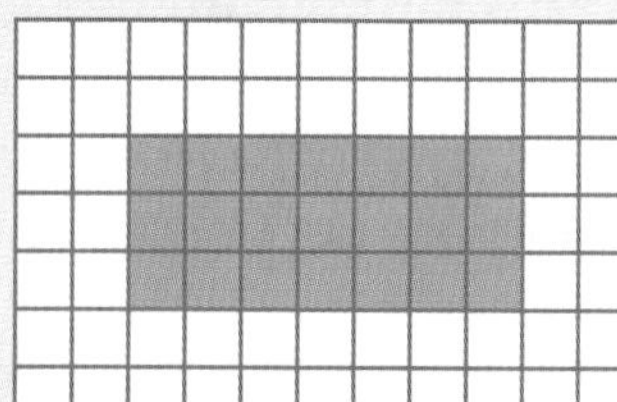

Method B

You can also use a formula.
Multiply the length by the width.

Formula for area (A) of a rectangle:
$A = \text{length} \times \text{width}$ or $A = \ell w$

Formula for area (A) of a square:
$A = \text{side} \times \text{side}$ or $A = s \times s = s^2$

$A = 69 \times 31 = 2{,}139$ square meters

Remember: ℓw means $\ell \times w$

Area is measured in square units, such as square inches ($in.^2$), square centimeters (cm^2), and square meters (m^2). A square centimeter, for example, is the area of a square with sides 1 centimeter long.

The Parthenon has an area of 2,139 square meters.

Note: The area and perimeter of rectangles are *not* related. An 8 unit by 6 unit rectangle has an area of 48 square units and a perimeter of 28 units. A 12 by 4 rectangle also has an area of 48 square units, but a perimeter of 32 units. Can you draw two rectangles with the same perimeter but different areas?

Try It

Find the area of each figure.

1. 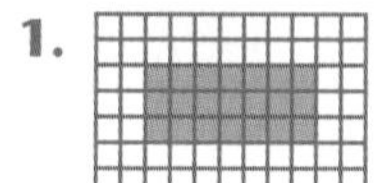

2. 5 ft by 6 ft

3. 4.1 cm by 8.7 cm

4. 

Sum it Up Explain how to find the area of a rectangle.

Practice

Find the area of each figure.

5. 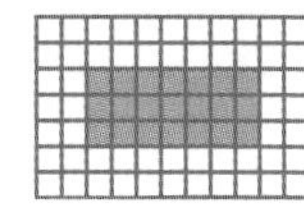

6. 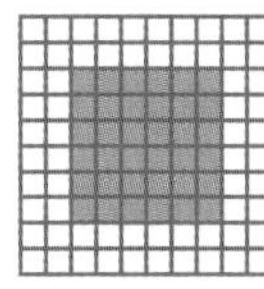

7. 13.4 m; 8.5 m

8. $6\frac{1}{2}$ in.; $6\frac{1}{2}$ in.

Algebra & functions

Find each missing measurement.

9. $A = 12\text{ cm}^2$

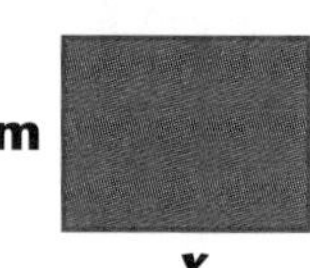

10. $A = 1\text{ in.}^2$

11. $A = 9\text{ cm}^2$

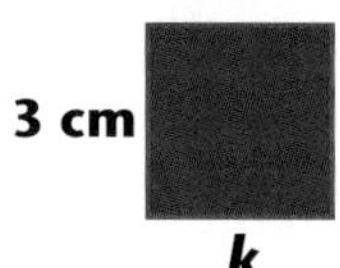

12. $A = 2\text{ in.}^2$

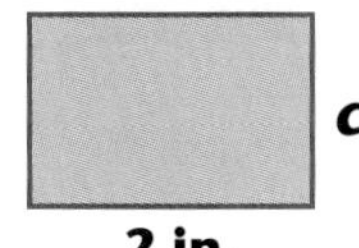

Problem Solving

13. A new building measures 42 feet by 30 feet. How much land does it cover?

14. What is the perimeter of a building measuring 42 feet by 30 feet?

15. **Summarize:** Write the formulas for the area of a rectangle and a square. Explain what each letter stands for.

16. **Create a problem** about a rectangular building. Solve it and give it to another student to solve.

★17. The door of a new building will be covered with large metal sheets. The door measures 7 feet by 3 feet. Each sheet of metal covers 1 square foot. If each sheet costs $15, how much will it cost to cover the door?

★18. **Spatial Reasoning:** You want to design a treehouse that has a rectangle or square shape. The area will be 36 square feet. What are the lengths of the sides of a rectangle or square that would have the greatest perimeter?

Spiral Review and Test Prep

Classify each angle.

19. 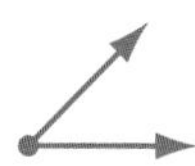

20. 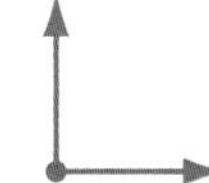

21. M, N, O

Choose the correct answer. Use data from the graph for problems 22–23.

22. How many votes did football get?

A. 4
C. 10
B. 8
D. 20

23. How many more votes did basketball get than hockey?

F. 2
G. 3
H. 6
J. 15

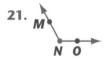

Our Favorite Sports

Sport	Vote
Baseball	6 baseballs
Basketball	10 basketballs
Football	8 footballs
Hockey	4 pucks
Soccer	2 soccer balls

1 object = 1 vote

Extra Practice, page 573

Objective: Identify the main idea and supporting details of a problem.

12•3 Problem Solving: Reading for Math
Distinguish Between Perimeter and Area

Future Architects Build Doghouses for Animal Shelter

Read

The Future Architects are building a 2-foot by 2-foot doghouse for the animal shelter. They must decide how much plywood is needed for the floor. Should they find the perimeter or area of the doghouse?

READING SKILL ▶ **Compare and Contrast**

The main idea of a word problem is the question that needs to be answered. Supporting details provide needed information.

- **What do you know?** The doghouse will be 2 feet by 2 feet
- **What do you need to decide?** Whether to find the perimeter or the area

MATH SKILL ▶ **Distinguish Between Perimeter and Area**

- Perimeter is a measure of the distance around a figure.
- Area is the number of square units inside the figure.

Plan

Sketch the doghouse floor and label the sides. Decide whether you need to find perimeter or area.

Solve

Use area to find the number of square units in the floor.
Area = length × width = 2 ft × 2 ft = 4 ft^2
The Future Architects need 4 square feet of plywood.

Look Back

How could you check your answer?

Explain how the architects would find how much wood they need to make a floor if they know its length and width.

State whether perimeter or area is needed. Then solve the problem.

1. The Future Architects want to put a fence around the yard of the shelter. The yard is 40 feet long and 50 feet wide.

2. The Future Architects want to cover the floor of a doghouse with a waterproof mat. The doghouse is 6 feet long and 6 feet wide.

Use data from the list for problems 3–8.

Doghouse Sizes

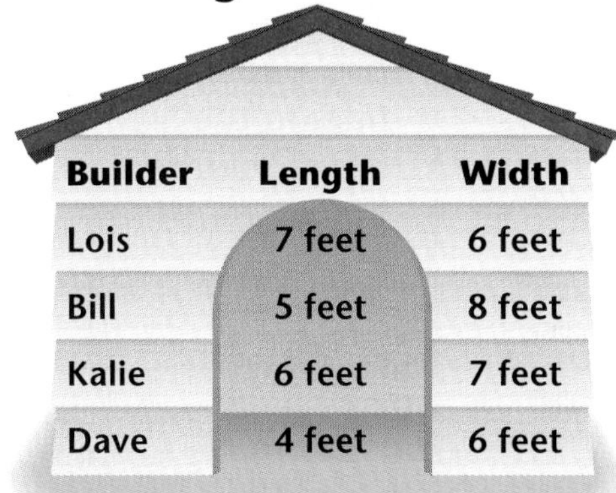

Builder	Length	Width
Lois	7 feet	6 feet
Bill	5 feet	8 feet
Kalie	6 feet	7 feet
Dave	4 feet	6 feet

3. Bill wants to put his doghouse in a shaded part of the yard. The shady spot is 44 square feet. How can Bill determine whether his doghouse will fit in this spot? Will it fit?

4. Lois wants to put a border along the outside of her doghouse. How can she determine how much border to buy? How much should she buy?

5. Dave will put a fence around the base of his doghouse. How can he determine the amount of fencing he needs? What is that amount?

6. A company gave the Future Architects 65 square feet of plywood. Bill and Dave want to use this plywood for flooring in their 2 doghouses. Is this possible? Explain.

7. Lois and Kalie put the doghouses they made side by side at the shelter. What is the area covered by these doghouses?

8. What is the difference in square feet between the largest and smallest doghouses in the list?

Spiral Review and Test Prep

Choose the correct answer.

Stacey's dog needs a doghouse with a floor that is at least 25 square feet. She plans to build a square doghouse that is 5 feet on each side. Will the house be large enough for the dog?

9. Which of the following statements is true?
   - A. The area of the doghouse is 10 square feet.
   - B. Stacey's doghouse will not be large enough for her dog.
   - C. The area of the doghouse is 25 square feet.
   - D. Stacey should build a doghouse 4 feet long.

10. When you find the area of a square, you need to know
    - F. that a square is a rectangle.
    - G. the length of all 4 sides.
    - H. the length of one side.
    - J. the perimeter.

Extra Practice, page 573

Objective: Find the area of parallelograms and rhombuses.

12·4 Explore Area of Parallelograms

Learn

Math Words

base a side of a polygon, usually the one at the bottom

height of a parallelogram the length of a line segment from one side to the side parallel to it, perpendicular to both of the sides

You can use graph paper to explore finding the area of a parallelogram.

Work Together

You Will Need
- **graph paper**
- **scissors**

▶ Use graph paper to draw and cut out a parallelogram like the one shown below. The width should be 5 units and the height 8 units. The bottom side starts 2 units to the left of the top side.

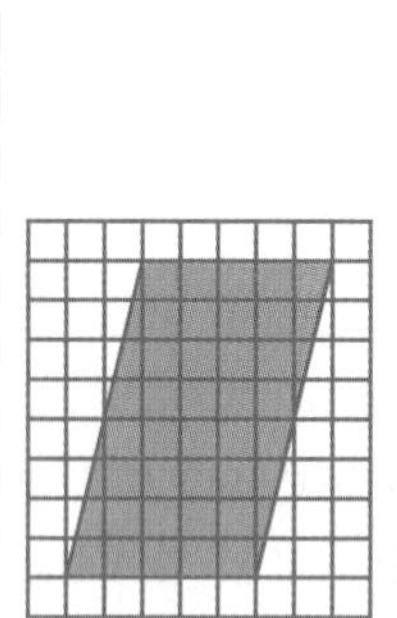

Cut out the parallelogram. Mark a triangle on the left side of the parallelogram as shown. Cut the triangle from the parallelogram.

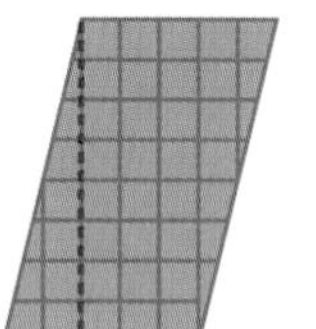

Then place the triangle that you cut out next to the right edge of the parallelogram. What do you notice about the new shape?

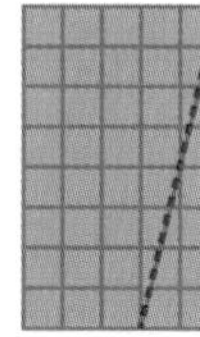

What is the relationship between the area of the original parallelogram and the area of the new rectangle?

▶ Make other parallelograms with different side lengths. Find the area of each parallelogram.

Make Connections

You can use the area of a rectangle to write a formula for the area of a parallelogram.

Using Models

Use the model of the rectangle that you made from the parallelogram.

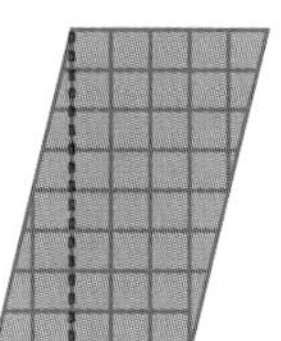

Using Paper and Pencil

The formula for the area of a parallelogram is the same as that for a rectangle. Any side can be considered a **base**. You must measure the **height** vertically from the base you choose to the opposite side.

Formula for the area of a parallelogram, where b is the base and h is the height

$A = b \times h$

$5 \times 8 = 40$

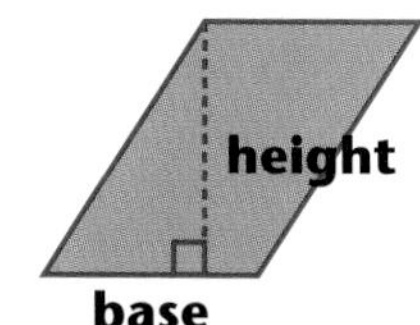

The area of the parallelogram is 40 square units.

Try It

Find the area of each figure.

1. 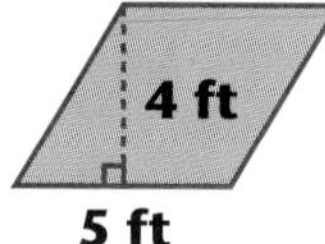

2. 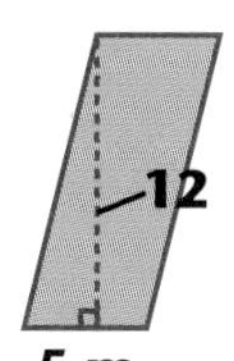

3. 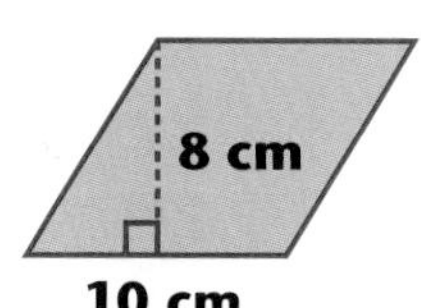

4. 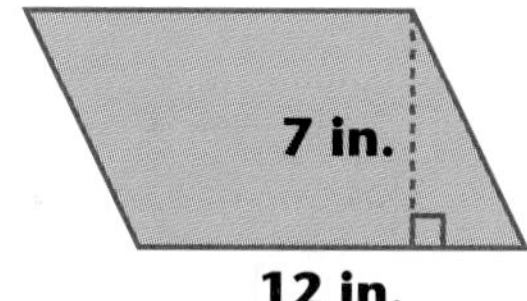

How is finding the area of a parallelogram similar to finding the area of a rectangle?

Practice

Find the area of each figure.

5. 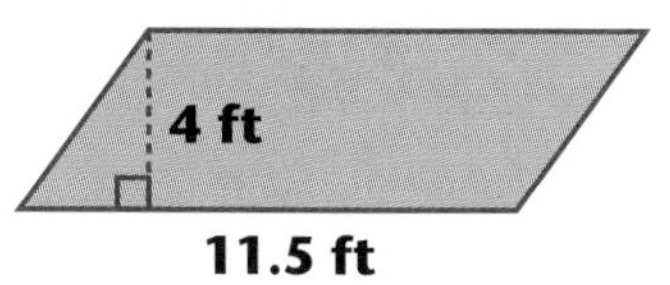

6. 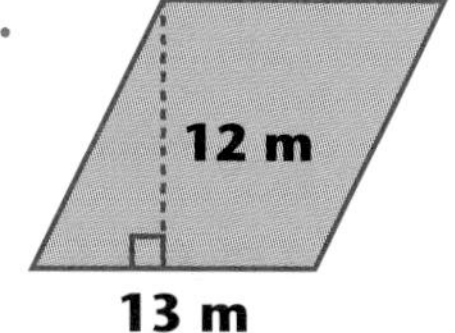

7. 

★8. 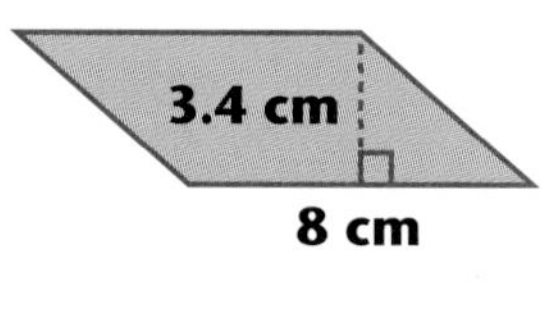

9. **Analyze:** Can two parallelograms with different shapes have the same area? Explain and give an example to support your answer.

Extra Practice, page 574

Objective: Find the area of triangles.

12·5 Explore Area of Triangles

Learn

You can use graph paper to explore finding the area of a triangle.

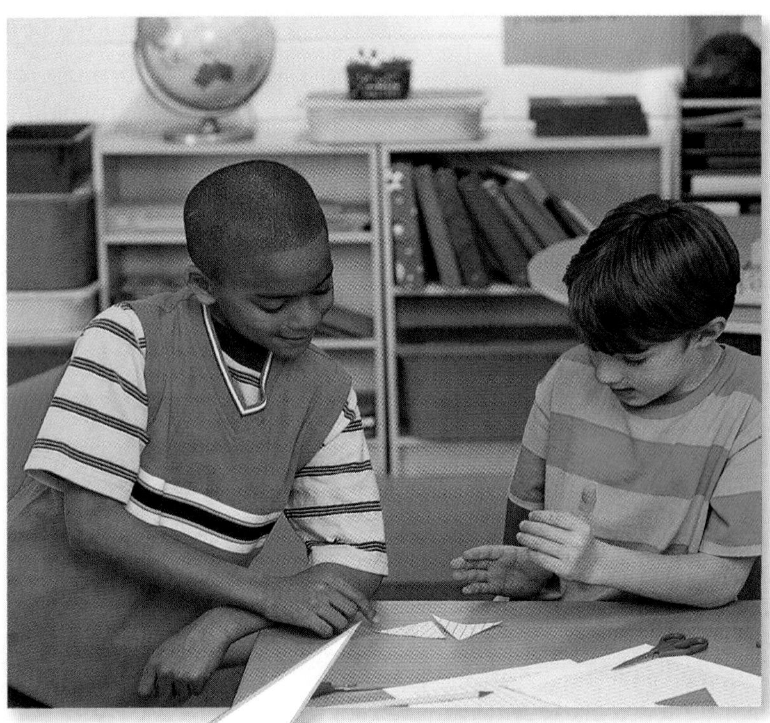

Work Together

You Will Need
- **graph paper**
- **scissors**

▶ Use graph paper to draw and cut out two identical isosceles triangles. Make the bases of the triangles 8 units and the heights of the triangles 6 units.

Fit the two triangles together to form a parallelogram.

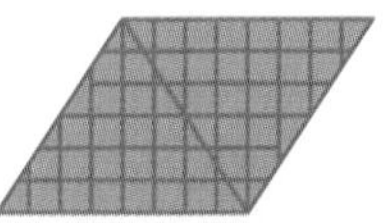

How many identical triangles are needed to form a parallelogram?

What is the relationship between the area of a triangle and the area of a parallelogram?

▶ Make your own pairs of identical triangles. Repeat the steps in the activity. Do two identical triangles always make a parallelogram?

Make Connections

You can use the area of a parellelogram to write a formula for the area of a triangle.

Using Models

Count the number of squares in the triangle. Add the half and partial squares as well.

6 units

8 units

Using Paper and Pencil

Use the formula to find the area of the triangle.

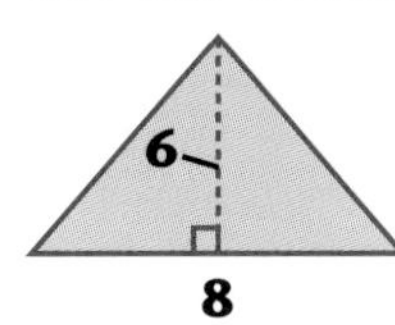

Area $= \frac{1}{2} \times$ base $\times$ height

$A = \frac{1}{2} \times b \times h$

$A = \frac{1}{2} \times 8 \times 6 = 24$

Remember: The area of a parallelogram is $b \times h$.

You can also count the number of square units in the parallelogram and divide by two. The parallelogram is 48 square units.

The area of the triangle is 24 square units.

Try It

Find the area of each triangle.

1. 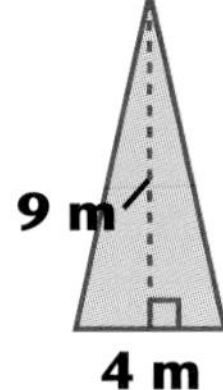

2. 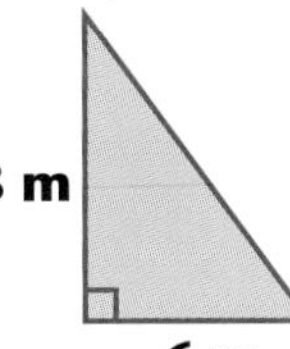

3. 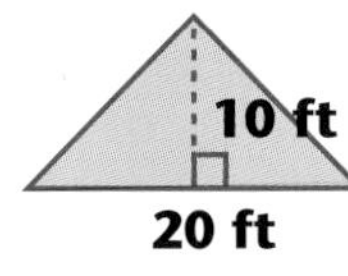

4. 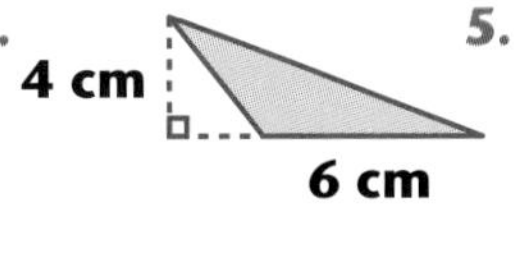

5. 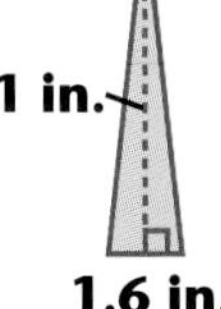

Explain how to find the area of a right triangle that is 7 centimeters along the base and 4 centimeters high.

Practice

Find the area of each triangle.

6. 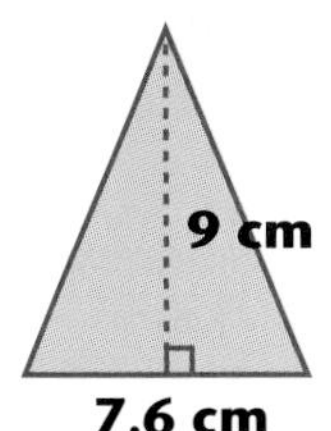

7. 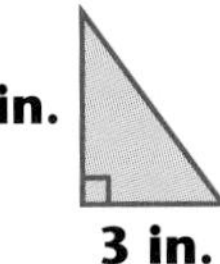

8. 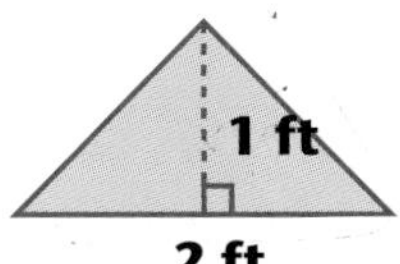

9. 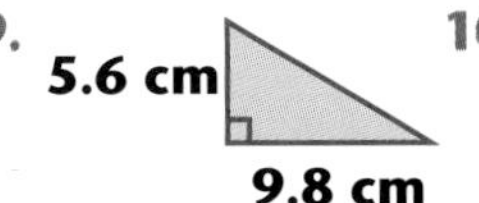

10. 

Journal

11. **Analyze:** Can two triangles of different shapes and sizes have the same area? Explain and give an example to support your answer.

Extra Practice, page 574

Objective: Find the circumference of circles.

12·6 Explore Circumference of Circles

Learn

Math Word

circumference the distance around a circle

You can use a variety of round objects to explore the circumference of a circle.

Work Together

You Will Need
- **string**
- **metric ruler**
- **round objects**

▶ You will measure the diameter and **circumference** of each round object.

- Copy and complete the table.

Object	Diameter (in Millimeters)	Circumference (in Millimeters)	Circumference ÷ Diameter

- Measure the diameter of each object to the nearest millimeter.
- Measure the circumference. Wrap string around the outside. Then measure the length of the string to the nearest millimeter.
- Divide the circumference by the diameter and round to the nearest hundredth.

▶ What do you notice about the quotients for each of the objects?

Make Connections

The circumference divided by the diameter gives a quotient that is always a little more than 3. Your quotients may have been a little different because the measurements were not exact.

> Ancient Greeks discovered that, if you divide the circumference of a circle by its diameter, you get 3.14156...They named this number π, a Greek letter that is read as "pi."
>
> Estimates for π include 3.14 and 3.1.

The formula for the circumference C of a circle is:

Think: The diameter is 2 times the radius.

Circumference $= \pi \times d = \pi \times 2 \times r$

You can write $\pi \approx 3.14$. The symbol $\approx$ means "almost equal to."

Find the circumference of a circle with a radius of 43 meters.	You can also approximate the answer by using $\pi \cong 3.14$.
$C = \pi \times d$ $= \pi \times 43$ $= 43\pi$	$C \approx 3.14 \times 43$ ≈ 135.02, or about 135 meters.

Try It **Find the approximate circumference of each circle. Use $\pi \approx 3.14$. Round to the nearest tenth, if necessary.**

1. 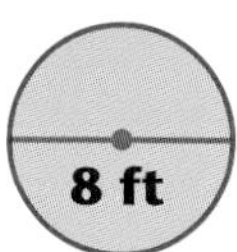

2. 

3. 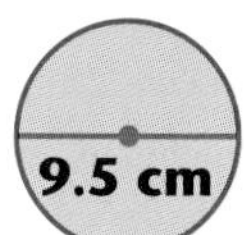

4. 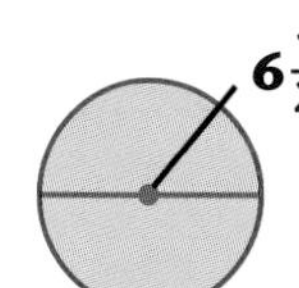

5. 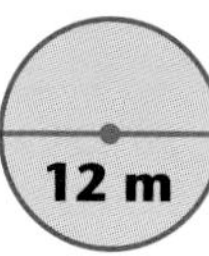

Sum it Up Explain how to find the circumference of a circle that has a diameter of 3 centimeters.

Practice **Find the approximate circumference of each circle. Use $\pi \approx 3.14$. Round to the nearest tenth, if necessary.**

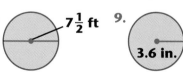

6. 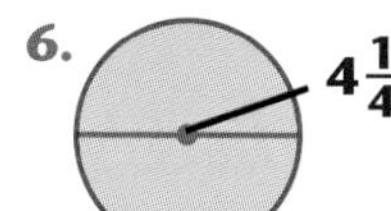

7. 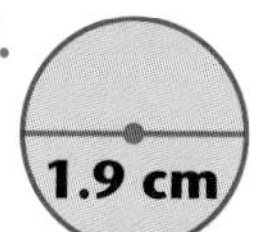

8. 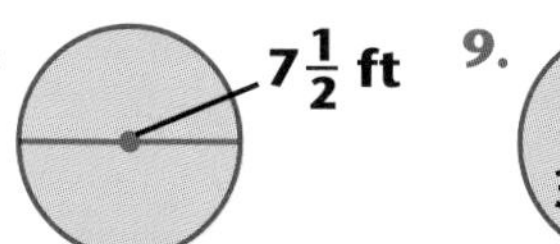

9. 3.6 in.

10. 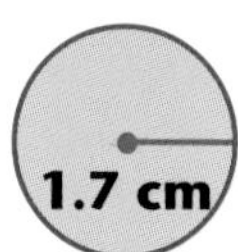

Journal

11. **Analyze:** How can you find the diameter of a circle if you know the circumference?

Extra Practice, page 574

Objective: Find the area of circles.

12•7 Explore Area of Circles

Learn

You can use a compass and graph paper to explore finding the area of a circle.

Work Together

You Will Need
- **graph paper**
- **compass**

▶ Use a compass to draw four different circles on the graph paper. The radius of each should be:

Circle A—2 units
Circle B—3 units
Circle C—4 units
Circle D—5 units

- Record the radius and radius squared for each circle in the table.
- Record an estimate for the area of each circle. You can put a square around the circle and count the number of squares.

Circle	Radius (r)	r^2	Estimate of Area of Circle	Estimate of Circle Area $\div r^2$
A				
B				
C				
D				

- Divide the estimate of the area by the radius squared. Round the quotient to the nearest hundredth.

▶ What do you notice about the quotients?

Make Connections

In the last lesson, you learned that the circumference and the diameter (or the radius) of a circle are related by the number π. The ancient Greeks made another major discovery when they found the relationship between the radius and the area of a circle. They are related by π.

Formula for the area of a circle:

The area, A, of a circle with radius r is

$A = \pi \times r \times r = \pi r^2$

> Remember: If you know the diameter, divide it by 2 to get the radius.

Find the area of a circle with a radius of 13 feet.

$$\begin{aligned} A &= \pi r^2 \\ &= \pi \times 13^2 \\ &= 169\pi \end{aligned}$$

You can also approximate the area using $\pi \approx 3.14$.

$$\begin{aligned} A &= \pi r^2 \\ &\approx 3.14 \times 13^2 \\ &\approx 530.66\text{, or about } 531 \text{ ft}^2 \end{aligned}$$

Try It **Find the approximate area of each circle. Use $\pi \approx 3.14$. Round to the nearest hundredth, if necessary.**

1. 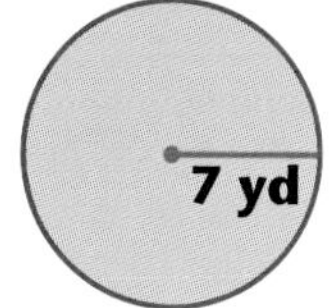

2. 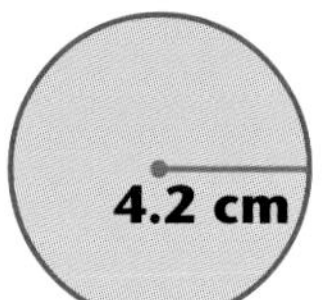

3. 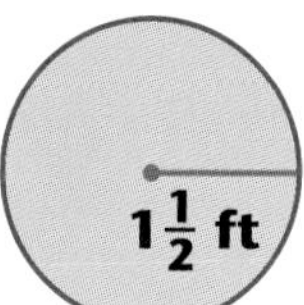

4. 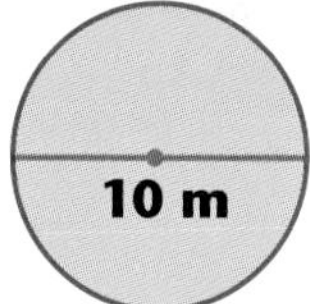

Sum it Up Explain how to find the area of a circle with a radius of 9 inches.

Practice **Find the approximate area of each circle. Use $\pi \approx 3.14$. Round to the nearest hundredth, if necessary.**

5. $r = 3.8$ m
6. $d = 8$ ft
7. $r = 2\frac{1}{2}$ in.
8. $d = 12$ cm
9. $r = 4.2$ in.
10. $d = 6.5$ m
11. $d = 3.1$ cm
12. $r = 6.5$ ft
13. **Compare:** How is finding the area of a circle different from finding the circumference? How is it the same?

Extra Practice, page 574

Check Your Progress A

Find the perimeter of each figure. **(pages 540–541)**

1. 9 in., 9 in., 9 in., 9 in., 9 in., 9 in.

2. 10 ft, 10 ft, 14 ft

Find the area of each figure. **(pages 542–543, 546–549)**

3. 9.4 mm, 9.4 mm

4. 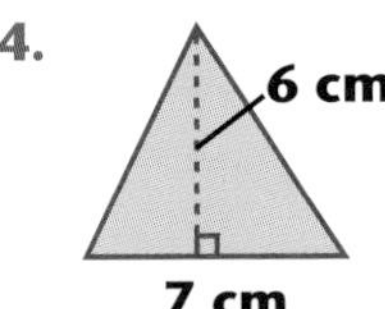

Find the approximate circumference of each circle. Use $\pi \approx 3.14$. Round to the nearest tenth, if necessary. **(pages 550–551)**

5. 15 m

6. $7\frac{1}{2}$ in.

Find the approximate area of each circle. Use $\pi \approx 3.14$. Round to the nearest hundredth, if necessary. **(pages 552–553)**

7. 8 ft

8. 3 yd

Solve. **(pages 540–553)**

9. Robert is building a doghouse for his new puppy. If the doghouse measures 2 feet by 3 feet, what is the area of the floor of the doghouse?

10. Robert wants to put a border around the doghouse. Does he need to know the perimeter or area? Explain.

Find Perimeter and Area of a Figure

Leon is designing a poster to advertise the school carnival. He wants to draw a parallelogram to show the placement of a picture on the poster. He then needs to find the perimeter and area of the parallelogram. Draw any parallelogram that could be used on the poster. Find the perimeter and area of the parallelogram.

You can use a drawing program with geometry tools to draw geometric figures.

- Click on the geometry tools.
- Click on Setup. Choose Show Labels.
- Choose the freeform polygon tool. Draw a parallelogram.
- Choose the segment tool. Draw the height of the parallelogram.
- Use the measurement tool. Find the lengths of the sides and the height of the parallelogram. Find the area of the parallelogram.

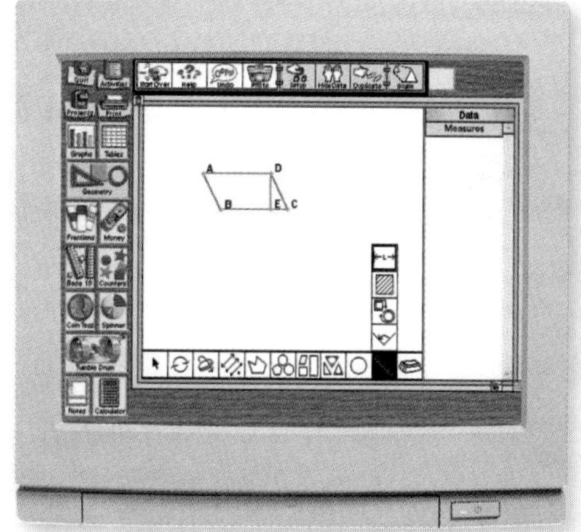

Find the perimeter and area of the parallelogram.

Use the computer to draw each figure. Then find the perimeter and area of the figure.

1. rectangle
2. right triangle
3. scalene triangle

Solve.

4. Cameron is designing a calendar. One of the pictures on the front of the calendar is a square. Cameron must draw a square to show the placement of the picture. Draw a square. Find the perimeter and area of the square.
5. Teresa is designing a book cover. She wants to put a photo shaped like a rhombus on the cover. Draw a rhombus. Find the perimeter and area of the rhombus.
6. **Analyze:** How do the geometry and measurement tools help you find the perimeter and area of figures?

For more practice, use Math Traveler™.

Objective: Solve problems by solving a simpler problem.

12•8 Problem Solving: Strategy
Solve a Simpler Problem

Read **Read the problem carefully.**

Math Word
compound figure
a shape that is made up of two or more shapes

The plan of the Pantheon in Rome from overhead looks like a circle attached to a rectangle. From the front, it looks like a triangle on top of a rectangle. How do you find the area of **compound figures**? Find the area of the plan shown below.

- **What do you know?** The length of the sides of the shape
- **What are you being asked to find?** The area of the shape

Plan One way to solve the problem is to think of it in simpler parts. You can find the area of shapes like squares, rectangles, triangles and circles. Then you can add those areas together to find the total area.

Solve

For the rectangle:

$A = \ell w$
$= 15 \times 12$
$= 180 \text{ ft}^2$

For the square:

$A = s^2$
$= 9 \times 9$
$= 180 \text{ ft}^2$

15 ft
9 ft
12 ft
9 ft

Add the two areas to get the total area.

$180 \text{ ft}^2 + 81 \text{ ft}^2 = 261 \text{ ft}^2$

The total area is 261 square feet.

Look Back Does your answer make sense?

Sum it Up! Explain how solving a simpler problem can make it easier to solve problems.

Practice Solve. Explain how you simplified each problem.

1. A backyard measures 50 feet by 60 feet and is covered with grass. A pool will be installed that covers 30 feet by 20 feet. How many square feet of grass will be left after the pool is built?

2. What is the area of the garden shown in the plan here?

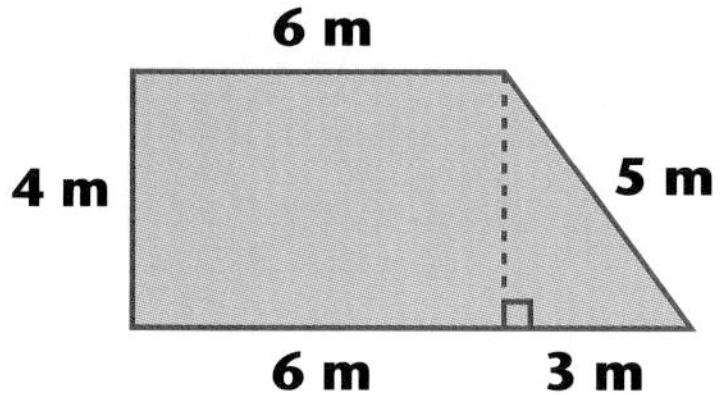

3. How much wood is needed to cover the front of the house shown in the plan?

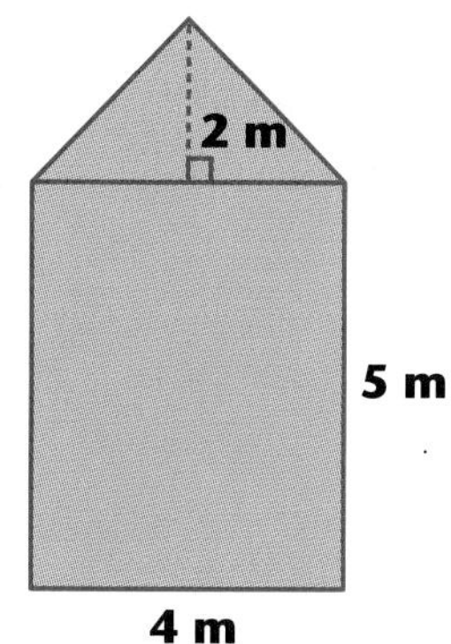

4. How much wood is needed to cover the area shown above?

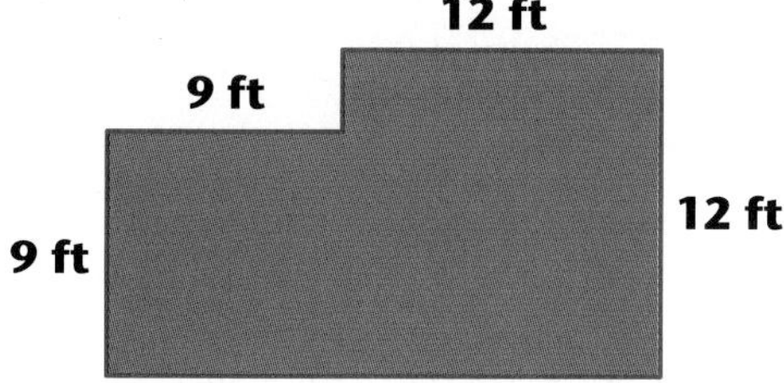

Mixed Strategy Review

5. Mitch needs 36 tiles to cover his bathroom floor. The tiles come in packages of 4, 8, and 10 tiles. Mitch wants to buy all of the same package sizes. Which package size should he buy so that he can tile his floor with no tiles left? Explain.

6. A shipping company charges the following rates to mail posters:

   \$1 for each poster for each of the first 5 posters

   \$0.50 for each poster after the first 5

   Bobby pays exactly \$8.50 for shipping. How many posters did he buy?

7. Jason is designing a rectangle-shaped garden. He wants the length of the garden to be twice the width. He wants the perimeter to be 84 feet. What length and width should Jason make the garden?

8. Chuck starts with 80 feet of wood. He uses half to build a table and half of the remainder to make a shelf. How much of the original wood is left?

CHOOSE A STRATEGY

- Logical Reasoning
- Draw a Diagram
- Make a Graph
- Make a Table or List
- Find a Pattern
- Guess and Check
- Write an Equation
- Work Backward
- Solve a Simpler Problem
- Conduct an Experiment

Extra Practice, page 574

Objective: Identify and describe 3-dimensional figures.

12•9 3-Dimensional Figures and Nets

Learn

Math Words

face a flat side of a 3-dimensional figure

edge a line segment where two faces of a 3-dimensional figure meet

vertex the common point of the two rays of an angle, two sides of a polygon, or three or more edges of a 3-dimensional figure

3-dimensional figure a figure that has length, width, and height

net a 2-dimensional pattern that can be folded to make a 3-dimensional figure

The Great Pyramids in Egypt are truly great. This 3-dimensional figure is 480 feet high. The base has sides of 748 feet, and is made of 2,300,000 limestone blocks weighing $2\frac{1}{2}$ tons each. How many faces, edges, and vertices does the pyramid have?

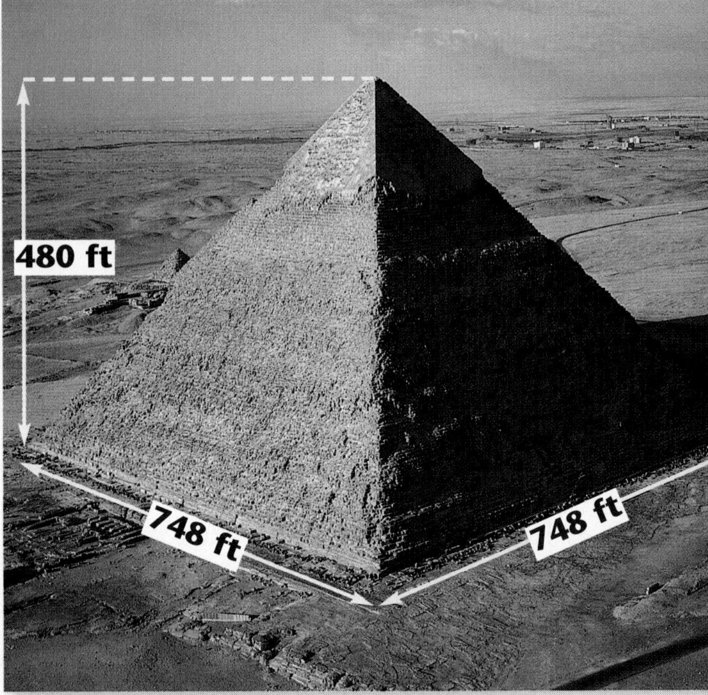

Example 1

Count the **faces**, **edges**, and **vertices** of the pyramid.

4 triangular faces + 1 square face = 5 faces
4 base edges + 4 other edges = 8 edges
4 base vertices + 1 other vertex = 5 vertices

Square Pyramid
vertex
edge
face
square base

The pyramid has 5 faces, 8 edges, and 5 vertices.

Here are examples of other 3-dimensional figures.

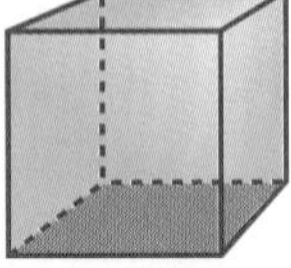
Cube

Rectangular Prism

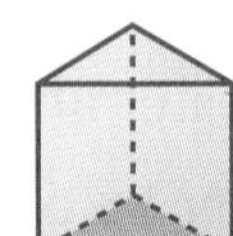
Triangular Prism

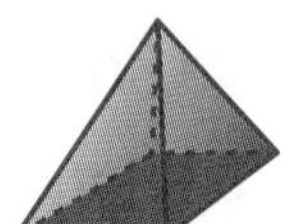
Rectangular Pyramid

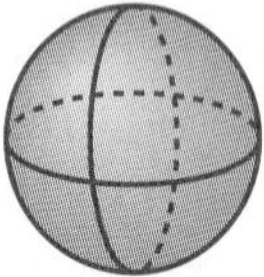
Sphere

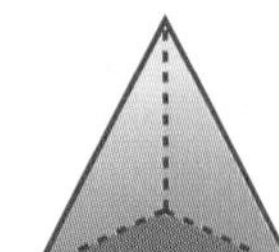
Triangular Pyramid

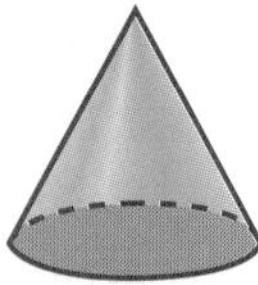
Cone

Cylinder

Example 2

Here is a net for a rectangular prism.

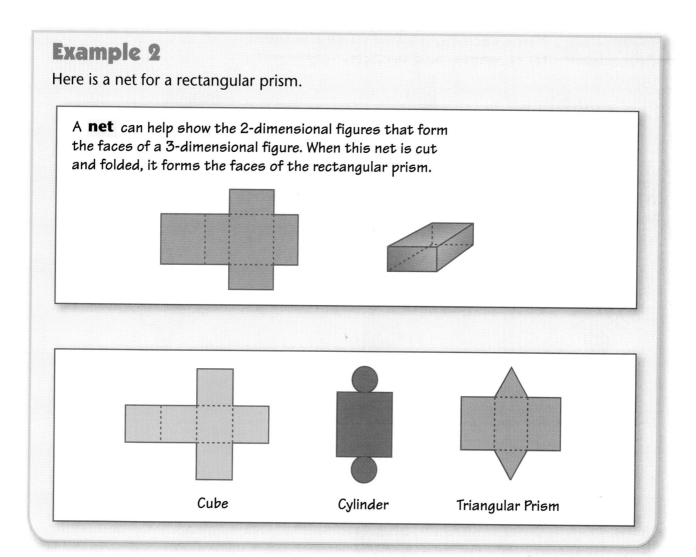

A **net** can help show the 2-dimensional figures that form the faces of a 3-dimensional figure. When this net is cut and folded, it forms the faces of the rectangular prism.

Cube

Cylinder

Triangular Prism

Try It **Write the number of faces, edges, and vertices for each figure.**

1. 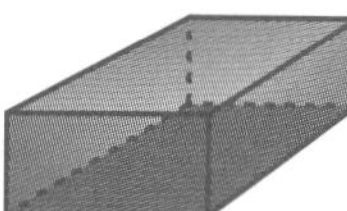

2. 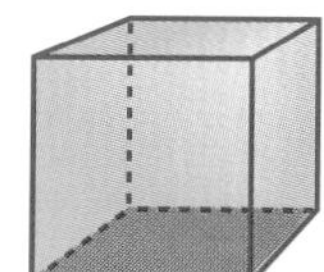

3. 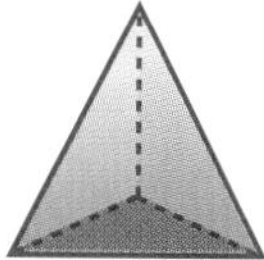

What 3-dimensional figure does each net make when cut and folded?

4. 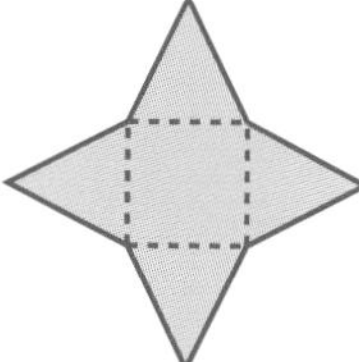

5. 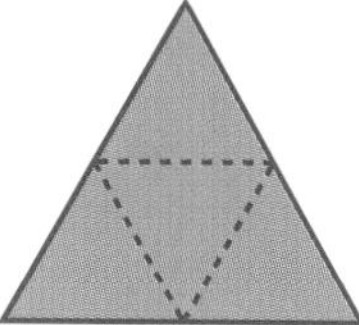

6. 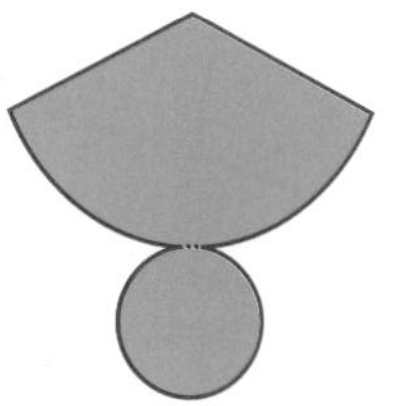

Draw a cube. Label an edge, a face, and a vertex.

Practice Name each figure and write the number of faces, edges, and vertices.

7. 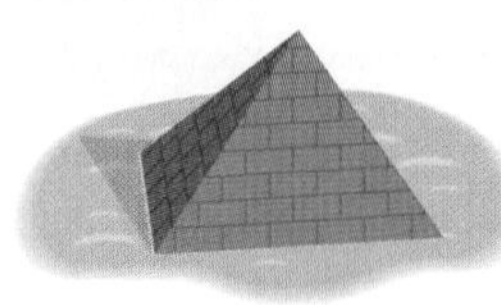

8. 

9. 

What 3-dimensional figure does each net make when cut and folded?

10. 

11. 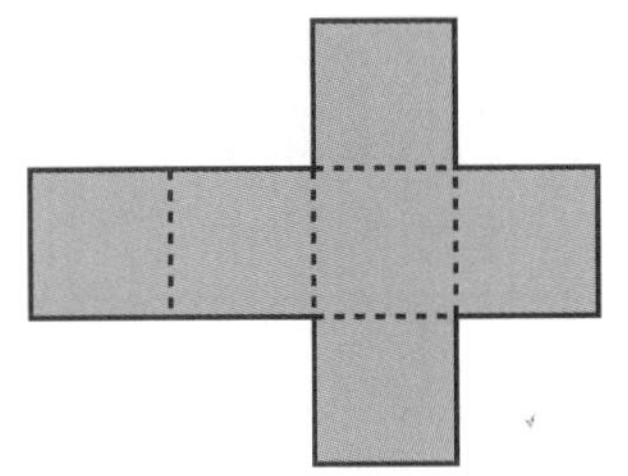

12. 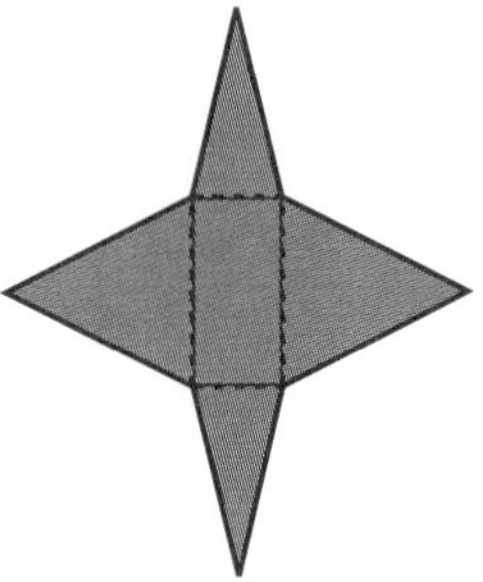

Draw the net for each 3-dimensional figure.

★13. 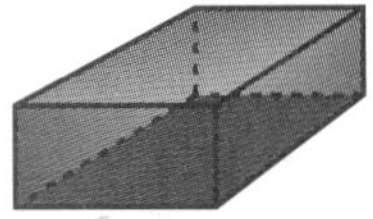

★14. 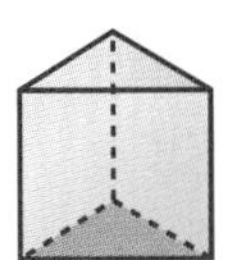

★15. 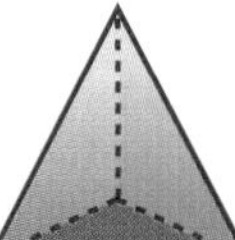

★16. 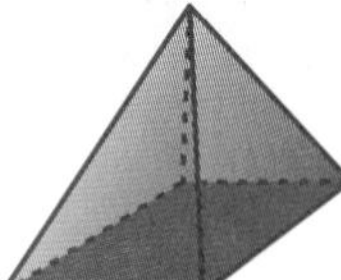

★17. 

★18. 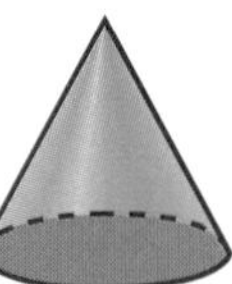

19. 

Here's how Lucilla drew a net for a cube. Tell what mistake she made. Explain how to correct it.

Problem Solving

20. **Science:** What shape is the earth?

21. **Summarize:** How many faces, edges, and vertices does a cube have?

Use data from the art for problems 22–23.

22. What shape was used for the top of the building?

23. How many square-shaped faces are part of the outside wall of the building?

24. **Literature:** In *Robinson Crusoe* by Daniel Defoe, the main character is shipwrecked and needs to survive on an island. He makes a tent using the cloth from the ship's sail. Draw the shape of the tent as a triangular prism.

★25. **Logical Reasoning:** A box of toy blocks has 12 triangular prisms, 20 cubes, 10 cylinders, and 5 square pyramids. In all, are there more square-shaped faces or triangle-shaped faces?

Use data from *Did You Know?* for problems 26–27.

26. What is the area of the floor of Olympic Cavern Hall?

27. If each person in the hall requires 4 square feet of space, how many people can fit inside the hall?

Did You Know?

The biggest public place inside a mountain is Olympic Cavern Hall in Norway. The exhibition center was built for the 1994 Winter Olympic Games in Lillehammer. It is 200 feet wide and 300 feet long.

Spiral Review and Test Prep

Find each missing angle.

28. 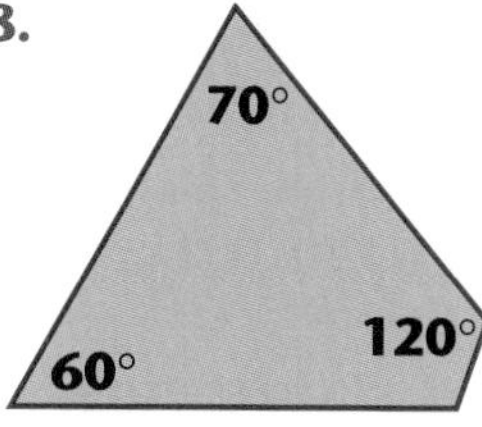

29. 

30. 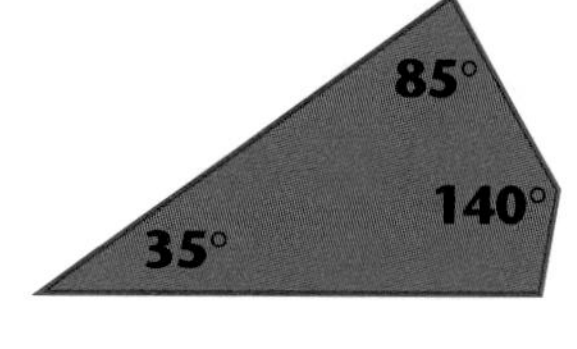

31. 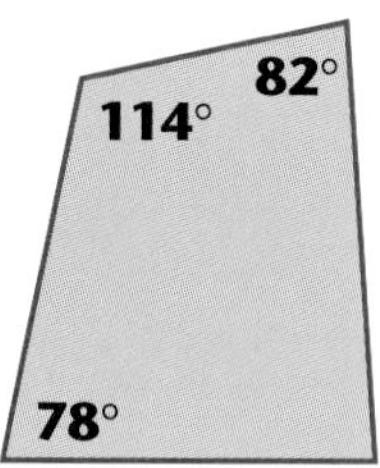

Choose the correct answer.

32. Which of the fractions below is the greatest?

A. $\frac{1}{4}$ C. $\frac{1}{10}$

B. $\frac{1}{7}$ D. $\frac{1}{6}$

33. Janna must read 48 pages. She reads $\frac{1}{4}$ of the pages before Friday and $\frac{1}{2}$ of the remainder over the weekend. How many pages does she have left to read?

F. 48 H. 18

G. 26 J. Not Here

Objective: Draw the top, front, and side views of a 3-dimensional object in a 2-dimensional drawing of the figure.

12·10 3-Dimensional Figures from Different Views

Architect Andrew Wittemore

Math Word

perspective drawing a drawing that shows a 3-dimensional object in a 2-D drawing

Learn

Architects often use models to show their building designs. How can you show models from above, from the front, and from the side?

Example

You need to find how the model would look from different places by using a **perspective drawing**. Since the drawings are 2-dimensional, only the faces of the 3-dimensional shapes are shown.

For the top view, think of how the shape would look if you were directly above it.

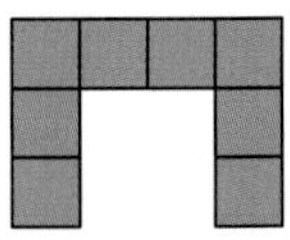
Top View

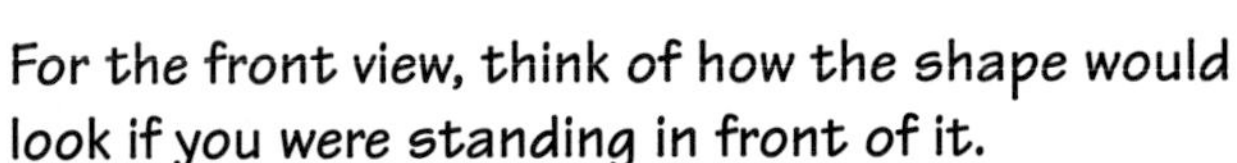

For the front view, think of how the shape would look if you were standing in front of it.

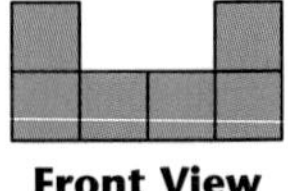
Front View

For a side view, think of how the shape would look if you were standing on one side of it.

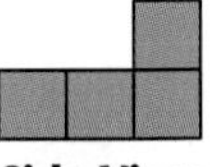
Side View

Try It

Draw the top view, front view, and a side view of each shape.

1. 

2. 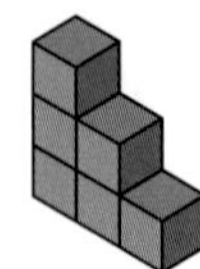

3. 

Explain why you can only see part of a 3-dimensional object from the top, front, or side.

Practice

Draw the top view, front view, and a side view of the shape.

4. 

5. 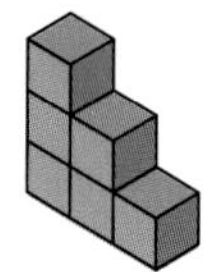

6. 

Problem Solving

7. This building is made from cubes. Sketch a side view of the building. How many square faces are on one side?

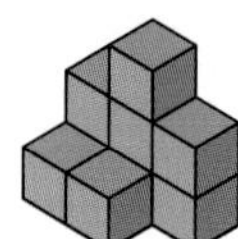

★8. Ellen made the building here using cubes. She wants to know the number of square faces that are rooftops. Sketch the top view of the building. How many square faces are on the top of the building?

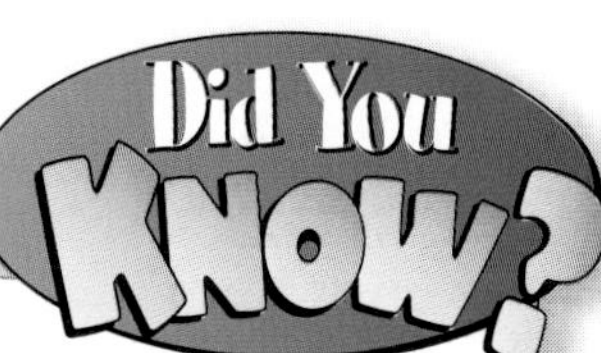

Use data from *Did You Know?* for problems 9–11.

9. What fraction of the total number of floors in the Hancock Center is occupied by businesses? Write your answer in simplest form.

10. If each floor of the building is the same number of feet tall, how many feet tall is each floor, to the nearest foot?

11. **Create a problem** using the information in *Did You Know?*

12. **Explain** how a shape can have more than one perspective.

Did You Know?

The tallest apartment building is the John Hancock Center in Chicago, Illinois. It is 1,127 feet tall. The building has 100 floors. Of the first 92 floors, 44 are occupied by businesses, and the rest are apartments where people live.

Spiral Review and Test Prep

13. $\frac{1}{5} \times 40$

14. $\frac{1}{10} \times 30$

15. $36 \div \frac{1}{3}$

16. $\frac{3}{5} \times 500$

Choose the correct answer.

17. What word describes the type of missing angle of the quadrilateral?

A. Acute
B. Obtuse
C. Right
D. Straight

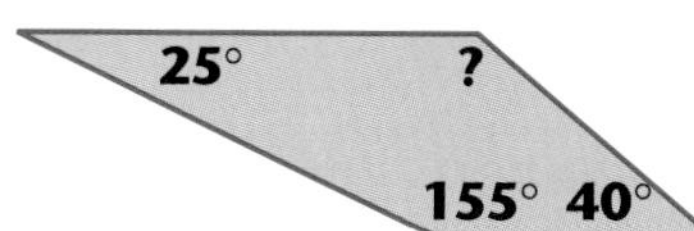

18. Which word describes the lines below?

F. Quadrilateral
G. Parallel
H. Perpendicular
J. Segments

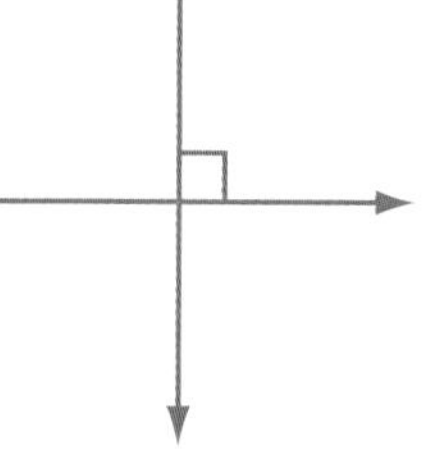

Extra Practice, page 575

Objective: Find the surface area of rectangular prisms.

Explore Surface Area of Rectangular Prisms

Math Word

surface area the total area of the surface of a 3-dimensional figure

Learn

You can use paper and tape to explore finding surface area.

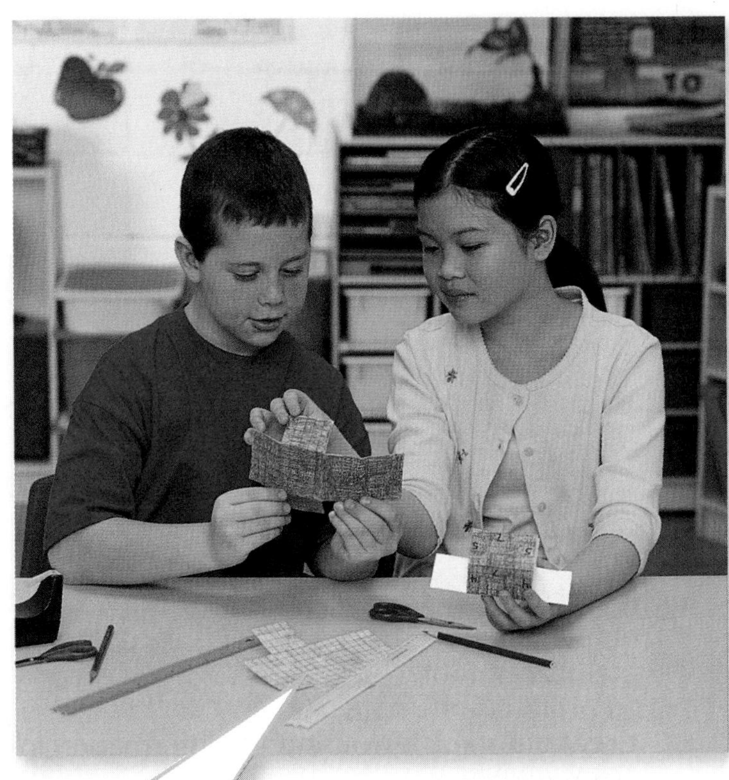

Work Together

You Will Need
- ruler
- paper
- tape

▶ Find the **surface area** of a rectangular prism. Measure and draw the net of a rectangular prism, using the lengths shown below.

- Find and record the area of each face of the rectangular prism. Add the areas of the faces to get the total surface area of the rectangular prism.
- Cut out the net. Form the net into a rectangular prism. Tape the edges.

▶ Make nets of rectangular prisms of different sizes and shapes. Find their surface areas.

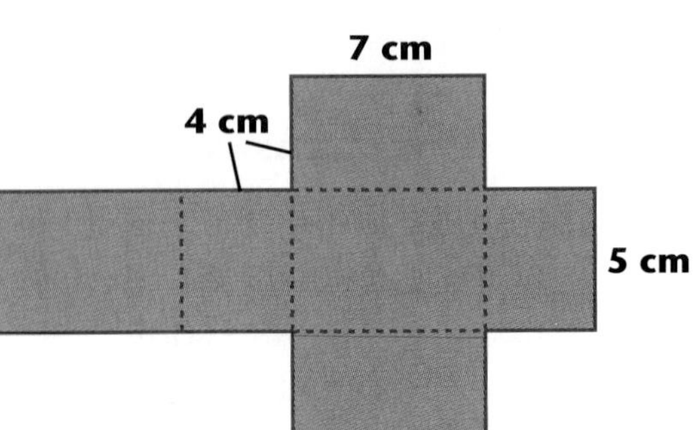

Make Connections

Find the surface area of a rectangular prism $7 \times 5 \times 4$ meters.

Using Models

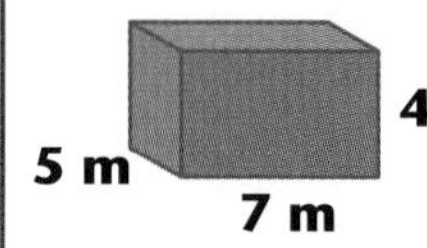

Draw the net on graph paper.

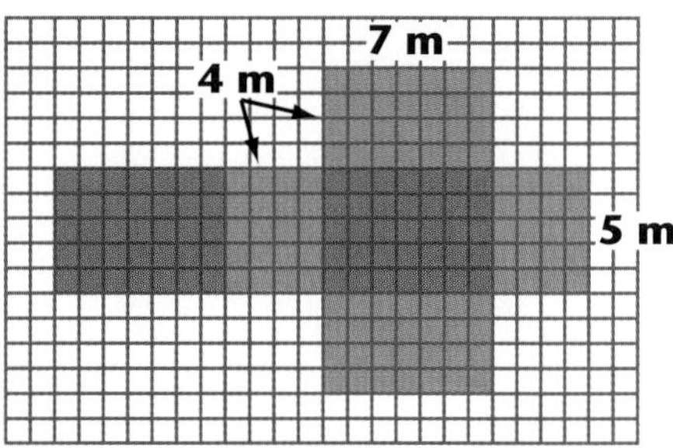

Count the number of units in each face. Then add the areas of the six faces.

$35 + 28 + 20 + 35 + 28 + 20 = 166$

Using Paper and Pencil

Use the formula to find the area of each face of the prism.

$A = lw$

$7 \times 5 = 35$ $7 \times 5 = 35$

$7 \times 4 = 28$ $7 \times 4 = 28$

$5 \times 4 = 20$ $5 \times 4 = 20$

The surface area of the rectangular prism is 166 square meters.

Try It

Find the surface area of each rectangular prism.

1. 

2. 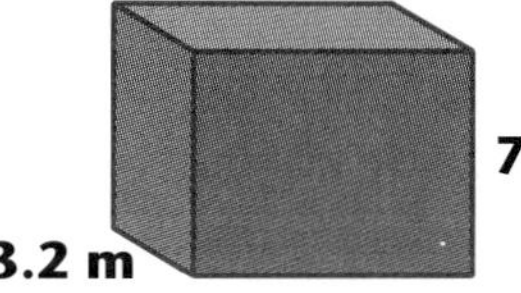

3. 

Sum it Up How is area like surface area? How is it different?

Practice

Find the surface area of each rectangular prism.

4. 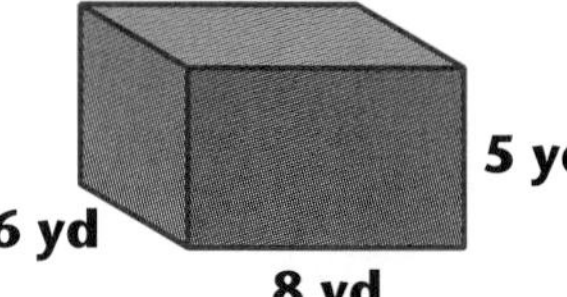

5. 

6. 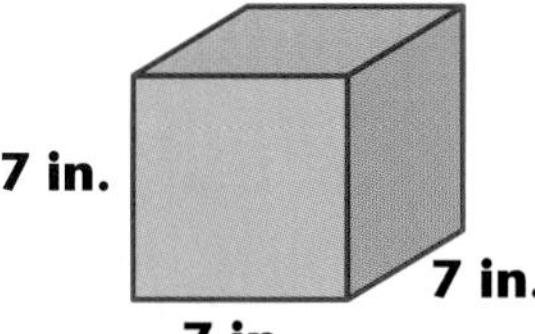

7. **Analyze:** How could you find the surface area of a cube without measuring each face?

Objective: Find the volume of rectangular prisms.

12·12 Explore Volume of Rectangular Prisms

Learn

Math Word

volume the amount of space that a 3-dimensional figure encloses, measured in cubic units

You can use boxes and centimeter cubes to explore finding volume.

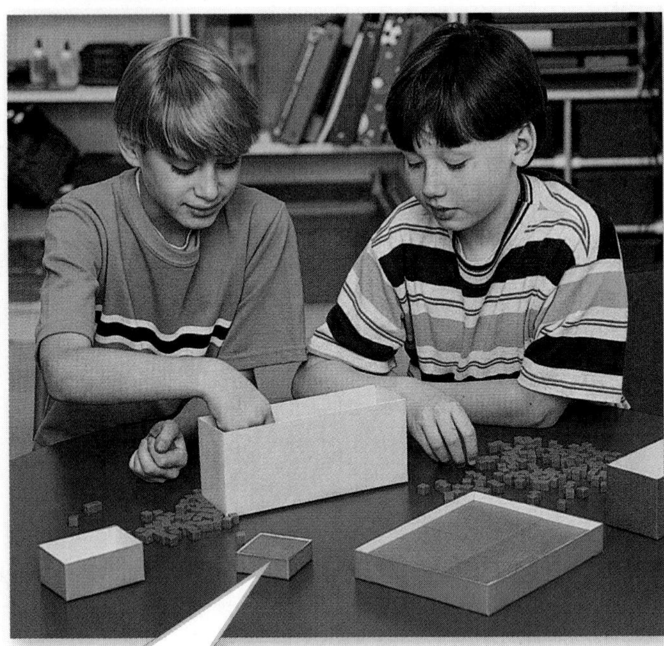

Work Together

You Will Need
- **boxes in various sizes**
- **centimeter cubes**

▶ Find the **volume** of a rectangular prism. You will fill a box with centimeter cubes to find how many cubes will fit inside.
- Copy and complete the table.

Rectangular Prism	Length of Box (in Cubes)	Width of Box (in Cubes)	Height of Box (in Cubes)	Total Number of cubes

- Fill a box with one layer of cubes. Record the length and width of the layer in terms of the number of cubes.
- Fill the box, and keep count of the number of layers. Record the height.
- Record the total number of cubes.
- Relate the length, width, and height of the cubes to the total number of cubes.

▶ Repeat the steps for each of your boxes.

Make Connections

Find the volume of a rectangular prism $2 \times 3 \times 5$ centimeters.

Using Models

Count the number of cubic units that the rectangular prism encloses.

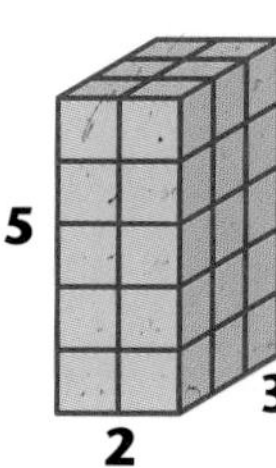

There are 30 cubic units.

Using Paper and Pencil

Use a formula to find the volume of a rectangular prism.

Volume is measured in cubic units, such as cubic centimeters (cm^3) or cubic inches ($in.^3$). A cubic centimeter, for example, is the volume of a cube that is 1 centimeter on each side.

Formula for the volume V of a rectangular prism:

$$V = \ell \times w \times h$$

where ℓ is the length, w is the width, and h is the height.

$$\begin{aligned} V &= \ell \times w \times h \\ &= 2 \times 3 \times 5 \\ &= 30 \end{aligned}$$

The volume of the box is 30 cm^3.

Try It

Find the volume of each rectangular prism.

1.

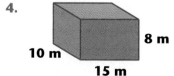

12 ft
14 ft
20 ft

2.

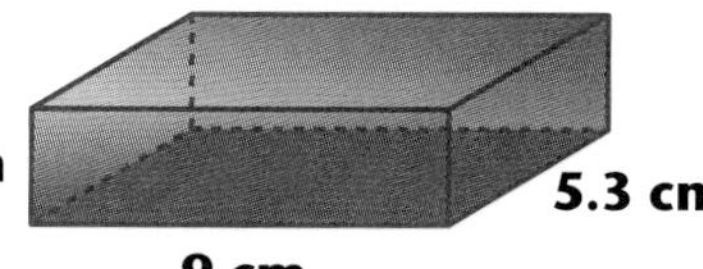

3.

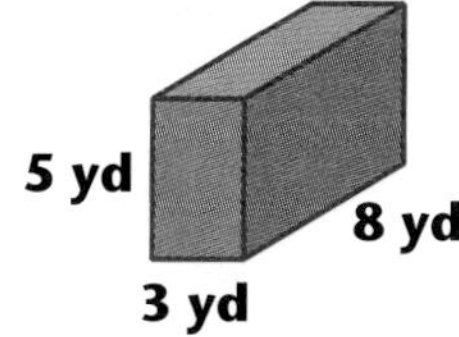

Define volume.

Practice

Find the volume of each rectangular prism. Round to the nearest tenth, if necessary.

4.

8 m
10 m
15 m

5.

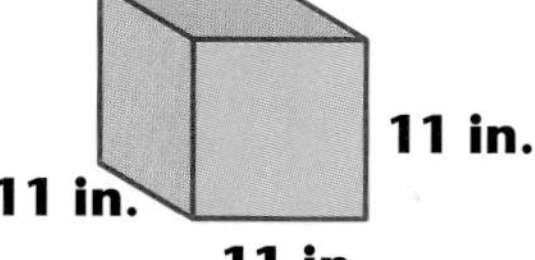

6.

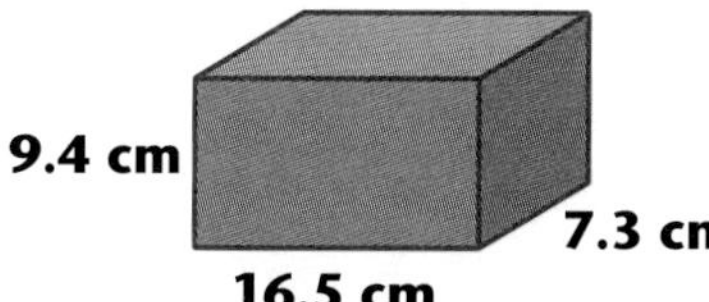

Journal

7. **Analyze:** If the volume of a cube is 216 $in.^3$, what is the length of each side?

Extra Practice, page 575

Objective: Apply perimeter, area, and volume to make decisions.

Problem Solving: Application
Decision Making

You want to design a swimming pool in a backyard that is 30 feet long and 20 feet wide. It will have a depth of 10 feet. It can be a square, rectangle, or compound shape.

You Decide!

- **What shape is the pool?**
- **What size is the pool?**
- **Which tile will you use? How many will you need?**
- **Which cover will you choose?**
- **Which pump filter will you choose?**

Franklin Pool Center

Pool Covers
For Rectangular Shaped Pools

Style	Size
Malibu	15–20 feet long x 8–10 feet wide
Bel Air	20–25 feet long x 10–15 feet wide
Augusta	25–30 feet long x 15–20 feet wide

Pool Tiles
Each package contains 30 tiles.

Style	Length
Alexandra	12 inches
Barcelona	6 inches
Caraous	4 inches

Pool Pump Filters

Style	For Water Volumes
Pure & Clean	Up to 2,000 ft^3
Krystal	2,000–3,000 ft^3
Mt. Spring	3,000–4,000 ft^3
Maxima	4,000–5,000 ft^3

Read for Understanding

1. What shape pool could you design? What compound shapes might you use?
2. What information do you need to decide how big to make your pool?
3. What information do you need to decide which pool tiles to buy?
4. What is the largest pool area that a Malibu pool cover will cover?
5. What is the smallest pool area that an Augusta pool cover will cover?
6. What is the greatest water volume that a Krystal pump filter can handle?

Problem Solving

Make Decisions

7. What is the area of a 25-feet long by 15-feet wide pool?
8. Which style of pool cover would cover the area of the pool in problem 7?
9. What is the area of a square pool with a 20-foot side?
10. Which style pool cover would cover the pool in problem 9?
11. What is the perimeter of a pool 19-feet long by 8-feet wide?
12. Which style of tile and how many packages could you buy for the pool in problem 11?
13. A pool has a length of 20 feet, a width of 15 feet, and a height of 6 feet. What is the volume of the pool?
14. Which style pump filter should you buy for the pool in problem 13?
15. If a pool has the compound shape of a rectangle with a length of 16 feet and a width of 9 feet, and a square with a side length of 8 feet, what is the area of the pool?
16. If the pool in problem 15 has a depth of 6 feet, what is the volume of the pool?
17. Draw several possible designs for the pool. Add labels that show the dimensions. Check that the designs will fit in the space available.
18. For each design you made in problem 17, decide which tiles, cover, and filter would work with the pool.

Your Decision!

What is your decision for the shape and size of your pool? Which tiles, cover, and pump filter did you choose?

Objective: Apply perimeter, area, and volume to investigate science concepts.

Problem Solving: Math and Science

Elbow Room: How close is too close?

Where would you rather be—at a crowded mall or music concert, or in a quiet park or yard?

You Will Need
- **meterstick**
- **masking tape or string**

Different people react to crowds in different ways. Your experience, family, culture, environment, or mood may affect how much close contact you can stand.

Hypothesize

How do you think you will feel as you become more crowded by other people?

Estimate how close another person must be to make you feel uncomfortable.

Procedure

1. Find the area of the classroom.
2. Let the class spread out all over the room.
3. Estimate, then measure, the distance between you and the nearest person.
4. Rate how comfortable you feel (3 = I feel fine, 2 = I feel a little crowded, 1 = I can't stand it!).
5. Divide the room in half and mark the middle with tape or string.
6. Find the area of half the room. Spread out in that half only.
7. Estimate the distance between you and the nearest person.
8. Rate how comfortable you feel.
9. Repeat the experiment with $\frac{1}{4}$ of the room.
10. Repeat the experiment with $\frac{1}{8}$, $\frac{1}{16}$, and $\frac{1}{32}$ of the room.

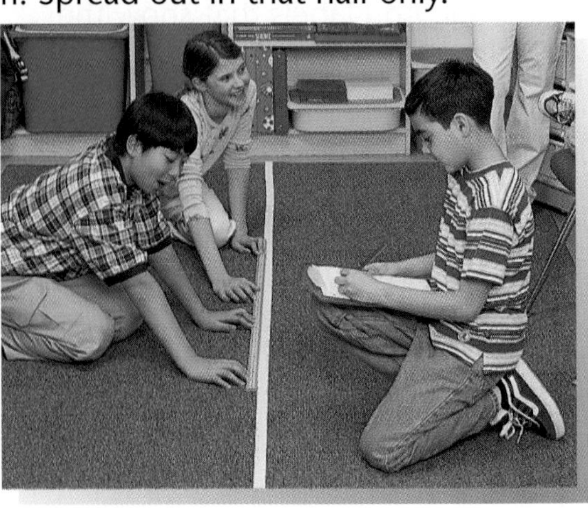

Data

Copy and complete the chart to record your observations.

Room Size	Area	Distance	Comfort Level
Full			
$\frac{1}{2}$			
$\frac{1}{4}$			
$\frac{1}{8}$			
$\frac{1}{16}$			
$\frac{1}{32}$			

Conclude and Apply

- At what distance did you decide that the nearest person was too close?
- What happens when you crowd people closer together?
- Using the data from your class, calculate the mean distance at which people feel uncomfortable. How do you compare to the mean?
- List and describe at least one job where you might need to study **proxemics.**

Did You
KNOW?
Scientists who study proxemics investigate the ways people react to being near other people.

Problem Solving

Going Further

1. Repeat the activity by crowding yourself with desks instead of people. Describe your experience. Compare and contrast your reaction to desks versus people.
2. Talk with someone in the class who reacted to crowding differently from you. Try to discover why you and that person had such different reactions. Consider your experience, family, and cultural backgrounds.

Check Your Progress B

What 3-dimensional figure does each net make when cut and folded? **(pages 558–561)**

1. 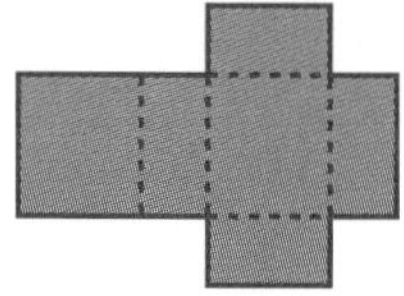

2. 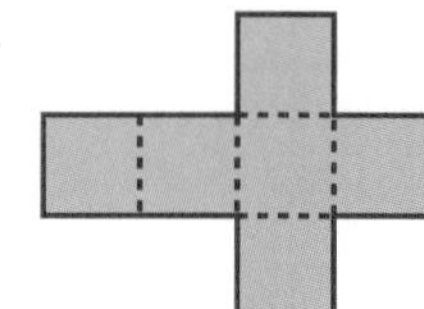

Draw the top view, front view, and a side view of the shape. **(pages 562–563)**

3. 

Find the surface area of each rectangular prism. **(pages 564–565)**

4. 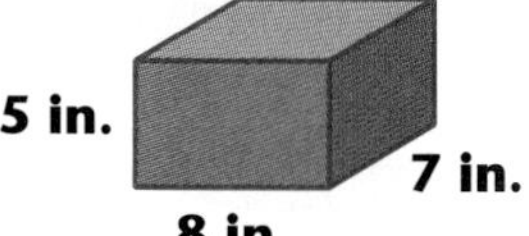

5. 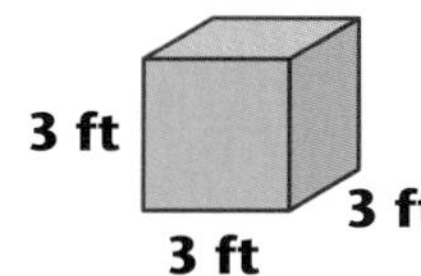

Find the volume of each rectangular prism. **(pages 566–567)**

6. 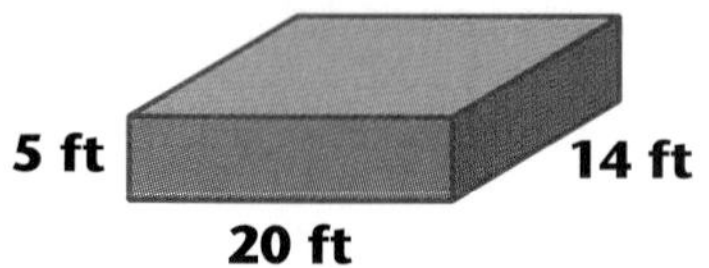

7. 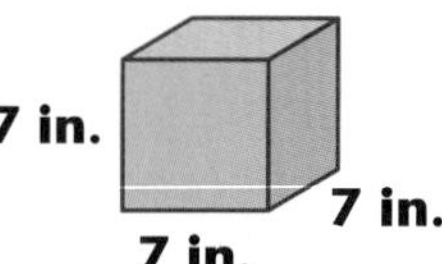

Solve. **(pages 556–567)**

8. Suni is painting the faces of a box. The box is 12 inches long, 6 inches wide, and 4 inches high. What is the surface area of the box that Suni is painting?

9. The floor of a new building is shaped like a rectangle with a square garden in the middle. The rectangle is 40 ft by 60 ft. The square has 10 feet on a side. What is the area of the floor?

10. **Summarize:** What steps would you use to measure and find the volume of a rectangular prism?

Extra Practice

Perimeter of Polygons (pages 540–541)

Find the perimeter of each figure.

1. 12 ft, 12 ft, 12 ft, 12 ft, 12 ft

2. 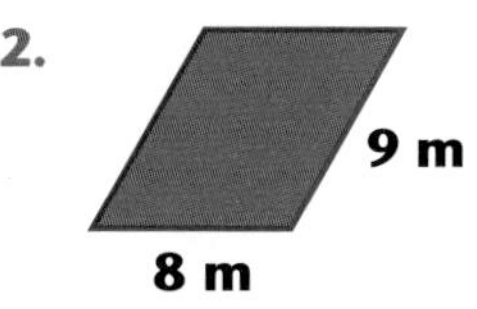
9 m
8 m

3. 4 in., 5 in., 3 in.

Solve.

4. Complete the table. What do you notice about the perimeter when the length and the width are doubled?

ℓ	w	P
2 in.	3 in.	10 in.
4 in.	6 in.	
8 in.	12 in.	
16 in.	24 in.	
32 in.	48 in.	

5. A rectangular building is 180 feet long and 156 feet wide. What is the perimeter of the building?

Area of Rectangles (pages 542–543)

Find the area of each figure.

1.

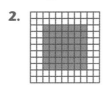

2.

3. 6.7 cm, 20.4 cm

4. $5\frac{1}{2}$ in., $5\frac{1}{2}$ in.

Solve.

5. Mavis is ordering some carpet for her family room floor. The room measures 16-feet square. What is the area of the carpet she should order?

6. Chet is buying some wallpaper for his dining room wall. The wall measures 18 feet long and 12 feet high. What is the area of the wallpaper Chet should buy?

Problem Solving: Reading for Math Distinguish Between Perimeter and Area (pages 544–545)

1. James is building a floor for his doghouse. To find how much wood to buy, should he calculate the area or the perimeter?
2. Nancy makes a fence in her yard. Is the length of the fence an example of perimeter or area?

Extra Practice

Area of Parallelograms and Triangles (pages 546–549)

Find the area of each figure.

1. 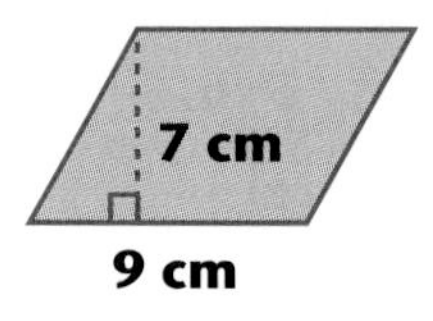

2. 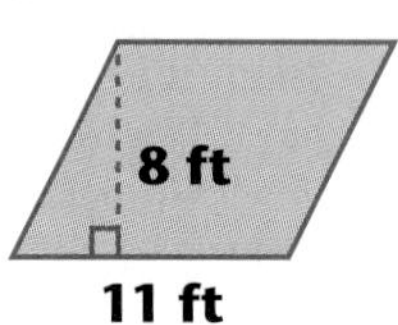

3. 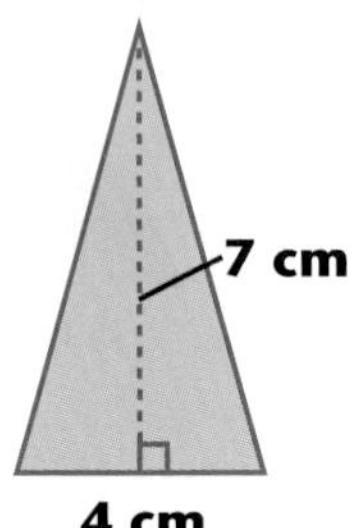

4. 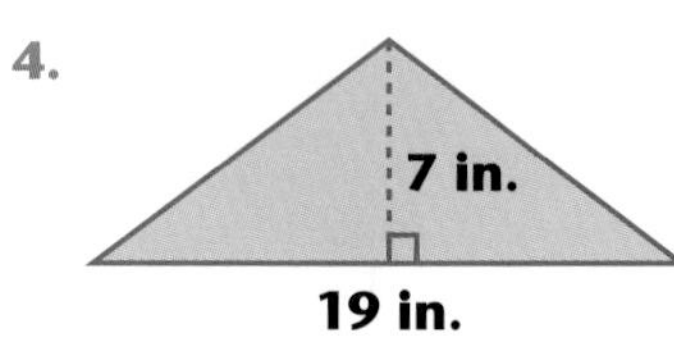

Solve.

5. Kendra is making a flag shaped as a right triangle. The triangle has a base of 20 inches and a height of 12 inches. How much cloth does Kendra need for her flag?

Circumference and Area of Circles (pages 550–553)

Find the circumference and area of each circle. Use $\pi \approx 3.14$. Round to the nearest hundredth, if necessary.

1. 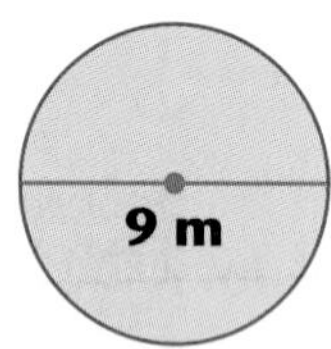

2. 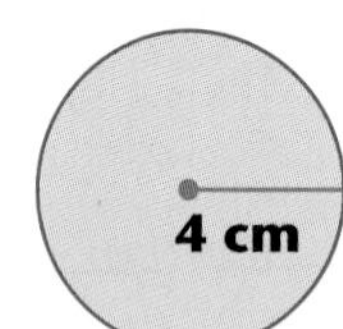

3. 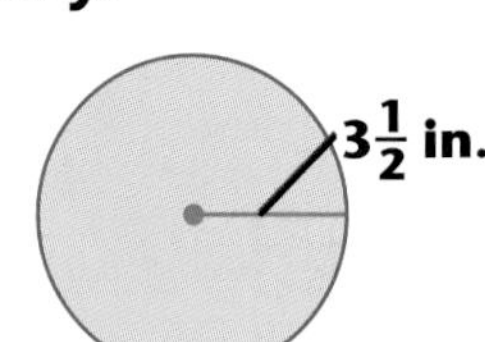

4. 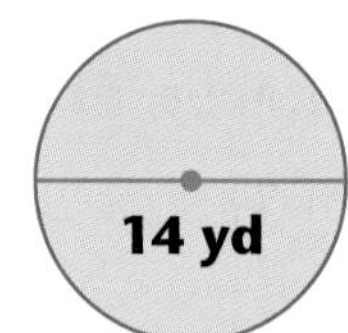

Solve.

5. Theo is fencing a round garden. The diameter of the garden is 15 feet. What is the length of fence Theo needs to form the garden?

Problem Solving: Strategy Solve a Simpler Problem (pages 556–557)

1. Nelson is using the floor plan shown below to design part of a doghouse. What is the area of the wood he needs for the shape?

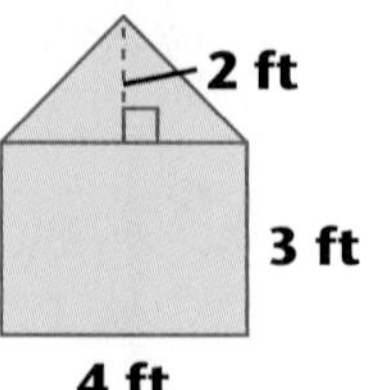

2. Merilee is covering the room shown in this floor plan with tiles. What amount of tile is needed to cover the room?

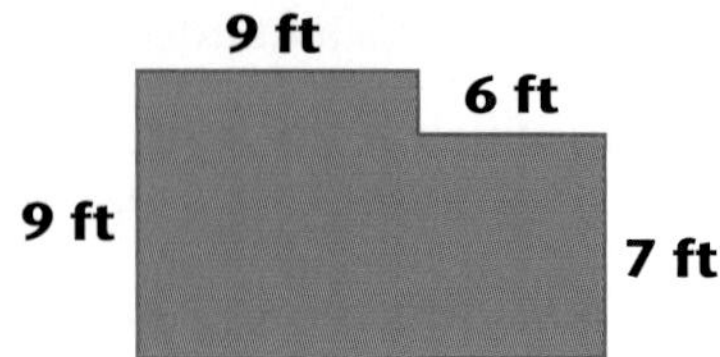

Extra Practice

3-Dimensional Figures and Nets (pages 558–561)

What 3-dimensional figure does each net make when cut and folded?

1. 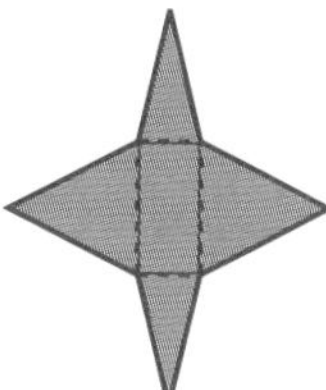

2. 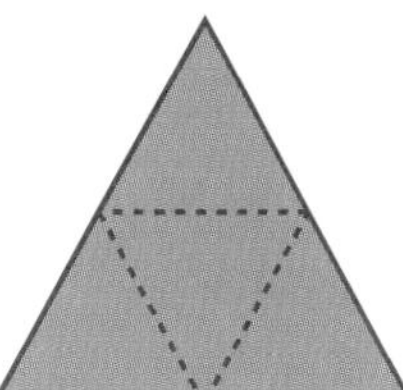

Solve.

3. A sculpture is made up of a rectangular prism, a cylinder, and a cone. How many circle-shaped faces does the sculpture have?
4. A building is made up of three different-sized cubes. The largest cube is at the bottom of the tower. The second largest cube is in the middle of the tower. The smallest cube is at the top of the tower. How many square-shaped faces make up the outside walls of the building?

3-Dimensional Figures from Different Views (pages 562–563)

Sketch the top view, front view, and a side view of the shape.

1. 

2. 

Solve.

3. Use cubes to make the letter H. The letter should lie flat on the table surface. Sketch a side view of the letter.

Surface Area of Rectangular Prisms (pages 564–565)

1. What is the surface area of a cube that measures 3 inches on each side?
2. A rectangular prism is 5 meters long, 4 meters wide, and 3 meters high. What is its surface area?

Volume of Rectangular Prisms (pages 566–567)

1. What is the volume of a cube that measures 3 inches on each side?
2. A rectangular prism is 5 meters long, 4 meters wide, and 3 meters high. What is its volume?

Chapter Study Guide

Language and Math

Complete. Use a word from the list.

1. The total area of the surface of a 3-dimensional figure is called its ____.
2. The distance around a square is its ____.
3. The amount of space that a 3-dimensional figure encloses is called its ____.
4. The number of square units needed to cover a region or figure is called the ____.

Math Words

- area
- base
- circumference
- perimeter
- surface area
- volume

Skills and Applications

Find the perimeter of polygons and the circumference of circles. (pages 540–541)

Perimeter of a square: $P = 4s$

Perimeter of a rectangle: $P = 2\ell + 2w$

Circumference of a circle: $C = \pi d = 2\pi r$

$\pi \approx 3.14$

Perimeter of any polygon: Add the length of all the sides.

Find the perimeter of each figure.

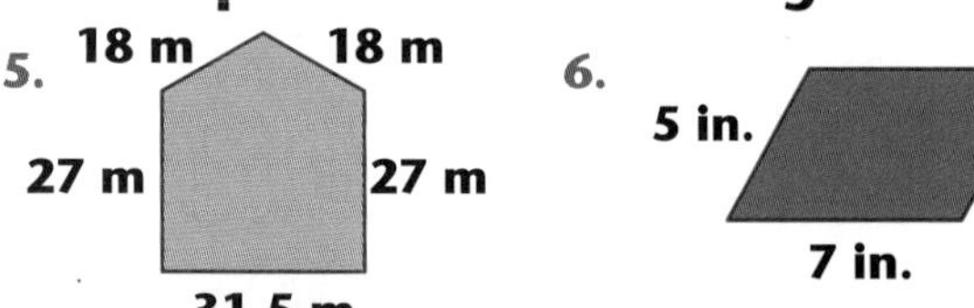

Find the circumference of each circle. Use $\pi \approx 3.14$. Round to the nearest tenth.

7. A rectangular building has a length of 64 feet and a width of 36 feet. What is the perimeter of the building?

Find the area of polygons and circles. (pages 542–543, 546–549, 552–553)

Area of a rectangle: $A = \ell w$

Area of a parallelogram: $A = bh$

Area of a triangle: $A = \frac{1}{2} \times bh$

Area of a circle: $A = \pi r^2$

Find the area of each figure.

10.

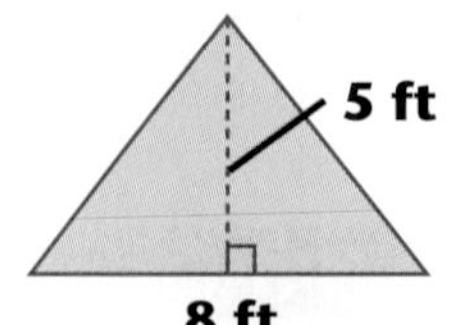

11.

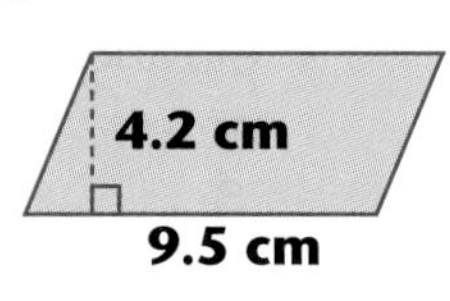

12.

13.

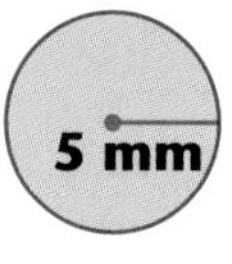

Find the surface area of rectangular prisms and cubes. (pages 564–565)

To find surface area: Find the area of each face. Use $A = \ell w$.
Add the areas of the faces.

Find the surface area.

14. 4 m, 7 m, 3.6 m

15. 8 ft, 8 ft, 8 ft

16. A cube is 4 feet long, 4 feet wide, and 4 feet high. What is the surface area of the cube?

Find the volume of rectangular prisms and cubes. (pages 566–567)

Volume of rectangular prisms.
$V = \ell \times w \times h$

Find the volume of each rectangular prism. Round to the nearest tenth, if necessary.

17. 5 ft, 13 ft, 6 ft

18. 3.2 m, 3.2 m, 3.2 m

Solve problems. (pages 544–545, 556–557)

Example

Find the area of the figure.

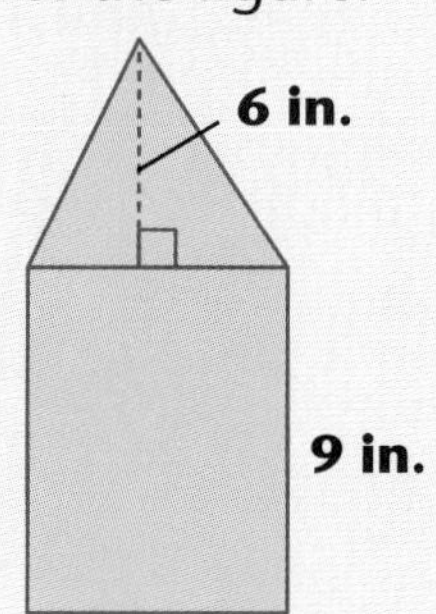

Solution

Find the area of each part of the figure.

For the area of the rectangle:
$A = \ell w = 7 \times 9 = 63 \text{ in.}^2$

For the area of the triangle:
$A = \frac{1}{2}(b \times h) = \frac{1}{2}(7 \times 6) = 21 \text{ in.}^2$

Add the two areas to get the total area.
$63 + 21 = 84 \text{ in.}^2$

Solve a simpler problem to solve.

19. Annette is using tile to cover the kitchen floor shown in the plan. What is the area of tile she needs?

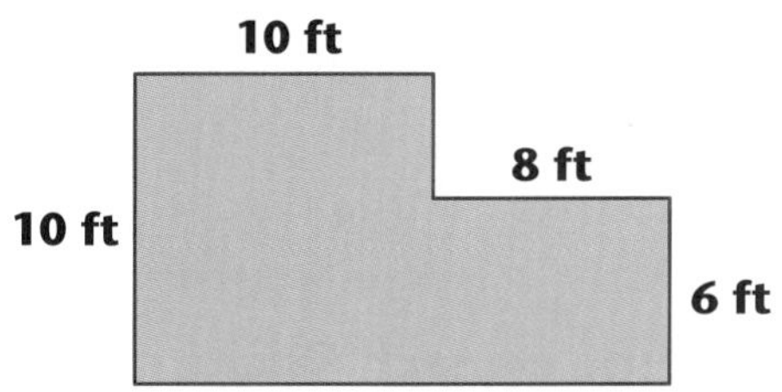

20. Explain how you would find the dry area of a rectangular building with a fountain in the middle.

Chapter Test

Find the perimeter of each figure.

1. 4 m, 4 m, 6 m, 6 m, 7 m

2. $9\frac{1}{2}$ in., $9\frac{1}{2}$ in.

3. 25 ft, 13 ft, 25 ft

4. 4.3 cm, 15.8 cm

Find the approximate circumference and area of each circle. Use $\pi \approx 3.14$. Round to the nearest hundredth, if necessary.

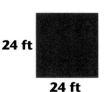

5. 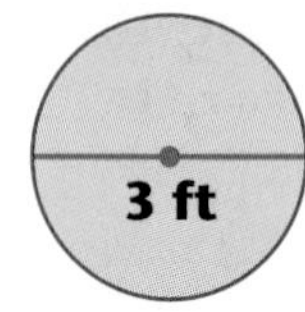

6. 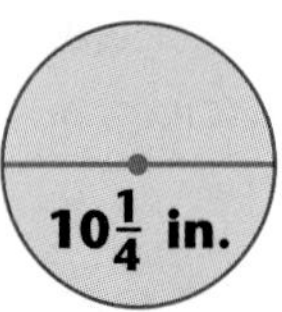

7. 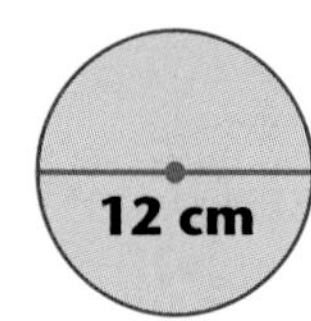

8. 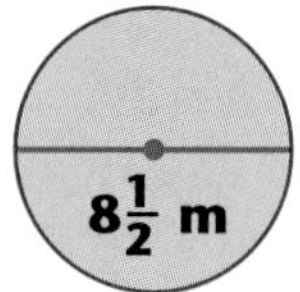

Find the area of each figure.

9. 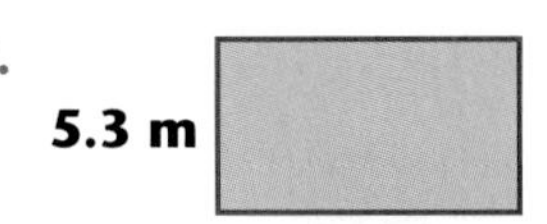

10. 

11. 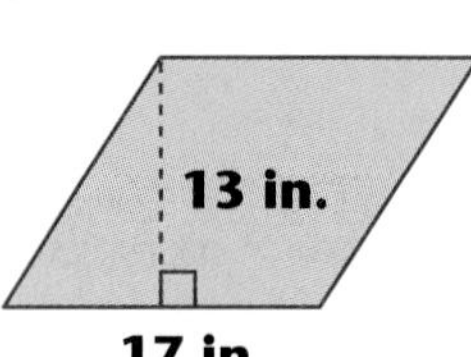

12. 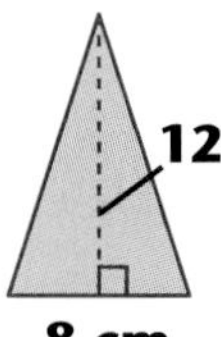

Find the surface area of each figure.

13. 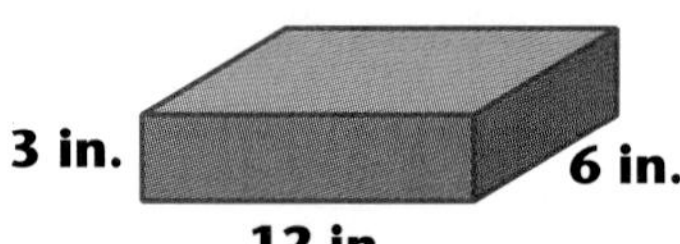

14. 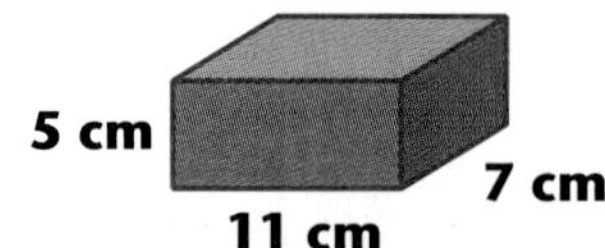

15. 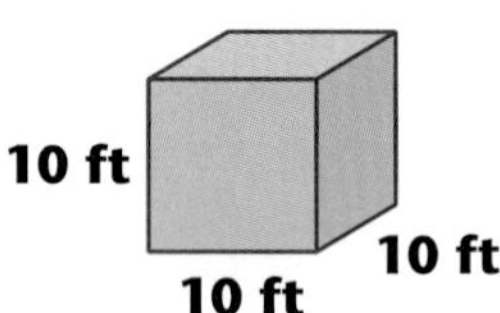

Find the volume of each figure.

16. 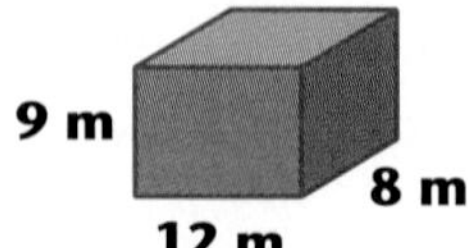

17. 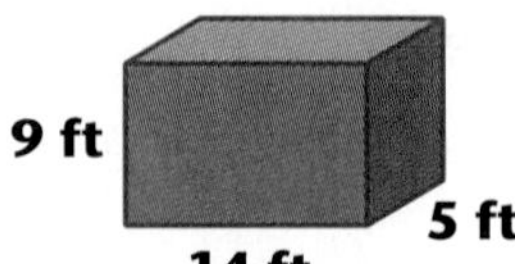

18. 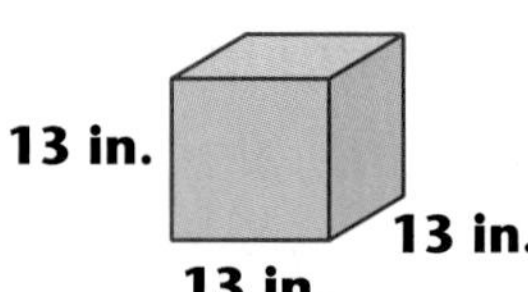

Solve.

19. Maggie designed this public plaza. What is the approximate area of the plaza?

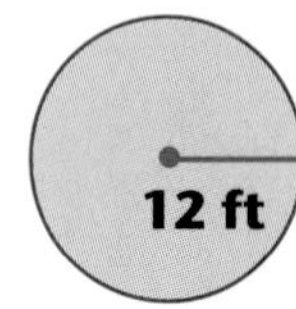

20. How much wood is needed to cover the area shown in the diagram?

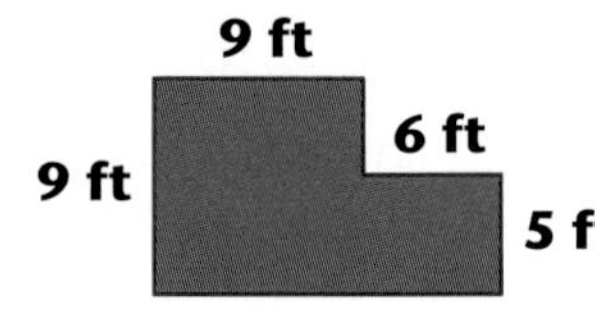

Performance Assessment

Be the architect! Design a building and draw your plan on graph paper.

For each shape in the building, tell the length, width, diameter, and height, where appropriate.

Find the area of each shape and the volume of each rectangular prism or cube. Where appropriate, find the surface area.

A Good Answer

- has a drawing of your building.
- has labels showing the length, width, diameter, and height of each figure, where appropriate.
- includes the area, surface area, and total volume of the figures, where appropriate.
- shows your calculations.

You may want to save this work for your portfolio.

Assessment

Enrichment

Area of a Trapezoid

Remember:
A trapezoid is a four-sided polygon with one pair of parallel sides.

The area of a trapezoid and a parallelogram are related.

A trapezoid can be copied and arranged to form a parallelogram. The parallelogram will have an area equal to the height times the mean of the base. The area of the trapezoid is half that number.

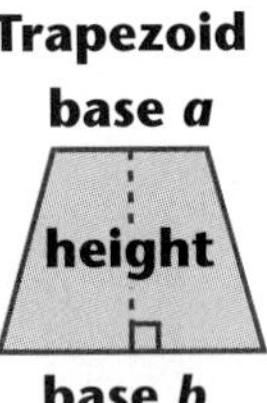

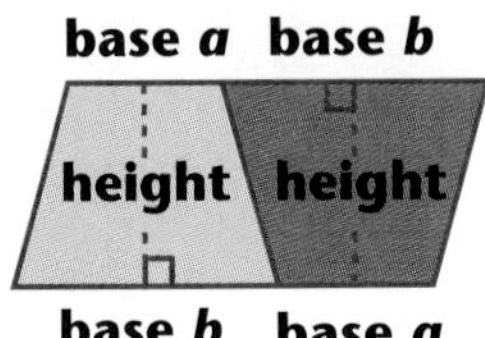

Remember:
The area for a parallelogram is $A = b \times h$.

You can use a formula to find the area of a trapezoid.

Formula for the area of a trapezoid:

$$A = \frac{1}{2} \times h \times (a + b)$$

where h is its height and a and b are the length of its two bases.

Example

Find the area of the trapezoid.

$$A = \frac{1}{2} \times h \times (a + b)$$
$$= \frac{1}{2} \times 4 \times (3 + 6)$$
$$= 18$$

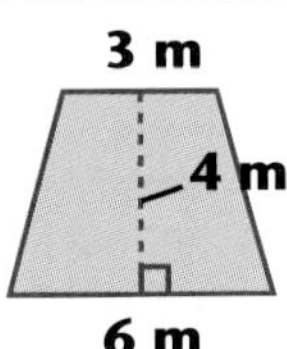

The area of the trapezoid is 18 m^2.

Find the area of each trapezoid.

1.

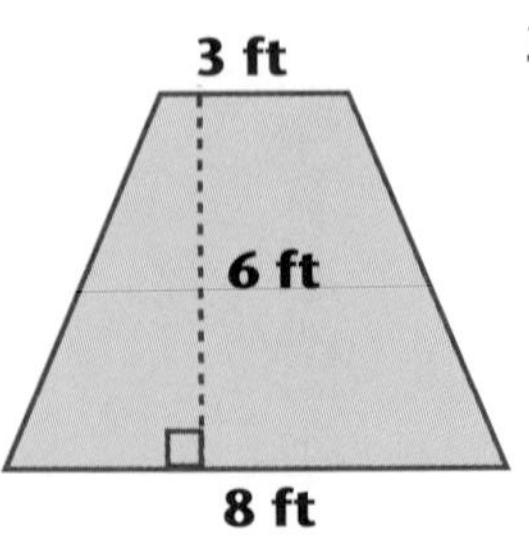

2.

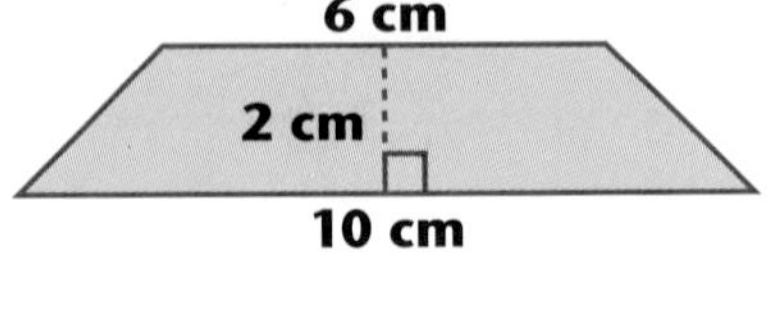

3.

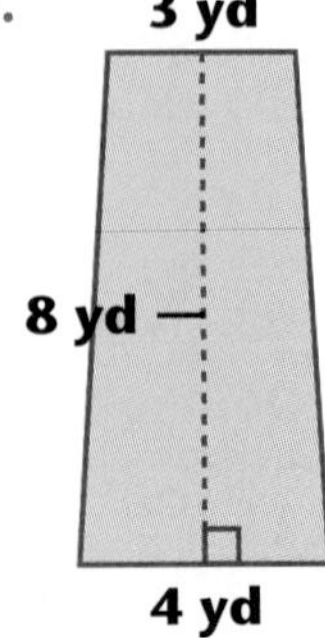

4.

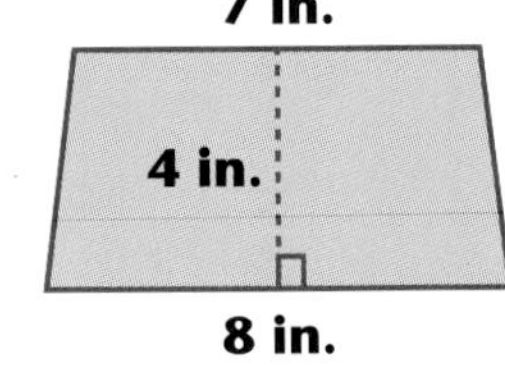

Test-Taking Tips

When taking a multiple-choice test, sometimes you must **make measurements** with a ruler, protractor, or other tool.

What is the area in cm^2 of the figure shown here?

A. 6 C. 10
B. 8 D. 16

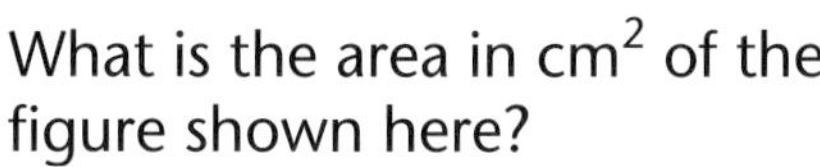

Read the problem carefully.

- What measurements must you make to find the answer?
- What tool do you need?
- What units should you use?

The length of the rectangle is 4 centimeters and the width is 2 centimeters. The area is 8 centimeters squared. The correct answer is choice B.

Check for Success

Before turning in a test, go back one last time to check.

- ☑ I understood and answered the questions asked.
- ☑ I checked my work for errors.
- ☑ My answers make sense.

Practice

Choose the correct answer.

1. What is the perimeter of this figure?

   A. 8 cm C. 16 cm
   B. 12 cm D. 20 cm

2. What is the area of the circle?

   A. π cm^2 C. 3π cm^2
   B. 2π cm^2 D. 4π cm^2

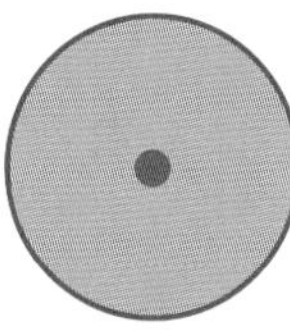

3. What is the area of this figure?

   F. 6 cm^2 H. 16 cm^2
   G. 15 cm^2 J. 24 cm^2

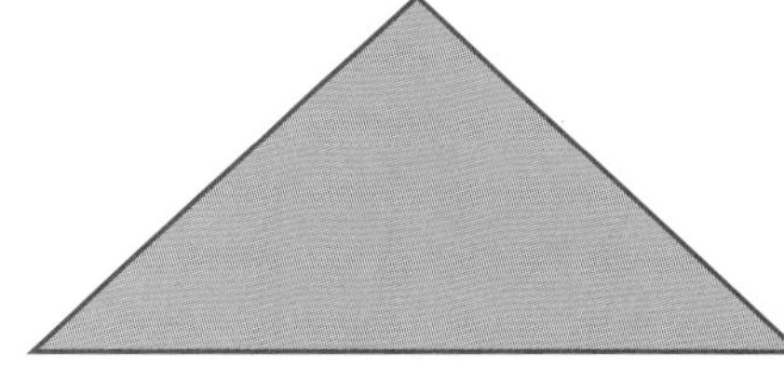

4. What is the measure of the angle shown here?

   F. 140° H. 45°
   G. 135° J. 40°

Spiral Review and Test Prep

Chapters 1–12

Choose the correct answer.

Number Sense

Use the table to answer problems 1–2.

Median Price of a Home		
Year	Akron, Ohio	Cincinnati, Ohio
1996	$98,800	$104,800
1997	$105,900	$110,500
1998	$106,200	$115,400

1. What was the difference in price of a home in Akron between 1998 and 1996?
   - A. $7,100
   - B. $7,400
   - C. $10,600
   - D. $205,000

2. How much greater was the price of a home in Cincinnati than in Akron in 1996?
   - F. $203,600
   - G. $104,800
   - H. $6,000
   - J. $5,000

3. In each package of assorted nails, $\frac{1}{4}$ of the 96 nails are 1 inch long. How many 1-inch nails are there?
   - A. $\frac{1}{4}$
   - B. 16
   - C. 24
   - D. 96

4. What is the value of 2^5?
   - F. 7
   - G. 10
   - H. 16
   - J. 32

Algebra and Functions

5. Which number goes in the blank to complete the table? The rule for this table is to multiply by 12.

In	Out
3	36
5	60
6	__
8	96

   - A. 39
   - B. 69
   - C. 72
   - D. 156

6. Which of the following values for t makes the expression true?

$$5 = t - 8$$

   - F. 3
   - G. 5
   - H. 5
   - J. 13

7. Tyra wants to save $8 each week for 12 weeks. How much money should she have after 9 weeks?
   - A. $17
   - B. $29
   - C. $72
   - D. $96

8. The perimeter of the figure is 18.4 feet. What is the missing measurement?

   - F. 1.9 feet
   - G. 2.5 feet
   - H. 3.8 feet
   - J. 11.1 feet

Mathematical Reasoning

9. Mr. Hill asked his 32 students to read *The Adventures of Huckleberry Finn.* After the first week, $\frac{3}{4}$ of the class had finished the book. After the second week, $\frac{1}{2}$ of the remainder had finished. How many students still must finish the book?

   A. 24 C. 8
   B. 16 D. 4

10. In August 14 days were only sunny and 9 days were only rainy. How many days in August had both rain and sun?

   F. 8 days H. 12 days
   G. 11 days J. 23 days

11. Phillip used peanut butter and jelly to make 10 sandwiches for the picnic. Of these sandwiches, 5 had only peanut butter on them and 2 had only jelly. How many sandwiches had both?

   A. 1 sandwiches C. 5 sandwiches
   B. 3 sandwiches D. 6 sandwiches

12. Ann wrapped gifts using 3 kinds of paper and two colors of ribbons. How many different ways can she combine paper and ribbon to wrap the gifts?

   F. 4 ways H. 6 ways
   G. 5 ways J. 9 ways

Measurement and Geometry

13. Tim made a design for a kitchen. What is the area of the kitchen?

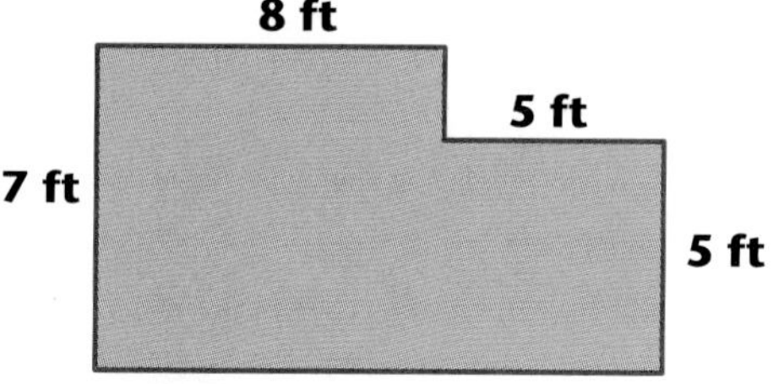

   A. 25 square feet C. 50 square feet
   B. 38 square feet D. 81 square feet

14. The computer room is square. What is the perimeter of the room?

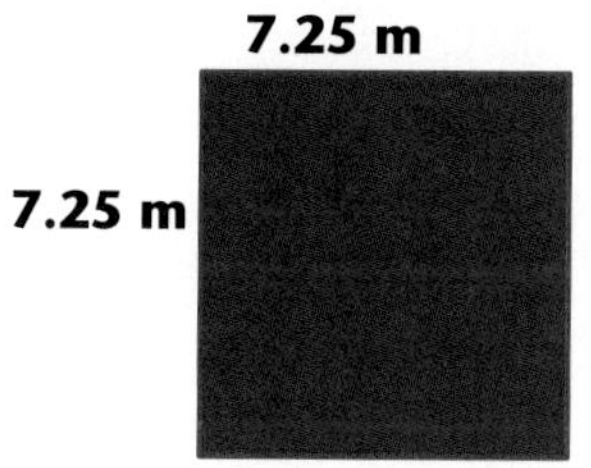

   F. 7.25 meters H. 29 meters
   G. 14.5 meters J. 52.6 square meters

15. The architect made a drawing of the playground. What is the area?

   A. 38 square meters C. 76 square meters
   B. 325 square meters D. Not Here

16. How many lines of symmetry does a square have?

Spiral Review and Test Prep

CHAPTER 13 Ratio and Probability

Theme: Running a Business

Use the Data

Top 3 Average American Expenses Each Year

Housing	$10,458
Transportation	$6,014
Food	$4,505
Total (including all expenses)	$32,264

Source: The Top Ten of Everything

- How do Americans spend their money? This table shows the top three ways the money is spent. What is the ratio of housing expenses to the total money spent? What is the rate of spending for the average person?

What You Will Learn

In this chapter you will learn how to

- find equivalent ratios.
- use scale drawings and maps.
- find the probability of an event.
- use strategies to solve problems.

Objective: Represent ratios in three different ways.

13•1 Explore Ratio

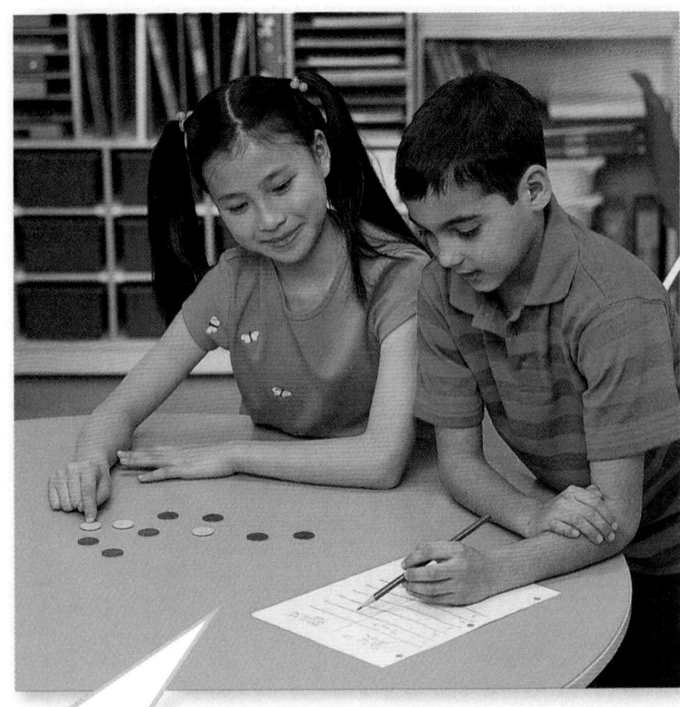

Learn

Math Words

ratio a comparison of two quantities

terms the numbers in a ratio

A ratio compares two quantities. You can use two-color counters to explore ratios. If you have 2 red counters and 4 yellow counters, what will the ratio of red counters to yellow counters be?

Work Together

You Will Need
- two-color counters

▶ Use two-color counters to model the **ratio**.

- Use red counters to model the number 2.
- Use yellow counters to model the number 4.

The model shows the ratio of red to yellow counters.
The ratio will be 2 red to 4 yellow counters.
The **terms** of the ratio are 2 and 4.

▶ Use two-color counters to model other ratios.

- Copy the table below. Drop 10 two-color counters on the table. Record the ratio of red to yellow and the ratio of yellow to red. Do this 5 times, using 10 counters each time.

	Ratio of Red to Yellow	Ratio of Yellow to Red
1	■	■
2	■	■
3	■	■
4	■	■
5	■	■

Make Connections

There are three kinds of ratios.

Each kind of ratio can be written in three different ways.

One way of writing a ratio is as a fraction. Both ratios and fractions show the relationship between two quantities.

	Using Models	Using Paper and Pencil
Part to Part	The ratio is 3 to 5.	3 to 5 3 : 5 $\frac{3}{5}$ Read: three to five
Part to Total	The ratio is 3 to 8.	3 to 8 3 : 8 $\frac{3}{8}$ Read: three to eight
Total to Part	The ratio is 8 to 3.	8 to 3 8 : 3 $\frac{8}{3}$ Read: eight to three

Try It **Write each ratio in three ways.**

1. red to yellow
2. yellow to red
3. red to total
4. yellow to total
5. total to red
6. total to yellow

Compare and contrast the ratio 3 : 5 and the ratio 5 : 3.

Practice **Write each ratio in three ways.**

7. red to yellow
8. yellow to red
9. red to total
10. yellow to total
11. total to red
12. total to yellow
13. **Analyze:** Why does the order of the terms in a ratio matter?

Objective: Make equivalent ratios; determine whether two ratios are equivalent.

13•2 Equivalent Ratios

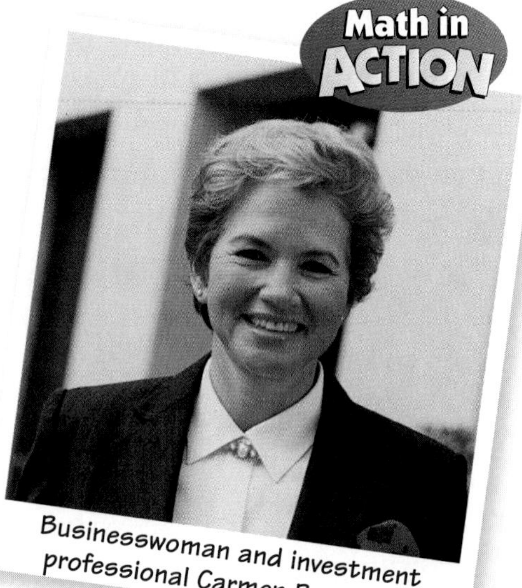

Businesswoman and investment professional Carmen Bermudez

Algebra & functions

Learn

Suppose that an investment manager buys the stocks of 3 internet businesses for every 5 retail businesses. What other ratios are equivalent to 3 : 5?

Math Words

equivalent ratios ratios that are represented by equivalent fractions

proportion an equation that contains equivalent ratios on each side

cross product the product of the numerator of one ratio and the denominator of another ratio

There's more than one way!

Equivalent ratios are the same as equivalent fractions.

Method A

1 Express the ratio as a fraction.

$$\frac{\text{internet}}{\text{retail}} \begin{matrix}\rightarrow \\ \rightarrow\end{matrix} \frac{3}{5}$$

2 Multiply the numerator and denominator by the same number. You can use any number except 0 and 1.

$$\frac{3}{5} = \frac{3 \times 7}{5 \times 7} = \frac{21}{35}$$

Method B

Use a table.

3	6	9	12	15	18	21
5	10	15	20	25	30	35

So 21 : 35 is an example of an equivalent ratio to 3 : 5.

Are $\frac{4}{6}$ and $\frac{6}{9}$ equivalent ratios?

Example 1

You can use a least common denominator (LCD).

$$\frac{4}{6} = \frac{4 \times 3}{6 \times 3} = \frac{12}{18} \qquad \frac{6}{9} = \frac{6 \times 2}{9 \times 2} = \frac{12}{18}$$

Since $\frac{4}{6}$ and $\frac{6}{9}$ are both equal to $\frac{12}{18}$, $\frac{4}{6}$ and $\frac{6}{9}$ are equivalent ratios.

An investment portfolio owns the following ratios of internet to retail stocks: January: 8 : 25
February: 24 : 75
March: 21 : 70

Has the ratio changed during these months?

Think: When you cross-multiply, you are actually putting both fractions over a common denominator that is the product of the two denominators. You then compare the size of the numerators.

Example 2

If two ratios form a **proportion**, then the ratio has not changed. You can use **cross products** to see if the ratios are equal.

Does 8 : 25 = 24 : 75?

$$\frac{8}{25} \stackrel{?}{=} \frac{24}{75}$$

Find the cross products.

$$8 \times 75 \stackrel{?}{=} 24 \times 25$$

$$600 = 600$$

The cross products are the same, so the ratios are equal.

Does 24:75 = 21:70?

$$\frac{24}{75} \stackrel{?}{=} \frac{21}{70}$$

Find the cross products.

$$24 \times 70 \stackrel{?}{=} 21 \times 75$$

$$1{,}680 \neq 1{,}575$$

The cross products are not the same, so the ratios are not equal.

The ratio changed in March.

Find a value for n that makes $\frac{6}{8} = \frac{n}{96}$ true.

Example 3

Solve for n.

$\frac{6}{8} = \frac{n}{96}$

	$6 \times 96 = 8 \times n$	← Use cross products.
	$576 = 8n$	← Multiply.
	$72 = n$	← Divide.

When $n = 72$, the statement is true.

Try It **Tell whether the ratios are equivalent. Write *Yes* or *No*.**

1. 1 : 2, 3 : 6 **2.** 2 : 3, 3 : 9 **3.** $\frac{4}{7}, \frac{7}{14}$ **4.** $\frac{8}{24}, \frac{9}{27}$ **5.** 8 to 20, 10 to 25

Find the missing number.

6. $\frac{1}{3} = \frac{x}{18}$ **7.** $\frac{2}{5} = \frac{y}{10}$ **8.** $\frac{c}{4} = \frac{18}{24}$ **9.** $\frac{5}{6} = \frac{30}{d}$

Explain how you know that $\frac{6}{9}$ and $\frac{14}{21}$ are equivalent ratios.

Practice Copy and complete each ratio table.

10.

3	6	■	12	■
8	■	24	■	40

11.

5	10	15	■	■
12	■	■	48	60

12.

10	■	30	■	50
7	14	■	28	■

13.

56	■	42	■	28
48	42	■	30	■

14.

1	■	■	4	5
6	12	18	■	■

★15.

13	■	■	■	65
19	■	■	■	95

Tell whether the ratios are equivalent. Write *Yes* or *No*.

16. $\frac{6}{9}, \frac{12}{18}$ **17.** $\frac{10}{7}, \frac{40}{28}$ **18.** $\frac{9}{21}, \frac{27}{42}$ **19.** $\frac{8}{5}, \frac{40}{25}$ **20.** $\frac{4}{12}, \frac{7}{36}$

21. 10 : 2, 5 : 1 **22.** 20 : 8, 5 : 2 **23.** 12 : 18, 1 : 2 **24.** 7 : 8, 21 : 24 **25.** 3 : 12, 1 : 4

Name three ratios equivalent to the given ratio.

26. $\frac{1}{2}$ **27.** $\frac{2}{5}$ **28.** $\frac{70}{90}$ **29.** $\frac{9}{2}$ **30.** $\frac{10}{3}$ **31.** $\frac{100}{75}$

Find the missing number.

32. $6 : 7 = n : 42$ **33.** $5 : 15 = 15 : d$ **34.** $5 : 7 = s : 35$ **35.** $1 : 6 = 6 : m$

36. 4 to 15 = 20 to g **37.** 18 to 24 = $k : 4$ **38.** 3 to 5 = $p : 30$ **39.** 20 to 40 = 1 to w

40.

Here is how Jim solved 6 : 15 = ■ : 60. Tell what mistake he made. Explain how to correct it.

Problem Solving

41. An investment manager uses a ratio of 1 to 2 to guide stock purchases. Find an equivalent ratio.

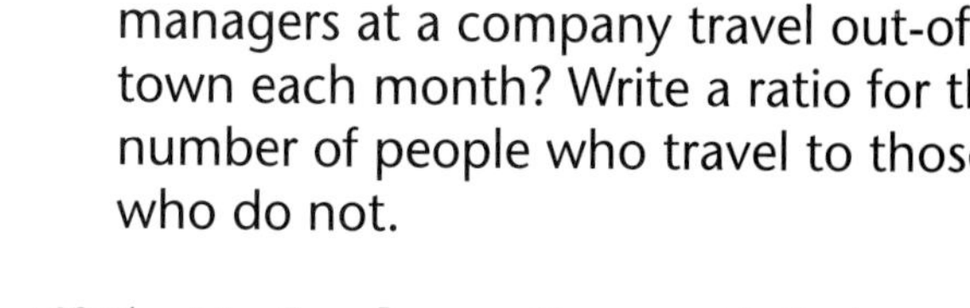

42. **What if** four of the 12 investment managers at a company travel out-of-town each month? Write a ratio for the number of people who travel to those who do not.

43. A new office building provides each employee with an office that is 12 feet long and 16 feet wide. How many square feet of space does each person have?

44. **Analyze:** One portfolio has a ratio of 6 new company stocks to 42 total stocks. Another portfolio has a ratio of 3 to 21. Are these ratios equivalent? Explain.

Use data from the pictograph to answer problems 45–46.

45. **Number Sense:** During this week, each manager comes to the office exactly once. How many managers are scheduled for the week?

46. What is the ratio of the number of managers for Tuesday to the number of managers for Friday?

Work Schedule for Investment Managers

Key: Each [symbol] represents 2 managers.

47. Dr. Cooke spent 2.5, 2.8, 2.5, and 2.4 hours doing research on her computer. What is the mean of these times?

48. **Collect Data:** Survey 20 students. Ask if they have ever seen or read a stock page in the newspaper. Graph the results.

★ 49. A portfolio consists of 3,000 stocks, 456 being Internet stocks. At that rate, about how many out of 500 stocks would be internet stocks?

★ 50. **Social Studies:** In 1891 the International Geographic Congress mapped the world on a scale of 1 : 1,000,000. If a distance on the map is 1 mm, how many kilometers is the actual distance?

Spiral Review and Test Prep

Name the place value for the 4 in each problem.

51. 54.02 52. 9.142 53. 8.463 54. 64,328 55. 40,197.3

Choose the correct answer.

56. A costume requires $2\frac{5}{8}$ yards of material to make. Robert needs 6 costumes. How much material will he need?

A. $15\frac{3}{4}$ yd
B. 7 yd
C. $8\frac{5}{8}$ yd
D. Not Here

57. Annabeth bought 8 pizzas for a total of $102.80. How much did each pizza cost?

F. $8.80
G. $10.88
H. $22.40
J. $12.85

Extra Practice, page 615

Objective: Solve problems by finding unit rates and unit prices.

13•3 Rates

Learn

Math Words

rate a ratio that compares measurements or amounts

unit rate a rate in which the second measurement is 1 unit

unit price the cost of a single item

Messenger services deliver packages to businesses within a town. If a messenger keeps up the same rate all day, how many messages can he deliver in a 6-hour workday?

Trevor delivers messages at a **rate** of 9 messages every 3 hours.

Messages Delivered

Time	Messages
8:00 - 11:00	9
12:00 - 3:00	
3:00 - 6:00	

There's more than one way!

Method A

Find an equivalent ratio to 9 to 3.

$$\frac{\text{messages}}{\text{hours}}\ \frac{9}{3} \xrightarrow{\times 2} \frac{18}{6}\ \frac{\text{messages}}{\text{hours}}$$

Method B

Divide the greater term by the lesser term to find the **unit rate**.

$\frac{9}{3} \div \frac{3}{3} = \frac{3}{1}$ messages per hour ← **per means "for each"**

Then multiply by 6 to find the number of messages delivered in 6 hours. $6 \times 3 = 18$ messages

Trevor can deliver 18 messages in 6 hours.

More Examples

Here are some other examples of unit rates.

A Scale on a Map: 1 inch to 100 miles

B Gas Mileage: 25 miles per gallon (mpg)

C Speed: 35 miles per hour (mph)

D Money Exchange: 9 pesos to 1 dollar

E Earnings: $5.25 per hour

F Sales Tax: $0.07 for every $1.00

Which box of pens is the better buy?

Example 1

Divide the total price by the number of items to find the **unit price**.

For the 12-pen box, $\$4.20 \div 12 = \$0.35$	The unit price is $0.35 per pen.
For the 20-pen box, $\$6.60 \div 20 = \$0.33$	The unit price is $0.33 per pen.

The box of 20 pens is the better buy since $\$0.33 < \$0.35$.

Trevor rides his bicycle 45 miles in 3 hours. What speed does he travel?

Think: Dividing the numerator by the denominator is the same as simplifying the fraction. You can then see how many miles would be traveled in one hour, a basic unit of time.

Example 2

1. Write the ratio of total miles to total hours as a fraction. $\frac{45 \text{ miles}}{3 \text{ hours}}$

2. Divide. $\frac{45 \text{ miles}}{3 \text{ hours}} = \frac{15 \text{ miles}}{1 \text{ hour}}$

Trevor travels 15 miles per hour.

Trevor's gas tank holds 12 gallons. He can drive 252 miles on a full tank. What is his car's gas mileage?

Example 3

Divide the total miles by the number of gallons. $\frac{252 \text{ miles}}{12 \text{ gallons}} = \frac{21 \text{ miles}}{1 \text{ gallon}}$

The gas mileage is 21 miles per gallon.

Try It **Copy and complete.**

1. 16 mi in 2 h = ■ mi in 1 h
2. $5.08 for 4 packages = ■ for 1 package
3. 8 orders per h = ■ orders for 3 h
4. 30 min per delivery = ■ min for 10 deliveries

Explain how to find the unit rate if 11 gallons of gas make a car go 143 miles. What is the unit rate?

Practice Copy and complete.

5. 250 mi in 5 h = ▯ mi in 10 h
6. 15 mi in 10 min = ▯ mi in 40 min
7. 280 stairs in 35 min = ▯ stairs in 105 min
8. 6 pages in 8 h = ▯ pages in 24 h
9. 16 calls in 8 h = ▯ calls in 32 h
10. 36 books in 1 y = ▯ books in 5 y
11. $41.65 in 7 h = ▯ in 49 h
12. 9 for $7.56 = 27 for ▯
★13. 24 seats per row = ▯ seats in 9 rows
★14. $106.75 for a wk = about ▯ for a mo

Find each unit rate.

15. 225 mi on 9 gal = ▯ mi per 1 gal
16. 15 in. of snow in 6 wk = ▯ in. per 1 wk
17. 640 mi to 4 in. = ▯ mi to 1 in.
18. 45 mi in 4 h = ▯ mi in 1 h
19. $29.50 for 10 books = ▯ for 1 book
20. $5.76 for 16 oz = ▯ per 1 oz
21. 10 for $75 = 1 for ▯
22. $13.08 for 12 lb = ▯ per 1 lb
★23. $2.88 per dozen = ▯ each
★24. $16.08 for 1 ft = ▯ per 1 in.

Decide which is the better buy.

25. 10 pencils for $0.45
8 pencils for $0.40
26. 12 deliveries for $96
15 deliveries for $135
27. 2 computers for $1,500
3 computers for $2,100
28. 8 bicycles for $2,712
5 bicycles for $1,375
29. 3 cars for $43,500
4 cars for $48,000
30. 6 helmets for $276
8 helmets for $300
31. $84 for 4 deliveries
$132 for 6 deliveries
32. $16 for 1 delivery
$54 for 4 deliveries
33. $8 every 3 miles
$10 every 4 miles

34.

Here is how Shelly found the unit rate for 232 miles in 8 hours. Tell what mistake she made. Explain how to correct it.

Problem Solving

35. **Time:** Trevor takes 45 minutes to ride across town to deliver a package. If he leaves at 2:00 P.M., what time will he return to his office?

36. Trevor earns $15 per hour. He works 8 hours a day Monday through Friday. How much money does he earn for the week?

Use data from the table for problems 37–38.

Wind Chill Factor				
Wind Speed (mph)	Temperature (°F)			
	60	50	40	30
10 mph	53	41	28	16
20 mph	47	33	18	4
30 mph	44	28	13	-2

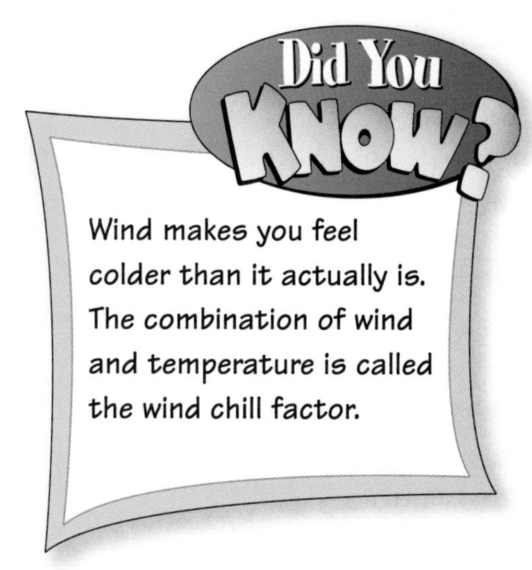

Did You KNOW?
Wind makes you feel colder than it actually is. The combination of wind and temperature is called the wind chill factor.

37. **Science:** What does the temperature feel like if it is 50°F with a 20 mph wind?

38. Does if feel colder when it is 40°F with a 30 mph wind or when it is 30°F with a 10 mph wind?

39. **Health:** Blood pressure is the ratio of the maximum to the minimum pressure. Ten minutes after a delivery, a messenger's maximum pressure was 131 and her minimum pressure was 80. How would you express her pressure as a ratio?

Use data from the chart for problems 40–41.

40. What is the unit cost per mile for a 4-pound package? for a 21-pound package? for a 48-pound package?

41. Trevor is delivering a 13-pound package and two 16-pound packages 9 miles from his office. How much is he earning for the deliveries?

TREVOR'S DELIVERY	
Package size	Price per mile
• less than 10 lb	$12
• 10 — 30 lb	$22
• more than 30 lb	$25

42. **Create a problem** that can be solved by finding a unit price. Solve it, then give it to another student to solve.

Spiral Review and Test Prep

Find the area.

43. 16 in. by 32 in.

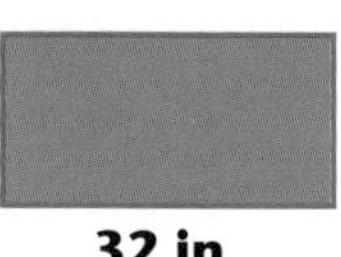

44. 29 cm by 87 cm

45. 31 yd

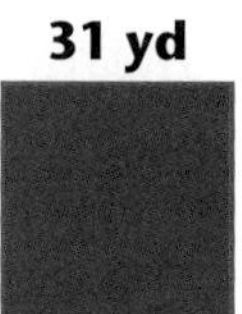

Choose the correct answer.

46. What is the sum of 3 and $^{-}4$?
   - A. 1
   - B. $^{-}1$
   - C. 7
   - D. 0

47. Which formula would help you find the circumference of a circle, given the radius?
   - F. $C = \pi$
   - G. $C = l \times w$
   - H. $C = 2 \times r$
   - J. $C = 2 \times \pi \times r$

Objective: Read for details to check whether a solution is reasonable.

13•4 Problem Solving: Reading for Math
Check the Reasonableness of an Answer

"It's a Dog's Life"

Read Ryan has a dog-walking business. He charges $4 per dog each day. His first 7 days, he walks two of the neighbors' dogs. He decides that he will make $28 for those days. Is his answer reasonable?

READING SKILL ▶ Read for Details

When you read for details, you notice the important details in the problem.

- **What do you know?** That Ryan charges $4 per dog each day; he walks 2 dogs; he expects to earn $28 for the week.
- **What do you need to find?** You need to know if the calculation is reasonable.

MATH SKILL ▶ Check for Reasonableness

- Something that is reasonable makes sense.
- An answer is reasonable if it fits with the facts you know.

Plan Decide if Ryan's estimate makes sense with the detail that he is going to charge $4 per dog each week.

Solve Ryan's estimate is not reasonable. You know that he will make about $28 for each dog during the week.

Look Back How can you check your answer?

How does checking the reasonableness help you solve problems?

Practice

Use data from the schedule for problems 1–6. Explain your answers.

1. Ryan calculates that he will earn a total of $6.25 for walking 5 dogs on Tuesday. Is his calculation reasonable?
2. Ryan is scheduled to wash 6 dogs next week. He calculates that he will earn a total of $10.50. Is his calculation reasonable?
3. Ryan calculates that he will earn $130 for all the walks on his schedule. Is his calculation reasonable?
4. Ryan told a friend that he will earn more than $10 for dog-sitting on Wednesday. Is his statement correct?
5. Ryan also stated that he will earn more than $35 for all the dog-sitting he does on Monday and Tuesday. Is his statement correct?
6. Ryan plans on earning more than $16 for washing dogs from Monday through Wednesday. Is his calculation reasonable?

Pet Care Schedule

Monday	**Wash 3 dogs** **Walk 2 dogs** **Dog-sit for 4 hours**
Tuesday	**Walk 5 dogs** **Dog-sit for 6 hours**
Wednesday	**Wash 1 dog** **Walk 4 dogs** **Dog-sit for 5 hours**

Charges:
Walking dog – $1.25 per walk
Dog sitting – $2.50 per hour
Dog baths – $4.50 per bath

Spiral Review and Test Prep

Choose the correct answer.

A bag of doggie treats costs $5.85. Ryan will buy 3 bags. He calculates the total cost will be about $18.

7. Which of following statements is true?
   - A. Since the difference between $6 and $3 is $3, the calculation is not reasonable.
   - B. Since the sum of $6 and $18 is $24, the calculation is not reasonable.
   - C. Since the product of $6 and 3 is $18, the calculation is reasonable.
   - D. Since the quotient of $6 and $3 is 2, the calculation is not reasonable.

8. When you check the reasonableness of an answer, you
   - F. always rework the problem from the beginning.
   - G. always draw a diagram.
   - H. determine if the answer makes sense.
   - J. redo all of your calculations with a calculator.

Extra Practice, page 616

Objective: Use scale drawings to solve problems.

13•5 Scale Drawings

Learn

Math Words

scale drawing a reduced or enlarged drawing of an actual object

scale the ratio that compares the distance on a map or scale drawing with the actual distance

An architect draws floor plans to show builders how to construct a building. What is the actual size of bedroom 1?

Bedroom 2

Bedroom 1

Bathroom

Kitchen

Family Room

Scale: 1 cm = 2 m

Example 1

Look at the **scale drawing**. Use the **scale**.

1 Set up a proportion.

scale given on the drawing → $\frac{1 \text{ cm}}{2 \text{ m}} = \frac{3 \text{ cm}}{y}$ ← distance on drawing ← actual distance

2 Solve for y.

$\frac{1 \text{ cm}}{2 \text{ m}} = \frac{3 \text{ cm}}{6 \text{ m}}$ (× 3, × 3)

The actual size of bedroom 1 is 6 meters by 6 meters.

A bedroom measures 8m by 8m. On a drawing, it is 2 cm. What is the scale?

Example 2

1 Set up a ratio in the form of a fraction. $\frac{8 \text{ m}}{2 \text{ cm}}$

2 Simplify. $\frac{4 \text{ m}}{1 \text{ cm}}$

Think: Make sure you have the number 1 in the numerator or denominator.

The scale is 4 meters equals 1 centimeter.

Try It

Use data from the architect's floor plan. Find the actual size of the following.

1. the kitchen
2. bedroom 2

Explain how the scale given on a drawing helps you find the actual size of objects seen on the drawing.

Practice **Use data from the architect's floor plan on page 598. Find each actual size.**

3. width of doorway from kitchen to family room
4. perimeter of the family room
5. perimeter of bedroom 1
6. length and width of the house

Find the scale.

7. an actual bedroom that is 12 feet is 4 inches on a drawing
8. an actual window that is 2 meters is 2 centimeters on a drawing

Problem Solving

9. An architect flies from Salt Lake City, Utah to Denver, Colorado, for a seminar. Her map shows a scale of 1 inch = 100 miles. The map distance from Salt Lake City to Denver is 4 inches. Find the distance from Salt Lake City to Denver.
10. **Art:** A home decorator plans to hang a replica of Paul Jenkins' *Phenomena Astral Signal* in a client's family room. The painting is $9\frac{2}{3}$ feet tall. The replica will be $\frac{2}{3}$ the height of the original. How tall is the replica?
11. An actual kitchen is 6 meters by 5 meters. Appliances cover 12 square meters of the floor. How much floor space is in the kitchen?
12. **Analyze:** The scale on Mr. Yan's drawing is 1 cm = 3 m. A bathroom is 1 cm on the drawing. On Ms. Carter's drawing the scale is 2 cm = 1 m. Her bathroom on the drawing is 2 cm. Whose actual bathroom is larger?

★13. **Measurement:** The width of a door is 80 centimeters. If about 2.54 centimeters = 1 inch, about how wide is the door to the nearest half inch?

★14. A map has a scale of 2 inches = 5 miles. There are $1\frac{3}{4}$ inches on the map between an architect's home and the airport. What is the actual distance to the nearest half mile?

Spiral Review and Test Prep

15. $\frac{3}{4} + \frac{1}{2}$
16. $\frac{3}{4} - \frac{1}{2}$
17. $4\frac{5}{8} + \frac{5}{6}$
18. $6\frac{7}{8} + 3\frac{3}{4}$

Choose the correct answer.

19. Phil's math test scores were 98, 91, 94, 92, and 98. What is the range of his scores?
    A. 94.6
    B. 98
    C. 94
    D. Not Here
20. A marching band marches with 2, 4, or 5 people in each row with no person left over. What is the fewest number of people in the band?
    F. 12
    G. 20
    H. 40
    J. Not Here

Check Your Progress A

Write each ratio in three ways. **(pages 586–587)**

1. red to yellow
2. yellow to red
3. total to red
4. yellow to total

Tell whether the ratios are equivalent. **(pages 588–591)**

5. 2 to 9, 8 to 36
6. 7 : 3, 14 : 9
7. $\frac{6}{4}, \frac{18}{8}$

Find the missing number. **(pages 588–591)**

8. $10 : 3 = 50 : n$
9. $\frac{5}{4} = \frac{h}{36}$
10. 7 to 9 = 56 to f

Find each unit rate. **(pages 592–595)**

11. 8 mi in 2 h = x mi per 1 h
12. \$4.56 for 12 bagels = m per 1 bagel

Use the unit rate of 21 miles per gallon to solve. **(pages 592–595)**

13. t mi with 10 gal
14. 168 mi with g gal

Use the map and a ruler. Find each actual distance. **(pages 598–599)**

15. Berryville to Hillview
16. Appleton to Hillview

Berryville **Appleton** **Hillview**

Scale: 1 cm = 3 mi

Solve. **(pages 586–599)**

17. Rita runs a gardening business. She feeds the plants with a solution that has a ratio of 1 teaspoon of fertilizer to 2 gallons of water. How much fertilizer does she use for 10 gallons of water?
18. One store sells 3 packs of paper towels for \$2.97. Another store sells 9 packs of the same paper towels for \$8.73. Which is the better buy? Why?
19. Marie is paid \$13 to baby-sit for 4 hours. Daniel is paid \$13.75 to baby-sit for 5 hours. Leonard wants to charge \$8 per hour to baby-sit. Is his fee reasonable? Explain.

Journal

20. Explain what a scale drawing is.

Additional activities at
www.mhschool.com/math

Find Probability

Anna is tossing a coin to conduct an experiment. She needs to toss the coin 50 times in each of 2 runs. Conduct the experiment and create a table of the results. What is the probability of tossing heads on the first run? on the second run?

You can use the coin toss tool to conduct the experiment.

- Set Trials to 50.
- Click on Toss Slow or Toss Fast.
- Click on the link at the bottom of the Data table.
- Choose Table. The table that shows the results of both runs is given.

What is the probability of tossing heads on the first run? the second run?

Use the computer to toss a coin the given number of times for 2 runs. Create a table of the results. Then find the probability of tossing heads on each run.

1. 25
2. 40
3. 75
4. 100

Solve.

5. Use a four-color spinner to conduct an experiment. Spin the spinner 25 times for 2 runs and create a table to show the results. Choose one color. What is the probability of spinning that color on the first run? on the second run?

6. Use a coin to conduct an experiment. Toss the coin 60 times for 3 runs and create a table to show the results. What is the probability of tossing tails on the first run? on the second run? on the third run?

7. **Analyze:** How do the probability tools help you conduct an experiment and create a table to show the results?

For more practice, use Math Traveler™.

Objective: Review probability. Record the results of a probability experiment; determine whether an outcome is likely or unlikely.

Explore Probability

Learn

Math Words

probability a number from 0 to 1 that measures the chances of an event happening

outcome the result of a probability experiment

likely an outcome is likely if it probably will happen

unlikely an outcome is unlikely if it probably will not happen

You can explore probability by studying the outcomes of a spinner.

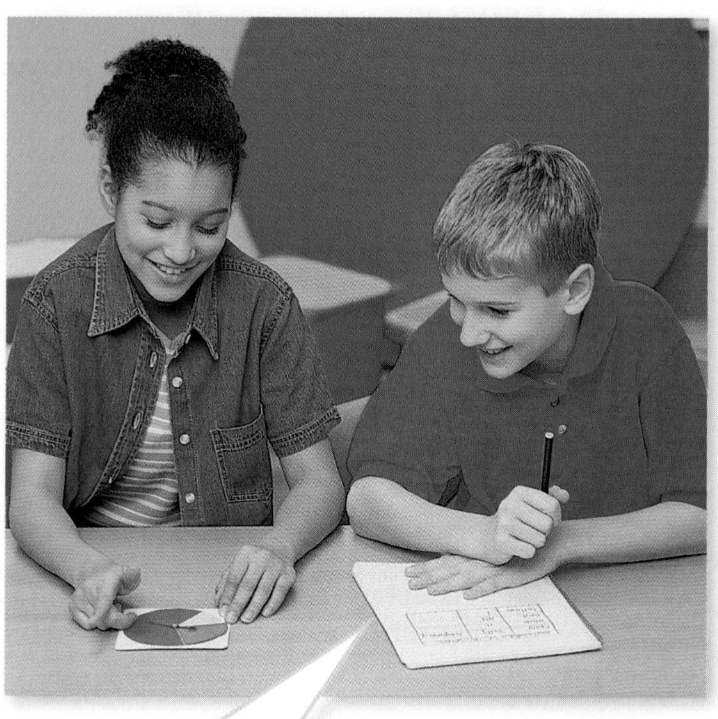

Work Together

You Will Need

- 8-section spinner
- markers or crayons

- ▶ Explore the **probability** of a spinner landing on each color.
  - Copy the table below.
  - Spin the spinner 40 times. Record the **outcomes** in the table.

Outcomes of 40 Spins		
Color	Tally	Frequency
Blue		
Red		
Yellow		

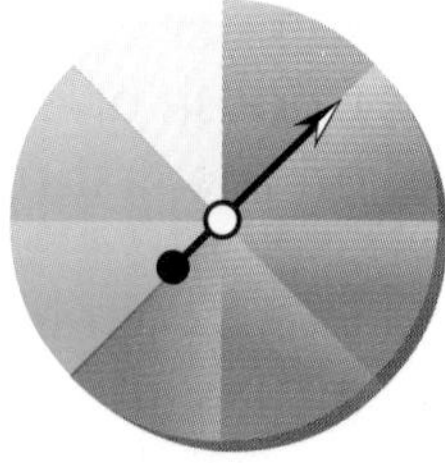

- ▶ Use your completed table for each question.
  - Which color did the spinner land on most often?
  - Why do you think you got that result?
  - What do you think will happen if you spin the spinner 40 more times? 80 more times? Explain

Make Connections

	Using Models	Using Paper and Pencil
There are 8 sections on the spinner. They are red, blue, and yellow.	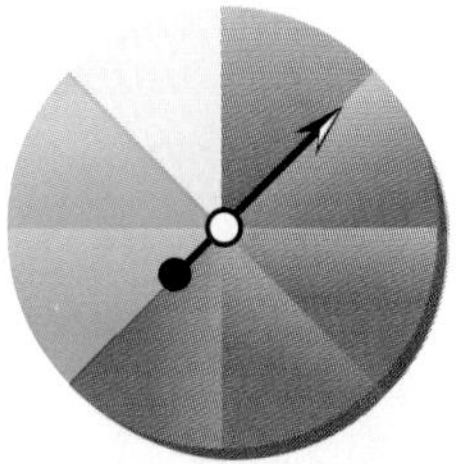 There are 5 red sections. There are 2 blue sections. There is 1 yellow section.	The possible results of spinning the spinner are red, blue, and yellow. Most of the sections are red. The outcome of red is very **likely**. Two sections are blue. Only 1 section is yellow. This outcome is **unlikely**.

Try It

Make a spinner like the one shown. Spin the spinner 40 times. Record the outcomes in a frequency table. Use the table for problems 1–6.

1. What are the possible outcomes?
2. Which outcome is most likely?
3. Which outcome is least likely?
4. Which outcome happened most often?
5. Which outcome happened least often?
6. What do you think will happen if you spin the spinner 20 more times?

Explain why some outcomes are most likely and others least likely.

Use the spinner for problems 7–10.

7. What are the possible outcomes?
8. Which outcome is most likely? least likely?
9. If you spin the spinner 40 times, which color do you think you will get most often?
10. **Analyze:** What if you make 3 of the yellow sections green, which outcome will be most likely? least likely?

Objective: Write a probability as the number of favorable outcomes over the number of possible outcomes.

Probability

Learn

Math Words

outcome a possible result in a probability experiment

sample space the possible outcomes in a probability experiment

equally likely outcomes are equally likely when they have the same probability

event a collection of one or more outcomes of a probability experiment

certain an event is certain when it will definitely happen

impossible an event is impossible when it will definitely not happen

more likely an outcome is more likely than another when its probability is greater

less likely an outcome is less likely than another when its probability is smaller

Educational companies often provide spinners, number cubes, and other materials to schools. Students use these materials in the classroom. Use a number cube to find the probability of rolling a 5 or 6.

Example 1

The possible **outcomes** are 1, 2, 3, 4, 5, and 6. These outcomes are called the **sample space**. The outcomes all have the same chance of happening so they are **equally likely**.

When the possible outcomes of a probability experiment are equally likely, you can express probability as a fraction.

Probability of an **event** $= \dfrac{\text{number of favorable outcomes}}{\text{number of possible outcomes}}$

There are 2 favorable outcomes: 5 or 6.
There are 6 possible outcomes: 1, 2, 3, 4, 5, or 6.

Probability $= \dfrac{\text{number of favorable outcomes}}{\text{number of possible outcomes}} = \dfrac{2}{6}$

Note: Favorable outcomes are the ones you are interested in.

So the probability of getting a 5 or 6 is $\frac{2}{6}$.
You can also write, $P(5 \text{ or } 6) = \frac{2}{6}$.

Note: When you have a choice of one outcome or the other, you add the favorable outcomes.

Example 2

You can use the terms **certain**, **impossible**, **more likely**, and **less likely** to describe probabilities of events.

An event that is certain has a probability of 1.

Spinning a number less than 10

Probability $= \frac{6}{6}$ $\frac{\text{favorable outcomes}}{\text{possible outcomes}}$

Remember: $\frac{6}{6} = 1$

An event that is impossible has a probability of 0.

Spinning a number greater than 9

Probability $= \frac{0}{6}$ $\frac{\text{favorable outcomes}}{\text{possible outcomes}}$

Remember: $\frac{0}{6} = 0$

An event is more likely than another event if it has a greater probability of happening.

If you pick a marble from the box without looking, you are more likely to pick yellow than blue.

An event is less likely than another event if it has a lesser probability of happening than the other event.

If you pick a marble without looking, you are less likely to pick red than blue.

Try It **Use the spinner to find the probability of each event.**

1. P (3)
2. P (an even number)
3. P (number greater than 6)

Suppose you roll a number cube. What is the probability of rolling an even number? Explain.

Practice

If you pick a marble without looking, what is the probability of each event?

4. picking a red marble
5. picking a blue marble
6. picking a white marble
7. picking a red or yellow marble
8. picking any marble
9. picking a yellow or blue marble

If you pick a marble without looking, what is the probability of each event? Write *certain* or *impossible* for each event.

10. picking a white marble
11. picking a yellow marble
12. picking a yellow, white, or brown marble
13. picking a red, blue, or green marble

Write *more likely than, less likely than,* or *equally likely as* to complete each sentence.

14. Spinning a 1 is ▒ spinning a 2.
15. Spinning a 2 is ▒ spinning a 3.
16. Spinning a 3 is ▒ spinning a 4.
17. Spinning a 4 is ▒ spinning a 1.

★18. Spinning a prime number is ▒ spinning a composite number.

19. **Make it RIGHT**

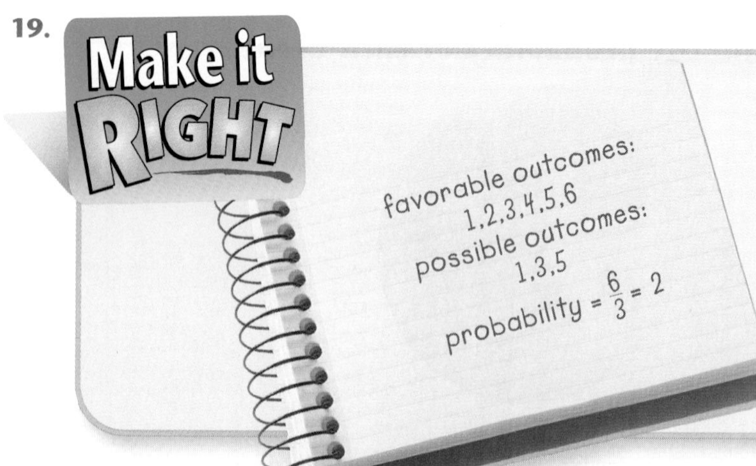

Here is how Lynn found the probability of rolling an odd number on a number cube. Tell what mistake she made. Explain how to correct it.

Problem Solving

The table shows an experiment of picking marbles from a bag without looking. Use data from the table for problems 20–22.

Marble Experiment		
Color	Tally	Frequency
Red	||	2
Blue	||	2
Yellow	||||	4
Green	~~||||~~ ~~||||~~ ||	12

20. Based on the data, what is the probability of picking a red marble?

21. What is the probability of picking a yellow or green marble?

22. Which color of marble do you think there are most of in the bag? Explain.

23. There are 8 blue sections and 6 red sections on a spinner. What is the greatest common factor of these two numbers?

24. **Analyze:** Can a probability ever be greater than 1? Explain.

★25. **Measurement:** A student activity board measures 18 inches by 24 inches. How many square feet is this?

26. **Create a problem** about probability using a spinner. Solve it and give it to another student to solve.

27. **Spatial Reasoning:** If you close your eyes and put your finger on this board, which color will you be most likely to touch? Why?

Spiral Review and Test Prep

Is the number prime or composite?

28. 51
29. 103
30. 213
31. 87
32. 485

Choose the correct answer.

33. Which of the following is not an equivalent fraction of $\frac{3}{4}$?

A. $\frac{9}{12}$ C. $\frac{6}{8}$

B. $\frac{15}{20}$ D. $\frac{10}{16}$

34. A group of friends go to a drive-in movie. They pay $6 for the car and an additional $2 for each person in the car. If there are 4 friends, how much do they pay?

F. $6 H. $12

G. $8 J. $14

Objective: Solve problems by conducting an experiment.

Problem Solving: Strategy
Do an Experiment

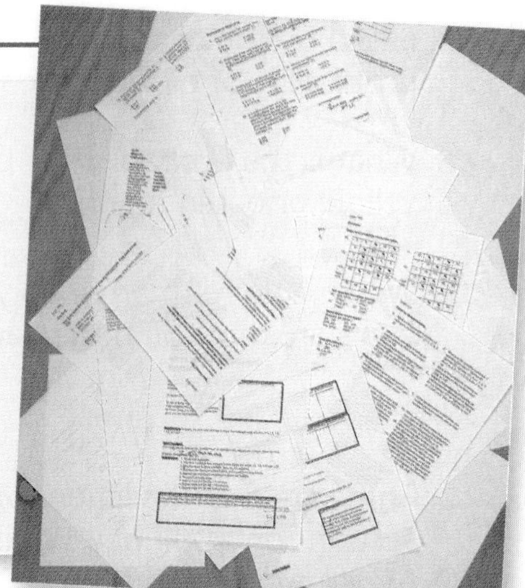

Read

Read the problem carefully.

An employee at a copy shop accidentally drops 50 papers that are printed on one side only. What is the probability of the papers landing printed side up?

- **What do you know?** 50 pages were dropped.
- **What do you need to find?** How many land face up

Plan

With some problems, you have no way to calculate the probability. You must do an experiment to get an idea of how likely an event is.

Solve

Draw an X on a blank paper. Hold the paper X-side up and drop it from 1 meter. Record whether it lands X-side up or X-side down. Repeat a total of 50 times.

Record the results in a frequency table.

Calculate the probability.

Paper Experiment

How it Lands	Tally	Frequency
X-side up	𝍸 𝍸 |||	13
X-side down	𝍸 𝍸 𝍸 𝍸 𝍸 𝍸 𝍸 ||	37

Look Back

How can you decide if your results are reasonable?

If you do this experiment again will you get the same results? Explain.

Do an experiment to solve.
Record the results in a frequency table.

1. **Language Arts:** Which letter is used most often to start a sentence? First make a prediction. Then choose 50 sentences from a book and record the first letter of each sentence to solve.

2. What is the probability that a paper cup will land on its side, right side up, or upside down? First make a prediction. Then record the results of dropping a paper cup 50 times.

3. **Language Arts:** Lauren wants to know which vowel is used the most in writing—A, E, I, O, or U. Predict which vowel you think is used the most. Then choose 20 lines of text from a book and count the numbers of each vowel to solve.

4. What is the probability that a dropped envelope will land with the flap up or with the flap down? First make a prediction, and then record the results of dropping an envelope 50 times.

Mixed Strategy Review

5. The book *Shark in School* by Patricia Reilly Giff was printed with 104 pages and 13 illustrations by Blanche Sims. If the book is reprinted with a larger type size, it will have the same number of illustrations and $1\frac{1}{2}$ the number of pages. How many pages will it have?

6. A box of envelopes contains 200 envelopes. Marty finds that there are 42 in the box after sending out a large group of letters. How many envelopes were used?

7. Postcards cost $0.20 to mail and letters cost $0.33. If Greg sends exactly 8 pieces of mail and spends $1.73, how many of each kind of mail did he send?

8. **Spatial Reasoning:** How many squares of all sizes are in the diagram?

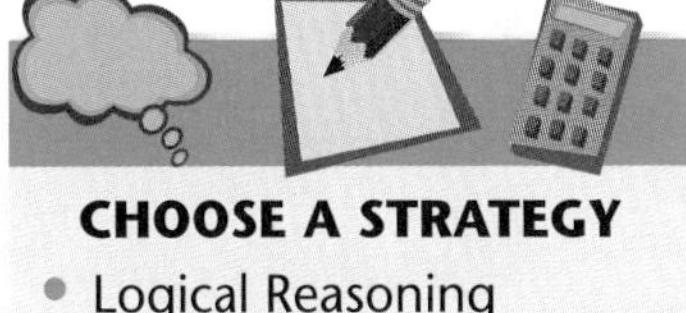

CHOOSE A STRATEGY
- Logical Reasoning
- Draw a Diagram
- Make a Graph
- Make a Table or List
- Find a Pattern
- Guess and Check
- Write an Equation
- Work Backward
- Solve a Simpler Problem
- Conduct an Experiment

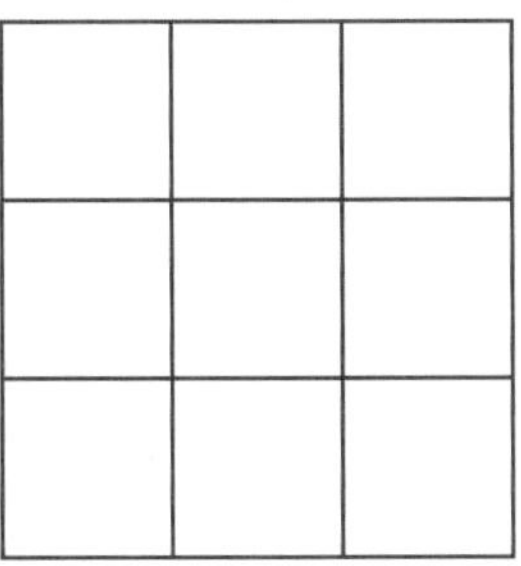

Extra Practice, page 617

Objective: Apply algebra to analyze data and make decisions.

13•9 A

Problem Solving: Application

Decision Making

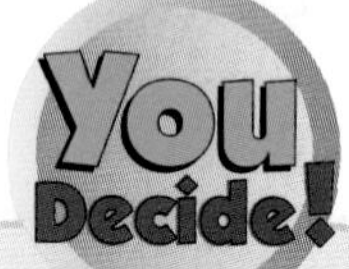

Should you choose spinner A, B, C, or D?

Your friends created the game *Spin, Toss, and Multiply*. You and some friends play the game. You want to win the game as much as possible.

Spin Toss and Multiply Game

1. Spin the spinner.
2. Roll the number cube.
3. Find the product of the two numbers.
4. If the product is odd, add 15 points.
5. Repeat steps 1-3 three more times.
6. Find the sum of the four products.
7. The person with the greatest sum wins.

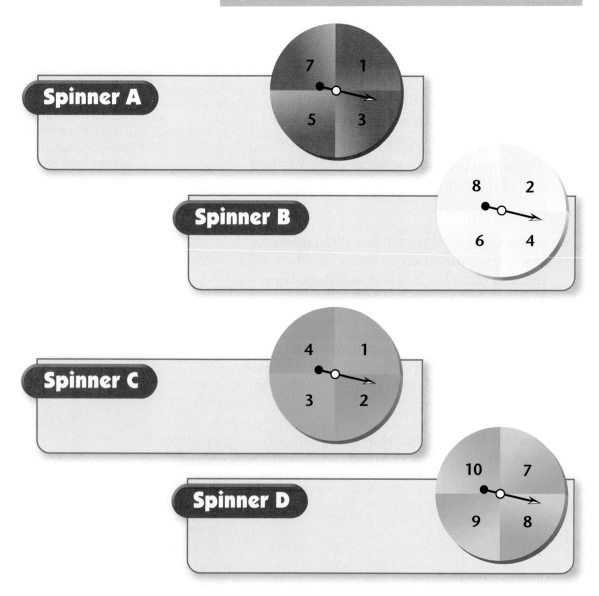

Spinner A: 7, 1, 5, 3

Spinner B: 8, 2, 6, 4

Spinner C: 4, 1, 3, 2

Spinner D: 10, 7, 9, 8

Read for Understanding

1. What are the possible outcomes of rolling the number cube?

2. What are the possible outcomes of spinning spinner A? spinner B? spinner C? spinner D?

3. What is the probability of rolling an even number on the number cube?

4. What is the probability of rolling an odd number on the number cube?

5. What is the probability of spinning an even number on spinner A? on spinner B? on spinner C? on spinner D?

6. What is the probability of spinning an odd number on spinner A? on spinner B? on spinner C? on spinner D?

Make Decisions

7. Is the product even or odd when you multiply two even numbers? when you multiply two odd numbers?

8. Is the product even or odd when you multiply an even number and an odd number?

9. When you toss the number cube and spin spinner A, what is the probability of getting an odd product? an even product?

10. When you toss the number cube and spin spinner B, what is the probability of getting an odd product? an even product?

11. When you toss the number cube and spin spinner C, what is the probability of getting an odd product? an even product?

12. When you toss the number cube and spin spinner D, what is the probability of getting an odd product? an even product?

13. If you get the greatest possible product each time, what will your total be after 4 spins with spinner A? spinner B? spinner C? spinner D?

14. If you get the greatest possible odd-number product each time, what will your total be after 4 spins with spinner A? spinner B? spinner C? spinner D? Remember to add points for each odd product.

Which spinner should you choose if you want the greatest chance of winning the game? Explain.

Problem Solving

Objective: Apply ratios to investigate science concepts.

Problem Solving: Math and Science
Which solution makes the best bubbles?

You have been invited to a bubble-making contest. Before you go, you want to decide which bubble solution makes the best bubbles.

In this activity, mix and study various soap solutions with different ratios of soap to water. Then you will decide which ratio gives you the best bubbles.

You Will Need

- **dish soap**
- **spoon**
- **four bowls**
- **bubble wand or chenille wires twisted into a wand**
- **timer or clock**

Hypothesize

Estimate the best ratio of soap to water for making a soap solution. Is it 1 : 1, 1 : 5, 1 : 10, or 1 : 20?

Procedure

1. Work with a partner.
2. Mix four solutions into separate bowls. Make the ratios of soap to water 1 : 1, 1 : 5, 1 : 10, and 1 : 20.
3. Use the wand to blow a bubble from the 1 : 1 solution.
4. Estimate the diameter of the bubble and record how long it lasts.
5. Record any important observations about the bubble.
6. Repeat four more times with the 1 : 1 solution.
7. Repeat steps 3–6 for the 1 : 5 solution.
8. Repeat steps 3–6 for the 1 : 10 solution.
9. Repeat steps 3–6 for the 1 : 20 solution.

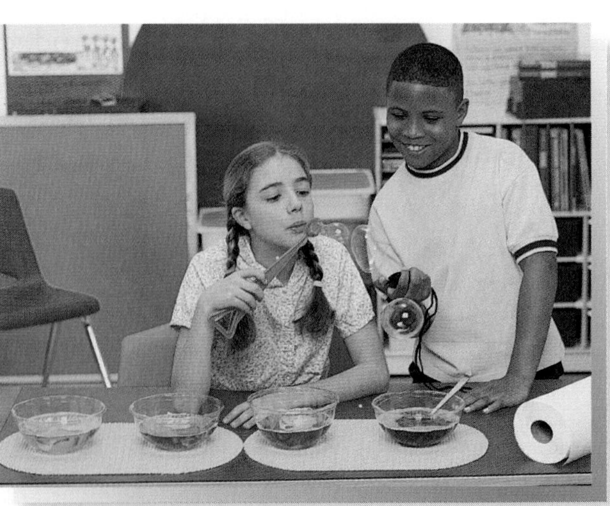

Data

Copy and complete the chart to record your data and observations.

1 : 1	Diameter	Lifetime	Observations
1			
2			
3			
4			
5			

1 : 5	Diameter	Lifetime	Observations
1			
2			
3			
4			
5			

1 : 10	Diameter	Lifetime	Observations
1			
2			
3			
4			
5			

1 : 20	Diameter	Lifetime	Observations
1			
2			
3			
4			
5			

Conclude and Apply

- Calculate the mean estimated diameter and lifetime for each solution.
- Which solution made the best bubbles? Explain your choice.
- Was your hypothesis correct?
- Rank the solutions from best to worst. What data did you use to make this list?
- Explain how bubbles are made using the idea of **surface tension**.

Did You Know?

All liquids experience surface tension, though some experience it more strongly than others. Surface tension occurs because the molecules underneath pull on the molecules at the surface.

Going Further

1. Some people add glycerine to their soap solution to make better bubbles. Design and complete an activity to compare solutions with and without glycerine. For the glycerine solution, add one tablespoon of glycerine to your favorite recipe and let it sit overnight.
2. Bend chenille stems into different shapes. Compare and contrast the bubbles made by the different shapes. Tie string across the middle of the shapes. What differences do you see in the bubbles now?

Check Your Progress B

Use the spinner to find the probability. **(pages 602–607)**

1. spinning a 10
2. spinning a 30
3. spinning a 55
4. spinning a 4
5. spinning a 15
6. spinning a 35
7. spinning a 10 or 15
8. spinning a 30 or a 35
9. spinning a 10, 15, 30, 35, or 55
10. spinning an even number
11. spinning an odd number
12. spinning a number greater than 10 and less than 55

Use the spinner to find the probability. **(pages 602–607)**

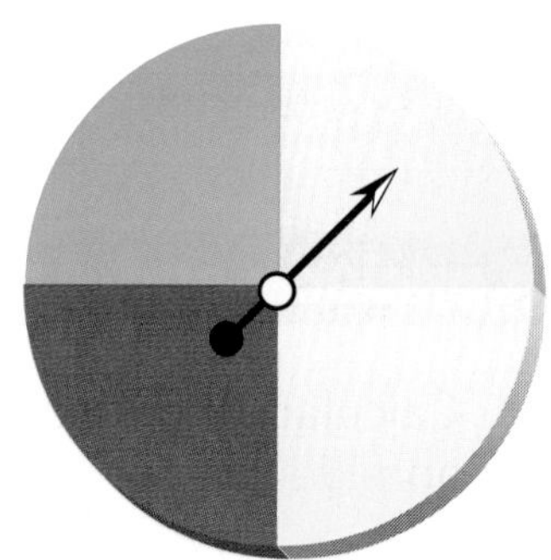

13. spinning red
14. spinning yellow
15. spinning red or blue
16. spinning yellow or blue

Solve. **(pages 602–609)**

17. Taylor drops a dime. What is the probability that the coin will land tails up?
18. Sally drops 1,000 thumbtacks on the floor. How can you find the probability of thumbtacks landing on their side or with their point up?
19. Wes tosses a number cube numbered 1 to 6. What is the probability that he will toss either a 2 or a 5?

20. **Compare:** Matt spins a 4-section spinner labeled 1, 4, 7, 10. Suzanne spins a 10-section spinner labeled 1, 2, 3, 4, 5, 6, 7, 8, 9, 10. Who has a greater chance of spinning an even number?

Extra Practice

Ratios (pages 586–591)

Copy and complete each table.

1.

6	12	▮	24	▮
4	▮	12	▮	20

2.

3	▮	9	▮	15
12	24	▮	48	▮

Copy and complete.

3. $5 : 1 = n : 9$
4. 6 to 7 = 24 to p
5. $\frac{3}{10} = \frac{27}{k}$
6. $4 : 9 = m : 72$
7. $8 : 12 = w : 48$
8. $\frac{40}{52} = \frac{10}{a}$
9. 14 to 8 = r to 72
10. $\frac{15}{12} = \frac{f}{4}$

Tell whether the ratios are equivalent.

11. 2 to 7, 8 to 35
12. 5 : 4, 60 : 48
13. $\frac{6}{11}, \frac{24}{44}$
14. 7 : 15, 21 : 30
15. $\frac{10}{3}, \frac{40}{12}$
16. 3 : 5, 10 : 18
17. $\frac{4}{6}, \frac{32}{50}$
18. 6 : 8, 36 : 48
19. $\frac{22}{55}, \frac{2}{5}$
20. 45 : 50, 18 : 20

Name four ratios equivalent to the given ratio.

21. $\frac{5}{6}$
22. 9 : 10
23. $\frac{7}{3}$
24. 1 : 2
25. $\frac{16}{4}$
26. 12 : 9

Rates (pages 592–595)

Find each unit rate.

1. 48 mi in 2 h = ▮ mi per 1 h
2. 63 mi in 7 d = ▮ mi per 1 d
3. 95 mi on 5 gal = ▮ mi per 1 gal
4. $270 for 40 h = ▮ per 1 h
5. $180 in 1 y = ▮ per 1 mo
6. 180 ft in 1 min = ▮ ft per 1 s
7. 6 books in 24 d = 1 book in ▮ d
8. $30 for 60 pens = ▮ for 1 pen

Use the unit rate of 35 miles per hour to solve.

9. d mi in 5 h
10. c mi in 7 h
11. g mi in 15 h
12. 70 mi in t h
13. 350 mi in z h
14. 420 mi in n h
15. x mi in 10 h
16. v mi in 3 h
17. d mi in 12 h

Solve.

18. A car travels 260 miles on 13 gallons of gas. What kind of mileage does the car get?
19. An office manager spends $4.65 for 5 rolls of tape at Al's Office Supply. He finds that The Supply Store sells packs of 6 for $5.34. Where can the manager find the better buy? Explain.

Extra Practice

Problem Solving: Reading for Math
Check the Reasonableness of an Answer (pages 596–597)

Solve.

1. Bill can read 2 pages in 3 minutes. Is it reasonable to expect that Bill will read a 200-page book within 2 hours? Explain.
2. A package of 12 pens costs $9.00. A package of 3 of the same kind of pens is marked $2.35. Does the smaller package have a reasonable price? Explain.
3. Samantha lives in Denver, Colorado. She purchased a roundtrip plane ticket to St. Louis, Missouri, for $230. Is it reasonable to expect that she can purchase a roundtrip ticket to Tokyo, Japan, for less than $250? Explain.
4. Greg went to a movie theater and paid $7 for admission. Donna went to a different movie theater and paid $6.50 for admission. Lynn is going to a movie theater that charges $15 for admission. Is this price reasonable? Explain.

Scale Drawings (pages 598–599)

Use the map and a ruler. Find each actual distance.

1. Furniture to Appliances
2. Furniture to Automotive
3. Appliances to Sporting Goods
4. Automotive to Household
5. Electronics to Household
6. Sporting Goods to Appliances to Furniture

Scale: 1 cm = 25 ft

Furniture ★ | ★ Automotive
Appliances ★ | ★ Sporting Goods
Electronics ★ | ★ Household

Solve.

7. The scale on a map shows 6 cm = 2 km. Bow Valley is 12 cm from Mapleton on the map. How far is it in kilometers?
8. Amanda is making a floor plan of an office. She is using the scale 2 cm = 1 m. A hall is 12 m long. How long should it be on her floor plan?
9. Randall is making a plan of his room. He is using the scale 2 in. = 5 ft. A wall is 7 in. on the plan. How long is the actual length in feet?
10. Winton is 3 in. from Grifton on the map. If the scale is 2 in. = 15 mi, how far is it in miles?
11. A map scale is $\frac{1}{2}$ in. = 2 miles. Greydon is $3\frac{1}{2}$ in. from Ashton on the map. How far is it in miles?

Extra Practice

Probability (pages 602–607)

Use the spinner to find the probability of each event.

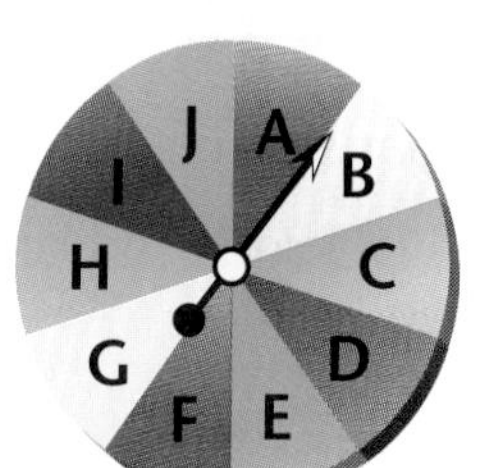

1. spinning G
2. spinning J
3. spinning A, B, C, or D
4. spinning E or F
5. spinning a vowel
6. spinning a consonant

Use the picture to find the probability of each event. Write *certain* or *impossible* for each event.

7. picking a white marble
8. picking a green marble
9. picking a blue, red, or yellow marble
10. picking a green or white marble

Use the spinner. Write *more likely than, less likely than,* or *equally likely as* to complete each sentence.

11. Spinning a 1 is ▒ spinning a 2.
12. Spinning a 4 is ▒ spinning a 3.
13. Spinning an even number is ▒ spinning an odd number.
14. Spinning a 3 is ▒ spinning a 5.
15. Spinning a number less than 4 is ▒ spinning a number greater than 3.
16. Spinning a 1 or 2 is ▒ spinning a 3 or 4.

Problem Solving: Strategy Do an Experiment (pages 608–609)

Do an experiment to solve.

1. What is the probability that a fork will land face down?
2. What is the probability that an eraser will land chalk side down?

Chapter Study Guide

Language and Math

Complete. Use a word from the list.

1. A comparison of two quantities is called ____.
2. A ____ is a reduced or enlarged representation of an actual object.
3. The ____ of tossing a 3 or 4 on a number cube is $\frac{2}{6}$.
4. To find the ____, you multiply the numerator of one ratio by the denominator of the other.
5. Ratios represented by equivalent fractions are called ____.

Math Words

ratio
terms
equivalent ratios
cross product
proportion
scale drawing
scale
probability
outcome

Skills and Applications

Find equivalent ratios. (pages 586–591)

Example

$1 : 2 = 6 : n$

Solution

Multiply: $\frac{1}{2} = \frac{1}{2} \times \frac{6}{6} = \frac{6}{12}$

So $1 : 2 = 6 : 12$.

Copy and complete.

6. $7 : 5 = 63 : p$
7. $6 : 4 = w : 48$
8. $3 : 10 = 36 : d$
9. $2 : 11 = u : 132$

Tell whether the ratios are equivalent.

10. 1 to 4, 2 to 8
11. $\frac{2}{3}, \frac{12}{18}$
12. 4 : 6, 5 : 7
13. 1 to 1, 2 to 2

Use scale drawings and maps. (pages 598–599)

Example

What is the actual distance from the computer to the printer?

Scale: 1 cm = 3 ft

Solution

The scale is 1 cm : 3 feet.

So the actual distance is 3 feet.

$$\frac{1 \text{ cm}}{1 \text{ ft}} = \frac{3 \text{ cm}}{x}$$

Use the scale drawing and a centimeter ruler. Find each actual distance.

14. from the phone to the answering machine
15. from the phone to the computer
16. from the printer to the phone
17. from the computer to the answering machine

Find the probability of an event. (pages 602–607)

Example

What is the probability of tossing a coin and landing on heads?

Solution

Probability $= \frac{\text{number of favorable outcomes}}{\text{number of possible outcomes}}$

favorable outcomes: heads
possible outcomes: heads, tails

Probability $= \frac{1}{2}$

Find the probability of each event.

18. tossing a 1 to 6 number cube and getting a number less than 5
19. picking a red marble from a bag with 2 green, 3 blue, and 5 red marbles
20. picking a green cube from a bag with 7 green, 7 red, and 1 white cubes
21. tossing a 1 to 6 number cube once and getting a number greater than 10
22. tossing a coin and getting heads

Solve problems. (pages 596–597, 608–609)

Example

Tom bought two cans of soup for \$2.70. He calculates that he can purchase 5 cans of soup for \$4. Are his calculations reasonable?

Solution

Write a proportion to solve.

$$\frac{2}{\$2.70} = \frac{5}{?}$$

$$\frac{2}{\$2.70} = \frac{5}{\$6.75}$$

\$4 is not enough for 5 cans of soup, so Tom's calculations are not reasonable.

Solve.

23. Nancy bought 6 apples for \$5.64. Is it reasonable to assume that she can buy 4 more apples with a five-dollar bill? Explain.
24. Lisa bought 3 notebooks for \$8.34. She needs 2 more notebooks. Is it reasonable to assume that she can pay for 2 notebooks with a five-dollar bill? Explain.
25. Do an experiment to find the probability of a plastic fork landing up or down.

Chapter Test

Copy and complete.

1. $2:5 = 20:f$
2. $3:4 = 45:u$
3. $9:7 = 27:b$
4. $3:1 = 75:z$
5. $8:6 = y:36$
6. $5:11 = r:220$
7. $19:15 = a:75$
8. $12:7 = k:77$

Use the scale drawing and a ruler. Find each actual distance.

9. West to Central
10. West to Park
11. Central to Park
12. East to Park

Elementary Schools

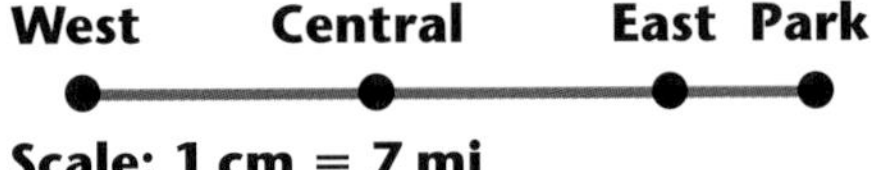

Scale: 1 cm = 7 mi

Find the probability of each event.

13. spinning a 10
14. spinning a 35
15. spinning an even number
16. spinning an odd number
17. spinning a 1-digit number
18. spinning a 2-digit number
19. tossing a 4 on a number cube numbered 1 to 6
20. tossing a 7 on a number cube numbered 1 to 6
21. tossing a number less than 7 on a number cube numbered 1 to 6

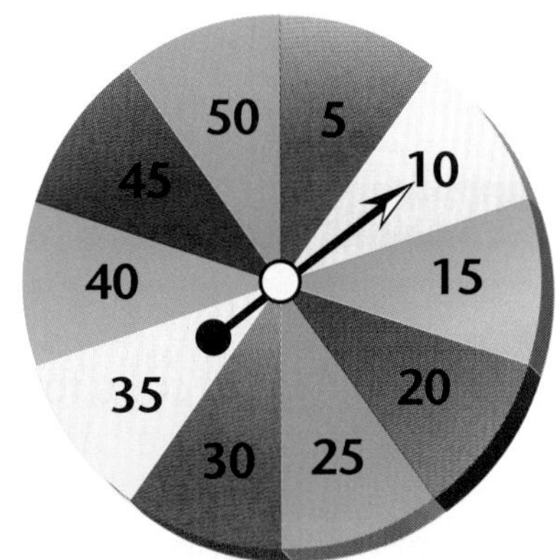

Solve.

22. The ratio of cats to total animals at Arnie's Pet Store is 8 to 32. At the animal shelter there are 16 animals and 5 are cats. Are these ratios equivalent? Explain.
23. Lewistown is 5 inches from Elliston on a map. The map scale is 2 inches = 9 miles. How far apart are the two cities?
24. Nick puts 12 identical cards in a bag. A month of the year is written on each card. If Nick pulls a card from the bag without looking, what is the probability that he will choose a month that begins with J?
25. An office supply store sells a box of 20 pens for \$4 and a box of 15 pens for \$3.30. Which box is the better buy?

Performance Assessment

You want to make copies of this picture. You want one larger copy for your wall and one 3-inch by 4-inch copy for your wallet.

You Will Need
- **ruler**

Measure the sides of the photo. Then use the dimensions to answer the questions.

- What scale will you choose for the copy that will go on the wall?
- What will be the dimensions for the copy that goes on the wall?
- What is the ratio of the length of the original picture to the length of the wallet copy?

Assessment

A Good Answer
- has all parts of the exercise completed and clearly marked.
- shows an appropriate scale for the wall copy.
- shows how the scale for the wall copy is used to find the dimensions of the copy.
- shows how the scale for the wallet copy is found.

You may want to save this work in your portfolio.

Enrichment

Tree Diagrams

What are the possible outcomes if you toss a quarter and a nickel?

Example

You can make a tree diagram to count all the possible outcomes.

In this tree diagram, *H* stands for heads. *T* stands for tails.

Quarter Toss **Nickel Toss** **Outcome: Quarter-Nickel**

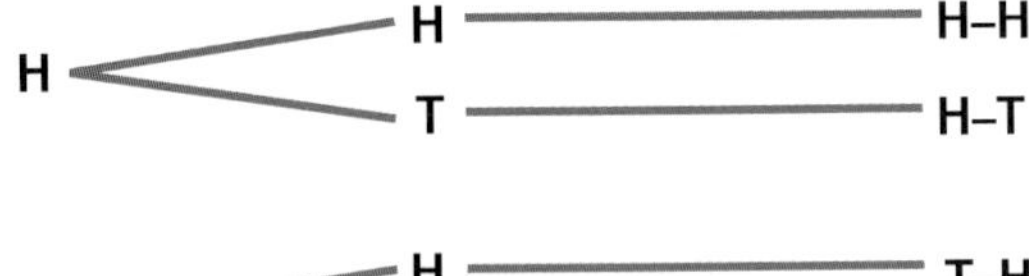

The possible outcomes are Heads-Heads, Heads-Tails, Tails-Heads, and Tails-Tails. So there are 4 possible outcomes.

You can use the number of possible outcomes to determine a probability. For example, the probability of getting at least one 'Heads' when you toss two coins is $\frac{3}{4}$.

Practice

Solve.

1. Use the tree diagram in the example. What is the probability of tossing two heads?

2. Use the tree diagram in the example. What is the probability of tossing one head and one tail?

3. A number cube numbered 1 to 6 is tossed with a nickel. Draw a tree diagram to show possible outcomes.

4. Use the tree diagram in problem 3. List all the possible outcomes.

5. Use the tree diagram in problem 3. What is the probability of tossing a 5 and a tail?

6. Use the tree diagram in problem 3. What is the probability of tossing an even number and heads?

7. Two number cubes are tossed. Each is numbered from 1 to 6. Draw a tree diagram to show all possible outcomes.

8. Use the tree diagram in problem 7. How many outcomes are there?

Test-Taking Tips

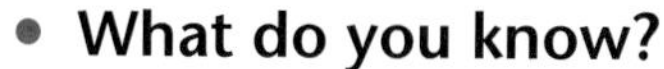

S.O.S.

When taking a test, you may not have answer choices. In this case, you must **find and explain your answer.**

A 10-section spinner has sections that are red, red, blue, yellow, red, green, yellow, green, red, and red. Which color is most likely to be spun?

- **What do you know?** The spinner colors
- **What do you need to find?** The most likely color

You can organize the data to see which color comes up most often.

Red 5	Blue 1
Yellow 2	Green 2

- Answer the question in complete sentences.
- Be sure to explain how you calculated your answer and why you think it is correct.

The most likely color is red. Red is the most likely because it covers more of the spinner than any other color. It covers five of the ten sections. The other colors only cover one or two sections.

Check for Success

Before turning in a test, go back one last time to check.

- ☑ I understood and answered the questions asked.
- ☑ I checked my work for errors.
- ☑ My answers make sense.

Practice **Solve.**

1. Francine spins a 6-section spinner. The sections are red, red, blue, blue, red, and green. Which color is least likely? Explain.
2. If Jan can travel 200 miles on 10 gallons of gas, what is her gas mileage? Explain.
3. A scale drawing has a scale of 1 inch equals 3 feet. If the drawing has a room that is 5 inches long, what is the actual length?
4. A cube is numbered from 1 to 6. What is the probability of tossing an even number?
5. A cube is numbered from 1 to 6. What is the probability of tossing a number greater than 10? Explain.
6. Store A offers pens in packs of 10 for \$3.30. Store B offers pens in packs of 15 for \$4.65. Which store offers the better buy? Explain.

Spiral Review and Test Prep

Chapters 1–13

Choose the correct answer.

Number Sense

1. Find the number that makes this sentence true.
$95 \times 307 = m$
A. 29,165 **C.** 4,298
B. 28,535 **D.** 4,208

2. Find the number that makes this sentence true. $6{,}201 \div 75 = v$
F. 8.268 **H.** 826.8
G. 82.68 **J.** 8,268

3. $8 : 11 = p : 143$
A. 11 **C.** 88
B. 19 **D.** 104

4. Leo buys 12 bagels for $4.08. What is the unit price per bagel?
F. $0.34 **H.** $12.24
G. $0.40 **J.** $48.96

Algebra and Functions

5. Solve for x.
$x + 25 = 1{,}042$
A. $x = 41.68$ **C.** $x = 1{,}067$
B. $x = 1{,}017$ **D.** Not Here

6. Solve for y.
$y \div 13 = 455$
F. $y = 35$ **H.** $y = 468$
G. $y = 442$ **J.** $y = 5{,}915$

7. Solve for z.
$28z = 131.6$
A. $z = 4.7$ **C.** $z = 159.6$
B. $z = 103.6$ **D.** $z = 3{,}684.8$

8. $3^3 + (12 + 59) - 11 \times 4 = h$
F. 54 **H.** 348
G. 231 **J.** Not Here

Mathematical Reasoning

9. Joy's dog weighs 720 ounces. How many pounds does it weigh?
   - A. 45 pounds
   - B. 90 pounds
   - C. 180 pounds
   - D. 360 pounds

10. Charlie has a fish tank that is 4 feet long, 2 feet wide, and 3 feet tall. What is the volume of Charlie's fish tank?
   - F. 24 cubic feet
   - G. 24 square feet
   - H. 9 cubic feet
   - J. 9 square feet

11. Cecilia buys $1\frac{1}{2}$ pounds of ground beef, $2\frac{1}{4}$ pounds of chicken, and $3\frac{1}{3}$ pounds of roast beef. How much meat does she buy in all?
   - A. $6\frac{1}{3}$ pounds
   - B. $6\frac{11}{12}$ pounds
   - C. $7\frac{1}{12}$ pounds
   - D. Not Here

12. A 3-digit number has a 3 in the hundreds place. The digit in the ones place is 3 times the digit in the hundreds place. The digit in the tens place is the difference between the hundreds and ones digits. What is the 3-digit number?
   - F. 396
   - G. 936
   - H. 369
   - J. 376

Statistics, Data Analysis, and Probability

Use data from the graph for problems 13–15.

Pat's Pet Wash

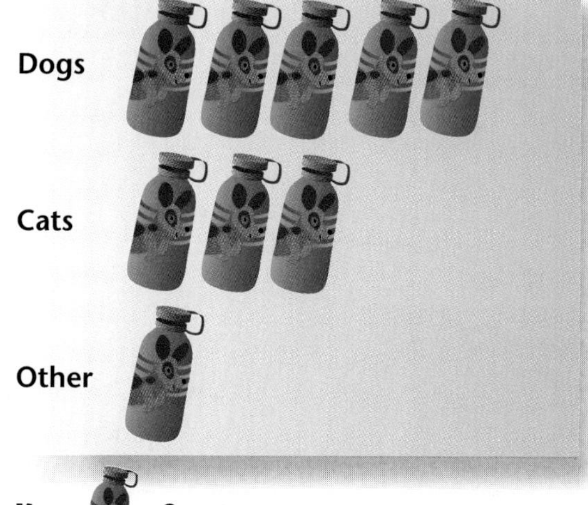

Key: = 2 pets

13. What is the ratio of cats washed to other pets washed?
   - A. 1 to 3
   - B. 2 to 6
   - C. 4 to 1
   - D. 6 to 2

14. What is the ratio of all pets washed to dogs washed?
   - F. 18 to 10
   - G. 10 to 18
   - H. 7 to 5
   - J. 5 to 9

15. How many more dogs than cats are washed?
   - A. 2 more dogs
   - B. 4 more dogs
   - C. 5 more dogs
   - D. 8 more dogs

16. Find the missing number

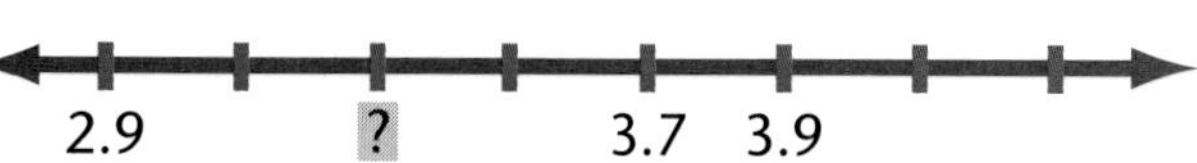

Spiral Review and Test Prep

#1

CHAPTER 14 Percents

Theme: Sports and Games

Use the Data

Recreation	Percentage of Time
Books, maps	7%
Magazines, newspapers, sheet music	8%
Toys and sports supplies	14%
Cars, boats, airplanes, sports, & photography equipment	14%
Video an audio products, computers, and musical instruments	28%
Flowers, seeds and plants	4%
Movie tickets	2%
Play and opera tickets	3%
Sporting event tickets	2%
Clubs	4%
Amusements	14%

Source: The World Almanac and Book of Facts

The table shows the percentage of time that people in the United States spend on the listed recreational activities. Which categories are the largest and smallest? How many categories have 14% of the total?

What You Will Learn

In this chapter you will learn how to

- write numbers as percents.
- change numbers between percents, decimals, and fractions.
- find a percent of a number.
- find the percent one number is of another.
- make circle graphs.
- use strategies to solve problems.

Additional activities at
www.mhschool.com/math

Objective: Understand percents and relate them to fractions, ratios, and decimals.

14·1

Explore the Meaning of Percent

Learn

Math Word

percent means per hundred, or part of a hundred

You can use graph paper to explore percents.

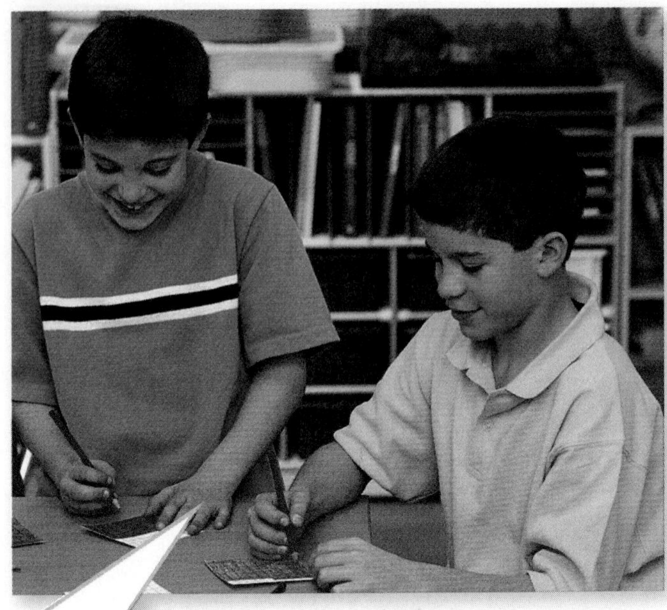

Work Together

▶ You will use graph paper to represent the **percents** of cotton and polyester in Crazy T's T-shirts.

You Will Need
- **graph paper**

Shirt	Cotton	Polyester
Crazy T's	85%	15%
Al's Shirts	75%	25%
Shirts 'n More	60%	40%

Crazy T's		
	Cotton	Polyester
Percent	85%	15%
Fraction	$\frac{17}{20}$	
Decimal	0.85	
Ratio	85:100	

- Make a 10-by-10 grid on graph paper. Each of the 100 small squares on the grid represents 1 percent.
- Label the grid Crazy T's.
- Shade the grid in one color to show the part of the shirt that is cotton. Use another color to shade the part that is polyester.
- Copy and complete the table. Record the cotton part and the polyester part using a fraction, a decimal, a ratio, and a percent. For each fraction, use simplest form.

▶ Repeat the activity for Al's Shirts and Shirts 'n More.

Make Connections

A shirt is 80% cotton. How can you show the percent as a fraction, a decimal, and a ratio?

Using Models

Each square represents 1%.
Shade 80 squares for 80%.

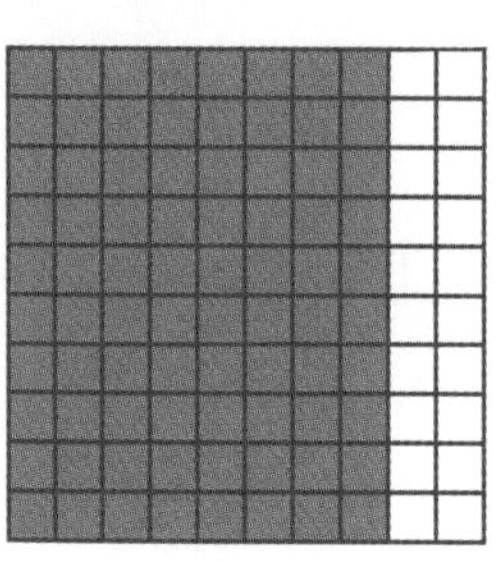

Using Paper and Pencil

Percent: 80%

Think: 80% means 80 parts of 100.

Fraction: $\frac{80}{100} = \frac{4}{5}$

Think: Write the 80 parts of 100 as a fraction and simplify.

Decimal: 0.80

Think: 0.80 is 80 hundredths or 80 parts of 100.

Ratio: 80 : 100

Think: There are 100 total squares and 80 are shaded.

Try It

Write a fraction in simplest form, a decimal, ratio, and percent to show the part shaded in each color.

1. 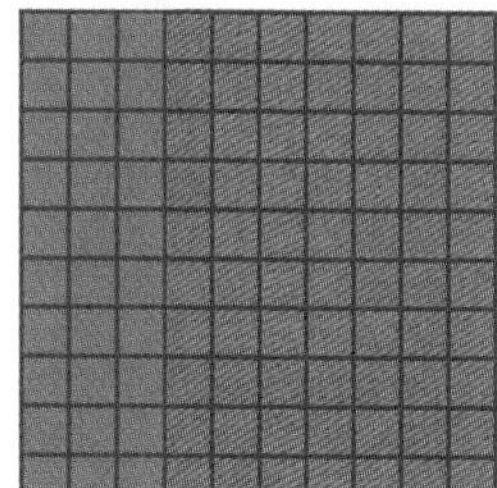

2. 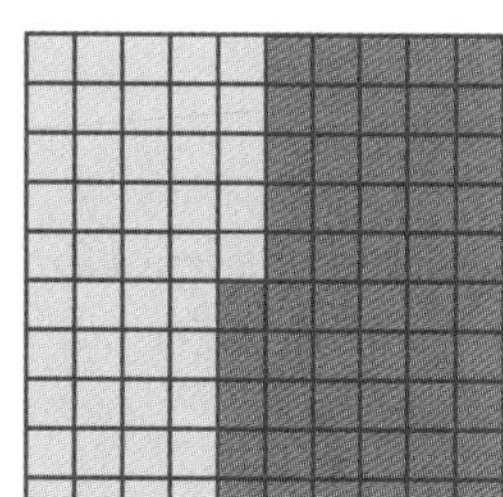

3. 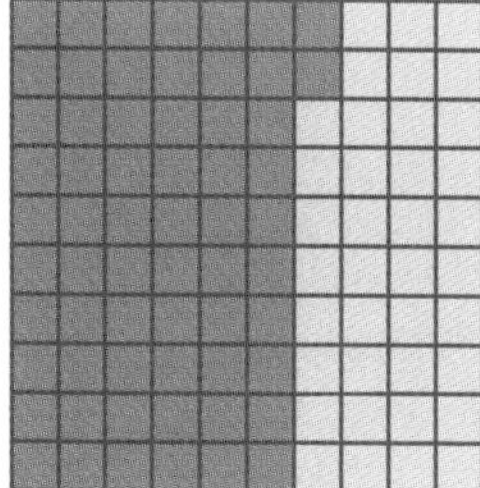

Sum it Up How are the numbers $\frac{25}{100}$, 0.25, 25:100, 25% alike? How are they different?

Practice

Write each fraction, decimal, or ratio as a percent.

4. $\frac{50}{100}$ **5.** 0.30 **6.** 45:100 **7.** $\frac{5}{100}$ **8.** 0.62 **9.** $\frac{75}{100}$

10. **Analyze:** A 10-by-10 grid is shaded in two colors—green and blue. If 65 percent of the grid is shaded green, what part of the grid is shaded blue? Explain.

Objective: Change percents to decimals and fractions, and change decimals and fractions to percents.

14·2

Percents, Fractions, and Decimals

Learn

Math Word

percent the ratio of a given number to 100, expressed with a percent sign (%)

People use numbers to record almost everything in sports. Here are the wins, losses, and percentages in a recent football season. How can you write the percent of the total games Denver won as a fraction and as a decimal?

National Football League Final Standings American Football Conference, Western Division

Team	Wins	Losses	Percent Won
Kansas City	13	3	81.3%
Denver	12	4	75%
Seattle	8	8	50%
Oakland	4	12	25%
San Diego	4	12	

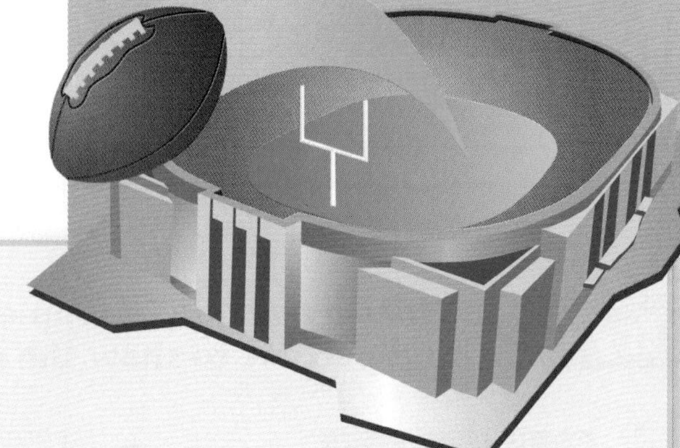

Example 1

Write 75% as a fraction in simplest form.

1. Write the **percent** as a fraction with a denominator of 100. $75\% = \frac{75}{100}$

2. Simplify the fraction. $\frac{75}{100} = \frac{75 \div 25}{100 \div 25} = \frac{3}{4}$

Think: 25 is the GCF of 75 and 100

Denver won $\frac{3}{4}$ of its games.

Example 2

Write 75% as a decimal.

1. Write the percent as a fraction with a denominator of 100. $75\% = \frac{75}{100}$

2. Then write an equivalent decimal. $\frac{75}{100} = 0.75$

Think: $\frac{75}{100}$ is 75 hundredths.

Denver won 0.75 of its games.

San Diego won $\frac{4}{16}$ or 0.25 of its games. How can San Diego's wins be written as a percent?

Example 3

Write 0.25 as a percent.

1 Write a fraction with 100 as the denominator. $0.25 = \frac{25}{100}$ **Think:** 0.25 is 25 hundredths

2 Rewrite the fraction as a percent. $\frac{25}{100} = 25\%$

San Diego won 25% of its games.

More Examples

A

Write 4% as a fraction in simplest form.

$4\% = \frac{4}{100} = \frac{1}{25}$

B

Write 8% as a decimal.

$8\% = \frac{8}{100} = 0.08$

C

Write 0.12 as a percent.

$0.12 = \frac{12}{100} = 12\%$

D

Write $\frac{1}{20}$ as a percent.

$\frac{1}{20} = \frac{5}{100} = 5\%$

Try It **Write each percent as a decimal and as a fraction in simplest form.**

1. 50%
2. 20%
3. 16%
4. 35%
5. 33%
6. 14%
7. 27%
8. 62%
9. 30%

Write each fraction or decimal as a percent.

10. $\frac{3}{4}$
11. 0.8
12. $\frac{4}{5}$
13. 0.9
14. $\frac{3}{10}$
15. 0.1
16. 0.65
17. $\frac{2}{10}$
18. 0.81
19. $\frac{2}{8}$
20. $\frac{26}{100}$
21. 0.28
22. $\frac{9}{25}$
23. 0.44
24. $\frac{17}{100}$

Sum it Up Explain how the numbers $\frac{3}{5}$, 0.6, and 60% are alike and different.

Practice

Write each percent as a decimal and as a fraction in simplest form.

25. 60%	**26.** 80%	**27.** 15%	**28.** 75%	**29.** 20%
30. 10%	**31.** 50%	**32.** 40%	**33.** 19%	**34.** 45%
35. 25%	**36.** 30%	**37.** 21%	**38.** 2%	**39.** 100%

Write each fraction or decimal as a percent.

40. $\frac{1}{5}$	**41.** $\frac{7}{10}$	**42.** 0.8	**43.** 0.21	**44.** 0.13
45. 0.6	**46.** $\frac{1}{4}$	**47.** 0.36	**48.** $\frac{3}{5}$	**49.** 0.17
50. 0.72	**51.** 0.22	**52.** $\frac{9}{10}$	**53.** 0.5	**54.** $\frac{1}{2}$
★**55.** $\frac{20}{200}$	★**56.** $\frac{20}{125}$	★**57.** $\frac{30}{150}$	★**58.** 0.95	★**59.** 0.92

Algebra & functions **Find each missing number.**

60. $\frac{n}{5} = 40\%$	**61.** $55\% = \frac{s}{20}$	**62.** $16\% = \frac{b}{25}$	**63.** $\frac{c}{4} = 75\%$
64. $\frac{x}{10} = 10\%$	**65.** $\frac{t}{100} = 22\%$	★**66.** $\frac{47}{d} = 47\%$	★**67.** $\frac{4}{z} = 80\%$

68.

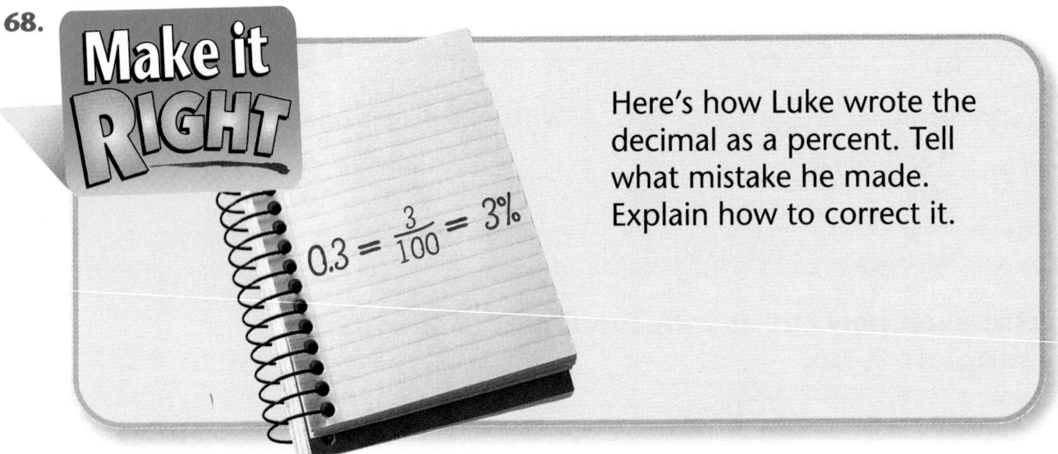

Here's how Luke wrote the decimal as a percent. Tell what mistake he made. Explain how to correct it.

Problem Solving

69. A football quarterback made 7 complete passes out of 10 attempts. How can you write this number as a percent?

70. **What if** a quarterback had an average of 54% completed passes? What is this percent as a fraction in simplest form?

71. Of 10 marbles in a closed bag, 5 are red. What is the probability of pulling out a red marble? What is this number as a percent?

★**72.** **Analyze:** George makes 6 of 8 field goals and Marvin makes 7 of 10. Who scored the higher percentage? Explain.

Use data from the table for problems 73–77.

73. How can you write the Cougars' wins as a percent?

74. How can you write the Bears' wins as a fraction in simplest form?

75. Which teams won more than 50 percent of their games?

76. Which team won about 90 percent of its games?

★77. What percent of their games did the Hawks lose?

Newton League Football Final Standings

Team	Games Won
Ravens	0.875
Bears	0.75
Cougars	0.65
Tigers	0.625
Dolphins	0.5
Hawks	0.25
Lions	0.2

78. **Measurement:** Tom Dempsey of the New Orleans Saints holds the record for the longest field goal ever. On November 8, 1970, Dempsey kicked a 63-yard field goal. How many feet is that?

79. **Social Studies:** The shortest war in history started over a cricket match in 1896. British warships moved into waters off Zanzibar so that the officers could watch the game. Zanzibar declared and lost the war in 37 minutes, 23 seconds. How many seconds did the war last?

80. **Analyze:** Joe says that the decimal 0.04 and 40% represent the same number. Is he correct? Explain.

81. A football field measures 100 yards. How many feet is that?

82. **Summarize** the steps you would take to change a decimal to a percent.

83. If a football game starts at 1:07 P.M. and runs 3 hours and 22 minutes. What time does it finish?

Spiral Review and Test Prep

84. 0.98 + 0.31

85. 2.04 + 0.07

86. 1.485 + 3.0012

87. 19.49 + 1.26

Choose the correct answer.

88. Last season the Marwick Melons won 0.875 of their games. This season they won 0.75 of their games. By what decimal did their record change?

A. 0.125
B. 1.25
C. 0.738
D. 1.563

89. Daniel ran the four laps of the race in these times: 12.8 seconds, 14.06 seconds, 13.95 seconds, 14.13 seconds. What was the total time of his race?

F. 14.13 seconds
G. 54.94 seconds
H. 55.48 seconds
J. Not Here

Objective: Change numbers between percents, decimals, fractions, and mixed numbers.

14·3

More About Percents

Learn

The Ridgemont School track-and-field team improved its wins by 125% over last season. How can that record be written as a decimal and mixed number?

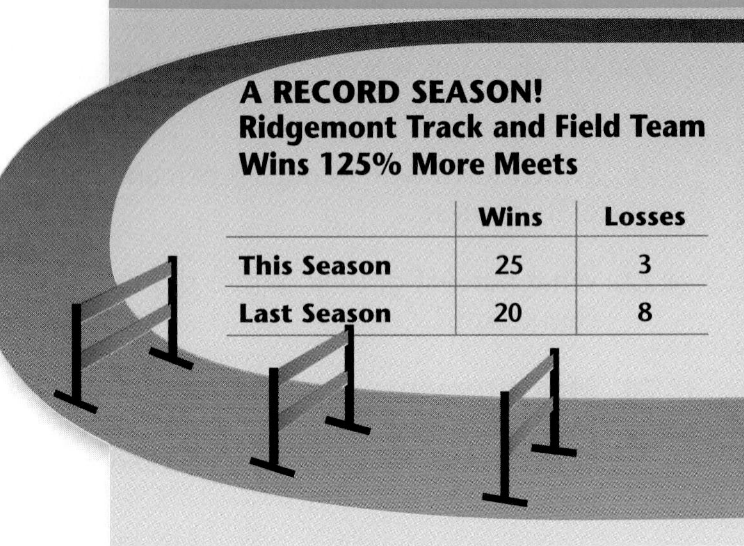
A RECORD SEASON!
Ridgemont Track and Field Team
Wins 125% More Meets

	Wins	Losses
This Season	25	3
Last Season	20	8

Example 1

Write 125% as a decimal.

Note: You can use phrases like "a 125% increase" or "20% decrease" to indicate if numbers are getting larger or smaller over time.

1 Write the percent as a fraction with a denominator of 100. $125\% = \frac{125}{100}$

2 Divide the numerator by the denominator. $100\overline{)125.00}$ = 1.25

The team won 1.25 times more games.

Example 2

Write 125% as a mixed number.

1 Write the percent as a fraction with a denominator of 100. $125\% = \frac{125}{100}$

2 Divide the numerator by the denominator and show the remainder. Write the answer as a mixed number in simplest form. $100\overline{)125}$ = 1 R25

$1 \text{ R}25 = 1\frac{25}{100} = 1\frac{1}{4}$

The team won $1\frac{1}{4}$ times more games.

The Ridgemont swim team won 19.5% of its meets last season. How can this percent be written as a decimal?

Example 3

Write 19.5% as a decimal.

Note: 19.5 percent is a percent with a decimal in it, not a whole number percent

1 Write the percent as a fraction with a denominator of 100. $19.5\% = \frac{19.5}{100}$

2 Write the fraction with a denominator of 1,000 to remove the decimal. $\frac{19.5}{100} = \frac{195}{1{,}000}$

Think: Multiply the numerator and denominator by the same power of 10.

3 Write an equivalent decimal. $\frac{195}{1{,}000} = 0.195$

Think: $\frac{195}{1{,}000}$ is 195 thousandths.

The Ridgemont swim team won 0.195 of its meets.

Example 4

Write 19.5 percent as a fraction in simplest form.

1 Write the percent as a fraction so that the numerator has no decimal points. $19.5\% = \frac{195}{1{,}000}$

2 Simplify the fraction. $\frac{195}{1{,}000} = \frac{195 \div 5}{1{,}000 \div 5} = \frac{39}{200}$

Think: 5 is the GCF of 195 and 1,000.

The Ridgemont swim team won $\frac{39}{200}$ of its meets.

Try It **Write each percent as a decimal and as a mixed number in simplest form, or as a whole number.**

1. 275%
2. 150%
3. 320%
4. 200%
5. 500%

Write each percent as a decimal and as a fraction in simplest form.

6. 12.5%
7. 22.5%
8. 16%
9. 62.5%
10. 35.2%

Explain how to write 165 percent as a decimal and mixed number.

Practice

Write each percent as a decimal and as a mixed number in simplest form, or as a whole number.

11. 325%	**12.** 250%	**13.** 100%	**14.** 400%	**15.** 375%
16. 350%	**17.** 120%	**18.** 180%	**19.** 600%	**20.** 550%
21. 640%	**22.** 160%	**23.** 425%	**24.** 875%	**25.** 900%
26. 125%	**27.** 500%	**28.** 110%	**29.** 225%	**30.** 150%

Write each percent as a decimal and as a fraction in simplest form.

31. 37.5%	**32.** 24%	**33.** 40%	**34.** 87.5%	**35.** 25%
36. 50%	**37.** 62.5%	**38.** 19%	**39.** 30%	**40.** 12.5%
★**41.** 11.2%	★**42.** 19.2%	★**43.** 84%	★**44.** 20.5%	★**45.** 98%

Algebra & functions **Find each missing number.**

46. 315% = 3.■5	**47.** 250% = 2.■	**48.** 48.5% = 0.■85	**49.** 80% = ■.8
50. 100% = ■.00	**51.** 20% = 0. ■	**52.** 33.3% = 0.33■	**53.** 112.5% = 1. ■25

54.

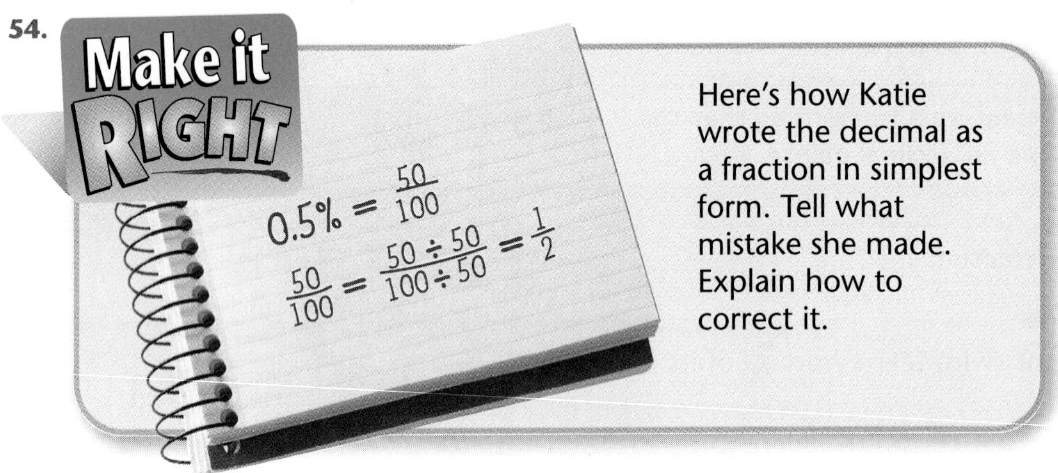

Here's how Katie wrote the decimal as a fraction in simplest form. Tell what mistake she made. Explain how to correct it.

Problem Solving

55. The Ridgemont gymnastics team won 0.744 of its meets this season. Write this decimal as a percent and as a fraction in simplest form.

56. The Culverton School lacrosse team improved its wins this year over last year by 150 percent. Write the percent as a decimal and as a mixed number in simplest form.

Journal

57. Generalize: Give an example of how a percent can be written as a decimal and as a fraction.

58. Health: 51.2 percent of the students at Ridgemont School scored above average in a fitness test. Have greater than or less than half of the school's students scored above average?

Use data from the table for problems 59–64.

59. Which school had the most wins during the season?

60. Round Clifton's wins to the nearest tenth.

61. How can you write Riverside's wins as a fraction in simplest form?

62. **Number Sense:** What percent of its games did Larkville lose?

63. Which teams won more than 50 percent of their games?

64. Which teams won about $\frac{1}{4}$ of their games?

Western County Schools Track and Field 1997–1998 Final Standings

Team	Meets Won
Redding	0.756
Clifton	0.683
Woodridge	0.549
Larkville	0.500
Summerton	0.244
Riverside	0.232
Highgrove	0.134

Use data from *Did You Know?* for problems 65–66.

65. Write Ty Cobb's batting average as a percent.

★ 66. What career batting average would a baseball player need to set a new record? Write the answer as a percent.

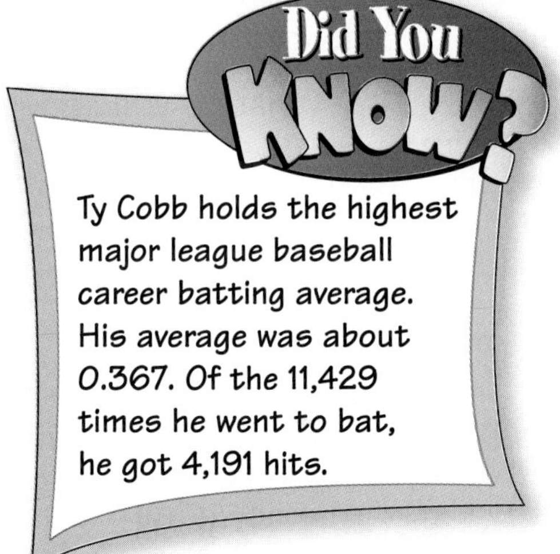

Did You Know?
Ty Cobb holds the highest major league baseball career batting average. His average was about 0.367. Of the 11,429 times he went to bat, he got 4,191 hits.

Spiral Review and Test Prep

67. 5.2×0.14

68. 1.37×2.19

69. 9.6×0.05

70. 0.24×0.38

71. $12 \div 0.5$

72. $1.24 \div 4$

73. $16.4 \div 0.4$

74. $108 \div 0.2$

Choose the correct answer.

75. Anton scored the following number of points in the last 5 games. What is the mean?

A. 19
B. 20
C. 21
D. 25

Game 1:	25 points
Game 2:	18 points
Game 3:	21 points
Game 4:	17 points
Game 5:	19 points

76. In the last basketball game, Milton scored 2-point baskets and 1-point foul shots. He made a total of 9 baskets and scored 15 points. How many of each kind of basket did he make?

F. 8 baskets and 1 foul shot
G. 6 baskets and 3 foul shots
H. 2 baskets and 7 foul shots
J. 4 baskets and 5 foul shots

Extra Practice, page 661

Objective: Compare and contrast information to choose a representation.

14·4 Problem Solving: Reading for Math

Represent Numbers

Hockey Player Reaches Her Goals

Read Alexa is trying to improve her rate of ice hockey goals per shot attempts. Last year 55 percent of her shots scored goals. This year she made 13 goals in 20 shots. Did Alexa improve her record?

READING SKILL ▶ **Compare and Contrast**

When you compare and contrast, you notice how items are alike and different.

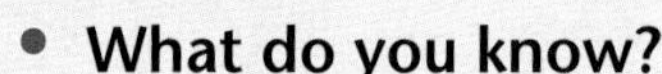

- **What do you know?** Percent of goals last year; number of goals and shots this year
- **What do you need to find?** Whether Alexa improved her record

MATH SKILL ▶ **Choose How to Represent Numbers.**

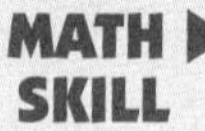

You can represent numbers as fractions, percents, or decimals. You should use the same representation when comparing amounts. Fractions should be compared with fractions, percents with percents, and decimals with decimals.

Plan Decide if you want to compare fractions or percents. Then change the percent to a fraction or the fraction to a percent.

Solve

Write $\frac{13}{20}$ as a percent.	Or write 55% as a fraction.
$\frac{13}{20} = \frac{65}{100}$ $\frac{65}{100} = 65\%$	$55\% = \frac{55}{100} = \frac{11}{20}$
Compare. $65\% > 55\%$	Compare. $\frac{13}{20} > \frac{11}{20}$

This season Alexa had a better scoring rate.

Look Back How could you check your answer?

Sum it Up Explain why you changed the numbers in the problem to have the same representation.

Practice

Solve.

1. Billy plays hockey. Last year 0.45 of his shots scored goals. This year he made 11 scores out of 20 shots. Did Billy improve his record? Explain.

2. A survey question asked residents what kind of sports arena the town should have: 0.3 said an ice hockey rink, $\frac{1}{3}$ said a basketball court, and 37 percent said a swimming pool. List these responses from greatest to least.

Use data from the table for problems 3–6.

3. Would more people use the pool for less than 3 hours or more than 6 hours?

4. Which time category did most people select?

5. List the choices from most responses to least.

6. Express the sum of all the responses shown in the table as a fraction, a percent, and a decimal.

Survey Results

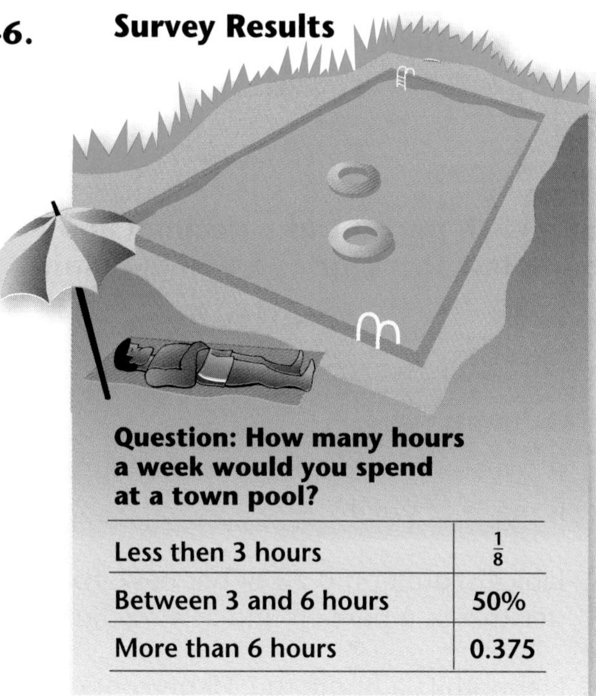

Question: How many hours a week would you spend at a town pool?

Less then 3 hours	$\frac{1}{8}$
Between 3 and 6 hours	50%
More than 6 hours	0.375

Spiral Review and Test Prep

Choose the correct answer.

Of the people who make up Oakville's town council, 42 percent were born in Oakville. So 0.58 of the council was born somewhere else.

7. Which of following statements is true?
   - A. Of the council members, $\frac{21}{50}$ were born in Oakville.
   - B. More town members were born in Oakville than somewhere else.
   - C. Only people born in Oakville can be members of the town council.
   - D. About 20 percent of the council was not born in Oakville.

8. When comparing a fraction and a percent,
   - F. always use fractions.
   - G. never use decimals.
   - H. use the same representation for both.
   - J. always use a percent.

Extra Practice, page 661

Check Your Progress A

Write each fraction, decimal, or ratio as a percent. **(pages 628–629)**

1. $\frac{35}{100}$
2. 0.45
3. 12 : 100
4. $\frac{9}{100}$
5. 0.15

Write each percent as a decimal and as a fraction in simplest form. **(pages 630–633)**

6. 40%
7. 90%
8. 32%
9. 80%
10. 16%

Write each percent as a decimal and as a mixed number in simplest form, or as a whole number. **(pages 634–637)**

11. 220%
12. 160%
13. 310%
14. 400%

Solve. **(pages 628–639)**

15. A sweater is made of $\frac{3}{4}$ wool. What percent of the sweater is made of wool?
16. Janice scored on 0.72 of her basketball shots. Write the decimal as a percent and as a fraction in simplest form.
17. Nelson hits a home run 15 percent of his times at bat. Write this number as a fraction in simplest form.
18. The Bradford Bears basketball team won 175% more games this year compared to last year. Write the percent as a decimal and as a mixed number in simplest form.
19. Last year Norm made 55% of his shots on goal. This year he made 15 scores out of 25 shots. Did he improve this year? Explain.

Journal

20. **Generalize:** Terence says that every decimal can be written as a percent and as a fraction. Do you agree or disagree? Explain. Give an example.

Additional activities at
www.mhschool.com/math

Use a Table to Change Fractions to Percents

A choir held a concert on four consecutive days. On the first day of the concert, 90 tickets were sold and 85 people attended the concert. On the second day, 120 tickets were sold and 90 people attended. On the third day, 119 tickets were sold and 96 people attended. On the fourth day, 124 tickets were sold and 108 people attended. On which day was the percentage of tickets used the greatest?

You can use a spreadsheet table to find the fraction of the tickets that were used and then change that fraction to a percent.

- Click on the Table key.
- Label the columns *Day, People Attending, Number of Tickets Sold,* and *Percent of Tickets Used.*
- In the column labeled *Day,* enter the 1, 2, 3, and 4.
- In the column labeled *People Attending,* enter the number of people who attended the concert each day.
- In the column labeled *Number of Tickets Sold,* enter the number of tickets sold for each day of the concert.

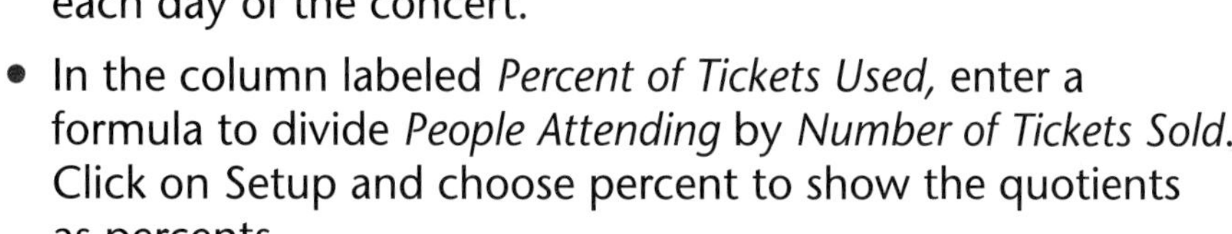

- In the column labeled *Percent of Tickets Used,* enter a formula to divide *People Attending* by *Number of Tickets Sold.* Click on Setup and choose percent to show the quotients as percents.

On which day was the percentage of tickets used the greatest?

Use the computer to create a table to change each pair of fractions to a percent. Then use your table to complete each sentence.

1. $\frac{3}{5} = ■\%$ **2.** $\frac{3}{8} = ■\%$ **3.** $\frac{6}{25} = ■\%$

4. $\frac{4}{5} = ■\%$ **5.** $\frac{5}{8} = ■\%$ **6.** $\frac{17}{25} = ■\%$

For more practice, use Math Traveler™.

Objective: Find a percent of a number.

14·5 Percent of a Number

Soccer Champion Brad Bahr

Learn

At age 11 Brad Bahr won the 1998 MLS Dribble, Pass & Shoot national championship in his age group. Brad played soccer with the Peoria Sporting Futbal Club 88 in Illinois. Suppose Brad scored 25% of the team's 32 goals in a tournament. How many goals would he score?

Example 1

Find: 25% of 32

1 Write the percent as a fraction in simplest form or as a decimal.

$$25\% = \frac{25}{100} = \frac{1}{4} = 0.25$$

2 Multiply the fraction or decimal by the whole number.

$$0.25 \times 32 = 8 \text{ or } \frac{1}{4} \times 32 = 8$$

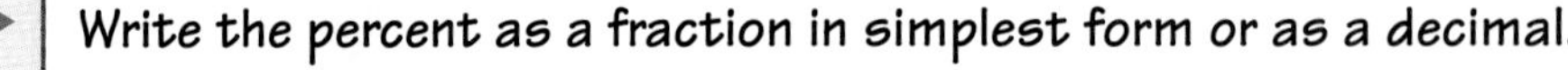

Brad would score 8 goals.

You can use the same steps for percents greater than 100%.

Example 2

Find: 150% of 32

$$150\% = \frac{150}{100} = \frac{3}{2} = 1.5$$

$$1.5 \times 32 = 48 \text{ or } \frac{3}{2} \times 32 = 48$$

So 150% of 32 is 48.

ACE Sporting Goods
SALE
Soccer Shirts
Sale Price: 80% of original price
Original Price: $9.50

What is the sale price of the soccer shirts?

Example 3

Find: 80% of $9.50

When you find the percent of a decimal, it is usually easiest to convert the percent to a decimal.

1. Rewrite the percent as a decimal.

   80% = 0.8

2. Multiply the decimal amounts.

$$\begin{array}{r} \$9.50 \\ \times \quad 0.8 \\ \hline \$7.60 \end{array}$$

The shirt will cost $7.60.

Example 4

Find: 175% of $8.20

1. Rewrite the percent as a decimal.

   175% = 1.75

2. Multiply the money amount by the decimal.

$$\begin{array}{r} \$8.20 \\ \times 1.75 \\ \hline \$14.35 \end{array}$$

So 175% of $8.20 is $14.35.

Try It **Find the percent of each number.**

1. 10% of 30
2. 25% of 36
3. 20% of 25
4. 30% of 90
5. 150% of $4.00
6. 175% of $4.20
7. 90% of $11.00
8. 35% of $8.20

Sum it Up Explain how to find 30% of 30.

Practice **Find the percent of each number.**

9. 10% of 40	**10.** 20% of 60	**11.** 250% of 80	**12.** 50% of 70
13. 40% of 90	**14.** 125% of 40	**15.** 30% of 30	**16.** 75% of 48
17. 45% of 20	**18.** 55% of 20	**19.** 60% of 70	**20.** 180% of 30
21. 70% of $5.00	**22.** 120% of $9.00	**23.** 90% of $8.00	**24.** 85% of $7.00
25. 35% of $4.00	**26.** 75% of $6.00	**27.** 150% of $10.00	**28.** 15% of $12.00
★**29.** 130% of $4.50	★**30.** 76% of $3.00	★**31.** 175% of $12.50	★**32.** 68% of $9.00

Algebra & functions **Find each missing number.**

33. 10% of ▒ = 10

34. ▒% of 30 = 15

35. 30% of ▒ = 18

36. ▒% of 80 = 8

37. ▒% of 40 = 8

38. 80% of ▒ = 40

39.

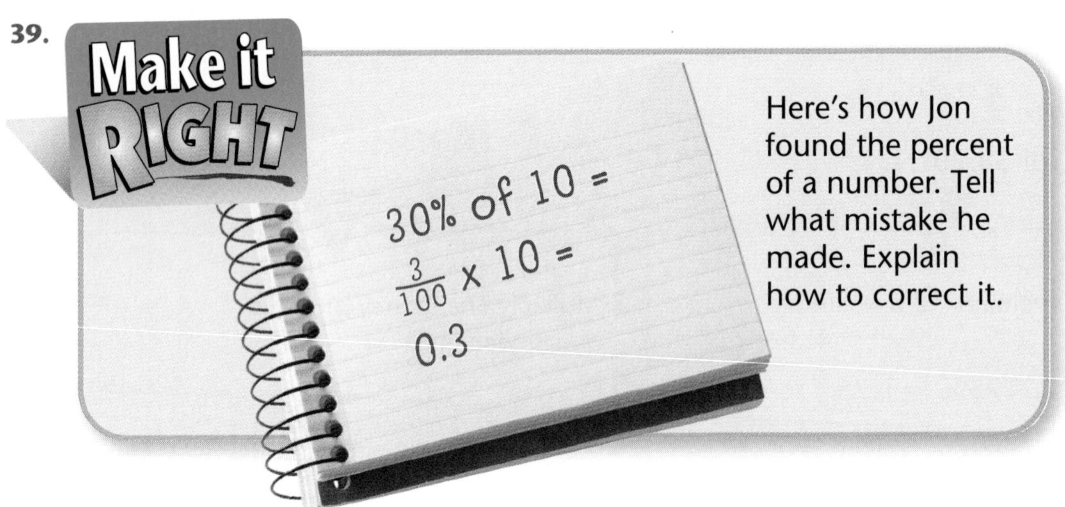

Here's how Jon found the percent of a number. Tell what mistake he made. Explain how to correct it.

Problem Solving

40. The Melville School soccer team won 80 percent of its 30 games. How many games did the team win?

41. Paula bought a soccer shirt for $9.50. She paid with a twenty-dollar bill. What should her change be?

42. The Pinetown School soccer team has won all of its games so far. It has played 75 percent of the 24 games on its schedule. How many games has the team won?

43. **Compare:** Show how to use multiplying by a fraction and multiplying by a decimal to find 50% of 34. How are the methods different from each other?

Practice

Use data from the sign for problems 44–46.

Reed's Sporting Goods
$15.00
$6.50
$9.00
$40.00
Sale Price
All Shirts and Shorts.....70% of original price
All Shoes and Socks.......80% of original price

44. Madeline buys a shirt. What is the sale price of the shirt?

45. Elena buys cleats. What is the sale price of the cleats?

46. The store has 35 pairs of socks in stock. Last month it had 220 percent of this amount in stock. How many pairs of socks did the store have in stock last month?

47. **Create a problem** about buying two items and their sale prices. Solve it, then give it to another student to solve.

48. **Health:** Playing soccer is a good way to exercise. For every 20 minutes of soccer played, 180 calories are used. If you play soccer for 60 minutes, how many calories do you use?

49. **Analyze:** To find 40% of 16, Fred multiplies 0.4×16 and Jen multiplies $\frac{2}{5} \times 16$. Who will get the correct answer? Explain.

50. **Analyze:** When would you change a percent to a fraction and when would you change it to a decimal to find the percent of a number?

★ 51. **Summarize:** Is the percent of a number always less than the number? Explain.

Spiral Review and Test Prep

Compare. Write >, <, or =.

52. $1\frac{4}{5}$ ● 1.75 53. $\frac{7}{8}$ ● 0.6 54. $\frac{3}{3}$ ● $\frac{9}{9}$ 55. $2\frac{3}{8}$ ● $2\frac{3}{4}$ 56. $\frac{3}{5}$ ● $\frac{7}{10}$

Choose the correct answer.

57. Ben took a survey of students' favorite winter sports. Which sport received exactly 10 more votes than figure skating?
    A. Ice hockey
    B. Sledding
    C. Skiing
    D. Snowboarding

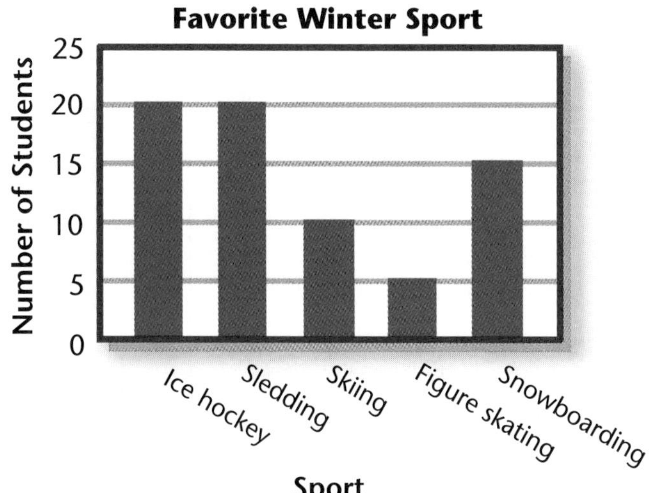

Extra Practice, page 662

Objective: Find the percent one number is of another.

14-6 Percent That One Number Is of Another

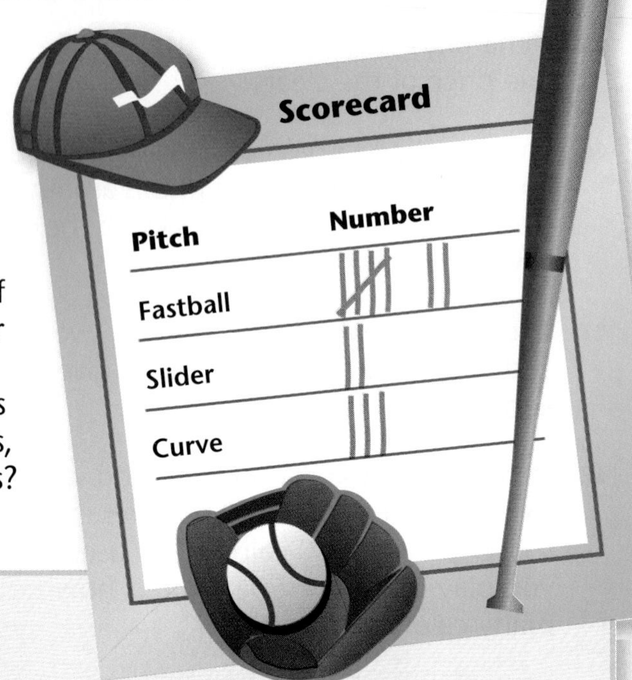

Learn

One of the things sports statisticians do is keep track of the kinds of pitches a pitcher throws during a game. If a pitcher has thrown 12 pitches and 3 of them are curve balls, what percent are curve balls?

Example 1

Find what percent 3 is of 12.

1 Think in terms of fractions. What part of 12 is 3?

$\frac{3}{12}$ ← part / ← whole

2 Divide the numerator by the denominator.

$12\overline{)3.00}$ = 0.25

3 Rewrite the decimal as a percent.

0.25 = 25%

Check: 25% of 12 = 0.25 × 12 = 3

25% of the pitches are curve balls.

Example 2

Find what percent 30 is of 20.

1 Think in terms of fractions. What part of 20 is 30?

$\frac{30}{20}$ ← part / ← whole

2 Divide the numerator by the denominator.

$20\overline{)30.0}$ = 1.5

3 Rewrite the decimal as a percent.

1.5 = 150%

So 150% of 20 is 30.

A pitcher threw 32 pitches in an inning. Six of the pitches were knuckleballs. What percent were knuckleballs?

Example 3

Find what percent 6 is of 32.

1 Think in terms of fractions. What part of 32 is 6?

$\frac{6}{32}$ ← part / ← whole

2 Divide the numerator by the denominator.

$32\overline{)6.000}$ = 0.1875

3 Write the decimal as a percent.

0.1875 = 18.75%

So 6 is 18.75% of 32.

You can round percents that do not terminate.

Example 4

What percent of 6 is 2, rounded to the nearest tenth?

Divide the numerator by the denominator to 3 more places than you are rounding to.

$6\overline{)2.0000}$ = 0.3333...

Note: Some decimals do not terminate, or end. In this problem, the decimal 0.3333... will repeat forever.

When the decimal does not terminate, you can round. 0.3333 ≈ 33.33%

0.3333 is equal to 33.3%, rounded to the nearest tenth. 33.33% → 33.3%

So 2 is about 33.3% of 6.

Find the percent each number is of the other. Round to the nearest whole number percent, if necessary.

1. What percent of 36 is 27?
2. Nine is what percent of 45?
3. Three is what percent of 17?
4. What percent of 20 is 24?

Explain how to find what percent 3 is of 20.

Practice

Find the percent each number is of the other. Round to the nearest whole number percent, if necessary.

5. What percent of 70 is 35?
6. Twelve is what percent of 48?
7. Nine is what percent of 90?
8. What percent of 85 is 17?
9. What percent of 30 is 45?
10. Forty-five is what percent of 50?
11. What percent of 60 is 75?
12. Thirty is what percent of 30?

★13. Twenty is what percent of 54?

★14. What percent of 150 is 20?

★15. What percent of 80 is 140?

★16. One hundred is what percent of 40?

Algebra & functions **Compare. Use >, < or =.**

17. 60% of 20 ● 40% of 20
18. 25% of 12 ● 25% of 16
19. 15% of 90 ● 16% of 90
20. 50% of 20 ● 100% of 10

Find each missing number.

21. ■ is 10% of 50
22. ■ is 20% of 45
23. ■ is 50% of 18

★24. ■ is 90% of 75

25.

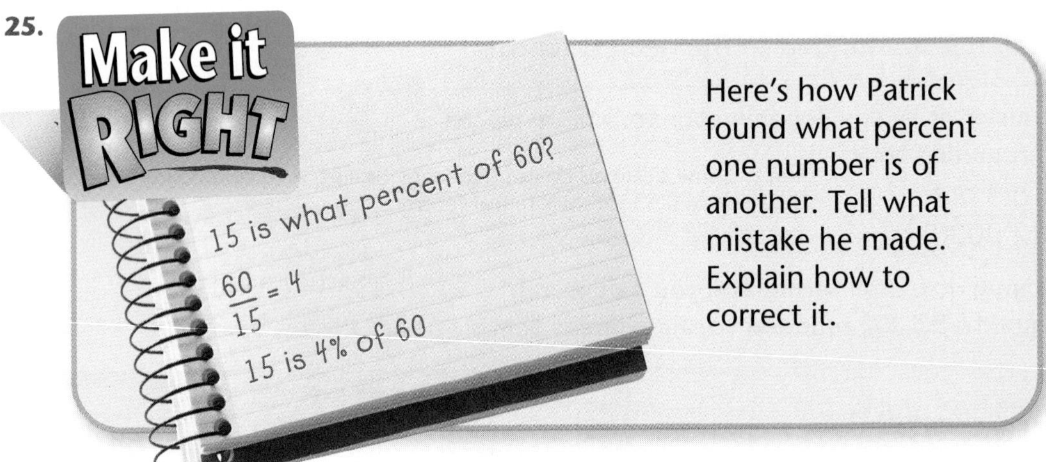

Here's how Patrick found what percent one number is of another. Tell what mistake he made. Explain how to correct it.

Problem Solving

26. Helen had 4 hits in a softball game. In the next game she had 5 hits. What percent of 4 is 5?

27. Dexter came to bat 60 times in the baseball season. He had 6 home runs. What percent of the time did he have a home run?

28. **Health:** When you exercise, you should try to get your heart rate to a target rate that depends on your age and fitness level. Suppose Pedro's minimum target rate is 140 and his maximum rate is 200. What percent of 200 is 140?

29. **Language Arts:** Write a word problem about sports that can be solved by finding what percent of 40 is 8.

30. The Atlanta Braves won 106 of their 162 baseball games in 1998. What percent of their games did they win, rounded to the nearest whole percent?

31. The San Diego Padres won 98 games and lost 64 games. What percent of the total games did the team win, to the nearest tenth of a percent?

32. **What if** the total number of games stays the same and the number of wins decreases? Does the percent increase or decrease? Explain.

33. **Science:** When a batter hits a baseball to the outfield, it travels about 295 feet in 4.3 seconds. About how many feet does the baseball travel each second?

Use data from *Did You Know?* for problems 34–35.

34. Express Williams' on-base percentage as a percent.

35. **What if** a player earned a lifetime on-base percentage of 48.6%. Would he beat Williams' record? Explain.

36. **Music:** Chicago Cubs broadcaster Harry Caray was famous for his performances of the song "Take Me Out to the Ball Game." Caray broadcast 8,326 games during his 53-year career. If he sang the song at each game, about how many times would he sing it each year?

★ 37. **Measurement:** In 1931 Joe Sprinz of San Francisco caught a ball dropped from a blimp 800 feet above the ground. What percent of a mile is 800 feet, rounded to the nearest whole percent?

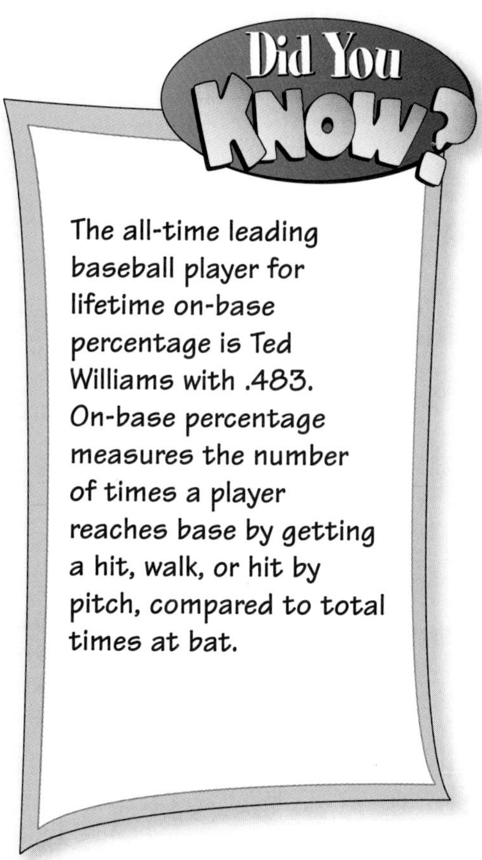

The all-time leading baseball player for lifetime on-base percentage is Ted Williams with .483. On-base percentage measures the number of times a player reaches base by getting a hit, walk, or hit by pitch, compared to total times at bat.

Spiral Review and Test Prep

38. $\frac{3}{5} \times \frac{1}{3}$

39. $1\frac{1}{4} \times \frac{1}{2}$

40. $2\frac{2}{5} \times 3$

41. $3\frac{1}{4} \times 4\frac{1}{2}$

Choose the correct answer.

42. A basketball player made a shot standing $5\frac{1}{2}$ feet from the basket. How many inches away was the player standing?
   A. 56 inches
   B. 60 inches
   C. 64 inches
   D. 66 inches

43. Which is the best unit to use to measure how much water a sink will hold?
   F. Centimeter
   G. Kilogram
   H. Liter
   J. Meter

Extra Practice, page 662

14·7

Objective: Solve problems by making Venn diagrams.

Problem Solving: Strategy
Use Logical Reasoning

Read

Read the problem carefully.

Of the 30 students in a fifth grade class, 15 play on the basketball team. Eighteen students play on the soccer team, and 3 students play on both teams. How many students play only on the basketball team? only on the soccer team?

- **What do you know?** The number who play on the basketball team, the soccer team, and both teams
- **What do you need to find?** The number who play only on the basketball team and only on the soccer team

Plan

A **Venn diagram** organizes data with overlapping circles. The overlap section shows data that fall into both groups.

You can find the number of students who only play basketball by subtracting the number who play both sports from the total number that play basketball. You can follow the same procedure to find the number of students who play only soccer.

Solve

So 12 students play only on the basketball team and 15 students play only on the soccer team.

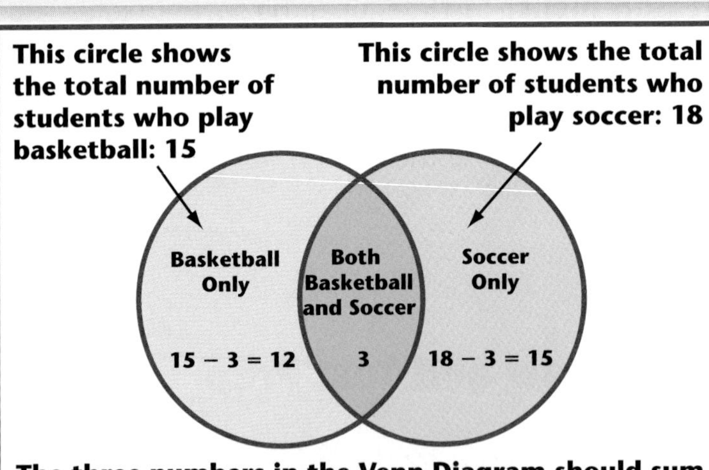
This circle shows the total number of students who play basketball: 15
This circle shows the total number of students who play soccer: 18
Basketball Only
15 − 3 = 12
Both Basketball and Soccer
3
Soccer Only
18 − 3 = 15
The three numbers in the Venn Diagram should sum to the total numbers of students: 12 + 3 + 15 = 30

Look Back How else could you solve this problem?

Sum it Up!

How can drawing a Venn diagram help you solve problems?

Practice

Use a Venn diagram to solve each problem.

1. Of 35 people surveyed, 28 said they go to baseball games and 14 said they go to hockey games. Seven of the people said they go to both. How many people said they go only to hockey games?

2. Of 24 students in a class, 18 students like to play volleyball, and 11 students like to play softball. Five of the students like to play both. How many students like to play only softball?

3. Of the 32 players on the All-City football team, 18 play defense and 16 play offense. Two play both offense and defense. How many only play defense?

4. Of the 12 players on the Hillford basketball team, 5 are forwards and 9 are guards. Two play both forward and guard. How many players are forwards, but not guards?

5. The 3 sections of a Venn diagram about people's favorite sports show the numbers 8, 5, and 11. How many people were surveyed?

6. A survey counts the number of people who like skiing, skating, and both sports. Which data belongs in the overlap section of a Venn diagram?

7. Make a Venn diagram that shows the following data: 14 students study karate after school, 10 students study gymnastics, and 4 students study both. How many students are there in all?

8. Explain how a Venn diagram organizes information.

Mixed Strategy Review

9. **Logical Reasoning:** The Briarton basketball team scored its greatest number of points in its last game. When the coach divided the score by 4 quarters, he found an average of 26 points for each quarter. How many points did the team score?

10. The Bradley family is at a baseball game. They have been at the game for 1 hour 50 minutes. The time is 5:20 P.M. At what time did they arrive?

11. The sum of the measure of the angles of a pentagon is 540°. If each angle measures the same amount, what is the measure of each angle?

12. Joy tells Harvey that she scored 4 less than 3 times as many points in Tuesday's game as she scored on Monday. She scored 29 points on Tuesday. How many points did she score on Monday?

CHOOSE A STRATEGY

- Logical Reasoning
- Draw a Diagram
- Make a Graph
- Make a Table or List
- Find a Pattern
- Guess and Check
- Write an Equation
- Work Backward
- Solve a Simpler Problem
- Conduct an Experiment

Extra Practice, page 663

Objective: Interpret and make circle graphs.

14·8 Circle Graphs

Learn

Jamie wants to know which board games students like most. She surveyed 120 students and made a circle graph to show the results. How many of the students chose backgammon as their favorite game?

Math Word

circle graph a graph in which data are represented by parts of a circle, also known as a pie graph or pie chart

Favorite Board Games

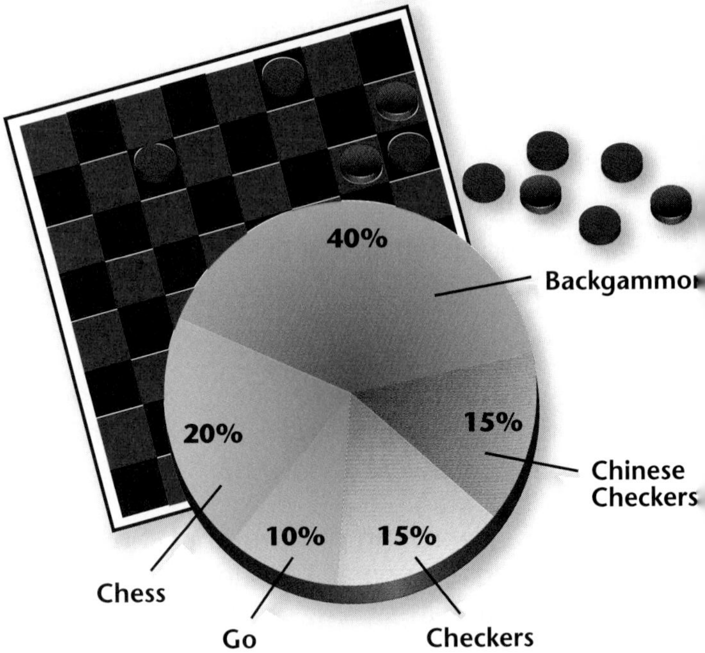

Example 1

The entire **circle graph** represents 100%. Each section of the graph tells you what percent of the total is represented.

- Circle graphs make it easy to compare parts of a whole. You can tell that backgammon was the favorite game because that is the largest part of the graph.
- You can read the actual percents from the graph.

  Chess: 20%
  Go: 10%
  Checkers: 15%
  Chinese Checkers: 15%
  Backgammon: 40%

  40% of the students prefer backgammon.

- You can find exactly how many students like backgammon.

Find: 40% of 120

$0.4 \times 120 = 48$

So 48 students prefer backgammon.

Example 2

The table lists the results of a survey about favorite kinds of games. How can you make a circle graph of the data?

Kind of Game	Percent of Total Responses
Board games	25%
Video games	50%
Puzzles	25%

Remember: The central angles of a circle sum to 360°.

1 Multiply 360° by each percent.

Board games: $25\% = 0.25$ $\quad 0.25 \times 360^\circ = 90^\circ$

Video games: $50\% = 0.50$ $\quad 0.50 \times 360^\circ = 180^\circ$

Puzzles: $25\% = 0.25$ $\quad 0.25 \times 360^\circ = 90^\circ$

2 Draw a circle. Draw each angle with the vertex at the center.

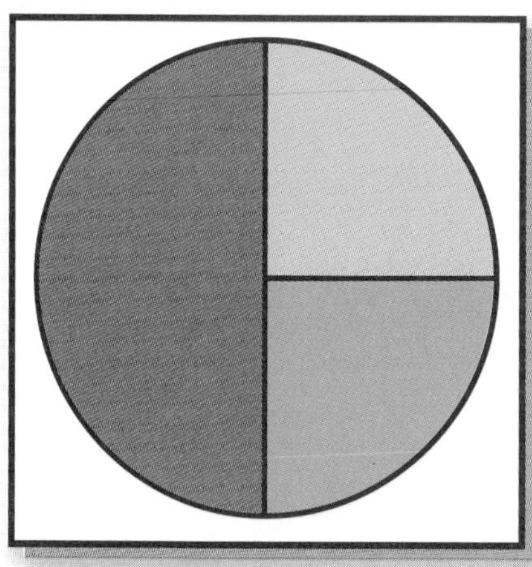

Label each section.
Write a title for each graph.

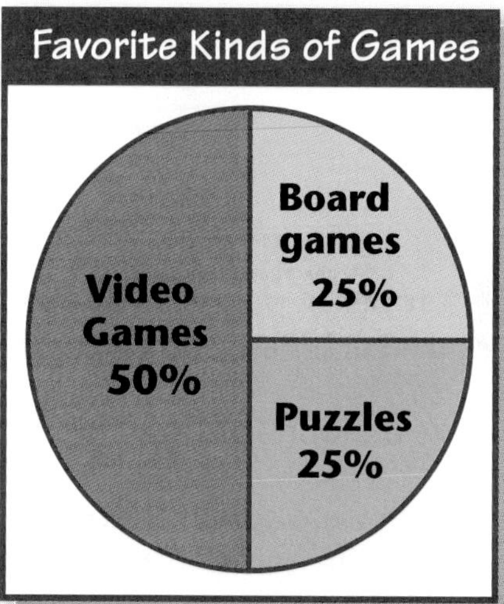

Try It **Make a circle graph to show each data set.**

1. Of the students surveyed, 55% like to play checkers, but 45% percent of the students do not like to play checkers.
2. Of the students surveyed, 30% like video games best; 50% like card games best; 20% like board games best.

Explain how a circle graph makes it easy to see the largest group quickly.

Practice **Use data from the circle graph for problems 3–7.**

3. List the games from favorite to least favorite.

4. What fraction of the total votes did bicycle riding receive?

5. If 160 people were surveyed, how many people chose races?

6. If 180 people were surveyed, how many people chose races?

7. **Generalize:** Write two statements that compare the results for favorite outdoor activities.

Which of these outdoor activities is your favorite?

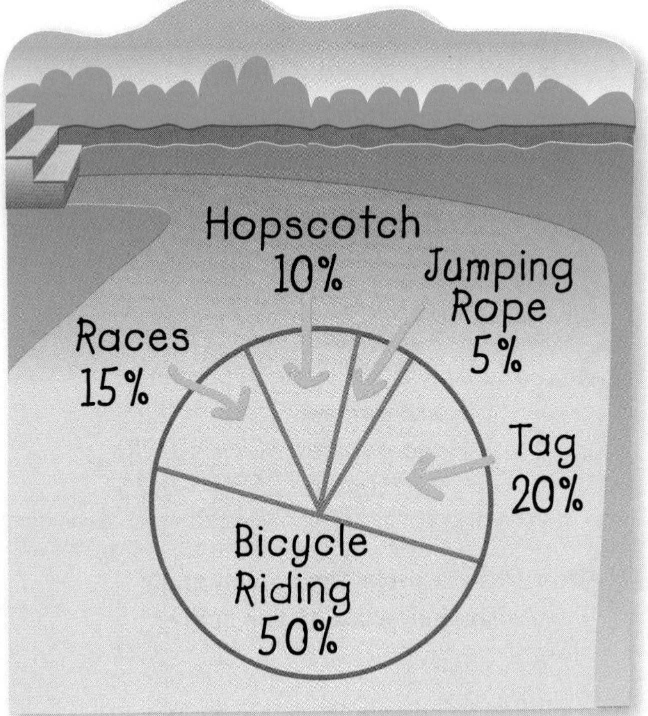

Use data from the table to answer problems 8–10.

Favorite Game	Percent of Total Responses
Chess	25%
Checkers	30%
Dominoes	20%
Backgammon	25%

8. List the number of degrees you would use to make each part of a circle graph.

9. Make a circle graph to show the data.

10. If 140 people were surveyed, how many people said checkers was their favorite game?

11.

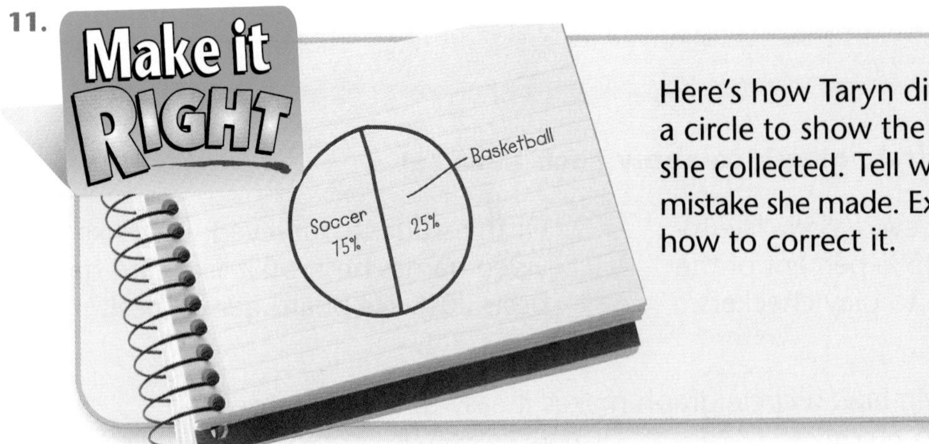

Here's how Taryn divided a circle to show the data she collected. Tell what mistake she made. Explain how to correct it.

Problem Solving

12. Explain why the angle measurements in a circle graph must have a sum of 360 degrees.

13. **Collect Data:** Take a survey about sports, games, or activities. Make a circle graph to show your data.

14. Carolyn is making a circle graph to show some data results. There are five parts in the circle graph. One part is 40 percent of the total. The other four parts are equal. What angle measurement should she draw for each of the four equal parts of the graph?

★15. **Literature:** In *The King's Chessboard*, by David Birch, the king wants to reward the wise man. The wise man asks for 1 grain of rice on the first square, 2 grains on the second square, 4 grains on the third square, 8 grains on the fourth square, and so on. How many grains of rice would the wise man ask for on the tenth square?

Use data from the table to answer problems 16–17.

16. Make a circle graph to show the data.

17. If the survey included 180 people, how many people chose each of the games or activities?

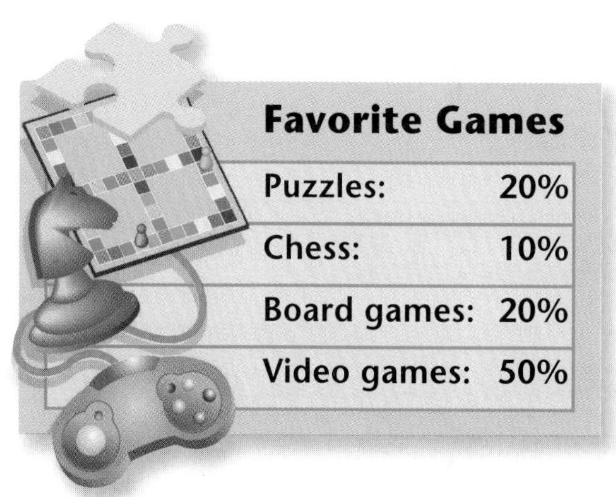

Favorite Games	
Puzzles:	20%
Chess:	10%
Board games:	20%
Video games:	50%

Spiral Review and Test Prep

Evaluate each expression.

18. $y + 9$ for $y = 13$

19. $c - 4$ for $c = 4$

20. $13 - a$ for $a = 5$

21. $2 + t$ for $t = 0$

Choose the correct answer.

22. What is the length of the string needed to enclose this circle? Use 3.14 as an approximation for *pi*.

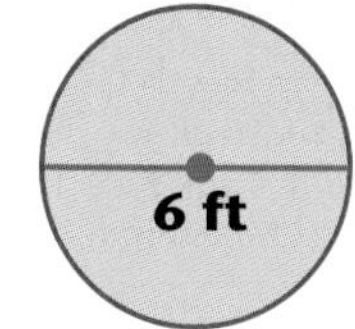

A. 9.14 feet
B. 18.84 feet
C. 37.68 feet
D. 113.04 feet

23. There are 3 blue cubes, 5 red cubes, 2 yellow cubes, and 1 green cube in a bag. If you pick a cube from the bag without looking, what is the probability you will pick a yellow cube?

F. $\frac{1}{2}$
G. $\frac{2}{9}$
H. $\frac{2}{11}$
J. $\frac{2}{1}$

Objective: Apply percents to analyze data and make decisions.

14·9 A

Problem Solving: Application

Decision Making

Which store will you buy the bicycle from? Which services will you choose?

You want to buy a new Cosmic Tour bicycle. You can choose from three different stores and several different services. Use the information in the signs to help make your decision.

Option 1

Parker's
Sporting Goods

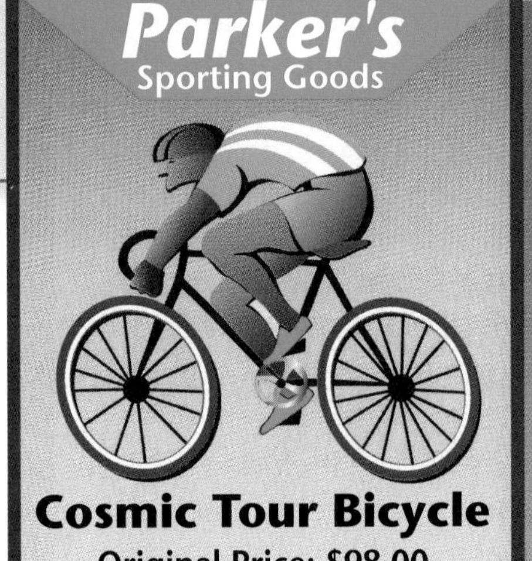

Cosmic Tour Bicycle
Original Price: $98.00
Sale Price: 80% of original price
Assembly: $15.00 Delivery: $10.00

Option 2

Rider's Rack

Cosmic Tour Bicycle
On Sale This Week!

Original Price: $94.00
You Pay 90% of Original Price
Assembly: $12.00 Delivery: $10.00

Option 3

HiLLtop Bicycles

All Cosmic Brand Bicycles on Sale

Cosmic Trail Bicycle – Originally $95.00
Cosmic Tour Bicycle – Originally $109.00
Cosmic Mountain Bicycle – Originally $129.00
Sale Price is 85% of Original Price
Assembly: $13.00 Delivery: $9.00

Read for Understanding

1. How many stores can you choose from to buy the bike?
2. Which services are available from the stores?
3. What information in the signs will be helpful in making a decision?
4. What information in the signs is not needed to make a decision?
5. What are the original prices for the bicycle at each store?
6. What are the percents of the original prices that you will use to find the sale price at each store?
7. What are the assembly prices at each store?
8. What are the delivery prices at each store?

Problem Solving

Make Decisions

9. Find the sale price for the bicycle at Parker's Sporting Goods.
10. Find the sale price for the bicycle at Rider's Rack.
11. Find the sale price for the bicycle at Hilltop Bicycles.
12. Find the sale price at Parker's Sporting Goods with delivery but no assembly.
13. Find the sale price at Parker's Sporting Goods with assembly, but no delivery.
14. Find the sale price at Parker's Sporting Goods with assembly and delivery.
15. Find the sale price at Rider's Rack with delivery, but no assembly.
16. Find the sale price at Rider's Rack with assembly, but no delivery.
17. Find the sale price at Rider's Rack with assembly and delivery.
18. Find the sale price at Hilltop Bicycles with delivery, but no assembly.
19. Find the sale price at Hilltop Bicycles with assembly, but no delivery.
20. Find the sale price at Hilltop Bicycles with assembly and delivery.

Where will you buy your bicycle? Will you choose delivery or assembly or neither?

Objective: Apply percents to investigate science concepts.

Problem Solving: Math and Science

Which paper towel would you buy?

Oh no! You spill a glass of juice and have no paper towels. You go to the market to buy more and find that there are many choices. How do you know which to buy?

In this activity you will investigate how to make a smart decision by researching brands of paper towels.

You Will Need

- **3 different kinds of paper towels (labeled A, B, and C)**
- **large bowl with water**
- **ruler**
- **measuring spoons**
- **connecting cubes**

Hypothesize

Study each paper towel and hypothesize which will be the best choice.

Procedure

1. Work in a group of three.
2. Record any three observations of each towel.
3. Measure each towel and find the area.
4. Wet Towel A as much as possible. Wring out the water and measure how much it could hold.
5. Repeat for Towel B and Towel C.
6. Wet and wring out Towel A. Hold it by four corners. Add cubes, one at a time, until the towel tears. Record how many cubes it could hold.
7. Repeat for Towel B and Towel C.
8. Given the price of a roll and the number of sheets in the roll, calculate the price per towel for each brand.

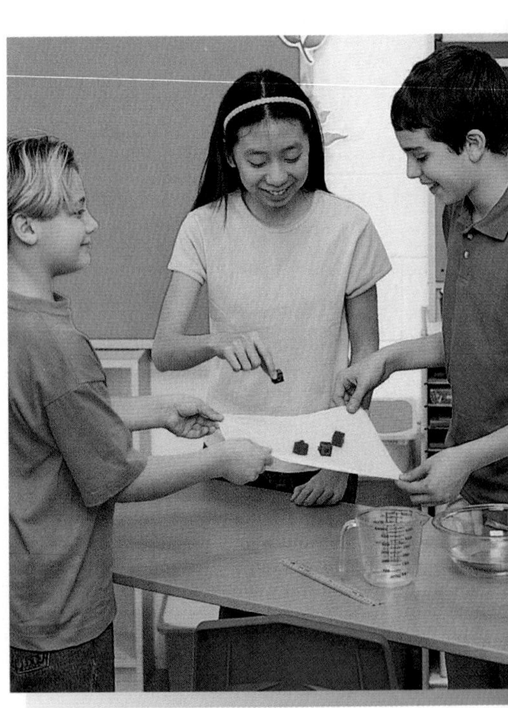

Data

Copy and complete the charts to record your observations.

Brand	Area	Water	Cubes	Price/Towel
A				
B				
C				

Brand	Observations
A	
B	
C	

Conclude and Apply

- Which paper towel has the largest area?
- Which paper towel held the most water?
- Which paper towel held the most cubes before tearing?
- Which paper towel costs the least per sheet?
- If you were shopping, would you choose A, B, or C? Explain.
- Is it possible to identify a best choice? Why or why not?
- Explain how labeling the towels A, B, and C helped make the activity a **blind study**. What might happen if a study were not blind?

A blind study is one where the investigators do not know the identity of the brands they are studying.

Going Further

1. Write a consumer report to summarize your results. Use graphs and data to support any claims you make.
2. Design and complete an activity that evaluates brands of soap.

Problem Solving

Check Your Progress B

Find the percent of each number. **(pages 642–645)**

1. 90% of 50
2. 15% of 60
3. 80% of $4.00
4. 110% of $6.50
5. 85% of 40
6. 45% of 80
7. 50% of $5.00
8. 150% of $9.00

Find the percent each number is of the other. Round to the nearest whole number percent, if necessary. **(pages 646–649)**

9. What percent of 50 is 35?
10. Sixty is what percent of 80?
11. What percent of 60 is 30?
12. Thirty-three is what percent of 40?
13. What percent of 20 is 25?
14. Thirty-six is what percent of 20?

Use data from the chart for problems 15–16.

15. Make a circle graph to show the data.
16. List the number of degrees for each part of the circle graph.

Which is your favorite summer camp activity?	
Activity	Percent of Total Responses
Arts and Crafts	10%
Hiking	25%
Music and Drama	50%
Swimming	15%

Solve. **(pages 642–655)**

17. The Pinetown soccer team has won all of its games. It has played 75 percent of the 16 games on its schedule. How many games has the team won?
18. Samuel is riding his bicycle on a 30-mile tour. He has ridden 21 miles so far. What percent of the total miles has he ridden?
19. A survey shows that some students like to play baseball only, some only play soccer and some play both. Which category would be found in the overlap section of a Venn diagram?

Journal

20. **Explain** why the percents in a circle graph always add up to 100 percent.

Additional activities at
www.mhschool.com/math

Extra Practice

Percents, Fractions, and Decimals (pages 628–633)

Write each percent as a decimal and as a fraction in simplest form.

1. 75%
2. 80%
3. 98%
4. 60%
5. 24%

Write each fraction or decimal as a percent.

6. $\frac{50}{100}$
7. 0.3
8. $\frac{1}{5}$
9. 0.92
10. $\frac{1}{4}$

Solve.

11. The Granville School soccer team won 85 percent of its games. How can the percent be written as a decimal? How can the percent be written as a fraction in simplest form?
12. A basketball player makes 9 of 12 shots. How can you express this as a percent?

More About Percents (pages 634–637)

Write each percent as a decimal and as a mixed number in simplest form, or as a whole number.

1. 300%
2. 475%
3. 625%
4. 260%
5. 800%
6. 140%

Write each percent as a decimal and as a fraction in simplest form.

7. 62.5%
8. 12%
9. 90%
10. 22.5%
11. 20%
12. 75%

Solve.

13. In the 1997–1998 season, the New Jersey Nets won 0.524 of their games. How can the decimal be written as a percent? How can the decimal be written as a fraction in simplest form?
14. The Larkston Tigers baseball team improved its wins this year over last year by 115 percent. How can you write the percent as a decimal and as a mixed number in simplest form?

Problem Solving: Reading for Math Represent Numbers (pages 638–639)

1. Last year Duncan made 60 percent of his shots on goal. This year he has made 26 of 40 shots. Did Duncan improve his record this year over last year? Explain.
2. A softball team had a 0.5 record this year and won $\frac{2}{5}$ of their games last year. Which year was the better season?

Extra Practice

Percent of a Number (pages 642–645)

Find the percent of each number.

1. 25% of 48
2. 30% of 90
3. 150% of 60
4. 80% of 30
5. 120% of 80
6. 75% of 64
7. 60% of 40
8. 125% of 100
9. 90% of $4.00
10. 130% of $7.00
11. 60% of $5.00
12. 75% of $3.00

Solve.

13. The Brentmor School baseball team has won all of its games so far. It has played 50 percent of the 18 games on its schedule. How many games has the team won?

14. The Silver Creek soccer team has played 75 percent of the 12 games on its schedule. It has won 6 of the games. How many games has the team lost?

15. Out of 20 shots Rick scored 12 soccer goals. Fred kicked 25 shots and made 14 shots. Who had a higher shot-making percent? Explain.

Percent That One Number Is of Another Number (pages 646–649)

Find the percent each number is of the other. Round to the nearest whole number percent, if necessary.

1. What percent of 80 is 60?
2. Thirty-eight is what percent of 90?
3. Eleven is what percent of 30?
4. What percent of 76 is 19?
5. What percent of 24 is 30?
6. What percent of 150 is 60?

Solve.

7. Nelson uses 50 tiles to cover a gym floor. Thirty-five of the tiles are black. The rest of the tiles are white. Was the number of black tiles greater or less than 50 percent of all the tiles?

8. The coach of a baseball team ordered 40 blue shirts and 24 white shirts for the team. What percent of all the shirts were white?

9. Of 36 basketball shots made, 27 were 2-point shots and the rest were 1-point shots. What percent were 2-point shots? What percent were 1-point shots?

Extra Practice

Problem Solving: Strategy Use Logical Reasoning (pages 650–651)

Use a Venn diagram to solve each problem.

1. Of 25 people surveyed, 12 said they get their sports news from TV, and 20 said they get their sports news from the newspaper. Seven of the people said they get their sports news from both. How many people said they get their sports news from TV, but not from the newspaper?
2. Of 20 people surveyed, 6 said they go to football games, and 17 said they watch football games on TV. Three of the people said they do both. How many people said they watch football games on TV, but do not go to football games?
3. Of 30 people surveyed, 19 said they exercise at a health club and 15 said they exercise at home. Four of the people said they do both. How many people said they exercise at home, but not at a health club?

Circle Graphs (pages 652–655)

Melanie took a survey of favorite outdoor games and activities. The table lists the results.

Use data from the table to answer problems 1–4.

Which is your favorite outdoor game or activity?	
Activity	Percent of Total Responses
Ball games	20%
Bicycling	55%
Hopscotch	5%
Jump rope	10%
Tag	10%

1. Make a circle graph to show the data.
2. List the number of degrees needed to make each part of the circle graph.
3. If 60 people were surveyed, how many people said bicycling was their favorite outdoor activity? hopscotch?
4. If 80 people were surveyed, how many people said bicycling was their favorite outdoor activity? hopscotch?

Chapter Study Guide

Language and Math

Complete. Use a word from the list.

1. A way to represent data as parts of a whole is by using a ____.
2. A number that means per hundred is called a ____.

Math Words

circle graph
decimal
percent
fraction
mixed number

Skills and Applications

Change numbers between percents, decimals, and factions. (pages 630–637)

Example

Rewrite the fraction $\frac{3}{5}$ as a percent.

Solution

Write an equivalent fraction with a denominator of 100.

$\frac{3}{5} = \frac{3}{5} \times \frac{20}{20} = \frac{60}{100}$

Then write the fraction as a percent.

$\frac{60}{100} = 60\%$

Write each fraction or decimal as a percent.

3. $\frac{1}{5}$
4. 0.85
5. $\frac{7}{100}$
6. 0.3

Write each percent as a decimal and fraction in simplest form.

7. 10%
8. 70%
9. 11%
10. 65%

Find a percent of a number. (pages 642–645)

Example

What is 40% of 30?

Solution

Write the percent as a fraction.

$40\% = \frac{40}{100} = \frac{2}{5}$

Multiply the fraction by the whole number.

$\frac{2}{5} \times 30 = 12$

So 40% of 30 is 12.

Find the percent of each number.

11. 70% of 60
12. 30% of 30
13. 125% of 40
14. 20% of $7.20
15. What percent of 25 is 5?
16. Carlos pays the sale price for a hockey jersey. The sale price is 80 percent of $9.20. What is the sale price of the jersey?

Find the percent one number is of another. (pages 646–649)

Example

What percent of 24 is 9?

Solution

Write a fraction showing the part and whole.

$\frac{9}{24}$ ← part / ← whole

Divide the numerator by the denominator.

Think: $\frac{9}{24}$ means $9 \div 24$ $\quad 24\overline{)9.000}$ = 0.375

Rewrite the decimal as a percent.

0.375 = 37.5%

So 9 is 37.5 percent of 24.

Find the percent each number is of the other. Round to the nearest whole number percent, if necessary.

17. What percent of 40 is 28?
18. What percent of 50 is 8?
19. What percent of 32 is 18?
20. The spinner lands on the color blue in 6 out of 16 spins. What percent of the spins land on blue?

Interpret and make circle graphs. (pages 652–655)

Example

Billy surveyed 160 students and made a circle graph. How many students said their favorite sport is gymnastics?

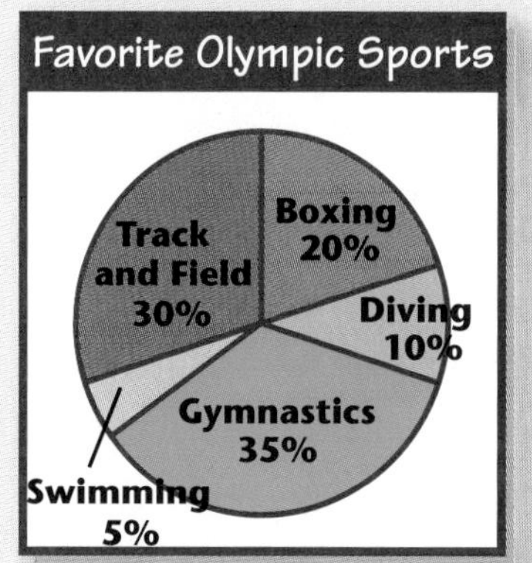

Solution

What is 35 percent of 160?

35% = 0.35 $\quad 0.35 \times 160 = 56.00$

So 56 students chose gymnastics.

Use data from the graph in the example for problems 21–23.

21. Which Olympic sport received the fewest number of votes? How many votes did it receive?
22. How many more votes did gymnastics receive than track-and-field?
23. What is the angle measurement of each of the parts of the circle graph?

Solve problems. (pages 638–639, 650–651)

Solve.

24. Out of 15 batters on a baseball team, 9 batters are right-handed and 8 batters are left-handed. Two of the batters are both right-handed and left-handed. How many batters are right-handed, but not left-handed?
25. Last year, a team had 10 wins out of 25 games. This year, the team won 35 percent of its games. Was the team's record better this year or last year?

Study Guide

Chapter Test

Write each fraction or decimal as a percent.

1. $\frac{3}{5}$ 2. 0.51 3. $\frac{1}{4}$ 4. $\frac{9}{10}$ 5. 0.7

Write each percent as a decimal and as a fraction in simplest form.

6. 80% 7. 75% 8. 24% 9. 140% 10. 36%

Find the percent of each number.

11. 70% of 80 12. 160% of 30 13. 90% of $7.00 14. 135% of $4.00 15. 35% of 40

16. What percent of 64 is 24?

17. Fifteen is what percent of 75?

18. What percent of 45 is 90?

19. Forty-two is what percent of 48?

Solve.

20. A shirt is $\frac{2}{5}$ cotton. What percent of the shirt is cotton?

21. The Treetop School volleyball team has improved its number of wins this year over last year by 150%. Last year the team won 8 games. How many games did the team win this year?

22. Trent is hiking a 12-mile trail. He has hiked 9 miles so far. What percent of the total miles has he hiked?

Use data from the table to answer problems 23–25.

23. Make a circle graph to show the data.

24. List the number of degrees you used to make each part of the circle graph.

25. Which sport received the greatest number of votes? the least? How does the circle graph show this?

Which of these is your favorite sport to play?

Activity	Percent of Total Responses
Baseball	20%
Basketball	35%
Soccer	25%
Tennis	5%
Volleyball	15%

Performance Assessment

As a sports statistician and football fan, you keep track of the records and final standings of football teams from year to year. You have collected the data for the AFC Western Division and want to organize it so you can compare the different teams. Each team played a total of 16 games.

Copy and complete the table. Write all fractions in simplest form.

National Football League Final Standings
AFC Western Division

Team	Wins	Fraction	Decimal	Percent
Kansas City	13	$\frac{13}{16}$	0.813	81.3
Denver	12	$\frac{3}{4}$	0.75	75
Seattle	8	$\frac{1}{2}$	0.5	50
Oakland	4	$\frac{1}{4}$	0.25	25
San Diego	4	$\frac{1}{4}$	0.25	25

Use the table to answer each question.

1. Which teams lost 75 percent or more of their games?
2. Which teams lost fewer than 50 percent of their games?
3. Which team had a win record that was 0.25 greater than Seattle's win record?

A Good Answer
- has a complete table.
- clearly shows how you found each decimal and percent.
- answers the questions correctly.

You may want to save this work for your portofolio.

Assessment

Enrichment

Find the Total Number

The Parkville Panthers scored 9 points by field goals. This was 25 percent of the total points they scored. What was the total number of points the team scored?

1 Write a statement showing what you need to find out.

Nine is 25 percent of what number?

2 Write a multiplication equation using a variable.

9 is 25% of what number?

↓ ↓ ↓ ↓ ↓

$9 = 25\% \times a$

3 Rewrite the percent as a decimal. Then use the decimal in the equation.

$$25\% = 0.25$$
$$0.25a = 9$$

4 Solve the equation.

$0.25a \div 0.25 = 9 \div 0.25$ $\quad a = \frac{9}{0.25}$ $\quad 0.25\overline{)9.00}$ with quotient 36 $\quad a = 36$

The team scored a total of 36 points.

Solve each equation.

1. $50\% \times b = 18$
2. $0.3c = 27$
3. $15 = 60\% \times m$

Find the total number in each problem.

4. Ten is 10% of what number?
5. Five is 50% of what number?
6. Six is 100% of what number?
7. Four is 25% of what number?
8. Three is 150% of what number?
9. Twenty is 200% of what number?
10. The Somerton Sharks scored 14 points by touchdowns. This was 70 percent of the total points the team scored. What was the total number of points the team scored?
11. The Carson Cobras scored 12 points by field goals. This was 30 percent of the total points the team scored. What was the total number of points the team scored?

Test-Taking Tips

When taking a multiple-choice test, you may sometimes find that a problem has more than one step. For these problems, you need to solve one part before you can solve another part. This method is called **break a problem into parts.**

The Parker School volleyball team won 75 percent of its 40 games. The Clifton School volleyball team won 150 percent of the games that Parker did. How many games did Clifton win?

A. 30 C. 45
B. 40 D. 60

Read the problem carefully.

- Find the question you need to answer.
- Break the problem into parts.
- Solve the first part. Then use the first solution to solve the second part.

Part 1

Find 75% of 40.

$0.75 \times 40 = 30$

Part 2

Find 150% of 30.

$1.5 \times 30 = 45$

Clifton won 45 games. The correct answer is C.

Check for Success

Before turning in a test, go back one last time to check.

☑ I understood and answered the questions asked.
☑ I checked my work for errors.
☑ My answers make sense.

Choose the correct answer.

1. The Jordan School soccer team won 50 percent of its 24 games. The Marlboro School soccer team won 125 percent of the games Jordan did. How many games did Marlboro win?
   A. 12 C. 24
   B. 15 D. 30

2. Ernesto scored a basket on 80 percent of his 25 shots in game one. In game two, he scored 110 percent of the number of scores in game one. How many times did he score in game two?
   F. 27.5 H. 22
   G. 25 J. 20

3. The tennis team has sold 40% of the 80 tickets for Saturday's match. They sold 60% of the 60 tickets for Sunday's match. How many more tickets were sold for Sunday than Saturday?
   A. 4 C. 12
   B. 8 D. 16

4. The Lakewood School basketball team lost 20 percent of its 30 games this season. Last season the team lost 20% of its 25 games. How many more games did the team lose this season than last season?
   F. 0 H. 2
   G. 1 J. 3

Spiral Review and Test Prep

Chapters 1–14

Choose the correct answer.

Number Sense

Use data from the table for problems 1–2.

The table shows the number of people who attended San Diego Padres baseball games in each of four years.

San Diego Padres	
Year	Attendance
1995	1,041,805
1996	2,187,886
1997	2,089,333
1998	2,555,901

1. In which year was the attendance nearest to two million people?
   A. 1995   C. 1997
   B. 1996   D. 1998

2. In which two years were the attendance numbers closest?
   F. 1995 and 1997   H. 1996 and 1998
   G. 1996 and 1997   J. 1997 and 1998

3. The Hillside School soccer team won 9 games and lost 6 games at the end of its season. What fraction of the total games, in simplest form, did the team win?
   A. $\frac{9}{6}$ C. $\frac{3}{5}$
   B. $\frac{6}{9}$ D. $\frac{9}{15}$

4. Which of the following statements is true?
   F. $15.3 > 15.33$ H. $15.39 > 16$
   G. $1.53 > 1.503$ J. $15.03 > 15.13$

Algebra and Functions

5. Which number could go in the blank to complete the table?

In	Out
8	32
6	24
9	■
2	8

   A. 13   C. 36
   B. 27   D. 45

6. Which of the following values for *t* makes the expression true?

$$\frac{5}{8} = \frac{t}{40}$$

   F. 10   H. 25
   G. 20   J. 37

7. Which expression is equivalent to $5 \times \frac{1}{9}$?
   A. $5 \div \frac{1}{9}$ C. 51×9
   B. $\frac{1}{9} + 5$ D. $\frac{1}{9} \times 5$

8. If the rule for the pattern below is multiply by 2 then add 8, what number comes next?

   4, 16, 40, 88, 184, ...

   F. 185   H. 376
   G. 196   J. 33,864

Statistics, Data Analysis, and Probability

Use data from the bar graph for problems 9–10.

Milton took a survey of 100 people. The results are shown in the graph.

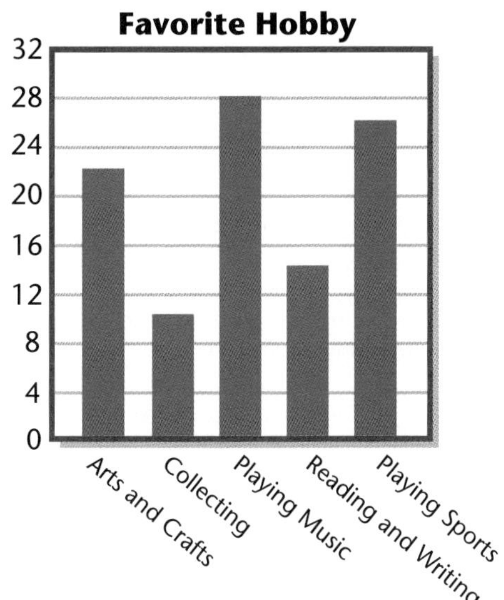

9. How many of the people surveyed said their favorite hobby is playing sports?
   A. 24 C. 26
   B. 25 D. 27

10. Which hobby had the closest amount of votes to reading and writing?
   F. Arts and Crafts H. Playing Music
   G. Collecting J. Playing Sports

Use the spinner for problems 11–12.

11. What is the probability of landing on an even number when you spin the spinner?
   A. $\frac{2}{3}$ B. $\frac{2}{4}$ C. $\frac{2}{5}$ D. $\frac{3}{5}$

12. What is the probability of landing on a number that is 3 or greater?
   F. $\frac{1}{3}$ G. $\frac{4}{5}$ H. $\frac{3}{5}$ J. $\frac{5}{3}$

Measurement and Geometry

13. How many obtuse angles does the figure have?

   A. 1 C. 3
   B. 2 D. 5

14. What is the surface area of the cube?

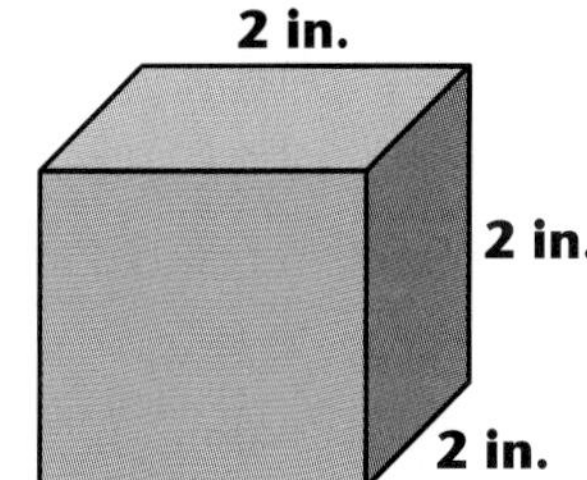

   F. 6 inches H. 24 inches
   G. 10 sq in. J. 24 sq in.

15. What is the area of the triangle?

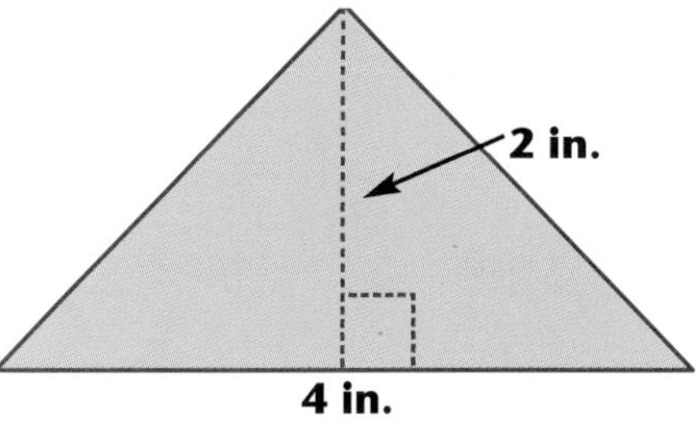

   A. 4 sq in. C. 8 sq in.
   B. 6 sq in. D. 16 sq in.

16. The Mustangs won 45% of their 20 games. The Red Rangers won 50% of their 16 games. Which team won more games? Explain.

Glossary

(*Italicized* terms are defined elsewhere in this glossary.)

A

acute angle An *angle* with a measure of less than 90°. (p 494)

acute triangle A *triangle* with 3 *acute angles.* (p 494)

addend A number that is to be added. (p 28)

algebraic expression A *variable* by itself or combination of one or more *variables,* one or more operations, and possibly one or more numbers. (p 434)
Examples: x, $6a$, $z - y$

angle A figure formed by two *rays* or *line segments* with the same *endpoint.* (p 490)

area The number of square units needed to cover the inside of a figure. (p 542)

array A group of objects separated into rows and columns. (p 52)

Associative Property of Addition When adding three *addends,* the grouping of the *addends* does not change the *sum.* (pp 28, 272)
Example: $16 + (14 + 89) = (16 + 14) + 89$

Associative Property of Multiplication The way *factors* are grouped does not change a *product.* (pp 58, 320)
Example: $20 \times (5 \times 77) = (20 \times 5) \times 77$

axis (plural: axes) A horizontal or vertical number line on a graph. (pp 161, 442)

B

bar graph A graph that compares *data* by using vertical or horizontal bars. (p 161)

base a. A *side* of a *polygon,* usually the one at the bottom. (p 546)

b. The number that is to be raised to a given *exponent.* (p 82)
Example: In the expression 3^5, 3 is the base.

biased sample A *sample* that is not representative of the entire *population.* (p 179)

C

capacity The *volume* of a container, measured in units of liquid measure. (p 354)

Celsius (C) A temperature scale in which water freezes at 0°C and boils at 100°C. (p 374)

center The *point* from which all *points* on a *circle* are the same distance. (p 516)

centiliter (cL) A metric unit of *capacity.* (See Table of Measures.)

centimeter (cm) A metric unit of length. (See Table of Measures.)

central angle An *angle* formed by two *radii* in a *circle.* (p 516)

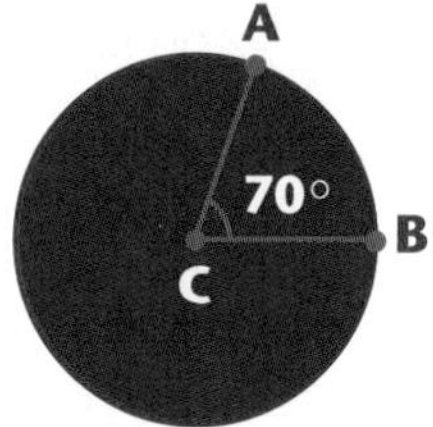

certain An *outcome* or *event* is **certain** if it has a *probability* of 1. (p 605)
Example: If a number cube with the numbers 1 to 6 on the faces is rolled, it is certain that a number less than 10 will be obtained.

chord A *line segment* that connects two *points* on a *circle.* (p 516)

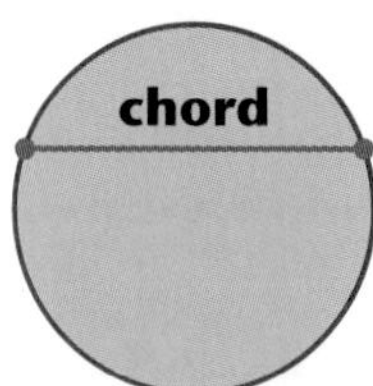

circle A *closed,* 2-dimensional figure that has all of its *points* the same distance from the *center.* (p 516)

circle graph A graph in which *data* are represented by parts of a *circle;* also known as a pie graph or pie chart. (p 652)

circumference The distance around a *circle.* (p 550)

closed figure A figure in a *plane* that can be traced with the same starting and stopping *points.* A figure in a *plane* that is not *open.* See *open.* (p 487)

clustering A way to *estimate* a sum by changing the *addends* that are close in *value* to one common number and multiplying by the number of *addends.* (p 63)

Example: $89 + 113 + 102 + 93 \approx$
$100 + 100 + 100 + 100 =$
$4 \times 100 = 400$

common denominator A **common denominator** of two or more *fractions* is a number which is a *multiple* of the *denominators* of the *fractions.* (p 252)

common factor A **common factor** of two or more *whole numbers* is a *whole number* that is a *factor* of all of the numbers. (p 204)

Example: 3 is a common factor of 6 and 15.

common multiple A **common multiple** of two or more *whole numbers* is a *whole number* that is a *multiple* of all of the numbers. (p 216)

Example: 24 is a common multiple of 4 and 6.

Commutative Property of Addition When adding, the order of the *addends* does not change the sum. (pp 28, 272)

Example: $44 + 13 = 13 + 44$

Commutative Property of Multiplication The order of the *factors* does not change a *product.* (pp 58, 320)

Example: $8 \times 11 = 11 \times 8$

compatible numbers Numbers that can be easily be added, subtracted, multiplied, or divided mentally. (p 115)

Example: 7,200 and 90 are compatible numbers for division because $72 \div 9 = 8$.

compensation A mental math technique for adding or subtracting two numbers, involving doing the same thing or the opposite thing to the two numbers.

Example: $298 + 236 =$
$(298 + 2) + (236 - 2) = 300 + 234 = 534$

composite number A *whole number* greater than 1 that is *divisible* by more numbers than just itself and the number 1. (p 202)

Example: 63 is composite because it is divisible by 1, 3, 7, 9, 21, and 63.

compound figure A shape that is made up of two or more shapes. (p 556)

congruent figures Figures that have the same shape and size. (p 506)

congruent line segments *Line segments* that have the same length. (p 486)

coordinate One of two numbers in an *ordered pair.* (pp 166, 442)

corresponding parts Matching parts of *congruent* or *similar figures.* (p 506)

cross product A **cross product** of two *fractions* is a *product* of the *numerator* of one of the *fractions* and the *denominator* of the other *fraction.* (p 589)

cup (c) A customary unit of *capacity.* (See Table of Measures.)

D

data Collected information. (p 152)

decimal A number with a decimal point in it, such as 8.37 or 0.05. (p 4)

degree (°) a. A unit for measuring temperature. See *Celsius* and *Fahrenheit.* (p 374)

b. A unit for measuring *angles.* (p 490)

denominator The number below the bar in a *fraction.* (p 206)

diagonal A *line segment,* other than a *side,* that connects two *vertices* of a *polygon.* (p 487)

diameter A *chord* of a *circle* that passes through the *center* of the *circle.* (p 516)

Distributive Property of Multiplication over Addition To multiply a sum by a number, you can multiply each *addend* by the number and add the *products.* (pp 53, 58, 320)

Example: $9 \times (8 + 7) = (9 \times 8) + (9 \times 7)$

Distributive Property of Multiplication over Subtraction To multiply a difference of two numbers by a third number, you can multiply each of the first two numbers by the third and then find the difference of the *products.* (p 58)
Example: $23 \times (11 - 5) = (23 \times 11) - (23 \times 5)$

dividend A number to be divided. (p 104)
Example: In the expression $48 \div 6$, 48 is the dividend.

divisible A *whole number* is divisible by another *whole number* if the *remainder* is 0 when the first is divided by the second. (p 200)
Example: 72 is divisible by 9.

divisor The number by which a *dividend* is divided. (pp 104, 324)
Example: In the expression $48 \div 6$, 6 is the divisor.

double-bar graph A *bar graph* that compares two related groups of *data.* (p 161)

edge A *line segment* where two *faces* of a *3-dimensional figure* meet. (p 558)

elapsed time The amount of time that passes from the start of an activity to the end of the activity. (p 347)

endpoint A *point* at the end of a *line segment* or *ray.* (p 486)

equally likely Two or more *outcomes* are **equally likely** if they have the same *probability* of occurring. (p 604)

equation A mathematical statement with an equal sign in it. (p 440)
Examples: $6 + 3 = 9$; $m + 2 = 29$

equilateral triangle A *triangle* with 3 congruent sides. (p 494)

equivalent decimals *Decimals* that name the same number. (p 7)
Example: 0.6 and 0.60

equivalent fractions *Fractions* that name the same number. (p 207)
Example: $\frac{1}{3}$ and $\frac{12}{36}$

equivalent ratios *Ratios* that are represented by *equivalent fractions.* (p 588)
Example: 3:5 and 12:20

estimate To find a number that is close to the exact answer. (p 23)

evaluate To find the value of an expression by performing the operation or operations. (p 434)

event A set of one or more *outcomes* in a *probability* experiment. (p 604)
Example: If a number cube with the numbers 1 to 6 on the faces is rolled, rolling an even number is an event. It consists of the three possible outcomes of 2, 4, and 6.

expanded form A way of writing a number as the sum of the *values* of its digits. (p 2)
Example: $638 = 600 + 30 + 8$.

exponent The number that tells how many times a *base* is used as a *factor.* (p 82)
Example: In the expression 3^5, 5 is the exponent.

face A flat side of a *3-dimensional figure.* (p 558)

fact family A group of related facts using the same numbers. (p 104)

factor a. A number that is multiplied to give a *product.* (p 50)
Example: In 3×5, 3 and 5 are factors.

factor b. A *whole number* is a **factor** of another *whole number* if the *remainder* is 0 when the second is divided by the first. (p 203)
Example: 5 is a factor of 245 because $245 \div 5 = 49$.

factor tree A way to write a number as a *product* of its *factors.* (p 202)

Fahrenheit (°F) A temperature scale in which water freezes at 32°F and boils at 212°F. (p 374)

fluid ounce (fl oz) A customary unit of *capacity.* (See Table of Measures.)

foot (ft) A customary unit of length. (See Table of Measures.)

formula An *equation* with at least two *variables,* showing how one *variable* depends on the other *variable* or *variables.* (p 540)

fraction A number that names part of a whole or part of a group. (pp 4, 206)

frequency The number of times a response occurs or something happens. (p 152)

frequency table A way of organizing a set of *data,* showing the number of times each item or number appears. (p 152)

function A relationship in which one quantity depends on another quantity. (p 440)

gallon (gal) A customary unit of capacity. (See Table of Measures.)

glide reflection A *transformation* that is a combination of a *reflection* and a *translation.* (p 508)

gram (g) A metric unit of mass. (See Table of Measures.)

greatest common factor (GCF) The **greatest common factor** of two or more numbers is the greatest *whole number* that is a *common factor* of the numbers. (p 204)

Example: 28 and 88 have common factors 1, 2, and 4. So, their greatest common factor is 4.

height of a parallelogram The length of a *line segment* from one side of the *parallelogram* to the side *parallel* to it, drawn *perpendicular* to both of the *sides.* (p 546)

height of a triangle The length of the *line segment* from a *vertex* of the *triangle* to the side opposite that *vertex,* drawn *perpendicular* to that *side.* (p 548)

hexagon A *polygon* with six *sides* and six *vertices.* (p 487)

histogram A *bar graph* that shows *frequency* of *data* for *intervals.* (p 164)

horizontal line A *line* that runs straight across. (p 486)

I

Identity Property of Addition When a number is added to 0, the sum is that number. (pp 28, 272)

Example: $8 + 0 = 8$

Identity Property of Multiplication The *product* of any *factor* and 1 equals the *factor.* (pp 58, 320)

Example: $8 \times 1 = 8$

impossible An *outcome* or *event* is **impossible** if it has *probability* of 0. (p 605)

Example: If a number cube with the numbers 1 to 6 on the faces is rolled, it is impossible that a number greater than 10 will be obtained.

improper fraction A *fraction* that has a *numerator* greater than or equal to its *denominator.* (p 226)

inch (in.) A customary unit of length. (See Table of Measures.)

integer A *whole number* or its opposite. (p 394)

Examples: 17, $^{-}9$, 0.

intersecting lines *Lines* that meet or cross at a common *point.* (p 491)

interval The distance between numbers on an *axis.* (p 160)

inverse operations Operations that undo each other. (p 456)

Example: Multiplying by 6 and dividing by 6 are inverse operations.

isosceles triangle A *triangle* with at least 2 *sides* of the same length. (p 494)

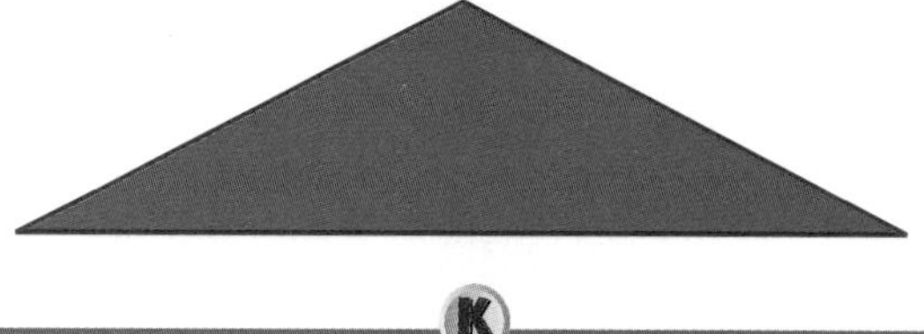

K

kilogram (kg) A metric unit of *mass.* (See Table of Measures.)

kilometer (km) A metric unit of length. (See Table of Measures.)

L

leaf A ones digit in a row of a *stem-and-leaf plot.* (p 176)

least common denominator (LCD) The **least common denominator** of two or more *fractions* is the *least common multiple* of the *denominators* of the *fractions.* (p 217)

least common multiple (LCM) The **least common multiple** of two or more *whole numbers* is the least *whole number* greater than 0 that is a multiple of each of the numbers. (p 216)

Example: 10 has multiples 10, 20, 30, 40, 50, ... and 8 has multiples 8, 16, 24, 32, 40, 48, 56, ... So, the least common multiple of 10 and 8 is 40.

less likely An *event* is **less likely** than a second *event* if it has a smaller *probability* of happening than the second *event.* (p 605)

like denominators *Denominators* that are the same number. (p 252)

likely An *outcome* is **likely** if it probably will happen. (p 602)

line A set of *points* that form a straight path that goes forever in both directions. (p 486)

line graph A graph that uses one or more *line segments* to show changes in *data.* (p 167)

line of symmetry A *line* that divides a figure into two parts that match when the figure is folded on that *line.* (p 512)

line plot A graph that uses columns of Xs above a number line. (p 152)

line segment A part of a *line* that connects two *endpoints.* (p 486)

liter (L) A metric unit of *capacity.* (See Table of Measures.)

M

mass The amount of matter in an object. (p 365)

mean The quantity that is found by adding the numbers in a set of numbers and dividing their sum by the number of *addends.* (p 154)

Example: The mean of the numbers 7, 8, 9, 6 and 9 is 7.8.

median The middle number in a set of numbers arranged in order from least to greatest. If the set contains an even number of numbers, the **median** is the *mean* of the two middle numbers. (p 154)

Example: The median of the numbers 6, 7, 8, 9, and 9 is 8.

meter (m) The basic unit of length in the metric system. (See Table of Measures.)

mile (mi) A customary unit of length. (See Table of Measures.)

milligram (mg) A metric unit of *mass.* (See Table of Measures.)

milliliter (mL) A metric unit of *capacity.* (See Table of Measures.)

millimeter (mm) A metric unit of length. (See Table of Measures.)

mixed number A number that combines a *whole number* and a *fraction.* (p 216)

Example: $3\frac{2}{5}$

mode The number that occurs most often in a set of numbers. (p 154)

Example: The mode of the numbers 7, 8, 9, 6 and 9 is 9.

more likely An *event* is **more likely** than a second *event* if it has a greater *probability* of happening than the second *event.* (p 605)

N

negative integer An *integer* less than 0. (p 394)

net A 2-dimensional pattern that can be folded to make a *3-dimensional figure.* (p 559)

numerator The number above the bar in a *fraction.* (p 206)

O

obtuse angle An *angle* with measure greater than 90° and less than 180°. (p 494)

obtuse triangle A *triangle* with 1 *obtuse angle.* (p 494)

octagon A *polygon* with eight *sides* and eight *vertices.* (p 487)

open figure A figure that starts and stops at different *points.* (p 487)

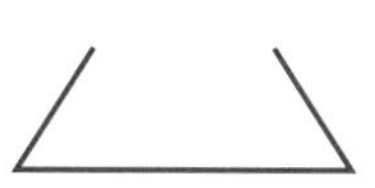

opposite integers Two different *integers* that are the same distance from 0 on a number line. (p 394)

Example: 5 and $^{-}5$

order of operations The agreed-upon order for performing operations. (p 438)

ordered pair A pair of numbers that gives the location of a *point* on a coordinate graph, map, or grid. (pp 166, 442)

Example: (4, 0)

origin The *point* on a *coordinate* graph where the vertical *axis* meets the horizontal *axis.* (p 442)

outcome A possible result in a *probability* experiment. (p 602)

Example: If a number cube with the numbers 1 to 6 on the faces is rolled, there are six possible outcomes. They are 1, 2, 3, 4, 5, and 6.

P

parallel lines *Lines* in the same *plane* that never *intersect.* (p 491)

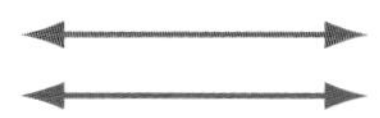

parallelogram A *quadrilateral* in which both pairs of opposite *sides* are *parallel.* (p 498)

pentagon A *polygon* with five *sides* and five *vertices.* (p 487)

percent Per hundred, or part of a hundred. (pp 628, 630)

perimeter The distance around a *closed figure.* (p 540)

period Each group of three digits in a *place value* chart. (p 2)

perpendicular lines *Intersecting lines* that cross each other at *right angles.* (p 491)

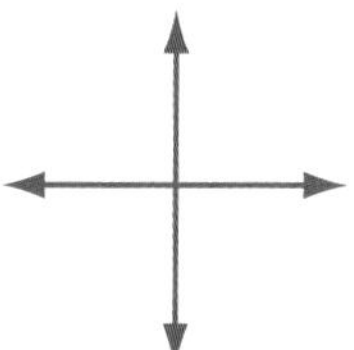

perspective drawing A drawing that shows a *3-dimensional* object in a 2-dimensional drawing. (p 562)

pictograph A graph that compares *data* by using picture symbols. (p 158)

pint (pt) A customary unit of capacity. (See Table of Measures.)

place The position of a digit in a number. (p 2)

plane A flat surface that extends forever. (p 491)

plot To graph a *point* on a *coordinate plane.* (p 166)

point An exact location in space. (p 486)

polygon A *closed figure* that can be drawn without lifting up your pencil, made up of *line segments* that do not cross each other. (p 487)

Examples: Squares and triangles.

population A group about which information is wanted. (p 178)

positive integer An *integer* greater than 0. (p 394)

pound (lb) A customary unit of weight. (See Table of Measures.)

power A number obtained by raising a *base* to an *exponent.* (p 82)

Example: $5^2 = 25$

power of 10 A number obtained by raising 10 to an *exponent.* (p 128)

Examples: $10^1 = 10$, $10^2 = 10 \times 10 = 100$

prime factorization A way of expressing a *whole number* as a *product* of its prime factors. (p 202)

Example: $120 = 2 \times 2 \times 2 \times 3 \times 5$

prime number A whole number greater than 1 that is only *divisible* by itself and the number 1. (p 202)

Examples: 2, 3, 127

probability A number between 0 and 1 that measures the chances of an *event* happening. (p 602)

product The answer in a multiplication problem. (p 50)

Example: In the number sentence $6 \times 11.2 = 67.2$, the product is 67.2.

proportion An *equation* that contains *equivalent ratios* on each side. (p 589)

Examples: $\frac{7}{8} = \frac{28}{32}, \frac{n}{10} = \frac{12}{5}$

quadrant One of the four sections on a *coordinate* graph formed by the horizontal and vertical *axes.* (p 446)

quadrilateral A *polygon* with four *sides* and four *vertices.* (p 487)

Examples: Parallelogram, rectangle.

quart (qt) A customary unit of *capacity.* (See Table of Measures.)

quotient The answer to a division problem. (p 104)

radius (plural radii) A *line segment* that connects the *center* of a *circle* to a *point* on the *circle.* (p 516)

random sample A *sample* where every member is chosen by chance, and everyone in the *population* has an equal chance of being chosen. (p 179)

range The difference between the greatest and the least number in a set of numbers. (p 154)

Example: The range of the numbers 7, 8, 9, 6, and 9 is 3.

rate A *ratio* that compares measurements or amounts. (p 592)

Example: 50 miles per hour.

ratio A comparison of two quantities. (p 586)

ray A part of a *line* that has one *endpoint* and continues in one direction without end. (p 486)

reciprocals Two numbers whose *product* is 1. (p 324)

Example: 3 and $\frac{1}{3}$ are reciprocals since $3 \times \frac{1}{3} = 1$; $\frac{2}{7}$ and $\frac{7}{2}$ are reciprocals since $\frac{2}{7} \times \frac{7}{2} = 1$.

rectangle A *parallelogram* with four *right angles.* (p 498)

reflection A *transformation* that creates a mirror image of a figure across a *line.* (p 508)

remainder In division, the number left after the *quotient* is found. (p 106)

Example: When 30 is divided by 7, the remainder is 2.

representative sample A *sample* of a *population* that gives you a good idea what the whole *population* is like. (p 179)

rhombus A *parallelogram* with four congruent *sides.* (p 498)

right angle An *angle* with measure 90°. (p 494)

right triangle A *triangle* with 1 *right angle.* (p 494)

rotation A *transformation* that turns a figure around a *point.* (p 508)

round To find the nearest value of a number based on a given *place.* (p 22)

Example: 6.38, rounded to the nearest tenth, is 6.4.

sample A part of a *population* used to get information about that *population.* (p 178)

sample space The set of all possible *outcomes* in a *probability* experiment. (p 604)

scale The *ratio* that compares the distances on a map or *scale drawing* with the actual distances. (p 598)

scale drawing A reduced or enlarged drawing of an actual object. (p 598)

scalene triangle A *triangle* in which no two *sides* are congruent. (p 494)

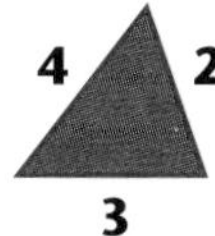

side of an angle The part of an *angle* formed by a *ray.* (p 490)

side of a polygon One of the *line segments* in the *polygon.* (p 487)

similar figures Figures that have the same shape but not necessarily the same size. (p 506)

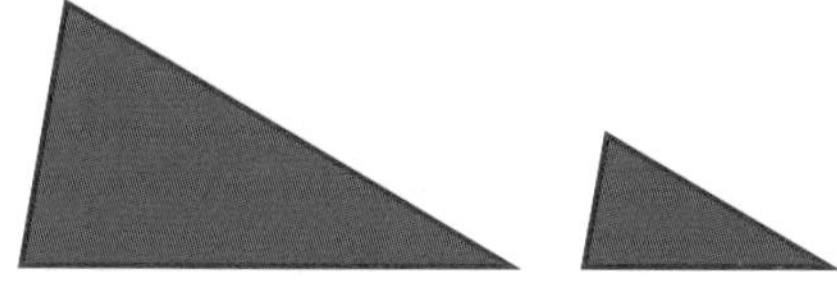

simplest form A *fraction* is in *simplest form* when 1 is the only *common factor* of the *numerator* and *denominator.* (p 214)

Example: $\frac{5}{12}$ is in simplest form because 5 and 12 have no common factor greater than 1.

square A *rectangle* with four congruent *sides.* (p 498)

standard form The usual or common way to write a number. (p 2)

stem The digit or digits to the left of the ones digits of a number in a *data* set. (p 176)

stem-and-leaf plot An arrangement of numerical *data* that separates the digits into columns. The digits to the left of the ones digits are called the *stems;* the ones digits for each *stem* are the *leaves.* (p 176)

surface area The total *area* of the surface of a *3-dimensional figure.* (p 564)

survey A method to gather *data* that involves asking people questions or observing events. (p 152)

symmetric about a line A figure is **symmetric about a line** if it can be folded along the *line* so that the two halves match exactly. (p 512)

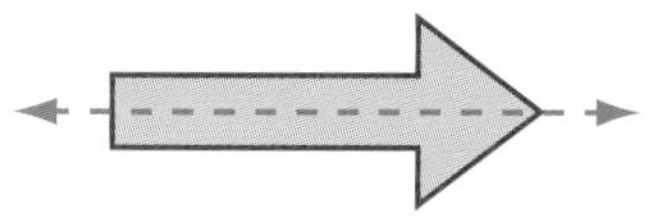

T

terms The numbers in a *ratio.* (p 586)

tessellation An arrangement of shapes that covers a region without any gaps or overlaps. (p 520)

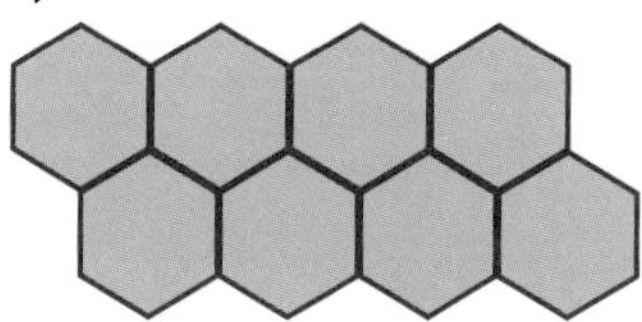

3-dimensional figure A figure that has length, width, and height. (p 558)

Examples: Prism, pyramid, cylinder.

ton (T) A customary unit of weight. (See Table of Measures.)

transformation A change of position of a geometric figure. (p 508)

Examples: Reflection, rotation, translation.

translation A *transformation* that moves a figure along a straight *line.* (p 508)

trapezoid A *quadrilateral* with exactly one pair of *parallel sides.* (p 498)

triangle A *polygon* with three *sides* and three *vertices.* (p 487)

U

unit price The cost of a single item or the cost per unit of *volume* or weight. (p 593)

unit rate A *rate* in which the second measurement or amount is 1 unit. (p 592)

unlikely An *outcome* is **unlikely** if it probably will not happen. (p 602)

V

value The *product* of a digit multiplied by its *place.* (p 2)

variable A symbol used to represent a number or numbers. (p 434)

Venn diagram A diagram that uses overlapping *circles* to organize and show *data.* (p 650)

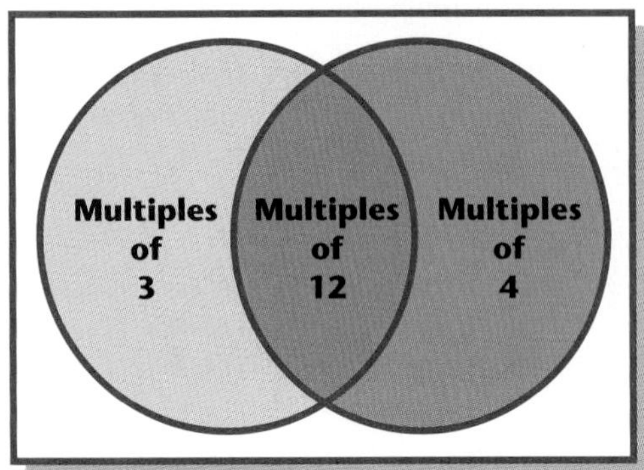

vertex (plural: vertices)

a. The *point* where two *rays* meet in an *angle.* (pp 487, 490)

b. The *point* where three or more *edges* of a *3-dimensional figure* meet. (p 558)

vertical line A *line* that runs straight up and down. (p 486)

volume The amount of space that a *3-dimensional figure* encloses. (pp 354, 566)

whole number Any one of the numbers, 0, 1, 2, 3, and so on. (p 2)

yard (yd) A customary unit of length. (See Table of Measures.)

Zero Property of Multiplication The *product* of any *factor* and 0 equals 0. (pp 58, 320)

Example: $67 \times 0 = 0$

Table of Measures

Customary

Length	Weight	Capacity
1 foot (ft) = 12 inches (in.)	1 pound (lb) = 16 ounces (oz)	1 cup (c) = 8 fluid ounces
1 yard (yd) = 3 feet, or 36 inches	1 ton (T) = 2,000 pounds	1 pint (pt) = 2 cups (c)
1 mile (mi) = 5,280 feet or 1,760 yards		1 quart (qt) = 4 cups
		1 gallon (gal) = 4 quarts

Area

1 square foot (ft^2) = 144 square inches ($in.^2$)

1 square yard (yd^2) = 9 square feet

Metric

Length	Mass	Capacity
1 millimeter (mm) = 0.001 meter (m)	1 milligram (mg) = 0.001 gram (g)	1 milliliter (mL) = 0.001 liter (L)
1 centimeter = 0.01 meter (m)	1 kilogram (kg) = 1,000 grams	1 centiliter (cL) = 0.01 liter
1 kilometer (km) = 1,000 meters		

Area

1 square centimeter (cm^2) = 100 square millimeters (mm^2)

1 square meter (m^2) = 10,000 square centimeters

1 square kilometer (km^2) = 1,000,000 square meters

Symbols

Symbol	Meaning	Symbol	Meaning	Symbol	Meaning
$<$	is less than	$^\circ$	degree	$\perp$	perpendicular
$>$	is greater than	°C	degree Celsius	2:5	ratio of 2 to 5
$=$	is equal to	°F	degree Fahrenheit	10^2	ten to the second power
$\neq$	is not equal to	$\overleftrightarrow{AB}$	line *AB*	$\lvert {}^{-}5 \rvert$	Absolute value of $^{-}5$ is 5
$\approx$	is approximately equal to	$\overline{AB}$	line segment *AB*	$^{+}4$	positive 4
$\cong$	is congruent to	$\overrightarrow{AB}$	ray *AB*	$^{-}4$	negative 4
%	percent	$\angle ABC$	angle	(5, 3)	ordered pair 5, 3
π	pi (approximately 3.14)	$\parallel$	is parallel to	P(B)	probability of event B

Formulas

$P = 2\ell + 2w$	Perimeter of a rectangle	$A = \frac{1}{2} \times b \times h$	Area of a triangle
$A = \ell \times w$	Area of a rectangle	$C = \pi \times d = 2\pi r$	Circumference of a circle
$A = s^2$	Area of a square	$A = \pi \times r^2$	Area of a circle
$A = b \times h$	Area of a parallelogram	$V = \ell \times w \times h$	Volume of a rectangular prism

Table of Random Numbers

14567	85552	63853	17961	95084	32354	96169	33718	64958	50892
36824	35568	40619	98350	84776	08468	98987	77942	64417	01258
48900	57979	89058	18031	39305	31613	54515	45030	24392	26950
46377	55250	70452	00358	22379	11677	20124	17022	55416	67563
99569	23616	79207	69433	51929	57159	42992	17628	01909	05579
65345	48005	90776	03764	48299	56175	19444	69264	21318	41562
62685	72874	64078	06039	06460	29268	37455	05432	60388	88402
57645	34425	23110	10669	55700	63433	28070	58797	03706	40359
70592	52388	39164	28982	83526	61569	09246	95487	33097	33474
13419	88293	44208	15009	25049	68554	28052	44052	44053	40966
12740	35726	76990	24143	81214	36165	32114	14450	83705	57864
05807	03935	18124	07339	98422	95568	93536	34497	67176	04777
83890	99567	16880	63324	23202	50981	23860	30786	29604	02234
28839	50442	62899	88837	06418	77444	88478	24429	75614	19595
80854	91845	77097	00640	33546	36394	43648	88287	17003	21621
85034	41782	07226	47949	76206	22756	33109	88145	16493	27729
78011	46960	17172	85728	98812	18187	10364	60159	73815	08067
10871	44769	61159	53631	37693	64670	68027	12222	76049	41616
55324	22373	47264	87243	87210	33145	49849	12500	15861	18241
93167	54306	46616	89912	77698	78150	09093	36699	83993	64905
25540	09394	25969	96174	68343	29837	26782	01386	18335	27003
18264	04292	93596	48923	71088	72696	77368	93470	49886	80758
13300	47319	40713	47995	71042	20419	19704	69294	91842	52536
99251	27623	05575	42635	56760	62621	25377	05922	61869	34973
90930	55497	41510	09581	29655	81422	40167	92845	52748	05038
42894	43222	89277	22957	95941	11870	66776	22343	25057	81607
33323	66020	31493	09030	73037	57315	69159	39221	03973	47602
91556	58706	38481	58565	85325	88040	31258	40215	38149	98434
88500	36675	75255	77222	46214	07743	68342	50214	58369	89552
15746	76626	41044	79115	64866	90886	09919	72949	90117	92967
26982	80667	36643	96978	37258	29086	32138	73214	36842	25997
86107	40694	29077	19597	47354	60641	56363	49393	88726	99502
31380	53818	02429	84916	05182	82042	81413	37889	63254	14732
06517	30069	36146	79693	26532	73842	33009	31912	04356	36761
92733	37810	88295	16143	66372	40009	94054	07499	52245	82487
92784	51817	40287	37391	87504	59934	91844	84964	66511	92789
16248	91101	54434	48128	77297	80098	85432	84714	30304	58121
92327	88047	26298	67017	17570	65731	50411	68635	83439	76788
87723	82601	21916	31523	92740	94779	52310	01346	26695	97914
73285	42494	37715	62479	09549	14557	99077	38740	57543	62846

Ray A. Waller, *Statistics: An Introduction to Numerical Reasoning*, 1979

Index

D

Credits

COVER PHOTOGRAPHY

David Muir for MHSD

PHOTOGRAPHY CREDITS

All photographs are by McGraw-Hill School Division (MHSD) and Ken Karp, Peter Brandt and Doug David for MHSD except as noted below.

Table of Contents xii: tr, Bob Daemmrich/Stock Boston • x: tr, Christopher Little/Christopher Little • vi: tr, Dave Watts/Tom Stack and Associates • xvii: tr, David Stoecklein/Stock Market • xi: tr, David Waitz for MHSD • xvi: tr, Estelle Carol and Bob Simpson • xiv: tr, Johns, Jasper, "Three Flags" 1958. © Jasper Johns/Licensed by VAGA, New York, NY. Whitney Museum of American Art/SuperStock • viii: tr, Mark E. Gibson/Gibson Color Photography • xiii: tr, Richard Hutchings for MHSD • ix: tr, Spencer Grant/Photo Edit • xv: tr, Stefano Cellai/Stock Market • iv: tr, Steve Powell/AllSport • v: tr, VCG/FPG International • vii: tr, Wright State University/The Wright Brothers Livensed by the Wright Family Fund. Represented by the Roger Richman Agency, Inc., Beverly Hills, CA; **Chapter 1** 2: tr, Allan Friedland/SuperStock • 2: all, Guy Charneau/Liaiaon • 4: tr, David Waitz for MHSD • 6: tr, Steve Powell/AllSport • 14: tr, Flip Chalfant/The Image Bank • 18: tr, Gary W. Meek/Gary Meek Photography • 22: tc, Comstock • 22: tr, Photodisk • 26: tr, Victah Sailer/Photo Run • 28: tr, Baiomys, Taylori/Photo Researchers • 31: cr, Keith Martin-Smith • 32: c, Ken Cavanagh for MHSD • 32: cl, Ken Cavanaugh for MHSD • 32: cr, Jean Higgins/Unicorn Stock Photos • 34: tr, Ken Cavanaugh for MHSD • 43: br, David Waitz for MHSD; **Chapter 2** 48: all, A. Ramey/Woodfin Camp and Associates • 52: tr, David Waitz for MHSD • 54: tr, Judi Wineland-Thomas/Thomas Safaris • 62: tr, Dan Guravich/Photo Researchers • 66: tr, Bonnie Kamin/Photo Edit • 70: tr, Liz Strenk/SuperStock • 70: cr, Jordan Information Bureau • 74: tr, David Waitz for MHSD • 76: tr, Spencer Swanger/Tom Stack and Associates • 80: tr, Miriam Austerman/Animals, Animals/Earth Scenes • 80: cr, Ron P. Jaffe/Unicorn Stock Photos • 82: tr, Luis Villota/Bruce Coleman, Inc. • 88: tr, VCG/FPG International • 88: br, David Waitz for MHSD • 97: tr, Richard Hutchings for MHSD; **Chapter 3** 102: all, Michael Newman/Photo Edit • 104: tr, Hans Reinhard/OKAPIA - Photo Researchers • 105: cr, Tom McHugh/Photo Researchers • 106: tr, David Waitz for MHSD • 108: tr, Dave Watts/Tom Stack and Associates • 110: tr, E. Widder/Harbor Branch Oceanographic 2000 • 113: cr, Ivor Fulcher/Stock Market • 114: tr, Aurora & Quanta • 118: tr, Lawerence Migdale/Lawrence Migdale Photography • 122: tr, Ken Cavanagh for MHSD • 124: tr, Brian Parker/Tom Stack and Associates • 127: cr, Hal Beral/VU • 128: tr, David Waitz for MHSD • 130: tr, Hans Reinhard/Bruce Coleman Inc. • 136: tr, Richard Hutchings for MHSD • 136: bc, David Waitz for MHSD • 137: br, Deborah Davis/Photo Edit • 145: tr, David Waitz for MHSD; **Chapter 4** 152: tr, David Waitz for MHSD • 152: all, Richard T. Nowitz/Folio Image Agency • 163: cl, D. Young-Wolff/Photo Edit • 164: tr, David Young-Wolff/Photo Edit • 169: c, Wright State University/The Wright Brothers Licensed by the Wright Family Fund. Represented by the Roger Richman Agency, Inc., Beverly Hills, CA. • 174: tr, Comstock • 178: tr, Paul Shoul • 184: tr, Robert Brenner/Photo Edit • 184: br, Richard Hutchings for MHSD • 193: tr, David Waitz for MHSD; **Chapter 5** 200: tr, Rhoda Sidney/Photo Edit • 202: tr, David Waitz for MHSD • 206: tr, Dottie Dillard • 210: tr, Mark E. Gibson/Gibson Color Photography • 222: tr, World Class Learning Materials • 226: tr, David Waitz for MHSD • 236: tr, Richard Hutchings for MHSD • 236: br, David Waitz for MHSD • 198: all, Mark E. Gibson/Gibson Color Photography; **Chapter 6** 252: tr, Jay Liebowitz • 256: tr, Richard Hutchings for MHSD • 258: tr, David Waitz for MHSD • 260: tr, David Waitz for MHSD • 268: tr, David Waitz for MHSD • 270: tr, Richard Hutchings for MHSD • 274: tr, Richard Hutchings for MHSD • 276: tr, David Waitz for MHSD • 278: tr, Stephen Ogilvy for MHSD • 280: tr, Photodisc • 280: tr, Spencer Grant/Photo Edit • 284: tr, RubberBall Productions/Picture Quest • 284: b, David Waitz for MHSD • 250: all, Index Stock; **Chapter 7** 298: all, Jeff Greenberg/Peter Arnold, Inc. • 300: tr, Richard Hutchings for MHSD • 301: cr, Greg Vaughn/Tom Stack and Associates • 305: cr, Catherine Karnow/Woodfin Camp and Associates • 310: tr, Ken Cavanagh for MHSD • 314: tr, Chris Little/Christopher Little • 322: tr, David Waitz for MHSD • 330: tr, David Waitz for MHSD; **Chapter 8** 344: all, Joseph Bailey/National Geographic Image Collection • 350: bl, Ken Cavanagh for MHSD • 350: bc, Ken Cavanagh for MHSD • 350: br, Eric Sander/Liaison International • 352: tr, Ken Cavanagh for MHSD • 354: tr, David Waitz for MHSD • 354: c, Ken Cavanagh for MHSD • 355: tl, Ken Cavanagh for MHSD • 355: tc, Ken Cavanagh for MHSD • 355: tr, Ford Motor/FPG International • 362: tr, David Waitz for MHSD • 362: c, Ken Cavanagh for MHSD • 363: tl, Ken Cavanagh for MHSD • 363: tr, Ken Cavanagh for MHSD • 363: cl, Gary A. Conner/Index Stock • 363: cr, Eric Sander/Liaison International • 364: tr, David Waitz for MHSD • 364: c, Ken Cavanagh for MHSD • 364: cl, Ken Cavanagh for MHSD • 364: cr, Ken Cavanagh for MHSD • 365: tl, Ron W. Perry • 365: tc, Stephen Myers/International Stock • 365: tr, Doug Martin/Photo Researchers • 365: cl, Ken Cavanagh for MHSD • 365: cr, Ken Cavanagh for MHSD • 368: tr, Richard Hutchings for MHSD • 372: tr, Lenore & Lionel Jean Baptiste • 378: tr, Richard Hutchings for MHSD • 378: br, David Waitz for MHSD • 387: tr, David Waitz for MHSD; **Chapter 9** 392: all, Bob Daemmrich/Stock Boston • 398: tr, David Waitz for MHSD • 404: tr, David Waitz for MHSD • 408: tr, David Waitz for MHSD • 418: tr, Richard Hutchings for MHSD • 418: br, David Waitz for MHSD; **Chapter 10** 432: all, David Young-Wolf/Photo Edit • 434: tr, David Waitz for MHSD • 436: tr, David Waitz for MHSD • 438: cr, YVA Momatiuk & John Eastcott • 440: tr, Richard Hutchings for MHSD • 445: br, Earth Imaging/Stone • 450: tr, Dusty Wilson/International Stock • 456: tr, Ken Cavanagh for MHSD • 460: tr, Don Romero/International Stock • 464: tr, Earth Imaging/Stone • 470: tr, David Waitz for MHSD • 470: br, David Waitz for MHSD; **Chapter 11** 484: all, Jim Cummings/FPG • 485: t, Herbin, Auguste. "Composition on the Word 'Vie' 2" 1950. Oil on canvas, 57 1/2 x 38 1/4" The Museum of Modern Art, New York. The Sidney and Harriet Janis Collection. Photograph © 2000 The Museum of Modern Art, New York. © 2000 ARS New York/ ADAGP, Paris • 486: tr, Snelson, Kenneth. "Free Ride Home" 1974. Aluminum & stainless steel, 30'x60'x60', Collection: Storm King Art Center. © Kenneth Snelson/Licensed by VAGA, New York, NY • 489: tr, Picasso, Pablo. "The Studio" Paris 1928. Oil on canvas, 59"x7'7". The Museum of Modern Art, New York. Gift of Walter P. Chrysler, Jr. Photograph © 2000 The Museum of Modern Art, New York. © 2000 Estate of Pablo Picasso/ARS New York • 489: br, Mondrian, Piet. "Composition with Red, Yellow, and Blue" 1937-42. Tate Gallery, London / Art Resource, © ARS, NY/Beeldrecht, Amsterdam • 490: tr, Lissitzky, Eleazer. "Victory Over the Sun: The New Man" 1923. Tate Gallery, London/Art Resource, New York • 491: tr, Johnson, William "Jitterbugs (IV)" © 1941 National Museum of American Art, Washington DC/Art Resource, New York • 493: tr, Hirshhorn Museum and Sculpture Garden, Smithsonian Institution, Gift of Joseph H. Hirshhorn, 1972. © 2000 Barnett Newman Foundation/ARS New York, photographer: Lee Stalsworth • 494: tr, Lichtenstein, Roy. "The Great Pyramids" 1969. Oil and magna on canvas; 129x 204 1/4" Purchased with funds from the Coffin Fine Arts Trust; Nathan Emory Coffin Collection of the Des Moines Art Center, 1970. © Estate of Roy Lichtenstein/photo by Michael Tropea, Chicago • 495: tr, Herbin, Auguste "Impasse" © 2000 ARS, NY/ADAGP, Paris, Bridgeman Art Library • 497: tr, Feininger, Lyonel. "Sailboats" 1929. Detroit Institute of Arts. © 2000 ARS, New York, VG Bild-Kunst, Bonn, Bridgeman Art Library • 498: tr, Leppien, Jean. "Composition" 1953. Musee National d'Art Moderne, Center, Paris © ARS New York, SuperStock • 499: tr, Van Gogh, Vincent, "The artist's room at Arles" 1889. Giraudon/Art Resource • 501: tr, Klein, Yves "Blue Sponge Relief" © ARS, New York/ADAGP, Paris. Wallfraf-Richartz-Museum, Cologne, Germany. Erich Lessing / Art Resource • 501: cr, Van Doesburg, Theo. "Simultaneous Counter-Composition" (1929-30), Oil on canvas, 19 3/4 x 19 5/8, The Museum of Modern Art, New York, The Sidney an Harriet Janis Collection. Photograph © 2000 The Museum of Modern Art, New York, © 2000 ARS NY/ Beeldrecht, Amsterdam • 502: tr, Kelly, Ellsworth, courtesy of the artist, "Yellow with Red Triangle", In the Collection of the Corcoran Gallery of Art, Washington, DC. Museum purchase with aid of funds from the Richard King Mellon Foundation. • 506: tr, Johns, Jasper, "Three Flags" 1958. © Jasper Johns/Licensed by VAGA, New York, NY. Whitney Museum of American Art/SuperStock • 508: tr, Newark Museum/Art Resource • 511: cr, Rivera, Diego, "Cactus on the Plains" aka "Hands" 1931. Oil on canvas 69.2 x84.5 cm. (Mexican 1886-1957). © Edsel & Eleanor Ford House, Grosse Pointe Shores, Michigan. photo: RH Hensleigh © 2000 Banco de Mexico Diego Rivera & Frida Kahlo Museums Trust. Av. Cinco de Mayo No.2, Col. Centro, Del. Cuauhtemoc 06059, Mexico, D.F. • 512: tr, John Running Studios/ McGraw-Hill • 513: c, Stockbyte • 513: br, Kelly, Ellsworth, "Two panels: Yellow, black" courtesy of the artist Ellsworth Kelly, Bridgeman Art Library • 514: tr, Albers, Josef "Homage to the Square" 1956. © 2000 ARS, NY, Bridgeman Art Library • 515: tr, Van Doesburg, Theo "Arithmetic Composition" 1930. Felix Witzinger © 2000 ARS NY/Beeldrecht, Amsterdam, Bridgeman Art Library • 516: tr, Noland, Kenneth. "Turnstole" 1961. Synthetic polymer paint on unprimed canvas, 7'10 1/8"x 7' 10 1/8", The Museum of Modern Art, New York, Blanchette Rockefeller Fund. Photograph © 2000 The Museum of Modern Art, New York.© Kenneth Noland/Licensed by VAGA, New York, NY • 517: tl, David Waitz for MHSD • 517: tc, David Waitz for MHSD • 517: tr, David Waitz for MHSD • 519: cr, Noland, Kenneth"Split" 1959. © Kenneth Noland/ Licensed by VAGA, New York, NY. National Museum of American Art / Art Resource • 520: tr, David Waitz for MHSD • 524: tr, Myrleen Ferguson/Photo Edit • 524: br, David Waitz for MHSD • 533: tr, Herbin, Auguste "Composition of the Word 'Vie'" Museum of Modern Art, Photograph © 2000 The Museum of Modern Art, © 2000 ARS, New York/ADAGP, Paris; **Chapter 12** 538: c, Kim MacDonald/Habitat for Humanity Intl. • 540: tr, 87 Tibor Bognar/Stock Market • 542: tr, Travelpix 1986/FPG International • 544: cr, Richard Hutchings for MHSD • 546: tr, David Waitz for MHSD • 548: c, David Waitz for MHSD • 550: tr, David Waitz for MHSD • 552: tr, David Waitz for MHSD • 556: tr, Stefano Cellai/Stock Market • 556: cr, William MacDonald • 558: tr, Sylvain Grandadam/Stone • 562: tr, Andrew Wittemore • 564: tr, David Waitz for MHSD • 566: tr, David Waitz for MHSD • 570: tr, Chad Ehlers/International Stock • 570: br, David Waitz for MHSD • 579: tr, David Waitz for MHSD; **Chapter 13** 584: all, David Young-Wolf/Photo Edit • 586: tr, David Waitz for MHSD • 588: tr, Mission Management & Trust Co. • 593: tr, Ken Cavanagh for MHSD • 595: cr, Richard Hutchings for MHSD • 596: tr, David Young-Wolf/Photo Edit • 602: tr, David Waitz for MHSD • 604: tr, Ken Cavanagh for MHSD • 608: tr, Ron W. Perry • 612: cr, Index Stock/Index Stock • 612: br, David Waitz for MHSD • 621: tr, Roy Morsch/Stock Market; **Chapter 14** 626: all, Chuck Savage/Stock Market • 628: tr, David Waitz for MHSD • 638: tr, David Stoecklein/Stock Market • 642: tr, Janet Bahr • 656: tr, Comstock • 658: tr, Richard Hutchings for MHSD • 658: br, David Waitz for MHSD.

ILLUSTRATION CREDITS

Kenneth Batelman: 216, 247 • Estelle Carol and Bob Simpson: xvi, 345, 346, 349, 374, 393, 414, 416, 585, 591, 592, 597, 610, 625, 627, 628, 630, 633, 634, 637, 639, 643, 645, 646, 652, 654, 656, 667 • Stephen Durke: 270, 282, 302, 306, 339, 442, 522, 534, 561, 605, 606, 617 • Colin Hayes: 50, 166, 262, 400, 410, 560

Contents

Calculator Handbook

ACTIVITY 1

Objective: Evaluate expressions that contain exponents.

Exponents

A caterer plans to seat 5 people at each of 5 tables. How many people total can he seat?

Using the TI-15

To answer the question, you can find 5×5 or 5^2.

The 5 is the base and the 2 is the exponent. It is read "5 squared" or "5 to the second power."

Exponential Form	Expanded Form	Standard Form
5^2	5×5	25
7^4	$7 \times 7 \times 7 \times 7$	2,401
2.5^2	2.5×2.5	6.25

Using the TI-15 to raise a number to a power, enter the following:

5 ^ 2 Enter = → 5^2= 25

7  4 Enter = → 7^4= 2401

2  5 ^ 2 Enter = → 2.5^2= 6.25

So, the caterer can seat 25 people.

Practice **Use your calculator to evaluate each.**

1. 5^4
2. 10^3
3. 9^5
4. 2.4^3
5. 6^6
6. 4^7
7. 3.1^3
8. 1^{25}
9. 10^7
10. 1.2^3
11. 23^3
12. 3.4^2
13. 2^{15}
14. 7^{10}
15. 6^{12}
16. 5.5^4
17. 9^9
18. 1.3^4

Solve.

19. A caterer has 12 tables he plans to seat with 12 people each. Find the total number of people he can serve.

20. Darlene painted 6 rectangles. Inside of each rectangle she painted 6 circles. Inside of each circle she painted 6 dots. Write an expression using exponents that could be used to solve this problem. How many dots did she paint?

Objective: Make corrections on the calculator using the backspace and clear keys.

Error Corrections

Lisa was using a calculator to add the following numbers: 19.75 and 48.72. She entered 19.75 + 48.62 before she realized that 48.62 was supposed to be 48.72. How can she correct the problem without starting over?

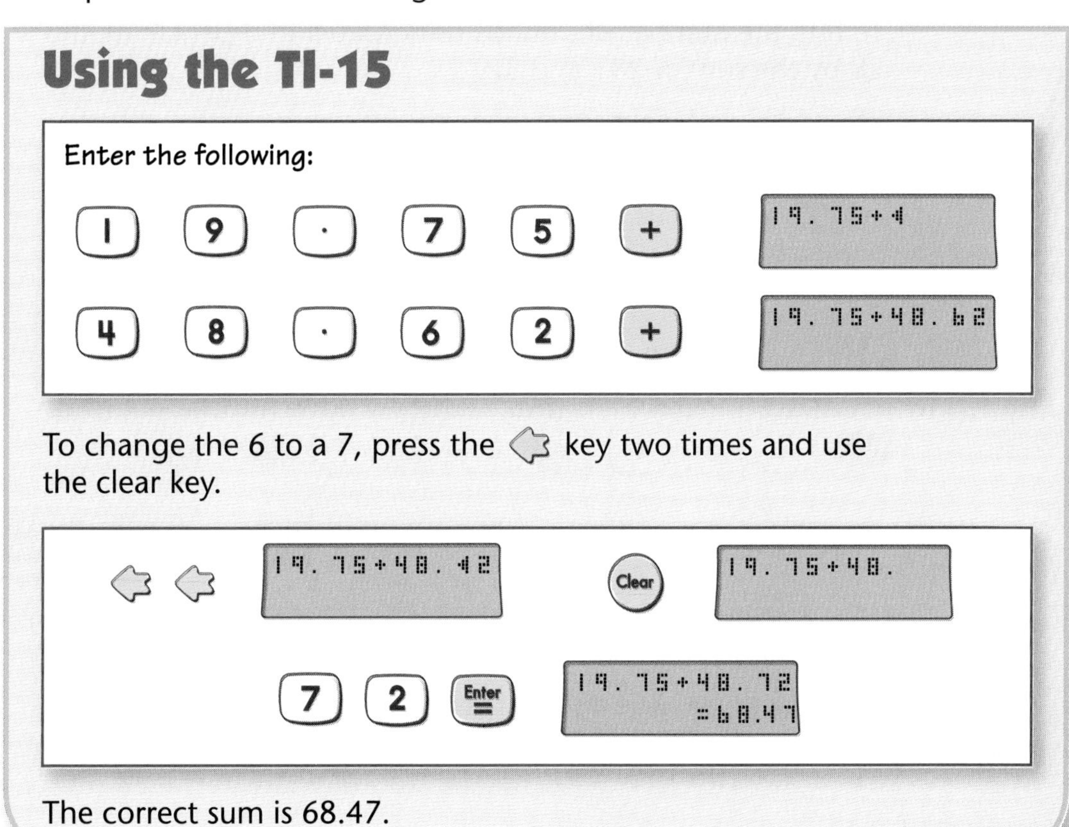

Practice

Enter the problem into your calculator, then correct the problem by entering the number in brackets. Find the sum.

1. 576 + 983 [953]
2. 1.32 [1.36] + 12.87 + 9.4
3. 428 [728] + 193 + 1,560
4. $95.32 + $54 + $8.03 [$8.43]

Solve.

5. Lisa entered 300 − 286.80 into her calculator. She should have entered 300 − 287.80. How many times must she press the left arrow key to correct the mistake? What is the correct answer?

ACTIVITY 3

Objective: Use parentheses and the operations to investigate order of operations.

Order of Operations

Mr. Jones and Mr. Lopez loaded cement blocks that weighed 28 pounds each onto a truck. Mr. Jones loaded 281 blocks and Mr. Lopez loaded 327 blocks. How many pounds of blocks did they load together?

To find the number of pounds using paper and pencil, multiply 28 by the sum of 281 and 327.

$28 \times (281 + 327) = 28 \times 608 = 17{,}024$

Using the TI-15

To find the number of pounds using the TI-15, enter the following:

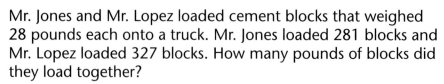

2 8 × — display: 28×

(2 8 1 + 3 2 7) — display: 28×(281+327)

Enter = — display: 28×(281+327) = 17024

$28 \times (281 + 327) = 17{,}024$

So, Mr. Jones and Mr. Lopez loaded 17,024 pounds of blocks.

Practice **Use mental math or paper and pencil to solve each problem. Check your answer using a calculator.**

1. $52 + 97 \times 18 + 46 \times 12$
2. $216 \div 12 + 59 \times 7 - 20 \times 15$
3. $12 \times (42 + 18 \times 16 - 9) + 31$
4. $20 + 50 \times 8 - 600 \div 30$
5. $6.2 \times 3.1 + 4.8 \times 0.2$
6. $4.2 \div 0.2 \times 8 + 17.5$

Solve.

7. Mr. Jones and Mr. Lopez helped a friend load bricks. Mr. Jones loaded 473 bricks and Mr. Lopez loaded 395 bricks. If each brick weighed 2.4 pounds, how many pounds of bricks did they load?

8. Christine bought 4 shirts that cost \$15.85 each and 2 pairs of pants that cost \$27.50 each. How much did she spend on clothes?

ACTIVITY 4

Objective: Use the Op1 key to divide varying quantities by a constant number.

Repeated Constants/Operations

Shelly is having a party for a total of 9 people. She can buy 25 party favors or 36 party favors. She wants to buy enough party favors so that everyone has an equal amount with none left over. Which should she buy?

You can answer the questions by dividing the amounts of party favors by 9.

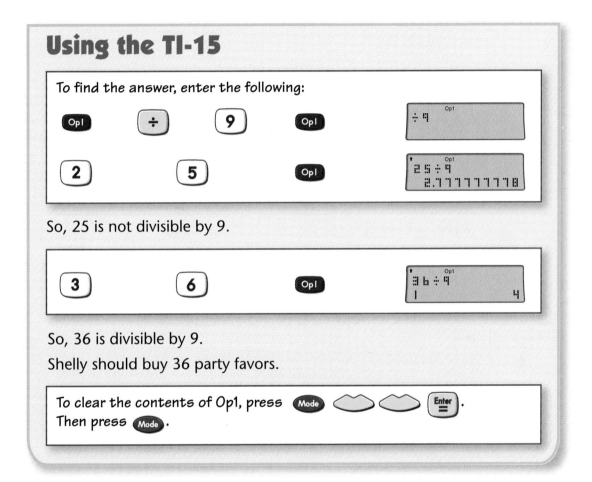

Using the TI-15

To find the answer, enter the following:

Op1 ÷ 9 Op1 — display: Op1 ÷ 9

2 5 Op1 — display: Op1 25 ÷ 9 / 2.777777778

So, 25 is not divisible by 9.

3 6 Op1 — display: Op1 36 ÷ 9 / 1 4

So, 36 is divisible by 9.

Shelly should buy 36 party favors.

To clear the contents of Op1, press Mode ▷ ▷ Enter =. Then press Mode.

Practice **Determine if each number is divisible by 6, by 8, or by neither.**

1. 58
2. 96
3. 144
4. 200
5. 340
6. 452

Solve.

7. Luke is making up table decorations for 35 tables. He has to decide between ordering 315 roses and 210 carnations or 250 roses and 280 carnations. If he wants to divide the flowers evenly, which should he order?

ACTIVITY 5

Objective: Use the F↔D key.

Fractions to Decimals and Decimals to Fractions

Denise and Mitchell work at a department store. Denise received a $\frac{3}{4}$ of a dollar per hour raise and Mitchell received a $0.41 per hour raise. What is $\frac{3}{4}$ written as a decimal? What is 0.41 written as a fraction?

Using the TI-15

To change $\frac{3}{4}$ to a decimal, enter the following:

3 n 4 d Enter → $3/4 = 3/4$

F↔D → 0.75

To change 0.41 to a fraction, enter the following:

0 . 4 1 Enter → 0.41 = 0.41

F↔D → $\frac{41}{100}$

So, Denise received a $0.75 per hour raise and Mitchell received a $\frac{41}{100}$ of a dollar per hour raise.

Practice **Change each fraction to a decimal.**

1. $\frac{3}{5}$ **2.** $\frac{3}{8}$ **3.** $\frac{3}{10}$ **4.** $\frac{4}{8}$ **5.** $\frac{7}{10}$

Change each decimal to a fraction.

6. 0.4 **7.** 0.32 **8.** 0.6 **9.** 0.73 **10.** 0.85

Solve.

11. John received a $\frac{2}{5}$ of a dollar per hour raise. What is $\frac{2}{5}$ written as a decimal?

12. Janice received a $0.61 per hour raise and Dan received a $\frac{3}{5}$ of a dollar raise. Who received the greater raise? How much more per hour is it? Write the difference as a fraction.

Objective: Use the memory keys.

Memory

Mr. Peters gave two different quizzes to 15 students. What is the mean score for each quiz?

Quiz 1: 80, 84, 84, 89, 72, 83, 84, 92, 98, 100, 68, 78, 80, 98, 100

Quiz 2: 82, 86, 88, 70, 72, 74, 100, 100, 100, 100, 92, 94, 98, 100, 100

To answer the question find the sum of the scores and divide the sum by the number of students.

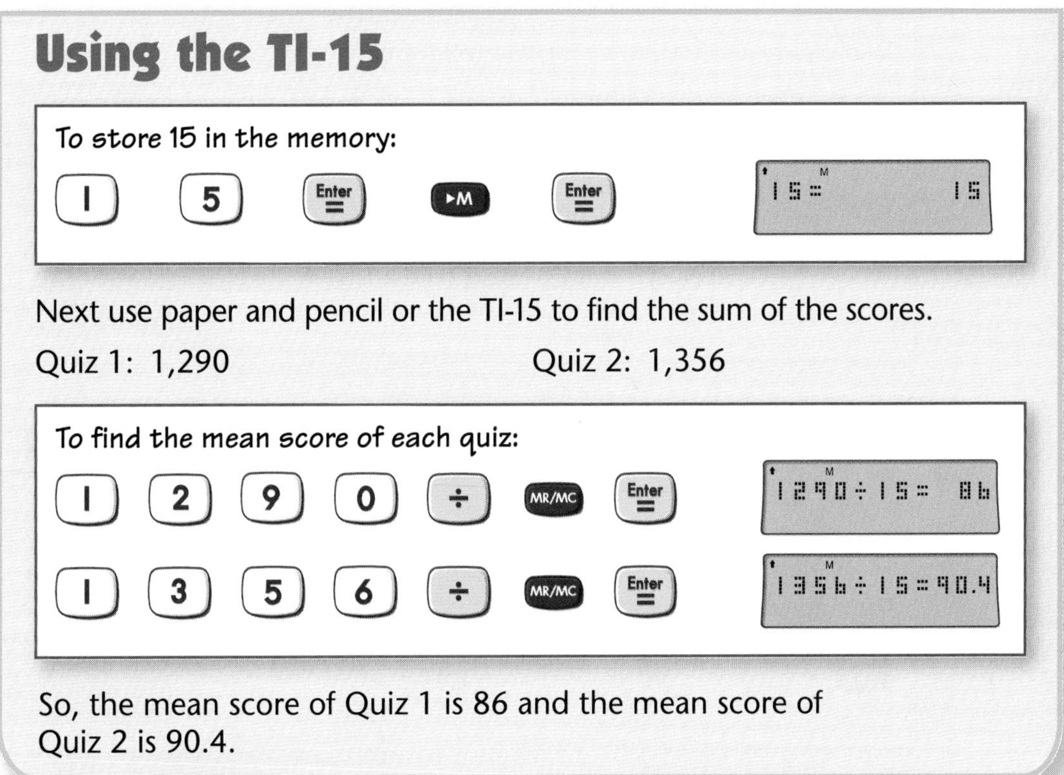

Using the TI-15
To store 15 in the memory:
1 5 Enter = ▸M Enter =
15 = 15
Next use paper and pencil or the TI-15 to find the sum of the scores.
Quiz 1: 1,290
Quiz 2: 1,356
To find the mean score of each quiz:
1 2 9 0 ÷ MR/MC Enter =
1290 ÷ 15 = 86
1 3 5 6 ÷ MR/MC Enter =
1356 ÷ 15 = 90.4
So, the mean score of Quiz 1 is 86 and the mean score of Quiz 2 is 90.4.

Practice **Find the mean for each set of data.**

1. A local newspaper stand recorded how many New York Times they sold each day for 30 days: 77, 68, 98, 64, 64, 97, 86, 82, 72, 75, 90, 80, 83, 72, 81, 88, 86, 70, 90, 95, 98, 65, 82, 82, 83, 88, 94, 92, 93, 95

2. The number of visitors to a museum at a given hour for 30 days: 96, 92, 93, 62, 64, 60, 64, 64, 62, 63, 60, 90, 98, 72, 71, 74, 79, 90, 80, 85, 82, 83, 81, 71, 84, 100, 92, 97, 91, 100

Solve.

3. Mr. Peters' class scored a mean of 98.75 on their last test. He has 20 students in class and 15 of them scored 100 on the test. If the rest all scored the same, what did they score?

ACTIVITY 7

Objective: Use the  *key to simplify fractions.*

Simplifying Fractions

Kyle surveyed his friends to find their favorite type of soda. Root beer was selected by 12 out of 16 of his friends. He wants to write the fraction in simplest form. He thinks that he can divide the numerator and denominator by either 3 or 4 to simplify the fraction. Which should he use?

Using the TI-15

To simplify a fraction, enter the following:

To divide the numerator and denominator by 3, enter the following:

The calculator shows the same fraction. This means that 3 is not a factor of 12 and 16. The $\frac{N}{D} \Rightarrow \frac{n}{d}$ in the display means the fraction can still be simplified.

To divide the numerator and denominator by 4, using the TI-15, enter the following:

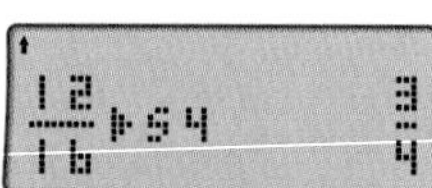

Since 4 is a common factor of 12 and 16, Kyle should use the common factor of 4 to simplify $\frac{12}{16}$ to $\frac{3}{4}$.

Practice **Write each fraction in simplest form.**

1. $\frac{20}{24}$
2. $\frac{12}{24}$
3. $\frac{12}{32}$
4. $\frac{12}{18}$
5. $\frac{18}{30}$
6. $\frac{7}{28}$
7. $\frac{13}{39}$
8. $\frac{15}{24}$
9. $\frac{12}{28}$
10. $\frac{9}{72}$

Solve.

6. Kyle surveyed 124 students in his school. He found that 35 of the girls surveyed selected purple and 45 of the boys selected purple as their favorite color. What fraction of the students have selected purple? Express the fraction in simplest form.

ACTIVITY 8

Objective: Add and subtract fractions using the $\frac{n}{\ }$ and $\frac{\ }{d}$ keys.

Adding and Subtracting Fractions

Janice cut a pan of brownies into 20 equal pieces. She gave $\frac{1}{3}$ to her neighbors and $\frac{1}{6}$ to her family. What fraction of the brownies did she give away?

You can answer the question by solving the following problem:

$\frac{1}{3} + \frac{1}{6} = \blacksquare$

Using the TI-15

To add fractions, enter the following:

1 n 3 d Enter

Simp 3 Enter

$\frac{1}{3} + \frac{1}{6} = \frac{3}{6} = \frac{1}{2}$

So, Janice gave away $\frac{1}{2}$ of the brownies.

Practice

Add or subtract. Write each answer in simplest form.

1. $\frac{2}{5} + \frac{1}{5}$
2. $\frac{2}{4} + \frac{1}{4}$
3. $\frac{2}{6} + \frac{2}{6}$
4. $\frac{3}{8} + \frac{4}{8}$
5. $\frac{3}{4} - \frac{2}{4}$
6. $\frac{4}{5} - \frac{2}{5}$
7. $\frac{3}{6} - \frac{1}{6}$
8. $\frac{5}{8} - \frac{4}{8}$

Solve.

9. Janice had $\frac{5}{20}$ of the brownies left. She ate $\frac{3}{20}$. What fraction of the brownies is left? Write your answer in simplest form.

10. Mark made 16 cookies to share with his friends. He gave $\frac{3}{16}$ to Paul and $\frac{5}{16}$ to Nikki. He ate $\frac{4}{16}$. What fraction of the cookies did he give away and eat? Write your answer in simplest form.

Objective: Add and subtract mixed numbers.

Adding and Subtracting Mixed Numbers

Veronica bought $8\frac{3}{4}$ pounds of compost for her garden. She already had $4\frac{3}{4}$ pounds at home. How many pounds of compost does she have altogether?

You can answer the question by solving the following problem:

$8\frac{3}{4} + 4\frac{3}{4} = \blacksquare$

Using the TI-15

To add mixed numbers, enter the following:

8  Unit  3  n  4  d +

$8\frac{3}{4} + 4$

4  Unit  3  n  4 d  Enter =

$8\frac{3}{4} + 4\frac{3}{4} = \quad 13\frac{2}{4}$

Simp 2 Enter =

$13\frac{2}{4}$ ▸S 2 $\quad 13\frac{1}{2}$

$8\frac{3}{4} + 4\frac{3}{4} = 13\frac{2}{4} = 13\frac{1}{2}$

So, Veronica has $13\frac{1}{2}$ pounds of compost.

Practice **Add or subtract. Write each answer in simplest form.**

1. $7\frac{1}{6} + 8\frac{4}{6}$
2. $9\frac{3}{8} + 4\frac{2}{8}$
3. $12\frac{3}{16} + 8\frac{5}{16}$
4. $7\frac{3}{20} + 6\frac{12}{20}$
5. $8\frac{3}{4} - 5\frac{1}{4}$
6. $6\frac{5}{8} - 4\frac{3}{8}$
7. $15\frac{5}{6} - 12\frac{3}{6}$
8. $20\frac{7}{16} - 8\frac{3}{16}$

Solve.

9. Veronica uses $7\frac{1}{4}$ feet of pipe to repair her irrigation system. She started with $12\frac{3}{4}$ feet. How many feet of pipe does she have left? Write your answer in simplest form.

10. Luke ran $6\frac{3}{8}$ miles on Monday and $3\frac{7}{8}$ miles on Tuesday. How many miles has he run altogether? Write your answer in simplest form.

ACTIVITY 10

Objective: Multiply whole numbers by fractions.

Multiplying Whole Numbers by Fractions

Mrs. Daly is making a border around her garden using logs. Each log is $\frac{3}{4}$ feet long. She has 58 logs. How many feet of logs does she have?

You have to find $58 \times \frac{3}{4}$ to solve this problem.

Using the TI-15

To multiply mixed numbers, enter the following:

5 8 × 3  4  Enter =

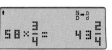

58 × 3/4 = 43 2/4

Simp 2 Enter =

43 2/4 ▸ S 2 43 1/2

$58 \times \frac{3}{4} = 43\frac{2}{4} = 43\frac{1}{2}$

So, Mrs. Daly has $43\frac{1}{2}$ feet of logs.

Practice

Multiply. Write each answer in simplest form.

1. $38 \times \frac{2}{5}$
2. $24 \times \frac{5}{8}$
3. $31 \times \frac{2}{3}$
4. $14 \times \frac{1}{8}$
5. $25 \times \frac{1}{4}$
6. $47 \times \frac{1}{6}$
7. $52 \times \frac{3}{8}$
8. $29 \times \frac{2}{6}$
9. $40 \times \frac{3}{10}$
10. $56 \times \frac{3}{4}$
11. $94 \times \frac{7}{8}$
12. $124 \times \frac{5}{6}$

Solve.

13. Mrs. Daly decided to put logs around her front yard. She needs 265 logs and each is $\frac{7}{8}$ feet long. How many feet of logs will she need?

14. Matthew is covering his wall using strips of oak wood $1\frac{3}{4}$ feet long. He figured that he needs 386 pieces of oak wood. How many feet of oak wood is he using?

ACTIVITY 11

Objective: Multiply and divide fractions using the n *key and the* d *key.*

Multiplying and Dividing Fractions

Maria and her brother must each paint $\frac{1}{2}$ of a fence. Maria has already painted $\frac{3}{4}$ of her half. How much of the total fence has she painted?

You can answer the question by solving the following problem:

$\frac{3}{4} \times \frac{1}{2} = \blacksquare$

Using the TI-15

To multiply fractions, enter the following:

3  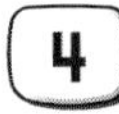  

1  2  

$\frac{3}{4} \times \frac{1}{2} = \frac{3}{8}$

So, Maria has painted $\frac{3}{8}$ of the fence.

Practice **Multiply or divide. Write each answer in simplest form.**

1. $\frac{3}{5} \times \frac{1}{4}$
2. $\frac{3}{4} \times \frac{1}{8}$
3. $\frac{5}{6} \times \frac{2}{9}$
4. $\frac{3}{8} \times \frac{5}{8}$
5. $\frac{1}{4} \div \frac{2}{4}$
6. $\frac{3}{5} \div \frac{4}{5}$
7. $\frac{1}{6} \div \frac{3}{6}$
8. $\frac{4}{8} \div \frac{7}{8}$

Solve.

9. Rashid had to paint $\frac{3}{4}$ of his bedroom walls. He has painted $\frac{2}{3}$ of that amount. How much of his bedroom has he painted? Write your answer in simplest form.

10. Gregg needs $\frac{1}{8}$ of a yard of material to make a book cover. He has $\frac{2}{3}$ of a yard. How many books can he cover?

ACTIVITY 12

Objective: Use the calculator to find patterns.

Patterns

Jeremy needs to find the rule that created the number pattern $\frac{1}{2}, \frac{1}{3}, \frac{2}{9}, \frac{4}{27}, \frac{8}{81}, \ldots$ and find the next term.

He started by finding the quotient of the first two terms in the pattern.

$\frac{1}{3} \div \frac{1}{2} = \blacksquare$

Using the TI-15

To find the answer and store it in memory, enter the following:

Since $\frac{1}{3} \div \frac{1}{2} = \frac{2}{3}$, Jeremy guessed that if you multiply a term in the pattern by $\frac{2}{3}$, you should get the next term in the pattern. He multiplied $\frac{2}{3}$ by $\frac{1}{3}$ to see if it equals $\frac{2}{9}$.

Since $\frac{1}{3} \times \frac{2}{3} = \frac{2}{9}$, he multiplied $\frac{8}{81}$ by $\frac{2}{3}$ to find the next term in the pattern.

So, the next term in the pattern is $\frac{16}{243}$.

Practice **Find a pattern. What is the next number according to your pattern?**

1. $\frac{1}{3}, \frac{1}{6}, \frac{1}{12}, \frac{1}{24}, \ldots$
2. $\frac{5}{6}, \frac{5}{24}, \frac{5}{96}, \frac{5}{384}, \ldots$
3. $\frac{1}{4}, \frac{3}{8}, \frac{9}{16}, \frac{27}{32}, \ldots$
4. $\frac{7}{8}, \frac{7}{6}, \frac{14}{9}, \frac{56}{27}, \ldots$

Objective: Add and subtract negative numbers.

Adding and Subtracting Integers

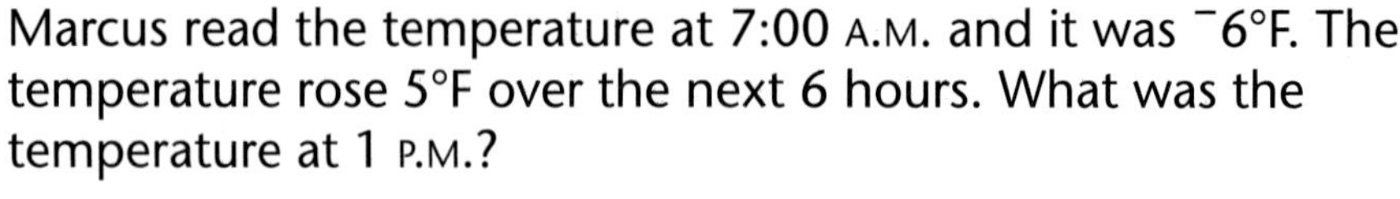

Marcus read the temperature at 7:00 A.M. and it was $^{-}6$°F. The temperature rose 5°F over the next 6 hours. What was the temperature at 1 P.M.?

You can find $^{-}6 + 5$ to solve this problem.

Using the TI-15

To add integers, enter the following:

$^{-}6 + 5 = {}^{-}1$

So, the temperature now is $^{-}1$°F.

When entering a negative into the calculator, make sure that you use the (−) key.

Marcus wanted to see if you get the same answer by solving $5 + {}^{-}6$.

Using the TI-15 to find the answer, enter the following:

$5 + {}^{-}6 = {}^{-}1$

So, $5 + {}^{-}6$ is the same as $^{-}6 + 5$.

Practice **Add.**

1. $^{-}7 + 9$
2. $^{-}6 + 13$
3. $^{-}12 + 16$
4. $^{-}9 + 15$
5. $12 + {}^{-}8$
6. $18 + {}^{-}3$
7. $23 + {}^{-}13$
8. $17 + {}^{-}14$
9. $^{-}12 + 6$
10. $^{-}15 + 8$
11. $^{-}22 + 14$
12. $^{-}24 + 17$

Solve.

13. The temperature was $^{-}12$°F at 4 A.M. and then it rose 23°F by 3 P.M. What was the temperature at 3 P.M.?

14. Jessica measured the temperature at 6:00 A.M. and it was $^{-}25$°F. By 8:00 A.M. the temperature had risen 5°F. At 10:00 A.M., the temperature had risen an additional 13°F. What was the temperature at 10:00 A.M.?

ACTIVITY 14

Objective: Use the calculator to check solutions to one-step equations.

Solving One-Step Equations

The temperature outside dropped 4°F. If the temperature is now $^{-}12$°F, what was the original temperature?

Nancy wrote the equation $x - 4 = {}^{-}12$ to answer the question. When she solved it, she found $x = 16$. To check her answer, she substituted 16 for x and used the calculator to see if $16 - 4$ equals $^{-}12$.

Using the TI-15

To check her answer to the equation, enter the following:

Since $16 - 4 = 12$, the answer is not 16.

Nancy solved the equation again and found $x = {}^{-}8$ for an answer. To check her answer, she calculated $^{-}8 - 4$ to see if it equals $^{-}12$.

Using the TI-15 to check the answer, enter the following:

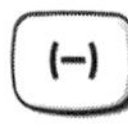

-8-4= -12

Since $^{-}8 - 4 = {}^{-}12$, $^{-}8$ is the answer. The temperature was $^{-}8$°F before it dropped.

Practice **Solve. Check your solution using the calculator.**

1. $x + {}^{-}9 = {}^{-}15$
2. $x + 13 = 6$
3. $x + {}^{-}21 = 15$
4. $x + 21 = {}^{-}13$
5. $x + {}^{-}28 = {}^{-}5$
6. $x + {}^{-}46 = 38$
7. $x - {}^{-}3 = {}^{-}27$
8. $x - 16 = 28$
9. $x - {}^{-}11 = {}^{-}18$

Solve.

10. The temperature rose 18°F. If the temperature is now $^{-}15$°F, what was it before it rose?

11. The temperature outside dropped 25°F. It is now $^{-}16$°F. What was the temperature before it dropped?

Calculator Activities

ACTIVITY 15

Objective: Use the ▸% key.

Percents

If Mr. Drake buys plants for his garden center for \$1.00 each, he adds \$0.75 to the price and sells them for \$1.75. He multiplies his cost by $\frac{3}{4}$ to decide how much extra to charge his customers.

What is $\frac{3}{4}$ written as a percent?

Using the TI-15

To change $\frac{3}{4}$ to a percent, enter the following:

      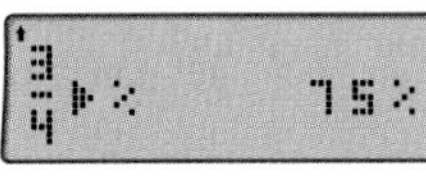

Since $\frac{3}{4}$ = 75%, Mr. Drake raises the price by 75%.

Mr. Drake buys shrubs and multiplies his cost by 0.85. What percent does he use?

You can answer the question by changing 0.85 to a percent.

To change 0.85 to a percent, enter the following:

 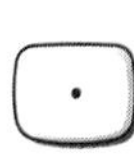 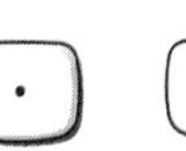    

0.85▸% 85%

Since 0.85 = 85%, Mr. Drake multiplies by 85%.

Practice

Change each fraction or decimal to a percent.

1. $\frac{1}{2}$	**2.** $\frac{1}{5}$	**3.** $\frac{1}{4}$	**4.** $\frac{2}{5}$
5. $\frac{1}{10}$	**6.** $\frac{7}{10}$	**7.** $\frac{3}{5}$	**8.** $\frac{4}{10}$
9. $\frac{17}{100}$	**10.** $\frac{23}{100}$	**11.** $\frac{4}{5}$	**12.** $\frac{73}{100}$

Solve.

13. Mr. Drake multiplies the cost of pots by $\frac{4}{5}$. What percent does he use?

14. Lisa got 98 out of 100 right on her test. She changed it to a decimal and got 0.98. What percent right did she get on her test?